DATE			

Environmental Analysis
of Transportation Systems

Environmental Analysis
of Transportation Systems

LOUIS F. COHN
Vanderbilt University

GARY R. McVOY
*New York State
Department of Transportation*

A Wiley-Interscience Publication
JOHN WILEY & SONS
New York   Chichester   Brisbane   Toronto   Singapore

Library of Congress Cataloging in Publication Data:

Cohn, Louis F. (Louis Franklin), 1948–
    Environmental analysis of transportation
systems.

    "A Wiley-Interscience publication."
    Includes index.
    1. Transportation—Environmental aspects.
I. McVoy, Gary R. (Gary Richard), 1951–
II. Title.
TD195.T7C63   380.5   81-14637
ISBN 0-471-08098-5   AACR2

Printed in the United States of America

10 9 8 7 6 5 4 3 2 1

To our wives,
Anita and Elaine,
whose understanding and support
made this work
much more pleasant
to accomplish

Preface

Transportation project development and implementation have evolved dramatically in recent times. Gone is the era when a government transportation agency simply and blindly put facilities into operation—not knowing or caring about potential indirect impacts.

NEPA—The National Environmental Policy Act—and other pieces of legislation changed all that. Today the agencies must concern themselves with an awesome and often intimidating array of regulations and specialized technical disciplines in trying to advance their projects.

In this book we attempt to assist transportation engineers and planners as they seek the "handles" to project development where the environment is concerned. These handles, of course, manifest themselves as legislation, regulations, process guidelines, modeling techniques, and analysis procedures.

Chapters 2 through 4 are devoted to the issues and questions relating to the Federal legislation and resulting regulations, and to the project development process itself. While much of this material may appear initially to be foreign to the field of transportation *engineering*, one need only spend some time working in a consulting engineer's office or government transportation agency to appreciate the importance of familiarity with the regulations and procedures for project development. We then move to rather technical discussions in the areas of noise analysis, air quality, and terrestrial and aquatic ecology. These discussions are based on predictive modeling techniques and should prove to be most challenging even to those technically oriented. Sufficient information and guidance are provided so that one could successfully perform the modeling studies called for by the Federal regulations.

This book should be well suited to courses for the advanced undergraduate or graduate student of engineering. The information gained thereby would be most appropriate for any civil engineering specialty, but would of course be most valuable to the student committed to a career in transportation engineering.

Consulting engineers and the government officials involved in transportation projects will also find the book helpful. Most often members of these two groups are the ones who must enforce and/or comply with confusing regulations and complex prediction models.

Our objective in undertaking this work will be accomplished if, after gaining familiarity with the subject matter, at least one (and hopefully many) engineer or student of engineering is able to come to understand and perhaps master transportation project development. Beyond that, it would be even better if such a student were able to improve significantly the environmental quality of a project.

LOUIS F. COHN

GARY R. McVOY

Nashville, Tennesse
Albany, New York
December 1981

Acknowledgments

We would like to thank many people whose efforts made completion of this text more efficient. Everett Smethurst, our editor, was most helpful in providing general guidance. William Bowlby and James Berka from the Federal Highway Administration provided early direction concerning technical matters. Thanks are also due to students Joe Serena and Jackie Serena, who helped with the typing, and to Marjorie Kay, who prepared the illustrations. A special thank you goes to Barbara Rich, whose work as manuscript supervisor was essential in the ultimate preparation of the text.

Dr. McVoy would also like to extend a special thank you to Dr. William E. Reifsnyder and others at the Yale School of Forestry and Environmental Studies, in hopes that the words contained in Chapters 6 and 7 do credit to their efforts on his behalf.

L.F.C.
G.R.M.

Contents

7. Terrestrial and Aquatic Impacts, 345

Environmental Analysis
of Transportation Systems

Introduction

A generation ago transportation project development was accomplished using a vastly different set of groundrules from those in effect today. The goals and objectives were much simpler then, and the constraints on the system were much less complex and numerous.

In those years prior to 1962, transportation projects were primarily tools used both to aid development through improving access into an area or between two or more areas and to relieve congestion. Given these as goals in most cases, the criteria for project development were limited principally to two: (*a*) minimized cost (maximized benefit/cost ratio), and (*b*) engineering feasibility.

Directly stated, projects were implemented in the cheapest way feasible. This philosophy, quite naturally, led to problems in terms of unexpected impacts, unplanned growth inducement, and, therefore, public opposition. In turn these problems produced a marked decrease in perceived credibility for the transportation agency.

As these results were becoming more acute (into the 1960s), other forces were coming to bear upon the process from the greatly enlarged bodies of knowledge in the areas of air quality, noise analysis, water quality, ecology, and social and economic impacts. A general awakening of the American public concerning transportation issues, as well as a new thrust in environmental legislation, were also major contributing factors in complicating transportation project development. The present criteria for project development are many and varied, concerning the *social*, *economic*, and *environmental* (SEE) effects of many alternatives, including the alternative of doing nothing (null option). Chapter 3 discusses these criteria in great detail.

The evolutionary nature of transportation project development since 1960 may be viewed from three perspectives.

1. Legislation and regulations
2. Project development process
3. Analytical modeling techniques

Tables 1-1 and 1-2 present chronologies of the Federal legislation and regulations in the areas of environment and process which have altered transportation project development since 1960. Each of these elements is discussed in detail in Chapters 2 (legislation), 3 (regulations), and 4 (environmental action planning), as appropriate. Similarly, Table 1-3 presents a chronology for the development of environmental modeling techniques for noise analysis (Chapter 5) and air quality (Chapter 6). While no models are included in Table 1-3 for water quality and ecology, these topics are discussed in detail in Chapter 7.

LEGISLATION

Each of the laws listed in Table 1-1 are important in the area transportation and environment, although two stand out as particularly important. These are the Federal Aid Highway Act of 1962 and the National Environmental Policy Act of 1969.

The 1962 Highway Act redirected the concepts of urban transportation problem solving by requiring the use of a *cooperative*, *continuing*, and *comprehensive* planning process. This "3-C" process was mandated for urban areas with populations of greater than 50,000. This concept is clearly an ancestor of the project development

TABLE 1-1.   Federal Environmental Legislation Influencing Transportation

Date	Legislation
Pre-1960	The Rivers and Harbors Act of 1899 Fish and Wildlife Coordination Act of 1958
1960	Federal Aid Highway Act of 1962 Clean Air Act of 1963
1965	Housing and Urban Development Act of 1965 Department of Transportation Act of 1966 Air Quality Act of 1967 Control and Abatement of Aircraft Noise and Sonic Boom Act of 1968 Wild and Scenic Rivers Act of 1968 National Flood Insurance Act of 1968 National Environmental Policy Act of 1969 (NEPA)
1970	Federal Aid Highway Act of 1970 Executive Order 11514, *Protection and Enhancement of Environmental Quality*, 1970 Environmental Quality Improvement Act of 1970 Airport and Airway Development Act of 1970 Clean Air Act Amendments of 1970 Noise Control Act of 1972 Federal Water Pollution Control Act of 1972 Coastal Zone Management Act of 1972
1975	Coastal Zone Management Act Amendments of 1976 Executive Order 11988, *Floodplain Management* Executive Order 11990, *Protection of Wetlands* Clean Air Act Amendments of 1977 Clean Water Act Amendments of 1977 Executive Order 11991, *Protection and Enhancement of Environmental Quality (amended)*, 1977 Quiet Communities Act of 1978
1980	

TABLE 1-2.   Federal Environmental Regulations and Directives Influencing Transportation

Date	Regulation
1965	USCG Section 9 Bridge Permit, 1967 FAR PART 36, Noise Standards: Aircraft Type and Airworthiness Certification, 1969
1970	FHPM 7-7-1, *Process Guidelines*, 1974
1975	USCOE/EPA Section 404, 1977[a] DOT Order 5660.1A, *Preservation of the Nation's Wetlands*, 1978 EPA/DOT, Transportation-Air Quality Guidelines, 1978 CEQ Guidelines, Regulations for Implementing the Procedural Provisions of NEPA, 1978[a] DOT Order 5610.1C, Procedures for Considering Environmental Impact, 1979[a] FAA Order 1050.1C, *Policies and Procedures for Considering Environmental Impacts*, 1979[a] DHUD, Noise Criteria and Standards, 1979[a] FHPM 7-7-9, Air Quality Guidelines, 1979[a] FHPM 6-7-3-2, Location and Hydraulic Design of Encroachments on Floodplains, 1979 DOT, F&W Compliance Procedures, 1979 (draft)[a]
1980	EPA, Noise Emission Standards for Interstate Rail Carriers, 1980 FHPM 7-7-2, Environmental Impact and Related Statements, 1980[a] UMTA, *Environmental Impact and Related Statements*, 1980[a]

[a] Represents revision of earlier version.

process in place today, which emphasizes impact analysis and public involvement.

The 1969 National Environmental Policy Act (NEPA) is without question the most significant piece of environmental legislation to influence transportation. This law has two basic provisions relevant to this discussion: (*a*) it requires a systematic, interdisciplinary approach to project development, and (*b*) it requires the preparation of an environmental impact statement (EIS) for any major Federal action significantly affecting the environment. These two provisions have dramatically altered the way in which transportation agencies deliver projects to implementation and, particularly the EIS requirement, have in some cases added years to the project schedule.

These two laws, as well as the others listed in

TABLE 1-3. Noise and Air Quality Models for Transportation

Date	Model
1965	NCHRP 78 (Noise), 1969
1970	NCHRP 117 (Noise), 1971 CALINE (Air), 1972 TSC Model (Noise), 1972 NCHRP 144 (Noise), 1973
1975	HIWAY (Air), 1975 NCHRP 173/174 (Noise), 1976 CALINE 2 (Air), 1977 FHWA Model (Noise), 1978 EPA Volume 9 (Air), 1978 MOBILE 1 (Air), 1978 INM (Noise), 1978 SNAP and STAMINA (Noise), 1979 CALINE 3 (Air), 1979 INM Version 2 (Noise), 1979
1980	HIWAY 2 (Air), 1980 MOBILE 2 (Air), 1980

Table 1-1, as mentioned earlier, are discussed and analyzed in Chapter 2.

REGULATION

The Federal Highway Administration's (FHWA) FHPM 7-7-1, Process Guidelines, is quite significant in that it provides the organizational and project development framework for implementation of the *systematic, interdisciplinary approach* for highway projects. Because of the highly decentralized nature of the highway program, it became necessary for the FHWA to formalize the process for project development that the state highway agencies must use. This decentralized nature is unique to the highway mode, and therefore the other modal agencies (i.e., agencies that are responsible for a mode of transportation, such as rail, highway, or aviation) have not found it necessary to adopt process guidelines.

Each of the modal agencies have, however, adopted guidelines for the consideration of environmental impacts and the preparation of environmental impact statements. These guidelines are based on Department of Transportation (DOT) Order 5610.1C, which is in turn based on the November 29, 1978 Guidelines from the President's Council on Environmental Quality (CEQ; see Chapter 3).

PREDICTIVE MODELING

The principal models in use today for transportation noise analysis are the FHWA model (highways) and the Integrated Noise Model, INM (aviation). The FHWA model represents the culmination of more than a decade of research and development in the area of highway noise prediction, much of which was sponsored by the National Cooperative Highway Research Program of the Transportation Research Board. The model is based upon energy equivalent sound levels, L_{eq}, and is best utilized in a Level 2 coordinate-system–based computer program called STAMINA.

The INM is also a coordinate-system–based model which relies quite heavily on a standardized data base for aircraft-type characteristics, stored within a computer program. Output may be obtained in either a contour or grid format, in any one of the following metrics.

1. Noise Exposure Forecast (NEF)
2. Day-Night Equivalent Level (L_{dn})
3. Equivalent Sound Level (L_{eq})
4. Community Noise Exposure Level (CNEL)
5. Time Above Threshold (TA)

Each of these metrics, as well as the models, is described in more detail in Chapter 5.

The two most commonly used prediction models in air quality analysis are CALINE 3, from the FHWA and the California Department of Transportation, and HIWAY 2 from the EPA. These models also rely on coordinate systems. Outputs from CALINE 3 and HIWAY 2 are in terms of parts per million (ppm) of carbon monoxide (CO). Chapter 6 contains detailed discussions of the models.

Legislative Actions at the Federal Level

The traditional delivery mechanism for transportation resources in the United States has been at the Federal level. While much of the planning and implementation activities have been at the state and even local levels, most of the funding of major transportation projects has been provided by the Federal government. There are several reasons for this, most of which have to do with the constitutional and governmental structure of the nation. The most important reason, for the purposes of discussion, is that Federal funding provides nationwide standardization and quality assurance.

For example, a state highway agency is reimbursed 90 percent of the cost of construction of a highway on the interstate system, provided the highway is designed and built according to Federal interstate standards and is located in a corridor approved by the FHWA. Similarly, an airport operator may have airport improvement costs paid mostly by the Federal Aviation Administration (FAA) provided the operator follows the FAA guidelines and priorities in determining improvements. Similar statements can be made concerning transit operators and railroad companies.

Basically, Federal laws and regulations must be met in order for state and local transportation providers to qualify for Federal assistance in planning and implementing their projects. Given the current framework of funding mechanisms, it is not usually realistic to consider major transportation improvements without Federal assistance. Thus, it is necessary to understand and abide by Federal direction. Accordingly, the remainder of this chapter is devoted to the discussion of those Federal laws and statutes having environmental-action effects upon the multimodal transportation project development process. Chapter 3 will discuss the Federal regulations which have resulted from these laws and statutes.

GENERAL ENVIRONMENTAL LEGISLATION

Federal Highway Act of 1962
(Title 23 of the U.S. Code)

This act is the foundation of present-day transportation planning legislation because of its specific requirements in the area of urban transportation problem solving. The act gave greater emphasis than ever before to planning and research activities and *required* cooperative, continuing, and comprehensive planning. This latter point helped open the way to increased public involvement and environmental consideration on urban transportation projects and programs.

In particular, the act required that urban highway systems be "an integral part of a soundly based, balanced transportation system for the area involved." It also required the lapsing of 1.5 percent of a state highway agency's Federal allocation unless those monies were set aside for planning and research (p & r) activities. Up until 1962, the states had the option, but were not required, to spend 1.5 percent for p & r activities. In addition, the act provided for an additional 0.5 percent of Federal highway funds for planning and research if a state highway agency so chose. Finally, the act required that effective

July 1, 1965, the Bureau of Public Roads (forerunner of the FHWA) not approve any highway program or project in an urban area of population greater than 50,000 *unless* the project was based on a continuing, comprehensive transportation planning process carried on cooperatively by the states and local communities. This "3-C" process serves as the basis for the project development process and gives rise to the consideration of the *impacts* of project implementation.

The National Environmental Policy Act of 1969 (42 USC 4321–4327)

Clearly the most important piece of environmental legislation enacted to date is the National Environmental Policy Act of 1969, or, as it is commonly referred to, NEPA. Because of its significance, the entire law, with the 1974 amendments, is reproduced in Appendix 2A.

Ten years before its enactment in 1969, elements of the NEPA package were under consideration in Congress. The ill-fated Resources and Conservation Act introduced in the Senate would have required the creation of an Environmental Advisory Council to the President and a joint Congressional resources and conservation comittee. In addition, this bill would have required an annual report to Congress concerning resources and conservation.

It is interesting to compare the statement of policy from this bill with that of NEPA (Section 101)

The Congress declares that it is the continuing policy and responsibility of the Federal Government with the assistance and cooperation of industry, agriculture, labor, conservationists, state and local governments, and private property owners, to use all practical means including coordination and utilization of all its plans, functions, and facilities for the purpose of creating and maintaining in a manner calculated to foster and promote the general welfare, conditions under which there will be conservation, development and utilization of the natural resources of the Nation to meet human, economic, and natural defense requirements, including recreational, wildlife, scenic, and scientific values and the enhancement of the national heritage for future generations.

Major comprehensive environmental legislation was not successfully reintroduced in Congress until February of 1969. In the intervening period, however, several congressional and executive departmental studies and reports repeatedly sounded the theme that the nation needed to have a comprehensive policy and executive accountability with respect to the environment.

These conclusions, plus the general mood of the nation in the late 1960s, made the way for the enactment of the NEPA legislation, which had been introduced on February 17, 1969, in the U.S. House of Representatives and on February 18 in the Senate. The respective versions had significant differences which were worked out over the course of the year. On January 1, 1970 NEPA was signed into law.

After setting forth the statement of national policy, Title I of NEPA outlines the requirements to be placed upon all the agencies of the Federal government undertaking or funding a major action which may have an impact on environmental quality. These requirements include the utilization of an interdisciplinary, systematic approach to planning and decision making; the development of procedures to address the unquantified environmental impacts of the action; and consultation with and receipt of comments from any Federal agency with jurisdiction or relevant expertise.

In addition, for any recommended or proposed Federal action significantly affecting the quality of the human environment, a detailed statement must be prepared by the sponsoring agency which delineates

1. The environmental impact of the proposed action
2. Any adverse environmental effects which cannot be avoided should the proposal be implemented
3. Alternatives to the proposed action
4. The relation between local short-term uses of man's environment and the maintenance and enhancement of long-term productivity
5. Any irreversible and irretrievable commitment of resources which would be involved in the proposal action should it be implemented

These fine points, of course, constitute the basic components of the Environmental Impact

Statement (EIS), the now commonplace document that has caused the long delay of many transportation projects. The ambiguities of these fine points have caused many Federal and state transportation agencies great difficulties in and out of court. Because the requirements are so general, NEPA has become a favorite tool of those groups who systematically seek to halt transportation projects. Accordingly, as the courts have sought to define the procedural intentions of NEPA, it has become one of the most litigated statutes of its kind in the U.S. Code.

Because many public works projects, particularly those in the transportation area, are initiated at the state or local level but are funded with Federal monies, Title I had to be clarified. Paragraph D. was added to Section 102 as an amendment permitting state agencies to prepare EISs on behalf of the sponsoring Federal agency. Typically, a state highway agency will perform the analyses required for determining environmental impact, and will circulate the EIS under FWHA signature. This fine point was challenged in the courts in the early 1970s with the argument that NEPA required *Federal preparation* of the EIS. Presently, however, under the amended NEPA, the state agency can prepare the EIS as long as (*a*) the project is fully within the state's jurisdiction; (*b*) the sponsoring Federal agency provides guidance and participation in the preparation of the EIS; (*c*) the Federal agency provides an independent evaluation of the EIS prior to its approval and adoption, and (*d*) the Federal agency solicits the input of other state or Federal land management agencies effected by the proposed project. The sponsoring Federal agency must also provide a written assessment of the expected impacts if so requested by the state or Federal land management agency involved.

Another extremely important feature of Title I is Section 103, which requires that all Federal agencies review their regulations, policies, and procedures to ascertain deficiencies which could prohibit full compliance with the act. Each agency was required to report the findings of its review to the President by July 1, 1971, along with proposals for attaining full compliance. This section precipitated major revisions in the transportation project development process, as it in effect mandated that each Federal agency modify its methods of operation to insure a sys-

tematic, multidisciplinary approach to project development, with emphasis on public participation and impact evaluation. Each of the modal transportation agencies, including the FWHA, FAA, and UMTA (Urban Mass Transportation Administration) have issued very detailed regulations, which are discussed in Chapter 3.

With respect to highways, NEPA, along with the Federal Highway Act of 1970, caused the FWHA to require the formalization of the project development process of each state highway agency. The FWHA issued a regulation entitled *Process Guidelines*, which outlined the procedures each state had to follow in modifying and documenting its project development process. The outcome of implementing the regulation is an approved document called the *Environmental Action Plan* (EAP). The development and implementation of the EAP is discussed in detail in Chapter 4.

Title II of NEPA is primarily concerned with the creation of the Council on Environmental Quality (CEQ) within the executive office of the President. This three-person body was patterned after the Council of Economic Advisors which was created by the Employment Act of 1946 to have ready access to the President in matters pertaining to the national economy.

It is the role of the CEQ to read environmental trends; to evaluate the programs and activities of the Federal agencies with respect to the implementation of Title I; to be responsive to the scientific, economic, social, aesthetic, and cultural needs and interests of the country; and to develop and recommend national policies for the improvement of environmental quality.

In addition, the CEQ is to conduct investigations and analyses on ecological systems and environmental quality, to document changes in the natural environment, to accumulate data necessary for a continuing analysis of these changes and other trends, to interpret the data as to underlying causes, and to perform special studies and recommendations as the President may direct.

The CEQ must prepare an annual Environmental Quality Report for the President to submit to Congress. This report discusses the current conditions of the atmospheric, aquatic, and terrestrial environments in the nation; outlines the national trends in the environment as they affect the social, economic, and other requirements nationally; evaluates population pressures in relation to the adequacy of available natural resources; reviews the programs, activities, and regulatory practices of the public and private sectors in relation to their effect on the environment and on the use of natural resources; and proposes remedies, including legislation for any deficiencies noted.

Obviously, a three-person group could not produce the information required by the CEQ. While NEPA did not make any provisions for a staff for CEQ, another piece of legislation enacted in 1970 did—the Environmental Quality Improvement Act, which is discussed after NEPA in this chapter.

The implementation of NEPA was initiated with the promulgation (from the President) of Executive Order 11514, *Protection and Enhancement of Environmental Quality*, March 5, 1970. This order, which is reproduced in Appendix 2C, spelled out in greater detail the responsibilities of the Federal agencies and of the CEQ. The agencies were told to develop programs to protect and enhance the quality of the environment and to develop procedures to insure maximum public input in determining environmental impact. Public hearings were specifically called for where appropriate. The agencies were also told to coordinate their activities with each other.

The CEQ was ordered, among other things, to provide continuing review of procedures used in developing and enforcing Federal environmental standards; to prioritize pollution control programs; to conduct public hearings or conferences on issues of environmental significance; and to coordinate Federal programs relating to environmental quality.

Originally, the CEQ was also given the task of approving all EISs prepared around the country. However, as the number of statements being prepared began to grow and the amount of data within each statement began to increase this activity became too burdensome for the staff of the CEQ. As a result, projects were delayed while awaiting CEQ approval. This was remedied when that function was given to the EPA for routine projects. Only when the EPA finds that a project is environmentally unsatisfactory does it get referred to the CEQ.

The order was amended by Executive Order 11991, May 24, 1977, to reflect concerns relating to the utility of the EIS. This order required the CEQ to issue guidelines to the Federal agencies for the purpose of streamlining the statements so they would focus on environmental issues and alternatives rather than on extraneous background data. The new guidelines were to emphasize the early preparation of the EIS and to spell out the procedures for the resolution of conflicts between Federal agencies. These new CEQ regulations were published on November 29, 1978 and caused the modal transportation agencies to revise their project development processes and regulations. Both the CEQ guidelines and the modal transportation agency responses are discussed in detail in Chapter 3.

Environmental Quality Improvement Act of 1970 (42 USC 4371–4374)

This relatively simple piece of legislation, which was enacted on April 3, 1970, declared that the primary agents for implementing environmental policy were the state, regional, and local government organizations that ordinarily initiate public works projects. As mentioned earlier, this concept was formalized in the 1975 amendments to NEPA when states were given the authority to actually prepare EISs.

This act also established within the Executive Office of the President an Office of Environmental Quality (OEQ). The act stipulated that the Chairman of the CEQ serve as director of this office. A Deputy Director of the OEQ is appointed by the President and is subject to Senate confirmation, as are all members of CEQ. The Director is then authorized to assemble a professional staff to assist him by

1. Providing the professional and administrative staff for the CEQ established by Public Law 91-190 [NEPA].
2. Assisting the Federal agencies and departments in appraising the effectiveness of existing and proposed facilities, programs, policies, and activities of the Federal government, and those specific major projects designated by the President which do not require individual project authorization by Congress, which affect environmental quality.

3. Reviewing the adequacy of existing systems for monitoring and predicting environmental changes in order to achieve effective coverage and efficient use of research facilities and other resources.

4. Promoting the advancement of scientific knowledge of the effects of actions and technology on the environment and encouraging the development of the means to prevent or reduce adverse effects that endanger the health and well-being of man.

5. Assisting in coordinating among the Federal departments and agencies those programs and activities that affect, protect, and improve environmental quality.

6. Assisting the Federal departments and agencies in the development and interrelationship of environmental quality and standards established through the Federal government.

7. Collecting, collating, analyzing, and interpreting data and information on environmental quality, ecological research, and evaluation.

Restating a point made in the discussion of NEPA, the EPA now handles the review of routine project EISs. Only when the EPA finds cause to rate a project as environmentally unsatisfactory is the CEQ (and thus the OEQ) called upon to arbitrate between the EPA and the sponsoring Federal agency. This change, which was part of Executive Order 11991, May 24, 1977, slightly modifies point 2 above. No longer does the CEQ have to appraise every proposed action which may affect environmental quality, but only those referred on by the EPA.

Federal Aid Highway Act (FAHA) of 1970
(23 USC 109)

Clearly this amended highway law is one of the most significant in terms of redirecting the project development process as it relates to environmental quality and urban transportation. The 1962 version of the FAHA introduced the concept of the "3-C" process—comprehensive, continuing, and cooperative, as discussed earlier in the chapter—providing the basis for *impact* evaluation.

Bridging the period between the passage of the landmark 1962 and 1970 versions of the FAHA was the 1966 Department of Transportation Act, which created the U.S. Department of Transportation (DOT). Seven functional organizations comprise the DOT.

1. Federal Highway Administration (FHWA)
2. Federal Aviation Administration (FAA)
3. Federal Railroad Administration (FRA)
4. Urban Mass Transportation Administration (UMTA)
5. National Highway Traffic Safety Administration (NHTSA)
6. St. Lawrence Seaway Development Corporation
7. United States Coast Guard (USCG)

A major feature of the 1966 DOT Act is Section 4(f), which states (as amended by the 1968 FAHA)

the Secretary [of DOT] shall not approve any program or project which requires the use of any publicly owned land from a public park, recreation area, or wildlife or waterfowl refuge of national, state, or local significance as determined by the Federal, state, or local officials having jurisdiction thereof, or any land from an historic site of national, state, or local significance as such determined by such officials unless (1) there is no feasible or prudent alternative to the use of such land, and (2) such program includes all possible planning to minimize harm to such park, recreation area, wildlife and waterfowl refuge, or historic site resulting from such use.

Approval of a Section 4(f) documentation report requires cooperation with Federal and local agencies, usually the U.S. Department of the Interior. This coordination requirement has been the cause of many delays in highway projects. The entire subject of Section 4(f) documentation is discussed in more detail in Chapter 3 as part of the analyses of FHPM 7-7-2, *Environmental Impact and Related Statements.*

Returning to the discussion of the FAHA of 1970, this piece of legislation formalizes the mandate to the FHWA concerning environmental analysis and criteria. The act required that

not later than July 1, 1972, the Secretary [of Dot], after consultation with appropriate Federal and state officials, shall submit to

Congress, and not later than 90 days after such submission, promulgate guidelines designed to assure that possible adverse economic, social and environmental effects relating to any proposed project on any Federal-Aid system have been fully considered in developing such project, and that the final decisions on the project are made in the best overall public interest, taking into consideration the need for fast, safe and efficient transportation, public services, and the costs of eliminating or minimizing such adverse effects as the following:

1. *Air, noise and water pollution*
2. *Destruction or disruption of synthetic or natural resources, esthetic values, community cohesion, and availability of public facilities and services*
3. *Adverse employment effects, and tax and property value losses*
4. *Injurious displacement of people, businesses, and farms*
5. *Disruption of desirable community and regional growth*

Thus, this act called for the adoption of guidelines and criteria for the evaluation of air, noise, and water pollution impacts from highway projects. This mandate obviously intended for these guidelines and criteria to be *quantitative* in nature, which was the FHWA interpretation. It may therefore be stated that the act was *technology-forcing*, because in 1970 there were no standardized techniques for estimating air, noise, and water pollution impacts from highways, nor were there any widely accepted evaluation criteria.

Working under the short time duration allowed by the act, the FHWA was able to develop regulations for noise and air quality analysis. The noise regulation, FHPM 7-7-3, includes quantitative design goals developed through consultation with other government agencies and the professional community, while the air quality guidelines, FHPM 7-7-9, rely on the EPA's National Ambient Air Quality Standards (NAAQS). No specific regulation was developed for water quality analysis because there were already several laws and regulations requiring permits from other Federal agencies, such as the U.S. Army Corps of Engineers and the U.S. Coast Guard, which were adequate to cause wa-

ter quality analysis and impact evaluation. These laws and regulations, as well as FHPM 7-7-3 and FPHM 7-7-9, are discussed later in this chapter and in Chapter 3.

Even with the standards and criteria in place for quantitatively evaluating noise and air quality impacts from highways, there existed no reliable and validated prediction methodologies for estimating these impacts. Accordingly, the following 10 years witnessed furious activity in model development, both in noise and air quality. As a result of many evolutions and refinements, brought upon by the investment of tremendous amounts of research and development funds, models now exist that are thought to perform with adequate stability and accuracy under proper conditions. Chapters 5 and 6 fully describe and give examples for application for the latest prediction models in noise and air quality, respectively.

The act also required that in the certification of highway projects,

such certification shall be accompanied by a report indicating the consideration given to the economic, social, environmental, and other effects of the plan or highway location or design and various alternatives which were raised during the hearing or were otherwise considered

The hearing referred to in this section is the required public hearing which is part of the citizen's and public participation process.

The report called for is the EIS that NEPA requires for any major Federal action which may affect environmental quality. The FAHA of 1970 simply requires that the EIS be part of the highway project approval process and that it document public hearing activities.

Because the EIS is now part of the approval process, it should be obvious that projects cannot be implemented without sucessfully completing the environmental studies. This concept is formalized in the act, which forbids the Secretary of Transportation from approving any project that does not comply with the guidelines developed for air, noise and water pollution. This is most important for noise impact guidelines. If a project violates the NAAQS, it will violate the State Implementation Plan (SIP) for air quality and will not be approved by the EPA under the Clean Air Act. Similarly, if the project does not meet the Corps of Engineers or Coast Guard requirements it will not receive the necessary permits to proceed. In other words, for the cases of air and water quality, outside agencies (other than the FHWA) will doom the project. But for noise impacts, only FHWA guidelines must be met.

Airport and Airway Development Act of 1970 (49 USC 1301)

This piece of legislation represents a fundamental revision of the landmark Federal Aviation Act of 1958. Several major programs and policies were implemented which have altered the course of aviation services delivery in this country. The policy statement in the 1970 act acknowledged that the nation's airport and airway system was inadequate to meet current and projected growth and that substantial improvement and expansion were required. The act spelled out the procedures and funding mechanisms to be used in providing improvement and expansion. As will become evident in this discussion, these procedures are totally consistent with the other environment-oriented laws related to transportation which were enacted during the period.

A major program implemented by the act was the formulation of a national airport system plan for the development of public airports. The development was generally to be in the form of improvements and expansion projects funded by grant agreement with the individual airport operator. The funds were to be (and are) allocated on a matching basis, with the Federal government supplying a majority of the funds. No project could be considered for funding under this program [the Airport Development Aid Program (ADAP)] unless it is included in the current revision of the national airport system plan formulated by the FAA. Thus it is incumbent upon airport operators to seek inclusion of their projects in the national plan.

In developing and revising the national airport system plan, the FAA is required to

> *consult with and consider the views and recommendations of the Secretary of the Interior, the Secretary of Health, Education and Welfare, the Secretary of Agriculture, and the National Council on Environmental Quality. The recommendations . . . with regard to the*

> *preservation of environmental quality shall, to the extent that the Secretary of Transportation determines to be feasible, be incorporated in the national airport system plan.*

The criteria that the Secretary of Transportation usually uses to determine this feasibility is related to the 1958 Federal Aviation Act. That is, any aviation activity in the Federal domain must not (*a*) interfere with interstate commerce, or (*b*) discriminate. These two provisions are often used by the FAA, in particular regarding safety issues, to reject recommendations by such agencies as the EPA.

The 1970 act goes on to state that no ADAP project will be funded unless fair consideration has been given to the interests of the communities in or near the project location. Specifically, the sponsoring public agency, that is, the airport operator, must certify that it has offered the opportunities for public hearings which are to consider the economic, social, and *environmental* effects of the airport location and "its consistency with the goals and objectives of such urban planning as has been carried out by the community." In other words, the projects should be rooted in the overall metropolitan transportation planning activities carried on by the community.

Section 16 of Title II, dealing specifically with airport development aid program, ADAP, states

> *it is declared to be national policy that airport development projects authorized persuant to this part shall provide for the protection and enhancement of the national resources and the quality of the environment of the Nation. In implementing this policy, the Secretary [of Transportation] shall consult with the Secretaries of the Interior and of Health, Education and Welfare with regard to the effect that any project involving airport location, a major runway extension, or runway location may have on national resources including, but not limited to, fish and wildlife, natural scenic and recreation assets, water and air quality, and other factors affecting the environment, and shall authorize no such project found to have adverse effect unless the Secretary shall render a finding, in writing, following a full and complete review, which shall be a matter of public record, that no feasible and prudent*

alternative exists and that all possible steps have been taken to minimize such adverse effect.

Consultation is now required with the administrators of the EPA rather than the Secretary of Health, Education and Welfare (HEW). The EPA was not yet established in 1970, so HEW held responsibility over some environmental areas.

It should be noted that this section does not prohibit an environmentally adverse project but simply requires proof that no feasible and prudent alternative exists. This concept of "prudence" provides a convenient escape tool for the FAA. Using this, coupled with the noninterference-with-interstate-commerce (and therefore safety) requirement from the Federal Aviation Act of 1958, the FAA can often forge projects ahead. Take, for example, the hypothetical case of a runway extension that would result in much lower approach altitudes (and correspondingly higher noise levels) in the vicinity of a residential development. It could be argued (successfully) by the airport operator and the FAA that anticipated growth in operations at the airport would be compromised unless the runway were lengthened. In that case, the noise problems, regardless of their severity, would be ignored as long as the airport operator promised to institute as many noise abatement operational procedures as possible.

This differs considerably from the Congressional mandate given the FHWA. According to the Federal Highway Act of 1970, all projects must comply with the guidelines required by the act to qualify for additional Federal funding. As will be demonstrated in Chapter 3 when FHPM 7-7-3 is discussed, the FHWA was able to circumvent this rigid guideline by providing for Design Noise Levels within this standard. It is permissible under the regulation as promulgated to receive an "exception" to the Design Noise Levels while still complying fully with the guidelines. It is unlikely that this "escape clause" was the intent of Congress when the 1970 highway act was passed. Such a mechanism, however, was clearly the intent of Congress in the Airport and Airway Development Act of 1970.

The reason behind the Congressional acquiescence on the issue of *airport* noise is evident when considering the Control and Abatement of Aircraft Noise and Sonic Boom Act of 1968,

which is discussed in the next section. This act has required a rather significant quieting of *aircraft*, or *source*, noise, which has greatly reduced aviation noise impacts. Thus it was the position of Congress that aviation noise was being adequately addressed and that airport development should not be unnecessarily hindered by noise considerations. By the end of the 1970s however, it became evident that additional source control was not feasible, so the FAA was mandated by the Secretary of Transportation in 1976 to initiate noise compatibility planning as part of the ADAP process. This entire issue will be discussed in the following section.

While Congress correctly anticipated a lessening of noise impacts resulting from the 1968 act, there was not a similar potential considered with respect to air and water quality impacts. Accordingly, the 1970 Airport and Airway Development Act specifically required that an ADAP project involving airport location, runway extension, or runway location *not* be approved unless

the Governor of the state in which such project may be located certifies in writing to the Secretary [of Transportation] that there is reasonable assurance that the project will be located, designed, constructed, and operated so as to comply with applicable air and water quality standards. In any case where such standards have not been approved or where such standards have been promulgated by the Secretary of the Interior or the Secretary of Health, Education and Welfare, certification shall be obtained from the appropriate Secretary. Notice of certification or refusal to certify shall be provided within sixty days after the project application is reviewed by the Secretary.

Further,

the secretary shall condition any such project application on compliance during construction and operation with applicable air and water quality standards.

The EPA now has jurisdiction over Federal air and water quality regulation.

It is interesting to note that there are no exceptions allowed under this provision. *All* applicable state and local (as well as Federal) air and water quality regulations and permit-granting procedures must be fully adhered to for the project to receive ADAP funding. In this case, the FAA cannot claim interference with interstate commerce, safety, or discrimination, and then override legally adopted standards.

NOISE-RELATED LEGISLATION

Housing and Urban Development Act of 1965 (PL 89-117)

This important piece of urban legislation contains one of the earliest statutory references at the Federal level to transportation noise. The Secretary of Housing and Urban Development (HUD) is directed to

determine feasible methods of reducing the economic loss and hardships of homeowners as a result of the depreciation in the value of their properties following the construction of airports in the vicinity of their homes, including a study of feasible methods of insulating homes from the noise of aircraft.

This mandate, coupled with a general provision in the Noise Control act of 1972 requiring Federal agencies to administer their programs in such a way as to reduce noise pollution, has been responsible for the development and distribution of a series of specific regulations applicable to not just aviation noise, but all areas of urban noise impact. The latest of these regulations is quite comprehensive in nature and basically states that applications from Community Development Block Grants and other HUD housing assistance (funding) may be jeopardized if the project is located in an area deemed "normally unacceptable" or simply "unacceptable." Criteria for determining acceptability are quite quantitative in nature and easily relate to all modes of transportation noise generation.

Whenever projects are proposed in the vicinity of highways or airports, the regulation requires noise assessments using accepted FHWA or FAA guidelines, respectively. More detail is provided concerning the HUD noise regulations in Chapter 4.

Control and Abatement of Aircraft Noise and Sonic Boom Act of 1968 (49 USC 1421-1430)

This is a major piece of legislation because it provides the statutory mandate for Part 36 of the Federal Aviation Regulations (FAR), which will be discussed in detail in Chapter 3. The enforcement mechanism for this law is rooted in the procedures for aircraft type certification required by the Federal Aviation Act of 1958. The certificate concerns the ability of the aircraft to meet FAA standards in safety and operational characteristics and must be obtained for each *type* or class of aircraft (DC-9, 727, etc.) before any of that class is allowed to carry passengers.

This 1968 act requires the administrator of the FAA to

prescribe and amend standards for the measurement of aircraft noise and sonic boom and prescribe and amend such rules and regulations as he may find necessary to provide for the control and abatement of aircraft noise and sonic boom, including the application of such standards, rules, and regulations in the issuance, amendment, modification, suspension or revocation of any certificate authorized by this title.

The first set of *Noise Standards: Aircraft Type and Airworthiness Certification* became effective as FAR Part 36, December 1, 1969. Any aircraft types certified after that date were required to meet the noise levels called for in the regulation. The result was that new aircraft, such as the 747, DC-10, and L1011, are significantly quieter than older jets like the 707, DC-8, and BAC-111.

The noise level requirements for aircraft type certified after November 5, 1975 are even more stringent than those certified before that date but after December 1, 1969. In fact, the FAA has determined that it is not feasible to reduce the noise level for new aircraft because of technology limitations. Accordingly, Congress has turned its attention to the retrofitting of the older aircraft, and has mandated that the entire fleet in operation meet the December 1, 1969 FAR Part 36 noise levels, regardless of certification date. Once again, a much more in-depth discussion of the FAR Part 36 measurement procedures and noise level certification requirements is presented in Chapter 3. A reading of the Chapter 5 sections dealing with aircraft noise theory and descriptors may be helpful prior to dealing with the FAR Part 36 material presented in Chapter 3.

Noise Control Act of 1972
(42 USC 4901)
as amended by
Quiet Communities Act of 1978
(PL 95-609)

This legislation created within the EPA an Office of Noise Abatement and Control (ONAC) with the mandate to identify major sources of noise; regulate those identified sources; propose aircraft noise standards to the FAA; label noisy products; engage in research, technical assistance, and dissemination of public information; and coordinate all Federal noise control activities. Several of these orders from Congress have had a direct impact on transportation noise, particularly at the source of the noise, the vehicle.

Section 5 of the act required the EPA to publish reports identifying major sources of noise in the environment, to provide noise control information on these sources, and to issue regulations covering those sources. As of mid-1979, the following sources had been identified

1. Wheel and crawler tractors
2. Truck-mounted solid waste compactors
3. Motorcycles and motorcycle replacement systems
4. Buses
5. Truck-mounted refrigerator units
6. Power lawn mowers
7. Pavement breakers and rock drills

In addition to these already formally identified, the EPA has been evaluating several other sources for possible identification. These include light-duty vehicles (automobiles and trucks), tires, chainsaws, and earth-moving equipment.

For those items identified as major sources of noise *and* distributed as products in interstate commerce, the EPA was required to determine the feasibility of noise emission standards. The act specifically stated that the following categories were to be studied: construction equipment; transportation equipment (including recreational vehicles and related equipment); motors and en-

gines; and electrical or electronic equipment. As a result, the EPA has published maximum emission level regulations for new portable air compressors, medium and heavy trucks, and several other products.

The act contained specific requirements for noise level regulations concerning highways (motor carriers), aircraft, and railroads. The motor carrier emission standard, which applies to trucks with a gross vehicle weight rating of more than 10,000 lbs. and used in interstate commerce, was issued in 1975. In addition to limiting noise levels, the regulation requires that mufflers be in good working order and bans "pocket" retread tires. Enforcement of this regulation is through the DOT, Bureau of Motor Carrier Safety (BMCS), or by state or local police in jurisdictions that have adopted identical regulations.

Because of the overriding issue of aircraft safety, the Noise Control Act of 1972 did not remove aircraft noise control responsibilities from the domain of the FAA. It did, however, require that the EPA complete a comprehensive report on the problems of aircraft and airport noise, and to *submit* regulatory proposals to the FAA. For each proposal not implemented by the FAA, the FAA had to publish detailed reasons for rejection. Through 1979, the FAA had adopted two relatively insignificant proposals out of nine received. In the 1978 Quiet Communities Act revision, the FAA was required to respond to EPA proposals within 90 days, rather than "in a reasonable time," in order to prevent FAA stalling tactics.

The development of railroad noise emission standards required by Section 17 of the 1972 act has proven to be a rather interesting and difficult challenge for the EPA. At the end of 1975, the EPA issued what it thought was a final regulation for locomotives and railcars operated by interstate rail carriers. Specifically excluded from that regulation was mention of railyard facilities and other additional equipment. After much study, it was the position of the EPA that

the health and welfare of the nation's population being jeopardized by railroad facility and equipment noise, other than locomotives and railcars, was best served by specific controls at the state and local level and not by Federal regulations, which would have to address rail-

road noise on a national and therefore on a more general basis. Where the Federal government establishes standards for railroad facilities and equipment, state and local noise control ordinances ordinarily are preempted unless they are identical to the Federal standards. For these reasons, we decided that it was best to leave state and local authorities free to address site-specific problems on a case-by-case basis, without unnecessary Federal hindrance. (45 FR 1252)

This seemingly noble gesture of calling for less Federal intervention was met with strong objection, however, from the Association of American Railroads (AAR). Court action was brought against the EPA by the AAR on the grounds that the regulation was not sufficiently comprehensive, and that the railroads were therefore not protected by Federal preemption from potentially conflicting state and local ordinances, as intended by the act. The litigation was successful, and the EPA was directed by the U.S. Court of Appeals in Washington, D.C. to significantly broaden its scope. This was an unusual case of a regulated industry calling for *more* Federal regulation than the government was initially willing to provide.

In response to the court order to provide a final source noise standard rule by January 23, 1980, the EPA issued the first of two additional regulations on January 4, 1980, to be effective January 15, 1984 (40 CFR 201). This directive provided maximum noise emission levels for four types of railroad noise sources: active retarders, switching locomotives, locomotive load cell test stands, and car coupling operations.

The second regulation required by the court order concerned property-line noise levels, which are in the form of time-averaged maximum sound level standards measured at the nearest property line of a property used for residential or commercial purposes. The regulation requires the application of "noise reduction technologies and techniques to all types of land-use classifications except undeveloped land." The term "land use" is not synonymous with zoning ordinances, but infers in-place activities.

Realizing that noise impact is primarily a localized problem and that the EPA was having a difficult time in providing an effective national noise control program, Congress enacted the Quiet Communities Act of 1978, which is simply a set of amendments to the Noise Control Act of 1972. The 1978 act authorized increased financial and other types of assistance to strengthen state and local noise control programs. The act also required the EPA to

administer a national Quiet Communities Program which shall include but not be limited to . . . developing abatement plans for areas around major transportation facilities (including airports, highways and railroads) and other major stationary sources of noise, and, where appropriate, for the facility or source itself.

These activities are to be carried out with the co-operation of other Federal agencies, particularly those having jurisdiction over the transportation modes. For example, the EPA is working with the FAA on noise abatement planning studies. As mentioned earlier, the FAA is becoming more involved with airport noise problems since the FAR Part 36 source noise reduction program was optimized. FAA efforts have included a pilot program entitled *Airport Noise Control and Land Use Compatibility* (ANCLUC) *Planning*, as part of its Planning Grant Program. Other EPA noise efforts under the 1978 act include a simple workbook procedure for predicting airport vicinity noise levels and an abatement planning guide for local citizen involvement.

Similar activities have been initiated for rail and highway noise planning assistance, although the FHWA has such a comprehensive and advanced noise program (mandated by the 1970 Federal Aid Highway Act) that the EPA efforts often become redundant. The EPA has, however, developed a useful highway noise level prediction model, which unlike the FWHA site-specific prediction model, yields regional and national assessment information.

AIR-QUALITY-RELATED LEGISLATION

The Clean Air Act of 1963 (42 USC 7401–7642) and Amendments

The earliest statutory activity at the Federal level began in 1955 with the passage of the Air Pollution Control Act. Congressional policy was determined *to preserve and protect the primary responsibilities and rights of state and local governments in controlling air pollution; to support and aid technical research to devise and develop methods of abating such pollution; and to provide Federal technical assistance and financial aid to state and local government air pollution control agencies and other public or private air pollution abatement programs.*

The Clean Air Act of 1963 began a shift toward more Federal involvement as HEW was authorized to develop air quality criteria for voluntary compliance. The act also gave HEW the power to intervene when a state government could not effectively handle a hazardous and dangerous air pollution problem. A funding mechanism in this act that provided grants-in-aid to states encouraged the development of state and regional air pollution control agencies as well as the enactment of state air pollution laws. However, because the criteria compliance was optional, the 1963 Clean Air Act was not in itself very effective in solving the worsening air pollution problems of the 1960s.

The act was amended for the first time in 1965, when HEW was authorized to develop and enforce motor vehicle emission standards with no input from state and local governments. In 1967, the act was again amended (under the title *Air Quality Act of 1967*) to require HEW to issue air quality criteria with compulsory compliance. The amendment also introduced the concept of the State Implementation Plan (SIP) which is the strategy states are to use in implementing Federally documented air pollution control techniques needed to *attain* the new criteria. Until this point primary responsibilities in enforcement still resided at the state and local levels.

A tremendously important set of amendments to the act was initiated in 1970. For all intents and purposes, the Clean Air Act Amendments of 1970 (see Appendix 2B) ushered in a new era, as the Federal government effectively took control of the air pollution problem from the state and local governments. The Reorganization Plan Number 3 from the Executive Office of the President created EPA, which, upon its implementation date of December 2, 1970, became the independent Federal agency charged with implementing the environmental laws of the nation. The 1970 Clean Air Act Amendments gave the EPA something significant to enforce in the area of air pollution.

As the remainder of this discussion is limited to transportation-related air quality considerations, two sections of the 1970 amendments are of particular importance: Section 110, dealing with implementation plans, and Section 202, dealing with the establishment of vehicular emission standards.

The 1967 amendments had required HEW to designate the air quality control regions (AQCR) within each state where air quality problems could exist. The 1970 amendments in effect designated the implementation plan (SIP) as the primary enforcement procedure for the attainment, maintenance, and enforcement of the National Ambient Air Quality Standards (NAAQS) within each AQCR. Preparation of the SIP by the state air pollution control agency was mandated by the 1970 amendments. Should a state fail to adopt an adequate SIP, the EPA was required to prepare one for it.

In responding to the legislative mandate to provide the NAAQS and guidance to the states, the EPA produced a detailed set of regulations on SIP preparation. These regulations are discussed in detail in Chapter 3. A basic principle in the EPA approach, however, is that each AQCR is classified separately for each pollutant having designated primary and secondary NAAQS. For those transportation-related pollutants—carbon monoxide, hydrocarbons, oxides of nitrogen, and photochemical oxidants—it was found that most AQCRs were in violation of the NAAQS. Since the 1970 amendments required that all the NAAQS be attained by May 31, 1975 it became necessary to develop control strategies and transportation control plans (TCPs).

A control strategy concerns controlling emissions from all sources, while, of course, a TCP deals only with transportation sources, which are "area sources." Transportation control strategies usually fall into two categories: measures to reduce emissions from individual vehicles, and measures to reduce vehicle use. Inspection and maintenance programs designed to insure that the proper functioning of pollution control devices is the primary mechanism to reduce individual vehicular emissions, while the following are used to reduce vehicle use: carpool programs; priority systems for carpools and buses; vehicle-free zones; vehicle-use prohibitions; gasoline supply limitations; parking programs; parking fee increases; bridge toll increases; transit improvement programs; bicycle lanes; and employer transit incentive programs.

Section 202 of the 1970 amendments, by the establishment of vehicular emissions standards, also has had a major impact on transportation. This section mandated standards for certain vehicle classes and engines which would achieve a 90-percent reduction in carbon monoxide and hydrocarbon emissions for the 1975 models, as compared to the 1970 models. For oxides of nitrogen, the 90-percent reduction was for the 1976 models over the 1971 models. Included in the legislation was the authority for the EPA to delay attainment for one year, which it did. In addition, the 1974 Energy Supply and Environmental Coordination Act suspended the 90-percent requirement for another year, as did a 1975 administrative order.

The period between the enactment of the 1970 Clean Air Act Amendments and the next major revision, in 1977, was quite tumultuous in the United States, particularly in the interrelationships between transportation, energy, and environment. The environmental movement gave way to the crises surrounding energy availability and cost. Questions concerning the proper role of government, especially at the Federal level, persisted, as did questions regarding the impact of environmental pollution control on the health of the national economy.

Consequently, even though the NAAQS attainment date had been pushed back to 1977 from 1975, it appeared that many areas were going to be unable to achieve attainment. This, and the other factors just discussed, plus several major court decisions, provided the motivation for Congress to enact a major and fundamental revision, the Clean Air Act Amendments of 1977.

The 1977 amendments called for the attainment of standards for carbon monoxide (CO) and other oxidants by July 1982. For those areas which were unable to do so, extension could be granted up to July 1987, although at a cost. To meet the new deadlines, the amendments also mandated formal revisions of the SIPs and the SIP preparation process.

Under the 1970 amendments, SIP preparation was strictly the responsibility of the *state* air pollution control agency, and, with respect to transportation, the plan relied primarily on the implementation of automobile emission standards (as discussed earlier). The 1977 amendments, however, required in Section 174 that for each AQCR a lead regional agency be designated to plan and implement the transportation portion (TCP) of the SIP. The intent was that the TCP be prepared by an organization of elected officials of local governments that would also be responsible for transportation planning and air quality maintenance planning for the region.

This designated lead agency is required to document existing responsibilities for transportation and air quality and to define and maintain the interrelationships between the agencies and programs involved in the TCP process. The lead agency must also insure the continued involvement of local elected officials by providing them with information and securing commitments of support.

Section 121 of the amendments required that TCPs and transportation-related air quality activities be integrated into ongoing planning functions, most likely through coordination with the related agencies. [The lead agency would have to be familiar with the Urban Transportation Planning and Transportation Improvement Program activities, as defined by the FHWA, and would therefore quite likely be the Metropolitan Planning Organization (MPO)]. This coordination and intergovernment relation create a continuous planning and consultation process for NAAQS attainment and maintenance through transportation planning in a manner similar to the "3-C" process mandated by the FAHA of 1962.

This continuous planning and consultation process required by Section 121 must involve, when appropriate, relevant state agencies (air pollution control, transportation, energy, community planning, and solid waste management); elected officials of local governments; Federal land managers, where Federal lands are affected; affected local and regional agencies; and public interest organizations with a major interest in the program.

As mentioned above, the 1977 amendments required that the SIP be revised for the attainment of the standards by 1982 or 1987. The procedure for the revision is the following (see Figure 2-1).

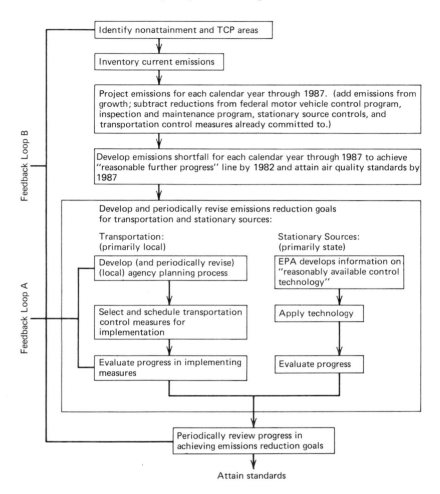

There are two "feedback loops." Loop A recognizes that implementation of transportation control measures will be highly dependent on the planning process developed by the lead agency. This planning process is depended on to develop public and political acceptance of the measures. The process should be continually evaluated and revised in light of the success of implementing the measures. Loop B emphasizes that the SIP must be periodically evaluated and revised in light of its success in maintaining reasonable further progress toward 1987 attainment. If progress for any year falls below the level required, the SIP must be strengthened to compensate for this shortcoming.

Figure 2-1.   Flow chart for SIP revision to meet oxidant and carbon monoxide standards by 1987. (Source: *County News*, June 19, 1978, "Report of NACOR's Air Quality Project")

1. Identification of nonattainment areas and areas subject to transportation control measures.

2. Current emissions must be inventoried to determine the extent to which they exceed the standards.

3. Population growth and other emissions-producing growth must be projected, and added to current emissions.

4. The amount that the standards will be exceeded by 1982 or 1987 may then be reduced by reductions resulting from new car emission factors.

5. For those NAAQS not met by 1982 or

1987, whichever date is selected, a package of control measures must be implemented.

(Taken together, items 3 and 4 are the *offset policy*; that is, emissions must be reduced to the level of the standards not only in view of current emissions but also in view of projected growth. Emissions growth is offset by emissions reductions.)

For those nonattainment areas unable to make the 1982 deadline, Section 108 of the amendments required that each of 18 specified *reasonably available control measures* (RACM) be analyzed to determine its feasibility and contribution to emissions reduction. The evaluation process requires a balancing of costs and benefits, and considers the following.

Impact on air quality

Positive and negative effects, besides air, on the environment

Energy consumption

Effects on employment, business activities, land-use patterns, regional and urban development, and other community goals

Ability to obtain funding

Capital and operating costs

Specific impacts on the local economy, by sector (public or private), income group, geographic area, and social group

Travel impacts, mainly in terms of convenience and service to communities and other travelers

Public acceptance (political feasibility)

Institutional feasibility, in terms of the existing or easily created agencies to carry out the measures

Other important local community values

The 18 measures to be evaluated under Section 108 are listed below. For each one the EPA was required by the amendments to provide informational documents on its air quality effectiveness on transportation systems and sources, and its environmental, energy, and economic impacts.

Reasonably Available Control Measures (RACM) Listed in the 1977 Amendments to the Clean Air Act

1. Programs for motor vehicle emission inspection and maintenance, I/M (I/M program required if extension to 1987 is granted).

2. Programs to control vapor emissions from fuel transfer and storage operations using solvents.

3. Programs for improved public transportation.

4. Programs to establish exclusive bus and carpool lanes and area-wide carpool programs.

5. Programs to limit portions of road surfaces or certain sections of the metropolitan areas to the use of common carriers, both as to time and place.

6. Programs to reduce emissions by improvements involving new transportation policies and transportation facilities or major changes in existing facilities.

7. Programs to control on-street parking.

8. Programs to construct new parking facilities for the purpose of park-and-ride lots and fringe parking.

9. Programs to limit portions of road surfaces or certain sections of the metropolitan area to the use of nonmotorized vehicles or pedestrian use, both as to time and place.

10. Provisions for employer participation in programs to encourage carpooling, vanpooling, mass transit, bicycling, and walking.

11. Programs for secure bicycle storage facilities and other facilities, including bicycle lanes, for the convenience and protection of bicyclists, in both public and private areas.

12. Programs of staggered hours of work.

13. Programs to institute road user charges, tolls, or differential rates to discourage single-occupancy automobile trips.

14. Programs to control extended idling of vehicles.

15. Programs to reduce emissions by improving traffic flow.

16. Programs for the conversion of fleet vehicles to cleaner engines or fuels, or to otherwise control fleet vehicle operations.

17. Programs to retrofit emission devices or controls on vehicles and engines other than light-duty vehicles.

18. Programs to reduce motor vehicle emissions which are caused by extreme cold start conditions.

The 1977 amendments to the Clean Air Act authorized the appropriation of $75 million for implementation. These funds were to cover 100 percent of the additional costs of developing the SIP revisions in each nonattainment area. Quite significantly, these funds were set aside specifically for use by regional and local government agencies. As mentioned above, previous amendments to the Clean Air Act funded activities by the *state* air pollution control agencies. Thus, the 1977 amendments clearly altered the direction and philosophies of air quality management as it relates to the transportation domain.

WATER-QUALITY–RELATED LEGISLATION

The Rivers and Harbors Act of 1899 (33 USC 401–403) as Amended

While actually predating the Federal highway program in the United States, this piece of legislation often has a major impact on the ability of a state highway agency and the FWHA to get a highway project implemented. This is because of the permission required from the U.S. Coast Guard and the U.S. Corps of Engineers when dealing with navigable rivers.

Section 9 (33 USC 401) states that

it shall not be lawful to construct or commence the construction of any bridge, dam, dike, or causeway over or in any port, roadstead, haven, harbor, canal, navigable river, or other navigable water of the United States until the consent of Congress to the building of such structures shall have been obtained and until the plans for the same shall have been submitted to and approved by the Chief of Engineers and by the Secretary of the Army: Provided, that such structure may be built under the authority of the legislature of a State across rivers and other waterways the navigable portions of which lie wholly within the limits of a single state, provided the location and plans thereof are submitted to and approved by the Chief of Engineers and by the Secretary of the Army, before construction is commenced: And provided further, that when plans for any bridge or other structure have been approved by the Chief of Engineers and by the Secretary of the Army, it shall not be lawful to deviate from these plans

either before or after completion of the structure unless the modification of said plans has previously been submitted to and received the approval of the Chief of Engineers and the Secretary of the Army.

When the Department of Transportation Act of 1966 (PL89-690) was implemented, this section of the Rivers and Harbors Act was modified significantly. All of the functions, powers, and duties vested in the Chief of Engineers and the Secretary of the Army related to the location of bridges and causeways in and over navigable waters were turned over to the U.S. Coast Guard, which is an agency of the DOT. Thus, when a state highway project has a project which interfaces (bridges) in any way with a navigable water in the United States, it must obtain a permit from the Coast Guard prior to construction. As a result of this section, the Coast Guard has developed a set of regulations to be followed in applying for the permit, so that potential harm to the navigable water is minimized. These regulations are discussed in detail in Chapter 4.

Section 10 of the Rivers and Harbors Act of 1899 (33 USC 403) concerns not the spanning or bridging of navigable waters, but the construction activities thay may take place within them.

The creation of any obstruction not affirmatively authorized by Congress to the navigable capacity of any water of the United States is prohibited; and it shall not be lawful to build or commence the building of any wharf, pier, dolphin, boom, weir, breakwater, bulkhead, jetty, or other structures in any port, roadstead, haven, harbor, canal, navigable river, or other water of the United States, outside established harbor lines, or where no harbor lines have been established, except on plans recommended by the Chief of Engineers and authorized by the Secretary of the Army; and it shall not be lawful to excavate or fill, or in any manner to alter or modify the course, location, condition, or capacity of any port, roadstead, haven, harbor, canal, lake, or refuge, or inclosure within the limits of any breakwater or of the channel of any navigable water of the United States, unless the work has been recommended by the Chief of Engineers and authorized by the Secretary of the Army prior to beginning the same.

This section represents the origin of the permit program for dredging and filling in navigable waters that have been mandated by Congress for the U.S. Army Corps of Engineers. While this section is focused primarily upon the maintenance and enhancement of navigation, the Section 404 permit required by the Clean Water Act (as amended) involves evaluation of impacts upon fish and wildlife, conservation, pollution, aesthetics, ecology, and other public interest parameters.

The Rivers and Harbors Act of 1899, in summary, *does* have a significant effect upon the transportation delivery system, in particular highways. Without the formal approval of the U.S. Coast Guard (for bridges) and/or the U.S. Corps of Engineers (for dredging and filling) it is not possible to construct a bridge that spans a navigable water or requires any rechannelization of that water.

The Clean Water Act Amendments of 1977 (33 USC 446 et seq.)

Originally enacted in 1948 as the Federal Water Pollution Control Act, the law was significantly amended in 1972 to greatly strengthen its provisions. This was consistent with the other pieces of environmental legislation adopted during the 1969 to 1972 period that gave the Federal government an increased role in enhancing environmental quality. The 1977 amendments, on the other hand, contained provisions which gave the states more jurisdiction than they previously held in certain programs, such as the Section 404 program.

While the Clean Water Act of 1977 (CWA77) is significant in improving water quality, two sections, more than any others, have considerable impact upon transportation. These are the Section 401 program dealing with *discharges* into navigable waters and the Section 404 program dealing with *dredging* and *filling* in navigable waters.

Although not as important as Section 404, Section 401 activities often become critical to the successful implementation of a transportation construction project. The section is aimed primarily at point sources and industrial applications, but may also include construction sites.

Any applicant for a Federal license or permit to conduct any activity including, but not limited to, the construction or operation of facilities which may result in any discharge into the navigable waters, shall provide the licensing or permitting agency a certification from the State in which the discharge originates or will originate or, if appropriate, for the interstate water pollution control agency having jurisdiction over the navigable waters at the point where the discharge originates, or will originate, that any discharge will comply with the applicable provisions of Sections 301, 302, 303, 306, and 307.

(Sections 301, 302, 303, 306, and 307 concern effluent limitations, water quality standards and implementation plans, national standards of performance, and toxic and pretreatment effluent standards.)

This section, then, would require that the state highway agency receive a certificate from the state water pollution control agency verifying that a proposed project or its construction will not violate any of the effluent standards and limitations or implementation plans currently in force. When a project is involved with a navigable water, this certification process can delay the project for up to one year after submission of the application, or even kill it.

Up until the 1977 CWA amendments, the U.S. Army Corps of Engineers had the exclusive authority to "issue permits, after notice and opportunity for public hearings, for the discharge of dredged or fill material into the navigable water at specified disposal sites." Also the EPA was vested with the authority to prohibit or restrict the specification of any area as a disposal site if it determines, that,

after notice and opportunity for public hearings, that the discharge of such materials into such area will have an unacceptable adverse effect on municipal water supplies, shellfish beds and fishery areas (including spawning and feeding areas), wildlife or recreational areas.

While the EPA still has this authority, the Corps of Engineers no longer holds exclusive authority over the permit program. Now involved in the program are the EPA (in a more direct role than before), the Department of the Interior's Fish and Wildlife Service (FWS), and the governments of the states.

The amendments allow the Corps of Engineers to issue general permits on a national, state, or regional basis, after public hearings, for any category of activities concerning the discharge of dredged or fill materials if it determines that the activities in the category will have only minimal adverse environmental effects, cumulatively. This permits the Corps to reduce the number of reviews of insignificant projects it has taken on in the past.

However, the CWA77 gave the states the option of administering their own dredge and fill programs, under certain conditions.

The Governor of any state desiring to administer its own individual and general permit program for the discharge of dredged or fill material into the navigable waters, within its jurisdiction may submit to the Administrator [of the EPA] a full and complete description of the program it proposes to establish and administer under State law or under interstate compact. In addition, such State shall submit a statement from the attorney general (or the attorney for the State agencies which have independent legal counsel), or from the chief legal officer in the case of an interstate agency, that the laws of such State, or the interstate compact, as the case may be, provide adequate authority to carry out the described program.

The amendments then require the EPA to solicit comments on the state's proposed program from the Corps and from the Department of the Interior (DOI) FWS. Within 120 days from receiving the proposed program from the state, the EPA is required, taking into account Corps and FWS comments, to determine whether the state has the authority to issue permits.

The responsibility to make sure that the state permit program is functioning properly and legally is clearly given to the EPA by the CWA77. Very detailed oversight guidance is given, which basically directs the EPA to turn the program back over to the Corps, should the state violate its agreement with the EPA. One area specifically mentioned in the amendments is for the state "to assume continued coordination with Federal-State water-related planning and review processes." Additional details on this coordination are included later in this section, and in other,

earlier Federal statutes (i.e., Fish and Wildlife Coordination Act, Endangered Species Act, and Wild and Scenic Rivers Act, which are discussed later in this chapter, and NEPA).

With respect to the Federal coordination requirements, the state must submit a copy of each permit application received to the EPA, which in turn must provide copies to the Corps and the FWS. In any written comments concerning the permit application, the EPA must take into consideration Corps and FWS comments. Whenever the EPA submits an objection to the granting of the permit by the state, it must conduct a public hearing, if the state so requires. However, if the state does not resubmit a revised permit or request a public hearing within a specified time, the decision reverts back to the Corps of Engineers. The amendments indicate that

if the state does not resubmit such permit revised to objection within 30 days after completion of the hearing or, if no hearing is requested within 90 days after the date of such objection, the Secretary [i.e., the Corps of Engineers] may issue the permit . . . for such source in accordance with the guidelines and requirements of this Act.

It would take, however, an unusual set of circumstances for the Corps to overrule serious objections by the EPA and FWS on a specific project.* This has been borne out in several instances of highway projects. Specific examples include sections of the Southern Tier Expressway in western New York State. While permission was finally granted to construct various portions of the projects, considerable discussion between the New York State Department of Transportation, the FWS, the EPA, and the New York State Department of Environmental Conservation was necessary before an acceptable plan of study and mitigation could be developed. Between the coordination requirement of the CWA77 and those in the Fish and Wildlife Coordination Act (discussed later in this chapter), the FWS is given substantial influence over highway construction in areas within its purview.

*Memorandums of Agreement between the Corps and other federal agencies cover this contingency (see the September 19, 1980 Federal Register PSS 62761–62771 for texts of the current agreements).

Safe Drinking Water Act
(42 USC 300A et seq.) as Amended

This relatively obscure law, which is part of Title 42 (Public Health and Welfare) of the United States Code, can, under certain circumstances, have a definite impact on the delivery of a transportation system. If a project, for example, is in the vicinity of a *sole source aquifer* (i.e., the principal supply of drinking water to a community), it must not inject contaminants into the aquifer which would exceed EPA maximum contaminant levels.

Each Federal agency having jurisdiction over any Federally owned or maintained public water system shall comply with all national primary drinking water regulations in effect . . . and each Federal agency shall comply with any applicable underground injection program, and shall keep such records and submit such reports as may be required under such program.

When a sole source aquifer is involved, Federal participation (funding) will not be allowed unless the maximum contaminant levels are met.

ECOLOGY-RELATED LEGISLATION

Fish and Wildlife Coordination Act
(16 USC 661–666)

This legislation, enacted in 1958, gives the FWS of the DOI considerable influence in cases where transportation projects may affect streams or wildlife habitats.

whenever the waters of any stream or other body of water are proposed or authorized to be impounded, diverted, the channel deepened, or the stream or other body of water otherwise controlled or modified for any purpose whatsoever, including navigation and drainage, by any department or agency of the United States, or by any public or private agency under Federal permit or license first shall consult with the United States Fish and Wildlife Service, Department of the Interior, and with the head of the Agency exercising administration over the wildlife resources of the particular State wherein the impound-

ment, diversion, or other control facility is to be constructed, with a view to the conservation of wildlife resources by preventing loss of and damage to such resources as well as providing for the development and improvement thereof in connection with such water resource development.

The important item to note concerning this law, unlike the Rivers and Harbors and Clean Water Acts, is that it is applicable to all streams and waters, and not just those which are navigable (although the Clean Water Act defines "navigable waters" as simply "the waters of the United States"). The emphasis on conservation of wildlife resources mandates a more thorough examination of habitat in the vicinity of a stream, which could be a wetland or a floodplain.

The consultation required with the FWS in the act, while not delegating veto power to the FWS, is intended to produce very specific recommendations from the FWS concerning wildlife conservation and development, and mitigating* or compensating measures designed to offset impacts on fish and wildlife. It should be easily seen that this requirement places considerable power into the hands of the FWS. Because it has a mandate to protect fish and wildlife, the FWS is legally justified in asking that the sponsoring agency conduct extensive environmental studies and/or incorporate extensive mitigation measures into project design (including the purchase of replacement lands) before FWS approval is granted. This is basically what happened on the Southern Tier Expressway projects mentioned earlier with respect to the Clean Water Act coordination requirements.

The Endangered Species Act of 1973
(16 USC 1533 et seq.)

The DOI was directed in this act to produce dynamic lists of endangered or threatened species of fish, wildlife, or plants. The criteria for inclusion on the lists, as set by Congress, were

1. the present or threatened destruction, modification, or curtailment of its habitat or range

*See the September 9, 1980 Federal Register for a copy of the current FWS statement on Mitigation Policy.

2. overutilization for commercial, sporting, scientific, or educational purposes

3. disease or predation

4. the inadequacy of existing regulatory mechanisms

5. other natural or man-made factors affecting its continued existence

The act stated that anyone could nominate a species for addition to the list, and that the DOI would have to conduct a review of the nomination, provided the nominator supplied substantial evidence to back up the nomination.

The DOI was further directed in the act to issue regulations for the conservation of the listed species, and was given the authority to prohibit by regulation any activity (Federal) jeopardizing them.

The Wild and Scenic Rivers Act of 1968 (16 USC 1271–1281)

Congress in this act authorized the DOI to protect certain rivers through a program of selective purchasing of adjacent properties to discourage development. It is the declared policy of Congress that the rivers, because of their outstanding scenic, recreational, geologic, fish and wildlife, historic, cultural, or other values, must be preserved in *free-flowing condition*. Further,

> the established national policy of dam and other construction at appropriate sections of the rivers of the United States needs to be complemented by a policy that would preserve the other selected rivers or sections thereof in their free-flowing condition to protect the water quality of such rivers and to fulfill other vital national conservation purposes.

A wild river area is a river free of impoundments and generally accessible only by trail, with primitive watersheds and shorelines and unpolluted water. Scenic rivers are similar except they may be accessible in places by roads. An interesting feature of this law is that rivers are designated by amendment to the law itself. In other words, it takes an act of Congress for a river to be placed on this system.

The act requires that

> each component of the national wild and scenic rivers systems shall be administered in such manner as to protect and enhance the values which caused it to be included in said system without, insofar as is consistent therewith, limiting other uses that do not substantially interfere with public use and enjoyment of these values. In such administration primary emphasis shall be given to protecting its esthetic, scenic, historic, archeologic, and scientific features.

Quite logically, the construction of a transportation system, particularly a highway, would not serve to protect and enhance a wild or scenic river. In most cases, it would work to the detriment of those values which caused the river to be included in the system originally. It would, therefore, be quite difficult for the highway agency to receive DOI approval for a project that would bridge or otherwise impact a river on the national system.

Protection of Wetlands
Executive Order 11990

During the Congressional debates concerning amendments to the Federal Water Pollution Control Act and subsequent development of the Clean Water Act of 1977 the issue of wetlands protection received much attention. As a result, the President's CEQ determined, in agreement with the Congress, that specific Federal direction was needed. It was further determined that the statutory authority necessary was already in place in the National Environmental Policy Act (NEPA) of 1969. Consequently, on May 24, 1977, President Carter issued Executive Order 11990, *Protection of Wetlands*.

The order defines wetlands as

> those areas that are inundated by ground or surface water with a frequency sufficient to support, and under normal circumstances does or would support, a prevalence of vegetative or aquatic life that requires saturated or seasonably saturated soil conditions for growth and reproduction. Wetlands usually include swamps, marshes, bogs, and similar areas such as sloughs, potholes, wet meadows, river overflows, mud flats, and natural ponds.

Deriving its authority from NEPA, the order requires that an integrated, public-oriented process be developed and that the Federal agencies "take action to minimize destruction, loss, or degradation of wetlands, and to preserve and enhance the natural and beneficial values of wetlands" when, among other things, providing Federally financed construction. Accordingly, all the modes of transportation, in nearly every case, would have to consider wetlands where appropriate because

> *each [Federal] agency, to the extent permitted by law, shall avoid undertaking or providing assistance for new construction located in wetlands unless the head of the agency finds (1) that there is no practical alternative to such construction, and (2) that the proposed action includes all practical measures to minimize harm to wetlands which may result from such use. In making this finding the head of the agency may take into account economic, environmental, and other pertinent factors.*

Federal agencies are directed by the order to revise their procedures (and accordingly promulgate regulations) to insure compliance. Evaluation factors to be used in the revised procedures include public health, safety, and welfare; water supply, quality, recharge, and discharge; maintenance of natural systems, including conservation and long-term productivity of existing flora and fauna, species and habitat diversity and stability, hydrologic utility, fish, wildlife, timber, food and fiber resources; recreational, cultural, and scientific uses; and other uses of the wetlands in public interest.

In response to this mandate, the Federal modal transportation agencies have issued appropriate regulations. Chapter 3 includes discussion of the FHWA guidelines concerning wetlands intrusion.

National Flood Insurance Act of 1968
(42 USC 4001 et seq.)

The purpose of this law is to restrict development of land within floodplains, thereby minimizing flood losses. The Department of Housing and Urban Development (HUD) was authorized to consider regulations concerning encroachment and obstruction of stream channels and floodways; orderly use and development of floodplains; building codes; subdivisions; and other building restrictions. In addition, the state and local governments of the nation were encouraged to modify land-use statutes to restrict floodplain development.

Obviously, this would affect transportation development where floodplains are concerned. Taken in conjunction with another directive, however, the Federal modal transportation agencies have specific instructions. On the same day President Carter issued the Wetlands Executive Order, May 24, 1977, he also issued Executive Order 11988, *Floodplain Management.* This mandate required the integrated approach to managing floodplain encroachments and to prevent uneconomic, hazardous, or incompatible floodplain use. The Federal agencies were directed to produce revised procedures for project development which were to include floodplain management, in a way analogous to the revised procedures required for wetlands protection. In response, the DOT issued an order to its modal agencies on April 26, 1979, DOT Order 5650.2, to insure compliance. This directive, as well as the corresponding FWHA regulation, FHPM 6-7-3-2, is discussed in Chapter 3.

Coastal Zone Management Act Amendments
of 1976
(33 USC 1451–1464)

Because Congress became concerned over the well-being of the coastal zones of the nation, it passed in 1972, and amended in 1976, this rather strong piece of legislation. The purpose is to encourage state, regional, and/or local government agencies to develop Coastal Zones Management (CZM) programs.

(As a point of information, coastal zones include the shorelines of the coastal and Great Lakes states, islands, transitional and intertidal areas, wetlands, salt marshes, beaches, bays, sounds, lagoons, bayous, estuaries, roadsteads, and harbors. These coastal zone waters must contain a measurable quantity or percentage of seawater. The zone extends inland only to the extent necessary to control shore lands whose uses have a significant and direct impact on the coastal waters.)

The act authorizes the U.S. Department of Commerce to fund 80 percent of the cost of a coastal state which develops a CZM program, so long as the program contains

1.   An identification of the boundaries of the

coastal zone subject to the management program.

2. A definition of what shall constitute permissible land and water uses within the coastal zone which have a direct and significant effect on the coastal waters.

3. An inventory and designation of areas of particular concern within the coastal zone.

4. An identification of the means by which the state proposes to exert control over the land and water uses referred to in item 2, including a list of relevant constitutional provisions, laws, regulations, and judicial decisions.

5. Broad guidelines on priorities of uses in particular areas, including specifically these uses of lowest quality.

6. A description of the organizational structure proposed to implement such management program, including the responsibilities and interrelationships of local, area-wide, state, regional, and interstate agencies in the management process.

7. A definition of the term "beach" and a planning process for the protection of and access to public beaches and other coastal areas of environmental, recreational, historical, aesthetic, ecological, or cultural value.

8. A planning process for energy facilities likely to be located in, or which may significantly effect the coastal zone, including, but not limited to, a process for anticipating and managing the impacts from such facilities.

9. A planning process for (a) assessing the effects of shoreline erosion (however caused), and (b) studying and evaluating ways to control or lessen the impact of such erosion and to restore areas affected by such erosion.

In a state that adopts an approved CZM plan, any Federal agency activities which involve coastal zones must conduct and support those activities in a manner consistent with the CZM plan. In addition, for those activities requiring Federal permits (i.e., Corps of Engineers Section 404, U.S. Coast Guard Section 9), a state-approved certificate of compliance with the CZM program must be included in the permit application.

The impacts of the CZM program upon trans-portation delivery can be significant. Highway and bridge projects planned in coastal areas could be effectively halted if the CZM plan were not conducive to such activity. Similarly, the extension or modification of runways at such airports as John F. Kennedy International in New York or Logan International in Boston could be difficult to implement because of CZM and other Federal permit requirements.

SUMMARY

Environmentally oriented statutes impacting upon the U.S. transportation system have existed in the United States Code for more than 80 years. The Rivers and Harbors Act of 1899, as an example, has a major impact on any transportation project which may affect a navigable water. Most of the enacted legislation, however, was implemented during the height of the environmental movement, around 1970.

Clearly the most significant, and one of the briefest, to be enacted was the National Environmental Policy Act of 1969 (NEPA), which requires the preparations of environmental impact statements on major Federal actions. NEPA also requires an interdisciplinary, scientific approach to planning and decision making and revised agency procedures for project development, which are to include unquantified environmental impacts. This requirement for revised agency procedures has produced major new regulations in most of the modal transportation agencies; the most important of these regulations are discussed in Chapter 3. The entire NEPA law, as well as Executive Orders 11514 and 11991 implementing it, are reproduced in Appendix 2A.

Other pieces of legislation having significant general impacts on the transportation development process were also enacted during this period. These include the Federal Aid Highway Act of 1970, the Environmental Quality Improvement Act of 1970, and the Airport and Airways Development Act of 1970.

Statutory consideration of transportation-related noise impacts began in 1965 when the Housing and Urban Development Act required the determination of methods to minimize the economic impacts of airport noise. The Noise Control Act of 1972 required considerable attention to transportation source noise control, while the 1978 amendments (called the Quiet Communities Act) called for more general noise abatement planning around transportation facilities. The Control and Abatement of Aircraft Noise and Sonic Boom Act of 1968 mandated the development of maximum noise levels of aircraft types in the certification process.

The Clean Air Act of 1963 as amended through 1977 is the major piece of air-quality–related legislation having an impact on transportation. Basically, this law requires that all transportation plans and projects be constant with the state's implementation plan (SIP) for attainment of the National Ambient Air Quality Standards (NAAQS) for several major pollutants. For those Air Quality Control Regions (AQCR) where the NAAQS are exceeded for the transportation-related pollutants, a series of 18 transportation control measures must be evaluated, with full attainment of the NAAQS by 1987.

The Rivers and Harbors Act of 1899 and the Clean Water Act of 1977 require that permits be obtained from the U.S. Coast Guard (navigable waters) and the U.S. Army Corps of Engineers (all waters in the nation) when a transportation project may have a water quality impact. Whenever bridges are planned over navigable waters, or dredging or filling is proposed, permits *must* be obtained.* Also, the Safe Drinking Water Act requires that a Federally funded project must not inject excessive contaminants into a community's sole source aquifer.

Relating to ecological impacts, the Fish and Wildlife Coordination Act has given the Fish and Wildlife Service (FWS) of the Department of Interior great power to delay transportation projects by requiring potentially enormous amounts of data on fish and wildlife conservation and development before signing off on a project. The Endangered Species Act of 1973 gave the Department of Interior authority to prohibit any activity jeopardizing a lifeform on the Endangered Species List. The Wild and Scenic Rivers Act of 1968 effectively prohibits activities which would effect the free-flowing,

wilderness character or river areas which have been designated by Congress as wild or scenic.

Executive Order 11990, deriving its authority from NEPA, required that the Federal agencies revise their project development processes to insure the adequate protection of the nation's wetlands. Similarly, the National Flood Insurance Act of 1968 restricted development of land within floodplains as a mechanism to reduce flood loss. Executive Order 11988, also deriving its authority from NEPA, mandated an integrated approach to minimize floodplain encroachment. Lastly, the Coastal Zone Management Act of 1972, as amended in 1976, required that a project proposal in a coastal zone must be in compliance with the state's coastal zone management program, if one exists.

There have been a very great number of agency regulations promulgated as a result of these laws. Chapter 3 presents and analyzes some of the most important and significant of these.

APPENDIX 2A

THE NATIONAL ENVIRONMENTAL POLICY ACT OF 1969, AS AMENDED*

An Act to establish a national policy for the environment, to provide for the establishment of a Council on Environmental Quality, and for other purposes.

Be it enacted by the Senate and House of Representatives of the United States of America in Congress assembled, That this Act may be cited as the "National Environmental Policy Act of 1969."

PURPOSE

Sec. 2. The purposes of this Act are: To declare a national policy which will encourage productive and enjoyable harmony between man and his environment; to promote efforts which will prevent or eliminate damage to the environment and biosphere and stimulate the health and welfare of man; to enrich the understanding of the ecological systems and natural resources important to the Nation; and to establish a Council on Environmental Quality.

TITLE I

DECLARATION OF NATIONAL ENVIRONMENTAL POLICY

Sec. 101. (a) The Congress, recognizing the profound impact of man's activity on the interrelations of all components of the natural environment, particularly the profound influences of population growth, high-density urbanization, industrial expansion, resource exploitation, and new and expanding technological advances and recognizing further the critical importance of restoring and maintaining environmental quality to the overall welfare and development of man, declares that it is the continuing policy of the Federal Government, in cooperation with State and local governments, and other concerned public and private organizations, to use all practicable means and measures, including financial and technical assistance, in a manner calculated to foster and promote the general welfare, to create and maintain conditions under which man and nature can exist in productive harmony, and fulfill the social, economic, and other requirements of present and future generations of Americans.

---

*Note that the Corps of Engineers maintains nationwide blanket permits that cover many projects with minor water and wetland impacts. See the September 19, 1980 Federal Register, pp. 62775–62777, for a listing.

*Pub. L. 91–190, 42 U.S.C. 4321–4347, January 1, 1970, as amended by Pub. L. 94–52, July 3, 1975, and Pub. L. 94–83, August 9, 1975.

(b) In order to carry out the policy set forth in this Act, it is the continuing responsibility of the Federal Government to use all practicable means, consistent with other essential considerations of national policy, to improve and coordinate Federal plans, functions, programs, and resources to the end that the Nation may—

(1) fulfill the responsibilities of each generation as trustee of the environment for succeeding generations;

(2) assure for all Americans safe, healthful, productive, and esthetically and culturally pleasing surroundings;

(3) attain the widest range of beneficial uses of the environment without degradation, risk to health or safety, or other undesirable and unintended consequences;

(4) preserve important historic, cultural, and natural aspects of our national heritage, and maintain, wherever possible, an environment which supports diversity, and variety of individual choice;

(5) achieve a balance between population and resource use which will permit high standards of living and a wide sharing of life's amenities; and

(6) enhance the quality of renewable resources and approach the maximum attainable recycling of depletable resources.

(c) The Congress recognizes that each person should enjoy a healthful environment and that each person has a responsibility to contribute to the preservation and enhancement of the environment.

SEC. 102. The Congress authorizes and directs that, to the fullest extent possible: (1) the policies, regulations, and public laws of the United States shall be interpreted and administered in accordance with the policies set forth in this Act, and (2) all agencies of the Federal Government shall—

(A) Utilize a systematic, interdisciplinary approach which will insure the integrated use of the natural and social sciences and the environmental design arts in planning and in decisionmaking which may have an impact on man's environment;

(B) Identify and develop methods and procedures, in consultation with the Council on Environmental Quality established by title II of this Act, which will insure that presently unquantified environmental amenities and values may be given appropriate consideration in decisionmaking along with economic and technical considerations;

(C) Include in every recommendation or report on proposals for legislation and other major Federal actions significantly affecting the quality of the human environment, a detailed statement by the responsible official on—

(i) The environmental impact of the proposed action,

(ii) Any adverse environmental effects which cannot be avoided should the proposal be implemented,

(iii) Alternatives to the proposed action,

(iv) The relationship between local short-term uses of man's environment and the maintenance and enhancement of long-term productivity, and

(v) Any irreversible and irretrievable commitments of resources which would be involved in the proposed action should it be implemented.

Prior to making any detailed statement, the responsible Federal official shall consult with and obtain the comments of any Federal agency which has jurisdiction by law or special expertise with respect to any environmental impact involved. Copies of such statement and the comments and views of the appropriate Federal, State, and local agencies, which are authorized to develop and enforce environmental standards, shall be made available to the President, the Council on Environmental Quality and to the public as provided by section 552 of title 5, United States Code, and shall accompany the proposal through the existing agency review processes;

(d) Any detailed statement required under subparagraph (c) after January 1, 1970, for any major Federal action funded under a program of grants to States shall not be deemed to be legally insufficient solely by reason of having been prepared by a State agency or official, if:

(i) the State agency or official has statewide jurisdiction and has the responsibility for such action,

(ii) the responsible Federal official furnishes guidance and participates in such preparation,

(iii) the responsible Federal official independently evaluates such statement prior to its approval and adoption, and

(iv) after January 1, 1976, the responsible Federal official provides early notification to, and solicits the views of, any other State or any Federal land management entity of any action or any alternative thereto which may have significant impacts upon such State or affected Federal land management entity and, if there is any disagreement on such impacts, prepares a written assessment of such impacts and views for incorporation into such detailed statement.

The procedures in this subparagraph shall not relieve the Federal official of his responsibilities for the scope, objectivity, and content of the entire statement or of any other responsibility under this Act; and further, this subparagraph does not affect the legal sufficiency of statements prepared by State agencies with less than statewide jurisdiction.

(e) Study, develop, and describe appropriate alternatives to recommended courses of action in any proposal which involves unresolved conflicts concerning alternative uses of available resources;

(f) Recognize the worldwide and long-range character of environmental problems and, where consistent with the foreign policy of the United States, lend appropriate support to initiatives, resolutions, and programs designed to maximize international cooperation in anticipating and preventing a decline in the quality of mankind's world environment;

(g) Make available to States, counties, municipalities, institutions, and individuals, advice and information useful in restoring, maintaining, and enhancing the quality of the environment;

(h) Initiate and utilize ecological information in the planning and development of resource-oriented projects; and

(i) Assist the Council on Environmental Quality established by title II of this Act.

SEC. 103. All agencies of the Federal Government shall review their present statutory authority, administrative regulations, and current policies and procedures for the purpose of determining whether there are any deficiencies or inconsistencies therein which prohibit full compliance with the purposes and provisions of this Act and shall propose to the President not later than July 1, 1971, such measures as may be necessary to bring their authority and policies into conformity with the intent, purposes, and procedures set forth in this Act.

SEC. 104. Nothing in section 102 or 103 shall in any way affect the specific statutory obligations of any Federal agency (1) to comply with criteria or standards of environmental quality, (2) to coordinate or consult with any other Federal or State agency, or (3) to act, or refrain from acting contingent upon the recommendations or certification of any other Federal or State agency.

SEC. 105. The policies and goals set forth in this Act are supplementary to those set forth in existing authorizations of Federal agencies.

TITLE II

COUNCIL ON ENVIRONMENTAL QUALITY

SEC. 201. The President shall transmit to the Congress annually beginning July 1, 1970, an Environmental Quality Report (hereinafter referred to as the "report") which shall set forth (1) the status and condition of the major natural, manmade, or altered environmental classes of the Nation, including, but not limited to, the air, the aquatic, including marine, estuarine, and fresh water, and the terrestrial environment, including, but not limited to, the forest, dryland, wetland, range, urban, suburban and rural environment; (2) current and foreseeable trends in the quality, management and utilization of such environments and the effects of those trends on the social, economic, and other requirements of the Nation; (3) the adequacy of available natural resources for fulfilling human and economic requirements of the Nation in the light of expected population pressures; (4) a review of the programs and activities (including regulatory activities) of the Federal Government, the State and local governments, and nongovernmental entities or individuals with particular reference to their effect on the environment and on the conservation, development and utilization of natural resources; and (5) a program for remedying the deficiencies of existing programs and activities, together with recommendations for legislation.

SEC. 202. There is created in the Executive Office of the President a Council on Environmental Quality (hereinafter referred to as the "Council"). The Council shall be composed of three members who shall be appointed by the President to serve at his pleasure, by and with the advice and consent of the Senate. The President shall designate one of the members of the Council to serve as Chairman. Each member shall be a person who, as a result of his training, experience, and attainments, is exceptionally well qualified to analyze and interpret environmental trends and information of all kinds; to appraise programs and activities of the Federal Government in the light of the policy set forth in title I of this Act; to be conscious of and responsive to the scientific, economic, social, esthetic, and cultural needs and interests of the Nation; and to formulate and recommend national policies to promote the improvement of the quality of the environment.

SEC. 203. The Council may employ such officers and employees as may be necessary to carry out its functions under this Act. In addition, the Council may employ and fix the compensation of such experts and consultants as may be necessary for the carrying out of its functions under this Act, in accordance with section 3109 of title 5, United States Code (but without regard to the last sentence thereof).

SEC. 204. It shall be the duty and function of the Council—

(1) to assist and advise the President in the preparation of the Environmental Quality Report required by section 201 of this title;

(2) to gather timely and authoritative information concerning the

conditions and trends in the quality of the environment both current and prospective, to analyze and interpret such information for the purpose of determining whether such conditions and trends are interfering, or are likely to interfere, with the achievement of the policy set forth in title I of this Act, and to compile and submit to the President studies relating to such conditions and trends;

(3) to review and appraise the various programs and activities of the Federal Government in the light of the policy set forth in title I of this Act for the purpose of determining the extent to which such programs and activities are contributing to the achievement of such policy, and to make recommendations to the President with respect thereto;

(4) to develop and recommend to the President national policies to foster and promote the improvement of environmental quality to meet the conservation, social, economic, health, and other requirements and goals of the Nation;

(5) to conduct investigations, studies, surveys, research, and analyses relating to ecological systems and environmental quality;

(6) to document and define changes in the natural environment, including the plant and animal systems, and to accumulate necessary data and other information for a continuing analysis of these changes or trends and an interpretation of their underlying causes;

(7) to report at least once each year to the President on the state and condition of the environment; and

(8) to make and furnish such studies, reports thereon, and recommendations with respect to matters of policy and legislation as the President may request.

SEC. 205. In exercising its powers, functions, and duties under this Act, the Council shall—

(1) Consult with the Citizens' Advisory Committee on Environmental Quality established by Executive Order No. 11472, dated May 29, 1969, and with such representatives of science, industry, agriculture, labor, conservation organizations, State and local governments and other groups, as it deems advisable; and

(2) Utilize, to the fullest extent possible, the services, facilities and information (including statistical information) of public and private agencies and organizations, and individuals, in order that duplication of effort and expense may be avoided, thus assuring that the Council's activities will not unnecessarily overlap or conflict with similar activities authorized by law and performed by established agencies.

SEC. 206. Members of the Council shall serve full time and the Chairman of the Council shall be compensated at the rate provided for Level II of the Executive Schedule Pay Rates (5 U.S.C. 5313). The other members of the Council shall be compensated at the rate provided for Level IV of the Executive Schedule Pay Rates (5 U.S.C. 5315).

SEC. 207. The Council may accept reimbursements from any private nonprofit organization or from any department, agency, or instrumentality of the Federal Government, any State, or local government, for the reasonable travel expenses incurred by an officer or employee of the Council in connection with his attendance at any conference, seminar, or similar meeting conducted for the benefit of the Council.

SEC. 208. The Council may make expenditures in support of its international activities, including expenditures for: (1) international travel; (2) activities in implementation of international agreements; and (3) the support of international exchange programs in the United States and in foreign countries.

SEC. 209. There are authorized to be appropriated to carry out the provisions of this chapter not to exceed $300,000 for fiscal year 1970, $700,000 for fiscal year 1971, and $1,000,000 for each fiscal year thereafter.

APPENDIX 2B

THE CLEAN AIR ACT § 309*

§ 7609. Policy review

(a) The Administrator shall review and comment in writing on the environmental impact of any matter relating to duties and responsibilities granted pursuant to this chapter or other provisions of the authority of the Administrator, contained in any (1) legislation proposed by any Federal department or agency, (2) newly authorized Federal projects for construction and any major Federal agency action (other than a project for construction) to which section 4332(2)(C) of this title applies, and (3) proposed regulations published by any department or agency of the Federal Government. Such written comment shall be made public at the conclusion of any such review.

(b) In the event the Administrator determines that any such legislation, action, or regulation is unsatisfactory from the standpoint of public health or welfare or environmental quality, he shall publish his determination and the matter shall be referred to the Council on Environmental Quality.

---

*July 14, 1955, c. 360, § 309, as added Dec. 31, 1970, Pub. L. 91–604 § 12(a), 42 U.S.C. § 7609 (1970).

APPENDIX 2C

Executive Order 11514. March 5, 1970
PROTECTION AND ENHANCEMENT OF ENVIRONMENTAL QUALITY
As amended by Executive Order 11991. (Secs. 2(g) and (3(h)). May 24, 1977*

By virtue of the authority vested in me as President of the United States and in furtherance of the purpose and policy of the National Environmental Policy Act of 1969 (Public Law No. 91–190, approved January 1, 1970), it is ordered as follows:

Section 1. *Policy.* The Federal Government shall provide leadership in protecting and enhancing the quality of the Nation's environment to sustain and enrich human life. Federal agencies shall initiate measures needed to direct their policies, plans and programs so as to meet national environmental goals. The Council on Environmental Quality, through the Chairman, shall advise and assist the President in leading this national effort.

Sec. 2. *Responsibilities of Federal agencies.* Consonant with Title I of the National Environmental Policy Act of 1969, hereafter referred to as the "Act", the heads of Federal agencies shall:

(a) Monitor, evaluate, and control on a continuing basis their agencies' activities so as to protect and enhance the quality of the environment. Such activities shall include those directed to controlling pollution and enhancing the environment and those designed to accomplish other program objectives which may affect the quality of the environment. Agencies shall develop programs and measures to protect and enhance environmental quality and shall assess progress in meeting the specific objectives of such activities. Heads of agencies shall consult with appropriate Federal, State and local agencies in carrying out their activities as they affect the quality of the environment.

(b) Develop procedures to ensure the fullest practicable provision of timely public information and understanding of Federal plans and programs with environmental impact in order to obtain the views of interested parties. These procedures shall include, whenever appropriate, provision for public hearings, and shall provide the public with relevant information, including information on alternative courses of action. Federal agencies shall also encourage State and local agencies to adopt similar procedures for informing the public concerning their activities affecting the quality of the environment.

(c) Insure that information regarding existing or potential environmental problems and control methods developed as part of research, development, demonstration, test, or evaluation activities is made available to Federal agencies, States, counties, municipalities, institutions, and other entities, as appropriate.

(d) Review their agencies' statutory authority, administrative regulations, policies, and procedures, including those relating to loans, grants, contracts, leases, licenses, or permits, in order to identify any deficiencies or inconsistencies therein which prohibit or limit full compliance with the purposes and provisions of the Act. A report on this review and the corrective actions taken or planned, including such measures to be proposed to the Presi-

---

*The Preamble to Executive Order 11991 is as follows:

By virtue of the authority vested in me by the Constitution and statutes of the United States of America, and as President of the United States of America, in furtherance of the purpose and policy of the National Environmental Policy Act of 1969, as amended (42 U.S.C. 4321 *et seq.*), the Environmental Quality Improvement Act of 1970 (42 U.S.C. 4371 *et seq.*), and Section 309 of the Clean Air Act, as amended (42 U.S.C. 1857h–7), it is hereby ordered as follows:

dent as may be necessary to bring their authority and policies into conformance with the intent, purposes, and procedures of the Act, shall be provided to the Council on Environmental Quality not later than September 1, 1970.

(e) Engage in exchange of data and research results, and cooperate with agencies of other governments to foster the purposes of the Act.

(f) Proceed, in coordination with other agencies, with actions required by section 102 of the Act.

(g) In carrying out their responsibilites under the Act and this Order, comply with the regulations issued by the Council except where such compliance would be inconsistent with statutory requirements.

Sec. 3. *Responsibilities of Council on Environmental Quality.* The Council on Environmental Quality shall:

(a) Evaluate existing and proposed policies and activities of the Federal Government directed to the control of pollution and the enhancement of the environment and to the accomplishment of other objectives which affect the quality of the environment. This shall include continuing review of procedures employed in the development and enforcement of Federal standards affecting environmental quality. Based upon such evaluations the Council shall, where appropriate, recommend to the President policies and programs to achieve more effective protection and enhancement of environmental quality and shall, where appropriate, seek resolution of significant environmental issues.

(b) Recommend to the President and to the agencies priorities among programs designed for the control of pollution and for enhancement of the environment.

(c) Determine the need for new policies and programs for dealing with environmental problems not being adequately addressed.

(d) Conduct, as it determines to be appropriate, public hearings or conferences on issues of environmental significance.

(e) Promote the development and use of indices and monitoring systems (1) to assess environmental conditions and trends, (2) to predict the environmental impact of proposed public and private actions, and (3) to determine the effectiveness of programs for protecting and enhancing environmental quality.

(f) Coordinate Federal programs related to environmental quality.

(g) Advise and assist the President and the agencies in achieving international cooperation for dealing with environmental problems, under the foreign policy guidance of the Secretary of State.

(h) Issue regulations to Federal agencies for the implementation of the procedural provisions of the Act (42 U.S.C. 4332(2)). Such regulations shall be developed after consultation with affected agencies and after such public hearings as may be appropriate. They will be designed to make the environmental impact statement process more useful to decisionmakers and the public; and to reduce paperwork and the accumulation of extraneous background data, in order to emphasize the need to focus on real environmental issues and alternatives. They will require impact statements to be concise, clear, and to the point, and supported by evidence that agencies have made the necessary environmental analyses. The Council shall include in its regulations procedures (1) for the early preparation of environmental impact statements, and (2) for the referral to the Council of conflicts between agencies concerning the implementation of the National Environmental Policy Act of 1969, as amended, and Section 309 of the Clean Air Act, as amended, for the Council's recommendation as to their prompt resolution.

(i) Issue such other instructions to agencies, and request such reports and other information from them, as may be required to carry out the Council's responsibilities under the Act.

(j) Assist the President in preparing the annual Environmental Quality Report provided for in section 201 of the Act.

(k) Foster investigations, studies, surveys, research, and analyses relating to (i) ecological systems and environmental quality, (ii) the impact of new and changing technologies thereon, and (iii) means of preventing or reducing adverse effects from such technologies.

Sec. 4. *Amendments of E.O. 11472.* Executive Order No. 11472 of May 29, 1969, including the heading thereof, is hereby amended:

(1) By substituting for the term "the Environmental Quality Council", wherever it occurs, the following: "the Cabinet Committee on the Environment".

(2) By substituting for the term "the Council", wherever it occurs, the following: "the Cabinet Committee".

(3) By inserting in subsection (f) of section 101, after "Budget,", the following: "the Director of the Office of Science and Technology,".

(4) By substituting for subsection (g) of section 101 the following:

"(g) The Chairman of the Council on Environmental Quality (established by Public Law 91-190) shall assist the President in directing the affairs of the Cabinet Committee."

(5) by deleting subsection (c) of section 102.

(6) By substituting for "the Office of Science and Technology", in section 104, the following: "the Council on Environmental Quality (established by Public Law 91-190)".

(7) By substituting for "(hereinafter referred to as the 'Committee')", in section 201, the following: "(hereinafter referred to as the 'Citizens' Committee')".

(8) By substituting for the term "the Committee", wherever it occurs, the following: "the Citizens' Committee".

CHAPTER 3

Regulative Actions at the Federal Level

The procedure for implementing enacted legislation in the United States is for the appropriate agency within the executive branch to develop compliance regulations. This chapter analyzes the regulations that have grown out of the laws discussed in Chapter 2. The format for this chapter is similar to that of Chapter 2, with a discussion of general environmental regulations followed by discussions of noise-, air-, water-, and ecology-related regulations.

A great number of regulations (and funding mechanisms) concerning public-sector–related activities have an effect on transportation delivery. However, in the environmental area, there are approximately 20 that must be considered as having or potentially having major transportation impacts.

GENERAL ENVIRONMENTAL REGULATIONS

The National Environmental Policy Act of 1969 (NEPA), which was discussed in detail in Chapter 2, has spawned an unusually large number of regulations, policies, and procedures to insure full compliance with the act. To provide guidance and direction to Federal agencies, the Office of the President issued Executive Orders 11514 (1970) and 11991 (1977). These orders, which were also discussed in Chapter 2, were closely followed by regulations issued by the Council on Environmental Quality (CEQ). The analysis presented in this chapter is limited to the most recent CEQ regulations, which were made public on November 29, 1978.

Following promulgation of the 1978 CEQ regulations, the DOT produced DOT Order 5610.1C, *Procedures for Considering Environmental Impacts*, on September 18, 1979, as specific instructions to its modal agencies. The FAA responded by issuing FAA Order 1050.1C, *Policies and Procedures for Considering Environmental Impacts*, on December 20, 1979. The FHWA and the UMTA issued, on October 30, 1980, a coordinated response entitled *Environmental Impact and Related Statements*. The FHWA version is found in 23 CFR 771 as Section 2, Chapter 7 of Volume 7 (FHPM 7-7-2) of the Federal Highway Aid Program Manual. The UMTA version is found in 49 CFR 662. All of these regulations, as well as FHPM 7-7-1, *Process Guidelines*, are discussed below.

CEQ Guidelines
Regulations for Implementing the Procedural Provisions of the National Environmental Policy Act
November 29, 1978
(40 CFR 1500-1508)

This directive serves as the basis for agency compliance with NEPA and is the foundation for DOT Order 5610.1C, FAA Order 1050.1C, FHPM 7-7-2, and the UMTA regulation. Accordingly, it is reproduced in its entirety in Appendix 3A.

The regulation contains nine parts, with three dealing with environmental impact statements (EISs), three dealing with processes, and three dealing with diverse topics such as policy, timing, and terminology. The headings of the nine parts are

Major Federal Action

Nepa required a detailed statement on major Federal actions signigicantly affecting the environment. The 1978 CEQ guidelines provide a great deal of refinement to this phrase in Part 1508. Actions targeted are those that are subject to Federal responsibility and may include *lack of action by responsible officials, where action is appropriate and reviewable by law.*

Actions included are those partly or wholly financed, assisted, conducted, regulated or approved by Federal agencies. Specifically excluded are actions funded by general revenue-sharing funds. Four categories of actions are defined:

1. Adoption of official policy, such as rules, regulations, and interpretations adopted pursuant to the Administrative Procedure Act, 5 USC 551 et seq.; treaties and international conventions or agreements; formal documents establishing an agency's policies which will result in or substantially alter agency programs.

2. Adoption of formal plans, such as official documents prepared or approved by Federal agencies that guide or describe alternative uses of Federal resources, upon which future agency actions will be based.

3. Adoption of programs, such as a group of concreted actions to implement a specific policy or plan; systematic and connected agency resources to implement a specific statutory program or executive directive.

4. Approval of specific projects, such as construction or management activities located in a defined geographic area. Projects include actions approved by permit or other regulatory decision as well as federally assisted activities.

Significantly Affecting

The word "major" has no meaning apart from "significantly." In other words, an action is "major" if it significantly affects the environment. The context of significance may include, on both a short-and long-term basis, the world, nation, region, or locale, depending on the nature of the action. Effects may be beneficial as well as adverse, and are to be evaluated based on their impacts on

1. Public health or safety
2. Unique geographical characteristics
3. Controversiality
4. Involvement upon unique or unkown risks
5. Precedent-setting potential
6. Historic Sites
7. Endangered or threatened species
8. Other environmental laws or requirements

In addition, a group of related actions which, taken individually, are insignificant, but when taken together are significant, must be reviewed for their "cumulative impact." Applying this principle to the time domain, cumulative impacts must be considered in view of past, present, and reasonably foreseeable future actions. This means that incremental impacts are not to be primarily considered. When a highway is widened, for example, absolute noise levels, as well as changes in noise levels, must be considered.

The Environment

Defined comprehensively, the environment includes the natural and physical domains, but not necessarily the economic or social ones. However, when an EIS is required, economic and social effects must be discussed and interrelated.

Direct effects of the action must be considered. Those effects which are indirect, either by chronology or geography, are also important. These include induced changes in growth, land-use patterns, population density, and natural systems and ecosystems.

The guidelines allow for entire categories or

classes of actions to be exempted from the NEPA requirements if they do not have individual or cumulative impacts which are significant. This procedure is known as "categorical exclusion"; agencies, however, are encouraged to perform *environmental assessments* on such actions. This will provide documentation that no significant effects are produced.

Policy

The guidelines intend to fully implement NEPA, but with minimum paperwork and delay. Many transportation projects in the 1970s were characterized by voluminous EISs and excessive delays owing to extended discussions on environmental issues. The 1978 guidelines, based on the 1977 Executive Order 11991, introduced several new concepts aimed at reducing paperwork and delay, including scoping and tiering, which are discussed later, and categorical exclusions. Encouraged is the use of a Finding of No Significant Impact (FONSI) when an action that is not otherwise excluded is found not to have a significant environmental impact. Adoption of a FONSI exempts an action from the requirement of EIS preparation.

Agency Planning, Decision Making, and Compliance

When more than one Federal agency is involved in an action, one is designated as the lead agency and the others as cooperating agencies. The agencies are required to use a systematic, interdisciplinary approach and to integrate NEPA activities early in the planning process. The lead and cooperating agencies, as well as other agencies, are to consult *prior* to EIS preparation in order to minimize adversary relationships.

The guidelines require that the lead agency apply "an early and open process for determining the scope of issues to be addressed and for identifying the significant issues related to a proposed action." This process is call *scoping*. The process must include the participation of affected Federal, state, and local agencies, as well as proponents *and* opponents of the action.

The lead agency is required to determine the significant issues to be analyzed in depth in the EIS and to determine the scope (range of ac-

tions, alternatives, and impacts to be considered in the EIS). When determining the scope of the EIS, three items must be considered.

1. Actions
    (a)   Connected actions
    (b)   Cumulative actions
    (c)   Similar actions
2. Alternatives
    (a)   No action
    (b)   Other reasonable courses of action
    (c)   Additional mitigation measures
3. Impacts
    (a)   Direct impacts
    (b)   Indirect impacts
    (c)   Cumulative impacts

The scoping process also requires the elimination of insignificant issues and previously studied issues from detailed study. Other related EISs and assessments must be identified in order to insure maximum integration into the EIS.

The lead agency retains responsibility for the EIS, but is to use the scoping process to allocate EIS preparation assignments among the cooperating agencies, where appropriate. The process is also to be utilized by the lead agency to integrate the environmental analysis preparation into the tentative planning and decision-making schedule.

The scoping process may be used to set page limits on environmental documents and to set time limits which may be requested by state or local agencies or members of the public. Normal final envirionmental impact statements (FEIS) are required to be less than 150 pages in length, while unusually complex proposals will normally be less than 300 pages for the FEIS.

In order to comply with the guidelines, all Federal agencies are now required to have modified their procedures to

utilize a systematic interdisciplinary approach which will insure the integrated use of the natural and social sciences and the environmental design arts in planning and in decision making which may have an impact in the human environment.

1. The environmental impact of the proposed action.
2. Any adverse environmental effects which cannot be avoided should the proposal be implemented.
3. Alternatives to the proposed action.
4. The relationship between short-term local uses of man's environment and the maintenance and enhancement of long-term productivity.
5. Any irreversible and irretrievable commitments of resources which would be involved in the proposed action should it be implemented.

This section is to include discussions of both direct and indirect effects, and their significance. Also, potential conflicts with land-use plans and policies are to be explored. The various alternatives studied are to be analyzed regarding their

1. Energy requirements
2. Energy conservation potential
3. Depletion of natural resources
4. Natural resource conservation potential
5. Design of the built environment, including
   (a) Urban quality
   (b) Historic and cultural resources
6. Means of mitigation not otherwise discussed

The appendix of the EIS may contain many of the details that have been excluded from the section on affected environment. However, this does not mean that all the supporting documents and reports prepared as part of the environmental analysis phase of the project study are to be included in the appendix. For example, a major highway project will generate noise study and air quality reports, each up to several hundred pages in length. Documentation to satisfy the State Historic Preservation Office under the National Historic Preservation Act can often require up to 1000 pages. In all, there can be more than 20 separate reports required on environmentally related issues on complex transportation projects. These reports can be called a "detached appendix," kept available for public inspection, but should not be circulated with the EIS.

The appendix that is circulated should contain only that material which is fundamental to the EIS, substantiating the analyses discussed and necessary for the understanding of the issues and decisions. That material included should be analytic in nature and highly relevant to the decision points.

The comments received during the circulation of the DEIS need to be addressed in and attached to the FEIS. Possible responses to comments include appropriate modifications of the alternatives or the development and serious consideration of new alternatives. Based on comments, it is appropriate to modify, supplement, improve, or otherwise correct the analyses reported in the DEIS. It is also appropriate to explain why certain comments are not incorporated. In this case, however, it is necessary to support that decision with authoritative documentation.

Minor changes from the draft to the final EIS can be made with errata sheets, rather than by rewriting sections of the DEIS. In those cases where all the changes in response to comments are minor, it is appropriate to evaluate only the comments, responses, and errata sheets (and not the entire DEIS) as the FEIS. However, it will still be necessary to file the DEIS, comments, responses, and errata sheets, along with a new cover sheet, as the FEIS. Currently, all FEISs are filed with the U.S. Environmental Protection Agency, Office of Federal Activities, A-104, 401 M Street SW, Washington, D.C.   20460.

The EPA, in turn, files one copy of the FEIS with the CEQ of the Office of the President of the United States. NEPA requires that the CEQ assist the President in making his annual Environmental Quality Report to Congress. This report is to contain a review of the "programs and activities" of the Federal government, as they affect the environment, conservation, and natural resources. This FEIS filing requirement assures the availability to the President and CEQ of all necessary and relevant information, as mandated by NEPA.

Department of Transportation Order 5610.1C Procedures for Considering Environmental Impact
September 18, 1979

The November 29, 1978 CEQ guidelines required that within eight months of its issuance, each Federal department had to produce compliance procedures. These procedures were not to *paraphrase* the CEQ guidelines, but were to *implement* them. In developing the procedures the agencies were to closely consult with the CEQ.

The DOT responded to the mandate by publishing its final regulation on September 18, 1979, as DOT Order 5610.1C., *Procedures for Considering Environmental Impacts*. It is interesting to note that the DOT considers its order *supplemental* to the CEQ guidelines, as specific application to transportation programs. Accordingly, the DOT requires in the order that full compliance is necessary with both the order *and* the CEQ guidelines.

The order itself consists of a 20-point directive involving the CEQ guidelines and several other environmental requirements to further the DOT objective of "one-step" environmental processing. That is,

> *to the maximum extent possible, a single process shall be used to meet requirements for environmental studies, consultations, and reviews*

In addition to the 20 points, the order contains two attachments. The first is simply a listing of all the states and localities that have enacted NEPA-type statutory or administrative requirements. The second is a rather comprehensive discussion of the recommended form and content of transportation-related EISs. This second attachment is discussed later in this section and is included as Appendix 3B.

The DOT order is in itself an intermediate document. It is further necessary for the modal agencies within the DOT to develop and implement appropriate regulations as part of their standard operating procedures. The implementing regulations for the FWHA, FAA, and UMTA are studied following the discussion of the DOT order.

As expressed in the order, it is the DOT position that the

> *assessment of the environmental impacts should be a part of regional transportation system planning and broad transportation system development.*

Accordingly, the scoping process is to be integrated into the existing procedures for early consultation and citizen participation. Assurances need to be made that all significant issues are identified early and that interested parties are given the opportunity to participate in the scoping process. Public input is to be solicited

> *through hearings, personal contact, press releases, advertisements or notices in newspapers, including minority or foreign language papers, if appropriate, and other methods. A summary of citizen involvement and any environmental issues raised should be documented in the EIS.*

Those actions considered covered by the order include construction, research activities, rule-making and regulatory actions, certifications, licenses, permits, approval of policies and plans, adoption or implementation of programs, DOT-proposed legislation, grants, and loans and loan guarantees.

Those actions considered to be categorical exclusions include administrative procurements, personal service contracts, personnel actions, project amendments (cost-related) not significantly altering the environmental impacts of the action, nonenvironment-related operating or maintenance subsidies, maintenance and modernization of existing facilities, minor safety improvements, equipment purchases, operating expenses, and planning grants that do not imply a project commitment.

When an action is clearly not categorically excluded, a preliminary environmental assessment is required to ascertain whether the action significantly affects the environment. If it does, a draft and final EIS must be prepared and fully circulated. If it does not significantly affect the environment, according to the assessment, the modal agency may prepare a Finding of No Significant Impact (FONSI), which is available for public inspection, but need not be circulated outside the originating office. The FONSI takes the place of the draft and final Negative Declaration which were required by previous CEQ guidelines.

The DOT order encourages the modal agencies to become lead or joint lead agencies whenever possible. If a project is initiated by a state agency, which is usually the case for highways, the Federal agency (usually the FHWA) is to serve as a joint lead agency.

It is expected that interested agencies will agree to serve as cooperating agencies and will be relied upon for consultation and input throughout the evaluation process. When an agency refuses a request to serve as a cooperating agency, the order requires that the DOT Assistant Secretary for Policy and International Affairs be so notified. If that agency

makes adverse comments on the draft EIS (including the adequacy of the EIS or consideration of alternatives or of mitigation measures), or if the agency indicates that it may delay or withhold action on some aspect of the proposal,

the matter shall be taken up with CEQ by the Assistant Secretary. This is a clear message to the Fish and Wildlife Agency (among others) that it must cooperate if it expects DOT modal agencies (particularly FHWA) to expand relevant activities in common areas. Political pressure will be brought to bear when cooperation in an official capacity has not been forthcoming. This feature is quite consistent with the CEQ guidelines, which seek to reduce the amount of conflict over environmental issues which has hampered project flow at the Federal level. A major purpose of Executive Order 11991 and the 1978 CEQ guidelines is to eliminate unnecessary project delays caused by NEPA-related activities.

The order contains a caution against *segmentation* of projects. This occurs when the scope has been narrowed to the extent that it is not possible to meaningfully evaluate impacts. However, the modal agencies are encouraged to *tier* their EISs whenever possible.

Preparation of tiered EISs should be considered for complex transportation proposals (e.g., major urban transportation investments, airport master plans, aid to navigation systems, etc.) or for a number of discrete but closely related Federal actions. The first tier EIS should focus on broad issues such as mode choice, general location, area-wide air quality and land-use implications of the alternative transportation improvements.

Environmental studies should be incorporated as part of the system (or area-wide) planning activities early in the process, and the first tier EIS

should use information from these system planning studies and appropriate corridor planning and other planning studies.

The second tier EIS is to be much more site-specific, with detailed discussions of project impacts and mitigation measures. Examples given for the second tier type project are detailed location, transit station location, and highway interchange configuration.

All final EISs are to be reviewed for *legal sufficiency* by the modal agency Chief Council. In addition, certain categories of projects must be approved by the DOT Assistant Secretary for Policy and International Affairs, as well as the modal agency administrator. These include

1. Highways and bridges
   (a) Any project located on new alignment in a standard metropolitan statistical area of more than 100,000 population
   (b) Any new controlled access highway
   (c) Any project where opposition on environmental grounds has been expressed by any Federal, state, or local agency.
2. Airports
   (a) Any new airport serving a metropolitan area
   (b) Any new runway or runway extension in a metropolitan area used by commercial operators
   (c) Any project where opposition on environmental grounds has been expressed by the Federal, state, or local agency

When a commitment is made in an EIS to provide mitigation measures, the order requires modal agency assurance that such measures are in fact implemented. Withholding funds otherwise due to the implementing agency is deemed to be a reasonable enforcement measure. It has been common to promise anything in an EIS in order to get it approved and then to ignore the promises during implementation in the hopes that bureaucratic inefficiencies would prevail.

The DOT order specifically directs the modal agencies to guard against this practice.

It may be recalled from Chapter 2 that section 4(f) of the Department of Transportation Act of 1966 prohibits the use of public land in a park, recreation area, significant waterfowl or wildlife refuge, or significant historic site, *unless* (*a*) there is no feasible or prudent alternative to the use of such land, and (*b*) the project includes all possible planning to minimize harm.

When a Section 4(f) involvement occurs, the particular site must be described by its size, available activities, use, patronage, unique or irreplaceable qualities, and relationship to other similarly used lands.

Measures to minimize harm include the replacement of land and facilities, providing for functional replacement of facilities, tunneling, cut and cover, cut and fill, treatment of embankments, plantings and screening, pedestrian or bicycle paths, and noise mitigation measures.

The Section 4(f) statement, whether part of an EIS or FONSI, must be reviewed for legal sufficiency by the modal agency Chief Council. In addition, it must include documentation of consultation with the DOI and, where necessary, the Departments of Agriculture and Housing and Urban Development.

The DOT order requires that a DEIS may become invalid after three years if no FEIS has been submitted. If, after three years from the approval of an FEIS, significant steps toward implementation (construction, acquisition, relocation) have not commenced, a written reevaluation of the adequacy, accuracy, and validity of the FEIS shall be prepared. When tiering is utilized, this FEIS reevaluation is not required until after five years. However, for projects implemented in stages, each requiring Federal approval, the reevaluation is required for each stage implemented more than three years after approval.

Several other items of lesser importance were considered in the DOT order. One item that is quite important, however, is Attachment 2, *Format and Content of Environmental Statements* (see Appendix 3B).

The format recommended in the CEQ guidelines is given as the format in the attachment for DOT EISs. Much of the discussion in the attachment simply amplifies the CEQ guidelines; however, there is a significant amount of information that is quite specific to transportation activities. For example, the problem of growth inducement is common to nearly all types of transportation projects and programs. The DOT order (in Attachment 2) makes note of that, indicating that secondary effects "may often be even more substantial than the primary effects of the original action itself." Land use and population growth induced by projects are to be assessed concerning their effect on water resources and public services. The EIS should contain comments from the agencies who provide resources and services.

Another problem common to many transportation solutions is community disruption and relocation resulting from eminent domain right-of-way purchase. The attachment requires that this issue be fully discussed in the EIS. Information specifically to be included is

1. Number of households displaced, including listing of
    (a) Minority groups
    (b) Income level
    (c) Tenure (length at residence)
    (d) Elderly
    (e) Unusually large families
2. Impact on human, or physical, environment
3. Impact on available housing supply
4. Number of businesses displaced and impact on the economy of the community
5. Results of consultation with local officials
6. Documentation of special assistance offered to
    (a) Illiterate
    (b) Elderly
    (c) Handicapped

In addition, the overall impact and particular effect of the proposed action upon the following list of social groups should be identified in the EIS.

1. Elderly
2. Handicapped
3. Nondrivers
4. Transit-dependent groups
5. Minorities

The attachment requires documentation that there has been consultation with the state water pollution control agency "as to conformity to standards and regulations regarding storm sewer discharge, sedimentation control, and other non-point discharges." Also, the EIS must reflect that the state air pollution control agency has found the project to be consistent with the air quality implementation plan for the attainment of the NAAQS. Conformance is specifically required for adopted noise levels and noise-compatible land-use programs.

Another directive that is unique to transportation projects is the requirement to consider impacts upon pedestrian and bicycle access, movement, and safety. This is to be emphasized in high density commercial and residential areas.

Many transportation projects run afoul and suffer long delays when they affect sites of historic or cultural significance. Accordingly, the attachment spells out in great detail the steps to be taken

to preserve and enhance districts, sites, buildings, structures, and objects of historical, architectural, archaeological, or cultural significance.

Whenever an affected property is included on or is deemed to be eligible (by the DOI) for inclusion upon the National Register of Historic Places, it is necessary to consult with the State Historic Preservation Office (SHPO) to determine and document the effect. If the project is determined to have an adverse impact on such a property, it is necessary to execute a Memorandum of Agreement with the Advisory Council on Historic Preservation (ACHP) as per 36 CFR 800. Quite often the coordination asked for by the SHPO requires extensive amounts of data and time to complete. Relations with the SHPO, ACHP, and local historic preservation officials can easily become strained because of the naturally divergent viewpoints of transportation delivery and historic preservation. It can be extremely difficult to obtain the required memorandum of agreement without a great deal of extra effort and compromise by the lead agency.

Encroachment upon a 100-year base floodplain mandates the analysis of the impacts upon that floodplain. In particular the impact of the action itself upon the floodplain, as well as the increased potential for development in the floodplain induced by the action, are to be studied. An evaluation of the alternatives to avoid floodplain encroachment is to be prepared.

Similar analyses of wetlands and coastal zones are required. Impacts are to be assessed in terms of construction *and* operation of the project, as they affect the wetlands, coastal zones, and associated wildlife. Measures to minimize adverse impacts, as well as documentation of consultation with the DOI, are also required discussion items in the EIS.

Impacts of the action upon energy supply and natural resources development are to be discussed where significant. Specifically, the affects on production or consumption of energy and other natural resources are to be addressed.

Lastly, the EIS is to consider the impacts of the action *during* construction. Three items are to be studied in this area: noise impacts; disposal of spoil and effect on borrow areas and disposal sites; and measures to minimize effects upon traffic and pedestrians.

With the information provided to the modal transportation agencies through the adoption of NEPA, as amended; Executive Orders 11514 and 11991; 11/29/78 CEQ Guidelines; and DOT Order 5610.1C specific guidance is available to them to develop and implement the appropriate procedures for considering environment impact. Not only is this guidance available, but each of these directives contain *mandates* to the agencies to comply. Therefore, the remainder of this section is devoted to analysis of agency responses from the FAA, the FHWA and the UMTA.

Federal Aviation Administration Order 1050.1C
Policies and Procedures for Considering
Environmental Impacts
December 20, 1979

The DOT order discussed above required that the operating (modal) administrations within the DOT issue implementation procedures. The administrations were given the option of simply using DOT Order 5610.1C without modification or issuing "detailed instructions or regulations which incorporate the points of this order and the CEQ regulations and provide guidance on applying the environmental process to the administration programs."

The FAA selected the latter course of action and issued a lengthy set of guidelines entitled *Policies and Procedures for Considering Environmental Impacts*. The guidelines, issued December 20, 1979, contain nine appendices and 115 pages of FAA-authorized instructions. Much of the information included, however, only provides rewording of the CEQ Guidelines and the DOT order. The remainder of this discussion will center upon those points unique to the FAA programs and will not restate those points already made in the previous two sections of this chapter.

The FAA order contains much greater detail than its predecessor documents relating to the characteristics of actions requiring EISs and those categorically excluded. According to the FAA order, an EIS is to be prepared if the proposed action

1. Has more than a minimal effect on (DOT ACT) Section 4(f) properties, or (Historic Preservation Act) Section 106 properties.

2. Has a significant impact on endangered species, wetlands, floodplains, or other natural, ecological, cultural, or scenic resources of significance.

3. Is highly controversial concerning the availability of relocation housing.

4. Causes substantial community disruption, or is not reasonably consistent with the adopted plans or goals of the community.

5. Significantly increases surface traffic congestion.

6. Significantly impacts noise levels of noise sensitive areas.

7. Significantly impacts air quality or violates any national, state, or local air quality standard.

8. Significantly impacts water quality or potentially contaminates any public water supply system.

9. Is not consistent with any individual Federal, state, or local environmental law.

10. Directly or indirectly creates a significant impact on the environment of any human beings.

11. Significantly impacts any prime or unique farmlands.

More than any other environmental parameter, the FAA order provides guidance in the area of *noise* impact. Noise is the overriding concern with respect to airport development and land-use compatibility, and is the one in which the FAA has invested the most effort to mitigate. The order formally defines *Noise-Sensitive Areas* as including

residential neighborhoods, educational, health, and religious structures and sites. A noise-sensitive area is one where noise may interfere with the usual activities associated with use of the land. Whether sound interferes with a particular use depends upon the level of noise exposure received and the type of activity involved. A site which is unacceptable for outside use may be acceptable for use inside a structure if adequate noise attenuation features are built into that structure.

Quite specifically, the order requires that the cumulative noise impact of each alternative be analyzed using the 24-hour energy-averaged Day-Night Level (L_{dn}). This descriptor considers, among other things, that noise made at night (10 p.m. to 7 a.m.) is more disruptive than that made during the day. The impacts must be described using the contour-type maps showing those areas exposed to L_{dn} values of 65 dBA or greater. The concepts of L_{dn} and dBA are explored in detail in Chapter 5.

The mandated responsibilities of the FAA are the most complex and diverse of any of administration with the DOT. In its implementing order the FAA therefore provided a series of guidelines for assessing the appropriateness of the categorical exclusion designation. In addition, several functional offices within the FAA included in the order long lists of specific project types deemed to be categorically excluded. The assessment guidelines to be used throughout the FAA are given below. (These classes of actions are categorically excluded from the EIS or FONSI requirement.)

1. Administrative and operating actions
   (a) procurements
   (b) organizational changes
   (c) personnel actions
   (d) legislative proposals

2. emergency measures regarding air or ground safety

3. planning grants which do not imply a project commitment

4. project amendments on costs, which do not alter environmental impacts

5. policy or planning documents not directly implementing project or system actions

6. provision of technical assistance, advice, or services in foreign countries

7. planning and developing projects and programs leading to
   (a) aeromedical applications and standards
   (b) personnel efficiency
   (c) performance

8. certification involving
   (a) medical examination
   (b) delegated authority
   (c) ground schools and other outside training

9. aircraft maintenance or repair not affecting noise, emissions, or wastes

Even though its class may be categorically excluded, a particular project significantly affecting the environment will still require an EIS, according to the FAA order. It would be necessary however, for the FAA to specifically mandate the EIS.

The principal activity of the FAA is to provide airport services. Accordingly, the FAA order devotes more attention to this, the most environmentally sensitive of its activities, than to any others.

Federal airport actions potentially applicable under the guidelines include the adoption of the National Airport System Plan, the approval of an airport location or layout plan, the approval of airport development funding, requirements for conveyances of government land for development or improvement of a public airport, and the approval of the release of airport land. Actions normally requiring an environmental assessment include airport location; runway construction, extension, or strengthening; or construction or expansion of passenger handling or parking facilities with Federal funding. The 11 points discussed above concerning EIS preparation are applicable for the assessement

requirement. Planning grants are not considered major Federal actions, although environmental considerations should be an integral part of airport master planning. (The airport layout plan, an *element* of the master plan, *is* subject to the guidelines.)

With respect to *airports*, the FAA order *categorically excludes* the following 16 actions.

1. Runway, taxiway, apron, or loading ramp construction or repair work including extension, strengthening, reconstruction, resurfacing, marking, grooving fillets, and jet blast facilities, except where such action will create environmental impacts off airport property.

2. Installation or upgrading of airfield lighting systems, including beacons and electrical distribution systems.

3. Installation of miscellaneous items including segmental circles, wind or landing direction indicators or measuring devices, or fencing.

4. Construction or expansion of passenger handling or parking facilities including pedestrian walkway facilities (without Federal funding).

5. Construction or repair of entrance and service roadways within airport property and relocation of these type roads except where they connect to a public highway or street.

6. Grading or removal of obstructions on airport property and erosion control actions with no off-airport impacts.

7. Landscaping generally, and landscaping or construction of physical barriers to diminish impact of airport blast and noise.

8. Land acquisition associated with any of the above items.

9. Acquisition of
   (a) noise suppression or measuring equipment
   (b) security equipment
   (c) snow removal equipment

10. Issuance of airport planning grants (as described above).

11. Airport Development Aid Program (ADAP) actions which are tentative and conditional and clearly taken as a preliminary action

to establish a sponsor's eligibility under the program.

12. Retirement of the principal of bond or other indebtedness for terminal development.

13. Issuance of airport policy and planning documents including advisory circulars on planning, design, and development programs not intended for direct implementation or issued by FAA as administrative and technical guidelines to the public.

14. Issuance of certificates and related actions under the Airport Certification Program.

15. Advisory actions.

16. Nonairport actions included in other FAA categorical exclusion listings which may be shown on airport layout plans or in an airport development plan.

Each of these actions is traceable to the generalized classes of actions categorically excluded, which were discussed earlier in this section. Similar lists, although not so extensive, are included in the FAA order for activities concerning systems research, engineering, and development; airway facilities; air traffic; aviation standards; and energy.

Airport-related actions are ordinarily initiated at the local level by the airport sponsor. (The sponsor is any public agency eligible to receive Federal financial assistance under the Airport Act, or anyone proposing an airport action for which Federal authorization is a requirement.) Sponsors are to begin the environmental evaluation process at about the same time they begin their other activities relating to airport development, site selection, layout, or master planning. The detail to which environmental issues are to be addressed at this early stage is to be commensurate with other planning analyses underway. With master planning studies, the order encourages the incorporation of noise-control land-use compatibility planning, as well as other environmental planning techniques, into the studies for subsequent environmental assessement.

The FAA order also encourages *tiering* of EISs with the caution "not to separate actions which are functionally related and have no independent utility." Applicable circumstances for tiering in the airports program are

1. Program EIS (for legislation or for a new National Airport System Plan), *followed by* site-specific EIS, as required.

2. Environmental documents resulting from master planning activities on short-term projects, in a long-term development context, *followed by* EISs on specific projects ripe for decision.

3. Environmental documents for airport location approvals, *followed by* specific project EISs as needs dictate; the subsequent EIS is to focus on the specific development proposed for decision, and is to exclude the issue of airport location.

4. Environmental documents for airport layout plan approvals.

Lastly, the FAA order gives considerably more detail on the issue of decision documentation than the CEQ guidelines of the DOT order. The Record of Decision (ROD) document required by CEQ section 1505.2 is to accompany the proposed FEIS during its internal review *prior* to FAA adoption and approval. Any mitigation measures that were commitments in the FEIS are to be included in the ROD. Any changes to these mitigation measures must be reviewed by all the FAA offices that reviewed the FEIS and must be approved by the FAA official who also approved the FEIS.

The ROD must be circulated in draft form for concurrence with the FAA review of the FEIS when the sponsor proposes to adopt an action which is (*a*) included in the range of alternatives of an approved EIS, but is (*b*) not the environmentally preferable alternative, or (*c*) the FAA's preferred alternative, as identified in the FEIS. In this case, the FAA reviewers may condition their concurrence upon the inclusion of specific mitigation measures to be incorporated, or may nonconcur. The FAA "shall not approve the Federal action over a nonconcurrence."

When the selected alternative involves a coordination requirement [Section 4(f), endangered species, fish and wildlife, wetlands, historic sites, and so on], that coordination must be accomplished prior to the adoption of an ROD. This includes the preparation and circulation of EIS supplements if required.

In summary, the FAA response to the Executive Order, CEQ, and DOT mandates is exceptionally detailed. As stated in its order,

the FAA's objective is to enhance environmental quality and avoid or minimize adverse impacts that might result from a proposed Federal action in a manner consistent with the FAA's principal mission *to provide for the safety of aircraft operations.* (emphasis added)

*Federal Aid Highway Program Manual,
Volume 7, Chapter 7, Section 2
(FHPM 7-7-2) Environmental Impact and
Related Procedures
and
Urban Mass Transportation Administration
Environmental Impact and Related Procedures
48 CFR 622
October 30, 1980*

For all intents and purposes, the FHWA is the agency most often involved in proposing major Federal actions significantly affecting the quality of the human environment. Since highway projects have been delayed by environmental issues more frequently than other kinds of public works projects, the concepts introduced in the 1978 CEQ guidelines concerning scoping, categorical exclusions, page limitations for an EIS, and tiering were most welcomed by the FHWA. Similarly, the UMTA is normally responsible for projects which are of sufficient magnitude and complexity to produce environmental controversy. Accordingly, these two modal agencies of the DOT have issued a joint regulation which applies to all surface transportation projects.

The regulation includes within its policy statement a direct commitment that reasonable measures required to mitigate adverse impacts resulting from projects are eligible for Federal-aid funding, over and above the cost of the project. The most frequent applications of this concept are noise barriers and water quality mitigation measures (erosion control and sediment retention).

As with FAA Order 1050.1C the regulation follows quite closely the CEQ guidelines and DOT Order 5610.1C. Much additional attention is given to the utilization of the categorical exclusion as a way to eliminate unnecessary paperwork and consultation in large numbers of routine projects. The Federal Highway Program Manual (FHPM) qualifies as categorical exclusions those actions:

which do not involve significant environmental impacts or substantial planning, time, resources, or expenditure. These actions will not induce significant foreseeable alterations in land use, planned growth, development patterns, or natural or cultural resources.

The following *types* of projects are categorical exclusions.

1. Planning and technical studies which do not fund the construction of facilities or acquisition of capital equipment.
2. Grants for training and research programs which do not involve construction.
3. Approval of a unified planning work program and certification of a state or local planning process. (23 CFR 450)
4. Approval of transportation improvement programs under 23 CFR 450, subpart C and statewide programs under 23 CFR 630, subpart A.
5. Approval of project concepts under 23 CFR 476.
6. Engineering when undertaken to define the elements of a proposal or alternatives sufficiently so that environmental effects can be assessed.
7. Federal-aid highway system revisions under 23 USC 103, which establishes classes of highways on the Federal-aid highway system.
8. Approval of utility installations on or across a transportation facility.
9. Reconstruction or modification of an existing bridge structure on essentially the same alignment or location (e.g., widening less than a single travel lane, adding shoulders or safety lanes, walkways, bikeways, or pipelines) except bridges on or eligible for inclusion on the National Register or bridges providing access to barrier islands. Reconstruction or modification of an existing one-lane bridge structure, presently

serviced by a two-lane road and used for two-lane traffic, to a two-lane bridge on essentially the same alignment or location, except bridges on or eligible for inclusion on the National Register or bridges providing access to barrier islands.

10. Construction of bicycle and pedestrian lanes, paths, and facilities.

11. Activity included in the state's "highway safety plan" under 23 USC 402.

12. Transfer of Federal lands pursuant to 23 USC 317 when the subsequent action is not an FHWA action.

13. Modernization of an existing highway by resurfacing, restoration, rehabilitation, widening less than a single lane width, adding shoulders, adding auxiliary lanes for localized purposes (e.g., weaving, turning, climbing), and correcting substandard curves and intersections. This classification is not applicable when the proposed project requires acquisition of more than minor amounts of right-of-way or substantial changes in access control.

14. Highway safety or traffic operations improvement projects including the correction or improvement of high hazard locations; elimination of roadside obstacles; highway signing; pavement markings; traffic control devices; railroad warning devices; and lighting. This classification is not applicable when the proposed action requires acquisition of more than minor amounts of right-of-way or substantial changes in access control.

15. Alterations to existing buildings to provide for noise reduction and the installation of noise barriers.

16. Ride-sharing activities and transportation corridor fringe parking facilities.

17. Landscaping.

18. Program administration and technical assistance to transit authorities to continue existing service or increase service to meet demand.

19. Project administration and operating assistance to transit authorities to continue existing service or increase service to meet demand.

20. Purchase of vehicles of the same type (same mode) either as replacements or to increase the size of the fleet where such increase can be accommodated by existing facilities or by new facilities which themselves are within a categorical exclusion.

21. Track and rail bed maintenance and improvements when carried out within the existing right-of-way.

22. Rehabilitation or reconstruction of existing rail and bus buildings and ancillary facilities where no additional land is required and there is no substantial increase in the number of users.

23. Purchase and installation of operating or maintenance equipment to be located within the transit facility and with no significant physical impacts off the site.

24. Installation of signs, small passenger and bus shelters, and traffic signs where no substantial land acquisition or traffic disruption will occur.

25. Construction of new bus storage and maintenance facilities in areas used predominantly for industrial or transportation purposes where such construction is not inconsistent with existing zoning and located on or near a street with adequate capacity to handle anticipated bus and support vehicle traffic.

26. Acquisition of land in which the property will not be modified, the land use will not be changed, and displacements will not occur. For projects other than UMTA advance land loans, this categorical exclusion is limited to the acquisition of minor amounts of land. This is undertaken for the purpose of maintaining the current land use and preserving alternatives to be considered in the environmental process. Advance land acquisition shall not limit the evaluation of alternatives, including shifts in alignment for a construction project, which may be required in the NEPA process.

27. Promulgation of rules, regulations, and directives for which a regulatory analysis is not required by Section 3 of Executive Order 12044.

28. Research activities as defined in 23 USC 307.

29. Emergency repairs under 23 USC 125 which do not substantially change the design and are commenced during or immediately after the occurrence of a natural disaster or catastrophic failure.

In previous times many project proposals certified for modernization, safety improvements, and bridge reconstruction were forced to include environmental analyses because of the ambiguity of the guidelines. The categorical exclusion allowance clearly eliminates this problem and reduces paperwork and delay.

Categorical exclusions represent Class II of a three-class categorization of projects, for the purpose of NEPA documentation. Class I projects are those which may significantly affect the environment, and therefore require an EIS. Examples of such projects are:

1. Any new controlled access freeway.
2. Any highway project of four or more lanes on a new location.
3. New construction or extension of fixed guideway systems (e.g., rapid rail, light rail, commuter rail, automated guideway transit, and exclusive busway). These projects would be expected to cause major shifts in travel patterns and land use.
4. Major transportation-related developments whose construction involves a large amount of demolition, displacement of a large number of individuals or businesses, or substantial disruption to local traffic patterns. This classification will take account of the condition of the buildings and the availability of comparable replacement facilities for displaced residences or businesses.

Class III projects are those which do not clearly fit into either one of the other classes. For these, a preliminary environmental assessment is to be made in order to resolve the classification question.

Ordinarily, an FEIS may be approved by the regional office of the appropriate administration without review by the Washington headquarters of the Office of the Secretary of the DOT. Exceptions to this are when (a) a highway is on new alignment in a metropolitan area of 100,000 population; (b) a highway is a new free-way; (c) a fixed guideway transit system is to be constructed or extended; (d) construction costs exceed $50 million in private money and Federal assistance exceeds $5 million; (e) a government agency has expressed opposition on environmental grounds; or (f) the headquarters in Washington requests a review. A Washington review, however, should not add to project delay because *prior concurrence* with the FEIS can be granted after the review of the DEIS, provided there is early coordination with the other Federal, state, and local government agencies, and the DEIS adequately identifies the environmental impacts of and the reasonable alternatives to the proposed project.

Whenever a major action is ready for implementation, it must be *reevaluated* by the applicant (state highway agency or local transit authority) and the appropriate administration to ascertain whether there have been substantial changes in the social, economic, or environmental impacts of the action.

An issue peculiar to transportation projects is Section 4(f) involvement as required by the 1966 Department of Transportation Act, when publicly owned park lands are potentially impacted. The joint regulation basically restates the guidance given in DOT Order 5610.1C concerning Section 4(f) involvement, except in two cases regarding exemptions to the requirement. The first is when the Federal, state, or local official with jurisdiction over the affected land determines that it is not significant, and the appropriate administration (UMTA or FHWA) agrees, Section 4(f) does not apply. It is unlikely that the clause would be frequently used, however, because few officials would willingly give up their leverage with the administration. Take, for example, the case where a proposed highway takes a small, relatively isolated piece of school playground. The school officials, unless they for some reason desire quick construction of the highway, would be in an ideal position to (a) cause delay in the project through forcing strict adherence to Section 4(f) requirements, or (b) barter their nonsignificance determination for other benefits, such as more noise barriers, insulation, or increased payment for damages.

In the second case, the Section 4(f) requirements need not be applied if the lands were acquired by the highway agency prior to a significance determination given to a particular park, recreation area, wildlife and waterfowl refuge, or historic site. This clause would be applied when a transportation agency purchased the right-of-way many years prior to construction. Even if highly significant lands were designated on either side of the right-of-way and the land included in the right-of-way was identical to the significant lands it could not be considered as anything but designated for project purposes (i.e., right-of-way). Section 4(f) would not apply as long as the highway agency stayed within the boundaries of its previously purchased lands. An exception to this exemption is the treatment of archaeological resources. This point is illustrated in Figure 3-1.

Unless the transportation agency can exercise one of these exemptive clauses, it must apply Section 4(f) requirements if a project is to "use land from a significant publicly owned park, recreation area, or wildlife refuge or any significant historic site," and it must determine that there is no *feasible* and *prudent* alternative to

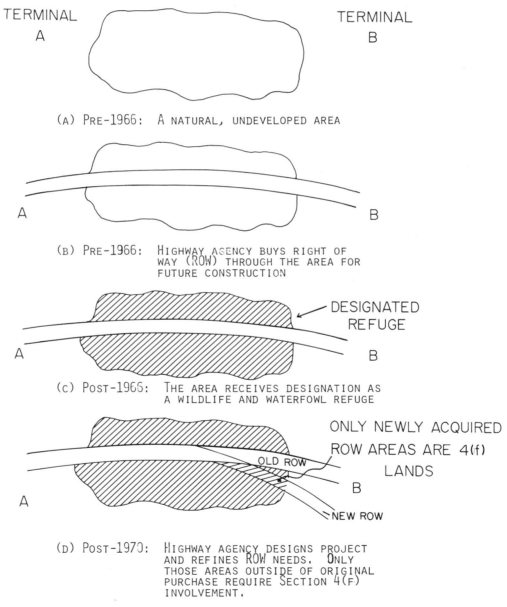

Figure 3-1.   Example of section 4(F) application.

the use of land from the property and the proposed action includes *all possible planning to minimize harm* to the property resulting from such use.

Information and data supporting these determinations must show that there are "unique problems or unusual factors involved in the use of the alternatives *and* that the cost, environmental impacts, or community disruption resulting from alternatives reaches extraordinary magnitudes." (emphasis added).

Just as DOT Order 5610.1C contains a detailed guide for the format and content of an EIS (see Appendix 3B), the draft version of the regulation (1979) provided a rather comprehensive view of the items that should be covered in an EIS on surface transportation. Particular emphasis is given to the section concerning environmental consequences, or impacts. These include the following.

1. Visual
    (a) Temporary
    (b) Permanent
2. Social and economic
    (a) Life-style changes
    (b) Travel patterns
    (c) School districts
    (d) Churches
    (e) Recreation
    (f) Businesses
    (g) Minorities and ethnic groups
    (h) Urban quality
    (i) Secondary impacts
3. Relocation
    (a) Number of households displaced
    (b) Neighborhood disruption
    (c) Available housing
    (d) Number of businesses displaced or impacted
    (e) Documentation of public participation activities
    (f) Unusual circumstances
4. Air quality
    (a) Microscale impacts
    (b) Mesoscale impacts
    (c) Analysis methodology
    (d) Documentation of early consultation
    (e) SIP consistency

5. Noise
    (a) Identification of sensitive receptors
    (b) Comparison of future noise levels with FHWA criteria
    (c) Comparison of future noise levels with existing
    (d) Noise abatement measures
    (e) Noise problem with no reasonable solution (exceptions to FHWA criteria)
6. Water quality
    (a) Erosion
    (b) Sedimentation
    (c) Deicing and weed control products
    (d) Chemical spills
    (e) Ground waste contamination
    (f) Stream modifications
    (g) Impoundment
    (h) Fish and wildlife
    (i) Documentation
7. Wetlands and coastal zones
    (a) Analyses summarized
    (b) Consultations undertaken
    (c) Practical measures to minimize harm
    (d) Documentation that there are no *practical alternatives*
8. Flood hazard
    (a) Impacts on beneficial floodplain values
    (b) Incompatible floodplain development
    (c) Measures to minimize flood risks
    (d) Evaluation of alternatives
9. Natural resources
    (a) Prime and unique farmlands
    (b) Threatened and endangered species
    (c) Natural landforms
    (d) Groundwater resources
    (e) Energy requirements
10. Land use
    (a) Growth-inducement
    (b) Factors which may influence development
    (c) State and/or local government plans or policies
    (d) Planned versus unplanned growth
    (e) Social, economic, and environmental impacts likely from induced growth or development

11. Historic sites
    (a) Historic, cultural, architectural, or architectural significance
    (b) Documentation of consultation
12. Construction
    (a) Air
    (b) Noise
    (c) Water
    (d) Detours
    (e) Safety
    (f) Spoil and borrow
    (g) Mitigation measures
13. Section 4(f) involvement
    (a) Project description and need [if Section 4(f) statement is a separate document]
    (b) Description of Section 4(f) properties
    (c) Alternatives (if a report document)
    (d) For each alternative, reasons why nonfeasible and/or nonprudent
    (e) Measures to minimize harm
    (f) Documentation of coordinations

FHPM 7-7-1
Process Guidelines for the Development of Environmental Action Plans
December 30, 1974

The FHWA has a unique role among the DOT modal agencies, as it delegates responsibilities to the state level. In typical situations, the FHWA channels matching funds to the 50 state highway agencies (SHA), who in turn are each responsible for providing the highway related services at a statewide level. Consistent with this method of operation, there are many SHAs with larger staffs and organizations than those of the FHWA.

Implementation of Sections 102(2) (A) and (B) of NEPA present peculiar problems to the FHWA as a result of its operational procedures. These sections, of course, call for the utilization of a "systematic, interdisciplinary approach," and the development of methods and procedures to "insure that presently unquantified environmental amenities and values may be given appropriate consideration in decision making." In order for the FHWA to adequately deal with these requirements, it must force the SHAs receiving matching funds to comply also.

The approach taken by the FHWA to obtain state compliance with NEPA Sections 102(2) (A) and (B) is to require each SHA to develop an Environmental Action Plan (EAP), which identifies and documents the necessary revisions to agency organization and project development processes for NEPA compliance. The EAP requirement has been formalized and fully defined in FHPM 7-7-1.

In the overall view of multimodal transportation, FHPM 7-7-1 is particularly significant, even though it is only a requirement in the highway mode. This is because the great majority (35 out of 50) of the states have followed the Federal example and created a state multimodal Department of Transportation, of which the SHA is an element. Therefore, the EAP, while mandated at the highway mode, has in effect provided the states with the incentive to formally review and document their procedures for consistency with NEPA in the *overall* transportation project development process.

FHPM 7-7-1 is applicable to the process

by which highway agencies plan and develop proposed projects, on any Federal-aid system, for which the FHWA approves the plans, specifications, and estimates [PS&E] or has the responsibility for approving a program. They apply to system planning decisions, including those made in compliance with 23 USC 134, and to project decisions made during the location and design stages.

In order to meet the requirements of FHPM 7-7-1, each state highway agency

shall operate under an approved Action Plan which describes the organization to be utilized and the process to be followed in the development of Federal and Federal-aid highway projects from the initial system planning through design.

The EAP for each state requires approval by the Governor of the state to assure a high level of interagency and intergovernmental coordination. In most cases, subsequent revision of the plan need only be approved by the Regional Federal Highway Administrator.

FHPM 7-7-1 is discussed in detail in Chapter 4. EAPs from several state departments of transportation are studied in order to gain insight into the project development process as it is affected by environmental issues.

NOISE-RELATED REGULATIONS

Federal Aviation Regulations
Part 36
Noise Standards: Aircraft Type and
Airworthiness Certification

One of the laws discussed in the last chapter was the *Control and Abatement of Aircraft Noise and Sonic Boom Act of 1968*, which required the FAA to "prescribe and amend" standards for aircraft noise measurement, control, and abatement. Aircraft type certifications were to be contingent upon these standards.

The FAA response to this mandate came on November 3, 1969, with an effective date of December 1, 1969, as FAR Part 36. This regulation contains seven subparts and six appendices.

Subpart A	General Provisions
Subpart B	Noise Measurement and Evalua-for Transport Category Large Airplanes and Turbojet Powered Airplanes
Subpart C	Noise Limits for Subsonic Transport Category Large Airplanes and Subsonic Turbojet Powered Airplanes
Subpart D	Noise Limits for Subsonic Transport Category Airplanes
Subpart E	Reserved
Subpart F	Propeller-Driven Small Airplanes
Subpart G	Operating Limitations and Information
Appendix A	Aircraft Noise Measurement
Appendix B	Aircraft Noise Evaluation
Appendix C	Noise Levels for Transport Category and Turbojet Powered Airplanes
Appendix D	Reserved
Appendix E	Reserved
Appendix F	Noise Measurement for Propeller-Driven Small Airplanes

Basically FAR Part 36 prescribes maximum noise levels for three types of aircraft (subsonic transport, supersonic transport, and small propeller-driven) under various operational modes as a function of (*a*) application date for type certification, and (*b*) date the individual aircraft first experienced flight. Depending upon (*a*) and (*b*) each aircraft is classified as Stage 1, Stage 2, or Stage 3, with Stage 3 having the most stringent requirement levels. The regulation also prescribes in detail measurement procedures to be utilized in determining the requisite noise levels.

Before discussing the particulars of the regulations, it would be interesting to note the *limitation* placed upon FAR Part 36:

Pursuant to 49 USC 1431(b)(4), the noise levels in this Part have been determined to be as low as is economically reasonable, technologically practicable and appropriate to the type of aircraft to which they apply. No determination is made, under the Part, that these noise levels are or should be acceptable or unacceptable for operation at, into, or out of, any airport.

Part 36 states that anyone applying for a type certificate or standard airworthiness certificate after the effective date (December 1, 1969) must show compliance with the appropriate noise level and measurement requirements. In addition (regardless of application date), anyone applying for a standard airworthiness certificate for a particular individual aircraft must show compliance with Stage 1 levels for large subsonic aircraft (more than 75,000 pounds), if there has been no flight time before December 1, 1973; Stage 1 levels for small propeller-driven aircraft (less than 75,000 pounds) with no flight time before December 31, 1974; or Stage 2 levels for Concorde (supersonic transport) airplanes with no flight time before January 1, 1980.

More stringent levels apply to small propeller-driven aircraft with no flight time before January 1, 1980. Also, for large aircraft powered by Pratt and Whitney Turbo Wasp JT3D series engines, the date is extended to December 31, 1974.

There is no single noise level value associated with Stage 1, because these are aircraft that do *not* comply with the values from Stage 2 or Stage 3. The Stage 1 value is the noise-level that the aircraft produces, in effect, when it comes *off*

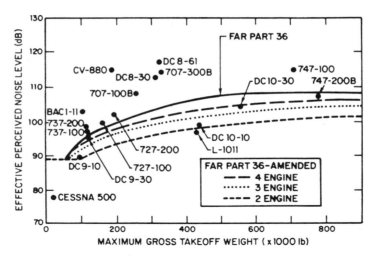

Figure 3-2.   Source: Federal Aviation Administration.

the assembly line. The point in assigning this value is to prevent future modifications to the aircraft that may raise its noise level. The aircraft types shown above the FAR Part 36 line (solid line) in Figure 3-2 are all Stage 1 aircraft.

Stage 2 and Stage 3 noise levels are applicable under three operating modes: takeoff, sideline, and approach (landing). The values are described in terms of *Effective Perceived Noise Levels* (EPNL), in *decibels* (EPNdB), which is a sound pressure level descriptor with adjustments for discrete frequency and time history (duration). Chapter 5 contains complete discussions of the meaning of EPNL and EPNdB.

From FAR Part 36, Stage 2 levels are listed here.

For takeoff—108 EPNdB for maximum weights of 600,000 pounds or more, reduced by 5 EPNdB per halving of the 600,000 pounds of maximum weight down to 93 EPNdB for maximum weights of 75,000 pounds or less.

For sideline and approach—108 EPNdB for maximum weights of 600,000 pounds or more, reduced by 2 EPNdB per halving of the 600,000 maximum weight down to 102 EPNdB for maximum weights of 75,000 pounds or less.

Figure 3-2 shows examples of Stage 2 aircraft types, in particular the DC10-30 and the 747-200B. Stage 2 aircraft were type-certified in the early 1970s, which was also a time when wide-body aircraft were introduced on a large

scale. Stage 2 levels apply to aircraft with the application date for type certification between December 1, 1969, and November 5, 1975.

Those aircraft types for which certification is applied for after November 5, 1975, must conform to the Stage 3 requirements, which are

For takeoff for airplanes with more than three engines—106 EPNdB for maximum weights of 850,000 pounds or more, reduced by 4 EPNdB per halving of the 850,000 pound maximum weight down to 89 EPNdB for maximum weights of 44,673 pounds or less.

For takeoff for airplanes with three engines—104 EPNdB for maximum weights of 850,000 pounds or more, reduced by 4 EPNdB per halving of the 850,000 pound maximum weight down to 89 EPNdB for maximum weights of 63,177 pounds or less.

For takeoff, for airplanes with fewer than three engines—101 EPNdB for maximum weights of 850,000 pounds or more, reduced by 4 EPNdB per halving of the 850,000 pound maximum weight down to 89 EPNdB for maximum weights of 106,250 pounds or less.

For sideline, regardless of the number of engines—103 EPNdB for maximum weights of 882,000 pounds or more, reduced by 2.56 EPNdB per halving of the 883,000 pound maximum weight down to 94 EPNdB for maximum weights of 77,200 pounds or less.

For approach, regardless of the number of engines—105 EPNdB for maximum weights of 617,300 pounds or more, reduced by 2.33 EPNdB per halving of the 617,300 pound maximum weight down to 98 EPNdB for maximum weights of 77,200 pounds or less.

Figure 3-2 shows examples of several Stage 3 aircraft, including the DC9-10, DC10-10, and L-1011. It should be noted that this figure is only for takeoffs. Similar figures could be developed for sideline and approach, for which each aircraft would also have to comply.

Figure 3-3 shows the measurement locations for the Stage 1, 2, and 3 noise level values. For takeoff, the location is 6500 m from the start of the takeoff roll on an extended center line of the runway. For approach, it is 2000 m from the runway threshold, on an extended center line. For sideline, the offset distance is 450 m opposite the point of highest noise level, except for aircraft with more than three turbojet engines. For these aircraft, the offset distance is 0.35 nautical mile.

For small propeller-driven aircraft with type certification application between October 10, 1973 and January 1, 1975 the maximum *flyover* sound pressure level at a height of 1000 ft is 82 dBA. For those with applications after January 1, 1975, the maximum sound pressure level is 80 dBA. The concepts of sound pressure level and dBA are explained fully in Chapter 5.

A January 1977 amendment to FAR Part 91 requires that all older-model aircraft still in service in the United States by January 1, 1983 be *retrofitted*. This means that these Stage 1 aircraft must be reengineered in such a way that their levels do not exceed Stage 2 (the solid line

on Figure 3-2). Aircraft utilizing four low-bypass ratio engines have until January 1, 1985.

It is the documented policy of the FAA that FAR Parts 36 and 91 have been extended to the limits for technologically and economically feasible aircraft noise *source* control. Further gains in aviation noise control will have to come in the areas of airport development and land-use compatibility. Accordingly, the FAA has issued several orders and advisory circulars aimed at assisting local airport proprietors in developing and implementing noise control plans. Included in this assistance is FAA Order 5100.33, *Instructions for Processing ADAP Requests for Land Purchase for Noise Compatibility Purposes*, which provides guidance for programming the acquisition of severely impacted land uses. The ADAP program, it may be recalled, was created by the Airport and Airway Development Act of 1970, for the purpose of airport planning and development.

U.S. Environmental Agency 40 CFR 201
Noise Emission Standards for Transportation
Equipment, Interstate Rail Carriers
January 4, 1980
(Effective Date: January 15, 1984)

The regulations required by court order for railroad noise levels are applicable nationwide and are preemptive over state and local laws. These points were the basis for successful litigation brought by the American Association of Railroads against the EPA and are discussed in Chapter 2. In that discussion it was noted that the lawsuit centered around *railyard* sources of noise, and in effect produced standards for these sources (switcher locomotives, locomotive load

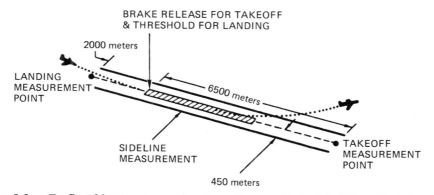

Figure 3-3. *Far* Part 36 measurement locations. Source: Federal Aviation Administration.

cell test stands, retarders, and car coupling operations). The standards were added to 40 CFR 201, which already included national standards for newly manufactured locomotives, as well as rail operations.

At a distance of 30 m from the geometric center of the locomotive along a line perpendicular to the track,

no carrier subject to this regulation shall operate any locomotive to which this regulation is applicable, and of which manufacture is completed after December 31, 1979, which produces A-weighted sound levels in excess of 87 dB[A] at any throttle setting except idle, when operated singly, or when connected to a load cell, or in excess of 70 dB[A] at idle when operated singly.

For rail purposes, no carrier

shall operate any rail car or combination of rail cars which while in operation produce sound levels in excess of (1) 88 dB[A] at rail car speeds up to and including 72 km/hr [45 mph]; or (2) 93 dB[A] at rail car speeds greater that 72 km/hr [45 mph] . . . at 30 meters (100 feet) from the centerline of any section of track which is free of special track work or bridge or trestles and which exhibits less than a two (2) degree curve [or a radius of curvature greater than 813 meters (2865 feet)].

Emphasis in this section is on rail *cars*, not locomotives. There is a separate standard for newly manufactured locomotives which are "moving at any time or under any condition of grade, load, acceleration, or deceleration," at a distance of "thirty meters [100 ft] from the centerline of any section of track having a two degree curve [or radius of curvature greater than 813 meters (2865)]." This standard is 90 dBA, which interestingly and paradoxically is less than the standard for (powered or unpowered) rail cars moving at speeds greater than 45 mph. This is an apparent inconsistency in the rail noise regulations.

From an enforcement standpoint, the standard concerning newly manufactured locomotives is a much better regulation because it encourages straightforward engineering solutions. Using the noise level requirement and a design

standard, locomotive manufacturers are able to build in noise reduction features into new models, with easily determinable cost differentials.

The standard concerning rail operations, however, is not a good regulation from the enforcement perspective because it does not consider the condition of the track and the trackbed, which have a significant effect on noise generation. The standard also does not consider the character of adjacent land use. It is entirely possible that a carrier could distribute noisy equipment in corridors of low population density in order to reduce or eliminate negative noise impacts.

The court-ordered standard for the first of the railyard sources, the switcher locomotive, is the same as for regular locomotives. Since that standard is for locomotives manufactured after December 31, 1979, however, there is an additional one for switcher locomotives manufactured prior to that date. For stationary switcher locomotives, the standard is 87 dBA for any throttle setting except idle and 70 dBA for idle. The measurement distance is 30 m. For *moving* switcher locomotives, the standard is 90 dBA at 30 m, with the same constraints on track curvature as in the other moving standards discussed.

Locomotive load cell test stands are also a source of railyard noise and are therefore regulated. At a perpendicular distance of 30 m, the maximum allowable level from a load cell test stand is 78 dBA. The other major sources of railyard noise, car coupling operations and retarders, have standards that are effective at the *nearest receiving property line*, rather than at 30 m. The car coupling operation maximum sound level is 92 dBA, unless the carrier can demonstrate that it cannot meet the standard at speeds less than 8 mph.

As discussed in Chapter 2, the sections of this regulation dealing with the railyard sources are effective on January 15, 1984. The standards for newly manufactured locomotives and rail operations have been in effect since December 31, 1976.

Procedures for Abatement of Highway Traffic Noise and Construction Noise
May 14, 1976
(FHPM 7-7-3)

Originally promulgated as Policy and Procedure Memorandum 90-2 in 1972, this regulation constitutes the noise *standards* mandated by the Federal-aid Highway Act of 1970. Conformance with the *standards* is mandatory, although conformance with the noise abatement criteria (which are discussed later) is not. The FHPM explicitly defines the noise *standards* as consisting of "the highway noise prediction requirements, noise analyses, noise abatement criteria, and requirements for informing local officials."

Two types of projects are included in the FHPM 7-7-3 instructions. *Type I projects* are projects which involve the construction of a highway on a new location or the significant altering of an existing highway. Compliance with FHPM 7-7-3 is mandatory for Type I projects. *Type II projects*, on the other hand, are voluntary proposals for adding noise abatement features to existing highways. Federal funding participation for Type II projects is the same percentage (share) as that for the system on which the project is located.

The FHPM requires for Type I projects that a five-step analysis procedure be utilized to "analyze expected traffic noise impacts and alternative noise abatement measures to mitigate these impacts." These steps are

1. Identification of existing activities, developed lands, and undeveloped lands for which development is planned, designed, and programmed which may be affected by noise from the highway.

2. Prediction of traffic noise levels.
3. Determination of existing noise levels.
4. Determination of traffic noise impacts.
5. Examination and evaluation of alternative noise abatement measures for reducing or eliminating the noise impacts.

The remainder of the FHPM provides illumination of these five steps, for the most part. Table 3-1, for example, gives the *Noise Abatement Criteria* (also known as Design Noise Levels) necessary for one of the methods used to determine impacts (step 4), as well as the guidance necessary to identify noise affected activities (commonly called sensitive receptors) (step 1).

To clearly define a point which is often confused in highway noise studies, the noise abatement criteria apply *only* to those activities which may be affected by noise from highway. This does *not* include those activities which are not affected by the noise, even though the highway noise levels may be high. FHPM 7-7-3 states that abatement will only be necessary "where frequent human use occurs and in which a lowered noise level would be of benefit." Most commercial and industrial areas do not meet these criteria because there is usually no significant benefit to lowered noise levels, at least in the range of most highway noise situations. It is therefore a mistake to identify commercial and industrial areas as Activity Category C properties and assign them the criteria of 72 dBA for

TABLE 3-1.   Noise Abatement Criteria

Activity Category	$L_{eq}(h)$	$L_{10}(h)^a$	Description of Activity Category
A	57 (exterior)	60 (exterior)	Lands on which serenity and quiet are of extraordinary significance and serve an important public need and where the preservation of those qualities is essential if the area is to continue to serve its intended purpose.
B	67 (exterior)	70 (exterior)	Picnic areas, recreation areas, playgrounds, active sports areas, parks, residences, motels, hotels, schools, churches, libraries, and hospitals
C	72 (exterior)	75 (exterior)	Developed lands, properties, or activities not included in categories A or B above
D	—	—	Undeveloped lands
E	52 (exterior)	55 (exterior)	Residences, hotels, motels, public meeting rooms, schools, churches, libraries, hospitals, and auditoriums

$^a L_{10}$ *is the sound pressure level exceed 10 percent of a given time period (see Chapter 5)*

L_{eq}(h) or 75 dBA for L_{10}(h). (The concepts of dBA, L_{eq}, and L_{10} are discussed in detail in Chapter 5.)

Activity Category E, interior levels, is to be applied

> *in those situations where there are no exterior activities to be affected by the traffic noise, or where the exterior activities are far from or physically shielded from the roadway in a manner that prevents an impact on exterior activities.*

Primary abatement consideration, however, is to be given to those situations where exterior benefit is to be gained. In other words, the FHWA puts a higher priority on noise *barrier* solutions than on noise insulation solutions.

Step 3 in the five-step analysis procedure requires the *prediction* of future traffic noise levels. Such predictions are based on several factors, including traffic volumes and mix, speeds, traffic flow conditions, roadway gradient, roadway to receiver distance, intervening topography, presence of barriers, and ground cover.

The principal methodology used to predict future levels is the FHWA Highway Traffic Noise Prediction Model (Report Number FHWA-RD-77-108), commonly referred to as the *FHWA Model*. Chapter 5 contains an exhaustive analysis of this model.

The determination of existing noise levels, step 3, is accomplished through one of two ways. If the existing noise environment is dominated by highways, it is acceptable to use a prediction technique such as the FHWA Model to estimate existing levels. However, when the proposed highway is on a new location in a primitive area, or if there are other major sources of noise (airport, railroad, industry) in the project vicinity, it is necessary to determine the existing levels by measurement. While this is an expensive and time-consuming activity, measurement does provide a degree of hard data for the noise study and is helpful in calibrating the prediction model to ensure its accuracy. Many state highway agencies have a policy to perform field measurements on all but minor projects.

As mentioned earlier, one method for determining impact is to compare the predicted future traffic noise levels with the noise abatement criteria (from Table 3-1). Whenever the future noise levels for a given land-use activity approach or exceed the noise abatement criteria, there is an impact. Also, whenever future noise levels exceed existing levels by a *substantial* amount there is an impact. While the FHPM does not define the term *substantial*, it is generally taken to mean 10 to 15 dBA.

For a project that includes noise impacts, the FEIS or FONSI will not be adopted by the FHWA unless the state highway agency identifies (*a*) noise abatement measures which are reasonable and feasible and which are likely to be incorporated into the project, and (*b*) noise impacts for which no apparent solution is available. In addition, the plans and specifications for the project will not be approved by the FHWA unless the reasonable and feasible noise abatement measures are incorporated.

There are six noise abatement measures given in the FHPM as available for use on FHWA-funded projects. These include

1. Traffic management measures (e.g., traffic control devices and signing for prohibition of certain vehicle types, time-use restrictions for certain vehicles types, modified speed limits, and exclusive lane designations).
2. Alterations of horizontal and vertical alignments.
3. Acquisition of property rights (either in fee or lesser interest) for construction of noise barriers.
4. Construction of noise barriers (including landscaping for aesthetic purposes) whether within or outside of the highway right-of-way.
5. Acquisition of real property or interests (predominantly unimproved property) to serve as a buffer zone to preempt development which would be adversely impacted by the traffic noise.
6. Noise insulation of public use or nonprofit institutional structures.

FHPM 7-7-3 includes two additional requirements that must be met. First, it is essential that the state highway agency *coordinate with local officials* in whose jurisdiction the project is located to inform them of the noise situation in order to prevent future traffic noise impacts.

The local officials must be provided with estimates of future noise levels for developed and undeveloped lands and other useful information, including the FHWA policy on Type II projects.

The other requirement in the FHPM concerns the analysis of construction noise. Three general steps are to be followed.

1. Identify activities which may be effected.
2. Determine the measures needed to minimize or eliminate adverse construction noise impacts.
3. Incorporate the needed abatement measures into the plans and specifications.

In many cases, step 1 will be the same as step 1 in the five-step analysis procedure for the traffic noise study. It should be noted that step 2 does not provide any guidance and/or methodologies for determining adverse construction noise impact or a listing of noise abatement measures. This lack of detail in the regulations leaves the state highway agencies in a potentially difficult situation if a project goes into litigation.

Department of Housing and Urban Development, Noise Criteria and Standards
August 13, 1979
(24 CFR 51)

This regulation implements the Department of Housing and Urban Development (HUD) policy toward funding assistance in areas of high noise levels. While the HUD standards are not concerned only with transportation-generated noise, they do recognize that the majority of noise problems in urban areas are caused by either highways or aircraft. Accordingly, the regulation is quite specific in its guidance concerning these two sources.

The HUD *Site Acceptability Standards* for noise are

L_{dn}	*Condition*
Less than 65 dBA	Acceptable
66 dBA to 75 dBA	Normally Unacceptable
Above 75 dBA	Unacceptable

L_{dn}, the day-night average sound level, is a 24-hour descriptor which is calculated by determining the hourly L_{eq} values for the 24-hour period, adding a 5 dBA penalty to nighttime levels (10:00 p.m. to 7:00 a.m.), and averaging the 24 values. L_{dn} is approximately equal to the design-hour L_{eq} for a highway situation, and is approximately 35 units less than the Noise Exposure Forecast (NEF) values. NEF is one of the more commonly used descriptors of airport noise.

The regulation allows for approval of projects in the Normally Unacceptable and Unacceptable zones, although with certain restrictions. For example, Normally Unacceptable situations will be approved if the building plans call for *additional* sound attenuation to reduce outdoor levels indoors, if the resulting L_{dn} is below 65 dBA. Sound attenuation measures to reduce Unacceptable levels to Acceptable levels, however, require the specific approval of the HUD Assistant Secretary for Community Planning and Development. This is because of the potentially significant costs required for the treatment, and because the analysis must document that exterior activities will not be adversely impacted by the high noise levels. Berms and/or barriers may be used as part of a plan to reduce both outdoor and indoor noise levels.

Any project located in a Normally Unacceptable zone must receive a *Special Environmental Clearance* permit, except when an EIS is being prepared on the project. In that case, FEIS approval would take the place of the permit. In an Unacceptable zone an EIS is required for the approval of any project. The EIS may be replaced by the Special Environmental Clearance permit, with the approval of the Assistant Secretary, where there is to be no sensitive exterior activity on the site and noise is the only environmental issue.

There is flexibility within the regulation to consider "nonacoustic benefits" of a project, and therefore to slightly relax the standards. This is to be done on a case-by-case basis, however, and allows the Acceptable zone to be shifted only from 65 dBA to 70 dBA for L_{dn}. This may be done if *all* of the following conditions are satisfied.

1. The project does not require an EIS, and noise is the only environmental issue.
2. The project has received a Special Environmental Clearance and has received the con-

currence of the Environmental Clearance Officer.

3. The project meets other program goals to provide housing in proximity to employment, public facilities, and transportation.

4. The project is in conformance with local goals and maintains the character of the neighborhood.

5. The project sponsor has set forth reasons, acceptable to HUD, as to why the noise attenuation measures that would normally be required for new construction in the L_{dn} 65 to 70 zone cannot be met.

6. Other sites which are not exposed to noise above L_{dn} 65 and which meet program objectives are generally not available.

It is the position of HUD then that an additional 5 dBA will be acceptable, but only when the project is clearly outstanding in every other way and there are no other satisfactory sites available. For sites with levels higher than L_{dn} 70 dBA, HUD funding is simply not a possibility. It is interesting to note that this L_{dn} 70 dBA value is slightly higher than the FHWA Noise Abatement Criterion of 67 dBA for design hour L_{eq} for residences, while the L_{dn} 65 dBA for acceptability is slightly lower.

AIR-QUALITY-RELATED REGULATIONS

Transportation-Air Quality Planning Guidelines, jointly issued by EPA and DOT June, 1978

Enactment of the Clean Air Act Amendments of 1977 produced a flurry of regulatory and procedural activity at all four levels of government—Federal, state, regional, and local—in response to the clear Congressional mandate to attain the National Ambient Air Quality Standards (NAAQS) by 1982 or 1987. Most of this activity has centered around developing and implementing a *revised* State Implementation Plan (SIP), a document designed to *require* the utilization of transportation measures and strategies as a *tool* to attain the NAAQS.

Congress, in the wording of the act, was very explicit in its intentions concerning the process to be utilized in revising and implementing the SIP and also in the specific transportation con-

trol measures to be used in its attainment. As a result, the discussion of the legislation in Chapter 2 (Air-Quality-Related Legislation) is quite detailed. The guidelines discussed here actually have not required a great amount of interpretation by either the EPA or DOT, but rather simply provide illumination of the act itself. This is quite a different situation from the circumstances surrounding NEPA, which was so brief that it has required a tremendous amount of interpretation, much of which has come through the courts.

The transportation portion of the SIP is to show attainment of the NAAQS for carbon monoxide (CO) and photochemical oxidants (O_x) by December 31, 1982 or is to demonstrate that an extension to December 31, 1987 is necessary *despite the implementation of all reasonable stationary and transportation control measures.* For nearly all of the urban areas in the country attainment for CO and O_x by 1982 is not possible through reliance on stationary source controls and Federal new-car emissions standards alone. Accordingly, these "nonattainment" areas must select one or more of the 18 transportation control measures listed in Chapter 2 (Air-Quality–Related Legislation) for implementation in order to meet the 1982 deadline. If there are no reasonable means to meet that deadline, extension to 1987 is granted by the EPA, but with a *very severe penalty*: the required adoption of an Inspection/Maintenance (I/M) program.

For those areas able to attain the NAAQS by the 1982 deadline, the revised SIP was to have been submitted to the EPA in 1979. For those seeking extension to 1987, the revision is required by December 31, 1982 with actual initiation control measures not later than that date.

According to the guidelines, the SIP must include

1. Identification of tasks and responsibilities of all participating agencies.

2. A schedule for developing and analyzing ambitious alternative packages of transportation measures.

3. Verification that such an analysis is underway

4. A schedule for adoption for package(s) of measures determined to be reasonably available.

5. A commitment to justify any decision not to adopt difficult measures.
6. A commitment to accelerate implementation of specific transportation control strategies.
7. A commitment to the incremental phase-in of additional strategies that appear reasonable and effective on the basis of a preliminary analysis.
8. Where required by extension, a commitment to a schedule of activities leading to the implementation of an I/M program.

The profundity of this law and these guidelines should be obvious—local and regional government (including elected) officials are being forced by a Federal agency (the EPA) to rethink and modify, where necessary, transportation delivery systems for the express and sole purpose of improving air quality.

The guidelines, as required by the act, include a rather involved procedure to ascertain that the revised SIP and the selected transportation control measures are developed using a highly integrated "3-C"-type planning process—continuous, comprehensive, and cooperative. Because the act was so explicit in this area, Chapter 2 contains an adequately detailed discussion on the process. The remainder of this section, therefore, will emphasize two other areas of the guidelines: specific pollutant requirements for CO and O_x, and the criteria for the evaluation of alternatives.

Photochemical oxidants, O_x, are a product of hydrocarbons (HC), nitrogen oxides, and sunlight, and are therefore organic. The revised SIP for O_x must be comprehensive and consider the emission of organic compounds from all sources, stationary as well as mobile (transportation). Oxidant plan development is to be regional in nature in that it is to address an entire urban area. Specifically,

the areas must be large enough to cover the entire urbanized area and adjacent to fringe areas of development. For nonattainment urban areas, the highest pollutant concentration for the entire area must be used in determining the necessary level of control. Additionally, uniform modeling techniques must be used throughout the nonattainment urban

area. These requirements apply to interstate as well as intrastate areas.

Each of the 18 transportation control measures are to be thoroughly analyzed for possible implementation in an *expeditous* manner. In addition to calling for attainment for CO and O_x by the target date (1982 or 1987), the guidelines call for *annual incremental reductions* in order to achieve progress in the period prior to attainment.

Therefore, not all transportation measure implementation activities should wait until the comprehensive analysis of control measures are completed. Demonstration studies are important and should accompany or precede full scale implementation of the comprehensive strategy. It is the EPA's policy that each area will be required to schedule a representative selection of transportation measures for implementation at least on a pilot or demonstration basis prior to the end of 1980.

The guidelines also state that the

EPA recognizes that the planning and implementation of very extensive air-quality related transportation measures can be a complicated and lengthy process, and in areas with severe carbon monoxide or oxidant problems completion of some of the adopted measures may extend beyond 1982. Implementation of even these very extensive transportation measures, however, must be initiated before December 31, 1982.

The EPA is quite adamant, as required by the act, in its position on expeditious implementation of the transportation control measures. Because of the requirement that all of the selected measures, even the most extensive, must be initiated before the end of 1982, there is no advantage in delaying implementation until 1987 (except in reductions due to vehicle emission controls). The disadvantage of such a delay, on the other hand, the mandated I/M program, is a most serious one. Nonattainment areas, therefore, have a great incentive to use all reasonable measures to attain the NAAQS for CO and O_x by 1982.

Another incentive to meet the 1982 date for oxidants is the EPA's policy on monitoring. Any revised SIP calling for an extension must contain a commitment to implement a complete O_x monitoring program in the urbanized area in order to adequately characterize the nature and extent of the problem as well as to ascertain the effectiveness of O_x control strategies.

The guidelines require, as part of the SIP revision process, a comprehensive analysis of the alternatives (the 18 transportation control measures) as part of the urban transportation planning process. Region-wide strategies are to be emphasized in the analysis of O_x levels, since oxidants represent a regional air quality problem. High CO concentrations, on the other hand, are a localized problem and therefore require emphasis on subarea studies and corrective measures.

This analysis of alternatives is to key on the appropriate attainment target date, 1982 or 1987, and is to closely parallel the level of detail used in the transportation planning activities in the urbanized area. Obviously, the accuracy obtained in calculating the transportation demand among the alternative scenarios will be one of the limiting factors in assessing the effects of the alternatives. In many cases, therefore, the data produced initially should only be to clarify critical issues and tradeoffs. In other words, the actual numbers from the alternatives should only be used for comparative purposes.

The guidelines are quite explicit in establishing the *criteria* for alternatives analysis. All potential impacts should be considered, not just air quality, but implementation feasibility is critical. Measures that would be likely to create serious hardships should not be selected just because they appear to improve air quality. Other considerations include transportation and urban development needs, as well as social, economic, and other environmental impacts.

For each alternative package of measures or control startegies under consideration the following factors should be considered qualitatively, where data or methodologies are available.

1. Air quality
   (a) Regional impacts for CO and O_x
   (b) Local impacts for CO and O_x

2. Energy consumption
   (a) Fuel consumed by each alternative
   (b) All other energy consumed by each alternative, if any
3. Community effects
   (a) Employment and employment patterns
   (b) Retail sales and other business indicators
   (c) Effects on the tax base
   (d) Changes in land-use patterns
   (e) Impacts on regional development
   (f) Urban development plans
   (g) Property acquisition requirements
   (h) Neighborhood disruption and displacement
   (i) Compatibility with community goals
4. Financial analysis
   (a) Funding sources and uses
   (b) Matching requirements
   (c) Opportunities forgone
5. Economic analysis
   (a) Present capital and operating costs
   (b) Future capital and operating costs
6. Economic impacts
   (a) Indirect present and future costs and benefits
   (b) Borne by public and private sector, income group, geographic area, social group
7. Travel impacts
   (a) Trip generation
   (b) Modal split
   (c) Travel time
   (d) Origin–destination
   (e) Level of service
   (f) Convenience
   (g) Accessibility
8. Political feasibility
   (a) Required public and elected official support
   (b) New legislation
   (c) Promotional efforts
   (d) Successful applications elsewhere
   (e) Potential controversy

9. Institutional feasibility
   (a) Assessment of need for new authority
   (b) Special interagency agreements
   (c) Extensive cooperation among agencies
   (d) Dependence upon other actions for successful implementation
10. Other factors considered important by the community

It is of course not by coincidence that this evaluation procedure is quite similar in parts to the requirements for the preparation of EISs as defined by NEPA and the CEQ guidelines. The similarities are also quite evident in the SIP development process, which is heavily dependent upon a systematic, integrated, interdisciplinary approach designed to maximize citizen and interagency involvement.

In summary, Congress, through the Clean Air Act of 1977, placed within the EPA an extraordinary degree of authority over the transportation programs in this country. There is no questioning the conclusion that Congress is convinced of the seriousness of the air quality problem and that the EPA is the lead Federal agency in solving the problem. In fact, the EPA has been given the power to impose *sanctions* upon any urban area that is unsuccessful in attaining the NAAQS by the target date. These sanctions may include the elimination of all Federal transportation funds in the urban area.

Air Quality Guidelines
November 19, 1979
(FHPM 7-7-9)

Implementation of the joint DOT and EPA guidelines as discussed above is necessary in order for urbanized areas to comply with the NAAQS and therefore not lose Federal urban transportation funding. Implementation of FHPM 7-7-9, on the other hand, is for a primarily different purpose: to insure that specific highway projects are consistent with the approved SIP. The FHPM says

it is the policy of the Federal Highway Administration [FHWA] that highway agencies responsible for the planning, location, and construction of highways persuant to 23 U.S.C. consult with the local, state and Federal air pollution control agencies as appropriate, and assure that decisions on highways are consistent with approved State implementation plans [SIPs] and that adequate consideration is given to preservation and enhancement of air quality.

In addition to consistency requirements for specific highway projects, the state highway agencies (SHA) and its designated metropolitan planning organization (MPO) must assess the consistency of their overall transportation plans and programs for the respective nonattainment urbanized areas. This is to be accomplished through a continuing review process which includes an annual solicitation of the state air pollution control agency for its evaluation of the consistency of SHA and MPO activities with respect to the SIP. Where any differences of opinion exist between the SHA and MPO and the state air pollution control agency, the SHA and MPO must take the initiative in resolving those differences.

Also as a part of this continuing review process, the SHA is to seek an annual assessment of its SIP consistency record from the Regional Federal Highway Administrator (in consultation with the Regional Administrator of the EPA) and from the appropriate *policy board*. This latter group is made up of local officials and representatives of agencies or organizations designated by the state for the purpose of providing "policy guidance and direction in the conduct of the urban transportation planning process in an urbanized area." Private individuals are also eligible for appointment to the policy board. The FHPM authorizes the Regional Federal Highway Administrator to withhold planning certification (and therefore Federal Aid Urban Systems funds) if the Administrator cites significant deficiencies and inconsistencies with respect to the SIP.

Concerning specific highway project proposals, the FHPM requires the preparation of an air quality analysis commensurate with several factors descriptive of the projects. These include project type and location, anticipated traffic volumes, existing air quality problems, the sensitivity of nearby receptors, and meteorological conditions.

Projects that are relatively minor and noncontroversial in nature can usually be satisfactorily addressed using simplified analysis techniques, without the use of on-site monitoring. However, higher volume projects in critical (nonattainment) areas may require a monitoring program and a rather sophisticated level of analysis. Chapter 6 discusses in significant detail the various methods available for analysis.

For any project whose impacts are such that it is classified as a major Federal action significantly affecting the quality of the environment, and therefore requires an EIS, the DEIS must contain

1. An identification of the air quality impact of the highway section [project].

2. An identification of the analysis methodology utilized.

3. A brief summary of the early consultation with the air pollution control agency, and where applicable, a brief summary of consultation with the indirect source review agency.

4. Any comments received from the air pollution control agency, and where applicable, any comments received from the indirect source review agency.

5. The highway agency's determination on the consistency of each alternative under consideration with the approved SIP.

It is implicit in this listing that the SHA must obtain from the state air pollution control agency a determination that the project is consistent with the SIP. This determination will have a major role in the final decision on consistency for the project, which is made by the Regional Federal Highway Administrator. The FEIS may not be adopted by the FHWA without the Regional Federal Highway Administrator's determination of consistency.

Requirements 3 and 4 listed above make mention of consultation with the *indirect source review agency*. This refers to a requirement imposed as a result of court action in 1973.* States must include in their implementation plans consideration of *mobile* source air quality impacts

*The 1977 Amendments to the Clean Air Act explicity forbade the EPA from *requiring* that states maintain an indirect source program.

which result from *stationary* source activities. The mobile, or *indirect*, sources are defined as highways and roads, shopping centers, commercial developments, industrial developments, recreation centers, parking lots and garages, sports stadiums, and airports.

WATER-QUALITY–RELATED REGULATIONS

Section 404 Permit for Dredge and Fill
33 CFR 323 (Corps)
40 CFR 230 (EPA)

A review of the discussions in Chapter 2 concerning water-quality–related legislation indicates that the U.S. Army Corps of Engineers has been involved in regulating construction-related activities in the navigable waters of the nation for more than 80 years. The law authorizing this role for the Corps was the Rivers and Harbors Act of 1899 (particularly Sections 9 and 10). In 1972 Section 404 was added to the Federal Water Pollution Control Act (FWPCA) which required a formalized permit procedure for activities involving fill or discharge into the navigable water.

A 1975 court decision held that the Corps had not been defining "navigable waters" broadly enough and interpreted the 1972 FWCPA as intending for the Corps to regulate "all of the waters of the United States" under its 404 program. This new definition greatly expanded the breadth of the Corps program and actually caused Federal encroachment into areas that had been traditionally under the jurisdiction of state agencies.

Being sensitive to issues involving Federal (versus state or local) domain, Congress specifically addressed Section 404 permit responsibilities in its 1977 amendments to the FWPCA, which was renamed the Clean Water Act.

As was discussed in Chapter 2 (Water-Quality-Related Legislation), the 1977 amendments provided the opportunity for the states to assume full regulative authority in certain Section 404 permit activities. In order to assume its authority, however, the state's water pollution control agency must put in place a program approved by the EPA, as well as a statewide plan for waste treatment management (Section 208, CWA), which also must be approved. The situation as it now stands, is that there are really *two* Section 404 permit programs: one administered by the Corps (33 CFR 323), and one administered by some states under the direction of the EPA (40 CFR 230).

Corps Program

In evaluating a permit application, the Corps considers conservation, economics, aesthetics, environmental concerns, fish and wildlife values, flood damage prevention, the welfare of the general public, historic values, recreation, land use, water supply, water quality, navigation, energy needs, safety, and food production.

The Corps permit process requires that an environmental assessment be prepared as part of the application package. The assessment is to discuss these considerations in such a way as to provide an overall view of the impact of the proposal.

The Corps ordinarily issues permits for individual activities. However, the regulations provide for *general* permits for *classes* of activities located within relatively small geographic areas. For such general issuance individual and cumulative impacts are to cause no more than minimal environmental harm. It is even possible for the Corps to issue a nationwide permit, provided the activities will affect (only minimally) very minor waters in the United States.

A Section 404 permit application to the Corps must include at least the following.

1. A detailed description of the project, including its purpose and use.
2. Types of structures involved.
3. Types and quantities of dredged or fill materials.
4. Names and addresses of affected and/or adjacent property owners.
5. Site information [including addresses, tax assessor's description, name of the waterway(s), and other information pertaining to property identification].
6. Current status of all necessary approvals and certifications.
7. Explanation of denials (if applicable) of any necessary approvals or certifications.
8. Signature of the applicant or authorized agent.

Decision on the permit application is made in most cases by the appropriate Corps District Engineer, after an opportunity is provided for public comment. In situations where another Federal agency has objections about the application, the approval decision is referred to the Corps Division Engineer level where attempts are made to resolve the objection through mediation. When this mediation is unsuccessful and unresolved objections still remain, the application may be referred to the Corps Chief of Engineers. Other circumstances which may require that the decision be made by the Chief of Engineers include situations when

1. A final determination by the Division Engineer is precluded by a statute or Memorandum of Agreement with another Federal agency. The memorandum of agreement will prescribe procedures for resolving objections.
2. The Corps position is contrary to the official position of the Governor of the State affected.
3. Relevant laws, regulations, and policies are in substantiated doubt.
4. The Chief of Engineers *requests* that the application be forwarded to him for decision.
5. The baseline used to determine the limits of the territorial sea would be affected.
6. Section 9 of the Rivers and Harbors Act of 1899 is involved (a bridge or other structure is proposed).

Because most transportation activities are non-point source in nature and usually require the construction of a bridge or other structure, Corps reviews of section 404 applications could come at the highest levels. This would be the case when a U.S. Coast Guard permit for Section 9 is also required. From the perspective of the Corps, the permit requirement is comprehensive under Section 404 in that activities related to Section 10 of the Rivers and Harbors Act, as well as Section 401 of the Clean Water Act are also provided under the Section 404 permit procedure. Thus, only one permit is required from the U.S. Corps of Engineers.

EPA/State Program

As already mentioned, the amendments to Section 404 passed in 1977 were designated to return a portion of the regulatory responsibility to the states. Congress was careful, however, not to modify the nature of the Section 404 program itself or in any way to relax the guidelines in allowing state involvement. Rather, the role of the states under the direction of the EPA is to *maintain* Federal water quality standards, and the state programs are to mirror the Corps program.

The opportunity for the states to administer the Section 404 program is strictly voluntary. In fact, a state desiring to exercise the option must present a letter from the Governor requesting program approval. The state must also document that it has in place the necessary legislation and regulations for full implementation of all aspects of the program. In addition, two very important memorandums of agreement are required. The first, between the state and the Regional Administrator of the EPA, is to describe the classes and categories of the applications and programs that are subject to Federal review and the scope of the possible waiver of Federal review. It also must describe reporting requirements and enforcement capability and review. The second memorandum of agreement is with the Corps. Very importantly, it is to identify which waters in the state are to come under *state* jurisdiction and which are to remain under the jurisdiction of the Corps. This agreement should also identify the processing procedure for both individual and general permits and delineate the classes or categories of permits for which Federal review has been involved. This agreement should also specify and prohibit those discharges (fill) which the Corps believe would impair anchorage and navigation.

Once a state Section 404 program has been approved and adopted, it can be modified at the request of either the EPA or the state. The program can also be terminated at any time by the state, as long as it gives the Corps at least six months notice and provides a plan for transfer of the function back to the Corps.

The primary operational requirement for a state Section 404 program is that a permit be *mandatory* for the regulated activities. The EPA guidelines for state programs, however, do provide that certain activities be *exempted* from regulation, as long as they do not involve the discharge of toxic substances. While the list of exempted activities is quite diverse, several are directly regulated to transportation. These include maintenance, including emergency reconstruction of currently serviceable structures, such as dikes, dams, levees, groins, riprap, breakwaters, causeways, bridge abutments or approaches, and transportation structures; construction of temporary sedimentation basins on construction sites; and construction or maintenance of forest and farm roads, or temporary roads for moving mining equipment, in accordance with best management practices in the approved state program and those necessary to protect water quality, aquatic life, wildlife, endangered species, and migratory, breeding, nesting, and feeding areas.

Once it is determined that a permit is required it is best to consult with the state water pollution control agency prior to the actual submission of the application. There are seven items that must be included in the application:

1. A complete project description
2. An identification of the source and type of material to be discharged and the method of dredging to be used
3. Specification of the use of structures to be erected on fill
4. For purposes of evaluation of the area—
   (a) Possible alternatives
   (b) Physical and chemical characteristics
   (c) Life which may be dependent on the water quality and quantity
   (d) Special characteristics requiring protection
   (e) Uses which may affect human health and welfare
5. A description of the technologies or management practices which could be used to minimize adverse environmental effects
6. A listing of the necessary approvals and any decisions already made
7. Appropriate drawings and maps

The application, when received, is generally distributed by the state for review and comment to the appropriate Federal, state, and local agencies and to the public. The Clean Water Act specifically requires review and consultation with the Corps, the EPA, and the Fish and Wildlife Service from the Department of the Interior.

The EPA regulations for state Section 404 programs are quite specific in what is to be in the permit, once a state determines to act favorably on an application. As a minimum, each permit must require the following.

1. The permittee comply with all terms of an existing permit.
2. The permit be reviewable, and may be modified, revoked, reissued, or terminated.
3. The permittee report any activity which would constitute cause for modification or revocation.
4. The permittee allow the state access to records and regulated operations and the right to sample any substances which the permittee is required to monitor.
5. The permittee furnish records to the state upon request.
6. The permittee maintain in good working order all facilities and treatment or control systems used to achieve compliance with the permit.
7. The permittee (in the event of noncompliance) provide the state with a description of and reasons for noncompliance and action taken or planned to reduce, eliminate, or prevent the noncompliance.
8. The permittee take all reasonable steps to minimize adverse environmental impacts from noncompliance.
9. The permittee cease or lessen its business activities if necessary to comply with the permit.
10. The permittee not falsify or knowingly tamper with any monitoring, reporting, or other required device or information.
11. The permitted discharge comply with the Section 404 guidelines, and be conducted so as to minimize adverse environmental impact.
12. Standards for toxic pollutants be at least as stringent as those in Section 307 (a) [from the 1977 Clean Water Act].
13. Approved best management practices be incorporated into the permit.
14. A detailed sketch with the location and boundaries and the type of material to be discharged be provided.

Once a permit has been issued, the state is to monitor and enforce the permit conditions. The regulations authorize the state to use court action to force cessation of unauthorized activity or to enjoin a threatened or continuing violation. The state may also file suit to recover damages incurred as a result of permit violations. In extreme cases, the state may seek criminal remedies to violations or falsified reporting.

Up to this point in the discussion it has been demonstrated what is to be in the permit application submitted to the state and precisely what is required to be in the permit which is issued. All that remains is to see where the EPA regulations *prohibit* issuance of a permit. Prohibition is required when

1. The permit would not comply with the statutes, regulations, or guidelines, including the Section 404 guidelines.
2. The Regional Administrator (of the EPA) objects and the issue has not been resolved.
3. The Corps has determined that anchorage or navigation would be substantially impaired.
4. The discharge would be into an area in which disposal is prohibited by the EPA.

In amending Section 404, Congress recognized that situations could occur when the EPA and states would be unable to resolve differences with respect to specific permit applications. The state has been given two options by the Clean Water Act to follow when faced with EPA objections on an application it wants to approve. First, it can resubmit the application within 90 days with a serious attempt to resolve the objections. Second, the state can *not* resubmit and thereby in effect defer the decision to the Corps, which would involve the Federal Section 404 process. After opportunities for review and comment, the Corps would have sole issuance or denial authority. As discussed in Chapter 2 (Water-Quality-Related Legislation), the intent of Congress in the 1977 amendment was not to strip the Corps of its authority over the waters of the United States, but to allow for state and local input into the authorizing process. Ultimate responsibility and jurisdiction still reside with the Corps.

The Corps, naturally, is bound by the legalities of the Clean Water Act when assuming the responsibility of an application that has unresolved EPA objections. The EPA regulations, therefore, delineate quite specifically the ground on which one of its Regional Administrators may object to the issuance of a permit. These include

1. Insufficient information to determine compliance with Section 404 guidelines.
2. Failure to assure compliance with the statutory and regulatory requirements.
3. Inadequate justification for the rejection of recommendations by another affected state.
4. Procedural inadequacies or errors.
5. Misinterpretation or misapplication of the statutory or regulatory requirements.
6. Inadequate procedures for reporting and monitoring.
7. Failure to carry out the statutory or regulatory requirements while EPA standards governing the activity have not been promulgated.
8. When issuance of the permit would be outside the statutory or regulatory requirements.

From the viewpoint of the transportation agency desiring to obtain a needed Section 404 permit for dredge or fill operations, it does not make a great difference whether there is a state program in operation. For all intents and purposes, the information required for submission and the application procedures to be followed are the same when dealing with the Corps or with the states.

Section 9 Bridge Permit
U.S. Coast Guard
December 12, 1967 (and amendments)
(33 CFR 114)

The Rivers and Harbors Act of 1899, as amended by the Department of Transportation Act of 1966, requires that the U.S. Coast Guard approve the plans for the construction of a bridge over any navigable waters in the United States. Unlike the Clean Water Act Section 404 process, however, "navigable waters" in this case are limited to those whose general character is "navigable, and which, either by themselves or by uniting with other water, form a continuous

waterway on which boats or vessels may navigate or travel between two or more states, or to or from foreign countries."

The courts have allowed this definition to stand because the purpose and scope of Section 9 are very narrow. Quite simply, the law in intended to protect *navigation* activities on the nation's waterways. Section 9 is in place strictly as means of preventing the construction of bridges (or other types of structures) which may obstruct the safe passage of vessels.

Section 9 activities have been interpreted in the form of implementing regulations in 33 CFR 114. The regulation states that Section 9 applies,

regarding construction of bridges, causeways, etc., to the extent that it relates generally to the location and clearances of bridges and causeways in the navigable waters of the United States.

While the regulation is not very extensive (for all intents and purposes it simply requires a permit), it does contain some interesting policy statements from the U.S. Coast Guard concerning permit issuance. For example,

the decision as to whether a permit will be issued must rest primarily upon the effect of the proposed work on navigation. However, in cases where the structure is unobjectionable from the standpoint of navigation but when state or local authorities decline to give their consent to work, it is not usual for the Coast Guard actually to issue the permit.

The reasoning behind this logic is that there is little chance for the construction of a bridge that is opposed by state or local officials, and that the permit simply expresses assent regarding the public rights of navigation. The regulation says that the issuance of a permit under such circumstances may be regarded as "an act of discourtesy." The applicant is told that the proposed bridge is unobjectionable from the standpoint of navigation, and that the permit would be issued if there was consent from the local authorities.

This is certainly a sensible approach for the Coast Guard to take and one that is conducive to good public relations with state and local agencies. However, it is clearly outside the scope of the legislation from which the regulation derives its authority. An examination of Chapter 2 (Water-Quality–Related Legislation) demonstrates that approval is to be provided on the basis of compatibility with navigation (as discussed above) and not on the popularity of the proposed project.

Another interesting policy statement in the regulation concerns the potential interference of a bridge with a proposed flood control project. In such a case, the Coast Guard is to advise the applicant that implementation of the flood control project may necessitate the removal or reconstruction of the bridge. However, the permit application itself will be evaluated strictly with regard to navigation impacts. To strengthen and protect its position concerning the possible removal or reconstruction of the bridge, the regulation stipulates that

the United States will in no case be liable for any damage or injuring to the structure which may be caused by or result from future operations undertaken by the government for the conservation or improvement of navigation, or for other purposes, and no claims or right to compensation will accrue from any such damage.

Neither the Rivers and Harbors Act of 1899, the Department of Transportation Act of 1966, nor 33 CFR 114 contains specific guidance as to acceptability criteria for bridges and their effects on navigation. Nor do they contain any guidance as to how a permit application should be prepared or what it should contain. The appropriate details are available, however, on the Coast Guard District level. For example, the Second Coast Guard District in St. Louis issued in June 1979 a comprehensive pamphlet entitled *Application for Coast Guard Bridge Permits*, from which the remainder of this discussion is drawn.

For the St. Louis District, the application is to come in the form of letter, with a series of attachments, to the District Commander. The letter is to include the following.

1. Name and address of the applicant(s). For interstate bridges, a copy of the agreement between the states laying out the division of responsibilities and authority should be discussed.

2. The name of the waterway to be bridged, river mile, location, nearest city, county and state.

3. A statement pertaining to the cost of bridges for
   (a) Estimated cost of the proposed bridge.
   (b) Estimated cost of a similar bridge without the navigational increment.

4. Documentation as to whether or not the bridge will have a significant impact on the environment.

5. A Section 4 (f) statement, if the project will effect or require the use of any wildlife and waterfowl refuges, recreation areas, public parks, or historic sites.

6. Citations of the state and Federal legislative authority for the bridge. (In most cases, the Federal authority will be the General Bridge Act of 1946).

7. A statement concerning the planned disposition of any bridge that is to be replaced by the proposed bridge. Documentation must be included that shows the consent of the bridge owner for its removal. In most cases, complete removal of all bridge parts is required including pier footings and bearing piles.

8. For movable bridges, like swing bridges, bascule bridges, and vertical lift bridges, a description is required as to how the bridge will be operated and attended.

In addition, a completed Coast Guard checklist is to be attached to the application letter. Table 3-2 presents that checklist.

Once an application is received by the Coast Guard, it undergoes an initial review for navigational and environmental impacts, site inspections, and coordination with other government agencies and special interest groups. This initial review ordinarily takes about two months, depending on the complexities involved. In most cases, the review turns up inadequacies in the application which must be corrected, thereby adding delay. The Coast Guard developed the checklist shown in Table 3-2 in response to the high percentage of unsatisfactory applications it receives.

Once an application has been reviewed and accepted as satisfactorily submitted, the Coast Guard initiates its public involvement process by

TABLE 3-2.   U.S. Coast Guard Permit Application Checklist

_____ Application letter and enclosures
_____ Checklist—Applications for USCG bridge permits
_____ Name of applicant
_____ Name of waterway to be bridged
_____ Bridge location (miles above the mouth of the waterway)
_____ At/nearest city, county, state
_____ Estimated cost of bridge
_____ Estimated cost of low-level bridge at this location

For Federal-Aid Projects of U.S. Coast Guard not Lead Agency

_____ Two copies FEIS, Negative Declaration, or Nonmajor Determination approved by lead agency
_____ Date FEIS filed with CEQ or EPA, as appropriate

For Nonfederal-Aid Projects, or U.S. Coast Guard Lead Agency for NEPA

_____ Environmental assessment concerning impact of bridge and causally related parts of the total project under Coast Guard jurisdiction on the human environment
_____ Statement concerning use of 4(f) lands in application letter. If properties are involved prepare assessment.
_____ Cite legal authority for bridge (usually General Bridge Act of 1946, as amended—See Bridge Administration Laws)
_____ Enclose all required state permits or statement that none are required (Permits from both states required for interstate bridges)
_____ Enclose water quality certificate(s) for projects, pursuant to FWPCA (WQC from both states required for interstate bridges)
_____ Applications signed by parties representing an applicant must include letter of evidence of authorization (i.e., consulting engineers, etc.)
_____ Statement concerning planned disposition of any bridge(s) to be replaced by proposed bridge
_____ Evidence of ownership of old bridge to be removed, or consent of owner(s) for removal
_____ Statement that old bridge will be completely removed

Note that the Coast Guard usually requires complete removal of bridge(s) to be replaced by the proposed bridge.

Exceptions:

_____ (1) Evidence (usually Section 10 permit) that appropriate District Engineer, Corps Engineer, has approved retention of structure or portion of structure for some purpose other than a bridge
_____ (2) If all portions of the old bridge are to be removed down to at least natural ground and/or the riverbed, proposed abutment and pier cut-off elevations may be submitted for approval
_____ (3) Plans of existing bridge; many bridges over minor waterways are not covered by Federal permits; for bridges to be replaced that are not covered by a Federal permit drawings showing the following should be submitted:
  _____ Show length of bridge
  _____ Show width of bridge and number of travel lanes
  _____ Dimension horizontal clearance in channel span(s)
  _____ Show elevations of low steel in channel span(s)
  _____ Graphic scale
  _____ North arrow
  _____ Name of bridge and year constructed
  _____ Owner of bridge

_____ PLANS
_____ Size $8 \times 10\frac{1}{2}$ in. (as few sheets as possible)
_____ Reproduction tracings (mylars preferred)
_____ Simple title block lower right hand corner each sheet; include proposal, i.e., proposed bridge, proposed reconstruction, proposed causeway, etc.; river; city; state; county; applicant; date plans prepared; sheet number, i.e., sheet No. 1 of 3

TABLE 3-2. (*Continued*)

_____ 1-in. margin top each sheet, for fasteners
_____ Vicinity map (small scale)
_____ Show major highways and rivers
_____ Show location of proposed bridge
_____ Show major communities
_____ Show 4(f) land, if any
_____ North arrow
_____ Graphic scale

_____ Location map (Large scale)
_____ Show all highways and rivers
_____ Show local communities
_____ Show existing bridges, docks, locks, dams, dikes, etc.
_____ Show 4(f) land, if any
_____ North arrow
_____ Graphic scale
_____ Flow arrow
_____ Soundings in feet below established government datum planes (usually normal pool)
_____ Label bridge(s) to be removed, if any
_____ Elevation view of proposed bridge from abutment to abutment
_____ Dimensions minimum vertical clearance in navigation span(s) above normal pool or record low water
_____ Indicate 2 percent flowline elevation and record high water; regulated high water elevation should be included when appropriate
_____ Graphic scale
_____ Show elevation of low steel, in figures, in channel span(s) at channelward faces of channel piers, 25 ft from each pier and at center of span
_____ Cross section of watercourse
_____ If bridge is movable, dimension vertical clearance in open and closed positions
_____ Identify datum used

_____ Plan view of proposed bridge from abutment to abutment.
_____ North arrow
_____ Graphic scale
_____ Flow arrow
_____ Length of bridge
_____ Width of bridge and number of travel lanes
_____ Dimension distance between bridges for dual bridges
_____ Show angle between axis of bridge and channel of flow or river, if applicable
_____ Dimension size and location of any proposed pier protection cells, sheer fences, etc.
_____ Dimension minimum horizontal clearance between channel piers—or flow of river
_____ Indicate river-mile location of bridge as measured upstream from mouth of waterway except Ohio River and Upper Mississippi River; Ohio River miles are measured downstream from Pittsburgh, Pennsylvania; mileage on the Upper Mississippi River is measured upstream from Cairo, Illinois

issuing a public notice. Comments are received on the proposal for a 30-day period. The Coast Guard attempts to provide a forum conducive to the resolution of adverse comments, but does not require resolution prior to making its decision. The Commandant of the Coast Guard formally makes the decision, after receiving a recommendation from the District Commander, who will recommend (*a*) issuance of the permit,

(*b*) denial of the permit, or (*c*) a public hearing be held to gather additional data.

As supplemental information in its bridge application package, the Coast Guard has prepared a series of appendices. Included in these appendices are detailed instructions concerning preparation of plans and maps, guide clearances, approval of falsework, construction procedures, instruction for fabrication and installation of vertical clearance gauges, and recommendation for installing navigation lights on bridges. Particular guidance is also provided in the area of environmental analysis. An appendix is included which presents the Coast Guard response to the 1978 CEQ guidelines and DOT Order 5610.1C, laying out an integrated approach for preparing for environmental assessments. Two additional appendices outline in detail the instructions and format to be used in preparing Section 4(f) statements (since the Coast Guard is an agency of the DOT).

Another appendix provides direction in making a determination as to whether a proposed project will be classified as a "major" action under NEPA, or a "nonmajor" action. Two types of circumstances are generally classified as major.

1. A new bridge in connection with a circumferential or arterial highway or new freeway or expressway, mainline railroad, major gas or petroleum pipeline or other major transportation system mode.
2. A new or substantially altered bridge which provides new access to an area and is likely to precipitate significant changes in land use, natural resource exploitation, or development use.

Nonmajor actions, on the other hand, include the following.

1. Replacement of an existing bridge on essentially the same alignment or location when the new bridge and approaches increase the existing highway capacity *less than one travel lane*.
2. Reconstruction or modernization of an existing bridge or approaches by widening less than a single travel lane, adding shoulders or safety lanes, walkways, bikeways, or pipelines.
3. Temporary replacement of a bridge which is commenced immediately after the occurrence of a natural disaster or catastrophic failure where such a bridge project is related to public safety, health, and welfare.
4. Time extensions for bridge construction or removal.
5. Approval of deviations from approved plans which do not significantly alter the approved location or plans.

When a bridge permit action is determined to be major, a full-scale EIS is required, unless the impacts are insignificant. In that case, a FONSI is sufficient.

It should be kept in mind that the Section 9 bridge permit process concerns primarily the effects on *navigation*. The information gathered in the environmental assessment phase is important, and could preclude the construction of a bridge. The bridge itself, however, could be totally acceptable from the Section 9 perspective. Conversely, a bridge project determined to be nonmajor by the FHWA, and therefore insignificant in impact, could be quite significant and major with respect to the Coast Guard. This is likely to arise when a bridge on a minor highway happens to cross over a stream or waterway that carries a significant amount of navigation. In that case the Coast Guard may demand that the project be deemed as a major action.

The Coast Guard and the FHWA have a formal Memorandum of Agreement which assigns the FHWA the *lead agency* role in environmental assessment when a proposed bridge is on the Federal-aid highway system. As a result, the FHWA is responsible for the major nonmajor determination. There are circumstances, as in the example just cited, where the Coast Guard preempts that responsibility.

(As a point of clarification, the phrase *nonmajor action*, which is used frequently in the Coast Guard instructions, has basically the same measning as *categorial exclusion* from the 1978 CEQ guideline. The *nonmajor action* phrase is simply a carryover from previous CEQ directives.)

ECOLOGY-RELATED REGULATIONS

Department of Interior
Fish and Wildlife Service
Fish and Wildlife Coordination Act
Uniform Procedures for Compliance
(50 CFR 410)

This most powerful regulation is actually jointly issued with the National Marine Fisheries Service of the U.S. Deaprtment of Commerce, National Oceanic and Atmospheric Administration. Its power and authority are rooted in the 1958 Fish and Wildlife Coordination Act, which, as discussed in Chapter 2, requires that a project that may modify any water in the United States cannot progress without first coordinating with the FWS, "with a view to the conservation of wildlife resources by preventing loss of such resources as well as providing for the development and improvement thereof."

This regulation clearly reflects that the FWS has taken an aggressive interpretation of the law. In the *Supplementary Information* released with the May 18, 1979 draft of the regulations, it is concluded that

the legislative history of the FWCA [Fish and Wildlife Coordination Act] shows that Congress was prepared to accept a reduction in the benefits of other project purposes in order to obtain the benefits of fish and wildlife conservation.

Whether or not Congress was in fact prepared to accept such a reduction, the FWS has issued its regulation as if it were. In the *Navigable Waters Handbook* portion of the regulation, for example, the FWS outlines the posture to be taken when negotiating with applicants or lead agency planners. FWS officials are to

1. Encourage acceptance of the validity of the national recognition of intensive high public value of shallow waters and wetlands habitat.
2. Avoid acceptance of monetary value as the full measure of significance of ecological and other environmental impacts.
3. Avoid expedient resolution of issues with the sponsor of the work or activity which do not satisfactorily resolve the environmental issues.

The regulation extends the concept of coordination to the point that it requires lead agencies to "regard wildlife conservation as a programmatic and project purpose or goal *equal* to other project purposes or goals" (emphasis added). The regulation interprets the FWCA mandate to provide for the *development and improvement* of wildlife resources as "enhancement" of the resource values as *beyond* those which would occur without the project.

While the FWS regulation stresses fairness and objectivity in its coordination procedures, its hard-line and strict interpretations can easily mean great difficulties for transportation agencies. The agencies should be prepared to compromise as much as possible toward FWS demands and to use political leverage when necessary.

Compliance Procedure

Equal consideration of wildlife resource values in project planning and approval is the essence of the FWCA compliance process. This compliance is accomplished through a four-step procedure.

1. Consultation
2. Reporting by wildlife agencies
3. Full consideration by the action agencies
4. Implementation of conservation measures

Consultation

It is incumbent upon the action (lead) agencies to consult with the wildlife agencies (the FWS and the appropriate state wildlife agency) upon the *initiation* of a project study which may require FWCA activities.. The wildlife agencies are then to be invited to actively participate throughout the planning process. The wildlife agencies are accordingly required to cooperate with the lead agencies in the development and preparation of analyses and recommendations on conservation measures. The lead agencies must allocate enough time in their project development schedules for the wildlife agencies to produce recommendations which can be incorporated into the EIS and then NEPA-related activities.

A *scoping* meeting must be held by the lead agency with the wildlife agencies upon initiating the compliance process. This is *not* the same scoping meeting required by the 1978 CEQ guidelines, although the regulation recommends combining the two when possible. The FWCA scoping meeting is for the purposes of

1. Developing plans of study which ensure full wildlife agency participation throughout each phase of the planning or approval process.
2. Determining who, as among the Federal and state agencies or the applicant, will undertake and oversee the required studies and investigations.
3. Establishing mutually acceptable target dates for the initiation and completion of

studies and the submission of FWCA reports and recommendations.

4. Coordinating FWCA compliance with other environmental review requirements.

5. Ensuring that conservation of wildlife resources is given equal consideration with other study or project purposes or goals.

6. Ensuring that action agencies provide wildlife agencies with adequate descriptions of alternative project plans under consideration.

Reporting

The studies, reports, and recommendations called for in step 3 above are to (*a*) describe project-related effects on wildlife resources, and (*b*) identify alternative measures which would conserve those resources. These effects and measures are to be both quantified *and* qualified.

More specifically, the reports from the wildlife agencies are to describe

1. Wildlife problems and needs and recommended fish and wildlife planning goals.

2. The positive and negative effects and impacts of alternative project plans upon wildlife and recommended conservation features.

3. The positive and negative effects and impacts of the construction and operation of the selected plan upon wildlife, the conservation measures identified during plan formulation, and specific recommendations for conservation measures that should be included in the selected plan.

4. The results and impacts expected from implementing these recommendations.

5. The plan, if any, which they prefer from the standpoint of wildlife conservation.

The regulation provides the wildlife agencies with the authority to initiate their own public participation process on projects where significant wildlife resource issues may be involved. It is therefore conceivable that a public hearing could be conducted by the FWS or a state wildlife agency on a project sponsored by a transportation agency.

In some cases the wildlife agencies may be unable to fully assess potential effects and impacts because certain aspects of a project are not suf-

ficiently developed. Under such circumstances, the wildlife agencies will make a list of additional studies needed to identify conservation measures. This process can be particularly troublesome to transportation agencies, who may not have the resources or time to develop the additional information requested and who may not share the position that wildlife resources conservation is a goal equal to transportation project implementation. It was pointed out above that FWA officials are to "avoid expedient resolution of issues" unless they are satisfied with the project effects, impacts, and mitigation measures.

Full Consideration

The lead agency must document in its official project records that it has fully considered each of the wildlife agency recommendations. In this documentation the lead agency is to justify any tradeoffs made between wildlife conservation and other project objectives and must identify any area where disagreement exists with the wildlife agency. In addition, there must be a finding as to whether there is full compensation for losses in wildlife resource productivity, measured in equivalent terms.

Neither the FWCA nor the regulations require that the lead agency adopt all or any of the wildlife agency recommendations but it is necessary to attempt to resolve any differences. The wildlife agency has the authority to request a public hearing on any unresolved issue, although the lead agency is not required to act favorably on such a request. Either agency, however, may demand that an unresolved issue be referred to higher levels for a decision.

As mentioned above, the basic decision criterion to be applied by the lead agency is that it must regard wildlife conservation as a project goal equal to other project goals and that certain benefits may be diminished in order to achieve this conservation.

In reacting to a wildlife agency recommendation, the lead agency must use substantive economic, environmental, and social reasons in its justification for adoption or rejection. Recommendations for wildlife resource loss compensation cannot be considered unjustified because

1. The lead agency or other agencies may not have adopted a habitat-based wildlife impact assessment and evaluation procedure.

2. Those measures (recommendations), either alone or collectively, do not have a favorable monetary benefit-cost ratio.

3. Project beneficiaries or other nonfederal entities are unwilling to fund the appropriate share of increased Federal project costs necessary to compensate for wildlife resource losses.

4. There are other procedures for land or waters recommended for wildlife compensation purposes, unless their proposed use is found to be more in the public interest than the proposed mitigation.

5. Recommended wildlife resource properties or compensation measures are outside the immediate project boundaries.

The regulations do make note of the situations where increased project cost due to implementation of the wildlife agency recommendations

is not justifiable because it would render the monetary benefit-cost ratio of the project unfavorable or because project beneficiaries or other non-Federal entities are unable to fund the appropriate share of increased Federal project costs necessary to mitigate/compensate for the wildlife resource losses involved.

In such cases the lead agency must fully document its situation, in the hopes that the wildlife agency will agree to maximizing overall project benefit.

Implementation

The lead agencies are not required by law to adopt all of the recommended mitigation measures from the wildlife agencies. They are, however, expected to implement those which are justifiable. The regulation does indicate that

all wildlife agencies should actively pursue such means as will ensure that necessary studies and recommended measures are undertaken and implemented.

In other words, the wildlife agencies are encouraged to resourcefully fight other agencies which may attempt to reject some of their recommendations. Transportation agencies and their projects are ideal targets for such fights.

Location and Hydraulic Design of Encroachments on Floodplains November 15, 1979 (FHPM 6-7-3-2)

In Chapter 2 there was a discussion of the National Flood Insurance Act of 1968, and Presidential Executive Order 11988, *Floodplain Management*, May 24, 1977. These directives caused the preparation of DOT Order 5650.2, which in turn produced FHPM 6-7-3-2.

Beginning with the Executive Order, each of these actions requires the utilization of an integrated and unified approach in floodplain management, for the purpose of minimizing incompatible or damaging use of the nation's floodplains. More specifically, the FHWA policy, as outlined in the FHPM, is to avoid significant encroachments (especially longitudinal encroachments) where practical and to avoid the support of incompatible floodplain development by others. A *significant* encroachment is one that has

1. A significant potential for interruption or termination of a transportation facility which is needed for emergency vehicles or provides a community's only evacuation route.

2. A significant risk.

3. A significant adverse impact on natural and beneficial floodplain values.

The FHPM has separate requirements for projects in the location (project planning) and design phases. Location phase studies, being earlier in the project life, are necessarily less detailed than those in design. Location studies are to include specific discussions (for each alternative) related to

1. The risks associated with implementation of the action.

2. The impacts on natural and beneficial floodplain values.

3. The support of probable incompatible floodplain development.

4. The measures to minimize floodplain impacts associated with the action.

5. The measures to restore and preserve the natural and beneficial floodplain values impacted by the action.

During this phase, the state highway agency is to complete its consultation and coordination activities with Federal, state, and local water resources and floodplain management agencies to ascertain that the project is consistent with floodplain management plans. Most states maintain an active program of floodplain mapping and "regulatory flooding" control. In addition, the public involvement activities (meetings, hearings, etc.) that are normally associated with the project development process are to clearly indicate and identify potential encroachments.

Very importantly, the location studies must evaluate and discuss the *practicality* of alternatives which minimize or eliminate encroachment or are unsupportive of incompatible floodplain development. For any project whose selected alternative includes a significant encroachment, the FEIS will not be approved by the FHWA unless it includes a formal *finding* that it is the only practical alternative. This finding must indicate the reasons why the project has to be located in the floodplain, and why the other alternatives considered were deemed impractical. The finding must also include a statement indicating whether the project conforms to state or local floodplain control standards.

Design Standards and Studies

When the highway agency progresses the project into and through the design phase, it must give consideration to the capital costs and to the risks involved, associated with the encroachment. This *risk analysis* is to be based upon the greater of the overtopping* flood or the 100-year flood, or the greatest flood which must flow through the highway drainage structure (when overtopping is not practical). For interstate highways, the actual *design flood* is the 50-year flood, for through lanes. Freeboard is to be provided where practical for all highways. (This means that the lowest structural member of a bridge superstructure is above the elevation of the overtopping flood.)

In addition to this information, the design study for the project must contain the appropriate hydrologic and hydraulic data and design computations. The actual project plans will show the magnitude, approximate probability of exceedence, and, at approximate locations, the water surface elevation associated with the overtopping flood, or the greatest flood which must flow through the drainage structure; and the magnitude and water surface elevation of the base flood, if larger than the overtopping flood.

The *risk analysis* is to be an *economic* comparison of the design alternatives to determine the one with the least expected cost to the public. The comparisons are to utilize total cost (construction, or capital, cost-plus-risk costs). These will include flood-related costs for highway operation, maintenance, and repair; highway-aggravated flood damage to other property; and additional or interrupted highway travel.

These costs are to be estimated for the service life of 20 years, the design flood is the 50-year flood, and the flood-related costs should not be prohibitive or greatly significant when annualized and compared with other project costs. However, as implied earlier, floodplain enroachment is to be avoided where possible, irrespective of cost.

Preservation of the Nation's Wetlands
August 24, 1978
(DOT Order 5660.1A)

On the same day that he issued the Executive Order on *Floodplains Management* (May 24, 1977) the President issued Executive Order 11990, *Protection of Wetlands.* Section 6 of the Wetlands Order required that the Federal agencies amend their procedures to insure compliance. Accordingly, on August 28, 1978 the DOT issued its own order to be implemented by the modal agencies. The wetlands definition included in the DOT order is basically the same as that from the Executive Order [see Chapter 2 (Ecology-Related Legislation)] except that the list of examples includes estuarine areas and shallow lakes and ponds with emergent vegetation, and excludes

> *areas covered with water for such a short time that there is no effect on moist-soil vegetation, [and] the permanent waters of streams, reservoirs, and deep lakes.*

The definition is further expanded.

> *The wetlands ecosystem includes those areas which affect or are affected by the wetlands*

---

*Overtopping occurs when the flood level (exceeds) is over the highway, over the watershed divide, or through structures provided for emergency relief.

itself; e.g., adjacent uplands or regions up and downstream. An activity may affect the wetlands indirectly by impacting regions up or downstream from the wetland, only disturbing the water table of the area in which the wetland lies.

The policy concerning wetlands to be enforced by DOT agencies is that new construction is to be avoided unless there is no *practicable alternative* (to the construction), and the proposed action includes *all practicable measures to minimize harm.*

The policy explicitly states that economic and environmental factors may be used as justifications for reaching a finding of no practicable alternatives. However, additional costs alone will not be a satisfactory basis to support such a finding, since it may be assured that there is a justified cost associated with meeting the national objective of wetlands protection. [As an aside, it should be noticed that there are great similarities in wording and policy between wetlands and Section 4(f) properties. It follows that the analyses needed for each would be similar and should even overlap.]

The DOT order provides specific procedures to be followed by the modal agencies to insure compliance with the Executive Order. Factors to be considered by the agencies when carrying out activities potentially affecting wetlands include

1. Public health, safety, and welfare, including water supply, water quality recharge and discharge, and pollution; flood and storm hazards; and sedimentation and erosion.
2. Maintenance of natural systems, including conservation and long-term activity of existing flora and fauna species and habitat diversity and stability, hydrologic utility, fish and wildlife, timber and food and fiber resources; and other uses of wetlands in the public interest, including recreational, scientific, and cultural uses as well as transportation uses and objectives.

A situation may arise where one of the modal agencies owns a wetland (or a portion of a wetland) and desires to sell or otherwise dispose of it. In that case, the agency should attach to the deed appropriate restrictions against uses of the wetland which may bring about damage. The order suggests that the agencies consider withholding the wetlands from disposal, as a means of protection.

The procedures outlined in the DOT order emphasize the necessity of maximum public participation and interagency consultation and coordination.

Appropriate opportunity for early review of proposals for new construction in wetlands should be provided to the public and to agencies with special interest in wetlands.

Specifically, any submissions made to the OMB Circular A-95 clearinghouse agencies should identify impacts on wetlands. By definition, *any* project expected to have a significant impact on a wetland *will require* the preparation of a draft and final EIS. In such cases, the DOT order mandates consultation with those agencies having particular expertise concerning wetland impacts. These include the DOI FWS, state wildlife agencies, and the U. S. Army Corps of Engineers. The EIS must reflect early coordination with these agencies, as appropriate.

Lastly, as mentioned above, the DOT order requires that any project which includes new construction located in a wetland must contain a formal finding that there is no practicable alternative to such construction, and that all practicable measures to minimize harm to the wetlands have been incorporated into the project. This finding is to be included in the FEIS for the project.

SUMMARY

A major role of the Executive branch of the Federal government is the provision of regulations necessary for the implementation of enacted legislation. There are many such regulations now in effect which concern the environmental impacts of transportation programs and projects.

Many of these regulations are rooted in the 1969 National Environmental Policy Act (NEPA), the most significant being the CEQ guidelines (40 CFR 1500–1508). Issued by the President's Council on Environmental Quality and amended on November 29, 1978, this regulation mandates the utilization of a systematic, interdisciplinary approach in the development of "major Federal actions significantly affecting the quality of the human environment." For such actions, the CEQ guidelines require the preparation of a two-phase Environmental Impact Statement (Draft and Final EIS) which receives wide circulation. In other cases, the preparation of a Finding of No Significant Impact (FONSI) is sufficient.

Whichever document is prepared, the CEQ guidelines encourage brevity and summarization so as to *minimize paperwork and avoid unnecessary project delay*. In an attempt to achieve these goals, the 1978 amendments introduced the concepts of categorical exclusion, scoping, and tiering.

In order to guarantee the attainment of the systematic, interdisciplinary approach in the project development process, the CEQ guidelines required that the Executive department and agencies revise their operating procedures. The U.S. Department of Transportation responded with the issuance of DOT Order 5610.1C, on September 18, 1979. This directive was intended to be *supplemental*, in the sense that the DOT also requires the full implementation of the CEQ guidelines by its modal agencies. The DOT order reflects the objective of the department to utilize "one-stop" environmental processing. In other words, the DOT would like to utilize a single process to meet the various requirements for environmental studies, consultations, and reviews. The order also includes a comprehensive recommendation for the format and content of transportation-related EISs.

The DOT order is in fact an intermediate document directing the modal agencies within the department to prepare their own specific procedures. The Federal Aviation Administration responded with the issuance of FAA Order 1050.1C on December 20, 1979. This order provides extensive listings of aviation-related activities that are categorically excluded from the environmental requirements. Since the most environmentally sensitive activity administered by the FAA is the provision of airport services, the order emphasizes airport development and related functions more than any other.

The Urban Mass Transportation Administration (UMTA) and the Federal Highway Administration (FHWA) jointly issued their implementing regulations on October 30, 1980. The UMTA regulations are codified in 49 CFR 622, while the FHWA guidelines are commonly referred to as FHPM 7-7-2.

NEPA and the CEQ guidelines have also caused the FHWA to issue a separate regulation dealing with the requirement of the systematic, interdisciplinary approach. FHPM 7-7-1, *Process Guidelines* was introduced as a way of forcing the state highway agencies (who actually perform most of the work in highways delivery) to modify and formalize their operating procedures to fully comply with NEPA. This process, called *Environmental Action Plan* development and implementation, is the subject of Chapter 4.

In addition to the general environmental regulations, there are many others that affect transportation activities in the four major areas of impact: noise, air quality, water quality, and ecology.

For noise impact, the major regulations include the Federal Aviation Regulations's (FAR) Part 36, which limits noise emissions from aircraft. Interstate rail carriers are regulated by the U.S. Environmental Protection Agency (EPA) in 40 CFR 201, which limits noise emissions from moving and idling trains, at railyards, and at property lines. Highway noise levels are controlled by FHPM 7-7-3, which includes noise abatement cirteria to be met by the state highway agencies when planning, designing, and constructing highways. The U.S. Department of Housing and Urban Development has a regulation 24 CFR 51, for the purpose of insuring that any housing project or program utilizing HUD funding meet the HUD Site Acceptability Standards.

The important regulations in the air quality area all relate to the Clean Air Act of 1977. In June 1978 the EPA and the DOT jointly issued guidelines concerning the revision of State Implementation Plans (SIP) for the attainment of the National Ambient Air Quality Standards (NAAQS) by 1982 or 1987. These guidelines provide direction in the evaluation of the 18 transportation control measures listed in the 1977 act. While these guidelines are for the purpose of region-wide attainment of the NAAQS, the FHWA issued FHPM 7-7-9 on November 19, 1979. This regulation provides guidance to the state highway agencies in determining the consistency of specific projects with the revised SIP.

The major regulation concerning water quality and transportation is the Section 404 permit program for dredge and fill in navigable waters mandated by the Clean Water Act of 1977. Section 401 "Water Quality Certification," in which the state environmental agency finds that the project will not generate violations of water quality standards, is a prerequisite to 404 permit issuance. The courts have defined navigable waters as simply "the waters of the United States." As a result, the U.S. Army Corps of Engineers no longer is required to directly oversee the 404 program; the 1977 act provides for state oversight for certain conditions though many states have yet to adopt such a program. Another major water quality regulation is the Section 9 permit program, required by the Rivers and Harbors Act of 1899 and administered by the U.S. Coast Guard. This program concerns the protection of navigation rights in the navigable waters and therefore regulates bridges and other crossings.

Ecology-related regulations are dominated by the Fish and Wildlife Coordination Procedures, 50 CFR 410. The Fish and Wildlife Service (FWS) of the DOI has interpreted the intent of Congress to be that wildlife resource conservation is a goal equal to any other in the development of a project. The coordination and consultation requirements in this regulation provide the FWS with extraordinary power and influence over transportation projects affecting fish and wildlife resource areas.

Regulations concerning the protection of floodplains and wetlands have been issued as a result of two Presidential Executive Orders released May 24, 1977. The floodplain requirements (DOT Order 5650.2 and FHPM 6-7-3-2) encourage the avoidance of encroachment where possible. Engineering solutions may often be used when encroachment is not possible. Construction in wetlands is prohibited unless there is a finding that there is no practicable alternative, and that the proposed project includes all practicable measures to minimize harm (DOT Order 5660.1A)

APPENDIX 3A: REGULATIONS FOR IMPLEMENTING THE PROCEDURAL PROVISIONS OF THE NATIONAL ENVIRONMENTAL POLICY ACT

TABLE OF CONTENTS

PART 1500—PURPOSE, POLICY, AND MANDATE

AUTHORITY: NEPA, the Environmental Quality Improvement Act of 1970, as amended (42 U.S.C. 4371 et seq.), section 309 of the Clean Air Act, as amended (42 U.S.C. 7609) and Executive Order 11514, Protection and Enhancement of Environmental Quality (March 5, 1970 as amended by Executive Order 11991, May 24, 1977).

§ 1500.1 Purpose.

(a) The National Environmental Policy Act (NEPA) is our basic national charter for protection of the environment. It establishes policy, sets goals (section 101), and provides means (section 102) for carrying out the policy. Section 102(2) contains "action-forcing" provisions to make sure that federal agencies act according to the letter and spirit of the Act. The regulations that follow implement Section 102(2). Their purpose is to tell federal agencies what they must do to comply with the procedures and achieve the goals of the Act. The President, the federal agencies, and the courts share responsibility for enforcing the Act so as to achieve the substantive requirements of section 101.

(b) NEPA procedures must insure that environmental information is available to public officials and citizens before decisions are made and before actions are taken. The information must be of high quality. Accurate scientific analysis, expert agency comments, and public scrutiny are essential to implementing NEPA. Most important, NEPA documents must concentrate on the issues that are truly significant to the action in question, rather than amassing needless detail.

(c) Ultimately, of course, it is not better documents but better decisions that count. NEPA's purpose is not to generate paperwork—even excellent paperwork—but to foster excellent action. The NEPA process is intended to help public officials make decisions that are based on understanding of environmental consequences, and take actions that protect, restore, and enhance the environment. These regulations provide the direction to achieve this purpose.

§ 1500.2 Policy.

Federal agencies shall to the fullest extent possible:

(a) Interpret and administer the policies, regulations, and public laws of the United States in accordance with the policies set forth in the Act and in these regulations.

(b) Implement procedures to make the NEPA process more useful to decisionmakers and the public; to reduce paperwork and the accumulation of extraneous background data; and to emphasize real environmental issues and alternatives. Environmental impact statements shall be concise, clear, and to the point, and shall be supported by evidence that agencies have made the necessary environmental analyses.

(c) Integrate the requirements of NEPA with other planning and environmental review procedures required by law or by agency practice so that all such procedures run concurrently rather than consecutively.

(d) Encourage and facilitate public involvement in decisions which affect the quality of the human environment.

(e) Use the NEPA process to identify and assess the reasonable alternatives to proposed actions that will avoid or minimize adverse effects of these actions upon the quality of the human environment.

(f) Use all practicable means, consistent with the requirements of the Act and other essential considerations of national policy, to restore and enhance the quality of the human environment and avoid or minimize any possible adverse effects of their actions upon the quality of the human environment.

§ 1500.3 Mandate.

Parts 1500-1508 of this Title provide regulations applicable to and binding on all Federal agencies for implementing the procedural provisions of the National Environmental Policy Act of 1969, as amended (Pub. L. 91-190, 42 U.S.C. 4321 et seq.) (NEPA or the Act) except where compliance would be inconsistent with other statutory requirements. These regulations are issued pursuant to NEPA, the Environmental Quality Improvement Act of 1970, as amended (42 U.S.C. 4371 et seq.) Section 309 of the Clean Air Act, as amended (42 U.S.C. 7609) and Executive Order 11514, Protection and Enhancement of Environmental Quality (March 5, 1970, as amended by Executive Order 11991, May 24, 1977). These regulations, unlike the predecessor guidelines, are not confined to Sec. 102(2)(C) (environmental impact statements). The regulations apply to the whole of section 102(2). The provisions of the Act and of these regulations must be read together as a whole in order to comply with the spirit and letter of the law. It is the Council's intention that judicial review of agency compliance with these regulations not occur before an agency has filed the final environmental impact statement, or has made a final finding of no significant impact (when such a finding will result in action affecting the environment), or takes action that will result in irreparable injury. Furthermore, it is the Council's intention that any trivial violation of these regulations not give rise to any independent cause of action.

§ 1500.4 Reducing paperwork.

Agencies shall reduce excessive paperwork by:

(a) Reducing the length of environmental impact statements (§ 1502.2(c)), by means such as setting appropriate page limits (§§ 1501.7(b)(1) and 1502.7).

(b) Preparing analytic rather than encyclopedic environmental impact statements (§ 1502.2(a)).

(c) Discussing only briefly issues other than significant ones (§ 1502.2(b)).

(d) Writing environmental impact statements in plain language (§ 1502.8).

(e) Following a clear format for environmental impact statements (§ 1502.10).

(f) Emphasizing the portions of the environmental impact statement that are useful to decisionmakers and the public (§§ 1502.14 and 1502.15) and reducing emphasis on background material (§ 1502.16).

(g) Using the scoping process, not only to identify significant environmental issues deserving of study, but also to deemphasize insignificant issues, narrowing the scope of the environmental impact statement process accordingly (§ 1501.7).

(h) Summarizing the environmental impact statement (§ 1502.12) and circulating the summary instead of the entire environmental impact statement if the latter is unusually long (§ 1502.19).

(i) Using program, policy, or plan environmental impact statements and tiering from statements of broad scope to those of narrower scope, to eliminate repetitive discussions of the same issues (§§ 1502.4 and 1502.20).

(j) Incorporating by reference (§ 1502.21).

(k) Integrating NEPA requirements with other environmental review and consultation requirements (§ 1502.25).

(l) Requiring comments to be as specific as possible (§ 1503.3).

(m) Attaching and circulating only changes to the draft environmental impact statement, rather than rewriting and circulating the entire statement when changes are minor (§ 1503.4(c)).

(n) Eliminating duplication with State and local procedures, by providing for joint preparation (§ 1506.2), and with other Federal procedures, by providing that an agency may adopt appropriate environmental documents prepared by another agency (§ 1506.3).

(o) Combining environmental documents with other documents (§ 1506.4).

(p) Using categorical exclusions to define categories of actions which do not individually or cumulatively have a significant effect on the human environment and which are therefore exempt from requirements to prepare an environmental impact statement (§ 1508.4).

(q) Using a finding of no significant impact when an action not otherwise excluded will not have a significant effect on the human environment and is therefore exempt from requirements to prepare an environmental impact statement (§ 1508.13).

§ 1500.5 Reducing delay.

Agencies shall reduce delay by:

(a) Integrating the NEPA process into early planning (§ 1501.2).

(b) Emphasizing interagency cooperation before the environmental impact statement is prepared, rather than submission of adversary comments on a completed document (§ 1501.6).

(c) Insuring the swift and fair resolution of lead agency disputes (§ 1501.5).

(d) Using the scoping process for an early identification of what are and what are not the real issues (§ 1501.7).

(e) Establishing appropriate time limits for the environmental impact statement process (§§ 1501.7(b)(2) and 1501.8).

(f) Preparing environmental impact statements early in the process (§ 1502.5).

(g) Integrating NEPA requirements with other environmental review and consultation requirements (§ 1502.25).

(h) Eliminating duplication with State and local procedures by providing for joint preparation (§ 1506.2) and with other Federal procedures by providing that an agency may adopt appropriate environmental documents prepared by another agency (§ 1506.3).

(i) Combining environmental documents with other documents (§ 1506.4).

(j) Using accelerated procedures for proposals for legislation (§ 1506.8).

(k) Using categorical exclusions to define categories of actions which do not individually or cumulatively have a significant effect on the human environment (§ 1508.4) and which are therefore exempt from requirements to prepare an environmental impact statement.

(1) Using a finding of no significant impact when an action not otherwise excluded will not have a significant effect on the human environment (§ 1508.13) and is therefore exempt from requirements to prepare an environmental impact statement.

§ 1500.6 Agency authority.

Each agency shall interpret the provisions of the Act as a supplement to its existing authority and as a mandate to view traditional policies and missions in the light of the Act's national environmental objectives. Agencies shall review their policies, procedures, and regulations accordingly and revise them as necessary to insure full compliance with the purposes and provisions of the Act. The phrase "to the fullest extent possible" in section 102 means that each agency of the Federal Government shall comply with that section unless existing law applicable to the agency's operations expressly prohibits or makes compliance impossible.

PART 1501—NEPA AND AGENCY PLANNING

AUTHORITY: NEPA, the Environmental Quality Improvement Act of 1970, as amended (42 U.S.C. 4371 et seq.), Section 309 of the Clean Air Act, as amended (42 U.S.C. 7609), and Executive Order 11514, Protection and Enhancement of Environmental Quality (March 5, 1970, as amended by Executive Order 11991, May 24 1977).

§ 1501.1 Purpose.

The purposes of this part include:

(a) Integrating the NEPA process into early planning to insure appropriate consideration of NEPA's policies and to eliminate delay.

(b) Emphasizing cooperative consultation among agencies before the environmental impact statement is prepared rather than submission of adversary comments on a completed document.

(c) Providing for the swift and fair resolution of lead agency disputes.

(d) Identifying at an early stage the significant environmental issues deserving of study and deemphasizing insignificant issues, narrowing the scope of the environmental impact statement accordingly.

(e) Providing a mechanism for putting appropriate time limits on the environmental impact statement process.

§ 1501.2 Apply NEPA early in the process.

Agencies shall integrate the NEPA process with other planning at the earliest possible time to insure that planning and decisions reflect environmental values, to avoid delays later in the process, and to head off potential conflicts. Each agency shall:

(a) Comply with the mandate of section 102(2)(A) to "utilize a systematic, interdisciplinary approach which will insure the integrated use of the natural and social sciences and the environmental design arts in planning and in decisionmaking which may have an impact on man's environment," as specified by § 1507.2.

(b) Identify environmental effects and values in adequate detail so they can be compared to economic and technical analyses. Environmental documents and appropriate analyses shall be circulated and reviewed at the same time as other planning documents.

(c) Study, develop, and describe appropriate alternatives to recommended courses of action in any proposal which involves unresolved conflicts concerning alternative uses of available resources as provided by section 102(2)(E) of the Act.

(d) Provide for cases where actions are planned by private applicants or other non-Federal entities before Federal involvement so that:

(1) Policies or designated staff are available to advise potential applicants of studies or other information foreseeably required for later Federal action.

(2) The Federal agency consults early with appropriate State and local agencies and Indian tribes and with interested private persons and organizations when its own involvement is reasonably foreseeable.

(3) The Federal agency commences its NEPA process at the earliest possible time.

§ 1501.3 When to prepare an environmental assessment.

(a) Agencies shall prepare an environmental assessment (§ 1508.9) when necessary under the procedures adopted by individual agencies to supplement these regulations as described in § 1507.3. An assessment is not necessary if the agency has decided to prepare an environmental impact statement.

(b) Agencies may prepare an environmental assessment on any action at any time in order to assist agency planning and decisionmaking.

§ 1501.4 Whether to prepare an environmental impact statement.

In determining whether to prepare an environmental impact statement the Federal agency shall:

(a) Determine under its procedures supplementing these regulations (described in § 1507.3) whether the proposal is one which:

(1) Normally requires an environmental impact statement, or

(2) Normally does not require either an environmental impact statement or an environmental assessment (categorical exclusion).

(b) If the proposed action is not covered by paragraph (a) of this section, prepare an environmental assessment (§ 1508.9). The agency shall involve environmental agencies, applicants, and the public, to the extent practicable, in preparing assessments required by § 1508.9(a)(1).

(c) Based on the environmental assessment make its determination whether to prepare an environmental impact statement.

(d) Commence the scoping process (§ 1501.7), if the agency will prepare an environmental impact statement.

(e) Prepare a finding of no significant impact (§ 1508.13), if the agency determines on the basis of the environmental assessment not to prepare a statement.

(1) The agency shall make the finding of no significant impact available to the affected public as specified in § 1506.6.

(2) In certain limited circumstances, which the agency may cover in its procedures under § 1507.3, the agency shall make the finding of no significant impact available for public review (including State and areawide clearinghouses) for 30 days before the agency makes its final determination whether to prepare an environmental impact statement and before the action may begin. The circumstances are:

(i) The proposed action is, or is closely similar to, one which normally requires the preparation of an environmental impact statement under the procedures adopted by the agency pursuant to § 1507.3, or

(ii) The nature of the proposed action is one without precedent.

§ 1501.5 Lead agencies.

(a) A lead agency shall supervise the preparation of an environmental impact statement if more than one Federal agency either:

(1) Proposes or is involved in the same action; or

(2) Is involved in a group of actions directly related to each other because of their functional interdependence or geographical proximity.

(b) Federal, State, or local agencies, including at least one Federal agency, may act as joint lead agencies to prepare an environmental impact statement (§ 1506.2).

(c) If an action falls within the provisions of paragraph (a) of this section the potential lead agencies shall determine by letter or memorandum which agency shall be the lead agency and which shall be cooperating agencies. The agencies shall resolve the lead agency question so as not to cause delay. If there is disagreement among the agencies, the following factors (which are listed in order of descending importance) shall determine lead agency designation:

(1) Magnitude of agency's involvement.

(2) Project approval/disapproval authority.

(3) Expertise concerning the action's environmental effects.

(4) Duration of agency's involvement.

(5) Sequence of agency's involvement.

(d) Any Federal agency, or any State or local agency or private person substantially affected by the absence of lead agency designation, may make a written request to the potential lead agencies that a lead agency be designated.

(e) If Federal agencies are unable to agree on which agency will be the lead agency or if the procedure described in paragraph (c) of this section has not resulted within 45 days in a lead agency designation, any of the agencies or persons concerned may file a request with the Council asking it to determine which Federal agency shall be the lead agency.

A copy of the request shall be transmitted to each potential lead agency. The request shall consist of:

(1) A precise description of the nature and extent of the proposed action.

(2) A detailed statement of why each potential lead agency should or should not be the lead agency under the criteria specified in paragraph (c) of this section.

(f) A response may be filed by any potential lead agency concerned within 20 days after a request is filed with the Council. The Council shall determine as soon as possible but not later than 20 days after receiving the request and all responses to it which Federal agency shall be the lead agency and which other Federal agencies shall be cooperating agencies.

§ 1501.6 Cooperating agencies.

The purpose of this section is to emphasize agency cooperation early in the NEPA process. Upon request of the lead agency, any other Federal agency which has jurisdiction by law shall be a cooperating agency. In addition any other Federal agency which has special expertise with respect to any environmental issue, which should be addressed in the statement may be a cooperating agency upon request of the lead agency. An agency may request the lead agency to designate it a cooperating agency.

(a) The lead agency shall:

(1) Request the participation of each cooperating agency in the NEPA process at the earliest possible time.

(2) Use the environmental analysis and proposals of cooperating agencies with jurisdiction by law or spe-

cial expertise, to the maximum extent possible consistent with its responsibility as lead agency.

(3) Meet with a cooperating agency at the latter's request.

(b) Each cooperating agency shall:

(1) Participate in the NEPA process at the earliest possible time.

(2) Participate in the scoping process (described below in § 1501.7).

(3) Assume on request of the lead agency responsibility for developing information and preparing environmental analyses including portions of the environmental impact statement concerning which the cooperating agency has special expertise.

(4) Make available staff support at the lead agency's request to enhance the latter's interdisciplinary capability.

(5) Normally use its own funds. The lead agency shall, to the extent available funds permit, fund those major activities or analyses it requests from cooperating agencies. Potential lead agencies shall include such funding requirements in their budget requests.

(c) A cooperating agency may in response to a lead agency's request for assistance in preparing the environmental impact statement (described in paragraph (b) (3), (4), or (5) of this section) reply that other program commitments preclude any involvement or the degree of involvement requested in the action that is the subject of the environmental impact statement. A copy of this reply shall be submitted to the Council.

§ 1501.7 Scoping.

There shall be an early and open process for determining the scope of issues to be addressed and for identifying the significant issues related to a proposed action. This process shall be termed scoping. As soon as practicable after its decision to prepare an environmental impact statement and before the scoping process the lead agency shall publish a notice of intent (§ 1508.22) in the FEDERAL REGISTER except as provided in § 1507.3(e).

(a) As part of the scoping process the lead agency shall:

(1) Invite the participation of affected Federal, State, and local agencies, any affected Indian tribe, the

proponent of the action, and other interested persons (including those who might not be in accord with the action on environmental grounds), unless there is a limited exception under § 1507.3(c). An agency may give notice in accordance with § 1506.6.

(2) Determine the scope (§ 1508.25) and the significant issues to be analyzed in depth in the environmental impact statement.

(3) Identify and eliminate from detailed study the issues which are not significant or which have been covered by prior environmental review (§ 1506.3), narrowing the discussion of these issues in the statement to a brief presentation of why they will not have a significant effect on the human environment or providing a reference to their coverage elsewhere.

(4) Allocate assignments for preparation of the environmental impact statement among the lead and cooperating agencies, with the lead agency retaining responsibility for the statement.

(5) Indicate any public environmental assessments and other environmental impact statements which are being or will be prepared that are related to but are not part of the scope of the impact statement under consideration.

(6) Identify other environmental review and consultation requirements so the lead and cooperating agencies may prepare other required analyses and studies concurrently with, and integrated with, the environmental impact statement as provided in § 1502.25.

(7) Indicate the relationship between the timing of the preparation of environmental analyses and the agency's tentative planning and decisionmaking schedule.

(b) As part of the scoping process the lead agency may:

(1) Set page limits on environmental documents (§ 1502.7).

(2) Set time limits (§ 1501.8).

(3) Adopt procedures under § 1507.3 to combine its environmental assessment process with its scoping process.

(4) Hold an early scoping meeting or meetings which may be integrated with any other early planning meeting the agency has. Such a scoping meeting will often be appropriate when the impacts of a particular action are confined to specific sites.

(c) An agency shall revise the determinations made under paragraphs (a) and (b) of this section if substantial changes are made later in the proposed action, or if significant new circumstances or information arise which bear on the proposal or its impacts.

§ 1501.8   Time limits.

Although the Council has decided that prescribed universal time limits for the entire NEPA process are too inflexible, Federal agencies are encouraged to set time limits appropriate to individual actions (consistent with the time intervals required by § 1506.10). When multiple agencies are involved the reference to agency below means lead agency.

(a) The agency shall set time limits if an applicant for the proposed action requests them: *Provided,* That the limits are consistent with the purposes of NEPA and other essential considerations of national policy.

(b) The agency may:

(1) Consider the following factors in determining time limits:

(i) Potential for environmental harm.

(ii) Size of the proposed action.

(iii) State of the art of analytic techniques.

(iv) Degree of public need for the proposed action, including the consequences of delay.

(v) Number of persons and agencies affected.

(vi) Degree to which relevant information is known and if not known the time required for obtaining it.

(vii) Degree to which the action is controversial.

(viii) Other time limits imposed on the agency by law, regulations, or executive order.

(2) Set overall time limits or limits for each constituent part of the NEPA process, which may include:

(i) Decision on whether to prepare an environmental impact statement (if not already decided).

(ii) Determination of the scope of the environmental impact statement.

(iii) Preparation of the draft environmental impact statement.

(iv) Review of any comments on the draft environmental impact statement from the public and agencies.

(v) Preparation of the final environmental impact statement.

(vi) Review of any comments on the final environmental impact statement.

(vii) Decision on the action based in part on the environmental impact statement.

(3) Designate a person (such as the project manager or a person in the agency's office with NEPA responsibilities) to expedite the NEPA process.

(c) State or local agencies or members of the public may request a Federal Agency to set time limits.

PART 1502—ENVIRONMENTAL IMPACT STATEMENT

AUTHORITY: NEPA, the Environmental Quality Improvement Act of 1970, as amended (42 U.S.C. 4371 et seq.), Section 309 of the Clean Air Act, as amended (42 U.S.C. 7609), and Executive Order 11514, Protection and Enhancement of Environmental Quality (March 5, 1970, as amended by Executive Order 11991, May 24, 1977).

§ 1502.1   Purpose.

The primary purpose of an environmental impact statement is to serve as an action-forcing device to insure that the policies and goals defined in the Act are infused into the ongoing programs and actions of the Federal Government. It shall provide full and fair discussion of significant environmental impacts and shall inform decisionmakers and the public of the reasonable alternatives which would avoid or minimize adverse impacts or enhance the quality of the human environment. Agencies shall focus on significant environmental issues and alternatives and shall reduce paperwork and the accumulation of extraneous background data. Statements shall be concise, clear, and to the point, and shall be supported by evidence that the agency has made the necessary environmental analyses. An environmental impact statement is more than a disclosure document. It shall be used by Federal officials in conjunction with other relevant material to plan actions and make decisions.

§ 1502.2   Implementation.

To achieve the purposes set forth in § 1502.1 agencies shall prepare environmental impact statements in the following manner:

(a) Environmental impact statements shall be analytic rather than encyclopedic.

(b) Impacts shall be discussed in proportion to their significance. There shall be only brief discussion of other than significant issues. As in a finding of no significant impact, there should be only enough discussion to show why more study is not warranted.

(c) Environmental impact statements shall be kept concise and shall be no longer than absolutely necessary to comply with NEPA and with these regulations. Length should vary first with potential environmental problems and then with project size.

(d) Environmental impact statements shall state how alternatives considered in it and decisions based on it will or will not achieve the requirements of sections 101 and 102(1) of the Act and other environmental laws and policies.

(e) The range of alternatives discussed in environmental impact statements shall encompass those to be considered by the ultimate agency decisionmaker.

(f) Agencies shall not commit resources prejudicing selection of alternatives before making a final decision (§ 1506.1).

(g) Environmental impact statements shall serve as the means of assessing the environmental impact of proposed agency actions, rather than justifying decisions already made.

§ 1502.3 Statutory requirements for statements.

As required by sec. 102(2)(C) of NEPA environmental impact statements (§ 1508.11) are to be included in every recommendation or report
On proposals (§ 1508.23)
For legislation and (§ 1508.17)
Other major Federal actions (§ 1508.18)
Significantly (§ 1508.27)
Affecting (§§ 1508.3, 1508.8)
The quality of the human environment (§ 1508.14).

§ 1502.4 Major Federal actions requiring the preparation of environmental impact statements.

(a) Agencies shall make sure the proposal which is the subject of an environmental impact statement is properly defined. Agencies shall use the criteria for scope (§ 1508.25) to determine which proposal(s) shall be the subject of a particular statement. Proposals or parts of proposals which are related to each other closely enough to be, in effect, a single course of action shall be evaluated in a single impact statement.

(b) Environmental impact statements may be prepared, and are sometimes required, for broad Federal actions such as the adoption of new agency programs or regulations (§ 1508.18). Agencies shall prepare statements on broad actions so that they are relevant to policy and are timed to coincide with meaningful points in agency planning and decisionmaking.

(c) When preparing statements on broad actions (including proposals by more than one agency), agencies may find it useful to evaluate the proposal(s) in one of the following ways:

(1) Geographically, including actions occurring in the same general location, such as body of water, region, or metropolitan area.

(2) Generically, including actions which have relevant similarities, such as common timing, impacts, alternatives, methods of implementation, media, or subject matter.

(3) By stage of technological development including federal or federally assisted research, development or demonstration programs for new technologies which, if applied, could significantly affect the quality of the human environment. Statements shall be prepared on such programs and shall be available before the program has reached a stage of investment or commitment to implementation likely to determine subsequent development or restrict later alternatives.

(d) Agencies shall as appropriate employ scoping (§ 1501.7), tiering (§ 1502.20), and other methods listed in §§ 1500.4 and 1500.5 to relate broad and narrow actions and to avoid duplication and delay.

§ 1502.5 Timing.

An agency shall commence preparation of an environmental impact statement as close as possible to the time the agency is developing or is presented with a proposal (§ 1508.23) so that preparation can be completed in time for the final statement to be included in any recommendation or report on the proposal. The statement shall be prepared early enough so that it can serve practically as an important contribution to the decisionmaking process and will not be used to rationalize or justify decisions already made (§§ 1500.2(c), 1501.2, and 1502.2). For instance:

(a) For projects directly undertaken by Federal agencies the environmental impact statement shall be prepared at the feasibility analysis (go-no go) stage and may be supplemented at a later stage if necessary.

(b) For applications to the agency appropriate environmental assessments or statements shall be commenced no later than immediately after the application is received. Federal agencies are encouraged to begin preparation of such assessments or statements earlier, preferably jointly with applicable State or local agencies.

(c) For adjudication, the final environmental impact statement shall normally precede the final staff recommendation and that portion of the public hearing related to the impact study. In appropriate circumstances the statement may follow preliminary hearings designed to gather information for use in the statements.

(d) For informal rulemaking the draft environmental impact statement shall normally accompany the proposed rule.

§ 1502.6 Interdisciplinary preparation.

Environmental impact statements shall be prepared using an inter-disciplinary approach which will insure the integrated use of the natural and social sciences and the environmental design arts (section 102(2)(A) of the Act). The disciplines of the preparers shall be appropriate to the scope and issues identified in the scoping process (§ 1501.7).

§ 1502.7 Page limits.

The text of final environmental impact statements (e.g., paragraphs (d) through (g) of § 1502.10) shall normally be less than 150 pages and for proposals of unusual scope or complexity shall normally be less than 300 pages.

§ 1502.8 Writing.

Environmental impact statements shall be written in plain language and may use appropriate graphics so that decisionmakers and the public can readily understand them. Agencies should employ writers of clear prose or editors to write, review, or edit statements, which will be based upon the analysis and supporting data from the natural and social sciences and the environmental design arts.

§ 1502.9 Draft, final, and supplemental statements.

Except for proposals for legislation as provided in § 1506.8 environmental impact statements shall be prepared in two stages and may be supplemented.

(a) Draft environmental impact statements shall be prepared in accordance with the scope decided upon in the scoping process. The lead agency shall work with the cooperating agencies and shall obtain comments as required in Part 1503 of this chapter. The draft statement must fulfill and satisfy to the fullest extent possible the requirements established for final statements in section 102(2)(C) of the Act. If a draft statement is so inadequate as to preclude meaningful analysis, the agency shall prepare and circulate a revised draft of the appropriate portion. The agency shall make every effort to disclose and discuss at appropriate points in the draft statement all major points of view on the environmental impacts of the alternatives including the proposed action.

(b) Final environmental impact statements shall respond to comments as required in Part 1503 of this chapter. The agency shall discuss at appropriate points in the final statement any responsible opposing view which was not adequately discussed in the draft statement and shall indicate the agency's response to the issues raised.

(c) Agencies:

(1) Shall prepare supplements to either draft or final environmental impact statements if:

(i) The agency makes substantial changes in the proposed action that are relevant to environmental concerns; or

(ii) There are significant new circumstances or information relevant to environmental concerns and bearing on the proposed action or its impacts.

(2) May also prepare supplements when the agency determines that the purposes of the Act will be furthered by doing so.

(3) Shall adopt procedures for introducing a supplement into its formal administrative record, if such a record exists.

(4) Shall prepare, circulate, and file a supplement to a statement in the same fashion (exclusive of scoping) as a draft and final statement

unless alternative procedures are approved by the Council.

§ 1502.10   Recommended format.

Agencies shall use a format for environmental impact statements which will encourage good analysis and clear presentation of the alternatives including the proposed action. The following standard format for environmental impact statements should be followed unless the agency determines that there is a compelling reason to do otherwise:

(a) Cover sheet.

(b) Summary.

(c) Table of Contents.

(d) Purpose of and Need for Action.

(e) Alternatives Including Proposed Action (secs. 102(2)(C)(iii) and 102(2)(E) of the Act).

(f) Affected Environment.

(g) Environmental Consequences (especially sections 102(2)(C) (i), (ii), (iv), and (v) of the Act).

(h) List of Preparers.

(i) List of Agencies, Organizations, and Persons to Whom Copies of the Statement Are Sent.

(j) Index.

(k) Appendices (if any).

If a different format is used, it shall include paragraphs (a), (b). (c), (h), (i), and (j), of this section and shall include the substance of paragraphs (d), (e), (f), (g), and (k) of this section, as further described in §§ 1502.11–1502.18, in any appropriate format.

§ 1502.11   Cover sheet.

The cover sheet shall not exceed one page. It shall include:

(a) A list of the responsible agencies including the lead agency and any cooperating agencies.

(b) The title of the proposed action that is the subject of the statement (and if appropriate the titles of related cooperating agency actions), together with the State(s) and county(ies) (or other jurisdiction if applicable) where the action is located.

(c) The name, address, and telephone number of the person at the agency who can supply further information.

(d) A designation of the statement as a draft, final, or draft or final supplement.

(e) A one paragraph abstract of the statement.

(f) The date by which comments must be received (computed in cooperation with EPA under § 1506.10).

The information required by this section may be entered on Standard Form 424 (in items 4, 6, 7, 10, and 18).

§ 1502.12   Summary.

Each environmental impact statement shall contain a summary which adequately and accurately summarizes the statement. The summary shall stress the major conclusions, areas of controversy (including issues raised by agencies and the public), and the issues to be resolved (including the choice among alternatives). The summary will normally not exceed 15 pages.

§ 1502.13   Purpose and need.

The statement shall briefly specify the underlying purpose and need to which the agency is responding in proposing the alternatives including the proposed action.

§ 1502.14   Alternatives including the proposed action.

This section is the heart of the environmental impact statement. Based on the information and analysis presented in the sections on the Affected Environment (§ 1502.15) and the Environmental Consequences (§ 1502.16), it should present the environmental impacts of the proposal and the alternatives in comparative form, thus sharply defining the issues and providing a clear basis for choice among options by the decisionmaker and the public. In this section agencies shall:

(a) Rigorously explore and objectively evaluate all reasonable alternatives, and for alternatives which were eliminated from detailed study, briefly discuss the reasons for their having been eliminated.

(b) Devote substantial treatment to each alternative considered in detail including the proposed action so that reviewers may evaluate their comparative merits.

(c) Include reasonable alternatives not within the jurisdiction of the lead agency.

(d) Include the alternative of no action.

(e) Identify the agency's preferred alternative or alternatives, if one or more exists, in the draft statement and identify such alternative in the final statement unless another law prohibits the expression of such a preference.

(f) Include appropriate mitigation measures not already included in the proposed action or alternatives.

§ 1502.15 Affected environment.

The environmental impact statement shall succinctly describe the environment of the area(s) to be affected or created by the alternatives under consideration. . The descriptions shall be no longer than is necessary to understand the effects of the alternatives. Data and analyses in a statement shall be commensurate with the importance of the impact, with less important material summarized, consolidated, or simply referenced. Agencies shall avoid useless bulk in statements and shall concentrate effort and attention on important issues. Verbose descriptions of the affected environment are themselves no measure of the adequacy of an environmental impact statement.

§ 1502.16 Environmental consequences.

This section forms the scientific and analytic basis for the comparisons under § 1502.14. It shall consolidate the discussions of those elements required by secs. 102(2)(C) (i), (ii), (iv), and (v) of NEPA which are within the scope of the statement and as much of sec. 102(2)(C)(iii) as is necessary to support the comparisons. The discussion will include the environmental impacts of the alternatives including the proposed action, any adverse environmental effects which cannot be avoided should the proposal be implemented, the relationship between short-term uses of man's environment and the maintenance and enhancement of long-term productivity, and any irre-

versible or irretrievable commitments of resources which would be involved in the proposal should it be implemented. This section should not duplicate discussions in § 1502.14. It shall include discussions of:

(a) Direct effects and their significance (§ 1508.8).

(b) Indirect effects and their significance (§ 1508.8).

(c) Possible conflicts between the proposed action and the objectives of Federal, regional, State, and local (and in the case of a reservation, Indian tribe) land use plans, policies and controls for the area concerned. (See § 1506.2(d).)

(d) The environmental effects of alternatives including the proposed action. The comparisons under § 1502.14 will be based on this discussion.

(e) Energy requirements and conservation potential of various alternatives and mitigation measures.

(f) Natural or depletable resource requirements and conservation potential of various alternatives and mitigation measures.

(g) Urban quality, historic and cultural resources, and the design of the built environment, including the reuse and conservation potential of various alternatives and mitigation measures.

(h) Means to mitigate adverse environmental impacts (if not fully covered under § 1502.14(f)).

§ 1502.17 List of preparers.

The environmental impact statement shall list the names, together with their qualifications (expertise, experience, professional disciplines), of the persons who were primarily responsible for preparing the environmental impact statement or significant background papers, including basic components of the statement (§§ 1502.6 and 1502.8). Where possible the persons who are responsible for a particular analysis, including analyses in background papers, shall be identified. Normally the list will not exceed two pages.

§ 1502.18 Appendix.

If an agency prepares an appendix to an environmental impact statement the appendix shall:

(a) Consist of material prepared in connection with an environmental impact statement (as distinct from material which is not so prepared and which is incorporated by reference (§ 1502.21)).

(b) Normally consist of material which substantiates any analysis fundamental to the impact statement.

(c) Normally be analytic and relevant to the decision to be made.

(d) Be circulated with the environmental impact statement or be readily available on request.

§ 1502.19 Circulation of the environmental impact statement.

Agencies shall circulate the entire draft and final environmental impact statements except for certain appendices as provided in § 1502.18(d) and unchanged statements as provided in § 1503.4(c). However, if the statement is unusually long, the agency may circulate the summary instead, except that the entire statement shall be furnished to:

(a) Any Federal agency which has jurisdiction by law or special expertise with respect to any environmental impact involved and any appropriate Federal, State or local agency authorized to develop and enforce environmental standards.

(b) The applicant, if any.

(c) Any person, organization, or agency requesting the entire environmental impact statement.

(d) In the case of a final environmental impact statement any person, organization, or agency which submitted substantive comments on the draft.

If the agency circulates the summary and thereafter receives a timely request for the entire statement and for additional time to comment, the time for that requestor only shall be extended by at least 15 days beyond the minimum period.

§ 1502.20 Tiering.

Agencies are encouraged to tier their environmental impact statements to eliminate repetitive discussions of the same issues and to focus on the actual issues ripe for decision at each level of environmental review (§ 1508.28). Whenever a broad environmental impact statement has been prepared (such as a program or policy statement) and a subsequent statement or environmental assessment is then prepared on an action included within the entire program or policy (such as a site specific action) the subsequent statement or environmental assessment need only summarize the issues discussed in the broader statement and incorporate discussions from the broader statement by reference and shall concentrate on the issues specific to the subsequent action. The subsequent document shall state where the earlier document is available. Tiering may also be appropriate for different stages of actions. (Sec. 1508.28).

§ 1502.21 Incorporation by reference.

Agencies shall incorporate material into an environmental impact statement by reference when the effect will be to cut down on bulk without impeding agency and public review of the action. The incorporated material shall be cited in the statement and its content briefly described. No material may be incorporated by reference unless it is reasonably available for inspection by potentially interested persons within the time allowed for comment. Material based on proprietary data which is itself not available for review and comment shall not be incorporated by reference.

§ 1502.22 Incomplete or unavailable information.

When an agency is evaluating significant adverse effects on the human environment in an environmental impact statement and there are gaps in relevant information or scientific uncertainty, the agency shall always make clear that such information is lacking or that uncertainty exists.

(a) If the information relevant to adverse impacts is essential to a reasoned choice among alternatives and is not known and the overall costs of obtaining it are not exorbitant, the agency shall include the information in the environmental impact statement.

(b) If (1) the information relevant to adverse impacts is essential to a reasoned choice among alternatives and is not known and the overall costs of obtaining it are exorbitant or (2) the information relevant to adverse impacts is important to the decision and the means to obtain it are not known (e.g., the means for obtaining it are beyond the state of the art) the agency shall weigh the need for the action against the risk and severity of possible adverse impacts were the action to proceed in the face of uncertainty. If the agency proceeds, it shall include a worst case analysis and an indication of the probability or improbability of its occurrence.

§ 1502.23 Cost-benefit analysis.

If a cost-benefit analysis relevant to the choice among environmentally different alternatives is being considered for the proposed action, it shall be incorporated by reference or appended to the statement as an aid in evaluating the environmental consequences. To assess the adequacy of compliance with sec. 102(2)(B) of the Act the statement shall, when a cost-benefit analysis is prepared, discuss the relationship between that analysis and any analyses of unquantified environmental impacts, values, and amenities. For purposes of complying with the Act, the weighing of the merits and drawbacks of the various alternatives need not be displayed in a monetary cost-benefit analysis and should not be when there are important qualitative considerations. In any event, an environmental impact statement should at least indicate those considerations, including factors not related to environmental quality, which are likely to be relevant and important to a decision.

§ 1502.24 Methodology and scientific accuracy.

Agencies shall insure the professional integrity, including scientific integrity, of the discussions and analyses in environmental impact statements. They shall identify any methodologies used and shall make explicit reference by footnote to the scientific and other sources relied upon for conclusions in the statement. An agency may place discussion of methodology in an appendix.

§ 1502.25 Environmental review and consultation requirements.

(a) To the fullest extent possible, agencies shall prepare draft environmental impact statements concurrently with and integrated with environmental impact analyses and related surveys and studies required by the Fish and Wildlife Coordination Act (16 U.S.C. Sec. 661 et seq.), the National Historic Preservation Act of 1966 (16 U.S.C. Sec. 470 et seq.), the Endangered Species Act of 1973 (16 U.S.C. Sec. 1531 et seq.), and other environmental review laws and executive orders.

(b) The draft environmental impact statement shall list all Federal permits, licenses, and other entitlements which must be obtained in implementing the proposal. If it is uncertain whether a Federal permit, license, or other entitlement is necessary, the draft environmental impact statement shall so indicate.

PART 1503—COMMENTING

Sec.
1503.1 Inviting Comments.
1503.2 Duty to Comment.
1503.3 Specificity of Comments.
1503.4 Response to Comments.

AUTHORITY: NEPA, the Environmental Quality Improvement Act of 1970, as amended (42 U.S.C. 4371 et seq.), Section 309 of the Clean Air Act, as amended (42 U.S.C. 7609), and Executive Order 11514, Protection and Enhancement of Environmental Quality (March 5, 1970, as amended by Executive Order 11991, May 24, 1977).

§ 1503.1 Inviting comments.

(a) After preparing a draft environmental impact statement and before preparing a final environmental impact statement the agency shall:

(1) Obtain the comments of any Federal agency which has jurisdic-

tion by law or special expertise with respect to any environmental impact involved or which is authorized to develop and enforce environmental standards.

(2) Request the comments of:

(i) Appropriate State and local agencies which are authorized to develop and enforce environmental standards;

(ii) Indian tribes, when the effects may be on a reservation; and

(iii) Any agency which has requested that it receive statements on actions of the kind proposed.

Office of Management and Budget Circular A-95 (Revised), through its system of clearinghouses, provides a means of securing the views of State and local environmental agencies. The clearinghouses may be used, by mutual agreement of the lead agency and the clearinghouse, for securing State and local reviews of the draft environmental impact statements.

(3) Request comments from the applicant, if any.

(4) Request comments from the public, affirmatively soliciting comments from those persons or organizations who may be interested or affected.

(b) An agency may request comments on a final environmental impact statement before the decision is finally made. In any case other agencies or persons may make comments before the final decision unless a different time is provided under § 1506.10.

§ 1503.2   Duty to comment.

Federal agencies with jurisdiction by law or special expertise with respect to any environmental impact involved and agencies which are authorized to develop and enforce environmental standards shall comment on statements within their jurisdiction, expertise, or authority. Agencies shall comment within the time period specified for comment in § 1506.10. A Federal agency may reply that it has no comment. If a cooperating agency is satisfied that its views are adequately reflected in the environmental impact statement, it should reply that it has no comment.

§ 1503.3   Specificity of comments.

(a) Comments on an environmental impact statement or on a proposed action shall be as specific as possible and may address either the adequacy of the statement or the merits of the alternatives discussed or both.

(b) When a commenting agency criticizes a lead agency's predictive methodology, the commenting agency should describe the alternative methodology which it prefers and why.

(c) A cooperating agency shall specify in its comments whether it needs additional information to fulfill other applicable environmental reviews or consultation requirements and what information it needs. In particular, it shall specify any additional information it needs to comment adequately on the draft statement's analysis of significant site-specific effects associated with the granting or approving by that cooperating agency of necessary Federal permits, licenses, or entitlements.

(d) When a cooperating agency with jurisdiction by law objects to or expresses reservations about the proposal on grounds of environmental impacts, the agency expressing the objection or reservation shall specify the mitigation measures it considers necessary to allow the agency to grant or approve applicable permit, license, or related requirements or concurrences.

§ 1503.4   Response to comments.

(a) An agency preparing a final environmental impact statement shall assess and consider comments both individually and collectively, and shall respond by one or more of the means listed below, stating its response in the final statement. Possible responses are to:

(1) Modify alternatives including the proposed action.

(2) Develop and evaluate alternatives not previously given serious consideration by the agency.

(3) Supplement, improve, or modify its analyses.

(4) Make factual corrections.

(5) Explain why the comments do

not warrant further agency response, citing the sources, authorities, or reasons which support the agency's position and, if appropriate, indicate those circumstances which would trigger agency reappraisal or further response.

(b) All substantive comments received on the draft statement (or summaries thereof where the response has been exceptionally voluminous), should be attached to the final statement whether or not the comment is thought to merit individual discussion by the agency in the text of the statement.

(c) If changes in response to comments are minor and are confined to the responses described in paragraphs (a) (4) and (5) of this section, agencies may write them on errata sheets and attach them to the statement instead of rewriting the draft statement. In such cases only the comments, the responses, and the changes and not the final statement need be circulated (§ 1502.19). The entire document with a new cover sheet shall be filed as the final statement (§ 1506.9).

PART 1504—PREDECISION REFERRALS TO THE COUNCIL OF PROPOSED FEDERAL ACTIONS DETERMINED TO BE ENVIRONMENTALLY UNSATISFACTORY

Sec.
1504.1 Purpose.
1504.2 Criteria for Referral.
1504.3 Procedure for Referrals and Response.

AUTHORITY: NEPA, the Environmental Quality Improvement Act of 1970, as amended (42 U.S.C. 4371 et seq.), Section 309 of the Clean Air Act, as amended (42 U.S.C. 7609), and Executive Order 11514, Protection and Enhancement of Environmental Quality (March 5, 1970, as amended by Executive Order 11991, May 24, 1977).

§ 1504.1 Purpose.

(a) This part establishes procedures for referring to the Council Federal interagency disagreements concerning proposed major Federal actions that might cause unsatisfactory environmental effects. It provides means for early resolution of such disagreements.

(b) Under section 309 of the Clean Air Act (42 U.S.C. 7609), the Administrator of the Environmental Protection Agency is directed to review and comment publicly on the environmental impacts of Federal activities, including actions for which environmental impact statements are prepared. If after this review the Administrator determines that the matter is "unsatisfactory from the standpoint of public health or welfare or environmental quality," section 309 directs that the matter be referred to the Council (hereafter "environmental referrals").

(c) Under section 102(2)(C) of the Act other Federal agencies may make similar reviews of environmental impact statements, including judgments on the acceptability of anticipated environmental impacts. These reviews must be made available to the President, the Council and the public.

§ 1504.2 Criteria for referral.

Environmental referrals should be made to the Council only after concerted, timely (as early as possible in the process), but unsuccessful attempts to resolve differences with the lead agency. In determining what environmental objections to the matter are appropriate to refer to the Council, an agency should weigh potential adverse environmental impacts, considering:

(a) Possible violation of national environmental standards or policies.

(b) Severity.

(c) Geographical scope.

(d) Duration.

(e) Importance as precedents.

(f) Availability of environmentally preferable alternatives.

§ 1504.3 Procedure for referrals and response.

(a) A Federal agency making the referral to the Council shall:

(1) Advise the lead agency at the earliest possible time that it intends to refer a matter to the Council unless a satisfactory agreement is reached.

(2) Include such advice in the referring agency's comments on the draft environmental impact statement, except when the statement does not contain adequate information to permit an assessment of the matter's environmental acceptability.

(3) Identify any essential information that is lacking and request that it be made available at the earliest possible time.

(4) Send copies of such advice to the Council.

(b) The referring agency shall deliver its referral to the Council not later than twenty-five (25) days after the final environmental impact statement has been made available to the Environmental Protection Agency, commenting agencies, and the public. Except when an extension of this period has been granted by the lead agency, the Council will not accept a referral after that date.

(c) The referral shall consist of:

(1) A copy of the letter signed by the head of the referring agency and delivered to the lead agency informing the lead agency of the referral and the reasons for it, and requesting that no action be taken to implement the matter until the Council acts upon the referral. The letter shall include a copy of the statement referred to in (c)(2) below.

(2) A statement supported by factual evidence leading to the conclusion that the matter is unsatisfactory from the standpoint of public health or welfare or environmental quality. The statement shall:

(i) Identify any material facts in controversy and incorporate (by reference if appropriate) agreed upon facts,

(ii) Identify any existing environmental requirements or policies which would be violated by the matter,

(iii) Present the reasons why the referring agency believes the matter is environmentally unsatisfactory,

(iv) Contain a finding by the agency whether the issue raised is of national importance because of the threat to national environmental resources or policies or for some other reason,

(v) Review the steps taken by the referring agency to bring its concerns to the attention of the lead agency at the earliest possible time, and

(vi) Give the referring agency's recommendations as to what mitigation alternative, further study, or other course of action (including abandonment of the matter) are necessary to remedy the situation.

(d) Not later than twenty-five (25) days after the referral to the Council the lead agency may deliver a response to the Council and the referring agency. If the lead agency requests more time and gives assurance that the matter will not go forward in the interim, the Council may grant an extension. The response shall:

(1) Address fully the issues raised in the referral.

(2) Be supported by evidence.

(3) Give the lead agency's response to the referring agency's recommendations.

(e) Interested persons (including the applicant) may deliver their views in writing to the Council. Views in support of the referral should be delivered not later than the referral. Views in support of the response shall be delivered not later than the response.

(f) Not later than twenty-five (25) days after receipt of both the referral and any response or upon being informed that there will be no response (unless the lead agency agrees to a longer time), the Council may take one or more of the following actions:

(1) Conclude that the process of referral and response has successfully resolved the problem.

(2) Initiate discussions with the agencies with the objective of mediation with referring and lead agencies.

(3) Hold public meetings or hearings to obtain additional views and information.

(4) Determine that the issue is not one of national importance and request the referring and lead agencies to pursue their decision process.

(5) Determine that the issue should be further negotiated by the referring and lead agencies and is not appropriate for Council consideration until one or more heads of

agencies report to the Council that the agencies' disagreements are irreconcilable.

(6) Publish its findings and recommendations (including where appropriate a finding that the submitted evidence does not support the position of an agency).

(7) When appropriate, submit the referral and the response together with the Council's recommendation to the President for action.

(g) The Council shall take no longer than 60 days to complete the actions specified in paragraph (f) (2), (3), or (5) of this section.

(h) When the referral involves an action required by statute to be determined on the record after opportunity for agency hearing, the referral shall be conducted in a manner consistent with 5 U.S.C. 557(d) (Administrative Procedure Act).

PART 1505—NEPA AND AGENCY DECISIONMAKING

Sec.
1505.1 Agency decisionmaking procedures.
1505.2 Record of decision in cases requiring environmental impact statements.
1505.3 Implementing the decision.

AUTHORITY: NEPA, the Environmental Quality Improvement Act of 1970, as amended (42 U.S.C. 4371 et seq.), Section 309 of the Clean Air Act, as amended (42 U.S.C. 7609), and Executive Order 11514, Protection and Enhancement of Environmental Quality (March 5, 1970, as amended by Executive Order 11991, May 24, 1977).

§ 1505.1 Agency decisionmaking procedures.

Agencies shall adopt procedures (§ 1507.3) to ensure that decisions are made in accordance with the policies and purposes of the Act. Such procedures shall include but not be limited to:

(a) Implementing procedures under section 102(2) to achieve the requirements of sections 101 and 102(1).

(b) Designating the major decision points for the agency's principal programs likely to have a significant effect on the human environment and assuring that the NEPA process corresponds with them.

(c) Requiring that relevant environmental documents, comments, and responses be part of the record in formal rulemaking or adjudicatory proceedings.

(d) Requiring that relevant environmental documents, comments, and responses accompany the proposal through existing agency review processes so that agency officials use the statement in making decisions.

(e) Requiring that the alternatives considered by the decisionmaker are encompassed by the range of alternatives discussed in the relevant environmental documents and that the decisionmaker consider the alternatives described in the environmental impact statement. If another decision document accompanies the relevant environmental documents to the decisionmaker, agencies are encouraged to make available to the public before the decision is made any part of that document that relates to the comparison of alternatives.

§ 1505.2 Record of decision in cases requiring environmental impact statements.

At the time of its decision (§ 1506.10) or, if appropriate, its recommendation to Congress, each agency shall prepare a concise public record of decision. The record, which may be integrated into any other record prepared by the agency, including that required by OMB Circular A-95 (Revised), part I, sections 6 (c) and (d), and part II, section 5(b)(4), shall:

(a) State what the decision was.

(b) Identify all alternatives considered by the agency in reaching its decision, specifying the alternative or alternatives which were considered to be environmentally preferable. An agency may discuss preferences among alternatives based on relevant factors including economic and technical considerations and agency statutory missions. An agency shall identify and discuss all such factors including any essential considerations of national policy which were balanced by the agency in making its decision and state how those considerations entered into its decision.

(c) State whether all practicable means to avoid or minimize environmental harm from the alternative selected have been adopted, and if not, why they were not. A monitoring and enforcement program shall be adopted and summarized where applicable for any mitigation.

§ 1505.3 Implementing the decision.

Agencies may provide for monitoring to assure that their decisions are carried out and should do so in important cases. Mitigation (§ 1505.2(c)) and other conditions established in the environmental impact statement or during its review and committed as part of the decision shall be implemented by the lead agency or other appropriate consenting agency. The lead agency shall:

(a) Include appropriate conditions in grants, permits or other approvals.

(b) Condition funding of actions on mitigation.

(c) Upon request, inform cooperating or commenting agencies on progress in carrying out mitigation measures which they have proposed and which were adopted by the agency making the decision.

(d) Upon request, make available to the public the results of relevant monitoring.

PART 1506—OTHER REQUIREMENTS OF NEPA

Sec.
1506.1 Limitations on actions during NEPA process.
1506.2 Elimination of duplication with State and local procedures.
1506.3 Adoption.
1506.4 Combining documents.
1506.5 Agency responsibility.
1506.6 Public involvement.
1506.7 Further guidance.
1506.8 Proposals for legislation.
1506.9 Filing requirements.
1506.10 Timing of agency action.
1506.11 Emergencies.
1506.12 Effective date.

AUTHORITY: NEPA, the Environmental Quality Improvement Act of 1970, as amended (42 U.S.C. 4371 et seq.), Section 309 of the Clean Air Act, as amended (42 U.S.C. 7609), and Executive Order 11514, Protection and Enhancement of Environmental Quality (March 5, 1970, as amended by Executive Order 11991, May 24, 1977).

§ 1506.1 Limitations on actions during NEPA process.

(a) Until an agency issues a record of decision as provided in § 1505.2 (except as provided in paragraph (c) of this section), no action concerning the proposal shall be taken which would:

(1) Have an adverse environmental impact; or

(2) Limit the choice of reasonable alternatives.

(b) If any agency is considering an application from a non-Federal entity, and is aware that the applicant is about to take an action within the agency's jurisdiction that would meet either of the criteria in paragraph (a) of this section, then the agency shall promptly notify the applicant that the agency will take appropriate action to insure that the objectives and procedures of NEPA are achieved.

(c) While work on a required program environmental impact statement is in progress and the action is not covered by an existing program statement, agencies shall not undertake in the interim any major Federal action covered by the program which may significantly affect the quality of the human environment unless such action:

(1) Is justified independently of the program;

(2) Is itself accompanied by an adequate environmental impact statement; and

(3) Will not prejudice the ultimate decision on the program. Interim action prejudices the ultimate decision on the program when it tends to determine subsequent development or limit alternatives.

(d) This section does not preclude development by applicants of plans or designs or performance of other work necessary to support an application for Federal, State or local permits or assistance. Nothing in this section shall preclude Rural Electrification Administration approval of minimal expenditures not affecting the environment (*e.g.* long leadtime equipment and purchase options) made by non-governmental entities seeking loan guarantees from the Administration.

§ 1506.2 Elimination of duplication with State and local procedures.

(a) Agencies authorized by law to cooperate with State agencies of statewide jurisdiction pursuant to section 102(2)(D) of the Act may do so.

(b) Agencies shall cooperate with State and local agencies to the fullest extent possible to reduce duplication between NEPA and State and local requirements, unless the agencies are specifically barred from doing so by some other law. Except for cases covered by paragraph (a) of this section, such cooperation shall to the fullest extent possible include:

(1) Joint planning processes.

(2) Joint environmental research and studies.

(3) Joint public hearings (except where otherwise provided by statute).

(4) Joint environmental assessments.

(c) Agencies shall cooperate with State and local agencies to the fullest extent possible to reduce duplication between NEPA and comparable State and local requirements, unless the agencies are specifically barred from doing so by some other law. Except for cases covered by paragraph (a) of this section, such cooperation shall to the fullest extent possible include joint environmental impact statements. In such cases one or more Federal agencies and one or more State or local agencies shall be joint lead agencies. Where State laws or local ordinances have environmental impact statement requirements in addition to but not in conflict with those in NEPA, Federal agencies shall cooperate in fulfilling these requirements as well as those of Federal laws so that one document will comply with all applicable laws.

(d) To better integrate environmental impact statements into State or local planning processes, statements shall discuss any inconsistency of a proposed action with any approved State or local plan and laws (whether or not federally sanctioned). Where an inconsistency exists, the statement should describe the extent to which the agency would reconcile its proposed action with the plan or law.

§ 1506.3 Adoption.

(a) An agency may adopt a Federal draft or final environmental impact statement or portion thereof provided that the statement or portion thereof meets the standards for an adequate statement under these regulations.

(b) If the actions covered by the original environmental impact statement and the proposed action are substantially the same, the agency adopting another agency's statement is not required to recirculate it except as a final statement. Otherwise the adopting agency shall treat the statement as a draft and recirculate it (except as provided in paragraph (c) of this section).

(c) A cooperating agency may adopt without recirculating the environmental impact statement of a lead agency when, after an independent review of the statement, the cooperating agency concludes that its comments and suggestions have been satisfied.

(d) When an agency adopts a statement which is not final within the agency that prepared it, or when the action it assesses is the subject of a referral under part 1504, or when the statement's adequacy is the subject of a judicial action which is not final, the agency shall so specify.

§ 1506.4 Combining documents.

Any environmental document in compliance with NEPA may be combined with any other agency document to reduce duplication and paperwork.

§ 1506.5 Agency responsibility.

(a) *Information.* If an agency requires an applicant to submit environmental information for possible use by the agency in preparing an environmental impact statement, then the agency should assist the applicant by outlining the types of information required. The agency shall independently evaluate the information submitted and shall be responsible for its accuracy. If the agency chooses to use the information submitted by the applicant in the environmental impact statement, either directly or by reference, then the names of the persons responsible for the independent evaluation shall be included in the list of preparers (§ 1502.17). It is the intent of this subparagraph that acceptable work not be redone, but that it be verified by the agency.

(b) *Environmental assessments.* If an agency permits an applicant to prepare an environmental assessment, the agency, besides fulfilling the requirements of paragraph (a) of this section, shall make its own evaluation of the environmental issues and take responsibility for the scope and content of the environmental assessment.

(c) *Environmental impact statements.* Except as provided in §§ 1506.2 and 1506.3 any environmental impact statement prepared pursuant to the requirements of NEPA shall be prepared directly by or by a contractor selected by the lead agency or where appropriate under § 1501.6(b), a cooperating agency. It is the intent of these regulations that the contractor be chosen solely by the lead agency, or by the lead agency in cooperation with cooperating agencies, or where appropriate by a cooperating agency to avoid any conflict of interest. Contractors shall execute a disclosure statement prepared by the lead agency, or where appropriate the cooperating agency, specifying that they have no financial or other interest in the outcome of the project. If the document is prepared by contract, the responsible Federal official shall furnish guidance and participate in the preparation and shall independently evaluate the statement prior to its approval and take responsibility for its scope and contents. Nothing in this section is intended to prohibit any agency from requesting any person to submit information to it or to prohibit any person from submitting information to any agency.

§ 1506.6 **Public involvement.**

Agencies shall: (a) Make diligent efforts to involve the public in preparing and implementing their NEPA procedures.

(b) Provide public notice of NEPA-related hearings, public meetings, and the availability of environmental documents so as to inform those persons and agencies who may be interested or affected.

(1) In all cases the agency shall mail notice to those who have requested it on an individual action.

(2) In the case of an action with effects of national concern notice shall include publication in the FEDERAL REGISTER and notice by mail to national organizations reasonably expected to be interested in the matter and may include listing in the *102 Monitor.* An agency engaged in rulemaking may provide notice by mail to national organizations who have requested that notice regularly be provided. Agencies shall maintain a list of such organizations.

(3) In the case of an action with effects primarily of local concern the notice may include:

(i) Notice to State and areawide clearinghouses pursuant to OMB Circular A-95 (Revised).

(ii) Notice to Indian tribes when effects may occur on reservations.

(iii) Following the affected State's public notice procedures for comparable actions.

(iv) Publication in local newspapers (in papers of general circulation rather than legal papers).

(v) Notice through other local media.

(vi) Notice to potentially interested community organizations including small business associations.

(vii) Publication in newsletters that may be expected to reach potentially interested persons.

(viii) Direct mailing to owners and occupants of nearby or affected property.

(ix) Posting of notice on and off site in the area where the action is to be located.

(c) Hold or sponsor public hearings or public meetings whenever appropriate or in accordance with statutory requirements applicable to the agency. Criteria shall include whether there is:

(1) Substantial environmental controversy concerning the proposed action or substantial interest in holding the hearing.

(2) A request for a hearing by another agency with jurisdiction over the action supported by reasons why a hearing will be helpful. If a draft environmental impact statement is to be considered at a public hearing, the agency should make the statement available to the public at least 15 days in advance (unless the purpose of the hearing is to provide information for the draft environmental impact statement).

(d) Solicit appropriate information from the public.

(e) Explain in its procedures where interested persons can get information or status reports on environmental impact statements and other elements of the NEPA process.

(f) Make environmental impact statements, the comments received, and any underlying documents available to the public pursuant to the provisions of the Freedom of Information Act (5 U.S.C. 552), without regard to the exclusion for interagency memoranda where such memoranda transmit comments of Federal agencies on the environmental impact of the proposed action. Materials to be made available to the public shall be provided to the public without charge to the extent practicable, or at a fee which is not more than the actual costs of reproducing copies required to be sent to other Federal agencies, including the Council.

§ 1506.7 Further guidance.

The Council may provide further guidance concerning NEPA and its procedures including:

(a) A handbook which the Council may supplement from time to time, which shall in plain language provide guidance and instructions concerning the application of NEPA and these regulations.

(b) Publication of the Council's Memoranda to Heads of Agencies.

(c) In conjunction with the Environmental Protection Agency and the publication of the 102 Monitor, notice of:

(1) Research activities;

(2) Meetings and conferences related to NEPA; and

(3) Successful and innovative procedures used by agencies to implement NEPA.

§ 1506.8 Proposals for legislation.

(a) The NEPA process for proposals for legislation (§ 1508.17) significantly affecting the quality of the human environment shall be integrated with the legislative process of the Congress. A legislative environmental impact statement is the detailed statement required by law to be included in a recommendation or report on a legislative proposal to Congress. A legislative environmental impact statement shall be considered part of the formal transmittal of a legislative proposal to Congress; however, it may be transmitted to Congress up to 30 days later in order to allow time for completion of an accurate statement which can serve as the basis for public and Congressional debate. The statement must be available in time for Congressional hearings and deliberations.

(b) Preparation of a legislative environmental impact statement shall conform to the requirements of these regulations except as follows:

(1) There need not be a scoping process.

(2) The legislative statement shall be prepared in the same manner as a draft statement, but shall be considered the "detailed statement" required by statute; *Provided,* That when any of the following conditions exist both the draft and final environmental impact statement on the legislative proposal shall be prepared and circulated as provided by §§ 1503.1 and 1506.10.

(i) A Congressional Committee with jurisdiction over the proposal has a rule requiring both draft and final environmental impact statements.

(ii) The proposal results from a study process required by statute (such as those required by the Wild and Scenic Rivers Act (16 U.S.C.

1271 et seq.) and the Wilderness Act (16 U.S.C. 1131 et seq.)).

(iii) Legislative approval is sought for Federal or federally assisted construction or other projects which the agency recommends be located at specific geographic locations. For proposals requiring an environmental impact statement for the acquisition of space by the General Services Administration, a draft statement shall accompany the Prospectus or the 11(b) Report of Building Project Surveys to the Congress, and a final statement shall be completed before site acquisition.

(iv) The agency decides to prepare draft and final statements.

(c) Comments on the legislative statement shall be given to the lead agency which shall forward them along with its own responses to the Congressional committees with jurisdiction.

§ 1506.9 Filing requirements.

Environmental impact statements together with comments and responses shall be filed with the Environmental Protection Agency, attention Office of Federal Activities (A–104), 401 M Street SW., Washington, D.C. 20460. Statements shall be filed with EPA no earlier than they are also transmitted to commenting agencies and made available to the public. EPA shall deliver one copy of each statement to the Council, which shall satisfy the requirement of availability to the President. EPA may issue guidelines to agencies to implement its responsibilities under this section and § 1506.10 below.

§ 1506.10 Timing of agency action.

(a) The Environmental Protection Agency shall publish a notice in the FEDERAL REGISTER each week of the environmental impact statements filed during the preceding week. The minimum time periods set forth in this section shall be calculated from the date of publication of this notice.

(b) No decision on the proposed action shall be made or recorded under § 1505.2 by a Federal agency until the later of the following dates:

(1) Ninety (90) days after publication of the notice described above in paragraph (a) of this section for a draft environmental impact statement.

(2) Thirty (30) days after publication of the notice described above in paragraph (a) of this section for a final environmental impact statement.

An exception to the rules on timing may be made in the case of an agency decision which is subject to a formal internal appeal. Some agencies have a formally established appeal process which allows other agencies or the public to take appeals on a decision and make their views known, after publication of the final environmental impact statement. In such cases, where a real opportunity exists to alter the decision, the decision may be made and recorded at the same time the environmental impact statement is published. This means that the period for appeal of the decision and the 30-day period prescribed in paragraph (b)(2) of this section may run concurrently. In such cases the environmental impact statement shall explain the timing and the public's right of appeal. An agency engaged in rulemaking under the Administrative Procedure Act or other statute for the purpose of protecting the public health or safety, may waive the time period in paragraph (b)(2) of this section and publish a decision on the final rule simultaneously with publication of the notice of the availability of the final environmental impact statement as described in paragraph (a) of this section.

(c) If the final environmental impact statement is filed within ninety (90) days after a draft environmental impact statement is filed with the Environmental Protection Agency, the minimum thirty (30) day period and the minimum ninety (90) day period may run concurrently. However, subject to paragraph (d) of this section agencies shall allow not less than 45 days for comments on draft statements.

(d) The lead agency may extend prescribed periods. The Environmental Protection Agency may upon a showing by the lead agency of compelling reasons of national policy reduce the prescribed periods and may upon a showing by any other Federal agency of compelling reasons of national policy also extend prescribed periods, but only after consultation with the lead agency. (Also see § 1507.3(d).) Failure to file timely comments shall not be a sufficient reason for extending a period. If the lead agency does not concur with the extension of time, EPA may not extend it for more than 30 days. When the Environmental Protection Agency reduces or extends any period of time it shall notify the Council.

§ 1506.11 Emergencies.

Where emergency circumstances make it necessary to take an action with significant environmental impact without observing the provisions of these regulations, the Federal agency taking the action should consult with the Council about alternative arrangements. Agencies and the Council will limit such arrangements to actions necessary to control the immediate impacts of the emergency. Other actions remain subject to NEPA review.

§ 1506.12 Effective date.

The effective date of these regulations is July 30, 1979, except that for agencies that administer programs that qualify under sec. 102(2)(D) of the Act or under sec. 104(h) of the Housing and Community Development Act of 1974 an additional four months shall be allowed for the State or local agencies to adopt their implementing procedures.

(a) These regulations shall apply to the fullest extent practicable to ongoing activities and environmental documents begun before the effective date. These regulations do not apply to an environmental impact statement or supplement if the draft statement was filed before the effective date of these regulations. No completed environmental documents need be redone by reason of these regulations. Until these regulations are applicable, the Council's guidelines published in the FEDERAL REGISTER of August 1, 1973, shall continue to be applicable. In cases where these regulations are applicable the

guidelines are superseded. However, nothing shall prevent an agency from proceeding under these regulations at an earlier time.

(b) NEPA shall continue to be applicable to actions begun before January 1, 1970, to the fullest extent possible.

PART 1507—AGENCY COMPLIANCE

Sec.
1507.1 Compliance.
1507.2 Agency Capability to Comply.
1507.3 Agency Procedures.

AUTHORITY: NEPA, the Environmental Quality Improvement Act of 1970, as amended (42 U.S.C. 4371 et seq.), Section 309 of the Clean Air Act, as amended (42 U.S.C. 7609), and Executive Order 11514, Protection and Enhancement of Environmental Quality (March 5, 1970, as amended by Executive Order 11991, May 24, 1977).

§ 1507.1 Compliance.

All agencies of the Federal Government shall comply with these regulations. It is the intent of these regulations to allow each agency flexibility in adapting its implementing procedures authorized by § 1507.3 to the requirements of other applicable laws.

§ 1507.2 Agency capability to comply.

Each agency shall be capable (in terms of personnel and other resources) of complying with the requirements enumerated below. Such compliance may include use of other's resources, but the using agency shall itself have sufficient capability to evaluate what others do for it. Agencies shall:

(a) Fulfill the requirements of Sec. 102(2)(A) of the Act to utilize a systematic, interdisciplinary approach which will insure the integrated use of the natural and social sciences and the environmental design arts in planning and in decisionmaking which may have an impact on the human environment. Agencies shall designate a person to be responsible for overall review of agency NEPA compliance.

(b) Identify methods and procedures required by Sec. 102(2)(B) to insure that presently unquantified environmental amenities and values may be given appropriate consideration.

(c) Prepare adequate environmental impact statements pursuant to Sec. 102(2)(C) and comment on statements in the areas where the agency has jurisdiction by law or special expertise or is authorized to develop and enforce environmental standards.

(d) Study, develop, and describe alternatives to recommended courses of action in any proposal which involves unresolved conflicts concerning alternative uses of available resources. This requirement of Sec. 102(2)(E) extends to all such proposals, not just the more limited scope of Sec. 102(2)(C)(iii) where the discussion of alternatives is confined to impact statements.

(e) Comply with the requirements of Sec. 102(2)(H) that the agency initiate and utilize ecological information in the planning and development of resource-oriented projects.

(f) Fulfill the requirements of sections 102(2)(F), 102(2)(G), and 102(2)(I), of the Act and of Executive Order 11514, Protection and Enhancement of Environmental Quality, Sec. 2.

§ 1507.3   Agency procedures.

(a) Not later than eight months after publication of these regulations as finally adopted in the FEDERAL REGISTER, or five months after the establishment of an agency, whichever shall come later, each agency shall as necessary adopt procedures to supplement these regulations. When the agency is a department, major subunits are encouraged (with the consent of the department) to adopt their own procedures. Such procedures shall not paraphrase these regulations. They shall confine themselves to implementing procedures. Each agency shall consult with the Council while developing its procedures and before publishing them in the FEDERAL REGISTER for comment. Agencies with similar programs should consult with each other and the Council to coordinate their procedures, especially for programs requesting simi-

lar information from applicants. The procedures shall be adopted only after an opportunity for public review and after review by the Council for conformity with the Act and these regulations. The Council shall complete its review within 30 days. Once in effect they shall be filed with the Council and made readily available to the public. Agencies are encouraged to publish explanatory guidance for these regulations and their own procedures. Agencies shall continue to review their policies and procedures and in consultation with the Council to revise them as necessary to ensure full compliance with the purposes and provisions of the Act.

(b) Agency procedures shall comply with these regulations except where compliance would be inconsistent with statutory requirements and shall include:

(1) Those procedures required by §§ 1501.2(d), 1502.9(c)(3), 1505.1, 1506.6(e), and 1508.4.

(2) Specific criteria for and identification of those typical classes of action:

(i) Which normally do require environmental impact statements.

(ii) Which normally do not require either an environmental impact statement or an environmental assessment (categorical exclusions (§ 1508.4)).

(iii) Which normally require environmental assessments but not necessarily environmental impact statements.

(c) Agency procedures may include specific criteria for providing limited exceptions to the provisions of these regulations for classified proposals. They are proposed actions which are specifically authorized under criteria established by an Executive Order or statute to be kept secret in the interest of national defense or foreign policy and are in fact properly classified pursuant to such Executive Order or statute. Environmental assessments and environmental impact statements which address classified proposals may be safeguarded and restricted from public dissemination in accordance with agencies' own regulations applicable to classified information. These documents may be organized so that classified portions can be included as annexes, in order that the unclassified portions can be made available to the public.

(d) Agency procedures may provide for periods of time other than those presented in § 1506.10 when necessary to comply with other specific statutory requirements.

(e) Agency procedures may provide that where there is a lengthy period between the agency's decision to prepare an environmental impact statement and the time of actual preparation, the notice of intent required by § 1501.7 may be published at a reasonable time in advance of preparation of the draft statement.

PART 1508—TERMINOLOGY AND INDEX

AUTHORITY: NEPA, the Environmental Quality Improvement Act of 1970, as amended (42 U.S.C. 4371 *et seq.*), Section 309 of the Clean Air Act, as amended (42 U.S.C. 7609), and Executive Order 11514, Protection and Enhancement of Environmental Quality (March 5, 1970, as amended by Executive Order 11991, May 24, 1977).

§ 1508.1 Terminology.

The terminology of this part shall be uniform throughout the Federal Government.

§ 1508.2 Act.

"Act" means the National Environmental Policy Act, as amended (42 U.S.C. 4321, et seq.) which is also referred to as "NEPA."

§ 1508.3 Affecting.

"Affecting" means will or may have an effect on.

§ 1508.4 Categorical exclusion.

"Categorical Exclusion" means a category of actions which do not individually or cumulatively have a significant effect on the human environment and which have been found to have no such effect in procedures adopted by a Federal agency in implementation of these regulations (§ 1507.3) and for which, therefore, neither an environmental assessment nor an environmental impact statement is required. An agency may decide in its procedures or otherwise, to prepare environmental assessments for the reasons stated in § 1508.9 even though it is not required to do so. Any procedures under this section shall provide for extraordinary circumstances in which a normally excluded action may have a significant environmental effect.

§ 1508.5 Cooperating agency.

"Cooperating Agency" means any Federal agency other than a lead agency which has jurisdiction by law or special expertise with respect to any environmental impact involved in a proposal (or a reasonable alternative) for legislation or other major Federal action significantly affecting the quality of the human environment. The selection and responsibilities of a cooperating agency are described in § 1501.6. A State or local agency of similar qualifications or, when the effects are on a reservation, an Indian Tribe, may by agreement with the lead agency become a cooperating agency.

§ 1508.6 Council.

"Council" means the Council on Environmental Quality established by Title II of the Act.

§ 1508.7 Cumulative impact.

"Cumulative impact" is the impact on the environment which results from the incremental impact of the action when added to other past, present, and reasonably foreseeable future actions regardless of what agency (Federal or non-Federal) or person undertakes such other actions. Cumulative impacts can result from individually minor but collectively significant actions taking place over a period of time.

§ 1508.8 Effects.

"Effects" include:

(a) Direct effects, which are caused by the action and occur at the same time and place.

(b) Indirect effects, which are caused by the action and are later in time or farther removed in distance, but are still reasonably foreseeable. Indirect effects may include growth inducing effects and other effects related to induced changes in the pattern of land use, population density or growth rate, and related effects on air and water and other natural systems, including ecosystems.

Effects and impacts as used in these regulations are synonymous. Effects includes ecological (such as the effects on natural resources and on the components, structures, and functioning of affected ecosystems), aesthetic, historic, cultural, economic, social, or health, whether direct, indirect, or cumulative. Effects may also include those resulting from actions which may have both beneficial and detrimental effects, even if on balance the agency believes that the effect will be beneficial.

§ 1508.9 Environmental assessment.

"Environmental Assessment":

(a) Means a concise public document for which a Federal agency is responsible that serves to:

(1) Briefly provide sufficient evidence and analysis for determining whether to prepare an environmental impact statement or a finding of no significant impact.

(2) Aid an agency's compliance with the Act when no environmental impact statement is necessary.

(3) Facilitate preparation of a statement when one is necessary.

(b) Shall include brief discussions of the need for the proposal, of alternatives as required by sec. 102(2)(E), of the environmental impacts of the proposed action and alternatives, and a listing of agencies and persons consulted.

§ 1508.10 Environmental document.

"Environmental document" includes the documents specified in § 1508.9 (environmental assessment), § 1508.11 (environmental impact statement), § 1508.13 (finding of no significant impact), and § 1508.22 (notice of intent).

§ 1508.11 Environmental impact statement.

"Environmental Impact Statement" means a detailed written statement as required by Sec. 102(2)(C) of the Act.

§ 1508.12 Federal agency.

"Federal agency" means all agencies of the Federal Government. It does not mean the Congress, the Judiciary, or the President, including the performance of staff functions for the President in his Executive Office. It also includes for purposes of these regulations States and units of general local government and Indian tribes assuming NEPA responsibilities under section 104(h) of the Housing and Community Development Act of 1974.

§ 1508.13 Finding of no significant impact.

"Finding of No Significant Impact" means a document by a Federal agency briefly presenting the reasons why an action, not otherwise excluded (§ 1508.4), will not have a significant effect on the human environment and for which an environmental impact statement therefore will not be prepared. It shall include the environmental assessment or a summary of it and shall note any other environmental documents related to it (§ 1501.7(a)(5)). If the assessment is included, the finding need not repeat any of the discussion in the assessment but may incorporate it by reference.

§ 1508.14 Human Environment.

"Human Environment" shall be interpreted comprehensively to include the natural and physical environment and the relationship of people with that environment. (See the definition of "effects" (§ 1508.8).) This means that economic or social effects are not intended by themselves to require preparation of an environmental impact statement. When an environmental impact statement is prepared and economic or social and natural or physical environmental effects are interrelated, then the environmental impact statement will discuss all of these effects on the human environment.

§ 1508.15 Jurisdiction By Law.

"Jurisdiction by law" means agency authority to approve, veto, or finance all or part of the proposal.

§ 1508.16 Lead agency.

"Lead Agency" means the agency or agencies preparing or having taken primary responsibility for preparing the environmental impact statement.

§ 1508.17 Legislation.

"Legislation" includes a bill or legislative proposal to Congress developed by or with the significant cooperation and support of a Federal agency, but does not include requests for appropriations. The test for significant cooperation is whether the proposal is in fact predominantly that of the agency rather than another source. Drafting does not by itself constitute significant cooperation. Proposals for legislation include requests for ratification of treaties. Only the agency which has primary responsibility for the subject matter involved will prepare a legislative environmental impact statement.

§ 1508.18 Major Federal action.

"Major Federal action" includes actions with effects that may be major and which are potentially subject to Federal control and responsibility. Major reinforces but does not have a meaning independent of significantly (§ 1508.27). Actions include the circumstance where the responsible officials fail to act and that failure to act is reviewable by courts or administrative tribunals under the Administrative Procedure Act or other applicable law as agency action.

(a) Actions include new and continuing activities, including projects and programs entirely or partly financed, assisted, conducted, regulated, or approved by federal agencies; new or revised agency rules, regulations, plans, policies, or procedures; and legislative proposals (§§ 1506.8, 1508.17). Actions do not include funding assistance solely in the form of general revenue sharing funds, distributed under the State and Local Fiscal Assistance Act of 1972, 31 U.S.C. 1221 et seq., with no Federal agency control over the subsequent use of such funds. Actions do not include bringing judicial or administrative civil or criminal enforcement actions.

(b) Federal actions tend to fall within one of the following categories:

(1) Adoption of official policy, such as rules, regulations, and interpretations adopted pursuant to the Administrative Procedure Act, 5 U.S.C. 551 et seq.; treaties and international conventions or agreements; formal documents establishing an agency's policies which will result in or substantially alter agency programs.

(2) Adoption of formal plans, such as official documents prepared or approved by federal agencies which guide or prescribe alternative uses of federal resources, upon which future agency actions will be based.

(3) Adoption of programs, such as a group of concerted actions to implement a specific policy or plan; systematic and connected agency decisions allocating agency resources to implement a specific statutory program or executive directive.

(4) Approval of specific projects, such as construction or management activities located in a defined geographic area. Projects include actions approved by permit or other regulatory decision as well as federal and federally assisted activities.

§ 1508.19 Matter.

"Matter" includes for purposes of Part 1504:

(a) With respect to the Environmental Protection Agency, any proposed legislation, project, action or regulation as those terms are used in Section 309(a) of the Clean Air Act (42 U.S.C. 7609).

(b) With respect to all other agencies, any proposed major federal action to which section 102(2)(C) of NEPA applies.

§ 1508.20 Mitigation.

"Mitigation" includes:

(a) Avoiding the impact altogether by not taking a certain action or parts of an action.

(b) Minimizing impacts by limiting the degree or magnitude of the action and its implementation.

(c) Rectifying the impact by repairing, rehabilitating, or restoring the affected environment.

(d) Reducing or eliminating the impact over time by preservation and maintenance operations during the life of the action.

(e) Compensating for the impact by replacing or providing substitute resources or environments.

§ 1508.21 NEPA process.

"NEPA process" means all measures necessary for compliance with the requirements of Section 2 and Title I of NEPA.

§ 1508.22 Notice of intent.

"Notice of Intent" means a notice that an environmental impact statement will be prepared and considered. The notice shall briefly:

(a) Describe the proposed action and possible alternatives.

(b) Describe the agency's proposed scoping process including whether, when, and where any scoping meeting will be held.

(c) State the name and address of a person within the agency who can answer questions about the proposed action and the environmental impact statement.

§ 1508.23 Proposal.

"Proposal" exists at that stage in the development of an action when an agency subject to the Act has a goal and is actively preparing to make a decision on one or more alternative means of accomplishing that goal and the effects can be meaningfully evaluated. Preparation of an environmental impact statement on a proposal should be timed (§ 1502.5) so that the final statement may be completed in time for the statement to be included in any recommendation or report on the proposal. A proposal may exist in fact as well as by agency declaration that one exists.

§ 1508.24 Referring agency.

"Referring agency" means the federal agency which has referred any matter to the Council after a determination that the matter is unsatisfactory from the standpoint of public health or welfare or environmental quality.

§ 1508.25 Scope.

Scope consists of the range of actions, alternatives, and impacts to be considered in an environmental impact statement. The scope of an individual statement may depend on its relationships to other statements (§§1502.20 and 1508.28). To determine the scope of environmental impact statements, agencies shall consider 3 types of actions, 3 types of alternatives, and 3 types of impacts. They include:

(a) Actions (other than unconnected single actions) which may be:

(1) Connected actions, which means that they are closely related and therefore should be discussed in the same impact statement. Actions are connected if they:

(i) Automatically trigger other actions which may require environmental impact statements.

(ii) Cannot or will not proceed unless other actions are taken previously or simultaneously.

(iii) Are interdependent parts of a larger action and depend on the larger action for their justification.

(2) Cumulative actions, which when viewed with other proposed actions have cumulatively significant impacts and should therefore be discussed in the same impact statement.

(3) Similar actions, which when

viewed with other reasonably fore- seeable or proposed agency actions, have similarities that provide a basis for evaluating their environmental consequencies together, such as common timing or geography. An agency may wish to analyze these actions in the same impact state- ment. It should do so when the best way to assess adequately the com- bined impacts of similar actions or reasonable alternatives to such ac- tions is to treat them in a single impact statement.

(b) Alternatives, which include: (1) No action alternative. (2) Other rea- sonable courses of actions. (3) Miti- gation measures (not in the pro- posed action).

(c) Impacts, which may be: (1) Direct. (2) Indirect. (3) Cumulative.

§ 1508.26 Special expertise.

"Special expertise" means statuto- ry responsibility, agency mission, or related program experience.

§ 1508.27 Significantly.

"Significantly" as used in NEPA requires considerations of both con- text and intensity:

(a) *Context.* This means that the significance of an action must be analyzed in several contexts such as society as a whole (human, nation- al), the affected region, the affected interests, and the locality. Signifi- cance varies with the setting of the proposed action. For instance, in the case of a site-specific action, signifi- cance would usually depend upon the effects in the locale rather than in the world as a whole. Both short- and long-term effects are relevant.

(b) *Intensity.* This refers to the se- verity of impact. Responsible offi- cials must bear in mind that more than one agency may make decisions about partial aspects of a major action. The following should be con- sidered in evaluating intensity:

(1) Impacts that may be both beneficial and adverse. A significant effect may exist even if the Federal agency believes that on balance the effect will be beneficial.

(2) The degree to which the pro- posed action affects public health or safety.

(3) Unique characteristics of the geographic area such as proximity to historic or cultural resources, park lands, prime farmlands, wetlands, wild and scenic rivers, or ecologically critical areas.

(4) The degree to which the effects on the quality of the human envi- ronment are likely to be highly con- troversial.

(5) The degree to which the possi- ble effects on the human environ- ment are highly uncertain or involve unique or unknown risks.

(6) The degree to which the action may establish a precedent for future actions with significant effects or represents a decision in principle about a future consideration.

(7) Whether the action is related to other actions with individually in- significant but cumulatively signifi- cant impacts. Significance exists if it is reasonable to anticipate a cumula- tively significant impact on the envi- ronment. Significance cannot be avoided by terming an action tempo- rary or by breaking it down into small component parts.

(8) The degree to which the action may adversely affect districts, sites, highways, structures, or objects listed in or eligible for listing in the National Register of Historic Places or may cause loss or destruction of significant scientific, cultural, or his- torical resources.

(9) The degree to which the action may adversely affect an endangered or threatened species or its habitat that has been determined to be criti- cal under the Endangered Species Act of 1973.

(10) Whether the action threatens a violation of Federal, State, or local law or requirements imposed for the protection of the environment.

§ 1508.28 Tiering.

"Tiering" refers to the coverage of general matters in broader environ- mental impact statements (such as national program or policy state- ments) with subsequent narrower statements or environmental analy- ses (such as regional or basinwide program statements or ultimately site-specific statements) incorporat- ing by reference the general discus- sions and concentrating solely on the issues specific to the statement subsequently prepared. Tiering is appropriate when the sequence of statements or analyses is:

(a) From a program, plan, or policy environmental impact statement to a program, plan, or policy statement or analysis of lesser scope or to a site-specific statement or analysis.

(b) From an environmental impact statement on a specific action at an early stage (such as need and site selection) to a supplement (which is preferred) or a subsequent statement or analysis at a later stage (such as environmental mitigation). Tiering in such cases is appropriate when it helps the lead agency to focus on the issues which are ripe for decision and exclude from consideration issues already decided or not yet ripe.

APPENDIX 3B: FORMAT AND CONTENT OF ENVIRONMENTAL IMPACT STATEMENTS (DOT 5610.1C, September 18, 1979, Attachment 2)

1. <u>Format.</u>

   a. The format recommended in CEQ 1502.10 should be used for DOT EISs:

      (a) Cover Sheet

      (b) Summary

      (c) Table of Contents

      (d) Purpose and Need for the Action

      (e) Alternatives Including the Proposed Action

      (f) Affected Environment

      (g) Environemntal Consequences

      (h) List of Preparers

      (i) List of Agencies, Organizations, and Persons to Whom Copies of the Statement Are Sent

      (j) Index

      (k) Appendices (if any)

   b. The cover sheet for each environmental impact statement will include the information identified in CEQ 1502.11 and will be headed as follows:

Department of Transportation

(operating administration)

(Draft/Final) Environmental Impact Statement Pursuant to Section 102(2)(C), P.L. 91-190

As appropriate, the heading will indicate that the EIS also covers the requirements of section 4(f) of the DOT Act, section 14 of the Mass Transportation Act, and/or sections 16 and 18 (a)(4) of the Airport Act.

2. Guidance as to Content of Statements.

    a. Environmental impact statements shall include the information specified in CEQ 1502.11 through 1502.18. The following paragraphs of Attachment 2 are intended to be considered, where relevant, as guidance regarding the content of environmental statements.

    b. Additional information contained in research reports, guidance on methodology, and other materials relating to consideration of environmental factors should be employed as appropriate in the preparation of EISs and environmental assessments. Examples of such materials include.

    U.S. Department of Transportation, Environmental Assessment *Notebook Series: Highways*, 1975, Report No. DOT P 5600.4, available from the U.S. Government Printing Office, Washington, D.C. 20402, Stock Number 050-000-00109-1;

    U.S. DOT, *Environmental Assessment Notebook Series: Airports*, 1978, Report Number DOT P 5600.5, available from the U.S. Government Printing Office, Washington, D.C. 20402, Stock Number 050-000-00138-5;

    U.S. DOT, FAA, *Environmental Assessment of Airport Development Actions*, 1977, available from the National Technical Information Service, 5284 Port

Royal Road, Springfield, Virginia 22161, NTIS Catalog Number ADA-039274; and

U.S. DOT, *Guidelines for Assessing the Environmental Impact of Public Mass Transportation Projects*, 1979, Report Number DOT P 79 001, available from the National Technical Information Service, Springfield, Virgina 22161.

3. General Content. The following points are to be covered.

    a. A description of the proposed Federal action (e.g. "The proposed Federal action is approval of location of highway . . ." or "The proposed Federal action is approval of a grant application to construct . . ."), and a statement of its purpose.

    b. Alternatives, including the proposed action, and including, where relevant, those alternatives not within the existing authority of the responsible preparing office. Section 102(2)(E) of NEPA requires the responsible agency to "study, develop, and describe appropriate alternatives to recommended courses of action in any proposal which involves unresolved conflicts concerning alternative uses of available resources." A rigorous exploration and an objective evaluation of the environmental impacts of all reasonable alternative actions, particularly those that might enhance environmental quality or avoid some or all of the adverse environmental effects, are essential. Sufficient analysis of such alternatives and their environmental benefits, costs, and risks should accompany the proposed action through the review process in order not to foreclose prematurely options which might enhance environmental quality or have less detrimental effects. Examples of such alternatives include: the alternative of not taking any action or of postponing action pending further study; alternatives requiring actions of a significantly different nature which would provide similar benefits with different environmental impacts, e.g. low capital intensive improvements, mass transit alternatives to highway construction; alternatives related to different locations or designs or details of the proposed action which would present different environmental impacts. In each case, the analysis should be sufficiently detailed to reveal comparative evaluation of the environmental benefits, costs, and risks of each reasonable alternative, including the proposed action. Where an existing impact statement already contains such an analysis, its treatment of alternatives may be incorporated, provided such treatment is current and relevant to the precise purpose of the proposed action.

c. Affected environment.

    (1) The statement should succinctly describe the environment of the area affected as it exists to a proposed action, including other related Federal activities in the area, their interrelationships, and cumulative environmental impact. The amount of detail provided in such descriptions should be commensurate with the extent and expected impact of the action, and with the amount of information required at the particular level of decision making (planning, feasibility, design, etc.).

    (2) The statement should identify, as appropriate, population and growth characteristics of the affected area and any population and growth assumptions used to justify the project or program or to determine secondary population and growth impacts resulting from the proposed action and its alternatives (see paragraph 3e(2)). In discussing these population aspects, the statement should give consideration to using the rates of growth in the region of the project contained in the projections compiled for the Water Resources Council by the Bureau of Economic Analysis of the Department of Commerce and the Economic Research Service of the Department of Agriculture (the OBERS projection).

d. The relationship of the proposed action and how it may conform to or conflict with adopted or proposed land use plans, policies, controls, and goals and objectives as have been promulgated by affected communities. Where a conflict or inconsistency exists, the statement should describe the extent of reconciliation and the reasons for proceeding notwithstanding the absence of full reconciliation.

e. The probable impact of the proposed action on the environment.

    (1) This requires assessment of the positive and negative effects of the proposed action as it affects both national and international human environment. The attention given to different environmental factors will vary according to the nature, scale, and location of proposed actions. Primary attention should be given in the statement to discussing those factors most evidently impacted by the proposed action.

    (2) Secondary and other foreseeable effects, as well as primary consequences for the environment, should be included in the analysis. Secondary effects, such as impacts on existing community facilities and activities inducing new facilities and activities, may often be even more substantial than the primary effects of the original action itself. For example, the effects of the proposed action on population and growth may be among the more significant secondary effects. Such population and growth im-

pacts should be estimated and an assessment made on their effects upon the resource base, including land use, water, and public services, of the area in question.

f. Any probable adverse environmental effects which cannot be avoided (such as water or air pollution, noise, undesirable land use patterns, or impacts on public parks and recreation areas, wildlife and waterfowl refuges, or on historic sites, damage to life systems, traffic congestion, threats to health, or other consequences adverse to the environmental goals set out in section 101(b) of NEPA). This should be a brief summary of those effects discussed in paragraph 3c that are adverse and unavoidable under the proposed action. Included for purposes of contrast should be a clear statement of how all adverse effects will be mitigated.

g. The relationship between local short-term uses of man's environment and the maintenance and enhancement of long-term productivity. This discussion should cover the extent to which the proposed action involves tradeoffs between short-term environmental gains at the expense of long-term losses, or vice versa, and a discussion of the extent to which the proposed action forecloses future options.

h. Any irreversible and irretrievable commitments of resources that would be involved in the proposed action should it be implemented. This requires identification of unavoidable impacts and the extent to which the action irreversibly curtails the range of potential uses of the environment. "Resources" means not only the labor and materials devoted to an action but also the natural and cultural resources lost or destroyed.

i. An indication of what other interests and considerations of Federal policy are thought to offset the adverse environmental effects of the proposed action identified pursuant to subparagraphs (e) and (f) of this paragraph.

The statement should also indicate the extent to which these stated countervailing benefits could be realized by following reasonable alternatives to the proposed action (as identified in subparagraph (b) of the paragraph) that would avoid some or all of the adverse environmental effects. In this connection, cost-benefit analyses of proposed actions, if prepared, should be attached, or summaries thereof, to the environmental impact statement, and should clearly indicate the extent to which environmental costs have not been reflected in such analyses.

j. A discussion of problems and objections raised by other Federal agencies, State and local entities, and citizens in the review process, and the disposition of the issues involved and the reasons therefor. (This section may be added to the final environmental statement at the end of the review process.)

(1) The draft and final statements should document issues raised through consultations with Federal, State, and local agencies with jurisdiction or special expertise and with citizens, of actions taken in response to comments, public hearings, and other citizen involvement proceedings.

(2) Any unresolved environmental issues and efforts to resolve them, through further consultations or otherwise, should be identified in the final statement. For instance, where an agency comments that the statement has inadequate analysis or that the agency has reservations concerning the impacts, or believes that the impacts are too adverse for approval, either the issue should be resolved or the final statement should reflect efforts to resolve the issue and set forth any action that will result.

(3) The statement should reflect that every effort was made to discover and discuss all major

points of view on the environmental effects of the proposed action and alternatives in the draft statement. However, where opposing professional views and responsible opinion have been overlooked in the draft statement and are raised through the commenting process, the environmental effects of the action should be reviewed in light of those views. A meaningful reference should be made in the final statement to the existence of any responsible opposing view not adequately discussed in the draft statement indicating responses to the issues raised.

(4) All substantive comments received on the draft (or summaries of responses from the public which have been exceptionally voluminous) should be attached to the final statement, whether or not each such comment is thought to merit individual discussion in the text of the statement.

k. Draft statements should indicate at appropriate points in the text any underlying studies, reports, and other information obtained and considered in preparing the statement, including any cost-benefit analyses prepared. In the case of documents not likely to be easily accessible (such as internal studies or reports), the statement should indicate how such information may be obtained. If such information is attached to the statement, care should be taken to insure that the statement remains an essentially self-contained instrument, capable of being understood by the reader without the need for undo cross reference.

4. Publicly Owned Parklands, Recreational Areas, Wildlife and Waterfowl Refuges and Historic Sites. The following points are to be covered:

a. Description of "any publicly owned land from a public park, recreational area or wildlife and waterfowl refuge" or "any land from an historic site" affected or taken by the project. This includes its size, available activities, use, patronage, unique or irreplaceable qualities, relationship to other similarly used lands in the vicinity of the project, maps, plans, slides, photographs, and drawings showing in sufficient scale and detail the project. This also includes its impact on park, recreation, wildlife, or historic areas, and changes in vehicular or pedestrian access.

b. Statement of the "national, State or local significance" of the entire park, recreation area, refuge, or historic site "as determined by the Federal, State or local officials having jurisdiction thereof."

(1) In the absence of such a statement, lands will be presumed to be significant. Any statement of "insignificance" by the official having jurisdiction is subject to review by the Department as to whether such statement is capricious.

(2) Where Federal lands are administered for multiple uses, the Federal official having jurisdiction over the lands shall determine whether the subject lands are in fact being used for park, recreation, wildlife, waterfowl, or historic purposes.

c. Similar data, as appropriate, for alternative designs and locations, including detailed cost estimates (with figures showing percentage differences in total project costs) and technical feasibility, and appropriate analysis of the alternatives, including any unique problems present and evidence that the cost or community disruptions resulting from alternative routes reach extraordinary magnitudes. This portion of the statement should demonstrate compliance with the Supreme Court's statement in the *Overton Park* case, as follows:

The very existence of the statute indicates that the protection of parklands was to be given paramount importance. The few green havens that are public parks were not to be lost unless there were truly unusual factors present in a particular case or the cost or community disruption resulting from alternative routes reached extraordinary magnitudes. If the statutes are to have any meaning, the Secretary cannot approve the destruction of parkland unless he finds that the alternative routes present unique problems.

d. If there is no feasible and prudent alternative, description of all planning undertaken to minimize harm to the protected area and statement of actions taken or to be taken to implement this planning, including measures to maintain or enhance the natural beauty of the lands traversed.

    (1) Measures to minimize harm may include replacement of land and facilities, providing land or facilities, or provision for functional replacement of the facility (see 49 C.F.R. 25.267).

    (2) Design measures to minimize harm: e.g. tunneling, cut and cover, cut and fill, treatment of embankments, planting, screening, maintenance of pedestrian or bicycle paths and noise mitigation measures, all reflecting utilization of appropriate interdisciplinary design personnel.

e. Evidence of concurrence or description of efforts to obtain concurrence of Federal, State or local officials having jurisdiction over the section 4(f) property regarding the action proposed and the measures planned to minimize harm.

f. If Federally-owned properties are involved in highway projects, the final statement shall include the action taken or an indication of the expected action after filing a map of the proposed use of the land or other appropriate documentation with the Secretary of the Department supervising the land (23 U.S.C. 317).

g. If land acquired with Federal grant money (Department of Housing and Urban Development open space or Heritage Conservation and Recreation Service land and water conservation funds) is involved, the final statement shall include appropriate communications with the grantor agency.

h. The General Counsel will determine application of section 4(f) to public interests in lands, such as easements, reversions, etc.

i. A specific statement that there is no feasible and prudent alternative and that the proposal includes all possible planning to minimize harm to the "section 4(f) area" involved.

5. <u>Properties and Sites of Historic and Cultural Significance.</u> The statement should document actions taken to preserve and enhance districts, sites, buildings, structures, and objects of historical, architectural, archaeological, or cultural significance affected by the action.

a. Draft environmental statements should include identification, through consulting the State Historic Preservation Officer and the National Register and applying the National Register Criteria (36 C.F.R. Part 800), of properties that are included in or eligible for inclusion in the National Register of Historic Places that may be affected by the project. The Secretary of the Interior will advise whether properties not listed are eligible for the National Register (36 C.F.R. Part 63).

b. If application of the Advisory Council on Historic Preservation's (ACHP) Criteria of Effect (36 C.F.R. Part 800) indicates that the project will have an effect upon a property included in or eligible for inclusion in the National Register of Historic Places, the draft environmental statement should document the effect. Evaluation of the effect should be made in consultation with the State Historic Preservation Officer (SHPO) and in accordance with the ACHP's Criteria of Adverse Effect (36 C.F.R. Part 800).

c. Determinations of no adverse effect should be documented in the draft statement with evidence of the application of the ACHP's Criteria of Adverse Effect, the views of the appropriate State Historic Preservation Officer, and submission of the determination to the ACHP for review.

d. If the project will have an adverse effect upon a property included in or eligible for inclusion in the National Register of Historic Places, the final environmental statement should include either an executed Memorandum of Agreement or comments from the Council after consideration of the project at a meeting of the ACHP and an account of actions to be taken in response to the comments of the ACHP. Procedures for obtaining a Memorandum of Agreement and the comments of the Council are found in 36 C.F.R. Part 800.

e. To determine whether the project will have an effect on properties of State or local historical, architectural, archaeological, or cultural significance not included in or eligible for inclusion in the National Register, the responsible official should consult with the State Historic Preservation Officer, with the local official having jurisdiction of the property, and, where appropriate, with historical societies, museums, or academic institutions having expertise with regard to the property. Use of land from historic properties of Federal, State and local significance as determined by the official having jurisdiction thereof involves section 4(f) of the DOT Act and documentation should include information necessary to consider a section 4(f) determination (see paragraph 4).

6. Impacts of the Proposed Action on the Human Environment Involving Community Disruption and Relocation.

a. The statement should include a description of probable impact sufficient to enable an understanding of the extent of the environmental and social impact of the project alternatives and to consider whether relocation problems can be properly handled. This would include the following information obtainable by visual inspection of the proposed affected area and from secondary sources and community sources when available.

(1) An estimate of the households to be displaced including the family characteristics (e.g. minorites, and income levels, tenure, the elderly, large families).

(2) Impact on the human environment of an action which divides or disrupts an established community, including, where pertinent, the effect of displacement on types of families and individuals affected, effect of streets cut off, separation of residences from community facilities, separation of residential areas.

(3) Impact on the neighborhood and housing to which relocation is likely to take place (e.g. lack of sufficient housing for large families, doublings up).

(4) An estimate of the businesses to be displaced, and the general effect of business dislocation on the ecomomy of the community.

(5) A discussion of relocation housing in the area and the ability to provide adequate relocation housing for the types of families to be displaced. If the resources are insufficient to meet the estimated displacement needs, a description of the actions proposed to remedy this situation including, if necessary, use of housing of last resort.

(6) Results of consultation with local officials and community groups regarding the impacts to the community affected. Relocation agencies and staff and other social agencies can help to describe probable social impacts of this proposed action.

(7) Where necessary, special relocation advisory services to be provided the elderly, handicapped and illiterate regarding interpretations of benefits, assistance in selecting replacement housing, and consultation with respect to acquiring, leasing, and occupying replacement housing.

b. This data should provide the preliminary basis for assurance of the availability of relocation housing as required by DOT 5620.1, Replacement Housing Policy, dated 6-24-70, and 49 C.F.R. 25.57.

7. Considerations Relating to Pedestrians and Bicyclists. Where appropriate, the statement should discuss impacts on and consideration to be given in the development of the project to pedestrian and bicycle access, movement and safety within the affected area, particularly in medium and high density commercial and residential areas.

8. Other Social Impacts. The general social groups specially benefitted or harmed by the proposed action should be identified in the statement, including the following:

a. Particular effects of a proposal on the elderly, handicapped, non-drivers, transit dependent, or minorities should be described to the extent reasonably predictable.

b. How the proposal will facilitate or inhibit their access to jobs, educational facilities, religious institutions, health and welfare services, recreational facilities, social and cultural facilities, pedestrian movement facilities, and public transit services.

9. Standards as to Noise, Air, and Water Pollution. The statement shall reflect sufficient analysis of the effects of the proposed action on attainment and maintenance of any environmental standards established by law or administrative determination (e.g. noise, ambient air quality, water quality), including the following documentations.

a. With respect to water quality, there should be consultation with the agency responsible for the State water pollution control program as to conformity with standards and regulations regarding storm sewer discharge, sedimentation control, and other nonpoint source discharges.

b. The comments or determinations of the offices charged with administration of the State's implementation plan for air quality as to the consistency of the project with State plans for the implementation of ambient air quality standards.

c. Conformity to adopted noise standards, compatible, if appropriate, with different land uses.

10. Energy Supply and Natural Resources Development. Where applicable, the statement should reflect consideration of whether the project or program will have any effect on either the production or consumption of energy and other natural resources, and discuss such effects if they are significant.

11. Floodplain Management Evaluation. When an alternative under consideration encroaches on a base (100-year) floodplain, the statement should describe the anticipated impacts on natural and beneficial floodplain values, any risk to or resulting from the transportation action, and the degree to which the action facilitates additional development in the base floodplain. The necessary measures to address floodplain impacts, including an evaluation of alternatives to avoid the encroachment in appropriate cases, should be described in compliance with Executive Order 11988, "Floodplain Management," and DOT Order 5650.2, "Floodplain Management and Protection."

12. Considerations Relating to Wetlands or Coastal Zones. Where wetlands or coastal

zones are involved, the statement should reflect compliance with Executive Order 11990, Protection of Wetlands, and DOT 5660.1A and should include:

a. Information on location, types, and extent of wetlands areas which might be affected by the proposed action.

b. An assessment of the impacts resulting from both construction and operation of the project on the wetlands and associated wildlife, and measures to minimize adverse impacts.

c. A statement by the local representative of the Department of the Interior, and any other responsible officials with special expertise, setting forth his views on the impacts of the project on the wetlands, the worth of the particular wetlands areas involved to the community and to the Nation, and recommendations as to whether the proposed action should proceed, and, if applicable, along what alternative route.

d. Where applicable, a discussion of how the proposed project relates to the State coastal zone management program for the particular State in which the project is to take place.

13. Construction Impacts. In general, adverse impacts during construction will be of less importance than long-term impacts of a proposal. Nonetheless, statements should appropriately address such matters as the following, identifying any special problem areas:

a. Noise impacts from construction and any specifications setting maximum noise levels.

b. Disposal of spoil and effect on borrow areas and disposal sites (include specifications where special problems are involved).

c. Measures to minimize effects on traffic and pedestrians.

14. Land Use and Urban Growth. The statement should include, to the extent relevant and predictable:

a. The effect of the project on land use, development patterns, and urban growth.

b. Where significant land use and development impacts are anticipated, identify public facilities needed to serve the new development and any problems or issues which would arise in connection with these facilities, and the comments of agencies that would provide these facilities.

15. (Deleted)

16. Projects under Section 14 of the Mass Transportation Act: Mass Transit Projects with a Significant Impact on the Quality of the Human Environment. The statement should include:

a. Evidence of the opportunity that was afforded for the presentation of views by all parties with a significant economic, social or environmental interest.

b. Evidence that fair consideration has been given to the preservation and enhancement of the environment and to the interests of the community in which the project is located.

c. If there is an adverse environmental effect and there is no feasible and prudent alternative, description of all planning undertaken to minimize such adverse environmntal effect and statement of actions taken or to be taken to implement the planning; or a specific statement that there is no adverse environmental effect.

CHAPTER 4

Environmental Action Planning

Discussions in Chapter 2 concerning the Federal Aid Highway Act (FAHA) of 1962 conclude that this was a major piece of legislation dealing with the *project development process.* Included in the act was the provision that projects proposed in major metropolitan areas (of population greater than 50,000) must utilize a *continuing, comprehensive, and cooperative* (3-C) planning process. In effect, this requirement meant that the state highway agencies would need to implement operational procedures which guaranteed a system with built-in evaluation mechanisms, including a public participation feature. It also meant that, in order to be comprehensive, there would need to be methods available to consider alternatives to the proposed action.

In urban areas many of the alternatives available to solve transportation problems are outside the domain of traditional highway agency activities. Primarily these include some form of transit (rail, bus, paratransit, and the like). Thus, at least for urban areas, the project development process for the state highway agency has become one with both highway *and* transit options.

In the 1960s it became apparent to state government officials that it would no longer be efficient from the administrative, management, and fiscal perspectives to keep the modal transportation functions separated. Most states, by 1980, did in fact follow the Federal example (DOT Act of 1966) and established a state department of transportation. A major result of the formation of the state DOT was to broaden the 3-C process concept to include transit as well as highway projects. Therefore, with a DOT there became a continuing, comprehensive, and

cooperative *transportation* project development process.

In most states, the aviation function, while merged into the DOT, operates relatively independently of the other modes. It may be recalled however, from the previous two chapters, that the Airport and Airways Development Act of 1970 placed 3-C–type planning requirements upon the states as an eligibility requirement for ADAP (Airport Development Aid Program) funds. Public involvement plays a significant role in these requirements.

NEPA AND FAHA OF 1970

Section 102 of NEPA requires that each agency of the Federal government is to

(A) utilize a systematic, interdisciplinary approach which will insure the integrated use of the national and social sciences and the environmental design arts in planning and in decision making which may have an impact on man's environment; [and] (B) identify and develop methods and procedures, in consultation with the Council on Environmental Quality established by Title II on this Act, which will insure that presently unqualified environmental amenities and values may be given appropriate consideration in decision making along with economic and technical consideration.

The fundamental issue in this section is the requirement for the utilization of a *systematic, interdisciplinary approach* to project development. Further, the agencies are required by Section 103 to bring their regulations and operating procedures into full NEPA compliance. As discussed in Chapters 2 and 3, these requirements have had a rather significant effect on the structure of the typical state transportation agency. Prior to NEPA there was little emphasis given to noncivil (highway) engineering disciplines; the 1962 Highway Act had, however, caused the states to introduce the elements of systematic thinking into their project development processes.

While NEPA established the framework for decision making, for all the Federal agencies, the 1970 FAHA set forth the specific mandates for change. As stated in Chapter 2 this act called upon the U.S. Secretary of Transportation to develop and implement detailed guidelines for analysis and attainment in the areas of air, noise, and water pollution. The act then called for the withholding of project approval from the state highway agencies *unless* compliance with the guidelines was documented. Because most of the state highway agencies did not at that time (July 1, 1972) have on staff personnel qualified in the analytical methods for air, noise, and water quality, it became necessary for them to significantly modify and broaden the character and expertise of their staffs. In summary, the 1970 Highway Act forced the FHWA and (indirectly) the states to attain the NEPA mandate for an *interdisciplinary* approach to project development. With the exception of projects on the Federal Aid Urban System (FAUS) however, the NEPA mandate for a *systematic* approach was not under implementation by the states. The FAUS projects were, of course, developed using the 3-C process.

Implementation of that mandate at the Federal level by the DOT and FHWA presented a peculiar problem resulting from the extraordinarily high degree of authority delegated to the states by the FHWA. The solution came in the form of FHPM 7-7-1,* *Process Guidelines for the Development of Environmental Action Plans* (see Chapter 3, page 48). It is this regulation that provides the basis for project development at the state level. As noted previously, the tendency for most states to maintain a multimodal

*FHPM 7-7-1 is reproduced in its entirety in Appendix 4.

DOT extends the impact of FHPM 7-7-1 beyond simply the highway mode. Succinctly stated, the *Process Guidelines* issued by the FHWA define the context for Federally funded transportation project development initiated at the state level. This, of course, where the majority of such activity occurs.

PROCESS GUIDELINES: FHPM 7-7-1

The FHPM was issued in final form on December 30, 1974, having been previously distributed in 1973 as Policy and Procedure Memorandum (PPM) 90-4, with the same title. Its purpose is to

assure that adequate consideration is given to possible social, economic, and environmental effects of proposed highway projects and that the decisions on such projects are made in the best overall public interest.

The mechanism to achieve this purpose is the Environmental Action Plan (EAP). A major objective of the EAP concept is "to merit public confidence in the highway agency." To achieve this objective, it is the *policy* of the FHWA that

(a) social, economic and environmental effects be identified and studies [be performed] early enough to permit analysis and consideration while alternatives are being formulated and evaluated, (b) other agencies and the public be involved in system planning and project development early enough to influence technical studies and final decisions, and (c) appropriate consideration be given to reasonable alternatives, including the alternative of not building the project and alternative modes.

This policy, of course, reflects the spirit of NEPA, which calls for the systematic interdisciplinary approach. By far the most effective method available to implement the policy at the *state* level is to require the modification of the operational procedures and then to monitor the success of integrating the modifications into standard practice. The responsibility for monitoring the utilization of the EAP (i.e., the modifications) belongs to the division offices of the FHWA. These offices are located in each state and are charged to work with each state highway agency on the project and system levels.

CONTENTS OF THE EAP

The EAP is basically a document which delineates staffing requirements and responsibilities, decision-making processes, public and outside-agency involvement responsibilities, and resource allocation. A basic intent of the EAP process is to identify as *early as possible* in the project's life the possible and negative effects of all the alternative courses of action.

Staffing

The EAP is to identify those organizational units given the responsibility to perform the relevant social, economic, and environmental (SEE) analyses on project alternatives. In some states these units of interdisciplinary professionals are housed in a headquarters office, while other states may have district-level expertise available for project assignment. Whichever organizational structure is used is strictly at the discretion of the state; however, the interdisciplinary nature of the unit(s) should be stressed. Also to be identified in the EAP is the organizational unit having technical quality control and state-of-the-art monitoring responsibilities. In virtually every state these functions are carried out by a headquarters-level group possessing the agency's most qualified staff in the SEE disciplines.

The educational background of these interdisciplinary SEE staffs varies from state to state, with a high degree of "recycled" civil engineers. These are usually professionals who entered the agency as planners or designers in the days before the environmental era, but who availed themselves of FHWA-and EPA-sponsored training courses. This route is particularly common in the air, noise, and water quality disciplines and offers a distinct advantage: the degree of communication between these SEE specialists and the current planners and designers is quite high because they share a common root discipline— civil engineering. Also, there is a good probability that at some point in the past the individuals involved functioned as co-workers. This helps reduce the all too common tense atmosphere

that can exist between environmental advocates and highway engineers.

The disadvantage of this route, however, is that the recycled civil engineers are often unable to fully integrate the philosophy of environmental advocacy into their psyches, and, as a result, the environmental position may not receive their full recognition and consideration in a tense atmosphere. This is the point where FHWA monitoring of EAP implementation is important.

Several disciplines in the SEE area simply do not lend themselves to the utilization of existing staff. Many state transportation agencies have recently created positions for archeologists so that relations with the State Historic Preservation Officer (SHPO) do not cause project delay. Other such disciplines include aquatic and terrestrial biologists, ecologists, sociologists, economists, and even regulatory analysts.

The EAP is to document the recruiting and training strategies used by the agency to assure that the SEE disciplines are adequately represented on staff. Included in the strategies should be well developed career ladders for the specialists, as a means of providing retention incentives.

Decision Making

A basic and fundamental criterion to be used in evaluating the relative merits of the various alternatives under consideration is the *option of no improvement*, otherwise known as the "do-nothing," or "null" alternative. This should be used as a reference point in determining the beneficial and adverse effects of other alternatives. It is quite significant to note that the option of no improvement is *not* the same as the existing case. Ordinarily the alternatives are evaluated at some point in the future, called the design year, which is the estimated Time of Completion (ETC) plus 20 years. The design year is usually selected early in the life of a project, and, for analysis purposes, does not usually change. Because most projects are initiated to solve an existing problem, use of the design year for analysis purposes almost always causes the option of no improvement to be unacceptable.

The EAP should take into consideration that various classes of projects may call for separate procedural plans. Accordingly, the state may *develop different procedures to be followed depending upon the economic, social, environmental, or transportation significance of the highway project to be developed.*

FHPM 7-7-1 suggests that the EAP identify *categories* of projects based upon the various degrees of effort which would normally be devoted to SEE activities. The New York State EAP utilizes this approach, and is discussed later in this chapter.

In a similar manner, the EAP is to allow for differences in geographic regions and how these differences may alter the decision making process. Extraordinary environmental areas or unusually structured local governmental organizations may give rise to such alterations. For example, the Adirondack Park Agency (APA) in upstate New York has special jurisdiction over a quite pristine, natural area of exceptional environmental sensitivity. Accordingly, the New York State DOT EAP calls for additional coordination with APA staff on any projects proposed within the limits of the park. Requirements for this additional coordination are formalized in an *Agreement in Principle* between the two agencies and contained in the EAP.

Discussions in Chapter 3 concerning the November 29, 1978 CEQ guidelines for EIS preparation included information on the subject of *tiering.* When applied in chronological sense, tiering allows for reconsideration at a later date of issues that are not yet "ripe." Although issued several years prior to the revised CEQ guidelines, FHPM 7-7-1 calls for the inclusion of a similar concept in EAPs. The FHPM calls for the EAP to include procedures to

(a) ensure that potential social, economic, and environmental effects are identified insofar as is practical in system planning studies as well as in later stages of location and design, and (b) provide for reconsideration of earlier decisions which maybe occasioned by results of further study, the availability of additional information, or the passage of time between decisions.

The purpose for introducing the tiering concept in the 1978 CEQ guidelines was different from the FHPM 7-7-1 logic in that tiering was meant to reduce paperwork and project delay. The FHWA was concerned, on the other hand, that SEE activities were not implemented early enough in the project life to receive maximum benefit in the decision-making process. The FHPM therefore directs that

decisions at the system and project stages shall be made with consideration of their social, economic, environmental, and transportation effects to the extent possible at each stage.

Public and Outside-Agency Involvement

The basic FHWA policy to be implemented in this area is that (from FHPM 7-7-1)

interested parties should have adequate opportunities to express their views early enough in the study process to influence the course of studies, as well as the action taken.

To implement this policy, the EAP is to identify procedures *in addition to* formal public hearings that are to be used to inform and involve the public and other agencies. Over the years there have been many tools utilized in efforts to fulfill this mandate. Many state transportation agencies have learned by experience that the most effective way to neutralize public opposition and therefore minimize project delay is to intimately involve neighborhood associations and similar groups very early in the project life, to give them opportunities to provide input, and to use that input. The groups then become part of the project team and in many cases opposition is transformed into support for an improved project. Table 4-1 lists the tools and techniques often used by states in eliciting public involvement.

Regarding outside agency involvement and coordination, the EAP is to identify the procedures used in obtaining appropriate input. It should be noted that these activities are generally required by other laws and regulations (eg., the Fish and Wildlife Coordination Act) and therefore in most cases do not represent a change in the project development process. The EAP is, however, to include specific information concerning involvement of the 3-C metropolitan

TABLE 4-1. Public Involvement Tools and Techniques

Public hearings
Information meetings
Legal (formal) notices
Mass media advertisements

Mailing lists
Citizens committees
Speaking engagements with interested parties
Circulation project reports

News releases
Prehearing and posthearing meetings
Surveys
Public workshops

Direct contact with affected property owners
Response forms
Newsletters
Personal interviews

Audio-visual presentations
Public forums
Project field office
Publication project development schedule

Telephone hotlines
Televised planning discussions
Project field review with citizens
Mass mail-outs

Citizen band radio announcements
Resource base analysis
Announcements on local bulletin boards
Public information displays

Billboard advertisements near project
Press conferences

Source: Public Involvement Techniques Outlined in Highway Agency Action Plans, DOT, FHWA Office of Environmental Policy, Washington, D.C., April 1, 1977.

(transportation) planning organization, for projects in areas of population greater than 50,000.

Resource Allocation

In an effort to verify that state transportation agency is taking its environmental responsibilites seriously, the EAP is to identify the resources of the agency (in terms of personnel and funding) that will be utilized in implementing and carrying out the Action Plan; the resources that are available in other agencies to provide necessary information on social, economic, and environmental effects; and the programs for the addition of trained personnel or fiscal or other re-

sources to either the agencies itself or other agencies.

As mentioned previously, many state transportation agencies "recycle" existing personnel, usually civil engineers, for use as environmental specialists. This practice is quite common for several reasons. First, because of shifting priorities and limited funding in the transportation program, many states curtailed their highway programs and as a result found themselves with an abundance of civil engineers. Second, the academic institutions were not, and still are not, geared to the production of graduates with the skills necessary to step into the environmental specialist positions and to function effectively. And third, the FHWA, through its National Highway Institute, has been very effective in offering practice-oriented training courses in almost all the areas of concern, including noise analysis, air quality, water quality, ecology, historical preservation, and EIS preparation. Many of these courses are offered in the headquarters offices of all or most of the state transportation agencies, who therefore are recipients of large amounts of free training.

CASE STUDIES OF TWO EAPs

Clearly the FHWA mandate to the state transportation agencies through FHPM 7-7-1 fulfills the spirit of NEPA in that it calls for the implementation of a systematic, interdisciplinary approach to project development. One must consider, at this point, the effectiveness of the mandate. Has *environmental action planning* been effectively integrated into the typical state project development process such that it is standard operating procedure? If so, how has it affected project flow, administration, and the overall quality of the product? Lastly, what could be done, if anything, to further improve the concept? To best answer these questions the remainder of this chapter will examine the EAPs from two states which represent divergent circumstances. The states are Kentucky and New York.

Kentucky is primarily rural in nature, with three major metropolitan areas (Louisville, Lexington, and Covington-Newport) and several smaller cities. The majority of the population resides in rural areas. The eastern third of the state is in the Appalachian Mountain Range and is therefore rugged in terrain and relatively inaccessible to transportation. Over the years the Kentucky DOT has made a substantial investment in attempting to improve accessibility to the region, which is rich in coal reserves.

New York State, on the other hand, is a major urban state, and includes the densest and most heavily populated metropolitan area in the nation: New York City (along with Long Island, Westchester County, southern Connecticut, and northern New Jersey). The Greater New York City area, with its unique form of government, obviously presents the New York State Department of Transportation (NYSDOT) with some special management situations that must be addressed in the EAP.

In addition to Greater New York City, the state has four major metropolitan areas (Albany-Schenectady-Troy, Syracuse, Rochester, and Buffalo). The remainder of the state, however, is quite rural in nature and includes some of the richest farm and dairy land in the nation. As mentioned earlier, the state also includes the Adirondack Park region, which is a mountainous, rugged territory rich in wildlife, virgin forests, lakes, recreational zones, and other environmentally sensitive entities. The region is also laden with government jurisdictions, which is characteristic of the entire state. Supplemental to the town, village, city, and county agencies is the Adirondack Park Agency, which, as mentioned earlier, has umbrella-type protective powers over the entire region. Again, projects in this area require special activities by the NYSDOT which need to be identified in the EAP.

Figures 4-1 and 4-2 show the administrative boundries for the states of Kentucky and New York, respectively.

AGENCY BACKGROUND

The DOTs for each of the states have evolved differently to reach their respective systematic, interdisciplinary approaches to project development.

Kentucky needed to radically transform its method of operation, based on the NEPA concept. Prior to 1970, the Kentucky DOT functioned *strictly* as a highway agency with a clear mandate to build as many roads as possible. The project development process was not at all interdisciplinary, with the technical staff being almost exclusively highway or civil engineers and the principal objectives for project initiation were congestion relief and growth inducement. Engineering feasibility and cost minimization were the project development guidelines.

All things considered, the Kentucky response to NEPA and FHPM 7-7-1 was quite positive. The first environmental specialists were brought on staff in 1971 and the agency was reorganized into a department of transportation in 1973. The Kentucky EAP reflects the successful evolution of the agency's project development process into one utilizing the systematic, interdisciplinary approach.

The NYSDOT, on the other hand, began implementing that approach *prior* to the enactment of NEPA. The agency became a department of transportation in 1967 and by that time included nonengineers in several of its career ladders. The department was the first in the nation to become a DOT and was very far ahead of the rest of the states in its transportation planning technique. In fact, many of the planning tools and models in use today throughout the nation were pioneered by the NYSDOT.

While the NYSDOT did not require a radical change to be consistent with NEPA and FHPM 7-7-1, the agency was molded to face other priorities resulting from the 1975 financial crises that struck New York City (and therefore the state). During the period of recovery following 1975, a declared policy of the state administration was to use the transportation program (particularly highways) to help revitalize the economy of the state. Goals were set and accomplished which more than doubled the capital construction budget within two years. As a result of the new thrust, the agency concentrated on the delivery of projects to be let, and accordingly deemphasized planning and development and environmental quality. Nevertheless, the agency by that time was (and in fact still remains) one whose project development process achieved consistency with the systematic, interdisciplinary approach.

(The EAPs in effect for both Kentucky and New York in 1980 were approved in 1977 and 1978, respectively. Therefore they do not reflect the concepts from the November 29, 1978 CEQ guidelines. It is anticipated that each EAP will be revised to so reflect the guidelines. However, the revision should not be significant.)

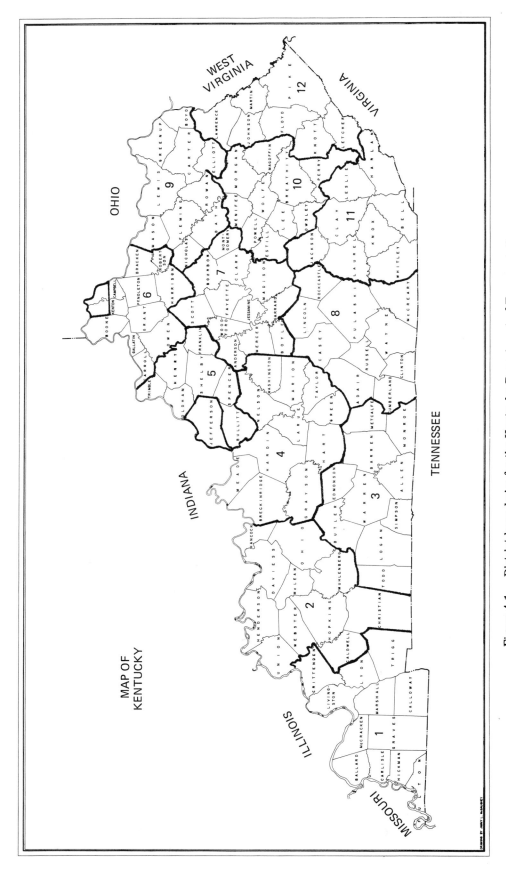

Figure 4-1.   District boundaries for the Kentucky Department of Transportation.

122

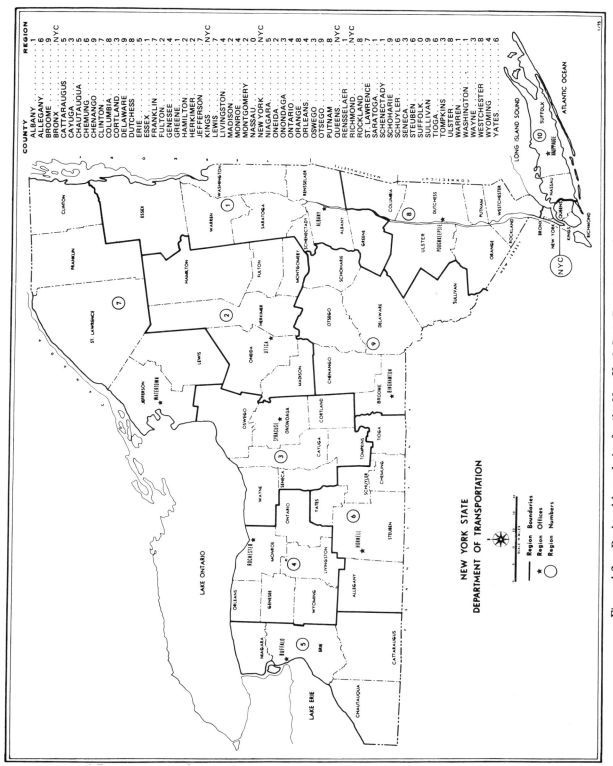

COUNTY	REGION
ALBANY	1
ALLEGANY	6
BROOME	9
BRONX	NYC
CATTARAUGUS	5
CAYUGA	3
CHAUTAUQUA	5
CHEMUNG	6
CHENANGO	9
CLINTON	7
COLUMBIA	8
CORTLAND	3
DELAWARE	9
DUTCHESS	8
ERIE	5
ESSEX	1
FRANKLIN	7
FULTON	2
GENESEE	4
GREENE	1
HAMILTON	2
HERKIMER	2
JEFFERSON	7
KINGS	NYC
LEWIS	7
LIVINGSTON	4
MADISON	2
MONROE	4
MONTGOMERY	2
NASSAU	0
NEW YORK	NYC
NIAGARA	5
ONEIDA	2
ONONDAGA	3
ONTARIO	4
ORANGE	8
ORLEANS	4
OSWEGO	3
OTSEGO	9
PUTNAM	8
QUEENS	NYC
RENSSELAER	1
RICHMOND	NYC
ROCKLAND	8
ST. LAWRENCE	7
SARATOGA	1
SCHENECTADY	1
SCHOHARIE	9
SCHUYLER	6
SENECA	3
STEUBEN	6
SUFFOLK	0
SULLIVAN	9
TIOGA	6
TOMPKINS	3
ULSTER	8
WARREN	1
WASHINGTON	1
WAYNE	3
WESTCHESTER	8
WYOMING	4
YATES	6

Figure 4-2. Regional boundaries for the New York State Department of Transportation.

123

THE KENTUCKY DOT EAP

The Kentucky EAP is quite straightforward in design, using one basic process for all types of projects. The department has decided *not* to formalize a project category concept for various levels of action (see FHMP 7-7-1, section 15). This is one area where the Kentucky EAP differs dramatically from that of New York State.

The approach selected by Kentucky is sequential in that it deals with each phase of the project development process as a separate unit, in the chronological order of the project life.

The phases discussed in the plan are

1. Statewide Systems Planning
2. Urban and Regional Systems Planning
3. Project Planning
4. Project Design
5. Construction
6. Operations

Figure 4-3 shows the summarization and general timetable for the stages involved in the Kentucky DOT EAP project development process.

Figure 4-3.   Kentucky Department of Transportation EAP, Summary of Process.

KENTUCKY DEPARTMENT OF TRANSPORTATION
ACTION PLAN SUMMARY FLOW CHART

PROJECT DESIGN PHASE — detailed construction plans are developed, property acquired and project let to contract

20. MOBILIZE PROJECT TEAM - IDENTIFY WORK TASKS & CITIZEN INPUTS NEEDED - START AND SCHEDULE WORK - RESTART LOCAL CITIZEN CONTACT

21. DEVELOP SCOPE OF STUDY FOR OPTIONS AND PROGRAM FOR PUBLIC INPUT - USE MULTI-DISCIPLINARY INPUTS - APPRAISE SKILLS AND RESOURCES AVAILABLE AGAINST NEEDS

22. INTERDISCIPLINARY TEAM REVIEW ON SCOPE OF STUDY, ON PROGRAM FOR PUBLIC PARTICIPATION, AND ON SIGNIFICANCE OF IMPACTS - CONTINUE LOCAL CITIZEN CONTACTS

23. /ORK LOCATION OR SITE PLAN STUDY ON ALIGNMENT & GRADE USING MULTIDISCI-

23. WORK LOCATION OR SITE PLAN STUDY ON ALIGNMENT & GRADE USING MULTI-DISCIPLINARY INPUTS - ESTIMATE TOTAL FUNDING NEEDS - SEEK APPROVAL FOR OVERRUN ON COSTS

24. INSEPCT LOCATION OF PRELIM. LINE & GRADE USING INTERDISCIPLINARY INPUTS - CONTINUE CITIZEN AND PROPERTY OWNER CONTACTS

25. SEEK APPROVALS ON CURRENT PREFERENCE FOR LINE & GRADE AND ON EXTENT OF CITIZEN AND COMMUNITY INVOLVEMENT

26. DEVELOP PLANS FOR APPROVED LINE & GRADE USING MULTIDISCIPLINARY INPUTS - CONTINUE CONTACTS WITH CITIZENS, UTILITIES & RAILROADS

27. INSPECT FINAL LINE WITH PLANS IN HAND, USING MULTIDISCIPLINARY INPUTS - VALIDATE SIGNIFICANCE OF IMPACTS

28. INTERDISCIPLINARY REVIEW & DECISION BY PROJECT REVIEW COMMITTEE ON VALIDITY OF IMPACTS ON FUNDS REQUIRED, ON PLANS FOR HEARING, ON CONFORMANCE WITH SYSTEM PLANNING

29. PREPARE FOR PUBLIC HEARING AND HOLD PRE-HEARING MEETINGS WITH CITIZENS

30. HEAR COMMENTS FROM CITIZENS, OFFICIALS, GROUPS & AGENCIES AT PUBLIC HEARINGS AS PREVIOUSLY ADVERTISED

31. FOLLOW-THRU AFTER HEARING WITH EVALUATION OF HEARING TRANSCRIPT - SCHEDULE CITIZEN CONTACTS TO CLARIFY ISSUES DISCLOSED

32. FINALIZE NEW OR REWORKED ENVIRONMENTAL IMPACT STATEMENT - SEEK APPROVALS - PUBLISH NOTICES ON APPLICATION FOR APPROVALS

33. COMPLETE PLANS FOR ROADWAY AND RIGHT-OF-WAY USING MULTIDISCIPLINARY INPUT - PUBLISH RELOCATION ASSISTANCE NOTICES

34. SEEK APPROVAL FOR RIGHT-OF-WAY PLANS AND AUTHORIZATIONS TO ACQUIRE PARCELS - PUBLISH NOTICES ON OUTCOME OF APPROVALS

35. MOBILIZE PRE-APPRAISAL OF RIGHT-OF-WAY AND START UTILITY NEGOTIATIONS - ISSUE 30 DAY NOTICES TO PROPERTY OWNERS AND UTILITIES

36. COMPLETE RIGHT-OF-WAY APPRAISALS AND COMPLETE UTILITY NEGOTIATIONS

37. RELOCATE UTILITY SERVICES

38. INSTITUTE LEGAL PROCEEDINGS TO CLEAR RIGHT-OF-WAY AND UTILITIES

39. CLEAR RIGHT-OF-WAY OF IMPROVEMENTS AND UTILITIES

40. SEEK FINAL APPROVAL OF COMPILED PACKAGE OF PLANS, SPECIFICATIONS, AND ESTIMATES OF COSTS FOR MOVING PROJECT TO CONSTRUCTION PHASE LETTING - <u>ACTION PLAN PROJECT DEVELOPMENT PROCEDURES COMPLETED</u>

CONSTRUCTION PHASE — the project is advertised, let to contract, awarded and constructed

41. MARK DETOURS, START CONSTRUCTION WORK, SEEK TO MINIMIZE ENVIRONMENTAL HARMS, CITIZEN DISCOMFORTS

42. INSPECT CONSTRUCTION WORK, MATERIALS & DETOURS, MONITOR PROGRESS AND REPORT ON ADEQUACY OF SPECIFICATIONS

43. OPEN PROJECT TO TRAFFIC AND COMPUTE FINAL PAYMENT - EVALUATE EFFECTIVENESS OF PRIOR PHASES FOR PROCEDURE CHANGES NEEDED

OPERATIONS PHASE — a continuous process to maintain the total highway system. Success and failures reported for improved planning of future system

44. TRAFFIC SIGNING & STRIPING AS NEEDED - SELECTED TRANSPORTATION IMPROVEMENTS MONITORED FOR SATISFACTION OF USERS AND CITIZENS

45. BUDGET & PERFORM PERIODIC MAINTENANCE, RECONSTRUCTIONS AND RESURFACING ANNUALLY

Figure 4-3. *(Continued)*

125

STATEWIDE SYSTEMS PLANNING

The first step in any transportation project development should be the analysis of the area transportation system to determine needs. Accordingly, the functions of this phase in the Kentucky EAP are to initiate and develop *study designs* for potential projects. Projects may be initiated through one of three ways.

1. Reaction to the results of the 3-C continuing planning process.
2. Reaction to Federal legislation and U.S. DOT regulations concerning transportation systems planning requirements.
3. Reaction to satisfy needs expressed through the public involvement process.

Once a decision to initiate a study design has been made, opportunities are provided for outside agencies and the public to make input into study design include the following.

1. Incorporation of applicable state and Fedderal guidelines.
2. Definition of study area and subunits within the area.
3. Development of data requirements for the study.
4. Development of detailed methodology for each phase of the study process.
5. Coordination with other agencies and states as necessary.
6. Development of detailed review and coordination process.
7. Preparation of study design document for review.
8. Advertisement for meetings with the Planning Review Committee through the media.
9. Solicitation of review and comment from all public and private sources.
10. Revision of study goals and objectives tentatively as a result of public input.
11. Finalization of study design.
12. Distribution of final study design to all interested participating parties.

The study to be produced in this system phase will be quite technical in that the necessary inventory of existing information will be completed. Based on these inventories, forecasts of impacts will be made for a finalized list of alternatives. The alternatives, in turn, will receive detailed analysis. A preferred alternative will then be selected. This preferred alternative will be in the form of a porposed *system* solution. Enough detail is available at this point to prioritize the project relative to other projects in the program so that a schedule of implementation can be determined for the project. After finalization, the preferred alternative for the systems solution is ready for sequential advancement to the next phase.

URBAN AND REGIONAL SYSTEMS PLANNING

This phase brings potential projects into a sharper focus as the Kentucky DOT begins to work more closely with regional agencies and Metropolitan Planning Organizations (MPO). Studies developed during this phase are to

provide an integration and analysis of social, economic, environmental and transportation elements responsible to the development of adequate facilities for the movement of people and goods. [Urban and regional] system planning provides long-range plans that identify transportation corridors and their interrelationships. Social, economic, and environmental impacts must be broadly identified in the system planning phase in order to determine the sensitivity of a particular impact and the possible necessary trade-offs or compromises.

This phase is designed to transition the potential project *and its impacts* into a position where a specific solution can receive consideration for planning initiation (i.e., the project planning phase). The study design (and study) produced in this phase is quite similar to that from the statewide system planning phase just discussed, but somewhat more detailed.

As noted above, there is particular emphasis in this phase on SEE (Social, Economic, and Environmental) impacts, especially as they concern area-wide bases. It is at this point in the process where the department begins to utilize some of the technical tools available from transportation planning analysis methods. For example, the study area (region) is broken into *traffic analysis zones* for purposes of social and economic data compilation, origin-destination surveys, travel pattern studies, physical inventories, and so on. Once all the necessary background information has been assimilated, the following forecasts are to be made.

1. Relationship between travel and socioeconomic characteristics.
2. Modal split.
3. Capacity of existing transportation system.
4. Future growth of travel and socioeconomic characteristics.
5. Environmental factors.

The analysis of alternatives is also refined, as is the selection of the preferred alternative. The following tasks are to be completed.

1. Conceptualize several alternative system plans that are designed to relieve existing transportation deficiencies.
2. Assign future traffic to conceptualized alternatives.
3. Analyze and refine alternative plans based on SEE effects and traffic impacts, including the "do-nothing" alternative.
4. Select a (new) preferred plan based on community goals and objectives.

Once a new preferred plan has been selected, it is necessary to more fully assess the SEE impacts, particularly as they relate to the improved travel conditions. It is also necessary to evaluate the fiscal implications of the preferred plan in relation to the capabilities of all the participating government agencies. More definitive prioritizing of the project versus other projects will then be possible, even to the details of the best rate of phased construction where necessary. At this point, the preferred system plan is ready for advancement to the next point.

PROJECT PLANNING

Prior to the NEPA-inspired changes in project development beginning in 1970 the project planning phase served as the starting point for high-

way projects in Kentucky. In other words *systems* planning, at either the statewide or regional levels, was not at all emphasized. As a result, there was little opportunity for public involvement given.

Under the Kentucky DOT EAP, however, there is a considerable amount of effort and outside input already invested in a project as it *enters* the project planning phase. In fact, there is enough information available so that the project may be programmed (i.e., placed on the official five-year Federal-aid program for the state). Only those projects which are programmed are activated in the project planning phase.

It is during this phase that the project first encounters major Federal requirements. Historically, the FHWA has referred to projects planning as the project *location* phase, with formal location approval required as one step in the process. (The product of this phase is recommended general highway location, which is usually a narrow corridor.)

Public participation requirements in this phase are quite extensive and include the possibility of a *corridor* public hearing. The EAP states that

at least one public hearing will be held or the opportunity for such a hearing afforded to give all interested persons, who have not already participated in the planning of the proposed project, an opportunity to become fully acquainted with highway proposals of concern to them and to express their views at those stages of a project's development while the flexibility to respond to these views still exists.

In order to receive location approval and therefore to advance to the design stage, the appropriate environmental documentation must receive FHWA concurrence and approval. If the decision is made that the project constitutes a Federal action either an EIS or FONSI must be prepared, depending on whether or not there is a finding of significant impact. When an EIS is required, both the draft and final need FHWA approval before the project may advance to the design phase.

The FEIS is ordinarily combined with the location phase report to form the project planning study report which recommends a preferred corridor alternative. Development of the information needed to produce this report, in addition to the public involvement, includes activities which

1. Gather geology and soil information
2. Gather additional traffic data
3. Determine final alternatives to be studied in detail
4. Finalize project geometrics
5. Determine preliminary profiles for each alternative
6. Obtain formal SEE reports from the KY DOT Division of Environmental Analysis
7. Address the applicability of Corps of Engineers and Coast Guard permits
8. Determine cost estimates for
   (a) Construction
   (b) Right-of-way
   (c) Relocation
   (d) Utility adjustments
9. Determine accident data on the existing facility
10. Determine level of service for each alternative (if applicable)
11. Compile complete cost estimates for each alternative
12. Determine whether Section 4(f) lands are involved.

Once this comprehensive report is completed and approved, it may be expected that the public participation and impact analysis activities would be fairly well finished. The only remaining task would appear to be the detailed design of the facility, which would seem to be a relatively straightforward assignment. However, the Kentucky DOT EAP calls for considerable SEE activities and coordination even after project planning concludes. This occurs when the Location Report/FEIS is approved by the FHWA and the project is progressed to the design phase.

DESIGN

The Kentucky DOT EAP says that

> *the design phase includes the establishment of a precise centerline location within an ap-*

> *proved corridor and the development of right-of-way, utility, and construction plans. The design also includes the acquisition of right-of-way, relocation assistance, utility adjustments, and other preconstruction activities.*

Such activities are often very sensitive and require intimate contact with the public. Accordingly, the EAP calls for regularly scheduled informational meetings with "local public officials, public agencies, and citizens, as necessitated by the type and scope of the project with positive effort to include any racial minority or disadvantaged group." In addition, the department is committed to at least *offering* the opportunity for a formal public hearing on all projects, except those minor projects which do not require the acquisition of significant right-of-way, do not have an adverse effect on abutting real property, and do not change the layout or function of connecting roads or streets of the facility being improved.

The EAP stresses the fact, as a mandate to the department decision makers, that alternative options are to be held open through final design. Frequent review is to be made of previously documented SEE effects, and, in the event of changes, more formal reassessments are to be made. Noise effects are often among those undergoing reanalysis in design, as more detailed data becomes available for input into prediction models. In fact, it is not uncommon to see noise barrier recommendations from previous phases extensively modified or even eliminated in design. It is important for the FHWA to make note of all commitments that a state highway agency has made in previous reports such as an FEIS and *require* that a full justification be made prior to allowing any modifications or eliminations.

The design phase of the Kentucky DOT project development process contains 14 general elements after project initiation. These are

1. Scope development
2. Alignment and grade studies
3. Work location of line and grade alternatives*
4. Preliminary line and grade inspection
5. Development of plans
6. Final inspections

7. Hold (or offer to hold) design public hearing*
8. Modify design based on comments*
9. Request design approval from FHWA
10. Complete right-of-way and roadway plans
11. Complete right-of-way appraisals
12. Complete utilities negotiations
13. Implement right-of-way relocation plans
14. Implement utilities relocation plans

Those elements marked by an asterisk (*) are those which require contact with the public concerning SEE activities. By the time the public hearing is held (8), plans for the preferred design alternative have been developed and the final inspection has been held. It would be reasonable to assume, therefore, that the flavor of the hearing and subsequent public participation would be to maintain the project scope, alignment, and grade, if at all possible. This quite often places the department in an adversary position with the same public it is trying to involve in the project development.

ENVIRONMENTAL ANALYSIS ACTIVITIES

The Kentucky DOT has decided to utilize a centralized approach to the organization of its environmental analysis function. In so doing, it has created a *Division of Environmental Analysis* to service the entire department in all phases of project development. This division houses the interdisciplinary specialists responsible for the preparation of technical studies in these areas.

1. Cultural resources
    (a) Socioeconomic
    (b) Historical
2. Archeology
3. Land and water ecology
4. Transportation noise
5. Air quality

The Kentucky DOT approach in utilizing its environmental staff in a centralized role to actually prepare technical studies in all phases of the project development process has one very significant advantage: strengthened environmental *advocacy*. Whenever there is a legislative or regulatory requirement for an impact analysis for any environmental issue, the Division of Environmental Analysis is brought into the project scheme in a very direct way. This allows the environmental specialists to forcefully voice their opinion on any phase of the project in areas where they have expertise. In fact, the Kentucky DOT EAP has made provisions for the creation of an interdisciplinary project team for each project. In addition to preparing the technical studies relating to the project, the Division of Environmental Analysis is represented by one of its staff on this interdisciplinary project team. Interestingly, the EAP calls for the division to hold interdisciplinary discussion meetings within itself on projects so as to develop an overall position on the project.

Once the technical analyses have been completed and the DEIS has been prepared, the role of the division reverts to one primarily of advising and consulting. Particular assistance is usually needed when the initiating division (usually the Project Planning or Design Division) must resolve comment on environmental issues raised in the review process.

The primary work of the Division of Environmental Analysis, then, is carried out in the pre-DEIS phase. The process by which the division evaluates a project in that phase is as follows.

1. Prepare impact analyses in each area
2. Schedule interdisciplinary discussion within division
3. Hold interdisciplinary discussion on impact analysis and level of environmental significance
4. Discuss possible mitigation measures
5. Discuss inputs to forthcoming project interdisciplinary team meeting
6. Discuss status reporting and scheduling constraints
7. Compile listing of environmental effects of each alternative
8. Compile listing of advantages and disadvantages for each alternative
9. Schedule meeting with division initiating the project
10. Assist in quantification and qualification of benefits and adverse effects of alternatives
11. Prepare element of pre-DEIS, including suggested mitigation measures

12. Validate or revise prior determination on level of environmental significance

As mentioned, the one great advantage of the Kentucky DOT approach is the manner in which the EAP *thrusts* the environmental staff into the midst of project development. There is, however, a significant disadvantage to the approach: because the planning and design staffs do not have to prepare technical environmental analyses, their skills and insights in such areas do not by necessity grow and deepen. As a result, it is more difficult to integrate systematic, interdisciplinary thinking into project flow than if this project staff also had environmental expertise. Nevertheless, the Kentucky DOT approach to project development as expressed in its EAP is quite consistent with the spirit of NEPA. It only remains to see how closely the department follows its own documented process. It is the responsibility of the FHWA to make sure that it does.

As a way of validating its interdisciplinary approach, the Kentucky DOT EAP contains a list of those professional disciplines and technical skills which the department maintains on its in-house staff. There are the following.

Agronomist
Airport development supervisor
Airport zoning committee members
Air quality engineer
Appraiser for right-of-way
Archeologist
Artist
Attorney
Biologist
Bridge inspector
Buyer for right-of-way
Chemist
Civil engineer
Computer specialist
Construction superintendent
Cultural resource specialist
Environmental specialist
Forester
Geologist
Historic resource specialist
Horticulturist

Human rights coordinator
Hydrologist
Land ecologist
Landscape planner/architect
Negotiator for right-of-way
Noise quality specialist
Paleontologist
Planning engineer or professional
Relocation assistance agent
Research analyst
Safety officer
Sociologist
Soils analyst
Systems analyst
Utility agent
Water Ecologist
Wildlife biologist
Writer

In summary, it may be restated that successful implementation of its EAP has altered the Kentucky DOT project development process. This is particularly true when one considers the pre-NEPA process employed by the department.

THE NEW YORK STATE DOT EAP

New York State represents the other end of the spectrum from Kentucky in terms of state characteristics and transportation needs. Accordingly, the respective state departments of transportation vastly differ in their histories, organizational structures, and appointed missions. One would expect, therefore, the project development processes and EAPs also to greatly differ. This turns out to be the case, within the limits of NEPA and FHPM 7-7-1 requirements.

The Kentucky EAP is primarily sequential in form, discussing the elements of the project development process in the order in which they occur: statewide planning; urban and regional system planning; and project planning, design, and implementation. Kentucky is heavily oriented toward the *highway* mode of transportation and has had over the years a clear mandate to provide access to rural areas of the state so that economic development may be encouraged.

The New York State DOT, on the other hand,

has long been multimodel in nature and has had to devote a large portion of its efforts in the multiagency struggle to meet the awesome transportation requirements of the New York City metropolitan area. A great deal of attention is also given to the upstate rural and urban areas, as well as the sensitive Adirondack Park and Finger Lakes regions.

The New York State DOT maintains significant activities in *five* modal components of transportation. These include

1. Highways—the department plans, designs, constructs, operates, and maintains a 14,000-mile state highway system.
2. Urban mass transit—the department assists in the planning, operating, and funding of the rail and bus transit facilities in the urban areas throughout the state.
3. Air—the department coordinates airport planning at the state level and provides a significant portion of the matching funds for Federally aided capital projects.
4. Rail—through legislatively authorized funding programs, the department is involved in coordination and funding of all aspects of the rail program in New York State.
5. Waterways—the department is responsible for operating and maintaining the New York State Barge Canal System.

Because of the many layers of government common in New York State, the department is continuously involved in interagency coordination and consultation, and has been since before NEPA. For example, in the New York City area, the agencies with primary responsibility for operation and maintenance are:

Airports	Port Authority of New York and New Jersey (PANYNJ)
Subways and buses	New York City Transit Authority (NYCTA)
Bridges and tunnels (interborough)	New York City Department of Transportation (NYCDOT)
Parkways	Various state parkway authorities
New York State Thruway	New York State Thruway Authority
Rail (intercity)	National Rail Passenger Corporation (AMTRAK)
Rail (commuter)	Long Island Railroad, PANYNJ, AMTRAK

A major portion of NYSDOT activity in relating to these agencies concerns funding. In order for the agencies to receive authorized state funds, it is often necessary for them to satisfy state DOT requests and regulations. In the particular area of aviation there is not a significant amount of state funding involved to warrant DOT intervention into PANYNJ activities. However, the department does involve itself at John F. Kennedy and LaGuardia Airports as the transportation "staff" of the governor of New York State. The governors of New York and New Jersey each appoint six members to the PANYNJ Board of Directors and also maintain veto power over certain PANYNJ actions. Upon request of the governor the NYSDOT may exert influence; in most cases, however, the Port Authority is in control of aviation activities (in concert with the Federal Aviation Administration) in Greater New York.

The Plan

The New York State DOT approach to environmental action planning adequately reflects the complexities of its various mandates. Rather than a completely sequential layout of the project development process elements, the EAP considers two basic components, each with several sub-components.

1. Systems planning
   (a) Regional
   (b) Interregional
   (c) Statewide
2. Project development
   (a) Location planning
   (b) Design
   (c) Real estate acquisition
   (d) Implementation

The EAP for New York utilizes the project category approach allowed in FHPM 7-7-1. During the initiation phase of the project the NYSDOT assigns a classification to the project based upon the following criteria.

Category I

Proposals for new freeways or expressways, or circumferential or belt highways.

Proposals for transportation facilities that include at least one feasible alternative that would be exclusively on proposed new right-of-way for much of its extent, when such alternative satisfies any one or more of the following:

1. Would provide new or improved access to an area and likely be a stimulus to or accompanied by substantial changes in travel patterns, land use, or development over those likely to occur otherwise without the project.
2. Would likely be accompanied by a substantial increase in growth, travel, or traffic over that likely to occur otherwise without the project.
3. Would, if implemented, likely require substantial modification to any current goals, land use, or development plans that have been adopted by a county, multicounty, or metropolitan area planning body or state agency.

Proposals that include one or more feasible alternatives that involve, as part of the proposal, significant changes in public transportation service or common carrier transportation service.

Category II

Includes all projects other than those in Category I that do not satisfy the criteria of Category III or that are of a scale or scope greater than that of Category III.

Category III

Includes the project proposals that satisfy *all* of the criteria listed below and are of a scale or scope illustrated by the examples below. Criteria for Category III include the following.

1. No acquisition of any occupied dwelling units or principal structures of business.
2. No significant changes in traffic volume, vehicle mix, local travel patterns, or access.
3. No more than minor social, economic, or environmental effects on occupied dwelling units, businesses, abutting properties, or other established human activities; some examples of types of effects that would ordi-

narily be considered to be "more than minor" and would preclude a project proposal from classification as Category III are:
   (a) Shifts of traffic substantially close to homes or other activities.
   (b) Substantial disruption of established parking patterns.
   (c) Removal of trees in residential areas.
   (d) Permanent adverse effects on pedestrian travel or access patterns.
   (e) Detours that may cause temporary significant adverse effects.
4. No acquisition or use of any property protected by Section 4(f) of the U.S. Department of Transportation Act.
5. No effect upon any property or resource protected by Section 106 of the National Historic Preservation Act.
6. No more than minor alteration of or adverse effect on any property, protected area, or natural or man-made resource of national, state, or local significance including, but not limited to:
   (a) Freshwater or tidal wetlands or associated areas,
   (b) Flood plain areas,
   (c) Prime or unique agricultural land,
   (d) Water resources,
   (e) Wild, scenic, and recreational rivers,
   (f) Unique natural, wooded, or scenic areas,
   (g) Rare or endangered species,
7. No requirement for an indirect source air quality permit;
8. No significant inconsistency with current plans or goals that have been adopted by local government bodies.

Note that a project that is likely to require a formal transportation project public hearing for any reason would not be classified as Category III.

Examples of Category III Projects include

1. Minor improvements to existing highways such as adding or widening shoulders, adding auxiliary lanes for weaving, climbing, turning, or speed change, or correcting substandard intersections.

2. Installation on existing highways of traffic control devices, surveillance systems, pavement markings, lighting signs, and other similar operational improvements.

3. Safety improvements to existing highways such as removal, relocation, or shielding of roadside obstacles; grooving; installation of impact attenuators, guide rails, atgrade protective devices, fencing, glare-screening, etc.

4. Reconstruction or rehabilitation at present sites of existing bridges, culverts, or other transportation structures, including railroad crossing structures, not involving substantial expansion of the structure.

5. Minor reconstruction or rehabilitation of existing highways within existing rights-of-way, or involving minimal right-of-way acquisition.

6. Aesthetic or user-convenience improvements to existing highways such as landscaping; removal of nonconforming outdoor advertising; screening of junkyards; improvements at existing rest areas.

7. Resurfacing or spot correction of deteriorated facilities or structures.

8. Minor expansion or alteration of an existing highway maintenance site or structure.

9. Construction of bus shelters and bays.

This listing of Category III projects contains primarily highway activities. Similar listings could be and in fact have been developed for other modal projects.

The EAP implemented by the New York State DOT allows for a "blanket" Category III determination for groupings of projects, with FHWA concurrence. Such projects would be deemed *nonmajor actions* and would be among those *categorically excluded* under the November 29, 1978 CEQ guidelines.

Under the *systems planning* component of the EAP, the two major activities for all categories of projects are project identification and definition. Ordinarily, potential projects will be produced through the conventional methods: the Urban Transportation Planning procedures which develop five year plans; recommendations for local governmental agencies; and input from private individuals and organizations. Once identified, the potential project is studied to determine the action necessary. If the project is likely to have a high enough priority to be included in the NYSDOT program it receives program approval and advances to the *location planning* subcomponent of the *project development* component. There, the question of categorical assignment is made. It is necessary to categorize the projects at this point because beginning in the location planning phase the project development process is quite different for Category I projects than for Category II and III projects. The major differences lie in the relative degree of effort devoted to SEE activities and the amount of public and outside agency coordination and consultation required.

Category I Process

Once the Category I determination has been made for a project in the beginning of the location planning phase, community interaction begins, with the notification of the public, specific groups, government agencies, and the Federal Office of Management and Budget Circular A-95 Clearinghouse organizations. Once the interested and appropriate project participants have been identified, a project mailing list is developed to keep them informed. The NYSDOT EAP terminology for this is *Stage I—Community Mobilization.*

During *Stage II—Assessment*, the department, utilizing its own expertise as well as that of other agencies and organizations, conducts a more detailed problem analysis and develops a wide range of solutions. An important aspect of the assessment is the identification of potential effects from any of the possible solutions. In this stage the NYSDOT has the option to conduct one or more "formal" public information meetings which would have two purposes: solicit information in an open forum, and provide the public with a sense of participation very early in the project life.

This second point is very important when the project is expected to be controversial or to encounter significant opposition. By providing this *sense of participation* it is often possible to neutralize such opposition.

Completion of the preliminary SEE analyses during this assessment phase does not provide the information necessary to produce the DEIS. However, substantial work has been done which indicates to the department the extent of its problems and the anticipated degree of public involvement necessary to expedite the project.

At this point in the Category I process the project enters either *Stage III—Evaluation and Location Recommendation* (if a combined location/design public hearing is to be held) or *Stage III A-D:* (A) Develop and Assess Location Alternatives; (B) Detailed Analysis of Location Alternatives; (C) Corridor Hearing Opportunity; and (D) Location Recommendation.

When the combined hearing process is used, the department as quickly as possible produces and distributes a report that is similar to a DEIS, but with much less detail. Based on the comments received from the circulation of this report, as well as other input, the NYSDOT selects the preferred alternative and prepares a second report which also responds to the comments received on the previous report. This process is preliminary to the actual DEIS and FEIS preparation. There has not yet been a formal public hearing on this project location phase and approval is not granted by the FHWA until the *combined* hearing is held during the design phase. This is nothing more than an administrative detail, however.

When a decision is made to conduct a separate location phase public hearing, a preliminary report is developed prior to DEIS preparation. Much more detail is involved in the analysis of location alternatives at the DEIS level because shortly after the public hearing is held a request for formal location approval is made. This request obviously contains a recommendation (preferred) corridor alternative.

Whether the combined or separate hearing process (Stage III or Stage III A-D) is used, the project is ready to proceed to the design subcomponent of the project development when the preferred corridor alternative has been selected. For highway projects, formal location approval will be granted at this time provided a corridor hearing has been offered and conducted if needed *and* the FEIS has received necessary approvals.

The design component has four phases: (I) Design Alternatives and Impact Identification; (II) Detailed Analysis of Design Alternatives; (III) Design/Combined Hearing Opportunity; and (IV) Design Alternative Recommendation.

Phase I includes highly specific data generation to develop the range of design alternatives and to assess their SEE impacts. By this time the technical analyses for air, noise, ecology, and so on will be well on their way to completion.

Using all available information, the design alternatives are fully analyzed in Phase II. A design report is prepared as a preliminary document to the formal design report which is submitted in the request for design approval. If the combined hearing process has been used, this preliminary report also serves as the DEIS. After distribution of this report, the opportunity to hold a combined or design public hearing is offered (Phase III) and comments analyzed.

The preliminary design phase ends as the design report (and FEIS, for combined hearing projects) is prepared, distributed, and approved. This document contains the recommendation for the preferred design alternative. For a combined hearing project, location and design approval are granted simultaneously.

In accordance with its EAP, the NYSDOT will, in effect, pause at this point in the life of a Category I project to perform a programming evaluation. Should the department determine that the project has sufficient priority and that resources (funds) are available to bring about implementation, the development of detailed design plans and the necessary real estate acquisitions take place. The only activity remaining prior to the letting of an implementation (usually construction) contract is the preparation and approval of plans, specifications, and estimates (PS&E).

Categories II and III

Obviously those projects determined by the NYSDOT to be classified in Category I are those that are the most complex, most controversial, and largest. Those projects of lesser scale are classified as Category II or III, have less impact on society and the environment, and have less extensive development processes.

Because of its decentralized organizational structure with relatively autonomous regional offices, the NYSDOT has deemed it necessary to maintain separate processes for Category II and III projects. The differences between the processes for all three categories are limited, however, by the various requirements of Federal and state laws and approvals.

It is not uncommon for Category II projects, for example, to require the preparation of an EIS or FONSI. Similarly, Category II projects often require a public hearing or information meeting prior to the preparation of the final design report/FEIS or FONSI. For Category II projects it is required that design *alternatives* be analyzed and impacts assessed as part of the process.

Category III projects, on the other hand, usually qualify as categorical exclusions and therefore *require* no SEE activity beyond that accomplished in the original category determination. The EAP does, however, allow for public involvement if the department believes that it would be useful. In most cases a preliminary design report is prepared as the first project document. Once the department is ready to proceed to detailed design, a final design report is prepared and design approval is requested. Unlike Category I or II projects, the department is not required to post formal notice when design approval is requested and obtained for Category III projects, although the option of public notification is still valid. Generally there is so little controversy associated with Category III projects that public notification presents no risk.

ENVIRONMENTAL ANALYSIS ACTIVITIES

The NYSDOT EAP states that

impact analyses of proposed projects are conducted in five steps: identification, measurements, analysis, prediction, and evaluation. Identification involves a determination of the potential impacts, both beneficial and adverse, that might occur should a given project alternative be implemented. Measurement involves collection of necessary data. Analysis concerns the investigation of acquired data to determine impact. Prediction extends the results of data analysis by forecasting the magnitude of probable impacts of each decision alternative. Finally, evaluation determines the relative importance of the impacts and their magnitudes, considers the cost implications of alternatives, and balances positive and negative impacts to facilitate project decisions.

Further,

measurement, analysis, and prediction are performed by professional staff. However, impact identification and value analysis involve

the individuals and groups directly affected by project decisions; successful accomplishment of these two steps depends to a large extent upon citizen participation.

These excerpts from the EAP provide the context through which the NYSDOT attempts to conduct its SEE activities. The department has available in its headquarters (main office) a small staff of highly trained professionals who provide environmental policy guidance, methods development, training, and project report review. Unlike their counterparts in the Kentucky DOT, however, these professionals are rarely involved in the day-to-day affairs relating to ongoing projects. Whereas the Division of Environmental Analysis *prepares* SEE reports and EISs in Kentucky, the NYSDOT Environmental Analysis Bureau *reviews* them. The actual preparation in New York is done at the regional level by lower-grade professionals who frequently deal directly with the individuals and groups directly affected by project decisions.

The EAP discusses a rather comprehensive listing of SEE effects usually analyzed in the course of a major transportation project development. The effects may be separated into seven broad areas. [The first, regional and community growth, is ordinarily evaluated early in the project life (systems and location planning) in qualitative terms. This type of data is of more immediate use to planners and others who provide the traffic projection information as input to other SEE analyses.]

1.   Regional and community growth
2.   Conservation and preservation
  (a)   Soil erosion and sedimentation
  (b)   Ecology of area
  (c)   Parks and recreation facilities
  (d)   Historic and natural landmarks
  (e)   Natural resources
  (f)   Prime and agricultural lands
  (g)   Wildlife and waterfowl areas
  (h)   Energy
3.   Public facilities and services
  (a)   Religious, health, and educational facilities
  (b)   Public utilities: major installations, minor installations

4. Community cohesion
   (a) Residential and neighborhood character and stability
   (b) Minorities and other special interest groups
   (c) Tax base property values
5. Displacement of people, businesses, and farms
   (a) Relocation assistance information
   (b) Availability of adequate replacement housing
   (c) Economic activity
   (d) Employment
6. Pollution
   (a) Air
   (b) Noise
   (c) Water
   (d) Solid waste disposal
   (e) Illumination
   (f) Flooding
   (g) Navigation
   (h) Wetlands
7. Aesthetics and other values
   (a) Aesthetics
   (b) Joint development

The EAP developed by the NYSDOT includes a rather significant discussion relating to the consideration of a wide range of alternatives. Of particular importance in this discussion is a commitment to maintain the low modal split concept.

System planning studies may not specify the development of one mode by completely excluding another. Mode choice may be subject to further study in the project development process.

The preferred location alternative will almost always include a specified modal choice, and will take one of three possible forms: (*a*) No improvement; (*b*) improvement to be implemented totally or partially by the department; or (*c*) improvement to be implemented solely by another agency.

This third point recognizes the fact that the NYSDOT does not have the primary responsibility in providing transportation services in the New York City area. Quite often, an obvious solution to a particular problem in that area will fall within the domain of a local or regional agency.

In an effort to summarize, it may be stated that unlike the case in Kentucky, implementation of the EAP did not have a profound effect on the project development process used by the NYSDOT. Because of the complexities and the diversity of both its clientele and constituency, the need for a *systematic*, interdisciplinary approach has long existed for the New York State department.

SIGNIFICANT DIFFERENCES BETWEEN THE EAPs OF KENTUCKY AND NEW YORK STATE

Each of the two plans discussed is designed to meet the needs of the particular organizational structure of the state department of transportation. Kentucky has a much more centralized approach to project development and therefore has an EAP that is *sequential* in nature. New York State, on the other hand, relies more heavily on a regional office concept, and therefore has a need to be very specific and detailed in its process definition. Accordingly, its EAP is *categorical* in nature. Because it is more centralized, the Kentucky EAP calls for the preparation of SEE analyses and reports to be accomplished at its headquarters by the Division of Environmental Analysis staff. In New York State these activities are carried out at the regional level, with the Environmental Analysis Bureau headquarters providing review and guidance.

Finally, the Kentucky EAP naturally reflects the highways-dominated characteristics of its department of transportation. New York State, however, is more involved in multimodal transportation activities than any other state in the country. Its EAP, accordingly, gives more consideration to the other modes of transportation, in addition to highways.

THE NATION

The basic differences between the Kentucky and New York State EAPs, as noted above, relate more to organizational structure than project development process. This is because the legislation and regulation (FHPM 7-7-1) mandating the systematic, interdisciplinary approach are in fact quite specific and constraining to the transportation agencies.

If one were to do an exhaustive study of the EAPs from *all* the states, the conclusion would be that there is not a significant amount of variation from state to state. Applications of specific requirements may vary as to the disposition of the interdisciplinary staff. Some states, like New York, maintain a small central environmental analysis staff which primarily reviews EISs and technical reports prepared by regional and district office personnel. Other states, like Kentucky, use a more centralized approach whereby the central environmental analysis staff actually *performs* and *prepares* the technical studies and EISs for the entire state. Whichever method is used, the outcome is the same: the interdisciplinary team of environmental professionals provides timely input into the project development process, thus fulfilling the requirement for the systematic, *interdisciplinary* approach.

Similarly, Table 4-1 has shown that the states have utilized many various tools and techniques in their efforts to achieve a common, mandated goal: maximized public involvement in the project, thus fulfilling the requirement for a *systematic*, interdisciplinary approach (where all possible input becomes available on all projects).

In summary, it may be stated that the EAPs from around the nation are quite similar, and resemble to varying degrees those of New York State and Kentucky. This similarity is because of the strong Federal role in the transportation project development process. This Federal role is in turn founded in the financial arrangement that exists between the Federal government and the states and local governments. Because the various administrations and agencies of the U.S. DOT fund the *majority* of the costs associated in providing transportation services, they have been directed by Congress and the Executive to effectively dictate project development.

CONCLUSION

Environmental Action Planning concerns the implementation of the systematic, interdisciplinary approach in the transportation project development process. This approach is mandated by Federal law through the National Environ-

mental Policy Act (NEPA) of 1969 and the Federal Aid Highway Act (FAHA) of 1970. Specific regulatory direction has been provided by the FHWA through the issuance of FHPM 7-7-1, *Process Guidelines.* While this regulation is aimed at only the highway mode, it has de facto application across the modes because states have instituted multimodal departments of transportation.

Prior to the adoption of the action plan concept, transportation projects were generally developed using only the criteria of cost minimization and engineering feasibility. These criteria were utilized to arrive at a satisfactory solution to a problem identified by the analysis of capacity, safety, sufficiency, growth inducement and potential, and so on. In most cases such projects were developed by civil engineers, with little input from other groups of professionals, outside agencies, or the public.

Institution of the NEPA-inspired EAP has added several additional criteria to the project development process. These include

1. Social effects
2. Economic effects
3. Environmental effects
4. Indirect effects
5. The public's desires
6. Expertise and views from other agencies
7. Alternative analysis
8. The option of no improvement

The revised process is to be truly *interdisciplinary* in nature, utilizing the skills of a wide range of professionals. The Kentucky DOT EAP, as an example, lists 39 classifications of professionals which are involved in project development.

There is no question that the EAP concept, as well as NEPA in general, have added to the cost and time required to bring a transportation project to implementation. There is also no question that project *quality* has been improved by the emphasis on the systematic, interdisciplinary approach. The only true question to be debated is whether the benefits, in terms of project quality, outweigh the costs, in terms of time and money. The answer can only be supplied by Congress and the President, who hold ultimate authority over NEPA legislation and funding.

APPENDIX 4

U. S. DEPARTMENT OF TRANSPORTATION

FEDERAL HIGHWAY ADMINISTRATION

FEDERAL-AID HIGHWAY PROGRAM MANUAL

VOLUME	7	RIGHT-OF-WAY AND ENVIRONMENT
CHAPTER	7	ENVIRONMENT
SECTION	1	PROCESS GUIDELINES (FOR THE DEVELOPMENT OF ENVIRONMENTAL ACTION PLANS)

Transmittal 107
December 30, 1974
HEV-10

Par.   1. Purpose
        2. Authority
        3. Definitions
        4. Policy
        5. Application
        6. Procedures
        7. Implementation and Revision
        8. Contents of the Action Plan
        9. Identification of Social, Economic, and Environmental
             Effects
       10. Consideration of Alternative Courses of Action
       11. Involvement of Other Agencies and the Public
       12. Systematic Interdisciplinary Approach
       13. Decisionmaking Process
       14. Interrelation of System and Project Decisions
       15. Levels of Action by Project Category
       16. Responsibility for Implementation
       17. Fiscal and Other Resources
       18. Consistency with Existing Laws, Regulations and
             Directives.

1. **PURPOSE**

    *To provide to highway agencies and the Federal Highway
    Administration (FHWA) field offices guidelines for the devel-
    opment of Action Plans to assure that adequate consideration
    is given to possible social, economic, and environmental
    effects of proposed highway projects and that the decisions
    on such projects are made in the best overall public interest.
    These guidelines identify issues to be considered in review-
    ing the present organization and processes of a highway
    agency as they relate to social, economic and environmental
    considerations, and in developing desirable improvements.
    The guidelines recognize the unique situation of each State
    and do not prescribe specific organizations or procedures.*

2. AUTHORITY

    a. 23 U.S.C. 109(h) directs the following: "Not later
than July 1, 1972, the Secretary, after consultation
with appropriate Federal and State officials, shall
submit to the Congress, and not later than 90 days
after such submission, promulgate guidelines designed
to assure that possible adverse economic, social, and
environmental effects relating to any proposed project
on any Federal-aid system have been fully considered
in developing such project, and that the final decisions
on the project are made in the best overall public
interest, taking into consideration the need for fast,
safe, and efficient transportation, public services,
and the cost of eliminating or minimizing such adverse
effects and the following:

       (1) air, noise, and water pollution;

       (2) destruction or disruption of manmade and natural
resources, esthetic values, community cohesion
and the availability of public facilities and
services;

       (3) adverse employment effects, and tax property value
losses;

       (4) injurious displacement of people, businesses and
farms; and

       (5) disruption of desirable community and regional growth.

Such guidelines shall apply to all proposed projects with
respect to which plans, specifications and estimates
are approved by the Secretary after the issuance of such
guidelines."

    b. 23 U.S.C. 128 stipulates those Federal-aid projects for
which the opportunity for public hearings must be afforded
and includes certain certification and reporting requirements for these projects.

    c. 42 U.S.C. 4321 et. seq. (the National Environmental
Policy Act of 1969) requires the utilization of a systematic interdisciplinary approach to ensure the integrated
use of the natural and social sciences and the environmental design arts in planning and decisionmaking. It
further requires that procedures be developed which will

ensure that presently unquantified environmental amenities and values may be given appropriate consideration in decisionmaking along with economic and technical considerations.

3. <u>DEFINITIONS</u> (As used in this directive)

  a. *<u>Highway Agency</u> - The agency with the primary responsibility for initiating and carrying forward the planning, design, and construction of Federal-aid highway projects.*

  b. *<u>Human Environment</u> - The aggregate of all external conditions and influences (esthetic, ecological, cultural, social, economic, historical, etc.) that affect human life.*

  c. *<u>Environmental Effects</u> - The totality of the effects of a highway project on the human and natural environment.*

  d. *<u>A-95 Clearinghouse</u> - Those agencies and offices in States, metropolitan areas, and multi-State regions which perform the coordination functions called for in Office of Management and Budget (OMB) Circular A-95.*

  e. *The following definitions are provided solely to clarify the terms "system planning stage," "location stage," and "design stage" as they are used in these guidelines. A highway agency may choose to use different definitions in responding to these guidelines. If not stated otherwise, the following definitions will be assumed to be applicable.*

    (1) *<u>System Planning Stage</u> - Regional analysis of transportation needs and the identification of transportation corridors.*

    (2) *<u>Location Stage</u> - From the end of system planning through the selection of a particular location.*

    (3) *<u>Design Stage</u> - From the selection of a particular location to the start of construction.*

  f. *<u>Major Design Features</u> - Those features required to describe a proposed highway improvement, including such elements as number of traffic lanes, access control features, general horizontal and vertical alignments, approximate right-of-way requirements, and locations of bridges, interchanges and other major structures, etc.*

4. <u>Policy</u>

    a. *It is the FHWA's policy that full consideration be given to social, economic, and environmental effects throughout the planning of highway projects, including system planning, location and design; that provisions for ensuring such consideration shall be incorporated in the decisionmaking process; and that decisions shall be made in the best overall public interest, taking into consideration the need for fast, safe, and efficient transportation, public services, and the cost of eliminating or minimizing possible adverse social, economic, and environmental effects.*

    b. *The process by which decisions are reached should be such as to merit public·confidence in the highway agency. To achieve this objective, it is the FHWA's policy that:*

        (1) *social, economic, and environmental effects be identified and studies early enough to permit analysis and consideration while alternatives are being formulated and evaluated,*

        (2) *other agencies and the public be involved in system planning and project development early enough to influence technical studies and final decisions, and*

        (3) *appropriate consideration be given to reasonable alternatives, including the alternative of not building the project and alternative modes.*

5. <u>APPLICATION</u>

    a. *These guidelines apply to the process by which highway agencies plan and develop proposed projects, on any Federal-aid system, for which the FHWA approves the plans, specifications and estimates or has the responsibility for approving a program. They apply to system planning decisions, including those made in compliance with 23 U.S.C. 134 and to project decisions made during the location and design stages.*

    b. *These guidelines and the Action Plan shall only be applied to the future development of ongoing projects and to future projects. They are not retroactive, and shall not apply to any step or steps taken in the development of a project prior to the time of the implementation of the parts of the Action Plan applicable thereto. Action Plan public hearing procedures, as defined in paragraph 11b(7), shall apply only to activities or stages of project development occurring subsequent to the FHWA approval*

*of the Action Plan containing such provision.
However, any project which has an initial (corridor)
public hearing opportunity in accordance with 23 CFR
790 shall also have a second (design) public hearing
opportunity if such hearing opportunity would have
been required by 23 CFR 790.*

6. **PROCEDURES**

    a. *To meet the requirements of these guidelines, each highway
agency shall operate under an approved Action Plan which
describes the organization to be utilized and the process
to be followed in the development of Federal and Federal-
aid highway projects from initial system planning through
design.*

    b. *The Action Plan should be consistent with the requirements
of all applicable FHWA regulations and directives.*

    c. *Involvement of the public and local, State and Federal
officials and agencies, including A-95 clearinghouses
and the 23 U.S.C. 134 metropolitan transportation planning
agencies, should be sought throughout the development of
the Action Plan. Comments should be solicited during the
draft and final stage of development of the Action Plan.*

    d. *The FHWA, through its division and regional offices, will
consult with the State in the development of the Action
Plan and, within the limits of its resources, will be
prepared to assist or advise.*

    e. *The Action Plan shall be submitted to the Governor of the
State for review and approval as a means of obtaining
a high degree of interagency and intergovernmental coordination. Approval by the Governor may occur prior to
submittal of the Action Plan to the FHWA, or, if desired
by the State, may occur concurrently with FHWA approval.*

    f. *The Action Plan submitted to the Governor of the State
and to the FHWA should be accompanied by a description
of the procedures followed in developing the Action Plan;
the steps taken to involve the public and other agencies
during development of the Plan; and a summary of comments
received on the Plan (including the sources of such
comments) and the State's disposition of these comments.*

    g. *Review and approval of the Action Plan and revisions
thereto will be the responsibility of the Regional Federal
Highway Administrator.*

h.   *The FHWA will not give location approvals unless the highway agency has an approved Action Plan.*

7.   IMPLEMENTATION AND REVISION

a.   *The FHWA shall review the States' implementation of their Action Plans at appropriate intervals. The FHWA may rescind approval of the Action Plan or take other action it deems appropriate if in its reviews it determines that the Action Plan is not being implemented or that the Action Plan is not achieving the objectives of this directive.*

b.   *The Action Plan shall be implemented as quickly as feasible. A program of staged implementation for the period up to November 1, 1974, shall be developed and described in the Action Plan. It is expected that all aspects of the Action Plan will be implemented by this date. If the highway agency believes that any provision in its Action Plan cannot be implemented prior to November 1, 1974, it shall present a schedule for the implementation of such provisions to the FHWA, which will consider the proposed schedule on a case-by-case basis.*

c.   *If the schedule for implementation set forth in an approved Action Plan is not met, the FHWA may withhold location approvals or take such other actions as it deems appropriate.*

d.   *An approved Action Plan may be revised to meet changed circumstances or to permit adoption of improved procedures or assignments of responsibilities.*

   (1)   *The Action Plan should identify the assignment of responsibility for developing Action Plan revisions.*

   (2)   *Paragraph 6f (Governor's approval) shall apply to revision of the Action Plan; except that the Highway Agency, with the Governor's approval, may include a provision in the Action Plan to allow all or some type of revisions in the approved Action Plan without review and approval by the Governor. In such instances, the Action Plan should include a description of the types of such revisions.*

   (3)   *The highway agency in consultation with the FHWA shall determine the extent to which involvement of the public and other agencies is necessary in the development of proposed Action Plan revisions.*

8. <u>CONTENTS OF THE ACTION PLAN</u>

*The Action Plan shall indicate the procedures to be followed
in developing highway projects, including organizational
structure and assignments of responsibility by the chief
administrative officer of the highway agency to positions or
units within the agency. Where participation of other
agencies or consultants will be utilized, this should be
so indicated. The topics to be covered by the Action Plan
are outlined in the following paragraphs of this directive.*

9. <u>IDENTIFICATION OF SOCIAL, ECONOMIC, AND ENVIRONMENTAL EFFECTS</u>

a. *Identification of potential social, economic, and
    environmental effects, both beneficial and adverse, of
    alternative courses of action should be made as early
    in the study process as feasible. Timely information
    on such effects should be produced so that the develop-
    ment and consideration of alternatives and studies can
    be influenced accordingly. Further, the costs, financial
    and otherwise, of eliminating or minimizing possible
    adverse social, economic, and environmental effects should
    be determined.*

b. <u>The Action Plan should identify</u>:

    (1)   the assignment of responsibility for;

        *(a)   providing information of social, economic, and
              environmental effects of alternative courses of
              action during system planning, location, and
              design stages,*

        *(b)   controlling the technical quality of social,
              economic, and environmental studies, and*

        *(c)   monitoring current social, economic, and
              environmental research; monitoring environ-
              mental effects of completed projects, where
              appropriate; and disseminating "state-of-the-art"
              information within the agency.*

    *(2)   procedures to be followed to ensure that timely
          information on social, economic, and environmental
          effects:*

        *(a)   is developed in parallel with alternatives
              and related engineering data, so that the*

development and selection of alternatives and other elements of technical studies can be influenced appropriately,

(b)   indicates the manner and extent to which specific groups and interests, including minority groups, are beneficially and/or adversely affected by alternative proposed improvements,

(c)   is made available to other agencies and to the public early in studies,

(d)   is developed with participation of staffs of local agencies and interested citizens, and

(e)   is developed sufficiently to allow for the estimation of costs, financial or otherwise, of eliminating or minimizing identified adverse effects.

10.   CONSIDERATION OF ALTERNATIVE COURSES OF ACTION

a.   *Alternatives considered should include, where appropriate, alternative types and scales of highway improvements and other transportation modes. The option of no improvement should be considered and used as a reference point for determining the beneficial and adverse effects of other alternatives. Appropriate alternatives which might minimize or avoid adverse social, economic, or environmental effects should be studied and described, particularly in terms of impacts upon specific groups and in relationship to 42 U.S.C. 2000d-2000d-4 (Title VI of the Civil Rights Act of 1964) and 42 U.S.C. 3601-3619 (Title VIII of the Civil Rights Act of 1968).*

b.   *The Action Plan should identify the assignment of responsibility and the procedures to be followed to ensure that:*

(1)   the consequences of the no-highway-improvement option are set forth, with data of a level of completeness and of detail consistent with that developed for other alternatives;

(2)   a range of alternatives appropriate to the stage is considered at each stage from system studies through final design;

(3) *Alternatives containing new transportation modes or improvements to existing modes are adequately considered, where appropriate.*

(4) *Nontransportation components, such as replacement housing, joint development, multiple use of rights-of-way, etc., are in coordination with transportation components.*

(5) *Suggestions from outside the agency are given careful consideration.*

11. <u>INVOLVEMENT OF OTHER AGENCIES AND THE PUBLIC</u>

a. *The President has directed Federal agencies to "develop procedures to ensure the fullest practicable provision of timely public information and understanding of Federal plans and programs with environmental impact in order to obtain the views of interested parties" (Executive Order 11514). Interested parties should have adequate opportunities to express their views early enough in the study process to influence the course of studies, as well as the actions taken. Information about the existence, status, and results of studies should be made available to other agencies and the public throughout those studies. Public hearings should be only one component of the agency's program to obtain public involvement.*

b. *The Action Plan should identify the assignment of responsibility and procedures to be followed.*

(1) *To ensure that information is made available to other agencies and the public throughout the duration of project studies, and that such information is as clear and comprehensible as practicable concerning:*

(a) *the alternatives being considered,*

(b) *the effects of alternatives, both beneficial and adverse, and the manner and extent to which specific groups and interests, including minority groups, are affected,*

(c) *right-of-Way and relocation assistance programs and relocation plans, and*

(d) *the proposed time schedule of project development, including major points of public interest.*

(2)   To clearly indicate the organizational unit or units
      within the highway agency to which the public can
      go for information outlined in paragraph 11b(1), and
      for assistance to clarify or interpret the information.

(3)   To ensure that interested parties, including local
      governments and metropolitan, regional, State and
      Federal agencies, and the public have an opportunity
      to participate in an open exchange of views through-
      out the system planning, location and design stages.

(4)   To utilize appropriate agencies with area-wide
      responsibilities to assist in the coordination of
      viewpoints during project development.

(5)   To consult with the responsible local public officials
      and involve appropriately the organization which is
      officially established to conduct continuing,
      comprehensive, cooperative transportation planning
      in urbanized areas of over 50,000 population (con-
      sistent with Vol. 4, Planning, Ch. 4, Urban
      Transportation Planning, Sec. 2, Urban Transportation
      Planning of the Federal-Aid Highway Program Manual.)

(6)   To select and coordinate procedures, in addition to
      formal public hearings, to be used to inform and
      involve the public.

(7)   To ensure adequate opportunity for public hearing(s)
      on the need for the proposed project; alternative
      courses of action; alternative project locations
      and major design features; social, economic, environ-
      mental and other effects of the alternatives; and
      the consistency of the project with local planning
      goals and objectives. The Action Plan shall
      include:

      (a)   Provisions for one or more public hearings to
            be held at a convenient time and place, or
            the opportunity for hearing(s) to be afforded,
            on any Federal-aid project which requires the
            acquisition of significant amounts of
            right-of-way, substantially changes the layout
            or function of connecting roadways or of the
            facility being improved, has a significant
            adverse impact on abutting real property, or
            otherwise has a significant social, economic,
            environmental or other effect.

    *(b) The stage(s) of project development at which
hearing opportunities will be afforded and
the function and coverage of each hearing,
including provisions that each hearing will be
held before the highway agency becomes committed
to any alternative presented at the hearing,
and that the alternatives presented at each
hearing will be developed to comparable levels
of detail.*

    *(c) Public notification procedures that will be
used to inform the public of hearing opportunities, including newspaper publication of
hearing notices, press releases and other
means that are likely to reach those interested
in or affected by proposed projects. Initial
hearing notices shall be published at least
30 days in advance of hearings.*

    *(d) A description of what information is presented
or made available to the public and the procedures for receiving verbal and written
commentary from the public to assure that the
public has adequate opportunity to participate
in the hearing process and to be informed of
the alternatives studied and their potential
effects. Information such as engineering,
social, economic and environmental studies,
draft environmental impact statements; noise
and air quality studies; and relocation program
descriptions should be made available before
the hearing(s) for inspection and copying and
should be provided at the hearing(s).*

    *(e) Provisions for additional hearing opportunities
when there has been (1) substantial change in
the proposal, or (2) substantial unanticipated
development in the area affected by the proposal, or (3) an unusually long lapse of time
since the last hearing, or (4) identification
of significant social, economic, or environmental effects not previously considered at
earlier hearings.*

  *(8) To provide for the submission of reports, certifi-
cations and, if appropriate, public hearing transcripts
as required by 23 U.S.C. 128 for each public hearing
opportunity.*

12. SYSTEMATIC INTERDISCIPLINARY APPROACH

    a. *42 U.S.C. 4332 (Section 102 of the National Environmental Policy Act of 1969) requires that agencies use "a systematic, interdisciplinary approach which will ensure the integrated use of the natural and social sciences and the environmental design arts in planning and in decisionmaking which may have an impact on man's environment."*

    b. *The Action Plan should indicate procedural arrangements and assignments of responsibilities which will be necessary to meet this requirement, including:*

        (1) the organization and staffing of interdisciplinary project groups which are systematic and interdisciplinary in approach, including the possible use of consultants and representatives of other State or local agencies,

        (2) recruitment and training of personnel with skills which are appropriate to add on a full-time basis, and the development of appropriate career patterns, including management opportunities, and

        (3) additional training for present personnel to enhance their capabilities to work effectively in an interdisciplinary environment.

13. DECISIONMAKING PROCESS

    a. *The process of reaching various decisions on projects should be reviewed to assure that it provides for the appropriate consideration of all economic, social, environmental and transportation factors as required by these guidelines.*

    b. *The Action Plan should identify:*

        (1) the processes through which other State and local agencies, government officials, and private groups may contribute to reaching decisions, and the authority, if any, which other agencies or government officials can exercise over decisions;

        (2) different decision processes, if any, for various cateogries of projects (e.g., Interstate, Primary, Secondary, TOPICS) and for various geographic

*regions of the State (e.g., in various urban and
rural regions) to reflect local differences in the
nature of potential environmental effects or in the
structure of local governments and institutions; and*

(3) *the processes to be used to obtain participation
in decisions by officials of appropriate agencies
in other States for those situations in which the
potential social, economic, and environmental
effects are of interstate concern.*

14. INTERRELATION OF SYSTEM AND PROJECT DECISIONS

a. *Many significant economic, social, and environmental
effects of a proposed project are difficult to anticipate at the system planning stage and become clear only
during location and design studies. Conversely, many
significant environmental effects of a proposed project
are set at the system planning stage. Decisions at the
system and project stages shall be made with consideration of their social, economic, environmental, and
transportation effects to the extent possible at each
stage.*

b. *The Action Plan should identify:*

(1) *Procedures to be followed to:*

(a) *ensure that potential social, economic, and
environmental effects are identified insofar
as practicable in system planning studies as
well as in later stages of location and
design, and*

(b) *provide for reconsideration of earlier decisions which may be occasioned by results of
further study, the availability of additional
information, or the passage of time between
decisions.*

(2) *Assignment of responsibility for ensuring that
project studies are effectively coordinated with
system planning on a continuing basis.*

15. LEVELS OF ACTION BY PROJECT CATEGORY

a. *A highway agency may develop different procedures to be
followed depending upon the economic, social, environmental,
or transportation significance of the highway project to
be developed. Different procedures may also be adopted*

for various categories of projects, such as TOPICS, new route locations, or secondary roads, and for various regions of the State, such as urban areas or zones of particular environmental significance.

b. *The Action Plan should identify:*

  (1) the categories which the highway agency will use to distinguish the different degrees of effort which under normal circumstances will be devoted to various types of projects;

  (2) assignment of responsibility for determining, initially and in periodic reviews, the category of each ongoing project; and

  (3) procedures to be followed for each category (including identification of impacts, public involvement, decision process, and other issues covered in these guidelines).

16. RESPONSIBILITY FOR IMPLEMENTATION

Assignment of responsibility for implementation of the Action Plan should be identified.

17. FISCAL AND OTHER RESOURCES

a. *An important component of the Action Plan is identification of resources of the highway agency and of other agencies required to perform the identified procedures and execute the assigned responsibilities.*

b. *The Action Plan should identify:*

  (1) the resources of the highway agency (in terms of personnel and funding) that will be utilized in implementing and carrying out the Action Plan;

  (2) resources that are available in other agencies to provide necessary information on social, economic, and environmental effects;

  (3) programs for the addition of trained personnel or fiscal or other resources to either the highway agency itself or other agencies;

18. <u>CONSISTENCY WITH EXISTING LAWS, REGULATIONS AND DIRECTIVES</u>

*The highway agency should identify and report, either in the
Action Plan or otherwise, areas where existing Federal and
State laws, regulations and administrative directives prevent
or hamper full compliance with these guidelines. Where
appropriate, recommendations and proposed actions to overcome
such difficulties should be described.*

CHAPTER 5

Transportation Noise Analysis

The problem of *noise* impact from transportation activities is unique among the pollutants in its spontaneity and lack of duration. In any given transportation situation, the noise generated by the sources involved *at the moment* is not affected by any previous activity, nor does it affect any future activity. Unlike air or water pollution, noise leaves no residual evidence to serve as a continuing reminder of its unpleasantness. This is the principal reason that, even though its effects are usually as severe as any transportation impact, noise is often the pollutant with the lowest priority for control. In the cases of highways and aviation, however, noise can, in certain situations, become *the* critical issue in project development. The DOT modal agencies (the FHWA and FAA) therefore have made provisions under the law to address noise where needed and to develop and utilize technical tools.

Specifically with regard to regulations, the FHWA has adapted FHPM 7-7-3, for the consideration of highway noise, and the FAA has adopted FAR Parts 36 and 91, as well as Order 5100.33, for aviation noise control. These regulations are discussed in Chapter 3.

The regulations, and their root legislative statutes, have had the effect of forcing technological advances in the area of prediction methodologies for impact analysis. In this chapter, the state-of-the-art methodologies for predicting highway noise and aviation noise levels will be discussed. Before proceeding with those discussions, however, it is first necessary to come to an understanding of the physical mechanisms involved in noise analysis, and to adequately define the various descriptors used in highway noise and aviation noise.

PHYSICAL MECHANISMS

In order to be fully understood, it is necessary to view noise as a problem of Source-Path-Receiver. As an aside, *all* problems of noise should be approached in this way, because solutions will invariably present themselves as solutions of source, path, and receiver. As the word implies, the source is simply that mechanism or device from which the noise is being emitted. In transportation noise, the source* is the aircraft, the traffic stream, or the locomotive. The path is the environment through which the emitted noise travels on its way to striking the receiver, which may be a person, a building, a group of buildings, or some other sensitive receptor.

Since noise is ordinarily a broad-banded source of acoustic energy, and since not all components of noise impact the *ultimate* receiver, the human, to the same degree, the goal of noise analysis should be to identify those parameters which will affect the emission, transmission, and reception of the noise by the human. These parameters include

1. *Temporal distribution* of the sound
2. *Magnitude* of the sound
3. Cyclic *frequency* of the sound
4. Coherence, or *time-variance* of the sound

---

*For the purposes of this discussion, the source is considered in the aggregate, or "macro" sense. In other words, it is the vehicle or vehicles emitting the noise. For a discussion of the source in the "micro" sense (monopole, dipole, quadrupole), see the section on Magnitude.

Temporal Distribution

This is an important consideration because the time of day, day of week, and month of year affect the condition of the receiver. For example, a heavy flow of truck traffic may not be offensive to an adjacent residential area if flow is concentrated in the afternoon hours, but will be very offensive if a large percentage of the trucks go by during the late night hours. Also, a church located in a departure path for a nearby airport will not ordinarily be bothered by a regularly scheduled departure at 11:30 a.m. unless Sunday is one of the days of the week that the flight is scheduled.

Magnitude

Emitted sound (or noise) travels by vibrating indivdual particles in an elastic medium back and forth along the direction of propagation, usually in a cylindrical or spherical manner. This type of sound wave may be classified as a longitudinal wave, capable of being propagated through solids, liquids, or gases. The net displacement for each particle within the transmitting medium is zero, even though the wave pulse moves at a high rate of speed, exceeding 340 m (1115 ft) per second in air at 20°C. Equation 5-1 gives the physical expression for speed of sound.

$$c = \sqrt{\gamma r T} \qquad (5\text{-}1)$$

where c = speed of sound (m/sec)
         γ = ratio of specific heats
         r = gas constant
         T = absolute temperature

The actual magnitude of the sound as perceived is caused by short-duration fluctuations in the atmospheric pressure. These fluctuations, called sound pressures, are extremely minute when compared to the atmospheric pressure, which is approximately 100,000 newtons per square meter (N/m^2), or pascals (1 Pa = 10 microbars, or 0.000147 psi). For example, a jet aircraft on takeoff may generate a sound pressure of up to 20 Pa. On the other hand, a very quiet sound, like the rustling of leaves, may cause a change in atmospheric pressure with an order of magnitude of only 0.00002 Pa, which is a millionfold smaller than that of the jet aircraft.

The most efficient method for analyzing and manipulating the magnitude component of sound is to examine the relationship between the physical stimulus and the corresponding physiological response by the human. This phenomenon was first studied in 1825 by E. H. Weber in connection with human estimates of weights of various objects. Conveniently, it works out that the mathematical relationship Weber observed also provides a mechanism for adequately condensing the magnitudes of the numbers involved such that they are relatively easy to work with. Basically, Weber noticed that the increase in stimulus required to produce a given increase in sensation is proportional to the preexisting stimulus.

Expressed mathematically,

$$ds = k \cdot \frac{dw}{w} \qquad (5\text{-}2)$$

where ds is the minimum perceptible increase in sensation, dw is the stimulus (in Weber's case, the weight) producing it, and w is the total stimulus originally present. Integration of the equation yields the relationship known as the Weber-Fechner Law:

$$s = k \cdot \log w \qquad (5\text{-}2a)$$

This logarithmic* relationship allows one to set the limits of integration at the extremities of the sound pressure spectrum of magnitude, and will still result in numbers of the same order (see below). The relationship also explains how the ear is able to respond to both small and large differences in sound pressure.

Transferring the concept of the Weber-Fechner Law to the commonly accepted acoustical terminology yields the widely used ratio of measure, the decibel (dB). Simply defined, *the decibel is the division of a uniform scale based on 10 times the logarithm of the relative intensity of sound intensities being compared.* In other words, the decibel is a dimensionless unit logarithmically relating two like quantities of different magnitudes, one of which is usually taken to be a reference magnitude (in this case, sound pressure). The most commonly accepted reference pressure is 0.00002 Pa, which corresponds to the threshold of human hearing at

---

*Throughout this chapter, base 10 logarithms are used exclusively. Thus "log" is an abbreviation for "$\log_{10}$."

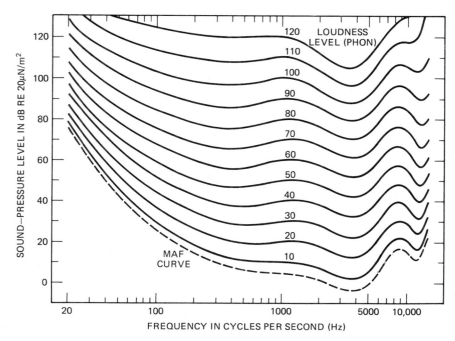

Figure 5-1. Equal-Loudness contours for pure tones. The number of phons on each curve is the sound pressure level (SPL) of the 1000-Hz tone used for comparison for that curve. To use the contours for determining the equally loud levels at other frequencies, find the point on the curve corresponding to the desired frequency and read the corresponding SPL at the ordinate. MAF means Minimum Audible Field, or the threshold of hearing.

1000 Hz*. The sound pressure level (SPL) equation, therefore, is expressed as

$$SPL = 10 \log \frac{p_0^2}{p_r^2} = 20 \log \frac{p_0}{p_r} \quad \text{(in dB)} \quad (5\text{-}3)$$

where p_0 is the sound pressure of the sound in question, and p_r is the reference pressure. [Both p_0 and p_r are root-mean-square (rms) pressures.] Substituting the reference pressure for p_0 yields SPL = $20 \log (p_r/p_r)$ = $20 \log (1)$ = 0 dB (threshold of hearing at 1000 Hz). Substituting the sound pressure of the jet aircraft mentioned earlier, 20 Pa, yields SPL = $20 \log (20/0.00002)$ = $20 \log (10^6)$ = 120 dB. Figure 5-1 shows the frequency-dependent limits of pure-tone SPL for humans.

It should be noted that the SPL equation could be written in terms of intensity, or energy flow per unit area. This energy flux ratio is given

*One Hz is one cycle per second. See the discussion on Frequency.

by Equation 5-4:

$$IL = 10 \log \frac{I}{I_r} \quad (5\text{-}4)$$

where IL = intensity level (dB)
   I = intensity of the sound in question (W/m²)
   I_r = reference intensity (10^{-12} W/m²)

Equation 5-4a utilizes the fact that the intensity I of a plane wave is related to the rms pressure p_0 of a plane wave by

$$I = \frac{p_0^2}{\rho_0 c} \quad (5\text{-}4a)$$

where $\rho_0 c$ is the characteristic impedance of the medium. For air at 20°C, $\rho_0 c$ is 415 MKS rayls. (1 MKS rayl = 1 kg/meter² sec and is a measure of specific acoustic impedance; it is named in honor of Lord Rayleigh.) The reference intensity I_r, is usually taken as 10^{-12} W/m². Because this intensity corresponds almost exactly to the reference pressure of 0.00002 Pa, IL is separated from SPL by only 0.2 dB. For the practical pur-

TABLE 5-1. Representative Sound Pressures and Sound Pressure Levels

P_{rms} (Pa)	SPL (dB)	
200.00	140	Threshold of pain
63.24	130	
20.00	120	Jet takeoff
6.32	110	
2.00	100	Jet landing
0.63	90	Heavy truck at 25 ft
0.20	80	Adjacent to major expressway
0.06	70	FHWA design noise levels (L_{10})
0.02	60	Automobile at 50 ft
0.006	50	Typical community
0.002	40	Quiet neighborhood
0.0006	30	
0.0002	20	
0.00006	10	
0.00002	0	Threshold of hearing (at 1000 Hz)

poses of transportation noise, it may be stated that *IL* equals SPL.

Table 5-1 below gives examples of transportation-related sound pressure levels, with corresponding sound pressures (rms) in Pascals (Pa).

The nature of human response to sound and noise is such that a 10 dB increase in sound pressure level, everything else being equal, will result in an apparent doubling of subjective loudness (above 40 dB). Likewise, a reduction of 10 dB will result in a sound that appears to be one half as loud. Obviously, this relationship does not correspond to the logarithmic nature of the decibel. For example, the one heavy truck listed in Table 5-1 has an SPL of 90 dB. Two trucks, then, would have an SPL of 93 dB, according to Equation 5-3. Four trucks would have 96 dB for an SPL, and so on. One-half of a truck, if there were such a thing, would have 87 dB for its SPL. The rule for decibel summation is that doubling the source strength will result in a 3 dB increase, and halving the source strength will result in a 3 dB decrease. This concept can be generalized to add any number of SPLs of different values to obtain a total SPL, by use of the Equation 5-5:

$$SPL = 10 \log (10^{10/SPL_1} + 10^{10/SPL_2} + \cdots$$

$$+ 10^{10/SPL_n}) = 10 \log \left(\sum_{i=1}^{n} 10^{10/SPL_i} \right) \quad (5\text{-}5)$$

One other concept regarding the magnitude of sound and noise needs to be discussed, and that is the relationship of SPL to distance from the source.* There are three basic types of sources found in transportation noise. The first is the *point* source, which would be represented by an individual vehicle, for example, a truck alone on a highway or an aircraft in flight. The second is the pure *line* source, which may be a railroad train or an extremely heavy and uniform traffic flow. The third type is the one most often found in typical highway traffic, the *modified line* source, which has characteristics of both point and line sources.

Point sources are subject to a phenomenon known as *spherical spreading*, which results (for a monopole source) from the so-called *inverse square law*. Basically, this means that the sound signal emanating from a source strikes an area A four times as large at a distance $2D$ as it does at a distance D from the source. Thus, the power per unit area, or intensity, I at $2D$ has reduced by a factor of four from its value at D. The acoustical effect of this is to reduce the sound pressure level (SPL) by 6 dB for the doubling of distance. Expressed mathematically

$$SPL_1 - SPL_2 = 10 \log I_1/I_r$$
$$- 10 \log I_2/I_r \ (D_2 = 2D_1)$$
$$= 10 \log I_1 - 10 \log I_r$$
$$- 10 \log I_2 + 10 \log I_r$$
$$= 10 \log I_1/I_2$$

but $I_1 = 4I_2$ because $A_2 = 4A_1$; therefore,

$$SPL_1 - SPL_2 = 10 \log (4I_2/I_2) = 10 \log 4 = 6 \text{ dB}$$

*The source of transportation noise, the motor vehicle, is actually an aggregate of several "micro" sources, including engine, exhaust, and tire-roadway interaction (among others). In turn, each of these "micro" sources can be classified as monopole, dipole, or quadrupole radiators of sound. A monopole source is one that produces sound waves through a change in mass outflow (or volume). A dipole source, on the other hand, has no volume change, because it includes two equal and opposite components. A quadrupole radiator is in effect two equal and opposite dipole radiators, with total dipole strength equal to zero. Thus a quadrupole has neither a volume change nor a change in the force on the medium. It may be assumed that motor vehicle noise is predominantly monopole in nature. A truck exhaust is an example of a monopole source, a rotating fan blade is a dipole source, and a turbulent jet is a quadrupole source.

The rule, then, for point sources is that the SPL decreases by 6 dB for every doubling of distance, and increases by 6 dB for every halving of distance.

The nature of the pure line source, however, is to conform to *cylindrical spreading* and obey the *inverse first power law*. According to this principle, the power flux (intensity) is reduced by one-half as the distance increases from D to $2D$ because the size of the area of impact of the sound power signal only doubles as the distance is doubled. Expressed mathematically

$$SPL_1 - SPL_2 = 10 \log I_1/I_2 \qquad (D_2 = 2D_1)$$

but $I_1 = 2I_2$ because $A_2 = 2A_1$.

$$SPL_1 - SPL_2 = 10 \log (2I_1/I_2) = 10 \log 2 = 3 \text{ dB}$$

For a line source, then, it may be stated that the SPL decreases 3 dB for every doubling of distance, and increases 3 dB for every halving of distance. (Note that these relationships only apply to SPL drop-off with respect to distance. They do not consider such factors as atmosphere, attenuation, absorption, and so on.)

Frequency

The cyclic frequency f of a sound or noise is determined primarily by the number of times per second that the sound pressures fluctuate between positive and negative values in a sinusoidal configuration. This quantitative measure uses the unit hertz (Hz) after H. R. Hertz (1857–1894). One Hz is equal to one cycle per second. Frequency is the reciprocal of temporal period T, which is the time required to complete one cycle on the sine curve. The practical range of human hearing extends from approximately 20 to 16,000 Hz, and is most sensitive at about 3000 Hz where the SPL actually becomes a negative quantity (see Figure 5-1).

Mathematically, frequency is defined as:

$$f = \frac{c}{\lambda} \qquad (5-6)$$

where f = cyclic frequency in Hz
c = speed of sound in the medium, in m/sec
λ = wavelength of the sound in m

As mentioned earlier, the speed of sound in air is 343 m/sec at 20°C. Thus a sound with a fre-

quency of 2000 Hz would have a wavelength of 0.17 m (0.56 ft); a frequency of 200 Hz would yield a wavelength of 1.72 m (5.6 ft); and a 20-Hz sound would have a wavelength of 17.2 m (55.8 ft).

Knowledge of wavelength as well as frequency is very important in transportation noise analysis for a number of reasons. First, the atmosphere has different absorption rates for different frequencies; second, barriers between the source and receiver are less effective against short-wavelength–dominated sounds; and third, humans simply respond differently to sounds of different frequencies.

Obviously, the noises found in the environment, especially those emanating from transportation sources, are not pure tone sounds having all their acoustic energy concentrated in a narrow frequency band. Instead, they are broad-banded in nature, meaning that acoustic energy is spread across the frequency spectrum. Transportation noises are complex composites of low frequency, mid-frequency, and high frequency sounds, but in most cases are dominated by one frequency range or another. For example, a diesel truck moving at slow speeds will emit a noise that appears to be low frequency in content because of heavy contributions from the engine and exhaust. On the other hand, an automobile moving at expressway speeds will ordinarily be dominated by the high frequency whine of its tires. If the diesel truck were moving at expressway speeds, its noise would be bi-nodal in nature, meaning that it would have large amounts of acoustic energy concentrated at the low frequencies (engine and exhaust related) and at the high frequencies (tire whine). The result would be an extremely high and offensive noise level. To adequately attenuate the truck noise, it would be necessary to attack *both* the power plant noise *and* the tire noise. If the power plant were quieted but tires allowed to whine, the truck would still be as loud as it would be if the tires were quieted but the power plant allowed to roar. The conclusion is that due to the logarithmic nature of sound pressure levels the entire vehicle must be designed for noise reduction. Transportation noise sources are by nature complex both in frequency content and in specific emission location points.

Pure tone sound sources can cause more problems than the broad-banded sources generally associated with transportation noise, especially when their acoustic energy is concentrated in the higher frequency bands (1000 Hz and above) where human hearing is more acute. A good example in transportation is the jet aircraft, which although not truly a "simple" source tends to concentrate extremely large amounts of energy in relatively narrow frequency bands in the 1000- to 10,000-Hz area. These acoustic energy concentrations are called *pure tones* and are so annoying to people that they receive special consideration in some of the more recent descriptive methodologies.

Because the frequency spectrum of noise is usually so broad, it can be very cumbersome to work with. Therefore, a method is needed to summarize the contributions of noise in the various bands and correlate the summaries with human response. This has been done quite effectively through the use of frequency weighting networks, which have the added benefit of being easily adaptable to sound measurement instrumentation. The three traditional weighting networks are the A, B, and C curves, which were designed to approximate the loudness level sensitivity of the human ear while listening to pure tones. The A curve is based on the 40-phon* contour from Figure 5-1, the B curve is based on the 70-phon contour, and the C curve is based on the 100-phon contour. It turns out that the A-weighting curve correlates very well with human response to noise, particularly in estimating the probability of hearing damage in industry, and in describing annoyance caused by traffic and aircraft noise. Table 5-2 shows the attenuations applied by the weighting networks for the frequency ranges of 10 to 20,000 Hz.

The utilization of the weighting curves is quite straightforward. A broad-banded noise in dB is separated into contributions in the various frequency ranges (octave, third, tenth-octave, narrow band, etc.), where the weighting attenuations given in Table 5-2 are applied for whichever weighting curve is desired. The newly attenuated contributions are then summed logarithmically to produce overall weighted sound levels. A sound level utilizing the A-weighting curve is expressed in terms of dB (A-weighted), or simply dBA. B-weighted sound levels are dBB,

*The number of phons is the SPL of a pure tone at 1000 Hz. See The Effects of Noise on Humans, this chapter.

TABLE 5-2. Third Octave Weighting Factors For A, B, and C Curves

Frequency (Hz)	Attenuations in (dB)		
	A	B	C
10	− 70.4	− 38.2	− 14.3
12.5	− 63.4	− 33.2	− 11.2
16	− 56.7	− 28.5	− 8.5
20	− 50.5	− 24.2	− 6.2
25	− 44.7	− 20.4	− 4.4
31.5	− 39.4	− 17.1	− 3.0
40	− 34.6	− 14.2	− 2.0
50	− 30.2	− 11.6	− 1.3
63	− 26.2	− 9.3	− 0.8
80	− 22.5	− 7.4	− 0.5
100	− 19.1	− 5.6	− 0.3
125	− 16.1	− 4.2	− 0.2
160	− 13.4	− 3.0	− 0.1
200	− 10.9	− 2.0	0
250	− 8.6	− 1.3	0
315	− 6.6	− 0.8	0
400	− 4.8	− 0.5	0
500	− 3.2	− 0.3	0
630	− 1.9	− 0.1	0
800	− 0.8	0	0
1,000	0	0	0
1,250	+0.6	0	0
1,600	+1.0	0	− 0.1
2,000	+1.2	− 0.1	− 0.2
2,500	+1.3	− 0.2	− 0.3
3,150	+1.2	− 0.4	− 0.5
4,000	+1.0	− 0.7	− 0.8
5,000	+0.5	− 1.2	− 1.3
6,300	− 0.1	− 1.9	− 2.0
8,000	− 1.1	− 2.9	− 3.0
10,000	− 2.5	− 4.3	− 4.4
12,500	− 4.3	− 6.1	− 6.2
16,000	− 6.6	− 8.4	− 8.5
20,000	− 9.3	− 11.1	− 11.2

and C-weighted, dBC. As implied earlier, transportation noises are usually expressed in terms of dBA, which best correlates human response to noise.

Time-Variance

Up until this point transportation noise has been characterized as having an intensity (magnitude) component, expressed in decibels (dB); a frequency component, expressed in hertz (Hz) and often *summarized* in A-weighting; and a temporal component, which describes the daily, weekly, monthly, and yearly fluctuations in its impact influence. The one other component that must be understood is time-variance, which attempts to describe and quantify the sporadic and random manner that transportation noises impinge on the acoustic environment. Does one, for example, use the average sound level emitted by the source as an indicator of its impact? If so, how is the one train per day or the two jet overflights per hour averaged in a meaningful way? If the peak sound level of the source is to be used, where is the significance of other slightly quieter sounds to be included? Also, do changes in human response correlate well with changes in peaks and averages? These are questions that need to be answered if transportation noise is to be completely and adequately analyzed.

Many schemes have been developed that attempt to provide the answers to the questions concerning the descriptors of time-variance, many of which have developed individualized solutions for specialized problems. The FHWA has adopted the concept of L_{10} (SPL exceeded 10 percent of a given time period), which relates to the peak condition, in describing highway noise. This is acceptable for most cases of highway noise, but there are drawbacks. First, when traffic volumes are extremely low, vehicular flow tends to become nonrandomized, causing statistical measures (L_x) like L_{10} to become unstable. Second, there is no reliable way to input nonhighway, intermittent sound sources into the L_{10} scheme.

This second drawback is not unique to the highway transportation area. Incompatibility between transportation noise source descriptors is a problem that has recently received some indirect attention at the Federal level. Congress mandated in Section 5(a) (1) of the Noise Control Act of 1972 that the EPA develop and publish criteria reflecting

the scientific knowledge most useful in indicating the kind and extent of all identifiable effects on the public health or welfare which may be expected from differing quantities and qualities of noise,

and in Section 5(a) (2) required the EPA to publish

information on the levels of environmental noise, the attainment and maintenance of which in defined areas under various conditions are requisit to protect the public health and welfare with an adequate margin of safety.

In attempting to meet these Congressional mandates, the EPA Office of Noise Abatement and Control (ONAC) has as its goal to characterize with reasonable accuracy the noise exposure of entire neighborhoods, where the range of existing noise levels is wide, "so as to prevent extremes of noise exposure at any given time, and to detect unfavorable trends in the future noise climate." Rather than develop a new descriptive system to attain this goal, the ONAC selected the concept of the equivalent sound pressure level, L_{eq} (usually A-weighted), which was developed both in the United States and Germany over a period of years. The L_{eq} was used by the U.S. Air Force in 1955 for its report on criteria for short-term exposure of personnel to high intensity jet aircraft noise, which spawned the 1956 Air Force Regulation on Hazardous Noise Exposure, and in 1957 by the Air Force in its Planning Guide for noise from aircraft operations.

Equivalent sound pressure level (L_{eq}) is formulated in terms of the equivalent steady-state noise level which in a defined period of time contains the same noise (acoustic) energy as a time-varying noise during the same period of time. The L_{eq} is an *energy summation integration*, and as such does not rely on statistical parameters. It is totally plausible to calculate an L_{eq} for a single locomotive operation in a given hour, an L_{eq} for two aircraft operations in the same hour, an L_{eq} for a steady highway traffic flow for the same hour, and an L_{eq} from some industrial noise sources for the same hour, and furthermore to determine an overall L_{eq} for all of these sources. This capability is a significant advantage over the FHWA's L_{10} scheme, which cannot adequately consider single-event noises.

Equivalent sound level has similar advantages over the collection of esoteric descriptive systems used in the recent past by the aviation industry to quantify aircraft noise impacts. The systems that describe noise emissions from multiple operations of aircraft, such as Composite Noise Rating (CNR), Noise Exposure Forecast (NEF), Aircraft Sound Description System

(ASDS), and Community Noise Equivalent Level (CNEL), as well as from single events like Perceived Noise Level (PNL) and Effective Perceived Noise Level (EPNL), are quite complex and difficult to compare. The L_{eq} and its corollary L_{dn} (day-night equivalent sound level), on the other hand, offer a system that is quite compatible with all aircraft operations and other sources.

Mathematically expressed, the *equivalent sound level* is

$$L_{eq} = 10 \log \left[\frac{1}{(t_2 - t_1)} \int_{t_1}^{t_2} \frac{p^2(t)}{p_r^2} \right] dt \quad (5\text{-}7)$$

where $p(t)$ is the time varying sound pressure, p_r is the reference pressure, and t_1 and t_2 are the limits of the time period in question. Performing the integration in Equation 5-7 and converting to SPL in dBA yields Equation 5-8.

$$L_{eq} = 10 \log \left[\frac{\sum_{i=1}^{n} f_i \cdot 10^{10/SPL_i}}{\sum_{i=1}^{n} f_i} \right] \quad (5\text{-}8)$$

where f_i is equal to the number of occurrences at SPL_i.

The day-night equivalent sound level L_{dn} is simply a 24-hour L_{eq} with a 10-dBA penalty added for nightime noise from the hours of 10:00 p.m. to 7:00 a.m. This is to account for the higher sensitivity of people to noise at night.

The Effects of Noise on Humans

Transportation noise has now been defined both quantitatively and, to a limited degree, qualitatively, through discussion of the concepts of time-variance. By knowing the physical mechanisms involved in the magnitude, frequency, temporal distribution, and time-variance of transportation noise, one has a preliminary view of the problem. It is necessary, however, to understand the physiological effects that transportation noise, and sound in general, have on people. Obviously this is quite a complex and involved topic and there are many physicians, engineers, and scientists who devote their entire careers to its study. There have been many volumes written concerning the health effects of noise, and it is not the intent of this chapter to add to those volumes. Therefore, a very brief summary of certain aspects is presented.

There are six basic effects of noise that can be quantitatively related to physical characteristics in ways that are fairly universal for all people. They are

1. The masking of unwanted sounds
2. Auditory fatigue and hearing damage
3. Excessive "loudness"
4. Bothersomeness, or "noisiness"
5. Startling noises
6. Infrasonic vibration

Transportation activities by their nature continually act as generators of each of these effects. For example, noise from highway traffic at close distances makes understanding speech difficult in most outdoor situations of work and recreation and is highly annoying where serenity and privacy are desirable (like backyards of residences). Jet aircraft noise levels are of sufficient magnitude as to cause pain and, sometimes, temporary threshold shift in communities adjacent to airports. Teachers and students in schools under flight paths have become accustomed to a phenomenon known as "jet pause," where teaching must stop while aircraft pass overhead.

The Human Ear

Figure 5-2 shows two interpretative schematic diagrams of the human ear. After being slightly displaced by the sound pressure wavefront, the air particles filling the auditory canal are driven against the tympanic membrane, which is stretched across the passage leading from the external ear toward the brain. The tympanic membrane then begins vibrating, transmitting motion to the ends of the auditory nerve. Traveling along the auditory nerve, the vibrations make their way to the brain, where they are converted to a sensation of sound.

The outer and middle ear have the function not only of transmitting the pressure wavefront to the inner ear, but also of protecting the inner ear from having to deal with sounds outside its capacity. The middle ear can prevent the transmission of pressure waves having rise times longer than 200 milliseconds by the action of the eustachian tube (or even by rupturing the eardrum). The mass and stiffness of the ossicles effectively prevent transmission of a pressure wave with a rise time less than 50 microseconds

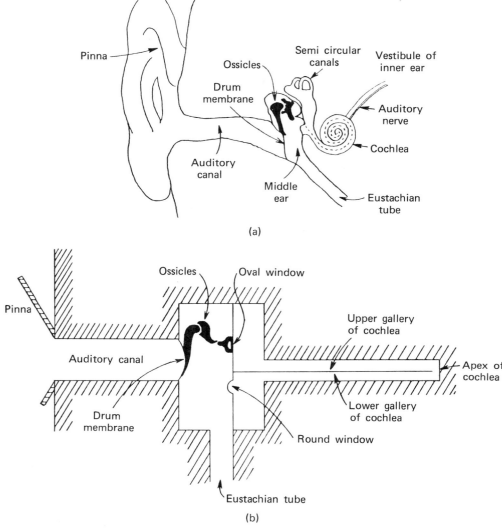

Figure 5-2. The human ear. (a) Sketch of hearing mechanism. (b) Schematic representation of hearing mechanism.

(μs). This 50-μs rise time sets the upper limiting frequency for humans at 20,000 Hz. The lower limiting frequency is approximately 5 Hz, which is in the transition region of velocity for the perilymphatic fluid in the cochlea. Typically, the human hearing range is taken to be 20 to 20,000 Hz.

The snail-shaped cochlea contains a longitudinal partition known as the basilar membrane in which the highly complex Organ of Corti rests. The Organ of Corti has imbedded in it approximately 23,500 evenly spaced sensory hair cells containing tiny cilia which are contained in the lower side of the basilar membrane. These hair cells are connected to nerve fibers which are joined to the auditory nerve, which in turn leads to the brain. Although the hair cells are evenly distributed along the basilar membrane, not all portions of the membrane have identical frequency response.

Human response to differing frequency ranges may be explained as follows. When a pressure wavefront impinges on the tympanic membrane, the stapes (one of the bones of the ossicles) moves inward. This action displaces the fluid in the cochlea, with the round window moving in response to fluid incompressibility. The vibratory movement of the stapes yields some deflection of the basilar membrane and expansion of the round window. If the movement of the stapes is very slow (1 Hz or so), almost no deflection will occur in the basilar membrane. Pressure will be relieved by expansion of the round window, since the impedance to fluid flow at the apex of the cochlea is very small. At higher frequencies, when the stapes moves inward, the basilar membrane deflects in a transverse manner. As frequency increases, the deflections occur nearer to the stapes, resulting in a type of hydraulic short ciruit. The net effect of all this is, as shown in Figure 5-1, human hearing is less sensitive at the lower frequencies, peaks in sensitivity in the 1000- to 3000-Hz range, and then trails off at the higher frequencies. This phenomenon is known as the Place Principle, and is discussed in detail in many standard references.

Loudness and Annoyance

Transportation noises, as well as the other sounds found in the environment, are very complex in nature and, as such, require some additional interpretation concerning impact on humans. Performing the A-weighting procedure on a sound pressure level gives a good approximation of how people receive sound, but it does not really indicate to what extent noise is judged to be loud or annoying. For example, if two sound levels of 60 dB are combined, the resultant level is 63 dB. However, a sample of human subjects would barely be able to discern any difference in the 63 or 60 dB levels, as far as "loudness" is concerned. Extensive testing has shown that it takes an increase of 10 dB before an apparent doubling of loudness is observed. To quantify this phenomenon, two measures of "loudness" have been developed: *loudness level* and *loudness*. Each is related to a reference sound pressure level at 1000 Hz.

Loudness level is defined by the American National Standards Institute as the median sound pressure level in dB of a free progressive wave of 1000 Hz as determined by a sample of qualified listeners in a number of trials to be equally loud. The units for loudness level are *phons*. Loudness, on the other hand, is expressed in *sones*. One sone is defined as the loudness level of 40 phons (40 dB at 1000 Hz). A loudness of 2 sones represents a loudness level (50 phons) deemed twice as loud as a 1-sone sound. The loudness of any sound that is judged to be n times as loud as

the one sone sound is n sones. Because of the tendency of human hearing to attenuate low and high frequencies, a pure tone of 40 dB at 1000 Hz is likely to be judged equally loud as an 89-dB tone at 20 Hz, a 52-dB tone at 100 Hz, and a 46-dB tone at 10,000 Hz. Equal loudness contours giving this type of information have been developed and are shown in Figure 5-1.

A major limitation on the concept of loudness is that it deals with pure tones, which are not characteristic of the sounds in the environment. There have been several procedures developed which attempt to relate the intensity and spectral content of noise to human response, which give an indication of the *annoyance*, or perceived noisiness, of the noise.

The primary difference between loudness and annoyance is assumed to be the spectral diversity and duration characteristics considered as annoyance. The five significant features of annoyance are

1. Spectrum content and level
2. Spectrum complexity
3. Duration of the total sound
4. Duration of the increase in level prior to the peak level of nonimpulsive sounds
5. The maximum level reached by the impulsive sounds

Equal noisiness contours, which are analogous to equal loudness contours, were developed in 1943 by S.S. Stevens to predict response to complex sounds. Equal noisiness values are expressed with the unit *noys*, and follow the same concept as sones do for loudness. That is, a sound of 2 noys is deemed twice as annoying as 1 noy, and so on.

Using similar methods as those converting sones to phons, the annoyance level, or *perceived* noise level (PNL), can be determined. The PNL is expressed in the units of PNdB, and was first used to correlate response to aircraft flyovers. The PNL has been refined to account for the apparently magnified annoyance of discrete frequency components of jet noise as well as the greater annoyance of longer duration flyovers. The modifications have brought into being the new name *Effective Perceived Noise Level* (EPNL), expressed in EPNdB. The PNL and EPNL range from 11 to 17 dB higher than the SPL (dBA) with an average of about 13 higher.

HIGHWAY NOISE

FHPA 7-7-3, *Procedures for Abatement of Highway Traffic Noise and Construction Noise* [see Chapter 3 (Noise-Related Regulations)] sets forth an analysis framework for considering highway noise impacts. The five steps of this framework are

1. Identification of existing activities, developed lands, and undeveloped lands for which development is planned, designed, and programmed which may be affected by noise from the highway.
2. Prediction of future traffic noise levels.
3. Determination of existing noise levels.
4. Determination of traffic noise impacts.
5. Examination and evaluation of alternative noise abatement measures for reducing or eliminating the noise impacts.

The principal problems in this framework are the predictions (2), and the abatement analysis (5).

Prediction of Highway Noise Levels

Prediction methodologies and models have evolved from the late 1960s, primarily through the funding efforts of the National Cooperative Highway Research Program (NCHRP). The NCHRP is the funded research arm of the Transportation Research Board (see below).

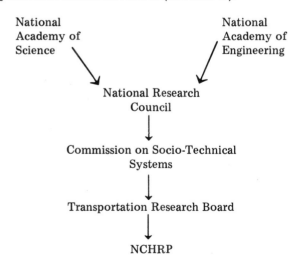

The following NCHRP reports represent the evolution of prediction methodologies and the expenditure of many thousands of research dollars.

NCHRP Report Number	Title (year of publication)
78	Highway Noise, Measurement, Simulation and Mixed Reaction (1969)
117	Highway Noise, A Design Guide for Highway Engineers (1971)
144	Highway Noise, A Field Evaluation of Traffic Noise Prediction Measures (1973)
173	Highway Noise, Generation and Control (1976)
174	Highway Noise, A Design Guide for Prediction and Control (1976)

The first prediction model used extensively was that found in NCHRP Report 117. The model utilized a statistical approach, in that L_x values (L_{50} and L_{10}) were the only descriptors found in the calculations. The noise source data base upon which the model was founded was quite small and did not adequately represent actual conditions. For example, the model assumed that all vehicles on a highway could be classified as either automobiles *or* trucks, with the following source emission levels.

$$L = 16 + 30 \log S^* \text{ dBA} \qquad \text{(automobiles)}$$

$$(5-9)$$

$$L = 82 \text{ dBA} \qquad \text{(trucks)} \quad (5-10)$$

Thus, the model assumed that automobile emission levels had a speed dependency of 9 dBA per doubling of speed and that truck emission levels were *independent* of speed. Later studies indicated that both of these assumptions were incorrect and also that it is not proper to assign all vehicles as either automobiles or trucks. A third category of vehicles, *medium trucks*, has since been documented, which is necessary for effective modeling of the highway traffic stream.

The experiences of many state highway agencies during the 1970s clearly demonstrated that additional work beyond that in NCHRP Report 117 was necessary. The FHWA became directly involved in the research effort and pro-

*S is speed in mph.

duced contributions which were quite significant in developing a new generation of prediction models.

The research effort sponsored by the NCHRP produced Report 174, a *Revised Design Guide* (RDG) which incorporated the medium-truck concept, replaced the L_x initial descriptor with L_{eq}, and generally laid the foundation for the new generation of models. The source emission levels used in the RDG were

$$L = 18 + 30 \log S \text{ dBA} \qquad \text{(automobiles)}$$
$$(5\text{-}11)$$

$$L = 28 + 30 \log S \text{ dBA} \qquad \text{(medium trucks)}$$
$$(5\text{-}12)$$

$$L = 86 \text{ dBA} \qquad \text{(heavy trucks)}$$
$$(5\text{-}13)$$

The RDG had some similarities with another model which was developed independently of the NCHRP effort. In 1972, the Transportation Systems Center (TSC), the research and development arm of the U.S. DOT, published its *Manual for Highway Noise Prediction*, popularly known as the TSC Model. This model was L_{eq}-based, but included only two types of vehicles: automobiles and trucks. The source emission levels used in the TSC model were

$$L = 5 + 38 \log S \text{ dBA} \qquad \text{(automobiles)} \quad (5\text{-}14)$$

$$L = 87 \text{ dBA} \qquad \text{(trucks)} \quad (5\text{-}15)$$

While the TSC Model was perhaps more technically sound than the NCHRP 117 model, it never gained wide acceptance by the state highway agencies because of its tendency to overpredict noise levels. It did, however, provide at least a part of the foundation for the new generation of models.

As a way of summarizing the experiences gained in highway noise prediction, the following needs were generally recognized as essential in the development of the new generation of models.

1. A large data base for source emission levels.
2. A mechanism to eliminate variable spatial decay rates as a function of traffic flow density.
3. A means to consider excess attenuation by absorptive ground covers.

4. An L_{eq}-based descriptor system to reduce statistical dependences.
5. A *fully* defined and validated theoretical equation for noise emission and propagation.

The FHWA Model

Realizing that several of these needs had not been met by the research efforts sponsored by the NCHRP, the FHWA undertook the task of developing the new generation of models as an in-house program. The result was the publication of Report FHWA-RD-77-108, *FHWA Highway Traffic Noise Prediction Model*, which is commonly referred to as the *FHWA Model*.

The basic emission and propagation equation for the FHWA Model is mathematically stated as

$$L_{eq}(h)\,i = (\overline{L_0})_{E_i} + 10 \log \left(\frac{N_i \pi D_0}{S_i T} \right)$$
$$+ 10 \log \left(\frac{D_0}{D} \right)^{1+\alpha}$$
$$+ 10 \log \left(\frac{\psi_\alpha(\phi_1, \phi_2)}{\pi} \right) + \Delta s$$
$$(5\text{-}16)$$

where $L_{eq}(h)\,i$ is the hourly equivalent sound level of the ith class of vehicles.

$(\overline{L_0})_{E_i}$	the reference energy mean emission level of the ith class of vehicles
N_i	the number of vehicles in the ith class passing a specified point during some specified time period (1 hour)
D	the perpendicular distance, in meters, from the centerline of the traffic lane to the observer
D_0	the reference distance, 15 m
S_i	the average speed of the ith class of vehicles, and is measured in kilometers per hour
T	the time period over which L_{eq} is computed (1 hour)
α	a site parameter whose values depend on site conditions
ψ	a symbol representing a function used for segment adjustments; i.e., an adjustment for finite-length roadways

ϕ_1, ϕ_2 roadway angles of acoustic influence which assist in locating roadway segments spatially

Δs the attenuation, in dBA, provided by some type of shielding such as barriers, rows of houses, densely wooded areas, etc.

The grouped parameters in Equation 5-16 represent

Reference Energy Mean Emission Level	$(\overline{L_0})_{E_i}$
+	
Traffic Flow Adjustment	$10 \log \left(\dfrac{N_i \pi D_0}{S_i T} \right)$
+	
Distance Adjustment	$10 \log \left(\dfrac{D_0}{D} \right)^{1+\alpha}$
+	
Finite Roadway Adjustment	$10 \log \left(\dfrac{\psi_\alpha(\phi_1, \phi_2)}{\pi} \right)$
+	
Shielding Adjustment	Δs

When sequentially added, these parameters produce an hourly L_{eq} value for the ith vehicle class. In practice, this means an L_{eq} value for automobiles, $L_{eq_{Au}}$; an L_{eq} value for medium trucks, $L_{eq_{MT}}$; and an L_{eq} value for heavy trucks, $L_{eq_{HT}}$. The overall L_{eq} for the traffic mix, $L_{eq_{ToT}}$, is then obtained by decibel, or *logarithmic*, addition.

$$L_{eq_{ToT}} = \sum_{sum}^{dB} L_{eq} (Au + MT + HT)$$

$$L_{eq_{ToT}} = 10 \log (10^{L_{eq_{Au}}/10} + 10^{L_{eq_{MT}}/10} + 10^{L_{eq_{HT}}/10}) \qquad (5\text{-}17)$$

See Equation 5-5.

$(\overline{L_0})_{E_i}$

In order to meet the need to have a large data base available for source emission level determination, the FHWA performed an extensive measurement program in four states spread across the country. The data gathered in this program is fully reported and analyzed in *Highway Noise Measurements for Verification of Prediction*

Models, DOT-TSC-OST-78-2/DOT-TSC-FHWA-78-1, and *Statistical Analysis of FHWA Traffic Noise Prediction Data*, FHWA-RD-78-64.

Actually, this measurement program was instrumental in modifying the direction in which highway noise prediction methodologies were heading. The concept of a *mean* emission level was introduced, which provided the mechanism to eliminate the variable spatial decay rate as a function of traffic density (flow rate). The previous models had utilized *maximum* (passby) emission levels for individual vehicles. As discussed earlier in this chapter, an individual vehicle is a *point* source, with a spatial decay rate of 6 dB per distance doubling. As flow rates increase, the traffic stream becomes a *line* source, with a spatial decay rate of 3 dB per distance doubling. In practice, most traffic stream densities are somewhere between point and line sources, with resultant decay rates of 6 to 3 dB. Some models, most notably the NCHRP 117, assumed a *modified* line source (4 to 4.5 dB); however, the issue of variability in decay rate had consistently been a problem in overall model accuracy and flexibility.

This problem was solved through the replacement of the *maximum emission level* with the *energy mean emission level*. This replacement meant that instead of developing the vehicle emission level L by measuring a series of maximum passby noise levels, energy mean emission levels $\overline{L_E}$ were to be developed by measuring equivalent sound levels (L_{eq}) of vehicular passby events. Consider for example Figure 5-3, which shows a typical vehicle passby event measured simultaneously at two distances, 50 ft and

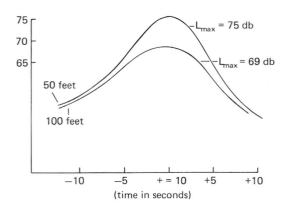

Figure 5-3.   Effects of distance on peak pass-by sound level.

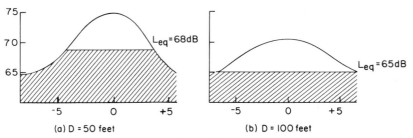

Figure 5-4.

100 ft. As one would expect the differences between the maximum (or peak) levels measured at time = 0 seconds is 6 dB (because one vehicle is a point source), or 75 dB to 69 dB.

Figure 5-4 shows the same vehicular passby, but with L_{eq} calculated for the highest 10-sec interval at each distance. The significant point to note is that while L_{max} dropped 6 dB as the distance doubled, the L_{eq}, or energy mean emission level, dropped by only 3 dB, 68 – 65.

The conclusion is that if a prediction model was developed upon a source data base of energy mean emission levels *the spatial decay rate would always be 3 dB per distance doubling*, notwithstanding traffic densities. The FHWA Model is based upon energy mean emission levels and therefore this conclusion applies to it.

The energy mean emission levels developed as part of the FHWA measurement program are termed *national reference* energy mean emission levels, because they are generally applicable to the entire country, and because they were measured at the reference distance of 15 m (approximately 50 ft). The values for the levels are

$$(\overline{L_0})_{E\,Au} = 38.1 \log S^* - 2.4 \text{ dBA}$$

$$\text{(automobiles)} \quad (5\text{-}18)$$

$$(\overline{L_0})_{E\,MT} = 33.9 \log S^* + 16.4 \text{ dBA}$$

$$\text{(medium trucks)} \quad (5\text{-}19)$$

$$(\overline{L_0})_{E\,HT} = 24.6 \log S^* + 38.5 \text{ dBA}$$

$$\text{(heavy trucks)} \quad (5\text{-}20)$$

Figure 5-5 is a graphical representation of Equations 5-18 through 5-20. A significant departure from previous source emission levels is the speed dependency of heavy trucks. Equation 5-20 indicates that this dependency is 7.4 dBA per speed doubling.

*S is in metric units, km/hr.

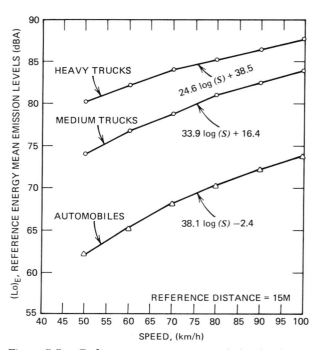

Figure 5-5.   Reference energy mean emission levels as a function of speed. Sources: ○, *Statistical Analysis of FHWA Traffic Noise Data*, FHWA-RD-64; △, *Update of TSC Highway Traffic Noise Prediction Code (1974)*, FHWA-RD-77-19.

$10 \log (N_i \pi D_0 / S_i T)$

Having now fully defined the noise emission characteristics of the individual vehicle, it is a relatively straightforward task to assimilate that vehicle into the traffic stream. This is accomplished through the application of the traffic flow adjustment. Three of the five subparameters in this adjustment are constants, with π representing an integration constant for the assumed infinite roadway segment (acoustic angle of influence is π, or 180 degrees). D_0 represents the reference distance of 15 m, and T, the time period, is 1 hr.

The remaining parts of the parameter, $10 \log \cdot (N_i/S_i)$, relate quite consistently with the physical mechanisms discussed at the beginning of the chapter. If the traffic volume, or source strength, N_i were to be doubled to become $2N_i$, the result would be a 3 dB increase in L_{eq}.

$$10 \log 2N_i = 10 \log N_i = 10 (.3) + 10 \log N_i$$

$$= 3 + 10 \log N_i$$

Conversely, if speed were doubled, and everything else held constant, the result would be a 3-dB *decrease* in L_{eq}.

$$10 \log \frac{1}{2S_i} = 10 \log \frac{1}{2} + 10 \log \frac{1}{S_i}$$

$$= 10 (-.3) + 10 \log \frac{1}{S_i}$$

$$= -3 + 10 \log \frac{1}{S_i}$$

The interesting reason for this decrease is that, with volume held constant, doubling the vehicular speed actually *reduces* the amount of time that each vehicle acoustically influences a given receiver of sound. This reduction would of course be more than offset by the increase in $(L_0)_{E_i}$ (11.5 dB per speed doubling for automobiles, 10.2 dB for medium trucks, and 7.4 dB for heavy trucks).

$10 \log (D_0/D)^{1+\alpha}$

The distance adjustment, or spatial decay rate, has been previously established to be 3 dB per distance doubling. Ignoring the subparameter α for the moment, if D is doubled,

$$10 \log \frac{1}{2D} = 10 \log \frac{1}{2} + 10 \log \frac{1}{D}$$

$$= 10 (-.3) + 10 \log \frac{1}{D}$$

$$= -3 + 10 \log D$$

This decay rate is applicable to only those effects from distance or geometrical spreading (diffusion of the sound source strength). There are situations, however, where other factors bring about *excess attenuation* of the sound, over and above distance considerations. The most important of these factors in the highway context is absorption due to a *soft* ground cover.

Experience has shown that this absorption adds an additional 1.5 dB per distance doubling to the decay rate. This is modeled in the parameter by assigning α a value of 0.5, thus providing

$$\left(\frac{D_0}{D}\right)^{1+.5} = 10 \log \left(\frac{D_0}{D}\right)^{1.5} = 15 \log \left(\frac{D_0}{D}\right)$$

Doubling the distance yields

$$15 \log \frac{1}{2D} = 15 \log \frac{1}{2} + 15 \log D$$

$$= 15 (-.3) + 15 \log \frac{1}{D}$$

$$= -4.5 + 15 \log \frac{1}{D}$$

The total spatial decay rate for an acoustically soft site, then, is ordinarily taken as 4.5 dB per distance doubling. It should be noted that the FHWA Model does allow for α to be assigned values other than 0 or 0.5, depending upon the facts at hand. Table 5-3 illustrates the criteria to be followed in determining whether a site is acoustically hard or soft.

$10 \log \psi_\alpha (\phi_1, \phi_2)/\pi$

The original assumption in the FHWA Model is that the vehicles are operating on a roadway of infinite length. Therefore, the acoustic angle of influence for any given observer would be 180 degrees, as shown in Figure 5-6a. For a finite-length highway segment, however, this angle would be *less than* 180 degrees (Figure 5-6b). Accordingly, an adjustment is needed to account for the *finiteness* of the segment.

The acoustic theory applicable in this case is found in Equation 5-4 which indicates that the intensity (or source strength) is related to intensity level (or sound level) logarithmically. That is, when source strength is halved, sound level is reduced by 3 dB. If an infinite highway ($\theta = 180°$) is assumed to have a source strength of 0.5. Thus,

$$\text{Adjustment} = 10 \log \frac{0.5}{1} = 10 \log (.5)$$

$$= 10 (-.3) = -3$$

$$\text{Adjustment} = 10 \log \frac{90°}{180°} = 10 \log (.5) = -.3$$

TABLE 5-3. Criteria for Selection of Drop-off Rate per Doubling of Distance

Situation		Drop-Off Rate	Site Condition
1.	All situations in which the source or the receiver is located 3 m above the ground or whenever the line-of-sight[a] averages more than 3 m above the ground	3 dBA ($\alpha = 0$)	Hard
2.	All situations involving propagation over the top of a barrier 3 m or more in height	3 dBA ($\alpha = 0$)	Hard
3.	Where the height of the line-of-sight is less than 3 m and		
	(a) There is a clear (unobstructed) view of the highway, the ground is hard and there are no intervening structures	3 dBA ($\alpha = 0$)	Hard
	(b) The view of the roadway is interrupted by isolated buildings, clumps of bushes, scattered trees, or the intervening ground is soft or covered with vegetation	4.5 dBA ($\alpha = \frac{1}{2}$)	Soft

[a]The line-of-sight (L/S) is a direct line between the noise source and the observer.

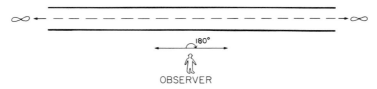

Figure 5-6(a). Infinite roadway noise source.

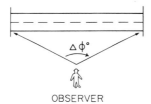

Figure 5-6(b). Finite roadway noise source.

A general relationship, then, may be stated (for hard site only):

$$\text{Finite length adjustment} = 10 \log \frac{\Delta\phi}{\pi}$$

(hard site only)   (5-21)

where $\Delta\phi$ = angle of acoustic influence.

When hard site conditions prevail, $\alpha = 0$, and the parameter $\psi_\alpha(\phi_1, \phi_2)/\pi$ becomes $\psi_0(\phi_1, \phi_2)/\pi$. As is seen below, $\Delta\phi = \phi_2 - \phi$, which allows the relationship to be written $\psi_0(\Delta\phi)/\pi$, or simply $\Delta\phi/\pi$.

Soft site conditions, however, greatly compli-

cate matters because of the excess attenuation resulting from ground surface absorption. In such cases, it is important to locate the finite segment spatially with respect to the observer in order to calculate this excess attenuation. It should be understood that excess attenuation accounted for in the distance adjustment discussed above [$10 \log (D_0/D)^{1+\alpha}$] concerns only the perpendicular distance between the observer and the segment (or its extension). The finite roadway adjustment, on the other hand, accounts for ground area directly between the observer and segment. Figure 5-7 attempts to illustrate this point.

The most convenient way to locate finite segments spatially is to adopt a sign (+ or −) notation for the angles ϕ_1 and ϕ_2. The FHWA

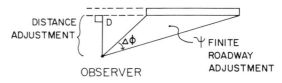

Figure 5-7. Distance and finite roadway adjustments.

Model notation defines ϕ_1 as the angle between the perpendicular and the left end of the segment and ϕ_2 as the angle between the perpendicular and the right end of the segment. Clockwise is positive (+), and counterclockwise is negative. As Figure 5-8 indicates, only three cases are possible: ϕ_1^-, ϕ_2^+; ϕ_1^-, ϕ_2^-; or ϕ_1^+, ϕ_2^+.

Once the angles ϕ_1 and ϕ_2 have been identified, the determination of the finite roadway adjustment (where $\alpha = \frac{1}{2}$) is a straightforward task. Figure 5-9 provides the chart from which the adjustment is derived.

As an example, Figure 5-10 shows a segment with angles $\phi_1 = +30°$ and $\phi_2 = +80°$. The finite roadway adjustment, from Figure 5-9, is -7 dBA.

Shielding Δs

The placement of an obstruction between the highway and the observer will *shield* the observer and therefore lower the sound level. Shielding may take the form of densely wooded vegetative strips, which will ordinarily yield attenuation values of 5 dBA per 100 ft of depth, up to a maximum of 10 dBA. To obtain this attenuation, the density must be such that there is no line of sight possible through the woods, and the trees must be at least 15 ft high.

In most instances where the shielding adjustment is used, solid barriers or walls are involved. The acoustic phenomenon governing *barrier attenuation* is known as *Fresnel* diffraction, which analytically defines the amount of acoustic energy loss encountered when sound rays are required to travel over and around a barrier. Figure 5-11 illustrates the concept of *path length difference*, δ.

The path length difference $\delta = A + B - C$, and is the extra distance the sound travels as a result of the barrier. Once δ is known, the Fresnel

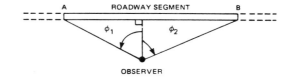

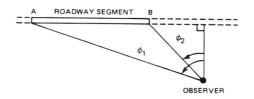

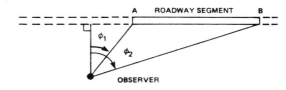

Figure 5-8.   Roadway segment angle designations.

number N may be calculated as

$$N = 2\frac{\delta}{\lambda} \qquad (5\text{-}22)$$

A composite wavelength λ for traffic noise is usually taken to be 2.2 ft. Thus, a barrier with $\delta = 3$ ft would have $N = 2.73$.

Given the Fresnel number N, barrier attenuation may be determined through the application of Equation 5-23, *for individual vehicles*. This limitation (for individual vehicles) must be enforced because N is dependent upon δ, which is the *maximum* path length difference. δ occurs when the vehicle is closest to the observer (at the perpendicular point). The Fresnel number corresponding to its maximum path length difference δ is designated N_0. Barrier attenuation at the perpendicular point for the individual vehicle is given as

$$\Delta = \begin{cases} 0 & N_0 < -0.63 \\[2ex] 5 \quad + 20 \log \dfrac{\sqrt{2\pi|N_0|}\,\phi}{\tan\sqrt{2\pi|N_0|}\,\phi} & -0.63 \leqslant N_0 \leqslant 0 \\[3ex] 5 \quad + 20 \log \dfrac{\sqrt{2\pi(N_0)}\,\phi}{\tanh\sqrt{2\pi(N_0)}\,\phi} & 0 < N_0 \leqslant 16.5 \\[2ex] 20 & N_0 > 16.5 \end{cases} \qquad (5\text{-}23)$$

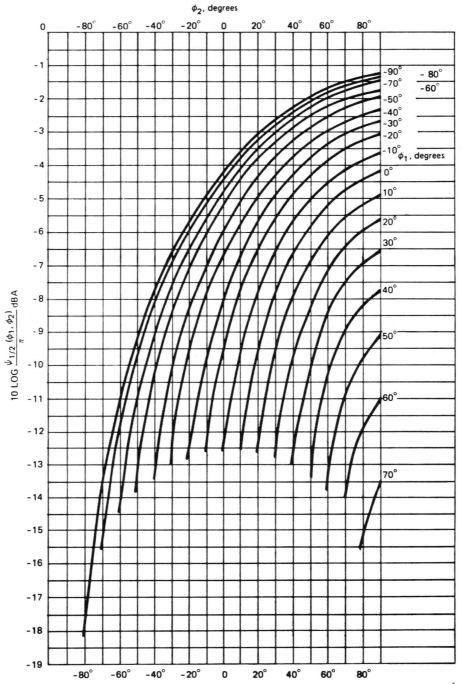

Figure 5-9. Adjustment factor for finite-length roadways for absorbing sites ($\alpha = \frac{1}{2}$).
Source: FHWA-RD-77-108.

Equation 5-23 is applicable to thin vertical barriers. Because natural earth berms are more effective in noise reduction, a supplemental 3 dBA attenuation is to be added to Δ when the barrier is a berm.

The value of N_0 varies significantly depending upon the type of vehicle involved, because source heights vary from 0 ft (autos) to 8 ft (heavy trucks). Accurate calculations, therefore, must be made for each source type in the traffic-mix (see Figure 5-12). Computer versions of the FHWA Model do this internally.

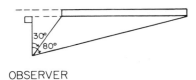

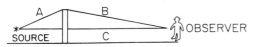

Figure 5-10. Finite roadway adjustment for angles $\phi_1 = +30°$ and $\phi_2 = +80°$ is -7 dBA (from Figure 5-9).

Figure 5-11. Path length difference.

Figure 5-12. Varying source heights.

In actual operating conditions, of course, the interest is in the effect of shielding upon the overall traffic stream and its L_{eq}, rather than the individual vehicle. Equation 5-23 is not adequate to address this situation, because it is based upon the idea of *maximum* path length difference, which occurs only at the perpendicular point. The solution to this problem is to examine simultaneously the attenuation values of all the vehicles up and down the roadway segment with regard to the receivers. This is accomplished through the integration of Equation 5-24, once each for automobiles, medium trucks, and heavy trucks.

$$\Delta_{B_i} = 10 \log \left[\frac{1}{\phi_R - \phi_L} \int_{\phi_L}^{\phi_R} 10^{-\Delta_i/10} \, d\phi \right]$$

(5-24)

where ΔB_i is the attenuation for the ith class of vehicles, and ϕ_R and ϕ_L are the angles measured from the perpendicular to the right and left ends of the barriers, respectively.

where Δ_i is the point source attenuation for the ith class of vehicles.

$N_i = (N_0)_i \cos \phi$

N_0 is the Fresnel number determined along the perpendicular line between the source and receiver

N_{0_i} is the Fresnel number of the ith class of vehicles determined along the perpendicular line between the source and receiver

An infinitely long barrier would have $\phi_L = -90°$ and $\phi_R = +90°$. Solutions of Equations 5-24 and 5-25 for such a barrier yield the curves shown in Figure 5-13. It may be deduced from those curves that when $N = 0$, $\Delta_B = 5$ dBA. That is, when the barrier *just grazes* the line between the source and receiver, a significant attenuation (due to diffraction) still occurs. In fact, part *b* of the figure shows that detectable attenuation still occurs when N is negative.

Rather than require the solution of the very complex and cumbersome Equation 5-24 for each possible set of angles Δ_L and Δ_R, the FHWA has computer-generated 60 pages of tabular results which appear in the appendix to the FHWA Model (Report FHWA-RD-77-108). Since effective barrier analysis and design ordinarily requires the utilization of a computer version of the FHWA Model, such as STAMINA, those tables will not be reproduced here.

Since the early 1970s, many state highway agencies and private developers have constructed highway noise barriers. The overwhelming majority of these barriers fall into one of these categories.

1. Concrete
   (a) Block
   (b) Cast-in-place
   (c) Precast post and panel or free standing

$$\Delta_i = \begin{cases} 0 & N_i < -0.63 \\[2mm] 5 + 20 \log \dfrac{\sqrt{2\pi |N_0|_i \cos \phi}}{\tan \sqrt{2\pi |N_0|_i \cos \phi}} & -0.63 \leqslant N_i \leqslant 0 \\[2mm] 5 + 20 \log \dfrac{\sqrt{2\pi (N_0)_i \cos \phi}}{\tanh \sqrt{2\pi (N_0)_i \cos \phi}} & 0 < N_i \leqslant 16.5 \\[2mm] 20 & N_i > 16.5 \end{cases}$$

(5-25)

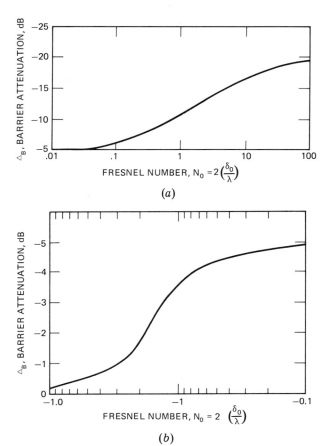

Figure 5-13. (*a*) Barrier attenuation vs. Fresnel Number, N_0, for *infinitely* long barriers. (*b*) Barrier attenuation vs. negative Fresnel Number, N_0, for *infinitely* long barriers.

2. Wood
    (a) Plywood
    (b) Glue-laminated
    (c) Tongue-in-groove
    (d) Ship-lap
3. Metal
    (a) Single skin
    (b) Double skin
    (c) Absorptive face
4. Berm
    (a) Earth only
    (b) Combination with concrete, wood, or metal

California, with approximately 70 miles constructed by the Department of Transportation and many more by developers, leads the nation in terms of mileage of noise barriers. Roughly, 90 percent of California's walls are concrete block. The state of Minnesota has the second largest barrier program.

Appendix 5 contains a series of photographs of selected barriers from around the nation.

Stamina 1.0

The FHWA Model has been computerized in three separate formats. The first is for use on a hand-held, programmable calculator such as the TI-59. These calculator programs are available from the FHWA and will not be discussed here.

The Level I version of FHWA Model computer methodology is called SNAP 1.0 (Simplified Noise Analysis Program). This version is quite limited in its ability to define site geometry and in its versatility in alternative abatement analyses. SNAP 1.0, therefore, is not recommended for use in many situations.

A much more powerful tool is the Level II version, STAMINA 1.0 (Standard Method In Noise Analysis), referred to here simply as STAMINA. The program is fully described in the report FHWA-RD-78-138, *User's Manual: FHWA Level 2 Highway Traffic Noise Prediction Model*. The manual, as well as the program itself, is available from the FHWA, Washington, D.C. 20590.

STAMINA is a coordinate-system–based program which simultaneously considers L_{eq} values at up to 15 receivers from as many as 20 separate roadways. Each of the roadways may contain as many as 10 straight-line segments. In addition, up to 20 noise barriers, each with as many as 10 straight-line segments, may be included.

Information is introduced into STAMINA through the use of six data blocks. These are

1. Program initialization parameters
2. Roadway parameters
3. Barrier parameters
4. Ground cover parameters
5. Receiver parameters
6. Alpha input parameters

Prior to supplying the information for the six data blocks, the user may insert an *option card*, which will modify certain standard assumptions in the program. These standard assumptions are that the input data and output results will be in the English system of units, and that all barriers will be reflective. These can be changed to metric in and/or out, and absorptive, respectively.

Program Initialization Parmeters. This data block may contain as many as nine cards. These are

Card Number	Description
1	Block identification (the number 1)
2	Receiver height adjustment (usually 5 ft)
3	Number of frequency bands (usually 1: A-weighted L_{eq})
4	Source height adjustment for automobiles (usually 0 ft)
5	Source height adjustment for heavy trucks (usually 8 ft)
6	Source height adjustment for medium trucks (usually 2.4 ft)
7	Source height for one additional vehicle class
8	Overall and octave band reference mean emission levels for optional vehicle class
9	Overall and octave band reference standard deviation of sound levels for optional vehicle class

In rare cases, the user may desire to include a fourth class of vehicle, such as buses or motorcycles, in the analysis. In these cases, the user must obtain or develop the data called for in cards 7, 8, and 9.

Roadway Parameters. This data block constitutes a critical part of the input required for STAMINA. The total number of cards in this data block is quite variable, but may be separated into two categories.

Category	Description
1	Traffic flow data cards—one card for each vehicle class, giving the hourly volume and speed for that class.
2	One card for each segment endpoint of the roadway. Two cards, thus, will give both endpoints of

one segment. Eleven cards are needed to identify the segment endpoints on a roadway with the maximum 10 segments.

As mentioned previously, there may be as many as 20 different roadways defined, representing a maximum of 200 roadway segments. Needless to say, this is sufficient to represent even the most complex situations.

The endpoint identification accomplished in this data block locates the segment spatially by indexing it to a three-dimensional grid system. Each endpoint is identified by an x-coordinate, a y-coordinate, and a z-coordinate (elevation). This notation is also used in identifying barriers (data block 4), absorptive strips (data block 4), and receivers (data block 5).

Barrier Parameters. Up to 20 barriers may be identified in this data block, through the use of endpoint coordinates, as described above. Each of these barriers may contain up to 20 segments. Thus, each barrier may have as many as 11 cards (one for each endpoint). Information concerning the absorptive or reflective characteristics may also be inserted in this data block.

Ground Cover Parameters. In situations where the site is otherwise hard, the user may insert rectangular strips which provide excess attenuation (4.5 dBA/distance doubling) for soft ground cover. For a maximum of 10 such strips, two cards are required for each. These cards provide the beginning and endpoint coordinates, the width of the strip and information as to whether the strip is composed of trees, high grass, or shrubbery.

Receiver Parameters. The three-dimensional coordinates (x, y, z) of each receiver, up to a maximum of 15, are needed for identification. It should be remembered that a receiver height adjustment was inserted in data block 1, Program Initialization Parameters. This adjustment brings the ground elevation up to ear height, and is usually taken as 5 ft. Thus, the z-coordinate elevation entered in data block 5 is taken as the ground or floor elevation.

This data block also allows for the establishment of a *criterion level*, above which the program prints a much more detailed analysis of

L_{eq}. For example, if a criterion level for a given receiver is established to be 45 dBA, a listing will be shown of each roadway segment (and its L_{eq} contribution) whose L_{eq} value exceeds (or comes within 5 dBA of) 45 dBA. Knowledge of these segment contributions is quite helpful in abatement analysis.

Alpha Input Parameters. Unless otherwise identified, STAMINA assumes that all sites are hard, the spatial decay rate is 3.0 dBA/distance doubling, and consequently the value of α (Alpha) in Equation 5-16 is zero. Therefore, when the user desires to assume soft ground cover (4.5 dBA/distance doubling), it is necessary to so inform the program. This is accomplished by identifying a roadway segment-receiver couple with the appropriate Alpha value, through the use of a table. For example, suppose a problem consisted of four roadways and five receivers. If the configuration and characteristics of the site were such that only roadway 2 propagated as *hard* to each receiver, the Alpha table would be:

Receiver	Roadway			
	1	2	3	4
1	0.5	0.0	0.5	0.5
2	0.5	0.0	0.5	0.5
3	0.5	0.0	0.5	0.5
4	0.5	0.0	0.5	0.5
5	0.5	0.0	0.5	0.5

It must be noted that whenever the program encounters a break in the geometric line of sight between a roadway and a receiver, in other words a barrier is present, it assumes that all excess attenuation is lost between the roadway and receiver. In those cases, Alpha becomes zero.

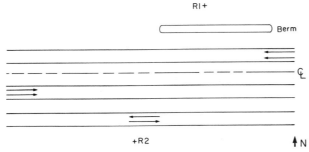

Figure 5-14. Example of problem for STAMINA application.

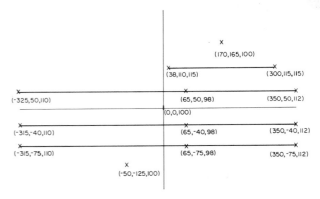

Figure 5-15.   Schematic of example problem.

As an example problem, consider the case of an expressway with a frontage road on the south size and a natural earth berm on the north side (Figure 5-14). The receivers are R1 and R2.

The site is shown schematically in Figure 5-15, with the appropriate coordinate points assigned. Note that while the roadways are straight, there is a segment break point approximated, halfway between the two receivers. This is because of a significant change in highway gradient.

For Figure 5-15 to be constructed, the following must be known or assumed.

1. The origin is taken to be at the approximate center of the figure. The base origin elevation is assumed to be 100 ft.

2. Each of the three sets of lanes (WB, EB, and FR, frontage road) has a 3 percent downgrade from west to east to a point 65 ft east of the origin. From that point on, there is a 5 percent upgrade.

Further information necessary for the solution to the problem is given as

1. Traffic Data
     —WB: 1000 Autos/Hr   55 mph
              75 medium trucks/hr   55 mph
              50 heavy trucks/hr   50 mph
     —EB: 800 Autos/hr   55 mph
              60 medium trucks/hr   55 mph
              40 heavy trucks/hr   50 mph
     —FR: 275 Autos/hr   35 mph
              20 medium trucks/hr   35 mph
              25 heavy trucks/hr   35 mph

2. Barrier—absorptive berm

3. Site—soft
    —no ground cover strips
4. Receivers—one-story houses (adjustment = 5 ft)
5. Criterion level—40 dBA

The input data file according to STAMINA specifications, and generated on a computer, is shown in Table 5-4. Table 5-5 shows the computer-generated output by STAMINA, once execution has been accomplished.

The first portion of the output is simply a restatement of the input data, except in a more self-explanatory format. The calculated sound levels are then shown for each receiver, for the different metrics.

$L_{E(A)}$	The A-weighted L_{eq} value
$L_{EOB(A)}$	The estimated A-weighted overall octave band sound level obtained by taking an intensity summation of the A-weighted octave band levels. Since no such octave band levels were used in this problem, this value is 0
L_{90}	The sound level exceeded 90 percent of the time

TABLE 5-4. Highway Noise/Stamna Example Problem

```
    1
        5.0   1                       RECEIVER HEIGHT ADJUSTMENT
        1.0   2                       NUMBER OF FREQUENCY BANDS
        0.0   3                       AUTO HEIGHT ADJUSTMENT
        8.0   4                       HEAVY TRUCK HEIGHT ADJUSTMENT
        2.4   5       L               MEDIUM TRUCK HEIGHT ADJUSTMENT
    2     3
      1000.        55.    1           AUTOS/HR
        50.        50.    2           HEAVY TRUCKS/HR
        75.        55.    3     L     MEDIUM TRUCKS/HR
      -325.        50.        110.    EXPRESSWAY
        65.        50.         98.    WESTBOUND LANES
       350.        50.        112.L
       800.        55.    1           AUTOS/HR
        40.        50.    2           HEAVY TRUCKS/HR
        60.        55.    3     L     MEDIUM TRUCKS/HR
      -315.       -40.        110.    EXPRESSWAY
        65.       -40.         98.    EASTBOUND LANES
      -350.       -40.        112.L
       275.        35.    1           AUTOS/HR
        25.        35.    2           HEAVY TRUCKS/HR
        20.        35.    3     L     MEDIUM TRUCKS/HR
       315.       -75.        110.    FRONTAGE ROAD
        65.       -75.         98.    BOTH DIRECTIONS
       350.       -75.        112.L
    3     1
        38.       110.        115.
       300.       115.        115.A   BERM N OF EB LANES, VIC R1
    5     2
       170.       165.        100.   40.   R1-N OF WB LANES
       -50.      -125.        100.   40.   R2-S OF FRONTAGE ROAD
      6     1
  0.5    0   1   2
      7
```

TABLE 5-5. Highway Noise/Stamna Example Problem

PROGRAM INITIALIZATION PARAMETERS

5.00000E+00	1	RECEIVER HEIGHT ADJUSTMENT
1.00000E+00	2	NUMBER OF FREQUENCY BANDS
0.00000E+00	3	AUTO HEIGHT ADJUSTMENT
8.00000E+00	4	HEAVY TRUCK HEIGHT ADJUSTMENT
2.40000E+00	5	MEDIUM TRUCK HEIGHT ADJUSTMENT

ROADWAY   1   MEDIUM TRUCKS/HR

NUMBER OF TYPE 1 VEH	VEH/H	MPH
1	1.0000E+03	5.5000E+01

NUMBER OF TYPE 2 VEH	VEH/H	MPH
1	5.0000E+01	5.0000E+01

NUMBER OF TYPE 3 VEH	VEH/H	MPH
1	7.5000E+01	5.5000E+01

SOURCE COORD IN FT

NUMBER	X	Y	Z	GRADE	COMMENTS
1	−3.2500E+02	5.0000E+01	1.1000E+02	0	EXPRESSWAY
2	6.5000E+01	5.0000E+01	9.8000E+01	0	WESTBOUND LANES
3	3.5000E+02	5.0000E+01	1.1200E+02	0	

ROADWAY   2   MEDIUM TRUCKS/HR

NUMBER OF TYPE 1 VEH	VEH/H	MPH
1	8.0000E+02	5.5000E+01

NUMBER OF TYPE 2 VEH	VEH/H	MPH
1	4.0000E+01	5.0000E+01

NUMBER OF TYPE 3 VEH	VEH/H	MPH
1	6.0000E+01	5.5000E+01

SOURCE COORD IN FT

NUMBER	X	Y	Z	GRADE	COMMENTS
1	−3.1500E+02	−4.0000E+01	1.1000E+02	0	EXPRESSWAY
2	6.5000E+01	−4.0000E+01	9.8000E+01	0	EASTBOUND LANES
3	−3.5000E+02	−4.0000E+01	1.1200E+02	0	

ROADWAY   3   MEDIUM TRUCKS/HR

NUMBER OF TYPE 1 VEH	VEH/H	MPH
1	2.7500E+02	3.5000E+01

NUMBER OF TYPE 2 VEH	VEH/H	MPH
1	2.5000E+01	3.5000E+01

NUMBER OF TYPE 3 VEH	VEH/H	MPH
1	2.0000E+01	3.5000E+01

SOURCE COORD IN FT

NUMBER	X	Y	Z	GRADE	COMMENTS
1	−3.1500E+02	−7.5000E+01	1.1000E+02	0	FRONTAGE ROAD
2	6.5000E+01	−7.5000E+01	9.8000E+01	0	BOTH DIRECTIONS
3	3.5000E+02	−7.5000E+01	1.1200E+02	0	

176

TABLE 5-5. (*Continued*)

BARRIER	1 (A)	BARRIER COORD IN FT		
NUMBER	X	Y	Z	
1	3.8000E+01	1.1000E+02	1.1500E+03	BERM N OF EB LANES, VIC R1
2	3.0000E+02	1.1500E+02	1.1500E+02	

RECEIVER		RECEIVER COORD IN FT				
NUMBER	X	Y	Z	LC	COMMENTS
1	1.7000E+02	1.6500E+02	1.0500E+02	40.0	R1-N OF WB LANES
2	−5.0000E+01	−1.2500E+02	1.0500E+02	40.0	R2-S OF FRONTAGE ROAD

ALPHA TABLE

NRC/NR	1	2	3
1	0.50	0.50	0.50
2	0.50	0.50	0.50

HIGHWAY NOISE/STAMNA EXAMPLE PROBLEM

RECEIVER		XRC	YRC	ZRC	
1		170.0	165.0	105.0	R1-N OF WB LANES

LE(A)	LEOB(A)	L90	L50	L10	SIGMA
55.1	0.0	43.9	51.3	58.6	5.7

ROADWAY SEGMENT SOUND LEVEL CONTRIBUTIONS EXCEEDING CRITERION LEVEL OF   40.0 DB

ROADWAY   SEGMENT

1	1	2
	53.5	47.7
2	1	2
	40.3	42.9

RECEIVER		XRC	YRC	ZRC	
2		−50.0	−125.0	105.0	R2-S OF FRONTAGE ROAD

LE(A)	LEOB(A)	L90	L50	L10	SIGMA
72.3	0.0	62.4	69.1	75.8	5.2

ROADWAY SEGMENT SOUND LEVEL CONTRIBUTIONS EXCEEDING CRITERION LEVEL OF   40.0 DB

ROADWAY   SEGMENT

1	2
62.6	57.5
1	2
67.5	67.6
1	2
64.7	52.9

STOP
END OF EXECUTION

L_{50} The sound level exceeded 50 percent of the time

L_{10} The sound level exceeded 10 percent of the time

SIGMA   The estimated standard deviation of the sound level variation.

Following the calculated sound levels is the table of roadway segment contributions for each receiver. It should be noted that the logarithmic (decibel) summation of the contributions from the six segments in each case equals the $L_{E(A)}$.

The $L_{E(A)}$ value for Receiver 2 is higher than that for Receiver 1 for two reasons. First, as the segment values for segment 2 of all three roadways shows, the berm is significant in noise abatement. Second, the frontage road has a much greater effect on Receiver 2 than Receiver 1, as demonstrated by its segment 1 (the frontage road has no effect at all on receiver 1).

Obviously, the complete instructions for using STAMINA have not been incorporated into this chapter. Rather, the salient points have been highlighted for the purpose of preliminary instruction. The reader is advised to obtain copies of the User's Manual (FHWA-RD-78-138) and the FHWA Model (FHWA-RD-77-108) prior to actual work with the program.

In addition, STAMINA has been combined with an iterating economic analysis program to form the Barrier Cost Reduction (BCR), program. At this writing, documentation for the BCR is in preparation for the FHWA and should be available by early 1982. When fully operational, BCR will be a most valuable tool. The computer program for the BCR will be named OPTIMA.

ABATEMENT OF HIGHWAY NOISE

The utilization of noise barriers is without question the most effective means of reducing noise impacts, given as fixed the horizontal and vertical alignments of the highway. The only other realistic method is the prohibition of truck traffic from sensitive areas during certain or all hours. Given the need to facilitate traffic flow, however, this method has limited applicability.

Appendix 5 contains a series of photographs of noise barrier installations on highways around the country.

AVIATION NOISE

The current methodology used to analyze aviation noise around airports is the *Integrated Noise Model* (INM). Version 2 of the INM (September, 1979) provides for the analysis of noise levels in any of five option metrics.

1. Noise Exposure Forecast (NEF), based upon Effective Perceived Noise Level, EPNL.
2. Equivalent Sound Level (L_{eq}).
3. Day-Night Average Sound Level (L_{dn})
4. Community Noise Exposure Level (CNEL), which is similar to L_{dn} except that it contains an intermediate weighting of 5 dBA for the evening hours (7 p.m. to 10 p.m.).
5. Time Above (TA), which is the amount of time that a threshold sound level in dBA is exceeded during a given time period.

The INM Version 2 is set up to execute as either batch or interactive (a question and answer session with the computer). Whichever execution mode is used, the program draws upon a standard data base of aircraft noise and performance characteristics. A total of 57 aircraft types and variations are included in the data base, including 34 in the commercial category, 13 in the general aviation category, and 10 in the military category.

Only the batch mode will be discussed here. The input data for this mode includes information in the following sections.

Section	Title
1	Airport
2	Aircraft Selection
3	Profile (Takeoff* and Approach)
4	Alternative Approach Parameters*
5	Alternative Noise versus Distance Tables*
6	Aircraft Mix
7	Takeoff Profile Modification*

Section 1: Airport

This section defines the physical description of the airport runways and their respective tracks. (A track is the projection of an aircraft's flight-path onto the ground.)

*Optional section.

Data is entered in this section via three cards, the first of which simply defines the altitude and average annual temperature of the airport. The second card (actually a series of cards) identifies the runways. Each runway requires two cards. One locates with x, y-coordinates the end of the runway where a departing aircraft starts its take-off roll and the far end of the runway as viewed from an approaching aircraft. The second card locates the end of the runway connecting with the track and is defined as the takeoff, flyover, and approach end. These cards also contain the runway direction numbers.

The final card (or series of cards) in this section delineates the track to be followed by the aircraft in the airport vicinity. Each track is broken up into segments which may be either curved or straight. For straight segments, only the segment length in nautical miles need be entered. For curved segments, the turn angle and turn radius must be entered. A track may utilize up to 15 segments.

Section 2: Aircraft Selection

Each aircraft type to be included in the scenario is defined by a combination of four sets of data:

1. Noise versus distance tables for EPNL and Noise Exposure Level (NEL).
2. Approach parameters describing performance during arrival.
3. Takeoff profiles.
4. Directivity parameters.

For each of the 57 aircraft stored in the standard data base, the INM has standardized configurations of data for the four combinations above. It is simply then a matter of matching the right numbered combinations with the aircraft type being used.

Section 3: Profile

The profile for each of the 57 aircraft in the INM is a table of altitude, velocity, and thrust as functions of ground distance from a runway end. The performance characteristics at any point along the profile are determined by means of interpolation.

As mentioned above, the INM, in its standard data base, includes configurations of takeoff profiles. As an option, users may incorporate different profiles if those stored in the data base do not suit their needs. It is necessary to use five cards to identify a new takeoff profile.

1. Profile Identification Card—indicates the units being used (feet or nautical miles) and a short narrative describing the option.
2. Ground Distance Card—identifies start of takeoff roll, point of liftoff (as the length of takeoff roll), and five additional points representing segment ends as the airplane leaves the airport.
3. Altitude Card—indicates the altitudes above the ground for each entry in the Ground Distance Cards.
4. Velocity Card—indicates the velocities in knots for each entry in the Ground Distance Card. Taxiing speed is 32 knots. In addition, the number of engines on the aircraft must appear as the eighth value in this card.
5. Thrust Card—indicates power in any acceptable unit, such as pounds per engine, for each entry in the Ground Distance Card. Also, the takeoff weight of the aircraft must appear as the eighth value in this card.

While the takeoff profile modifications discussed above are optional, insertion of approach profile data is mandatory, since each airport uses its own approach procedures. The data is inserted through five cards which are analogous to and titled the same as the takeoff profile. The ground distances divide the profile into at least five connected segments. The first data entry on the Ground Distance Card is the point where the aircraft finishes its landing, while the last entry represents the most remote point in the approach.

Section 4: Alternative Approach Parameters

Once the approach profile data for each aircraft has been inserted into the program via Section 3, it may be modified. Once the aircraft to be modified has been identified through a description card, the following approach parameters may be changed as part of a Performance Card.

1. Stop distance (landing roll)
2. Approach velocity
3. Thrust per engine for:
   (a) 3° glide slope with landing flaps
   (b) 6° glide slope with landing flaps

(c) Level flight with approach flaps

(d) 3° glide slope with approach flaps

(e) Level flight with maneuver flaps

(f) 500 ft/n.m. descent with maneuver flaps

(g) Idle

(h) Reversal

Section 5: Alternative Noise versus Distance Tables

The standard data base contains sets of data for each aircraft type giving EPNL and NEL values at eight slant range distances: 200, 400, 600, 1000, 2000, 4000, 6000, and 10,000 ft. When modifying this data, the appropriate unit (EPNL or NEL) must be identified as well as the power setting (thrust per engine). Once this is accomplished, the new noise values are inserted for the eight slant range distances.

Whenever alternate noise curves are utilized, the Time Above (TA) threshold sound level unit is not available. This is because the TA data sets are missing.

Section 6: Aircraft Mix

This data set identifies the daily activity at the airport in terms of aircraft type, volume, and schedule. Once the particular aircraft type, track, and approach profile identification numbers have been identified on the Mix Card, the following operation volumes are defined for day (7 a.m. to 7 p.m.), evening (7 p.m. to 10 p.m.), and night (10 p.m. to 7 a.m.).

1. All arrivals

2. Departures for trip lengths of (in nautical miles)

(a) 0 to 500

(b) 500 to 1000

(c) 1000 to 1500

(d) 1500 to 2500

(e) 2500 to 3500

(f) 3500 to 4500

(g) Greater than 4500

Section 7: Takeoff Profile Modification

In certain cases the standard data base takeoff procedures may be restricted at some point for one reason or another. When that is the case it is not necessary to go through the extensive modification procedures discussed in Section 3. Instead, a portion of the profile can be changed through the Modification Identification Card in one of five ways:

1. Altitude restriction.

2. Takeoff power is full power.

3. Climb power is maximum continuous climb power.

4. Engine-out flightpower (power per engine to maintain flight if one engine is lost).

5. Specified climb gradient.

Following the modification number, the card requires the identification of the starting and ending points of the modification. These are either in altitudes above the runway or distances from the start of the takeoff roll. This card also requires the insertion of the track identification numbers for the tracks (up to 10) for which the modification applies.

It is also possible for a particular aircraft type to override any or all of the modifications, should the need arise. This is accomplished through an Override Card which is coded to accept any modification, accept no modification, accept engine-out power only, or accept takeoff or climb power only.

INM Output

The program will generate data output in either one of two ways: contour analysis or grid analysis. The contour analysis option will produce x, y-coordinate points for any one of NEF, L_{dn}, L_{eq}, and CNEL. These coordinate points represent equi-noise contours for preselected metric values such as NEF 30 and 40. The output may be produced as either a listing of coordinate points (Figure 5-16), or a computer-generated plot (Figure 5-17).

The grid analysis output option allows the user to calculate noise levels at specific locations in the airport vicinity, through the introduction of a coordinate grid system. The metrics produced by the grid analysis option are TA (65, 75, 85, 95, 105, and 115), L_{eq}, L_{dn}, NEF, and CNEL. Figure 5-18 is an example output for the grid analysis option.

In a manner similar to the STAMINA program

Figure 5-16. Federal Aviation Administration Integrated Noise Model 2.6 (Example Airport Scenario)

PNT	X COORD.	Y COORD.	NEF DECIBELS	CONTOUR AREA SQ. MI.	FLTS USED	ITERATIONS
1	19843.8	0.0	29.95	0.00	14	14
2	20938.2	−373.9	29.99	.13	14	7
3	22035.6	−735.0	30.01	.26	14	7
4	23169.1	−1004.0	29.99	.35	14	5
5	24301.0	−1280.0	29.96	.45	14	5
6	25429.6	−1569.0	29.92	.55	14	5
7	26522.6	−1950.1	30.06	.69	14	7
8	26902.2	−2391.9	30.05	.89	14	10
9	26327.8	−2488.5	30.10	.96	14	11
10	25162.8	−2477.0	29.94	1.00	14	5
11	24007.9	−2354.0	30.01	1.00	14	7
12	22848.6	−2239.2	29.98	1.00	14	5
13	21690.9	−2109.1	29.95	.99	14	5
14	20535.5	−2078.8	29.97	1.03	14	7
15	19382.2	−2014.7	29.97	1.04	14	7
16	18225.■	−1878.8	29.96	1.04	14	5
17	17068.■	−1788.2	29.99	1.05	14	7
18	15915.■	−1689.0	29.98	1.06	14	7
19	14759.■	−1544.4	29.97	1.05	14	5
20	13604.2	−1438.7	30.00	1.05	14	7
21	12440.3	−1388.1	30.01	1.07	14	5
22	11276.2	−1343.9	30.01	1.09	14	5
23	10111.7	−1308.5	30.10	1.11	14	5
24	8956.7	−1233.5	29.94	1.12	14	7
25	7803.4	−1298.2	29.94	1.16	14	7
26	7272.7	−1504.6	29.98	1.20	14	10
27	7163.6	−2076.8	30.06	1.28	14	10
28	7636.9	−3141.3	29.90	1.40	14	7
29	8270.4	−4108.3	29.97	1.49	14	7
30	9009.9	−4996.5	29.98	1.57	14	7
31	9877.5	−5774.0	29.95	1.62	14	5
32	10253.9	−6866.7	29.99	1.77	14	7
33	10467.7	−8007.2	29.99	1.96	14	7
34	10801.9	−9113.5	29.98	2.12	14	7
35	11298.9	−10160.8	29.99	2.24	14	7
36	11894.5	−11156.4	30.00	2.33	14	7
37	12502.2	−12139	29.99	2.42	14	7
38	13282.4	−12998.5	30.00	2.44	14	7
39	14092.7	−13835.5	29.99	2.45	14	5
40	14720.9	−14816.6	30.09	2.55	14	5
41	15543.0	−15632.2	30.00	2.54	14	7
42	16332.8	−16488.6	29.95	2.56	14	5
43	16796.1	−17557.6	30.00	2.74	14	7
44	16235.1	−17714.5	30.09	2.96	14	11
45	15080.0	−17724.8	30.01	3.33	14	7
46	14537.0	−17872.4	29.99	3.54	14	9

Figure 5-16. (*Continued*)

PNT	X COORD.	Y COORD.	NEF DECIBELS	CONTOUR AREA SQ. MI.	FLTS USED	ITERATIONS
47	14492.9	−18439.6	29.96	3.70	14	11
48	14848.7	−19538.5	29.95	3.87	14	7
49	15273.7	−20623.2	30.06	4.01	14	5
50	15727.5	−21696.2	30.00	4.14	14	5

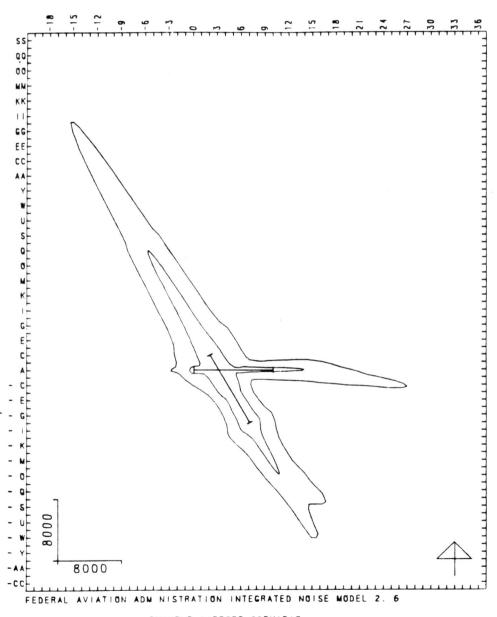

FEDERAL AVIATION ADMINISTRATION INTEGRATED NOISE MODEL 2. 6

EXAMPLE AIRPORT SCENARIO
NEF   30.0 40.0

Figure 5-17.   A sample NEF contour plot.

Figure 5-18. Federal Aviation Administration Integrated Noise Model 2.6 (Example airport scenario grid analysis without aircraft 101)[a]

INTER-SECTION	OFF SET	PERIOD	TIME IN MINUTES ABOVE INDICATED DRA LEVEL						LEQ	LDN	NEF	CNEL
			65	75	85	95	105	115				
0, B	.0,.0	24 HOUR	74.8	31.0	12.0	2.7	.1	0.0	77.4	83.5	46.6	83.6
		EVENING	9.4	4.1	1.6	.2	0.0	0.0				
		NIGHT	17.1	6.8	2.7	1.0	.0	0.0				
1, B	.0,.0	24 HOUR	81.2	37.5	16.7	3.7	.2	0.0	77.6	83.8	47.4	83.9
		EVENING	10.3	5.1	2.1	.2	0.0	0.0				
		NIGHT	18.7	8.1	3.9	1.1	.1	0.0				
0, C	.0,.0	24 HOUR	60.7	34.1	9.8	1.7	0.0	0.0	72.3	77.7	42.2	77.9
		EVENING	7.8	4.6	.6	0.0	0.0	0.0				
		NIGHT	13.8	7.4	2.8	.7	0.0	0.0				
1, C	.0,.0	24 HOUR	58.5	35.7	16.3	2.4	0.0	0.0	74.5	79.9	45.6	79.7
		EVENING	7.4	4.7	1.5	0.0	0.0	0.0				
		NIGHT	13.2	8.0	4.4	.7	0.0	0.0				
0, D	.0,.0	24 HOUR	59.5	32.0	9.2	.3	0.0	0.0	71.0	75.2	41.7	75.4
		EVENING	7.6	3.8	.2	0.0	0.0	0.0				
		NIGHT	13.7	7.2	2.9	0.0	0.0	0.0				
1, D	.0,.0	24 HOUR	56.0	30.4	11.6	2.2	0.0	0.0	75.2	41.1	47.8	79.2
		EVENING	7.1	3.5	.4	.1	0.0	0.0				
		NIGHT	12.8	7.0	3.6	.4	0.0	0.0				
0, E	.0,.0	24 HOUR	55.7	27.1	9.8	.3	0.0	0.0	71.3	74.9	43.1	75.0
		EVENING	6.7	2.4	.3	.0	0.0	0.0				
		NIGHT	13.1	6.8	2.8	.0	0.0	0.0				
1, E	.0,.0	24 HOUR	51.8	26.1	10.6	2.0	.4	0.0	77.5	81.7	51.4	82.0
		EVENING	6.2	2.3	.4	.1	.0	0.0				
		NIGHT	12.0	6.7	3.1	.4	.1	0.0				
0, F	.0,.0	24 HOUR	49.4	24.5	8.5	1.4	0.0	0.0	73.6	77.6	47.3	77.8
		EVENING	5.4	1.8	.3	.1	0.0	0.0				
		NIGHT	12.0	6.5	2.2	.3	0.0	0.0				
1, F	.0,.0	24 HOUR	51.5	23.4	8.8	.9	0.0	0.0	71.5	74.9	44.1	75.1
		EVENING	5.8	1.5	.3	.1	0.0	0.0				
		NIGHT	12.4	6.3	2.3	.2	0.0	0.0				
			X-START	Y-START	X-STEP	Y-STEP	NX	NY	OPTIONS			
			0.00	1000.00	1000.	1000.	2	5	00000			

[a]The user has provided his own aircraft definition(s), approach parameter(s), and takeoff profile(s).

for highways, the INM restructures as part of its output the input data, for the convenience of the user in data interpretation. Figure 5-19 provides an example INM input, in this case for NEF contours.

The actual application of the INM for a given airport situation is a complex and intensive effort. In addition to providing tapes of the program for a nominal fee, the FAA will provide detailed documentation to assist the user. It would not be prudent to attempt to utilize the INM without the aid of such documentation. The most important document currently available is Report FAA-EE-79-09, *INM-Integrated*

Figure 5-19. Example Airport Scenario

NEF

100		1	AIRPORT SECTION								
	0.	15.0									
1	10000.	0.		0.	0.	27	9	T.O.	RWY	27	
2	0.	0.		10000.	0.	9	27	T.O.	RWY	9	
3	7000.	-7000.		2000.	2000.	31	13	T.O.	RWY	31	
4	2000.	2000.		7000.	-7000.	13	31	T.O.	RWY	13	

1	1	1	50.								
1	2	3	.5	45.	1.5	50.					
3	3	1	50.								
2	4	5	.5	90.	-1.5	1.5	0.	45.	-1.5	50.	
2	5	1	50.								
2	6	3	.5	10.	1.5	50.					
4	7	3	.5	30.	-1.5	50.					
4	8	3	1.0	30.	-1.5	50.					
4	9	1	50.								

107			AIRCRAFT SELECTION SECTION
3.	5.	8.43	

101   PROFILE SECTION

301   STANDARD 3 DEGREE APPROACH

-1.0	-.165	2.975	9.255	12.395	18.675
0.0	0.0	1000.	3000.	4000.	5000.
32.	-2.	-2.	-2.	-2.	-2
-10.	-3.	-6.	-6.	-6.	

302   STANDARD 3 DEGREE APPROACH WITH LEV. SEGMENT

-1.0	-.165	2.975	9.255	12.	15.14
0.0	0.0	1000.	3000.	3000.	4000.
32.	-2.	-2.	-2.	-2.	-2.
-10.	-3.	-6.	-5.	-6.	

303   GA. 3 DEGREE APPROACH

-1.0	-.165	2.975	9.255	12.395	18.675
0.0	0.0	1000.	3000.	4000.	5000.
32.	-2.	-2.	-2.	-2.	-2.
-3.	-3.	-3.	-3.	-3.	

Figure 5-19. (*Continued*)

```
100        3           AIRCRAFT MIX SECTION
  3  7                  3.  1.  1.  2.1.5
  3  8                             3.  1.  1.  2.      1.5
  3  9301  9.  4.  4.
  5  6302  4.  3.  2.  2.  1.      2.  1.      2.  1.
  8  330110.  2.  5.  5.  1.  3.  2.      1.  3.      1.  1.
 43  4                  25.  5.  10.
 43  230325.  5.  10.
```

CONTOUR
30.
-40.
END

Noise Model Version 2, User's Guide, September, 1979. This report is the source document for the preceding discussion on the INM, as well as for Figures 5-16 through 5-19.

TRANSPORTATION NOISE MEASUREMENT

There are ordinarily two situations which would call for the measurement of noise levels in transportation. These are (*a*) to establish an ambient, or "before," condition in order to facilitate the analysis of impacts from a proposed transportation action, and (*b*) to document noise levels generated by in-place transportation systems.

The ambient measurement situation (*a* above) is most often associated with new highway construction. In that case, the analyst makes a series of short-duration (usually 10 to 15 minutes) measurements in the project vicinity as a data base for developing existing noise level contours. It is good practice to make measurements at each site on at least two separate occasions as a check on statistical reliability.

The type and quality of the data gathered during the measurement phase is strictly dependent on the equipment used. For example, if only a simple sound level meter (SLM) with either a digital display or sweep arm is used, the only metrics attainable are L_{50} and L_{10}. It is not likely that 95 percent confidence limits tighter than ± 3 dBA will be obtained. If the SLM has a storage capacity, it would be possible to obtain a precise L_{eq} value for the duration; however, the L_{50} and L_{10} values would still not be improved.

The next level of sophistication in instrumentation would allow for the precise determination of not only L_{eq} but also L_{10}, L_{50}, L_{max}, and L_{90}, among others. This is the dosimeter/analyzer single interval system which stores data in memory cells for the duration of the measurement period, and then "dumps" the data into a statistical analyzer-printer.

Increasing sophistication a step further would allow for determination of multiple-interval, long-term (24 hours or more) measurements. This is the unattended monitor, which is usually housed in a rugged, weatherproof field case and which utilizes a special outdoor microphone. The monitor includes a clock, so that a series of 24 one-hour L_{eq} values can be weighted internally by the microprocesser by 10 dBA for nighttime (10 p.m. to 7 a.m.) to obtain an L_{dn} value in dBA.

The most complex and sophisticated level of instrumentation used in short-duration, highway-oriented measurements is the audio recorder/real time analyzer system. While this system will not provide a much larger variety of useful metrics, it will produce a spectral analysis across the frequency range which may be necessary in research applications. This system is not convenient for day-to-day measurement activities, however, for several reasons. The cost, for example, of a high quality, dual-channel recorder with an additional cue channel is likely to run from $7,000 to $10,000. The real time analyzer costs an additional $15,000 to $20,000. (The real time analyzer is a signal processing system which, with the aid of a computer, performs complete spectral analysis on a signal in one pass of that signal through the system.) Also, utilization of the audio recorder/real time analyzer system is very labor-intensive; after the data is gathered in the field, it must be played back at the same speed in the laboratory. Lastly, operation and maintenance of the system requires more highly trained personnel than do the less sophisticated systems. In fact, many agencies and organizations which regularly use audio recorders and real time analyzers maintain full-time laboratory personnel just for those instruments.

The second situation where measurements may be appropriate is to document noise levels generated by in-place transportation systems. One such common application is in the analysis of levels from existing highways where barrier retrofit projects may be needed. These measurements are of short duration and the measurement techniques discussed above are typically utilized.

The other common application is the continuous monitoring of airport noise levels. Many of the larger airports, such as John F. Kennedy, LaGuardia, and Newark, all in the metropolitan New York City area, National Airport in Washington, D.C., Logan Airport in Boston, and the Los Angeles International Airport have installed permanent monitoring stations throughout the airport environs. These stations are connected to computers which provide a custom-designed array of data. It is custom-designed because there are no Federal guidelines or requirements that must be met. For example, the New York City and Newark Airports are governed by the Port Authority of New York and New Jersey (PANYNJ), which has adopted a maximum single-event level of 112 PNdB (perceived noise). Therefore, all monitors at those airports are programmed to measure in terms of PNdB. California airports, on the other hand, are under state statute to monitor in terms of CNEL.

The data taken from these continuous airport monitors may be used to identify specific aircraft operations in terms of noise level, as in the case of PANYNJ, and thus be an enforcement tool. Conversely, the data may be used, as in the case of the California CNEL requirements, to develop long-term noise exposure values. In either case, the information gained is quite useful in airport planning and overall noise reduction at the aviation facility.

BIBLIOGRAPHY

The Audible Landscape: A Manual for Highway Noise and Land Use, DOT, FHWA, Washington, D.C., 1974.

Barry, T. M. and Reagan, J. A., *FHWA Highway Traffic Noise Prediction Model*, FHWA-RD-77-108, Washington, D.C., 1978.

Beranek, L. L., *Acoustic Measurement*, Wiley, New York, 1949.

Beranek, L. L., ed., *Noise and Vibration Control*, McGraw-Hill, New York, 1971.

Berry, J. C., and Overgard, D. L., *Sound Attenuation Kit for Diesel-Powered Buses*, Final Report, DOT, Washington, D.C., 1976.

Bowlby, W. J., *Noise Measurement Systems Operating Instructions*, NYSDOT, Materials Bureau, Albany, 1976.

Brock, J. T., *Acoustic Noise Measurements*, Bruel and Kjaer, Copenhagen, 1971.

Burns, W., *Noise and Man*, Lippincott, Philadelphia, 1973.

Buses: Noise Emission Standards for Transportation, EPA, 40CFR Part 205, *Federal Register*, September 12, 1977.

Chalupnik, J. D., ed., *Transportation Noises*, Univ. of Washington Press, Seattle, 1970.

Forrest, D. E., Knox, R. F., and Spielberg, D. C., *A Guide to Noise Control at the Municipal Level in California*, Stanford Environmental Law Society, Stanford, CA, 1976.

Fundamentals and Abatement of Highway Traffic Noise, DOT, FHWA Rep. No. DOT-FH-11-7978, Washington, D.C., 1973.

Galloway, W. E., et al., *Highway Noise, Measurement, Simulation, and Mixed Reaction*, NCHRP Rep. 78, Transportation Research Board, 1969.

Gordon, C. G., et al., *Highway Noise, A Design Guide for Highway Engineers*, NCHRP Rep. 117, Transportation Research Board, Washington, D.C., 1971.

Hajek, J. J., *Ontario Highway Noise Prediction Method*, RR197, Ministry of Transportation and Communications, Toronto, Canada, 1975.

Highway Noise: Generation and Control, NCHRP Rep. 173, 1977. Also see Fox, G., *The Cost of Quieting Heavy Caliber-Engine Diesel Tractors*, BBN Rep. 2563, Bolt Beranek and Newman, Cambridge, MA, (unpublished).

Highway Traffic Noise Prediction Methods, Transportation Research Circular 175, Transportation Research Board, 1976.

Information on Levels of Environmental Noise Requisite to Protect Public Health and Welfare with an Adequate Margin of Safety, EPA, Office of Noise Abatement and Control, Washington, D.C., 1974.

Kinsler, L. E., and Frey, A. R., *Fundamentals of Acoustics*, Wiley, New York, 1962.

Kryter, K. D., *The Effects of Noise on Man*, Academic, New York, 1970.

Kugler, B. A., Commins, D. E., and Galloway, W. J., *Design Guide for Highway Noise Prediction and Control*, vol. 1 of NCHRP Project 3-7/3.

Kugler, B. A., et al., *Highway Noise Propagation and Traffic Noise Models*, vol. 3, *Establishment of Standards for Highway Noise Levels*, Transportation Research Board, NCHRP Project 3-7/3, 1974.

Lyon, R. H., *Lectures in Transportation Noise*, Grozier, Cambridge, MA, 1973.

Model Community Noise Control Ordinance, EPA, Washington, D.C., EPA 55019-75-003, September 1975.

Morse, P. M., and Ingard, K. U., *Theoretical Acoustics*, McGraw-Hill, New York, 1968.

Mosback, E. J., Goodrow, J. P., and Kester, W. C., *Policy and Techniques for Highway Noise Compensation and Valuation*, NCHRP Project 11-6 Final Report, July 1975.

Peterson, A. P. G. and Gross, E. E., *Handbook of Noise Measurement*, General Radio Company, West Concord, MA, 1972.

Piersol, A. G., and Winfrey, R., *Economic Evaluation of Highway Noise Reduction Strategies*, vol. 5 of NCHRP Project 3-7/3.

Public Health and Welfare Criteria for Noise, EPA, Office of Noise Abatement and Control, Washington, D.C., 1973.

Rentz, P. E., and Pope, L. D., *Description and Control of Motor Vehicle Noise Sources*, vol. 2, NCHRP Project 3-7/3.

Rettinger, M., *Acoustic Design and Noise Control*, Chemical Publishing, New York.

Rudder, F. F., Lam, D. E., and Chueng, P., *User's Manual: FHWA Level 2 Highway Traffic Noise Prediction Model*, STAMINA 1.0, FHWA-RD-78-138, Washington, D.C., May 1979.

Snow, C. N., *Highway Noise Barrier Selection Design and Construction Experiences*, FHWA Implementation Package 76-8.

Taylor, C. A., *The Physics of Musical Sound*, Elsevier, New York, 1965.

Tyndall, J., *The Science of Sound*, Philosophical Library, New York, 1964.

Vaughan, R. J. and Huckins, L., *The Economics of Expressway Noise Pollution Abatement*, Rand Corporation, Rep. P-5475, 1975.

Werner, V. A. and Boyce, W., *Truck Noise XI—Evaluation and Reduction of Heavy-Duty Truck Noise*, Final Report, DOT-TSC-OST-76-21, DOT, Washington, D.C., 1976.

Wesler, J. E., *Manual for Highway Noise Prediction*, DOT, Transportation Systems Center, Cambridge, MA, Rep. DOT-TSC-FHWA-72-1, 1972.

White, F. A., *Our Acoustic Environment*, Wiley, New York, 1975.

APPENDIX 5: PHOTOS OF HIGHWAY NOISE BARRIER INSTALLATIONS

Figure A1.   I-210, Los Angeles. Source: FHWA-IMP-76-8.

Figure A2. Typical ARMCO metal wall installation. Courtesy ARMCO, Inc.

Figure A3. Typical ARMCO metal wall installation. Courtesy ARMCO, Inc.

Figure A4.   I-35W, Minneapolis. Source: FHWA-IMP-76-8.

Figure A5.   I-405, Bellevue, Washington. Source: FHWA-IMP-76-8.

Figure A6.   I-84, West Hartford, Connecticut. Source: FHWA-IMP-76-8.

Figure A7.   I-15 and US 101, Escondido, California. Source: FHWA-IMP-76-8.

Figure A8.   I-86, Vernon, Connecticut. Courtesy Fanwall Corp., Framingham, Mass.

Figure A9.   Los Angeles International Airport. Courtesy Fanwall Corp., Framingham, Mass.

CHAPTER 6

Transportation Air Quality

AIR QUALITY

Highway vehicles are often the primary source of local carbon monoxide problems and are thought to be a major cause of excess regional photochemical oxidant concentrations. Airports can also generate local exceedences of the ambient carbon monoxide standards and to a lesser extent contribute to regional photochemical oxidant problems. Rail systems are usually not associated with significant air quality impacts and air quality impact analyses are usually not performed for rail traffic. In this chapter the fundamentals of pollutant emission and dispersion are discussed together with observations and suggestions as to how transportation air quality impact analyses are (or should be) accomplished in the real world of Environmental Impact Statement (EIS) preparation, review, and approval.

Air quality impact analysis for transportation systems is an interesting blend of science, engineering, administrative procedures, and professional guesswork. Air quality impacts are judged with respect to ambient concentration standards. Thus, if one is to analyze the impact of a proposed transportation project, it is necessary to

1. Project the amount of traffic expected to result from the project.
2. Calculate the quantity of pollutant(s) which will be emitted by the projected traffic.
3. Estimate the resultant concentration of the pollutant(s) of interest for particular receptor sites, using a dispersion model or some other analysis tool.
4. Add this traffic-generated pollutant concentration to an expected background con-

centration generated by other pollutant sources.
5. Compare this result to the ambient standard for various project alternatives.

Each step in the process carries with it a degree of uncertainty and the reliability of the final result is largely a matter of professional judgment, so transportation air quality impact analyses are often controversial. As a result, a considerable body of administrative dogma and custom has evolved over the past several years and continues to evolve today. The science in this chapter reflects the state of the art in 1980 and will probably continue to do so for at least the next few years. How long current administrative procedures for assessing impacts will endure, however, is hard to say.

Air Pollutants

The pollutant species most often of concern with respect to transportation facilities are carbon monoxide (CO), hydrocarbons (HC), photochemical oxidants (O_3), nitrogen oxides (NO_x), particulates, and lead. The U.S. Environmental Protection Agency (EPA) has promulgated ambient air quality standards for these and other pollutants, as have most states. In this section a brief discussion of the various pollutants is offered.

Carbon Monoxide

Carbon monoxide (CO) is a colorless and odorless gas formed through the incomplete combustion (oxidation) of fossil fuels which contain carbon [complete combustion results in the production of carbon dioxide (CO_2), a more stable molecule]. While natural and industrial sources do contribute to ambient CO concentrations, mobile sources (primarily gasoline-powered internal combustion engines) account for most of the carbon monoxide present in the atmosphere. Carbon monoxide sinks (removal mechanisms) are not well understood but probably include migration to the upper atmosphere, absorption and oxidation on various surfaces, metabolism by plants and animals, and others. The mean residence time of atmospheric CO is thought to be between one month and five years.*

Carbon monoxide is the most ubiquitious air pollutant. It is measured in terms of milligrams per cubic meter, mg/m^3, $(10^{-3}$ grams per cubic meter) while other pollutants are measured in micrograms per cubic meter, $\mu g/m^3$, $(10^{-6}$ grams per cubic meter). CO is not especially toxic to plants or harmful to materials. It does, however, combine readily with hemoglobin, the blood protein most responsible for oxygen transport within the body. The affinity of hemoglobin for CO is over 200 times its affinity for oxygen, and carboxyhemoglobin is a more stable compound than oxyhemoglobin. Thus, increasing exposure to CO leads to increasing displacement of oxygen by carbon monoxide in the blood with a resulting decrease in the availability of oxygen to the cells. Excessive exposure to CO in humans can result in impairment of vision and judgment, cardiovascular changes, and, at extreme concentrations, death. However, lethal concentrations occur only under special conditions such as in a closed garage containing an idling automobile. The ambient air quality standards for CO are designed to provide an adequate margin of safety from the effects of carbon monoxide. The Occupational Safety and Health Administration (OSHA) standard designed to protect workers is some five times higher than the national ambient eight-hour standard.

Hydrocarbons, Nitrogen Oxides, and Photochemical Oxidants

These three air pollutants are discussed together because their chemistries are interrelated. Two of the pollutants, hydrocarbons (HC) and nitrogen oxides (NO_x), are considered primary pollutants because they are emitted directly by a

*See AP-62 *Air Quality Criteria for Carbon Monoxide* published by HEW in 1970, for further details on this and other issues relating to carbon monoxide.

source such as an automobile. Photochemical oxidants, which are comprised principally of ozone (O_3) and peroxyacetyl nitrate (PAN), are formed in the atmosphere through reactions involving HC, NO_x, sunlight, and other chemical species and factors (e.g., temperature, humidity, etc.) whose interactions are not well understood.

The HC emitted by mobile sources result primarily from unburned fuel passing through the engine and fuel which evaporates before it passes through the engine. Aside from odor problems, HC in and of themselves are considered relatively inoffensive at ambient concentrations. In fact, the national ambient HC standard is not really a standard at all but a guideline to be used in meeting the photochemical oxidant standard. Some HC are apparently more critical than others with regard to the formation of photochemical oxidants. Methane (CH_4) for example, is relatively inert and is not currently considered to be a serious problem with respect to photochemical oxidant production. Since all carbon bonds in methane are single bonds, the molecule is said to be saturated, that is, no additional hydrogen atoms can be accommodated and the molecule tends to be relatively stable. Aldehydes, by contrast, are considered to be highly reactive, important photochemical oxidant precursors. They are unsaturated HC containing a double-bonded oxygen atom bonded to a carbon atom. This double bond is more easily broken than the single bonds in a saturated molecule; thus, an aldehyde molecule tends to be more reactive than a methane molecule.

For the purposes of this discussion the two most important oxides of nitrogen are nitric oxide (NO) and nitrogen dioxide (NO_2). Most mobile source emissions of nitrogen oxides (NO_x) are caused by the oxidation of atmospheric nitrogen (N_2) to NO, which occurs at high temperatures. Nitric oxide can in turn be oxidized to NO_2 in the atmosphere. At ambient concentrations nitrogen oxides, especially NO_2, for which the ambient standards have been promulgated, can corrode materials (through the formation of acids), kill plant foliage, and damage lung tissue. Nitrogen dioxide is also strongly colored and absorbs light over the entire visible spectrum, especially over the shorter, more energetic, wavelengths. This absorption of light can reduce visibility. In absorbing light, NO_2 also makes available at least some of the energy

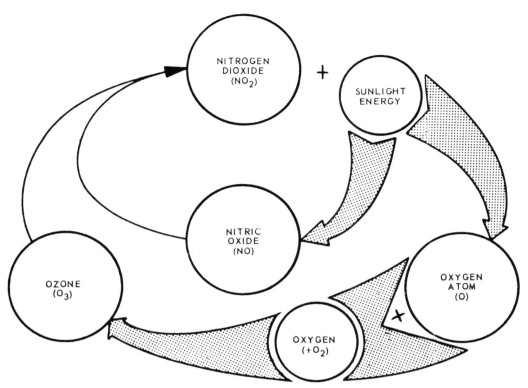

Figure 6-1.   Atmospheric nitrogen dioxide photolytic cycle. Source: HEW.

required to drive the photochemical oxidant cycle (see Figure 6-1). Note that the irradiation of NO_2 can result in its disassociation to $NO + O$. The combination of this free oxygen atom with an oxygen molecule results in the formation of an ozone molecule (O_3). Ozone is a highly re-active substance (a very strong oxidizer) and is highly corrosive. As a strong oxidizer, O_3 can oxidize materials and tissue (e.g., lung tissue) and is considered quite toxic to both plants and animals. Being a strong oxidizer, ozone will oxidize any available nitrogen oxide to nitrogen dioxide:

$$O_3 + NO \longrightarrow NO_2 + O_2$$

and thus return to the stable form of molecular oxygen (O_2). If nitrogen oxides, oxygen, and sunlight were the only factors involved in the photochemical oxidation process, ozone would be consumed rapidly through the reaction with NO (formed through the disassociation of NO_2 which released the oxygen atom required to form O_3) and high concentrations of ozone would never be generated. As illustrated by Figure 6-2, however, it is believed that HC are somehow involved in the photochemical oxidant

formation process, serving to prevent the consumption of O_3 by NO and thus providing for the buildup of ozone and other products of photochemical oxidation such as PAN and other organic species which can be highly toxic to plants and animals.

The photochemical oxidant formation process is an area of much active research and consider-able debate and uncertainty. There are, however, at least a few points upon which most in the professional community agree.

1. The photochemical oxidant formation process requires at least a few hours to proceed from precursor to oxidant.
2. Interstate transport of oxidant problems (through transport of oxidants and/or pre-cursors) can and does occur, especially in the eastern United States.
3. Photochemical oxidant formation is limited to the warmer months.
4. Morning HC emissions seem to have at least some influence on maximum downwind oxidant concentrations, which tend to occur around midday.

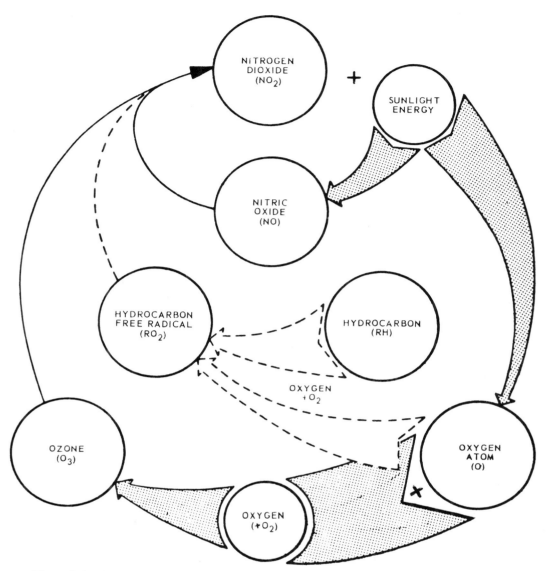

Figure 6-2. Interaction of hydrocarbons with atmospheric nitrogen dioxide photolytic cycle. Source: HEW.

5. Oxidant scavenging in the wake of significant NO sources can occur.

6. Maximum photochemical oxidant concentrations tend to occur during episodes which may last for several days and cover an entire region of the country, e.g., the Northeast. The occurrence of these episodes is apparently related to the prevailing meteorological conditions.

7. Much research regarding the formation of photochemical oxidants remains to be done.

At the present time, the EPA's strategy for photochemical oxidant control is concentrated mainly upon the control of HC emissions. The effectiveness of this strategy has not been conclusively demonstrated.

Lead

Lead is a well-known metabolic poison which when ingested over a period of time can cause a variety of toxic effects including anemia, brain disease, and a wide range of metabolic disorders.

Lead emissions from transportation-related activities arise primarily from the use of leaded gasoline. Although the use of leaded gasoline is decreasing due to its incompatibility with the catalytic converter, automobiles are still a significant source of lead emissions which cannot always be ignored.

The lead contained in leaded gasoline is not destroyed during the combustion process. Some of it is emitted directly to the atmosphere in fine particulate form, some agglomerates to form larger particulates, some adheres to the inside of the engine and exhaust system, and some is suspended in the engine oil. In general, the more leaded fuel an engine consumes, the more lead it emits. However, there is a marked tendency for lead to adhere to the exhaust system when the engine is operating at low speed, and for this same lead to be blown out of the system under heavy acceleration. For this reason lead emissions are often excessive in the vicinity of heavily traveled acceleration ramps.

Current methods of calculating lead emissions can be quite tedious, taking into consideration the age distribution of the vehicle fleet and its average fuel efficiency. The EPA guideline document EPA-450/2-78-038, *Supplementary Guidelines for Lead Implementation Plans* contains procedures for the calculation of highway lead emissions.

Sulfur Dioxide and Particulates

Sulfur dioxide (SO_2) and particulates are not generally considered to be important transportation-related pollutants. They are, however, emitted by transportation sources and are discussed here for completeness.

Sulfur dioxide is a colorless gas which is soluble in water, has a pungent and irritating odor, and is toxic to both plants and animals. It can react in the atmosphere to form sulfuric acid and other sulfates involved in the "acid rain" phenomenon. Sulfur dioxide emissions are produced when fossil fuels containing sulfur are burned and the sulfur is then oxidized. The highly refined petroleum fuels used by motor vehicles and aircraft contain very little sulfur. Representative SO_2 emission rates for transportation sources can be found in AP-42, the EPA's *Compilation of Air Pollutant Emission Factors*.

Particulate material is individual bits of dispersed matter, either liquid or solid, ranging in size from 0.002 to 500 microns (μm) in diameter. As with SO_2, particulates are usually considered to be a problem only as they relate to stationary sources like power plants. However, particulates can be generated by mobile sources through a variety of mechanisms. Particulates in and of themselves can be toxic to humans depending on their chemical composition and can cause plant damage through interference with stomata functions. However, it is their potentially synergistic interaction with other pollutants such as SO_2 that appears to be of most concern from the public health standpoint.

Particulates are emitted by mobile sources as droplets of unburned hydrocarbon, bits of rubber, metal, asbestos from brake shoes, lead particles, and entrained dust. Representative emission rates for most particulates generated by mobile sources are presented in Appendix 6A. Problems relating to the generation of particulates through the entrainment of highway dust remain somewhat intractable. While ambient levels of lead and asbestos are sometimes of concern in special cases, like that of a heavy volume of accelerating and decelerating vehicles in an enclosed area such as a tunnel, they are not routinely addressed in air quality analyses and routine procedures for their evaluation under such conditions have not been developed.

The Ambient Air Quality Standards

Table 6-1 is a listing of the National Ambient Air Quality Standards (NAAQS) as promulgated by the EPA. Most states have promulgated standards for these pollutants which are the same as or more stringent than the Federal standards. Note that these are primary standards, the attainment of which are considered necessary for the maintenance of public health. Secondary standards are designed to protect public welfare. The distinction between public health and public welfare is more often explained by referring to the particulate standard, where the primary (less stringent) standard is considered a minimum level for health reasons, and the secondary (more stringent) standard is designed to prevent the soiling of buildings, restriction of visibility, degradation of materials, and so on. The distinction between public health and public welfare is, however, somewhat nebulous as evidenced by the fact that the primary standards in some instances are the same as the secondary standards, as is the case with CO. Presumably, CO is thought to have no adverse effects save those on health.

It is important to note the statistical basis for

TABLE 6-1. National Ambient Air Quality Standards

Pollutant	Averaging Time	Primary Standard Levels	Secondary Standard Levels
Particulate matter	Annual (geometric mean)	75 $\mu g/m^3$	60 $\mu g/m^3$
	24 hours[b]	260 $\mu g/m^3$	150 $\mu g/m^3$
Sulfur oxides	Annual (arithmetic mean)	80 $\mu g/m^3$ (0.03 ppm)	—
	24 hours[b]	365 $\mu g/m^3$ (0.14 ppm)	—
	3 hours[b]	—	1300 $\mu g/m^3$ (0.5 ppm)
Carbon monoxide	8 hours[b]	10 mg/m^3 (9 ppm)	10 mg/m^3 (9 ppm)
	1 hours[b]	40 mg/m^3 (35 ppm)	40 mg/m^3 (35 ppm)
Nitrogen dioxide	Annual (arithmetic mean)	100 $\mu g/m^3$ (0.05 ppm)	100 $\mu g/m^3$ (0.05 ppm)
Ozone	1 hours[b]	235 $\mu g/m^3$ (0.12 ppm)	235 $\mu g/m^3$ (0.12 ppm)
Hydrocarbons (nonmethane)[a]	3 hours (6 to 9 a.m.)	160 $\mu g/m^3$ (0.24 ppm)	160 $\mu g/m^3$ (0.24 ppm)

Source: Council on Environmental Quality.
[a] A non-health–related standard used as a guide for ozone control.
[b] Not to be exceeded more than once per year.

measuring the various standards. In this discussion the term "averaging time" will be used to describe the exposure duration of interest and the term "return period" will be used to describe the frequency with which the specified concentration can be exceeded without violating the standard. For example, the CO standard is actually two standards. The one-hour ambient CO standard is 35 ppm (40 mg/m³) not to be exceeded more than once per year (a return period of six months). The eight-hour CO standard is 9 ppm (10 mg/m³) not to be exceeded more than once per year.* Many urban areas currently experience at least occasional violations of the eight-hour standard; however, violations of the one-hour

*The August 18, 1980 issue of the Federal Register proposed draft revisions to the CO standards(s). The proposed one-hour primary standard is 25 ppm (28.6 mg/m³). The level of the eight-hour primary standard is to remain the same, and there is to be no secondary ambient CO standard. The standards are to be exceeded on an average of less than one *day* per year (i.e., two exceedences on the same day count as one exceedance).

standard are relatively rare. In other words, if an area exhibits no violations of the eight-hour standard, violations of the one-hour standard would not be expected (barring some unusual circumstances such as extremely heavy traffic for only a few hours of the day). For these reasons the current eight-hour standard is usually considered the critical or controlling standard.

The term "ambient concentration," used in reference to the NAAQS, is simple and straightforward, but has been the subject of numerous misunderstandings. Ambient means surrounding, and concentration is a ratio of volume of pollutant to volume of air in parts per million, ppm, or, more commonly, mass per unit volume of air in milligrams per cubic meter, mg/m³ (thousandths of a gram per cubic meter) or micrograms per cubic meter, $\mu g/m^3$ (millionths of a gram per cubic meter). The NAAQS theoretically apply to that portion of the ambient atmosphere which the general public breathes. Misunderstandings arise when one attempts to define what constitutes the atmosphere (for example, the NAAQS are not usually applied inside buildings) or who is a member of the general public (for example, a toll collector working in a toll booth is considered an employee and is thus subject to the OSHA standard of 50 ppm of CO over eight hours). One can raise questions which confuse matters even more. Are persons riding in automobiles members of the general public? Is the air inside cars part of the atmosphere? Is a person smoking a cigarette a member of the general public? Is the air going into a smoker's lungs (containing hundreds of ppm CO) part of the atmosphere? Clearly the definition of where and when the NAAQS apply is not as straightforward as one might hope. In reality the NAAQS apply where the EPA (and the courts) say they apply, and it is prudent for the analyst to bear this in mind when citing the standards.

With regard to reasonable CO receptor sites which implicitly define the term ambient as used in reference to air quality standards, the EPA in EPA-450/4-78-001, *Guidelines for Air Quality Maintenance Planning and Analysis*, Vol. 9 (Revised), *Evaluating Indirect Sources* lists the following as reasonable CO receptor sites: sidewalks, vacant lots, portions of parking lots, building entrances, and air intakes. Unreasonable receptor sites include median strips of roadways, areas within the right-of-way of a limited access highway, areas within intersections, tunnel approaches, areas within toll booths, and portions of parking lots which the general public is not likely to have access to continuously.

Emissions

Air quality impacts are judged by comparison with the ambient air quality standards. Consequently, emission rates for transportation sources are determined for those pollutants to which the standards apply. Liberal doses of judgment, experience, and guesswork go into the selection of an acceptable emission factor.* Keep in mind

---

*Emission rates (to which pollutant concentrations are related in a linear fashion, as opposed to atmospheric conditions which can affect concentrations to a much greater degree) are usually the most controversial component of an air quality analysis. Reviewers tend to question an emission assumption that might affect the final result by one percent while ignoring a meteorologic assumption that might affect the final result by a factor of two.

that when questions arise regarding the acceptability of an emission factor, or for that matter any important component of an air quality analysis, the final decision regarding acceptability lies with the reviewing agency(s). Thus it is wise for the analyst to contact the reviewers (i.e., state and/or Federal officials) regarding the reasonableness of an emission rate when questions arise. This type of foresight will forestall many problems and often expedite review and acceptance of the completed analysis.

In assessing the impact of a transportation facility upon air quality, one is actually evaluating the impact of engines which burn refined low-sulfur petroleum fuel, that is, gasoline or some form of diesel fuel. Regardless of whether the vehicle under consideration is an automobile, jet aircraft, or locomotive, emissions are the by-products of the oxidation of hydrocarbons in the presence of various additives (e.g., lead) and atmospheric gases (e.g., nitrogen). The basic reaction is

$$\text{Hydrocarbon} + O_2 \longrightarrow CO_2 + H_2O + \text{energy}$$

However, since the reaction often occurs in the presence of excess carbon and complications arise from the effects of the walls of the combustion chamber, the reaction becomes

$$\text{Hydrocarbon} + O_2 \longrightarrow CO_2 + H_2O$$
$$+ \text{energy} + CO + \text{unburned hydrocarbons}$$

Depending on the temperature of the reaction and the volume of air passing through the engine, some fraction of the molecules of nitrogen present in the atmosphere will be oxidized. Thus,

$$\text{Hydrocarbon} + O_2 + N_2 \longrightarrow CO_2 + H_2O$$
$$+ \text{energy} + CO + \text{unburned hydrocarbons}$$
$$+ N_2 + NO_x$$

If other substances are present in the fuel (e.g., lead) they may pass through the engine more or less intact to be emitted as air pollutants.

The relative amounts of the various species of pollutants emitted by an engine vary as a function of engine type and the engine's mode of operation, as well as in response to ambient conditions (e.g., temperature, humidity, atmospheric pressure, etc.). Since CO and hydrocarbons result from the incomplete combustion of fuel, increasing the efficiency of combustion tends to reduce the rate at which these pollutants are emitted. For example, an automobile cruising at 10 mph emits more CO and hydrocarbons on a per-mile basis than the same vehicle operating at 40 mph. Conversely, as engine temperature increases, the fraction of atmospheric nitrogen oxidized to NO_x (mostly NO to be converted to NO_2 after emission) increases.

Emission Factors for Highway Project Analysis

Calculation of emission rates is one of the earlier tasks performed in completing an air quality impact analysis for a highway. Emission rates are developed for the various pollutant species in different formats depending on the analysis to be performed.

Carbon Monoxide

CO emissions are usually calculated on a peak-hour basis to yield a g/m-sec (gram per meter per second) emission rate for subsequent use in a dispersion model run which will yield a concentration value for comparison with an ambient standard. CO emissions may also be calculated on a total daily or yearly basis for use in adjusting background concentrations, developing emissions burdens for rollback-type calculations, or selecting a critical year for analysis.

Hydrocarbons

HC emissions are usually calculated on a daily basis for a total-burden analysis to demonstrate conformity with the State Implementation Plan (SIP). However, it makes more sense to calculate total 6:00 a.m. to 9:00 a.m. summertime HC emissions since this is believed by the EPA to be the critical time period with respect to photochemical oxidant formation. (Recall that because HC in and of themselves are considered harmless, they are important only as photochemical oxidant producers.)

Nitrogen Oxides

Like HC, NO_x emissions are often calculated on a daily or yearly basis. Though nitrogen oxides are involved in the formation of photochemical oxidants, they are not considered to be a limiting factor. Thus, NO_x emission rates often are carefully calculated, total emissions tabulated, and the results ignored. At this writing there is a possibility that a short-term NO_x standard will be developed. If a short-term NO_x standard is promulgated, or if nitrogen oxides are deemed a limiting factor in the photochemical oxidant reaction, the calculation of NO_x emissions may assume more importance.

Particulates and Sulfur Oxides

Because of their low emission rates, highway vehicles are not considered important sources of particulates or sulfur oxides. Therefore, emissions of these pollutant species are not usually considered in highway analyses.

Lead

Since highway vehicles are presently significant sources of ambient lead, there is a need to evaluate lead impacts from highway projects. Consequently, there is a need to calculate average lead emissions.

Mobile 1 and Mobile 2*

Proceeding on the assumption that improving the precision with which emissions can be calculated will significantly improve air quality impact assessments for highways, the EPA has refined the process of calculating CO, HC, and NO_x emission rates for highways to the point that a computer is needed to perform the calculation. In addition to improving the precision with which emissions for CO, HC, and NO_x can be made, the advent of the Mobile 1 has introduced a whole new set of assumptions into the highway air quality impact analysis procedure, and fostered countless disagreements over the exact values which should be used as inputs to the model. At this writing Mobile 1 is the method of determining highway emissions. Other sources of emissions data generally are not acceptable to the reviewing agencies.

Mobile 1 is a computer model developed by the EPA for the calculation of vehicle emission factors. The user's guide, EPA-400/9-78-007, *User's Guide to Mobile 1: Mobile Source Emissions Model* was published in August of 1978. It calculates emission of CO, HC, and NO_x for automobiles, two similar classes of light-duty trucks, heavy-duty gasoline powered vehicles, diesel trucks, and motorcycles. The model, together with the document EPA 400/9-78-005,

---

*At this writing, final release of Mobile-2 is imminent. Preliminary indications are that Mobile-2 will be essentially the same as Mobile-1 except that a few new features will be added and vehicle deterioration rates may be somewhat lower.

Mobile Source Emission Factors Final Document, and the user's guide may be obtained from the EPA Office of Mobile Source Air Pollution Control, Emission Control Technology Division, Characterization and Application Branch, 2565 Plymouth Road, Ann Arbor, Michigan 48105. Telephone (313) 668-4306. The user's manual also invites questions concerning model use to this office.

The Mobile 1 consists of a main program and 19 subroutines and data sets, and obviously cannot be used with a hand calculator. Because use of the computer may not be convenient for an individual emissions calculation on a minor project, listings of the more commonly used vehicular emissions factors are available in Vol. 9, *Guidelines for Air Quality Maintenance Planning and Analysis*, from *Evaluating Indirect Sources* EPA-450/4-78-001, 1978. Appendix 6A also contains some representative emission rates.

To use Mobile 1 the analyst must first set sixteen "flags" specifying the types of input/output desired, the choice of default values, the consideration of inspection and maintenance, and so on. With this accomplished, the user supplies "one-time data" relating to vehicle miles travelled (VMT) mix, mileage and registration distributions, emission factor modification data, and inspection and maintenance data. The one-time VMT mix information pertains to the breakdown of the vehicle fleet into automobiles/light-duty vehicles, two classes of light trucks, heavy gasoline trucks, heavy diesel trucks, and motorcycles. Mileage and vehicle registration data relate to the age distribution of the vehicle population (i.e., the percentage of the fleet that is one-year-old automobiles, two-year-old automobiles, one-year-old heavy trucks, etc.). The emission factor modification feature allows one to use emissions factors which differ from those contained in the program. Since the use of factors other than those contained in the program is almost certain to elicit questions from reviewers together with inevitable delays in acceptance of the analysis, the use of this feature is discouraged unless some compelling reason prompts its use.

Inspection and maintenance information is used if the vehicles being modeled will be or are subject to emissions inspections. If inspection and maintenance is a factor to be considered the following information must be supplied.

1. Year of I/M (Inspection and Maintenance) implementation—1982 for many states.

2. Stringency level, that is, what percentage of the vehicles will fail the inspection and require readjustment. Ten percent of the vehicles is a reasonable value.

3. Mechanic training flag: 0 = no, 1 = yes. Many I/M programs will involve the training of mechanics in vehicle maintenance techniques to reduce emissions.

4. Earliest model year included in I/M program; that is, will older vehicles be exempt ("grandfathered") from the program?

5. Latest model year included—unless the program is expected to expire, use 99 (1999) as the value.

Note that specification of inspection and maintenance will serve to reduce expected emissions. If doubt exists as to the applicability of this provision, it may be helpful to contact the state air pollution control agency or department of transportation. As with most factors considered in air quality analyses, one should always "err to the conservative," that is, make emissions higher than expected so that if the completed analysis shows compliance with the standard, no one can suggest that "more reasonable" assumptions would have shown violations.

With the one-time data supplied, the user can proceed with the description of the scenario under study. The inputs are as follows.

1. Region—usually low altitude (high altitude is defined as greater than 4000 ft).

2. Year of analysis—note that emission rates are assumed to decrease every year until well into the 1990s when uncontrolled vehicles will no longer constitute a significant fraction of the vehicle fleet.

3. Speed—CO and HC emissions tend to decrease on a per-mile basis with increasing speed. NO_x emissions tend to increase with increasing speed.

4. Temperature (F°)—emissions tend to increase with decreasing temperature. $20^\circ F$ is often used in "worst-case" analyses because this used to be the lowest temperature Mobile 1 would use. ($0^\circ F$ could be entered but the value output was the same as the $20^\circ F$ value.)

5. Percent of noncatalyst equipped LDV (light-duty vehicles) VMT in the cold start mode—the cold start mode for noncatalytic vehicles

is defined as the first 505 seconds of operation after the engine has been turned off for four hours or more. Twenty percent cold starts are often assumed when site-specific data is not available.

6. Percent of catalyst-equipped LDV in the hot start mode—the hot start mode for catalytic vehicles (not a factor for non-catalytic equipped vehicles) is defined as the first 505 seconds of operation follow-in a nonhot start, that is, less than four hours engine rest. Depending on the situation, 10–30 percent hot starts are often assumed.

7. Percent of catalyst-equipped LDV in the cold start mode—for catalytic vehicles the cold start mode is defined as the first 505 seconds of operation following a cold start. For these vehicles a cold start occurs after a "cold soak" (i.e., the engine not running) of one hour. A value of 20 percent is often assumed for this value.

The FHWA has published a procedure for deriving the percent of cold starts, *The Determination of Vehicular Cold and Hot Operating Conditions for Estimating Highway Emissions*, by Ellis, Camps, and Treadway, dated September 1978. Unfortunately, unless a breakdown of VMT by trip purpose is known (generally it is not), the techniques presented in the document are of limited value. However, an earlier document (August 1977), EPA-450/3-77-023, *Determination of Percentages of Vehicles in the Cold Start Mode*, lists cold start percentages by location (e.g., central business districts, expressways, fringe areas) and by time of day (e.g., morning peak, morning off peak, afternoon peak, etc.) making it a more effective document. See Table 6-2.

In addition to these input variables already described, Mobile 1 accepts inputs relating to: the fraction of LDV using air conditioning , the fraction of LDV carrying an extra 500-lb loading, the fraction of LDV towing trailers, the ambient humidity, average gross weight for heavy-duty gasoline vehicles, the average gross weight for diesel trucks, and the average displacement of both gasoline and diesel heavy trucks. In light of the difficulties associated with obtaining this type of detailed information for a highway project, they are usually ignored by the practicing professional and default values are used.

Mobile 1 Sensitivity

Since air quality analyses are usually performed under some sort of time or money constraint, it is useful to know the relative importance of the various inputs to Mobile 1 so that efforts to determine their proper values can be allocated accordingly. It would make little sense, for example, to spend thousands of dollars determining the percent of vehicles operating in the hot start mode if one were reasonably certain that it was less than 30 percent, if all agreed that 30 percent was a conservative value, and if the difference between zero and 30 percent hot starts amounted to an insignificant difference in emission rates.

The usual object of an air quality analysis is to determine compliance with the NAAQS and to develop a basis for comparison between alternatives. Accordingly, the most efficient approach to performing an analysis is to make what are obviously conservative assumptions concerning the various scenarios, perform the necessary calculations, and compare the results with the standards. If the results approach or exceed the standards, the analysis can be refined by determining more precise values of the most sensitive parameters first and proceeding in the direction of reality until further refinements are not possible or not required.

In Mobile 1, the most sensitive parameters (in rough order of importance) are

1. Year of analysis
2. Speed
3. Percent cold starts
4. Ambient temperature
5. Vehicle mix
6. Inspection and maintenance
7. Percent hot starts

As previously noted, factors related to air conditioning, trailer towing, humidity, gross and net vehicle loading, and engine displacements are usually not too important. Generalizations concerning the sensitivity of Mobile 1 are somewhat difficult to make since model sensitivity is dependent on the pollutant species, the values assumed for fixed parameters (e.g., cold starts with a large fraction of heavy-duty gasoline vehicles versus cold starts assuming a small fraction of heavy-duty vehicles), and the possible range of parameter values (e.g., a 20-percent range in

TABLE 6-2. Suggested Ranges of Values of the Percentage of Vehicles Operating in the Cold Mode for Various Conditions of Time and Location

Case[a]	General Location	Morning Peak Hours (%)	Midday Off-Peak Hours (%)	Evening Peak Hours (%)	Evening and Early Morning Off-Peak Hours (%)	Total Day (%)
I	CBD	10–20	20–50	40–70	25–50	25–55
	Fringe areas	10–20	25–60	40–65	20–45	25–50
	Outer arterials	15–25	30–50	30–60	25–60	30–40
	Local/collector streets	10–20	35–50	35–55	20–70	30–45
	Expressways					
	Within core area and fringes: inbound[b]	3–5	15–20	20–30	10–15	15–20
	Within core area and fringes: outbound[b]	1–3	15–20	15–20	5–10	10–15
	Outer portion of urban area: inbound[b]	3–5	2–4	2–4	4–6	3–5
	Outer portion of urban area: outbound[b]	3–5	2–4	15–20	10–15	10–15
	Special generators outside the CBD	25–40	30–50	45–60	50–65	40–60
II	CBD	5–15	15–45	30–50	20–35	20–40
	Fringe areas	5–15	20–25	30–45	15–45	20–35
	Outer arterials	10–20	15–25	20–45	15–45	20–30
	Local/collector streets	5–20	15–35	25–40	20–70	25–30
	Expressways					
	Within core area and fringes: inbound[b]	2–4	10–20	15–25	10–15	10–20
	Within core area and fringes: outbound[b]	1–3	10–20	10–20	5–10	10–15
	Outer portion of urban area: inbound[b]	2–4	2–4	2–4	3–5	3–5
	Outer portion of urban area: outbound[b]	2–4	2–4	10–20	10–15	10–15
	Special generators outside the CBD	15–25	20–25	30–35	35–40	25–35
III	CBD	1–6	5–20	25–40	15–25	15–25
	Fringe areas	1–15	10–20	15–40	10–40	10–30
	Outer arterials	5–15	10–15	15–30	10–35	15–20
	Local/collector streets	5–15	10–15	15–25	10–60	10–25
	Expressways					
	Within core area and fringes: inbound[b]	1–3	10–15	10–20	10–15	10–15
	Within core area and fringes: outbound[b]	1–3	10–15	10–15	5–10	10–15
	Outer portion of urban area: inbound[b]	1–3	1–3	1–3	2–4	2–4

202

TABLE 6-2. (*Continued*)

Case[a]	General Location	Morning Peak Hours (%)	Midday Off-Peak Hours (%)	Evening Peak Hours (%)	Evening and Early Morning Off-Peak Hours (%)	Total Day (%)
	Outer portion of urban area: outbound[b]	1-3	1-3	10-15	10-15	10-15
	Special generators outside the CBD	15-20	10-20	20-30	25-35	20-30

Source: *Determination of Percentages of Vehicles Operating in the Cold Start Mode*, EPA-450/3-77-023, August 1977.

[a]Case I—no access time added; Case II—1-minute additional access time; Case III—2.5-minute additional access time.
[b]With respect to the CBD.

speed might be possible for a project, but a 20-percent range in vehicle mix might be unusual).

For those interested in more detail concerning the sensitivity of Mobile 1, an analysis developed by the FHWA is presented in Appendix 6F. Note that this document also contains some representative emission rates for highway vehicles. EPA document EPA-400/9-78-006, *Mobile Source Emission Factors for Low Altitude Areas Only*, published in March of 1978 should be consulted for detailed information on the Mobile 1 emission factors.

Aircraft and Rail Emissions

Emissions from airplanes and locomotives follow the same general patterns discussed earlier in this section. That is, they both tend to emit less CO and HC with cruising than while idling, with the inverse being true for NO_x. Emission rates for these sources taken from the Environmental Protection Agency's *Compilation of Air Pollutant Emission Factors*, AP-42, are presented in Appendix 6B. Other emission sources peculiar to airports, such as, working losses from aircraft fueling activities, are discussed in the section on airport modeling. Note that aircraft and locomotives emit somewhat more sulfur oxides and particulates than highway vehicles, depending upon the types of fuel used. For this reason these pollutants are sometimes considered in impact analyses.

Aircraft emission rates are expected to decrease in future years in response to Federal regulations; unfortunately, future emission rates have yet to be published. The analyst may wish to contact the FAA regarding its most recent projection of future emission rates before conducting an analysis or review.

CARBON MONOXIDE MONITORING

This section will discuss why, when, and how one might choose to monitor CO in connection with an air quality analysis for a particular highway project. These same principles also apply to airport developments. There are two basic reasons why CO monitoring is done in connection with the development of an environmental assessment for a transportation project. The primary reason is usually to establish a background CO level for the project area. Monitoring studies may also be used to gather data which can be used to calibrate a dispersion model should such an undertaking prove necessary or desirable. Care must be taken in both the design and execution of an air quality monitoring study if the results are to prove useful. As in so many aspects of air quality analysis, there are commonly accepted methods and procedures which are used, not all of which can be found in the most current set of EPA regulations (e.g., 40 CFR part 58). Furthermore, these dogmas change from time to time and an early consultation with the state air quality control agency may serve to prevent problems further along in the study.

In designing an air quality monitoring study it is important to first establish for what purpose the data will be used. If a rural background level is desired, it may suffice to use a single CO monitor (e.g., a Beckman NDIR or other instrument certified by the EPA) with ancillary equipment (span gas, pump, recorder, etc.) housed in a shelter where constant temperature can be maintained, far from local sources. In a more suburban area one might wish to record wind direction with the CO data so that the effects of local sources on observed concentrations can be assessed. If data were needed for calibration of a dispersion model, one would seek to establish a sampling location utilizing several probes spread across the highway. Traffic counts would be recorded, along with wind speed, wind direction, horizontal and possibly vertical stability, temperature, and insolation.

As used here, the definition of "background level" is quite simple: the concentration of the pollutant species of interest immediately upwind from the source under consideration. Unfortunately, its value varies through time and space; herein lies the problem. If one is to assess the impacts of a highway segment that is perhaps five miles long and which will not even be built for four years, how can one determine a single "representative background value" which will be added to predicted concentrations generated by the highway for subsequent comparison with the ambient CO standards? Prediction of the precise background concentration at a point along the proposed highway during the second worst pollution episode* for the project's critical year (the year when CO concentrations are expected to be highest, usually the year of completion) is nearly impossible. Since background at different locations in the project corridor is likely to vary, precise specification of a unique background concentration is not possible. One is left with the problem of determining a background concentration that will enable the analyst to derive a value which most will agree is conservative (i.e., higher than the actual value) for comparison to the standard.

The first problem to be addressed is a test of the spatial variability of background concentrations. Since background concentrations will vary in different locations within the project corridor, one could site monitoring equipment in many different locations up and down the corridor. The different background values derived from these sites could then be used to predict ambient concentrations at different receptors. This approach may be warranted if one has the resources to commit to such an expensive program.

In deciding how many monitoring sites to commit to a program, one should be guided by several factors, one of which should be the degree of homogeneity within the project corridor. If a project affects both urban and rural areas, it would be advisable to establish monitoring stations within each type of area. However, it may become necessary to apply some judgment in deciding where to commit the usually limited resources available for the project monitoring. Since the final air quality analysis will likely undergo some critical and adverse reviews, it is wise for the analyst to monitor those places where the highest background concentrations can be expected in order to answer the inevitable criticisms regarding the degree of objectivity of the analysis.

There are two schools of thought regarding the placement of CO monitors with respect to local sources. One favors placement far away from the influence of any potential source so that the background concentration, that is, that uniform level of pollutant concentration which is not generated by any identifiable source, can be measured without interference from nearby sources. This approach has the advantage of needing only a CO monitor and a recorder. There is no need to measure wind direction since it does not matter from which direction the pollutant originates. This in turn simplifies the analysis of the data. One needs only to scan the record to select the highest or second highest values to determine background concentration at the monitoring site. Unfortunately, many highways are built in urban areas where it is difficult to find remote sites. And, if a remote site could be found, it would not be a location where maximum background concentrations would be expected. There is also the problem of obtaining access to a site which is removed from potential sources (i.e., roads that will be required in order to transport the monitoring equipment). Finally, these various sources which one tries to avoid in setting up a remote site may actually constitute the sources of the background concentration which is the object of the monitoring study. (Recall that background concentration is defined here as the concentration upwind from the source and *not* some constant

*It is possible that the *worst* episode is the result of a nonrepeatable act of nature. Such a possibility is much less for the *second* worst episode.

global value derived from the sum total of all regional sources and sinks.) Use of this "global background value" would be appropriate and preferable if one were able to effectively calculate (i.e., model) contributions from all significant local sources.

Another approach to the siting of ambient CO monitors requires the concurrent measurement of wind direction. With a record of both CO concentrations and wind direction one can speculate as to the origin of the observed concentrations. Thus the monitor can be sited alongside an existing highway and the concentrations observed while winds blow from the highway to the monitor can be ignored if concentrations generated by the highway are not to be considered in the determination of a background concentration. This approach allows for a more precise determination of background concentrations while providing greater flexibility in monitoring. If other parameters are recorded, for example, time of day, wind speed, temperature, and so on, the analyst has more of an opportunity to critically examine the data and ignore those records that appear to be spurious. Moreover, the costs of site setup, periodic service, and system removal do not increase dramatically with the addition of a few simple wind instruments, a thermometer, and a few extra channels on the recording device. The time of day and date should always be a part of the monitoring record, even if only a single-probe ambient CO monitor is being deployed.

One often measures maximum ambient CO concentrations in the predawn hours. If the dispersion modeling analysis is to assume peak-hour traffic, which may occur sometime in the late afternoon, one may not wish to use maximum concentrations characteristic only of the late night conditions to represent background concentrations. Consequently, care should be taken to accurately record time of day on the CO record so that these hours can be positively identified.

With a single CO probe located near a highway, observed concentrations will reflect contributions from the highway about half the time. If the project for which monitoring is being conducted involves improvements to the nearby highway, those data containing an unknown fraction of highway-generated pollutant will probably not be used to determine a background

concentration. One is left with a data set for which only half of the entries are of potential value. This may present a special problem for the determination of an eight-hour average background concentration if wind directions fluctuate from hour to hour (as they tend to do at low speeds, which are associated with maximum pollutant concentrations). The use of multiple CO probes located on either side of the highway offers at least a partial solution to this problem. However, problems associated with stringing tubing across a highway or setting up separate sites do contribute to the time and money required to successfully complete a monitoring effort.

If one is going to commit the resources required to set up and maintain a multiprobed monitoring site to determine background concentration, one might be well advised to take the program one step further and provide for the acquisition of data that could be used for dispersion model calibration. Calibration data can be very useful since the commonly used dispersion models tend to be inaccurate and conservative. The models are generally accurate only within a factor of two or three* and tend to overpredict.

These facts can present quite a problem for an agency intent upon building a highway. Since the attainment of the NAAQS by 1982 was mandated by the 1977 Amendments to the Clean Air Act, construction of a highway which would result in violations of the CO standards would not be consistent with the state air quality implementation plan (SIP). Consequently, the acquisition of state and/or Federal monies for highway construction would be difficult, if not impossible. Since the highway construction agency is usually the sponsor of the analysis, the analyst will often find that project managers are somewhat skeptical concerning the results of an analysis which shows that the proposed project is in violation of the standards. This is especially true if the violation is due to the conservatism of the dispersion model, when in fact no violation may actually occur.

One way to avoid this problem is to use a dispersion model which has been calibrated for the site in question to reduce the degree of uncer-

---

*This makes one wonder if it is worth the trouble to calculate emission rates to the nearest percent using Mobile 1.

tainty (and conservativeness) associated with un-calibrated model results. To calibrate a dispersion model one collects data at the site in question that conforms to the input requirements of the model, runs the model for the existing conditions, and compares model output with current observed data for the site in question. For example, if *observed* CO limits were 50 percent of those *predicted* by the model, one would adjust predicted values by a calibration factor of 0.5 to better conform with observed concentrations.

To design a monitoring system that will yield data lending itself to calibration, several factors should be considered, among them the parameters to be measured, the time of year during which the monitoring is to be done, and the location of the monitoring site. The design of an effective system involves tradeoffs between these various factors in an effort to conduct an optimal, if not perfect, monitoring study.

As in any well designed experiment, it is important to define the intended use of the desired data. When designing an ambient air quality monitoring system for use in calibrating a dispersion model it is important to know which model will be used and in which situations and specifically which parameters should be measured. This seems a trivial observation, but calibration studies have been performed which failed to record, for example, traffic counts, or some other variable. When the analyses on such data sets are completed, the conclusions almost always attribute the low degree of correlation between observed and predicted ambient concentrations (which seem characteristic of dispersion models in general) to uncertainties associated with unmeasured parameters. While this practice does provide a built-in, convenient, and credible explanation for the disappointing lack of correlation that often results from calibration studies, it does little to enhance the analyst's professional credibility.

If one intends to calibrate a Gaussian plume model such as HIWAY-2 at a site which is suitable for dispersion modeling (see the section on dispersion modeling) as well as determine a "representative background value," one could incorporate the following into the monitoring system.

1. A right-angle transect across the highway with 4 to 8 CO probes at various distances from the highway, preferably at breathing height (1-2 m), though EPA* criteria suggest 2-3 m.

2. A meteorological tower of perhaps 10 m containing wind instrument(s) to measure wind speed (with a threshold of less than 1 m), wind direction, and the horizontal and/or vertical deviation of the wind angle. Temperature should be monitored.

3. Traffic counters (induction loops often work best) to record traffic on a lane-by-lane basis if possible.

If strip charts are used to record the data in a continuous manner there is no need to worry about the averaging time of the various parameters. However, if the increasingly popular electronic averagers are to be used in connection with either strip charts or magnetic tape the analyst should give some thought to the averaging time for the various parameters. Wind direction is especially critical in this regard. If wind direction is only recorded on an hourly basis, the analyst may experience difficulty in discriminating between hours characterized by fairly constant fluctuations about some mean and hours of "identical" recorded wind direction and stability characterized by nonrandom changes in the mean wind direction (e.g., two distinct wind directions). The results may show a poor relationship between observed and predicted values.[†] Unless the analyst has made provisions for recording wind directions on something less than a one-hour basis, it may not be possible to adequately screen the data to select "nicely behaved" periods for use in model calibrations.

Using a monitoring system as described, one can easily discern background concentrations under a wide range of wind regimes by simply identifying the upwind probe(s). Because there is generally more than one instrument functioning at any given time and the other meteorological and traffic data aid in determining what is happening during the period of observation, one can also identify incorrect readings resulting from equipment malfunction. It

---

*40 CFR 58 Appendix E: *Probe Siting Criteria for Ambient Air Quality Monitoring*, Section 4.1.

[†]See the dispersion modeling section of this chapter for more on this subject.

should always be kept in mind that of the months of monitoring data acquired, relatively few hours of data (in some cases one) representing worst-case conditions will actually be used in further analysis. Thus, it is wise for the analyst to insure that this worst-case hour is a result of conditions that occurred on the site and not some undetected equipment malfunction.

There seems to be no clear consensus regarding when and for how long one should perform ambient air monitoring studies for the purpose of determining a background CO level. Ideally one would establish a monitoring site in some suitable area and collect data for some years so the return period for the various background levels could be firmly established. Indeed, since the Continuous Air Monitoring Station (CAMS) network usually maintained by the state air quality control agency provides such a record, every effort should be made to use CAMS data when appropriate. Unfortunately, one seldom finds a CAMS station located in just the right place, nor does one usually have the time and resources required to conduct a multiyear CO monitoring study. Obviously, some compromises must be made.

Given some additional information regarding CO concentrations, it is generally possible to arrive at a representative background concentration corresponding to the second-highest annual CO concentration upwind of the source of interest. (Whether or not this concentration will occur during the worst-case traffic and meteorologic conditions is questionable; however, in the absence of a better method this is how the analyses are performed—see the other sections of this chapter for further discussion of assumptions implicit in the typical CO analysis.)

It is useful to note that maximum CO levels tend to occur between October and February. Thus, if one conducts monitoring between October and February, one is reasonably well assured of recording a maximum annual concentration. NCHRP report 200 (Maisel and Dushang, 1978) takes this one step further and suggests that monitoring may be conducted for one month during the "CO season" and the maximum eight-hour value observed during the test month be used as an estimate for the second-highest annual value, provided that a sufficient number of adverse days occurred during the month in question. An adverse day is defined as a day during

which one of the 73 (20 percent of 365) highest daily eight hour CO concentrations occurred at a CAMS-type station (with a full year's data). This station must, through time, exhibit CO patterns similar to those recorded at the background monitor. A sufficient number of adverse days is defined as six. In other words, sampling for one month and calling the maximum observed eight hour concentration the second annual maximum is acceptable as long as six of the 73 worst days of the year occurred while sampling was being done. If a CAMS-type station is not available for the determination of adverse days, one can assume that a sufficient number occurred, provided sampling was conducted for at least 30 days between the beginning of October and the end of January. Other methods of determining adverse days are also presented in NCHRP Report 200; however, they are somewhat less satisfactory than these mentioned above. NCHRP Report 200 suggests that a one hour second-highest value can be estimated from the derived eight hour second-highest annual level using the following expression:

$$CO_{1-hour} = (1.26 \times CO_{8-hour}) + 4.4 \qquad (6-1)$$

A simplified approach to the determination of background levels which enjoys at least occasional use involves the acquisition of a reasonable background monitoring record (e.g., three months) preferably during the CO season with the maximum observed concentration used as a background level. If the data cannot be acquired during the CO season it can be adjusted for seasonality through comparison with the nearest CAMS station whose whole environs resemble those of the background monitor. (For example, if monitoring were conducted from May through July and the local CAMS station showed a maximum concentration during the period which was one-half the second highest annual value, the seasonally adjusted background level would be twice the observed background value.)

Clear direction regarding the optimal length of a background CO monitoring study cannot be offered here, as acceptable practices vary from state to state. Accordingly it is recommended that the state air pollution control agency be consulted before time, equipment, and manpower are committed to a background CO monitoring study. Not only can the state offer advice regarding what it considers to be acceptable monitoring and analysis procedures, it may already have data for the project area which could eliminate the need for project monitoring.

POLLUTANT DISPERSION

Given a system of pollutant sources and receptors, how does one predict the pollutant concentrations to which the sources will be exposed? One could begin by examining the concentration (mass, $\mu g/m^3$, or volume, ppm) and performing a dimensional analysis. That is, if the mass of pollutant is known or can be derived using known emission rates, determine the volume or air into which the mass of pollutant will be mixed to derive an average concentration value. For example, if a room contains 100 m^3 of air into which 50 μg of CO is released, the concentration of CO in the room would approach 0.5 $\mu g/m^3$ after the pollutant has had a chance to diffuse throughout the entire volume of air. The problem is made slightly more complex if the hypothetical room is equipped with a ventilation system which exchanges room air for clean air at a rate of 1 m^3 per second. A steady-state concentration estimate can still be made if the emission rate of the pollutant is known. That is, if the emission rate is 5 μg per second and 1 m^3 of air is exchanged for clean air every second, eventually (i.e., at steady-rate) the amount of pollutant emitted per unit time should equal the amount of pollutant lost per unit time. Thus, the 1 m^3 of air lost every second must contain an average of 5 μg of pollutant. Therefore, if the pollutant concentration is equal throughout the entire room (as it must be, assuming diffusion is the only pollutant dispersion mechanism) then the concentration of pollutant throughout the room must be the same as the concentration of pollutant in the room exhaust (5 $\mu g/m^3$). This line of reasoning is central to the development of so-called box models discussed later in this section.

Consider what would happen to the box model room above if the intake valve for the pollutant were located near the exhaust duct through which room air was expelled. In this situation the assumption that the pollutant is diffused equally throughout the room breaks down. One could easily imagine a situation in which the movement of air to the room exhaust (advection) would sweep the entire volume of pollutant emission (or worse yet, some unknown fraction of pollutant emission) along with it so that

it was exhausted (lost to the system) before it diffused throughout the room. In this case one could only predict that pollutant concentration within the room would average somewhere between zero and 5 $\mu g/m^3$, hardly a definitive prediction.

Unfortunately for those who must attempt to predict concentrations of pollutants into the atmosphere, the uniform dispersion of pollutant throughout some known volume of air is an assumption which can rarely, if ever, be completely justified. In the atmosphere, the process of advection moves pollutants around at a rate much higher than simple diffusion.* Thus, if one wishes to explain pollutant dispersion in the atmosphere it is necessary to examine the process of advection (i.e., winds) in the atmosphere. In addition to advection, other factors at work in the atmosphere which can affect pollutant concentrations include deposition, chemical reactions, and confinement of an air mass through the effects of topography and/or the presence of an inversion.

The movement (advection) of air across the surface of the earth can occur in one of two distinct modes: laminar or turbulent flow.† Laminar flow is characterized by parallel movement of fluid parcels as they are transported from point to point. An example of laminar flow may be found in a slow moving stream with a smooth bottom. Turbulent flow, by contrast, is characterized by violent swirling motions and the presence of eddies. Turbulent flow might be observed in a swiftly moving brook with a rough stony bottom.

In the atmosphere the movement of air is almost always turbulent. The degree of turbulence is affected by such things as wind speed, surface roughness, and surface temperature. One can easily imagine how the movement of air is typified by more violent eddies as wind speed increases, and also how any tendency for laminar flow could be disrupted by the presence of

---

*As used here, diffusion refers to a molecular process by which the random (kinetic) motion of individual molecules serves to uniformly mix two dissimilar chemical species.

†A detailed discussion of turbulence (or meteorology in general) is beyond the scope of this book. A brief and rather simplified discussion of this topic is offered here in the hope that the reader will consult a more complete discussion of the topic as can be found in meterological texts.

obstacles (e.g., trees, buildings, powerlines) that increase the roughness of the earth's surface and thus impede the smooth flow of air.

Perhaps less obvious but nonetheless highly effective in generating atmospheric turbulence is the effect of air parcels rising from the heated surface of the earth which tend to disrupt and confuse the smooth movement of air across the surface. When the sun shines on the earth's surface, especially on surfaces which have a low albedo (percent reflected light) such as concrete, rooftops, and plowed fields, the surface absorbs energy from the sun and its temperature increases. An air parcel in contact with the heated surface will be warmed through conduction and its temperature will increase. As the temperature of this parcel increases it will expand; that is, its molecules will be pushed farther from one another due to an increase in kinetic energy, and it will become less dense than parcels above it due to its elevated temperature. Eventually the more dense, cooler parcels, lying above the warmed parcel, will displace the warmed parcel, causing it to rise, or float up into the atmosphere. This vertical convective motion, when superimposed on the horizontal flow of the winds, tends to disrupt horizontal flow and leads to the generation of turbulence. The atmosphere's tendency for vertical motion, regardless of cause, is termed stability. An unstable atmosphere has a strong tendency for vertical motion and a stable atmosphere does not.

The upward movement of a heated parcel is, of course, affected by the temperature of the parcels above it. As a parcel is lifted up (or rather pushed, or buoyed up by more dense parcels) into the higher and less dense (i.e., lower pressure) levels of the atmosphere, it will expand in response to the lower ambient pressure. In expanding its molecules it will give up kinetic energy and the parcel will cool. This process will continue until the parcel has been lifted to a point where it exhibits the same temperature (and thus the same density) as its neighbors. The rate at which a parcel cools as it rises in the atmosphere as the result of adiabatic cooling (no exchange of energy with surrounding parcels) is called the adiabatic lapse rate. For dry parcels the adiabatic lapse rate is approximately $1°C$ per 100 vertical meters. Some thought on this topic (and/or reference to an adiabatic chart, found in most meteorologic texts) should convince the reader that if the thermal structure

of the atmosphere is such that ambient temperature decreases with height at a rate of less than $1°C$ per 100 m, a dry parcel in vertical motion will tend to cool with height at a rate which is less than the observed lapse rate (rate of temperature change with height). Thus the moving parcel will always be warmer and less dense than its neighbors and it will tend to keep moving vertically. Note that if some parcels are moving up, others must be moving down. Thus the atmosphere tends to be "well-stirred," that is, unstable, when the observed lapse rate is "superadiabatic," that is, decreasing in temperature with height at a rate greater than $1°C$ per 100 m. Similarly, when the lapse rate is subadiabatic, or an inversion occurs (i.e., temperature increases with height instead of decreases), parcels rising from the surface tend not to go far before they have cooled to a point where they are no longer warmer than their neighbors and vertical motion is suppressed. Thus subadiabatic activity occurs in the more extreme case of an inversion, when air parcels tend not to move vertically (i.e., remain at the surface if that is where they started) and stable conditions result. When the lapse rate is approximately equal to the adiabatic lapse rate* the atmosphere's tendency for vertical motion is neither enhanced nor suppressed. Such conditions are said to exhibit neutral stability.

Occasionally, because of the downward movement (i.e., compression) of air associated with a high pressure system, the cooling of layers in contact with the ground on a clear calm night, or some geographic anomaly, an inversion aloft is formed. Such an inversion can form a functional lid over an area trapping pollutants below. The classic scenario for the formation of a nocturnal inversion begins with the radiational cooling of the ground surface. This phenomenon is especially prevalent on clear nights when clouds (i.e., water vapor) are not present to absorb infrared radiation emitted from the ground surface and reradiate this energy back to the surface.[†] With the cooling of the ground surface, air lying above the ground is cooled by conduction. As this process proceeds through the evening a layer

---

*Note that there is also a pseudoadiabatic lapse rate of approximately $0.6°C/100$ m for moist parcels which condense water as they cool.

[†]Note that this absorption and reradiation of terrestrial radiation by the atmosphere is known as the greenhouse effect—even though real greenhouses do not operate in this fashion.

of very cool air overlaid by successively warmer layers is formed.

In valleys the formation of a nocturnal inversion can be exacerbated by the action of slope, or valley, winds. When air next to cool earth is cooled it becomes more dense than the air above it. When this happens on a slope this dense air flows down the slope (in the absence of some overriding regional wind regime) and tends to collect in the valley below forming a deep pool of cool air. This deep pool of air is of course stratified with the coolest (most dense) air at the bottom overlaid by warmer (less dense) layers above, thus forming an inversion.

In the morning following formation of a nocturnal inversion, solar energy (to which the atmosphere is more or less transparent) warms the earth's surface and parcels lying on the surface are warmed by conduction. These warmed parcels will be displaced upward by cooler parcels (expanding and cooling as they go) until they reach a level where they are at the same temperature (and the same density) as the surrounding parcels. Since the lapse rate in this nocturnal inversion is inverted, that is, temperature increases with height, and the parcels cool as they are lifted, the first few parcels will not get far and will be trapped very near the surface. As the day progresses more and more of the nocturnal inversion will be destroyed from below by the addition of energy supplied by the rising parcels. However, until the entire inversion is destroyed, air (and pollutants) below the bottom of the inversion will not be mixed with the air above, and the inversion layer will act as a lid, trapping air (and pollutants) beneath it. Figure 6-3 illustrates the formation and destruction of a nocturnal inversion.

The implications of an inversion trapping pollutants below it are relatively straightforward. Recalling the earlier discussion concerning the dispersion of pollutants within a room, if the

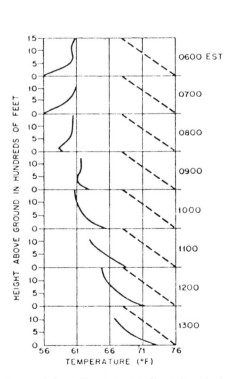

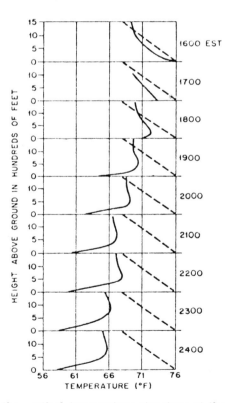

Figure 6-3.   The average diurnal variation of the vertical temperature structure at the Oak Ridge National Laboratory during the period September–October, 1950. The data were obtained from captive-balloon temperature soundings. The dashed line in each panel represents the adiabatic lapse rate. (Holland, 1953). Source: Slade, D./H., ed., *Meteorology and Atomic Energy, 1968*, U.S. Atomic Energy Commission, July 1968.

volume of air in the room (or within the atmosphere) through which pollutants can disperse is reduced, then the resultant concentration will be increased. To offer an obvious example, given equal volumes of pollutants, one would expect concentrations within a room of 50 m³ to be twice that in a room enclosing 100 m³. Similarly, one would expect pollutant concentrations measured while an inversion was present at 100 m (a mixing height of 100 m) to be greater than concentrations measured while an inversion was present at 300 m, assuming that equal amounts of pollutants were dispersed uniformly throughout the available air column. The trapping phenomenon associated with inversions can be especially troublesome when it occurs in a valley (where nocturnal or "ground-based" inversions are likely to occur) in that the valley walls can serve to restrict lateral pollutant dispersion while an inversion aloft prevents vertical dispersion.

Sea (or lake) breezes, like valley (or slope) winds, are rather weak local air movements generated by variations in temperature (and consequently density) of adjacent air parcels at or near the earth's surface. Sea breezes occur when one portion of the earth's surface is cooler than an adjacent portion. In temperate areas this often happens in the spring and early summer months when the greater thermal inertia of a large body of water causes it to increase in temperature more slowly than an adjacent land area. When soil surfaces near a large cool water body are warmed by the sun, air parcels warmed by contact with the soil tend to be displaced by the cooler air parcels which overlay the cold water. This convective movement creates a breeze from the cold water to the warm land. Since the parcels moving from the water to the land must be replaced by something, air parcels above the land surface tend to be displaced toward the water, forming a closed cell. This type of circulation tends to be most vigorous on calm sunny days when the temperature differential between land and water surfaces is the greatest. This closed convective cell can extend several miles inland and generate wind speeds of several miles per hour. It can also operate in the reverse direction at night. In addition to the influence this circulation can have on a local wind regime, it is important to note that the sea breeze is a closed system and pollutants introduced into the cell will remain trapped until the system breaks

down as the day ends with the nocturnal cooling of the land mass or when a more vigorous regional wind pattern overrides the seabreeze system.

At this point, the reader should have some appreciation of the mechanisms which affect the degree of turbulence with which the invisible, compressible, fluid air is moved across the earth. Whether induced by the speed of the wind, which is basically a function of the strength of the regional pressure gradient (i.e., regional high and low pressure areas), the stability of the atmosphere, which is a function of the lapse rate (vertical temperature structure of the atmosphere), surface roughness, or, more typically, some combination of these factors, turbulence is virtually always present in the atmosphere. It is the degree of turbulence which determines the rate at which pollutants are dispersed. The following discussion presents the relationship between turbulence and dispersion from the standpoint of the mechanics of the Gaussian Plume Model. Such a discussion is appropriate because the Gaussian Plume Model is by far the most commonly used technique for calculating pollutant concentrations. However, the reader should not assume that it constitutes the only viable method for modeling dispersion nor is it necessarily the most satisfactory method of conceptualizing the dispersion process.

Consider a single isolated point source, such as the smoke stack of a power plant. Upon emission, the plume rises because it is warmer (i.e., less dense) than the surrounding air. As the plume is advected downwind, the effects of atmospheric turbulence are immediately apparent. Small eddies, that is, those contained within the plume, force the plume to diffuse. Its cross-sectional area may increase from 1 to 5 m² within a kilometer of the stack. Larger eddies, that is, those too large to be contained within the plume, tend to move the entire plume up and down and/or side to side. (This causes the "looping" behavior of plumes on bright, sunny (unstable) days as large eddies generated by vigorous convection occasionally sweep the entire plume down to the ground or high into the air.) These up-and-down and side-to-side perturbations seem to occur at random. By analogy one could compare these motions with the familiar random coin toss experiment in which a professor seated at the head of a classroom flips a coin and passes it forward to the student on his right or left, depending on the outcome of the toss. The student receiving the coin flips it, and passes it to a student behind him over his shoulder to the left or right, depending on the outcome. This procedure is repeated by the coin recipient in the second row of students and so on for many coins. When the coins are collected in the back of the room the students seated in the middle of the room tend to receive the most coins and those seated at the sides of the room tend to receive relatively few. Upon further reflection it will be noted that the distribution of coins across the back of the room approximates a "normal" (or bell-shaped) distribution (or curve).

A similar phenomenon may be observed for plumes wafted from side to side (and up and down) by atmospheric turbulence. If a set of monitors were set up to measure pollutant concentrations across the axis of a plume, it could be observed that the maximum pollutant concentrations were recorded at the plume center line, that pollutant concentrations decrease with increasing distance from the center line, and that distribution of pollutant concentrations across the plume axis approximates a normal distribution (see Figure 6-4). Note that as the duration of monitoring observations across the plume and increased from say ten minutes to one hour the plume tends to become more "spread-out," center-line concentrations decrease, and the

values recorded at the plume margins tend to increase. Such is the effect of increasing the averaging time of the observations (again see Figure 6-4). A rather graphic illustration of the effects of averaging time on plume shape (and concentration) can be seen by comparing "snapshots" of plumes with time-lapse photographs of the same area which show a smoother, larger plume outline.

The two descriptors of the normal distribution are the mean and standard deviation. The mean defines the center point of the distribution and the standard deviation describes the spread of the curve (note that the "bell-shaped" shape of the curve remains constant). Applying this to plume spreading, an increase in plume spread can be described in terms of an increase in the standard deviation of the concentration distribution across the plume.

With some appreciation for the effects of turbulence superimposed on wind direction in the "spreading" and "wafting" of plumes conveyed, the effects of other aspects of wind dynamics on pollutant dispersion can be examined. Consider a smoke stack that emits one pollutant particle per second. At a constant wind speed of 1 m/sec, one would expect the mean distance between particles being transported downwind to be on the order of 1 m. If wind speed were to increase to 2 m/sec and particle releases were to continue at a rate of one per second, one would expect the mean distance between the particles to in-

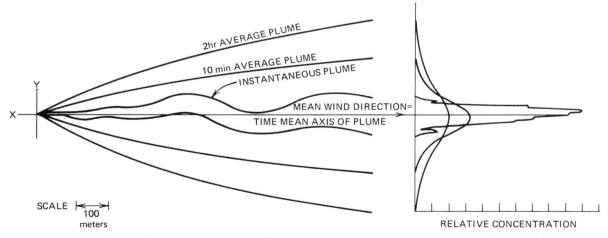

Figure 6-4. The diagram on the left represents the approximate outlines of a smoke plume observed instantaneously and of plumes averaged over 10 minutes and two hours. The diagram on the right shows the corresponding cross-plume distribution patterns. Source: Slade, D./H., ed., *Meteorology and Atomic Energy, 1968*, U.S. Atomic Energy Commission, July 1968.

crease to 2 m. Following this line of reasoning, it is apparent that pollutant concentrations tend to be inversely proportional to wind speed.

The effects of stability and mixing height have already been discussed to some degree. As the stability (tendency against vertical motion) decreases, the more intense and vigorous is the degree of atmospheric turbulence. This in turn tends to spread the plume more rapidly (to increase the standard deviation, σ, of the concentration distribution across the plume). If the plume has spread vertically to a point where the upper margin of the plume is contained by an inversion, the lower the mixing height, the higher the average pollutant concentration between the ground and the base of the inversion will be.

Emission height can also play a significant role in determining ground level concentrations. The greater the height of emission, the greater the vertical plume spread required before significant concentrations will be observed at ground level, and the lower ground level concentrations will be. If the plume is emitted close to the ground, it will have less of a chance to disperse (to increase its cross-sectional area) before affecting ground-based receptors at some point downwind.

The Gaussian Plume Model

This discussion utilizes the axis system shown in Figure 6-5, making the following assumptions.

1. Continuous emission from the source or emission times equal to or greater than travel times to the downwind location under consideration, so that the diffusion in the direction of transport may be neglected.

2. The material diffused is a stable gas or aerosol (less than 20 μm diameter) which remains suspended in the air over long periods of time.

3. The equation of continuity

$$Q = \int_0^{+\infty} \int_{-\infty}^{+\infty} \chi\, u\, du\, dz$$

is fulfilled, that is, none of the material is removed from the plume as it moves downwind and there is complete reflection at the ground.

4. The mean wind direction specifies the x-axis and a mean wind speed representative of the diffusing layer is chosen.

5. Except where specifically mentioned, the plume constituents are distributed normally in both the cross-wind and vertical directions.

6. Standard deviations (σ) used to quantify plume spread are consistent with averaging time of the concentration estimate.

It can be shown that the concentration of a pollutant at a point (x, y, z) generated by a

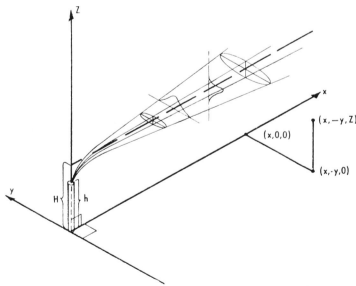

Figure 6-5. Coordinate system showing Gaussian distributions in the horizontal and vertical. Source: Turner, D./B., *Workbook of Atmospheric Dispersion Estimates*, EPA, 1970.

source at a height H can be estimated using the expression

$$\chi(x, y, z; H) = \frac{Q}{2\pi\sigma_y \sigma_z u} \exp\left[-\frac{1}{2}\left(\frac{y}{\sigma_y}\right)^2\right]$$

$$\left\{\exp\left[-\frac{1}{2}\left(\frac{z-H}{\sigma_z}\right)^2\right]\right.$$

$$\left.+ \exp\left[-\frac{1}{2}\left(\frac{z+H}{\sigma_z}\right)^2\right]\right\}$$

(6-2)

where χ = pollutant concentration
(x, y, z) = coordinates of the receptor point
H = height of emission
u = wind speed
Q = the emission rate
σ_y, σ_z = standard deviation of plume concentration distribution across the horizontal and vertical dimensions of the plume at the downwind distance x

However imposing this equation may seem at first glance, the placement of the various terms in the expression do make some sense intuitively. For example, Q is the numerator of the first part of the expression. That is, concentration (x, y, z: H) is directly proportional to the emission rate. Thus the expression indicates that if emissions are doubled, then concentrations will double. Since pollutants are transported passively by the atmosphere, if twice as many are released at the source, then twice as many should appear at the receptor regardless of the route they followed getting there.

Wind speed u appears in the denominator of the first part of the expression. Recalling the earlier discussion regarding the spacing of successively emitted particles as a function of wind speed, it should not be surprising that the expression shows concentration to be inversely proportional to the wind speed.

Horizontal and vertical sigmas (standard deviations, σ_y and σ_z) also appear in the denominator of the first part of the expression. This would indicate an inverse relationship between plume spread and concentration; that is, the greater the plume spread the lower the concentration at the plume centerline. In light of the earlier discussion, this should not seem strange to the reader.

The exponential terms in the equations are most simply considered adjustments necessary for the prediction of concentrations at receptor points off the centerline. This will become clearer later in the discussion. The remaining terms in the expression are constants.

For ground level receptors ($z = 0$) the Gaussian Plume expression becomes

$$\chi(x, y, 0; H) = \frac{Q}{\pi\sigma_y \sigma_z u} \exp\left[-\frac{1}{2}\left(\frac{y}{\sigma_y}\right)^2\right]$$

$$\cdot \exp\left[-\frac{1}{2}\left(\frac{H}{\sigma_z}\right)^2\right] \quad (6\text{-}3)$$

Additional simplification results when off-centerline concentrations are not considered (maximum concentrations occur at the centerline); and concentrations become a function of distance downwind, emission height, emission rate, plume spread (stability), and windspeed.

$$\chi(x, 0, 0; H) = \frac{Q}{\pi\sigma_z \sigma_z u} \exp\left[-\frac{1}{2}\left(\frac{H}{\sigma_z}\right)^2\right] \quad (6\text{-}4)$$

Finally, for ground level emissions

$$\chi(x, 0, 0; 0) = \frac{Q}{\pi\sigma_y \sigma_z u} \quad (6\text{-}5)$$

and concentrations at the ground along the plume centerline are a direct function of emission rate, and an inverse function of plume spread (stability) and wind speed.

Thus, given wind speed, emission rate, emission height, and receptor location, it would seem that if one had some system for determining plume spread (σ_y, σ_z) as a function of stability, calculating pollutant concentrations would be a simple matter.

One possible method of predicting plume spread on the basis of meteorological observations could involve the measurement of fluctuations in the vertical and horizontal component of the mean wind direction. Horizontal and vertical vector vanes can be used to measure the fluctuations in the wind direction on a continuous basis. These observations can be analyzed, for example, to derive a mean horizontal direction with some measure of the standard deviation of the wind angle (σ_θ). From σ_θ one could estimate σ_y, given the downward distance x through simple trigonometry (i.e., $\sigma_y = x \tan \sigma_\theta$, or, if σ_θ is expressed in radians, $\sigma_y \simeq \sigma_\theta$). Of course, the same basic technique could be used to estimate σ_z.

However, this technique is of limited utility if one wishes to investigate hypothetical situations involving, for example, a west wind under very stable conditions at a site where the standard deviation of the horizontal and vertical components are not known. Obviously if air quality experts are to perform analyses for specified conditions, some convention for describing stability must be adopted along with standard σ_y and σ_z functions. Turner (1970) has done much to promote this and a portion of his *Workbook of Atmospheric Dispersion Estimates* is included in this volume as Appendix 6C.

The standard stability classes (often referred to as the Pasquill-Gifford curves or classes) involved six classes, A to F. A is the most unstable and is expected to occur with light winds and high isolation (bright sunshine); that is, those kind of conditions which promote strong convective mixing. B and C stabilities occur at more moderate wind speeds and insolations. D, or neutral stability (characterized by the adiabatic lapse rate) occurs with stronger winds (3-6 m/sec) depending on the degree of cloudiness (the more cloudy the more the tendency for vertical stability). D stability can occur day or night. E and F stability are used to denote stable conditions such as would be found during a ground-based inversion and are expected to occur only during relatively calm nighttime hours. Note that the descriptions provided here are rather grossly oversimplified and that stability can be influenced by such other factors as surface roughness, height above the surface at which dispersion is occurring, and averaging time. The 10-minute Pasquall-Gifford Curves as presented by Turner (1970) which plot σ_y and σ_z versus distance downwind x for the various stability classes are contained in Appendix 6C.

Though it may be the most widely used method of air pollution impact analysis, the Gaussian Plume Model does have some inherent limitations. Assuming for the moment that the line sources of interest (e.g., highways, aircraft taxiways, runways, approach and departure patterns, railroad tracks, etc.) can be approximated as a series of point sources (which they are in most current dispersion models), one can arrive at a reasonable assessment of the limitations of most pollutant models by examining the assumptions implicit in the Gaussian Plume Model.

The assumption regarding continuous emission for a time equal to or greater than the aver-aging time of interest may be well approximated during a one-hour period along a busy highway. However, if one attempted to model emissions from a railroad or lightly traveled highway, this assumption might tend to break down if a large "slug" of pollutant material were emitted from the source during a period when the instantaneous wind direction did not happen to match the mean wind direction for the hour of interest.

The stable gas assumption is well approximated by carbon monoxide (CO), the pollutant most often of interest. However, some pollutants [e.g., hydrocarbons (HC) and nitrogen oxides (NO_x)] do undergo chemical transformations over the course of hours, and a regional modeling exercise which might involve travel times exceeding an hour should consider reactions (photochemical oxidation) which would change the total amount of pollutant in the system.

The continuity expression which calls for complete reflection of the plume from the ground surface is generally well approximated by the gaseous pollutants (CO, NO_x). Hydrocarbon droplets may tend to stick to the ground surface, but the problem pollutant in this regard is lead. Lead particles, especially large flakes emitted under heavy acceleration, exhibit a high settling velocity (a measure of a particle's tendency to stick to a surface, usually expressed in terms of centimeters per second). This issue has been addressed by the EPA in the development of a highway lead model (PBLSQ). However the model has not yet been released, reportedly due to problems concerning the proper technique for treating pollutant deposition. Note that a worst-case assumption of no deposition would yield concentration estimates that would tend to be conservative (too high).

The assumption regarding the specification of a mean wind direction causes a great deal of trouble in actual practice. If, for example, the wind blows across a highway from the north for half an hour and then shifts and blows from the south for half an hour, one could say that the average wind direction was from the east (or west). Unfortunately a Gaussian Plume calculation based on an easterly wind would not yield an accurate estimate for this condition. Marked wind shifts are not at all consistent with the concept of a well behaved conical plume spreading uniformly downwind from a constant source. To make matters worse, frequent shifts in wind direction are more the rule than the exception at the low wind speeds assumed in most analyses.* Unfortunately, high pollutant concentrations, worst-case conditions, and potential violations of the ambient standards tend to occur under light (and variable) winds. Consequently most dispersion calculations made for transportation sources using the Gaussian Plume Model to calculate expected pollutant concentrations for comparison to the ambient standards assume atmospheric conditions for which the model is not especially well suited.[†]

The assumptions regarding the Gaussian (normal) distribution of plume constituents in the crosswind and vertical directions also tend to break down under fluctuating wind directions (low wind speeds). The Gaussian assumptions are also highly time-dependent. The standard deviations (σ's) listed in the Turner workbook were originally developed to represent a ten-minute averaging time. When HIWAY (the EPA's original highway dispersion model) was developed in the mid 1970s, the Turner σ values were applied directly to the calculation of one-hour pollutant concentrations. The Turner workbook states that due to the increased meandering of wind direction, σ_y tends to increase with time, and a one-fifth power law of σ_y with time is mentioned for periods between 3 and 30 minutes. (σ_z also increases with time, though the constraints on σ_z imposed by the distance between the ground surface and the base of the inversion limit the growth of σ_z within a relatively short time.) At this writing, the EPA has observed that the σ's chosen for HIWAY are too low to represent a one-hour average, particularly at low wind speeds, when σ_y tends to be large due to a meandering wind. The σ values for HIWAY have been revised in the new version of HIWAY, HIWAY-2, which was released in May of 1980.

The idea of using a Gaussian Plume Model to estimate eight-hour pollutant concentrations is occasionally forwarded by newcomers to the field. However, problems associated with specifying σ's and a mean wind direction over an eight-hour period make this a somewhat impractical idea. The Gaussian Plume Model seems to work best for averaging times between ten minutes and a few hours. Long-term averages (e.g., monthly or annually) can be estimated by assuming uniform lateral diffusion within a given sector in accordance with wind direction frequency as listed on a wind rose such as the STAR output (a stability wind rose generated by the U.S. Department of Commerce listing wind speed/direction frequencies as a function of stability). Vertical diffusion can be calculated basically as for the one-hour case. See Appendix 6C for details.

For the calculation of pollutant concentrations of intermediate duration (eight hours), one usually proceeds by calculating a one-hour concentration for subsequent conversion to an eight-hour concentration through the use of an empirical persistence factor.

Numerical Models

Given the limitations associated with the application of the Gaussian Plume Model to air quality impact assessment problems involving short-term ambient air standards, one might think that a more satisfactory method of predicting pollutant concentrations would be available. Numerical models do possess several advantages over Gaussian Plume Models; many of the assumptions implicit in the Gaussian Model are not required for a numerical formulation.

Consider a three-dimensional array of boxes occupying the space above a highway right-of-way and its immediate environs. A numerical model could operate by breaking dispersion into two components: diffusion and advection. One could introduce a pollutant source to the series of boxes directly overlying the highway in accordance with the emission rate for the vehicles on the highway. The pollutant material would disperse within these boxes by diffusion at some given rate. Since the boxes are purely conceptual in nature the material would also diffuse into adjacent boxes. At the same time pollutant material would be advected from box to box by the local wind field. If one could define the local wind field as a function of time, and diffusion and emissions were reasonably well behaved functions of time (e.g., constant), one could easily predict the movement of pollutant ma-

---

*In the absence of a strong pressure gradient, wind speeds tend to be low and wind direction tends to be variable.

[†]To further complicate the situation, the return period of the atmospheric conditions specified for worst-case analyses is never known, and comparisons with the ambient standards are made more on the basis of faith than science.

terials from box to box with successive time increments. If one chose small enough boxes, an assumption of uniform concentrations within each box could be made. In this manner concentration estimates could be made for any point of interest within the three-dimensional gridwork. Given the power of a modern computer, one could keep track of pollutant concentrations in many small boxes for many very short increments of time, thereby arriving at a very precise estimate of pollutant concentrations. One could even simulate pollutant deposition and/or reactions within the various boxes. Indeed, this has been done with success for photochemical oxidant models for cities such as Los Angeles.

Unfortunately, the data requirements of even a simple numerical model are often overwhelming. One obviously needs detailed information concerning the local wind field during the period of interest. Other information concerning diffusion and emission rates must also be obtained. Some of this data can be derived from other models (like Mobile 1, for emissions). Given information concerning local topography and obstructions, it is possible to derive estimates concerning local wind field behavior, but such estimates tend to be somewhat undependable. Add to this the problem of specifying some sort of worst-case wind field for use in developing pollutant concentrations for comparison with CO standards, and one soon begins to wonder whether the additional efforts to run a numerical model actually produce better results than the more pedestrian Gaussian Plume Model with its built-in assumptions and limitations.

Box Models

In contrast to numerical models, box models assume uniform dispersion throughout a single large volume or box. The discussion of pollutant diffusion within a room presented the basic idea behind the box models. Take, for example, an area such as a small city in which pollutant sources are more or less equally distributed throughout the "box" (i.e., the horizontal confines of the city from the ground surface up to the average mixing height). Reasonable long-term average pollutant concentrations can be calculated using the average wind speed and the average total city-wide pollutant emission rate. For example, if the city covers an area 3×3 km (9×10^6 m^2), exhibits an annual average mixing height of 1000 m, and has average wind speed of 5 m/sec, it will take approximately 600 seconds for a pollutant particle emitted at one edge of the city to be blown across the city and out of the box. Thus, on the average, the box enveloping the city will contain the pollutants emitted during 300 seconds (the approximate average time required for a particle emitted in the city to be transported out of the city). If 90 kg of pollutant (90,000 g) were emitted every 300 seconds and dispersed evenly throughout the city up to the mixing height, the average concentration of pollutant would be 10 μg/m^3 (or 9×10^4 g dispersed throughout 9×10^9 m^3).

The assumptions upon which box models are based are seldom satisfied at any specific receptor site within the box, especially for short averaging times. For example, the FAA has a box model* which is used to assess air quality impacts at airports. Unfortunately, the pollutant concentration of interest at airports is CO (which has a one-hour and an eight-hour standard). The receptor sites of interest are passenger loading areas, which are located in the areas in which most ground level emissions occur; i.e., apron areas, where ground level emissions from aircraft and ground service vehicles are concentrated, and ground traffic pick up and loading areas, where vehicular traffic emissions are concentrated. To state that short-term maximum concentrations in these areas are equivalent to the long-term average concentrations throughout the entire airport area as predicted using a box model reveals bias and/or inexperience on the part of the analyst.

Air Pollutant Dispersion Models for Impact Analysis

General Remarks

This section will discuss the application of currently available dispersion models from a user's standpoint. However, since it is likely that new models, or new versions of existing models, will be in use within the next few years, this section also contains guidance of a more general nature in the hope that it will enable the reader to effectively utilize an unfamiliar model with a minimum of difficulty.

*DOT, FAA, February 1976, *Revision of the Box Model Method for Ascertaining Aircraft Emissions at Airports.*

Computer models are often complex in nature and may be difficult to manage. When a new model is received,* the first step one should take (after studying the user's manual) is to compile the computer program and prepare to run some sort of test case. Generation of test data is very important and deserves careful attention.

Many problems can arise in compiling a model for the first time on a system. First of all, the card deck or tape containing the code may be defective. Experience has shown that one can spend days debugging a program containing almost all of the necessary cards. Computer models have also been known to develop quirks when tested on one system and used on another. Many problems can be detected and still others avoided by taking the time to run a test case before attempting to perform useful work with a new model. It can be upsetting to find that the model used for the past few years contained a serious bug which caused it to produce spurious results—an error which could have (should have) been caught when the test case was first run.

Computer costs usually constitute an insignificant fraction of the dollars spent on air quality impact report preparation and, if the program has optional features that might prove to be useful, the extra money should be spent to test the program to its full capability. Some thought should always be given to sensitivity analysis. Note that shifts in wind angles of even a few degrees can often produce dramatic changes in results. One should always be prepared to answer questions such as "What if winds were from the south?" or "What if the percentage of cold starts were 25 percent instead of 20 percent?" The best way in which one can prepare to provide definitive answers to questions such as these is to perform a sensitivity analysis for the specific application under consideration.

In running air quality models, one should be aware that mistakes are easy to make and sometimes hard to detect. Some mistakes will prevent the model from running. These are easy to detect. Others are more subtle. The model will run, the results will pass the "test of reasonable-ness," but another investigation using the same input assumptions will get a different answer. If by chance the program will reproduce the input data set, the analyst should study it carefully to see if it corresponds to the intended input.

Sensitivity analyses can also be helpful in detecting input errors. If comparison of two separate model runs yields unexpected results for which no clear explanation can be developed, chances are that one or both of the model runs were in error. Conversely, if the sensitivity analysis shows model outputs to be "well-behaved," one tends to have more confidence in the validity of the model results. Finally, the performance of a sensitivity analysis will provide the analyst with an indication as to the relative importance of various parameters that go into the analyses. Efforts to determine precisely the values of the various parameters used in the analysis can then be allocated accordingly.

HIWAY

HIWAY is a short-term (one-hour) line source dispersion model. The *User's Guide for HIWAY, A Highway Air Pollution Model*, EPA-650/4-74-008, was released by the EPA in February, 1975.[†] The model is written in FORTRAN (as are virtually all of the more common dispersion models.[‡])

The model works through a numerical integration of the Gaussian Plume point-source equation (i.e., Turner's workbook, Appendix 6C) by breaking the line source into a series of point sources, calculating the pollutant concentration from each point at each receptor, and summing the contributions from each point source. The model then performs the same calculation again but with twice the number of point sources. The result of this calculation is then compared with that of the first calculation. If the result of the second estimate is within 2 percent of the previous concentration estimate, the result is reported and the process stops. If the result of the second estimate is *not* within 2 percent of the first estimate, the number of point sources is

---

*If attempts to secure a copy for free from a government agency or other user prove fruitless, most air quality models can be obtained from the National Technical Information Service (NTIS), Springfield, VA, 22161.

[†]HIWAY 2 was released in 1980.
[‡]The reader who tends to use dispersion models is encouraged to familiarize himself with the FORTRAN language. Knowledge of the language is not absolutely essential for successful model use, but is extremely useful when things go wrong.

again doubled and another estimate is made. This procedure of doubling the number of point sources is repeated until a stable solution (i.e., two successive estimates within 2 percent of one another) is achieved.

The original version* of HIWAY is commonly thought to overestimate pollutant concentrations by a factor of two, especially when applied to high-stability, low-wind speed, parallel wind/roadway angle situations; that is, the worst-case situation considered in most microscale CO analyses. This is a rather obvious and serious shortcoming of the model. The only sound method of bringing estimates made with the HIWAY model into line with reality is to take the time and effort to calibrate the model for the situation under consideration. However, since the situation under consideration often involves a highway which has yet to be built, calibration data can sometimes be difficult to obtain.

Table 6-3 lists the input parameters for HIWAY as reported in the *User's Guide*. The determination of appropriate values for most of the parameters is relatively straightforward. The alphanumeric data for the heading can be almost anything—project title and run number is often appropriate. Source coordinates can be expressed in almost any convenient units, though kilometers are sometimes found to be the simplest with which to work. Note that the model really doesn't care where the northerly direction is oriented. It is usually convenient to arbitrarily let one leg of the intersection (or the highway itself if no intersection is involved) define "due north" and enter all other coordinates accordingl.† The user should choose a coordinate system which simplifies the task to the greatest degree possible. When modeling an intersection it is often easiest to assign a value of, say, 5.000 km to one of the corners of the intersection.

The height of the line source is often a subject of disagreement between analysts and reviewers. A good assumption is that a line source height

of 2 m can be considered as a conservative emission height for moving vehicles which emit their exhaust into the turbulent wake of their passage. The 2-m emission height is also considered to be a reasonably conservative value to be specified for highway vehicles idling at intersections and generating heated exhausts in winter.

Total highway width is obviously the width of the travel lanes (both directions). If the highway under consideration does not have a median, or center strip, the width of the center strip should, of course, be set equal to zero.

Note that the HIWAY model does not acknowledge the existence of three-lane highways. The model will only perform for highways with 1, 2, 4, 6, 8, . . . , 24 lanes. One way to account for highways with an odd number of lanes is to tell the model that the highway has an even number of lanes, specify the *actual* highway width, and apportion emissions among these "pseudo" lanes. Note that the model numbers traffic lanes from left to right as viewed from endpoint 1 toward endpoint 2.

Card 3 of the HIWAY input sequence calls for emission rates by lane in grams per meter-second. Note that the format for this card(s) is actually 8F10.0, that is, the emission rate for lane 1 is to be listed in columns 1–10, the rate for lane 2 in columns 11–20, lane 3 in columns 21–30, and so on. As a practical matter it is usually a good idea for nonprofessional programmers/key punchers to include a decimal point when inputting real, or floating-point, numbers (as opposed to integer "I" format numbers, i.e., those than can only assume whole values, 0, 1, 2, 3, . . .).

As indicated in the input sequence listing, HIWAY does contain some provisions for modeling depressed highway sections. However, the model cannot provide concentration estimates within the depressed section itself.

As previously noted, wind direction should be specified in degrees from the north axis of the coordinate system used in the modeling application. Wind speed will usually be specified at one m/sec for worst-case analyses. For roadway applications in which the receptor(s) is located within a few hundred meters (and greater than at least a few meters—the model will provide estimates at a minimum distance of 0.1 m) specification of almost any reasonable mixing height will not affect the results of the calculation. The

---

*See Rao, S. T., and Keenan, M. T., Suggestions for Improvement of the EPA-HIWAY Model, *J. Air Pollution Control Assoc.*, 30:247–256.

†If a highway oriented 25° east of north were assumed to be oriented due north and one wished to specify a wind direction perpendicular to the highway, one would use a 90° or 180° wind as input to the model and *not* 115° or 205° wind.

TABLE 6-3. Input Data Cards for HIWAY

Name	Columns	Format	Form	Variable	Units
Card type 1 (1 card)					
Head	1–80	20A4	AAAA	Alphanumeric data for heading	— —
Card type 2 (1 card)					
REP1	1–10	F10.0	XXXX.XXX	East coordinate, point 1	Map units
SEP1	11–20	F10.0	XXXX.XXX	North coordinate, point 1	Map units
REP2	21–30	F10.0	XXXX.XXX	East coordinate, point 2	Map units
SEP2	31–40	F10.0	XXXX.XXX	North coordinate, point 2	Map units
H	41–50	F10.0	XX.X	Height of line source	Meters
WIDTH	51–60	F10.0	XX.	Total width of highway	Meters
CNTR	61–70	F10.0	XX.	Width of center strip	Meters
XNL	71–80	F10.0	X.	Number of traffic lanes	—
Card type 3 (up to 3 cards)					
QLS	1–80	F10.0	.XXXXXXXXX	Emission rate for each lane	g/m-s
Card type 4 (1 card; can be blank for at grade)					
CUT	1–10	F10.0	X.	1, if cut; 0, if at grade	—
WIDTC	11–20	F10.0	XX.	Width of top of cut section	Meters
Card type 5 (1 card)					
THETA	1–10	F10.0	XXX.	Wind direction	Degrees
U	11–20	F10.0	XX.X	Wind speed	m/sec
HL	21–30	F10.0	XXXX.	Height of mixing layer	Meters
XKST	31–40	F10.0	X.	Pasquill stability class	—
Card type 6 (1 card)					
GS	1–10	F10.0	X.	Scale factor[a]	—
Card type 7 (any number of cards)					
XXRR	1–10	F10.0	XXXX.XXX	East coordinate of receptor[b]	Map units
XXSR	11–20	F10.0	XXXX.XXX	North coordinate of receptor	Map units
Z	21–30	F10.0	XX.	Height (above ground) of receptor	Meters

Source: Zimmerman, John R., and Thompson, Roger S., *User's Guide for HIWAY, A Highway Air Pollution Model*, U.S. EPA-650/4-74-008, 1975.

[a]The scale factor converts map units to kilometers: if map units in kilometers, scale factor = 1.0; if map units in meters, scale factor = 0.001; if map units in feet, scale factor = 0.000305; if map units in miles, scale factor = 1.61.

[b]To begin again with another set of data, a value of 9999. is punched for XXRR (card type 7) following the last receptor card.

HIWAY user's manual suggests that a value of 5000 m be used when the user wishes to insure that the specification of a height will not affect the results.

Sample scale factors are listed in the table. Note that almost any set of linear units can be used as long as a scale factor is provided so that the model "knows" how to convert the selected units into kilometers.

Specification of receptor location(s) is fairly straightforward. Note that the model can predict concentrations for several receptor locations and that the breathing height of most receptors is about 1.5 m.

Despite its many shortcomings, some of which are rectified by the updated version, HIWAY is simple to use and affords the user a great deal of flexibility. If one wishes to model on each leg a traffic circle or intersection with several different approaches, left-turn lanes, and queues, or a line of idling vehicles waiting to enter a parking garage, it can be done using HIWAY. One can simply run the model for each line source (e.g., each queue, each approach lane, etc.) to predict the contribution from each separate source at the receptor(s) of interest, and sum the results to yield an estimate of the total concentration generated by the source assemblage. Of course this method can become quite complex and time-consuming—one has to determine queue lengths, emission rates, and geometries for each separate source. Since much of this effort is largely mechanical, especially for highway intersections, the EPA has developed the Intersectional Midblock Model (IMM), a new (1978) model designed to model intersections.

HIWAY-2

As suggested by its name, HIWAY-2 is an updated version of the HIWAY model released by the EPA in May of 1980 (Peterson, W./B., *User's Guide for HIWAY-2, A Highway Line Source Model* EPA-600/8-80-018). The main difference between HIWAY and HIWAY-2 is that HIWAY-2 gives more realistic (lower) concentration estimates, due to an updated dispersion algorithm. Instead of using the six Pasquill-Gifford dispersion curves presented by Turner (1970), HIWAY-2 uses only three stability regimes (unstable, neutral, and stable) for which new distance-dispersion curves have been developed. However, as indicated in Table 6-4, one still specifies one of the six Pasquill-Gifford stability classes in the input sequence (of course one gets the same answers regardless as to which of the two stable classes, E or F, is specified). HIWAY-2 also contains more sophisticated treatment of the initial dispersion which occurs in the turbulent wake of moving vehicles, considering such variables as wind angle and wind speed. Unfortunately, vehicular speed, a significant factor in the generation of traffic-induced turbulence, is not considered in the initial dispersion formulation, which was based on data extracted from experiments involving vehicles moving at considerable speeds.* Whether this might tend to cause

*Note that most "worst case" traffic situations, i.e., those commonly studied in air quality impact analyses, involve vehicles moving very slowly, or not at all, thus tending to generate less of a turbulent wake, and less initial dispersion.

the model to underpredict under low *vehicular* speeds seems unclear at this time.

HIWAY-2 allows the user to simulate multiple highways and miltiple hours thereby facilitating the modeling of intersection situations and the performance of sensitivity analyses. Unfortunately the program still does not acknowledge the existence of three-lane or five-lane highways.

Despite its shortcomings, HIWAY-2 represents a significant improvement over HIWAY, and its use is recommended. Future research should resolve questions regarding HIWAY-2's performance under low vehicular speed conditions, but in the meantime it should be noted that HIWAY-2 does tend to *over*predict under the conditions examined by Rao et al. (1980).

IMM—The Intersectional Midblock Model

The EPA's Intersectional Midblock Model (IMM)[†] is based at least in part on the premise that computers should be used to make routine and repetitive calculations. Until this model became available, the calculation of pollutant concentrations generated by intersections was often a tedious and time-consuming procedure. One needed to determine queue lengths using computer or manual techniques such as those mentioned in the *Highway Capacity Manual* published in 1965 by the Highway Research Board (now Transportation Research Board) as Special Report 87. Emission rates could be determined using the Mobile 1 Model, and pollutant dispersion estimated using another model such as HIWAY. With the development of the IMM, the EPA has combined these separate operations into a single package. Instead of using a computer model such as Mobile 1 to develop data which had to be processed and coded for input into another computer model such as HIWAY, the middle step (which carried with it additional opportunities for error) has been eliminated. This approach enables the user to deal with a single unified model requiring a single input data set.

Figure 6-6 defines the general structure of the IMM. From this flow diagram it is obvious that the IMM does a lot of things: calculates cycle times, queue lengths, and delay times; esti-

[†]EPA-450/3-78-037, *Carbon Monoxide Hot Spot Guidelines Volume V: User's Manual for Intersection Midblock Model,* August 1978.

TABLE 6-4.   Input Data Cards for HIWAY-2

Name	Columns	Format	Form	Variable	Units
Card type 1 (1 card)					
Head	1–80	20A4	AAAA	Alphanumeric data for heading	—
Card type 2 (1 card)					
THETA	1–10	F10.0	XXX.	Wind direction	Degrees
U	11–20	F10.0	XX.X	Wind speed	m/sec
HL	21–30	F10.0	XXXX.	Height of mixing layer	Meters
XKST	31–40	F10.0	X.	Pasquill stability class	—
Card type 3 (1 card)					
GS[a]	1–10	F10.0	X.	Scale factor	—
Card type 4 (up to 50 cards)					
XXRR[b]	1–10	F10.0	XXXX.XXX	East coordinate of receptor	Map units
XXSR	11–20	F10.0	XXXX.XXX	North coordinate of receptor	Map units
Z	21–30	F10.0	XX.	Height (above ground) of receptor	Meters
Card type 5 (any number of cards					
REP1[c]	1–0	F10.0	XXXX.XXX	East coordinate, point 1	Map units
SEP1	11–20	F10.0	XXXX.XXX	North coordinate, point 1	Map units
REP2	21–30	F10.0	XXXX.XXX	East coordinate, point 2	Map units
SEP2	31–40	F10.0	XXXX.XXX	North coordinate, point 2	Map units
H	41–50	F10.0	XX.X	Height of line source	Meters
WIDTH	51–60	F10.0	XX.	Total width of highway	Meters
CNTR	61–70	F10.0	XX.	Width of center strip	Meters
XNL	71–80	F10.0	X.	Number of traffic lanes	—
Card type 6 (up to 3 cards)					
QLS	1–80	F10.0	.XXXXXXX	Emission rate for each lane	g/m-s
Card type 7 (1 card, can be blank for at grade)					
CUT	1–10	F10.0	X.	1, if cut; 0, if at grade	—
WIDTC	11–20	F10.0	XX.	Width of top of cut section	Meters

Source: Peterson, William B., *User's Guide for HIWAY-2, A Highway Air Pollution Model*, EPA 600/8-80-018, May 1980.

[a] The scale factor converts map units to kilometers: If map units in kilometers, scale factor = 1.0; if map units in meters, scale factor = 0.001; if map units in feet, scale factor = 0.000305; if map units in miles, scale factor = 1.61.

[b] To begin again with another set of data, a value 9999. is punched for XXRR (card type 4) following the last receptor card. A value of −9999. for XXRR will cause the program to terminate after data set.

[c] Any number of sources can be input. Card types 5–7 must be used for each source. If REP1 = 9999. end of source data, card types 6 and 7 should not follow.

mates emission factors; assigns emission rates; and performs dispersion calculations. Unfortunately, it does many of these things badly. The model becomes unreliable as intersections approach capacity, predicting absurd queue lengths and delay times and CO concentrations in the hundreds of parts per million. Pollutant dispersion is simulated with the obsolete version of

HIWAY or the Street Canyon Model described in Volume 9 (EPA-450/4-78-001). Incredibly, this "state of the art" intersection model is not directly applicable to situations involving three lanes of traffic nor can it handle a three-phase (left turn lane) signal intersection. In short, the EPA has gone to great expense to develop a model for the assessment of CO concentrations

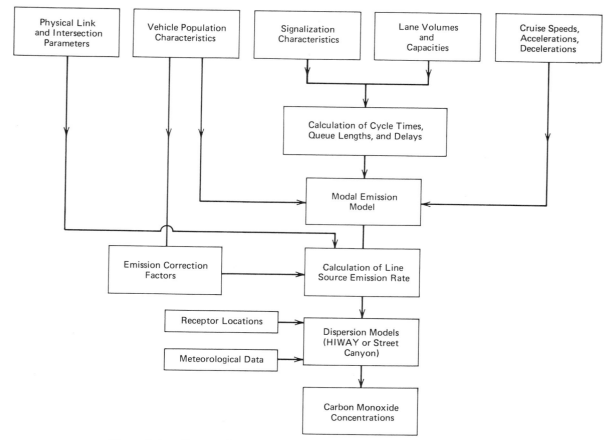

Figure 6-6.   General flow diagram for the IMM (from the user's manual).

generated by intersections which does not work well for intersections that might generate violations of the standard; that is, those that have either left turn lanes, three lanes of traffic, or a volume of traffic approaching capacity.*

Table 6-5 is a listing of the input data required to run the IMM. The potential user is advised to allocate a few days for familiarization with the model and for deciphering the rather cryptic instructions provided in the user's manual before attempting to apply the model to a real-life situation.

In using the IMM (or for that matter any model) to calculate pollutant concentrations generated by an intersection, note the importance of a sensitivity analysis. Predicted concentrations tend to be very sensitive to parameters such

*The New York State DOT and others are currently attempting to improve the IMM by incorporating HIWAY-2, making allowance for left turn lanes, and improving the queue length calculation.

as wind direction. The IMM lends itself well to sensitivity analyses by providing the user with an hourly scenario option. The ability to predict hour-by-hour CO concentrations is, for reasons discussed elsewhere in this chapter, of limited utility for its intended purpose (the prediction of eight-hour concentration estimates for comparison with the ambient air standard). However, the hourly scenario feature does provide a convenient method of simulating the same one-hour scenario for several different wind directions in a single model run.

The IMM output format is quite useful. Initially it lists all the relevant input data, thus providing the user with a convenient record of the data input to the model. The IMM will then display the results of intermediate calculations, for example, emission rates, queue length, delay time, and so on. Finally the IMM output lists not only the concentration calculated for each receptor point but also the percent contri-

TABLE 6-5. Input Data to Intersection Midblock Model (IMM)

Card	Columns	Format	Variable[a]	Description	Units
	1-5	I5	IPRSW1	If 1, print immediate emission data	—
	6-10	I5	IPRSW1	If 1, print 50A, HOA, EMAD	
	11-15	I5	IPRSW5	If 1, read in observed queue and delay	
	16-20	I5	IPRSW1	If 1, print MOBILE 1 emission estimates	
1	1-5	I5	NHOURS	Number of hours	—
	6-10	I5	NREC	Number of receptors	—
	11-13	I5	NINSEC	Number of intersections	—
2	1-10	I10	IFREE(INS)	0=free flow; 1=interrupted flow	—
	11-20	F10.0	XC(INS)	X-coordinate of the center of the intersection	km
	21-30	F10.0	YC(INS)	Y-coordinate of the center of the intersection	km
3	1-5	I5	ISIG(INS)	Type of intersection 0=unsignalized 1=vehicle actuated 2=fixed time	—
	6-10	I5	NPHASE(INS)	Number of phases	—
	11-15	F5.0	GAP(INS)	Gap acceptance time for unsignalized intersection	seconds
3a	1-10	F10.0	CY(INS)	Cycle time for fixed time intersection	seconds
	11-20	F10.0	G(INS,J)	Green time for each phase, Approach 1	seconds
	21-30	F10.0	G(INS,J)	Green time for each phase, Approach 2	seconds
4	1-5	I5	LINK(I,J,INS)	Link identification code	—
5[a]	1-10	F10.0	X1(L)	X-coordinate of the beginning of the link	km
	11-20	F10.0	Y1(L)	Y-coordinate of the beginning of the link	km
	21-30	F10.0	X2(L)	X-coordinate of end of the link	km
	31-40	F10.0	Y2(L)	Y-coordinate of end of the link	km
	41-50	F10.0	WLINK(L)	Width of the link	meters
	51-60	F10.0	HLINK(L)	Emission height	meters
	61-70	F10.0	ICUT(L)	0=grade section 1=cut section	—
	71-75	F5.0	WIDTC(L)	Width of top of cut section	meters
6	1-10	F10.0	CS(I,J,INS)	Lane capacity	vehicles/hr
	11-20	F10.0	VOL(I,J,INS)	Volume of link	vehicles/hr
	21-30	F10.0	VIN(I,J,INS)	Velocity into intersection	mph
	31-40	F10.0	VOUT(I,J,INS)	Velocity out of intersection	mph
	41-50	F10.0	AIN(I,J,INS)	Deceleration into intersection	mph/s
	51-60	F10.0	AOUT(I,J,INS)	Acceleration out of intersection	mph/s
7	1-10	F10.0	NL(L)	Number of lanes for the link	—
	11-50	−F10.0	VFRACT(LANE,L)	Fraction of volume for each lane	—

Repeat cards 4 to 7 for each phase, and for the two approaches to the intersection.
Repeat cards 2 to 7 for each intersection.

Card	Columns	Format	Variable	Description	Units
8	Same as card 5				
9	1-10	F10.0	VOLP(L)	Volume	vehicles/hr
	11-20	F10.0	VP(L)	Velocity	mph
10	Same as card 7				

Repeat cards 8 to 10 for each link departing from the intersection.

TABLE 6-5. *(Continued)*

Card	Columns	Format	Variable	Description	Units
11	1-10	F10.0	XX(IR)	X-coordinate of receptor	km
	11-20	F10.0	YX(IR)	Y-coordinate of receptor	km
	21-30	F10.0	Z(IR)	Z-coordinate of receptor	m
	31-40	I10	ISTR(IR)	I=street canyon	—
11a	1-5	I5	NLDUM	Number of links adjacent to street canyon	—
	6-15	2I5	ISTLIN(IR,M)	Link adjacent to street canyon	—
11b	1-10	F10.0	AST(IR)	Street heading from north	degrees
	11-20	F10.0	WST(IR)	Canyon width	meters
	21-30	F10.0	BUILDH(IR)	Building height	meters
	31-40	I10	IRSIDE(IR)	1=right side of street 2=left side of street	—

Repeat cards 11 to 11b from all receptors.

Card	Columns	Format	Variable	Description	Units
12	1-10	F10.0	THETA(K)	Wind direction	degrees
	11-20	F10.0	U(K)	Wind speed	meters/s
	21-30	F10.0	HL(K)	Height of mixing layer	meters
	31-40	I10	KST(K)	Stability code	—
	41-50	F10.0	TEMPF(K)	Ambient temperature	°F
	51-60	F10.0	FHOT(K)	Percentage of hot starts	—
	61-70	F10.0	FCOL(K)	Percentage of cold starts	—

Repeat card 12 for each hour of simulation.

Card	Columns	Format	Variable	Description	Units
13	1-80	7F10.0 F5.0	FAC(K)	Ratio of hourly volume to volume Specified on card 6	—
14[b]	1-5	I5	NYEAR	Year being modeled	—
	6-10	I5	IREG	Region (1=low, 2=Calif., 3=high)	—
	11-20	F10.0	MS(1)	Proportion of LDV	—
	21-30	F10.0	MS(2)	Proportion of LDT1	—
	31-40	F10.0	MS(3)	Proportion of LDT2	—
	41-50	F10.0	MS(4)	Proportion of HDV-C	—
	51-60	F10.0	MS(5)	Proportion of HDV-D	—
	61-70	F10.0	MS(6)	Proportion of MC	—
15[b]	1-5	I5	ALHFLG	Flag for optional data on card (1=yes, 0=no)	
	6-15	F10.0	AC	Fraction of vehicles using air conditioning)	
	16-25	F10.0	XLOAD(1)	Fraction of LDV with additional 500 lbs load	
	26-35	F10.0	XLOAD(2)	Fraction of LDT1 with additional 500 lbs load	
	36-45	F10.0	XLOAD(3)	Fraction of LDT2 with additional 500 lbs load	
	46-55	F10.0	TRAILR	Fraction of LDV with 1000 lbs trailer	qr/lb
	56-65	F10.0	ABSHUM	Absolute humidity	—
16[b]	1-5	I5	TRKFLG	Flag for optional data on card (1=yes, 0=no)	
	6-15	F10.0	HGHGT	Vehicle weight, gas HDV	pounds
	16-25	F10.0	HDWGT	Vehicle weight, diesel HDV	pounds
	26-35	F10.0	HGCID	Displacement, gas HDV	in.
	36-45	F10.0	HDCID	Displacement, diesel HDV	in.

TABLE 6-5. *(Continued)*

Card	Columns	Format	Variable	Description	Units
17[b]	1–5	I5	IMFLG	Flag for optional data on card (1=yes, 0=no)	
	6–10	I5	ICYIM	Year of implementation of I/M	Last two digits
	11–15	I5	ISTRING	L/M stringency	Percentage
	16–20	I5	IMTFLG	Mechanics training (1=yes, 0=no)	
	21–25	I5	MODYR1	First model year I/M applies to	Last two digits
	26–30	I5	MODYR2	Last model year I/M applies to	Last two digits

If IPRSW3 = I, repeat Card 18 for each approach I during phase J at intersection INS. Otherwise omit.

Card	Columns	Format	Variable	Description	Units
18	1–10	F10.0	QLENGTH(I,J,INS)	Queue length	meters
	11–20	F10.0	DELAY(I,J,INS)	Delay	seconds

Source: Benesh, Frank, *Carbon Monoxide Hot Spot Guidelines Volume V: User's Manual for Intersection Midblock Model*, EPA-450/3-78-037, August 1978.
[a] See HIWAY for more detail.
[b] See MOBILE 1 for more detail.

bution generated by each link along with other information which can be very helpful to the user who is trying to determine whether or not the results of the calculations make sense. The generous amount of information provided by the IMM output can also be useful in the development of mitigation measures designed to reduce pollutant concentrations or in the preparation of sensitivity analyses to be used as an aid in determining maximum concentrations.

The CALINE Models

The California DOT has long been a leader in the development of dispersion models for highways. The first nationwide distribution of a CALINE model was in 1972. The original model applied only to highways which could be considered infinitely long [i.e., the endpoints of a line source (queue) could not be modeled] and exhibited a discontinuity at a wind/roadway angle of 12.5 degrees. It was superseded by CALINE-2.* Unfortunately, CALINE-2 also applied only to long, straight highway sections and thus did not lend itself to intersection situations (where CO problems tend to occur). An improved version, CALINE-3, was released in 1980.

CALINE-3 can be considered a state-of-the-art Gaussian Plume line source model. An FHWA interim report dated November 1979 (FHWA/

CA/TL-79/23, *CALINE-3—A Versatile Dispersion Model For Predicting Air Pollutant Levels Near Highways and Urban Streets*) states that the model allows for the specification of up to 10 finite-length line sources and up to 20 receptors. The model will automatically sum the contribution to each receptor from each link.

Table 6-6 is an input sequence listing for CALINE-3. Note that this model has features not found in the HIWAY models. Among these are explicit considerations of averaging time, surface roughness, deposition velocity, elevated highway sections, ambient background concentrations, and mixing cell volume.

CALINE-3 is also very well documented. The Interim Report contains sections dealing with model sensitivity and model verification data, as well as the usual model description and user instructions. The model is available in either FORTRAN or BASIC.

A VAP—Airport Vicinity Air Pollution Model

The AVAP is a useful tool for the assessment of short-term (one-hour) CO concentrations generated by airport sources.[†] Figure 6-7 denotes the general structures of the model.

The AVAP Model considers an exhaustive list of potential emission sources including runways, taxiways, take-off and approach paths, access

---

*FHWA Report FHWA-RD-77-74, *CALINE-2—An Improved Microscale Model For the Dispersion of Air Pollutants From a Line Source*, June 1977.

[†]AVAP is available from NTIS as EPCIDIC Tape #AB-A031027/6WC FAA RD-73-113, *Airport Vicinity Air Pollution Study*, December 1973.

vehicle highways, service vehicle routes, terminal areas, point sources, and even off-airport line and area sources. The model is quite powerful in that the user need only supply data regarding emission rates, traffic volumes, approach angles, and so on to perform the calculations required for the generation of source strengths and geometries. The model generates concentration esti-

TABLE 6-6. CALINE-3 Input

Card Sequence Number	Variable Name	Variable Description[a]
1	JOB	Current job title[b]
	ATIM	Averaging time, minutes[c]
	ZO	Surface roughness, cm
	VS	Settling velocity, cm/s
	VD	Deposition velocity, cm/s; if the settling velocity is greater than 0 cm/s, the deposition velocity should be set equal to the settling velocity
	NR	Number of receptors; NR_{max} = 20 (Integer)
	SCAL	Scale factor to convert receptor and link coordinates and link height and width to meters.
2	RCP	Receptor name
	XR	X-coordinate of receptor
	YR	Y-coordinate of receptor
	ZR	Z-coordinate of receptor

Note that card sequence 2 must appear NR times.

3	RUN	Current run title
	NL	Number of links; NL_{max} = 20 (Integer)
	NM	Number of meterological conditions; no maximum (Integer)
4	LNK	Link title
	TYP	Section type
		AG = At grade
		FL = Fill
		BR = Bridge
		DP = Depressed
	XL1, YL1	Coordinates of link endpoint 1
	XL2, YL2	Coordinates of link endpoint 2
	VPHL	Traffic volume, vehicle/hr
	EFL	Emission factor, g/mi
	HL	Source height
	WL	Mixing zone width

Note that card sequence number 4 must appear NL times.

5	U	Wind speed, m/s
	BRG	Wind angle with respect to positive Y-axis in degrees; may range between 0° and 360°, inclusive.
	CLAS	Atmospheric stability class, in numeric format (1–6 = A–F) (Integer)
	MIXH	Mixing height, meters
	AMB	Ambient concentration of pollutant, ppm

Note that card sequence number 5 must appear NM times.

Source: CALINE-3 user's manual.

[a] Real variables, except titles, must contain a decimal point, and integer variables are right-justified.

[b] Data type real unless specified otherwise.

[c] See restrictions and limitations for additional information on variable limits.

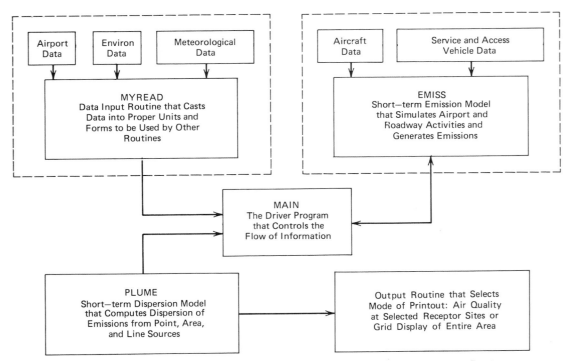

Figure 6-7. Overall structure of Airport Vicinity Air Pollution model (AVAP). Source: Report DOT-FAA 71 WI-223.

mates for a receptor grid of up to a 12 × 14 points plus special receptors using Gaussian Plume dispersion algorithms.

Volume 9 and the Hot Spot Guidelines

Volume 9* and the *Hot Spot Guidelines*† are both self-contained procedures which can be used to estimate highway-generated pollutant concentrations without the aid of a computer. Both these procedures are based on the original HIWAY model. Volume 9 has been characterized as a shortcut tabular version of an intersection modeling process based upon the Modal Model,‡ Mobile 1, and HIWAY — as per the IMM model. The *Hot Spot Guidelines*, which

_____

*EPA document EPA-450/4-78-001, *Guidelines for Air Quality Maintenance Planning and Analysis*, Vol. 9 (Revised), *Evaluating Indirect Sources*, September 1978.

†The Carbon Monoxide Guidelines is a series of seven volumes dated August 1978, designed to "provide state and local agencies with a relatively simple yet accurate procedure for assessing carbon monoxide potential on urban street networks." Most applicable to this discussion are Volumes II, *Rational*, and III, *Workbook*, EPA-450/3-78-034 and EPA-450/3-28-035, respectively.

‡An emissions model which considers acceleration and deceleration.

were developed as a shortcut version of Volume 9, contain two separate analysis procedures. The simpler of the two, the so-called "screening process," is designed to indicate whether or not an intersection might generate a CO violation and thus warrant detailed analysis. Unfortunately, the *Hot Spot Screening Procedure* is so conservative that is "screens out" virtually everything and is thus quite useless as a screening tool. The other hot spot analysis technique, the so-called *Verification Procedure*, is somewhat less conservative and does offer significant advantages over the Volume 9 procedure (for intersections), which has been characterized as cumbersome at best. It should be noted that neither Volume 9 nor the *Hot Spot Guidelines* are written in a manner which makes it especially easy for the user to get through the procedure without some confusion.

Not every situation lends itself to the application of these techniques. The tables and figures used in these documents to arrive at a concentration estimate can be adapted to only a finite number of situations, though with a little imagination, interpolation, and occasional guesswork the diligent user can usually derive an estimate for most situations. Note that in developing procedures that can produce an estimate of highway-generated pollutant concentrations it is necessary to make simplifying assumptions. Since these procedures are to be used in protecting public health, these assumptions tend to be conservative. As more assumptions are made, the simpler the analysis becomes and the more likely it is to predict violations where none will in fact occur. Hence the Volume 9 procedure, which is unwieldy and usually takes a few days or more to use, provides what can be considered realistic (if somewhat conservative) concentration estimates. The *Hot Spot Verification Procedure* can be accomplished in a few hours yielding very high (conservative) but useful, estimates. Finally, the *Hot Spot Screening Procedure* can be accomplished in a few minutes (provided one has already compiled the required data), but yields estimates that are so conservative that the procedure is of limited utility.

AIR QUALITY IMPACT ANALYSIS FOR TRANSPORTATION SYSTEMS

In performing an air quality impact analysis for a highway or an airport* one should determine whether or not the proposed project is likely to cause a violation of the ambient air quality standards; compare the relative impacts of the various project alternatives, including the null (or do-nothing) alternative; make an informal determination regarding consistency with the State Implementation Plan (SIP);[†] and plan to defend the analysis against criticism from professionals with a vested interest in opposing (or supporting) the project.

In preparing an air quality impact report it is seldom necessary to produce page after page of general information concerning the various pollutants, mechanics of dispersion, air pollution law, and so on. While it is essential to clearly and expressly state and/or reference the various assumptions and data used in the analysis, an air quality report should not attempt to provide the uninformed reader with the education necessary to comprehend fully the details of analysis any more than a piece of sheet music should contain instructions for playing the piano.

An air quality impact analysis should not take a week to perform and a month to write up. The many assumptions which go into an analysis (e.g., percent cold starts, ambient temperature, wind speed, wind direction, stability, distance to the receptor, etc.) often need not be discussed and presented in narrative form; rather, they can be presented in tables, figures, or left as computer printouts and included as an appendix. This approach makes the technical information more accessible to the professional reviewer who will not have to wade through page after page of text in order to find a specific piece of information.

There are two basic approaches used in assessing the air quality impacts of highways and airports. One of these involves the use of a dispersion model to predict concentrations at critical receptor sites.[‡] The other involves an "emissions burden" calculation which is a comparison of the total emissions for various project alternatives and is most often used in connection with an assessment of photochemical oxidant impacts as required by many SIPs.

Microscale Analysis

The object of a microscale analysis is to assess the air quality impact of a proposed action upon a particular receptor (or more typically, receptors) and generally involves the use of a dispersion model. The pollutant of interest in a microscale analysis is usually carbon monoxide, though lead emissions occasionally warrant a microscale investigation.

---

*Air quality impact analyses are usually not performed for rail systems due to their relatively low emissions. Also, increased rail activities tend to reduce the growth of highway traffic emissions to a degree that more than offsets any direct or indirect rail emissions that might result.

[†]The state's plan for achieving and/or maintaining the NAAQS. SIPs often call for an absolute reduction of hydrocarbon emissions to achieve the photochemical oxidant standard.

[‡]The FAA's box model for airports yields an airport-wide average concentration estimate (which is, of course, almost always infinitesimal because the volume for which the average is calculated is so very large). However, particular receptor sites on the airport (such as the ground traffic loading areas) may well exhibit high CO concentrations that are averaged away by the FAA model. Consequently, most airport impact assessments should be considered incomplete unless these particular sites have been specifically addressed using a line source model to consider ground-based emissions. Note that aircraft emissions which occur at heights greater than 100 m are so well dispersed by the time they reach the ground that they can usually be ignored.

Motor vehicles (and to a somewhat lesser extent, aircraft) generally do not emit enough sulfur dioxide or particulate material to significantly influence ambient concentrations. Nitrogen oxide and hydrocarbon emissions are generally considered potentially significant to the extent that they might influence photochemical oxidant concentrations. As previously suggested, the calculation of photochemical oxidant concentrations for a specific receptor site cannot be routinely accomplished with accuracy, given the current state of the art. Consequently, these three pollutants are not usually addressed in a microscale analysis. (Techniques for assessing the impacts of these pollutants as they relate to a specific project will be presented in the mesoscale, or emissions burden, section of this chapter.)

The accepted procedures for conducting a microscale analysis vary somewhat from state to state and evolve with time. The procedures presented here should be acceptable to most reviewers, although it can by no means be guaranteed. Contacting the state air pollution control agency and perhaps other reviewing agencies (e.g., EPA, FAA, state and Federal DOT, local agencies, state health departments, etc.) before commencing an analysis is a wise action. Many analysts have learned the hard way that in spite of the "perfect logic" behind their analyses, the acquisition of necessary approvals can be a long, tedious, and frustrating process if the analysis in question differs from "the way we usually do it." Since the values to be selected for many parameters included in a microscale analysis are determined largely on the basis of judgment (professional guesswork), it is a good practice for the analyst to use the generally accepted values whenever possible. Otherwise the analyst may be forced to convince skeptical reviewers of the validity of the rationale for selecting a particular value simply because it differs from the norm.

Receptor Site Selection

There is no officially sanctioned "cookbook" technique for the selection of microscale (i.e., carbon monoxide, or in some cases lead) receptor sites. Unfortunately, this is one of the more critical phases of the analysis and often does not receive the attention warranted. The quickest and easiest way to have an air quality impact

analysis sent back for additional work is to point out a few reasonable receptor sites where the NAAQS might be violated, for which no analysis was performed. While reasonable professionals may disagree on any number of issues until a hearing officer is completely perplexed, the straightforward question, "Did you consider pollutant concentrations at receptor X?" is readily understood by most people. If the answer to the question is an unqualified "No," many hearing officers will then take the easy way out and rule that more study is needed because the analyst failed to consider a particular receptor and this receptor must be of some importance or the opposition would not raise it as an issue. The receptor site issue can be argued at little or no cost to the opposition while imposing long, costly, and frustrating delays for the analyst. Consequently, the analyst is advised to give careful consideration to the selection of receptor sites and to avoid the temptation to just pick a few "representative sites" and get on with the real work of the analysis.

Obviously, it is impossible to analyze every reasonable receptor site for a given project. How then can one prepare an analysis that will not be susceptible to the "But you didn't consider this one" technique of attack? Several key observations will help at this point. First, pollutant concentrations tend to decrease with increasing distance from the highway (or airport taxiway, runway, apron etc.). Second, similar highway segments carrying similar traffic levels with similar operating characteristics will yield similar worst-case predicted pollutant levels. Thus, if one were assigned the task of conducting a microscale analysis for a limited access highway between two exits, one could proceed by selecting the single closest receptor and predicting concentrations for only that one point. A reviewer could perhaps cite hundreds of reasonable receptors not considered in the analysis. However, the *worst-case* highway-generated pollutant levels at these other points would be less than those predicted at the selected receptor site (assuming a uniform background concentration). Hence, if the standard were achieved at the selected receptor, clearly it would be achieved at all others. While it might be useful and perhaps interesting to compare the pollutant levels generated by other highway configurations at some of these other potential receptor sites, most hearing officers would not deem it essential since the central issue is compliance with the ambient air standards.

In situations involving simple highway segments with fairly uniform traffic levels, it is often best to predict worst-case concentrations for the various project alternatives at varying distances from the highway. A quick inventory of receptor sites (e.g., number of dwellings, schools, hospitals, etc.) at the various distances can then be performed or simply indicated on a map in isopleth (contour) style. In this manner the analyst considers every potential receptor to be affected by the highway segment, and the receptor selection portion of the analysis becomes difficult to criticize.

Unfortunately, many highway projects involve something more than a single uniform segment of roadway, and the analyst must consider secondary impacts resulting from traffic increases and diversions, as well as pollutant levels to be generated at intersections.* Suppose, for example, that a two-lane suburban highway is upgraded to a four-lane limited access facility and that projections show an increase of 30 percent in traffic levels. An analysis which was limited to the confines of the proposed right-of-way would probably conclude that improvements in traffic flow associated with the proposed project would more than offset the effects of increased traffic and that a net air quality improvement would result from construction of the proposed project. However, a perceptive reviewer will eventually pose the question, "Where does all this traffic go?" Upon inspection it will sometimes be found that this newly-widened highway will serve to dump additional traffic into an already congested intersection or network of urban streets. It is here, perhaps far removed from the actual site of the proposed construction, that the project will generate potential CO violations, and it is here that the bulk of the resources allocated to the performance of a microscale analysis should be committed.

As a general rule, if a highway project is going to generate a violation of the ambient CO stand-

ards, the violation will occur in the vicinity of an intersection. More vehicles spend more time at lower speeds at intersections (thus generating CO at a higher rate) than they spend on free-flow segments of almost any given highway. To further compound the emissions density problem associated with project intersections, emissions from the intersecting highways are mixed with those from the project highway at intersections, and any microscale modeling analysis performed for the intersection should consider the combined emissions from both highways.

Modeling CO at intersections is, by comparison with the efforts required to model free-flow highway segments, a painstaking task made more difficult by the lack of clear directives from regulatory agencies. Even the selection of potential receptor locations is complicated. Current ambient air standards for CO are designed to protect members of the general public from one-hour concentrations of 40 mg/m^3 † and eight-hour concentrations of 10 mg/m^3 not to be exceeded more than once per year. 40CFR 58, Appendix E, *Probe Siting Criterion for Ambient Air Quality Monitoring*, Section 4.3, states that for purposes of compliance with the ambient CO standards monitoring probes should not be placed within 10 m of an intersection and that midblock locations are preferable. The regulation goes on to state that for street-canyon–type areas, CO probes should not be placed closer than 2 m nor farther than 10 m from the nearest traffic lane at a height of approximately 3 m. There appears to be no distinction drawn between reasonable receptor locations for the one- and eight-hour standards.

With respect to street corners the regulation apparently assumes that anyone standing within 10 m of an urban street corner for more than an hour must be engaged in some sort of employment (and is thus protected by the OSHA standards). This does, however, ignore the possiblity that air intakes (e.g., windows) might be located at or near the roadway intersection. Thus it would seem that these locations are not considered part of the ambient atmoshpere in much the same manner that the air inside motor vehicles is not considered part of the ambient atmosphere.

On the basis of the available information, it

---

*As noted in a bulletin dated June 18, 1980 (see Appendix 6F), the FHWA does not feel that microscale analyses should be performed for intersections. However, most regulatory agencies feel, and rightly so, that if a project is going to generate a violation, it will occur at an intersection.

†The proposed one-hour standard is 25 mg/m^3.

would seem that for intersections, the EPA has defined the worst-case receptor as being located 2 m off the nearest traffic lane of the most heavily traveled leg of the intersection at a distance of 10 m back from the junction of the two highways. It is recommended that the analyst evaluate the reasonableness of this receptor location when dealing with an intersection before going on to consider other, presumably less critical, potential receptor sites.

Finally, as a matter of prudence, the analyst should check with the cognizant air pollution control agency regarding the selection of the receptor sites before the analysis is complete. To do otherwise is to risk needless delays in the approval of the analysis.

Meteorologic Conditions

Current ambient CO standards are expressed in terms of one- and eight-hour averages not to be exceeded more than once per year.* The format of the CO standard has caused countless disputes concerning standards compliance because there is currently no generally accepted method of determining how often predicted concentrations will occur. McVoy (1979) has suggested the use of Monte Carlo Simulation Techniques in this regard; however, the technique has yet to gain wide acceptance.

The basic problem is that one can predict CO levels at virtually any receptor site of interest for almost any specified set of traffic (emissions) and meteorologic conditions. Unfortunately, there is no accepted way to tell whether or not any chosen set of conditions will reoccur once per year, twice per year, every day, or never. Until this can be accomplished there will be no statistically valid technique for demonstrating whether or not microscale modeling results establish compliance with the ambient CO standards.

In a sense, the analyst does not model CO concentrations that reoccur twice a year but performs a worst-case analysis which it is hoped everyone will agree will not reoccur more than once per year. If it can be shown that these worse-case conditions will not generate a violation, then the analyst, for all practical purposes, has demonstrated compliance with the standard.

If, however, the worst-case scenario suggests that a violation will occur, the typical response would be to relax these "unnecessarily conservative assumptions" until compliance can be demonstrated. At this point the issue becomes one of establishing a return period for the estimate [i.e., every six months as specified by the standards, more frequently (i.e., a violation), or less frequently (i.e., a conservative estimate)]. Since neither side can support its contention regarding the return period of the estimate with a sound statistical analysis, hearings on projects where CO standards may be violated tend to center on "professional judgment" and as such are drawn out, confusing, heated, and involve a good deal of discussion regarding the qualifications and motives of those making the conflicting professional judgments.

To aid the professional in selecting the proper meteorological inputs to a model such as HIWAY, IMM, or one of the CALINE Models, the EPA has set forth certain guidelines in EPA-450/4-74-001, *Guidelines for Air Quality Maintenance Planning and Analysis*, Vol. 9 (Revised), *Evaluating Indirect Sources*. Additional information which may or may not have been superseded by the September 1978, revision is contained in the original Volume 9, EPA-450/4-75-001, published in January of 1975. In Appendix E of the revised Volume 9, the EPA suggests that HIWAY does not perform well at wind speeds of less than 1 m/sec. Recalling the discussion regarding the Gaussian Plume Model presented earlier in this chapter, it should be noted that windspeed, u, appears in the denominator of the Gaussian Plume expression. Hence, as wind speeds approach zero, concentrations approach infinity. Given the fact that HIWAY tends to break down as wind speeds are reduced below 1 m/sec, the EPA apparently has concluded that a wind speed of 1 m/sec is appropriate for a worst-case scenario which will reoccur twice per year.

Appendix E of the revised Volume 9 goes on to mention that HIWAY (the original version) tends to overpredict under parallel wind conditions. Thus, according to Appendix E, concentration estimates should not be made for a highway with a wind angle of less than about 5° to 8°,† or with wind speeds less than 1 m/sec.

---

*Proposed revisions to the standards call for not more than an average of one daily exceedance per year.

†Note that HIWAY-2 performs better under parallel wind conditions than the original HIWAY model. Thus it would seem that a change in the definition of worst-case conditions may be anticipated.

Obviously, these conditions can occur even if HIWAY does not handle them well. However, the EPA is correct in suggesting that winds tend not to blow parallel to highways at 1 m/sec continuously for one hour. In fact, in the absence of some overriding peculiarities, such as a drainage wind, winds driven by a pressure gradient so weak that speeds in excess of 1 m/sec are not realized tend to have no definite direction when observed for periods approaching one hour in duration. The fact that winds tend to waft about at low speeds can be at least partially accomodated in a Gaussian Plume Model such as HIWAY by increasing the value of σ_y to reflect the influence of variable wind direction.

In selecting a wind direction for use in a microscale analysis, one should choose the wind direction that produces the maximum concentration at the receptor. This is providing that it is not within 5° to 8° of the highway orientation, because the EPA has apparently determined that such a wind direction cannot occur. Obviously if it did occur, it would have to be analyzed. However, since parallel winds cannot be analyzed with HIWAY (without predicting violations for most projects), the EPA cannot insist that analyses of parallel wind conditions be done when using other dispersion models without conceding that the specification of worst-case conditions is really quite arbitrary.* If the EPA were to admit that the specification of worst-case conditions was arbitrary, it would have to admit that the concentration estimates made on the basis of these arbitrary conditions really might (or might not) occur more than once per year. This leaves one to conclude that the results of microscale analyses in general might (or might not) suggest violations of the ambient CO standards (and leads to awkward questions regarding the utility of performing an analysis).

With regard to stability, worst-case conditions usually call for the specification of D (neutral) or E (stable) conditions as input to a Gaussian Plume Model.† Since urban areas tend to exhibit a high degree of surface roughness and radiate a significant amount of heat energy, experience suggests that stable conditions seldom occur in urban areas. Thus, worst-case stability conditions

are usually defined as E stability in rural areas (note that stable conditions are expected to occur only at night) and as D stability in urban areas.

Since dispersion calculations for highway projects are usually performed for source-receptor distances of less than 100 m or so, specification of a mixing height is usually not critical to the analysis. Any mixing height greater than 50 m will have no effect on the outcome of the calculation since the plume generally will not disperse to that height within 100 m of its source under worst-case conditions. Hence, almost any mixing height (e.g., 500 m) can be used in a worst-case analysis for assessing highway impacts. This is, however, not so for airports. Since airports have sources at various heights, it is possible to prevent aircraft emissions from reaching ground level by assuming that there is an inversion layer between the aircraft source and the receptor on the ground. This mistake is not as grievous as it might appear since by the time aircraft emissions from high altitudes have reached ground level, they are so dispersed as to be almost insignificant in terms of ambient concentrations.

To summarize, for purposes of assessing compliance with the ambient one-hour CO standards, the following meteorologic assumptions may be used as input to a Gaussian Plume Model, assuming that they agree with current regulatory policy.

Wind speed	1 m/sec
Wind direction	Whichever direction will produce the maximum concentrations provided it is not within 5° to 8° of the highway alignment.
Stability	D (neutral) or E (stable) depending on whether the site is of an urban or rural nature.
Mixing height	500 m

Some models call for the specification of an emission height and/or an initial dispersion (σ_y). Since vehicles generate a turbulent wake when moving and pollutants emitted into this turbulent zone will be quickly dispersed through the zone, one could specify values up to several meters for these parameters depending upon the speed and type of vehicle under considera-

---

*i.e., different "worst case" conditions for different models.

†HIWAY-2 will give the same answers for E or F stability.

tion. For a traffic stream of passenger vehicles traveling at 30 mph, one might specify an emission height of 2 m and an initial dispersion equal to the width of the highway; however, if traffic were flowing 55 mph and buses and tractor-trailers constituted a significant portion of the vehicle mix, one might choose to increase these values by a few meters. In the case of vehicles queueing at a traffic signal, it should be remembered that worst-case conditions usually assume winter temperatures for purposes of emissions calculations. Thus, it would be expected that the heated exhaust from idling vehicles would rise to a height of at least a few meters. As always, one should consult with the state air pollution control agency when making assumptions such as this, to avoid potential problems with reviewers.

Emissions Calculations

As with other calculations made in connection with a CO microscale analysis, the derivation of appropriate emissions rates is usually based on the assumption that if the worst conceivable situation will not give rise to a violation of the ambient air standard, a violation is not likely to occur. Note that if the analysis shows that the worst conceivable situation may give rise to a violation, no one is quite sure of what to do; but most analysts relax the worst-case assumptions to reflect conditions that are more likely to occur. Assumptions are relaxed "in the direction of reality" until the project no longer shows a violation, or the scenario under consideration is so "realistic" that the probable generation of a violation is conceded. Note that the inputs to Mobile 1 allow for considerable latitude in the specification of inputs discussed earlier in this chapter and in Appendix 6A. Accordingly, one should always opt for the more conservative scenario when questions arise. For example, one generally assumes winter temperatures (i.e., 20°F, because it was at one time the coldest temperature considered in the Mobile 1 program, though lower temperatures can now be specified), a defensibly high proportion of cold starts, trucks, low operating speeds, a high volume of traffic (i.e., the peak hour), an early year for project completion and so on.

Background CO Concentrations

The monitoring section of this chapter presents a general approach to the determination of back-

ground CO concentrations together with suggestions as to when, where, and how monitoring should be done. As with most aspects of a defensible microscale analysis it is important to be able to demonstrate that the value chosen to represent background concentrations (i.e., pollutant concentration *upwind* of the source under consideration) is valid. Thus, if project data is not representative of a full year's monitoring, it may be necessary to adjust the data for seasonality through comparison with data from the local CAMS station or through techniques described in NCHRP Report 200. Other adjustments which might be warranted involve the year of analysis and local traffic levels (see monitoring section for details).

For less controversial projects it is often permissible to assume a reasonable background level based on information from CAMS data, monitoring data for other projects, or the experience and judgment of professionals in the state air pollution control agency. The EPA *Hot Spot Guideline Series* (EPA-450/3-78-034, *Carbon Monoxide Hot Spot Guidelines*, Vol. II: *Rationale*, August 1978) suggest that values of 4.1 $\mu g/m^3$ (3.6 ppm), one-hour, and 2.9 $\mu g/m^3$ (2.5 ppm), eight-hour, represent reasonable worst-case CO background levels for the 1982–1983 CO season (October, November, December, January, February). These values might also be considered conservative worst-case background concentrations for rural projects as well. Of course, whatever method is used to arrive at background concentrations (note that different values could, and sometimes should, be used for different sections of a project corridor), it is important to document clearly the derivation of the values in the project report.

Deviation of Eight-Hour CO Concentrations

Thus far this discussion has dealt with the projection of worst-case one-hour CO concentrations which might be generated by a project for comparison with the one-hour ambient air standard. However, projected and/or observed violations of the one-hour standard are rather rare.* As previously mentioned, attaining the eight-hour CO standard is often a problem (i.e., the eight-hour standard is the limiting factor; if the one-hour standard is violated, the eight-hour standard is almost invariably exceeded. However, violations of the eight-hour CO standard

*This may change if the new standard is adopted.

often occur without a corresponding violation of the one-hour standard). As explained in the dispersion section of this chapter, the Gaussian Plume Model does not work well for eight-hour average meteorological conditions. Any attempt to break an eight-hour period into consecutive one-hour episodes involves questions as to what might constitute eight consecutive one-hour meteorological conditions that might be expected to occur on the average of twice per year, and what corresponding traffic and background conditions would be appropriate for use in such a scenario. Since direct calculation of an eight-hour average CO concentration suitable for comparison to the ambient air standard seems hopeless [although Monte Carlo techniques (McVoy, 1979) might provide a convenient method of doing this], eight-hour CO concentrations are generally derived from the projected one-hour worst-case concentration (which itself is nothing but an educated guess). There are various methods of accomplishing this one-to-eight-hour conversion. The simplest method involves the use of a direct ratio between observed second annual one- and eight-hour CO concentration values. In the revised Volume 9 (EPA-450/4-78-001), and in the *Hot Spot Guidelines* (EPA-450/3-78-034), the EPA lists a value for this ratio, called a "persistance factor," as being on the order of 0.6 to 0.7.

In the revised Volume 9, the EPA suggests a procedure for deriving an eight-hour second annual maximum concentration. This procedure involves the use of observed hour-by-hour meteorologic conditions which give rise to a maximum observed eight-hour concentration over some period of observations at a local or regional background CO monitoring site. This approach would seem to have some merit if there were several years of data collected at the receptor site of interest while the source under consideration was in operation. Given such a data base, one could examine the record to determine on an annual average basis that series of one-hour conditions which gave rise to the observed second annual maximum CO concentration for a particular receptor. One could then use this sequence of one-hour conditions to examine "what if?" questions involving different emission rates on the subject highway.

Note the importance of source-receptor geometry in this situation. If this spatial relationship were altered, then the conditions which gave rise

to the historical maximum concentrations would not necessarily have any bearing upon the maxima expected from the new configuration. For example, suppose a receptor were located to the northeast of an intersection and a year of continuous hourly observations showed the maximum concentrations occur when the wind blows from the northeast for five out of eight hours under conditions of D stability. If the source receptor geometry were to change, that is, if one wished to consider a receptor located southwest of the intersection, then the observed worst-case scenario involving winds from the northeast could no longer be expected to produce second annual maximum eight-hour concentrations. It is unclear as to how the EPA observed-worst-case approach accounts for this source-receptor geometry versus wind-direction problem, especially in light of the fact that any highway project involving the intersection would almost certainly change the balance of traffic on the various legs of the intersection or otherwise disturb the source-receptor geometry.

The EPA's original Volume 9 describes a procedure for the estimation of second annual maximum eight-hour CO concentrations, which is among the more logical and practical approaches to the problem yet devised. The procedure begins by observing that the ratio between concurrent maximum one- and eight-hour concentrations can be considered to be the combined product of two independent factors: emissions and meteorology. If meteorologic conditions (and background concentration) were to remain constant for an eight-hour period (e.g., 1 m/sec. wind, D stability, wind-roadway angle of $8°$) and highway emissions were also constant over this period, then the eight one-hour average concentrations should all be the same (i.e., equal to the eight-hour average concentration). If, in this scenario, all traffic on the subject highway were to occur during a single hour, then the eight-hour average downwind concentration would be equal to one-eighth of the peak one-hour concentration (assuming zero background). Clearly, under constant meteorologic conditions the ratio of highway-generated CO concentrations is equal to the one-hour peak to eight-hour average emissions ratios. Thus, if eight-hour average traffic levels involve average hourly volumes that are one-third less than the peak-hour volume, then the peak-hour highway-generated CO concentration should be approximately one-third higher than the eight-hour average, under constant meteorologic conditions.

However, worst-case one-hour meteorologic conditions are not likely to persist for eight straight hours (indeed, there is some question as to whether they might regularly persist for a full hour during periods of maximum traffic flow). Thus the one-hour/eight-hour concentration ratio should reflect the fluctuation in meteorologic conditions in some sort of "meteorologic persistence factor." For example, if worst-case meteorology were to somehow persist for five out of eight hours with a 180° wind shift for the other three hours, one would expect the meteorologic persistence factor for this case to be on the order of five-eighths. In EPA-450/4-75-001 (Volume 9, the original) an equation for the one-hour/eight-hour meteorologic persistence factor is presented as

$$p = \left(\frac{8 \text{ hour maximum } [CO]}{1 \text{ hour maximum } [CO]^*}\right)\left(\frac{V_1}{V_8}\right) \quad (6\text{-}6)$$

where p = the one-hour/eight-hour meteorologic persistence factor
   V_1 = traffic volume in vehicles per hour (vph) during the hour when the maximum CO concentration was observed
   V_8 = traffic volume (in vph) during the eight-hour period.

The EPA goes on to state that the maximum meteorologic persistence factor, p, observed during an EPA sponsored study was 0.6 and that in the absence of better data this value may be used.

This approach appears to have some real advantages over the straight-ratio approach and the eight consecutive one-hour episodes approach. It is sensitive to the traffic volumes involved. If the project under consideration involves very high one-hour peak volumes with low traffic levels during other periods (e.g., a sports complex or factory) eight-hour concentrations will not tend to be overestimated as they would under the straight-ratio approach, which assumes that the one-hour/eight-hour peaking characteristics of this project are the same as those observed over an entire region. It does, however, incorporate the assumption that the

*For periods when the wind speed is less than 2 m/sec.

relationship between worst-case one-hour meteorology and worst-case eight-hour meteorology will be constant when considered over the course of some years. The assumption is borne out to at least some degree by observed data (see Larsen, 1971, and others).

Therefore, given that the one-hour scenario chosen was appropriate for the one-hour condition, the eight-hour value derived from the one-hour value corrected for variations in emission rate and meteorologic conditions over eight hours should be appropriate for comparison with the eight-hour standard. Note that the greatest opportunity for gross errors in the analysis involves the specification of an appropriate one-hour worst-case scenario for which *no* theoretical or empirical basis for choice exists. Clearly it is better to rely on an empirically derived relationship between one- and eight-hour second annual maximum concentrations for the derivation of an eight-hour value rather than to pick one-hour scenarios and thereby increase the chances for error by a factor of eight.

There is some question as to whether the procedures presented in revised Volume 9 and the *Hot Spot Guidelines* are better than those referenced in the original Volume 9. Through its failure to present this methodology in subsequent publications on the subject, it would seem that the EPA is suggesting that this "persistence factor approach" should be discarded in favor of more recently developed procedures that appear to offer no significant advantages over this relatively straightforward approach. Until this meteorological persistence factor approach is officially banned in favor of something which is clearly superior in both theory and practice, its use should be continued with the advice and consent of the appropriate air pollution control agency.

Mesoscale Analysis

A mesoscale, or emissions burden, analysis involves the calculation of total emissions generated by the various project alternatives. Total emissions are usually calculated on a daily average or total annual basis for CO, total HC (Hydrocarbons and/or nonmethane HC), and nitrogen oxides. For highway projects, emissions from the project highway as well as from the surrounding highway network which might experience changes in traffic levels as a result of the proposed project are usually considered in the derivation of total project emissions. For a large highway project, a comprehensive meso-scale analysis might involve the calculation of emissions for hundreds of individual highway segments for each of several project alternatives for three or four years of analysis (e.g., year of completion, ten years after, and twenty years after). Mesoscale analyses of this magnitude are often performed with the aid of a computerized traffic model linked to the Mobile 1 package.

The estimation of total HC emissions for various project alternatives provides the analyst with a basis for the determination of the relative impacts of the various project alternatives (including, of course, the null, or do-nothing, alternative) as they relate to photochemical oxidant generation. If it is assumed that nonmethane HCs are the limiting species in the photochemical oxidation process,* then it can be concluded that the project may result in the production of higher photochemical oxidant concentrations. Conversely, if it can be shown that the project construction will expedite traffic flow to such a degree that overall net HC emissions will decrease, then it can be concluded that the project will serve to mitigate the photochemical oxidant problem.

Since many states currently experience violations of the photochemical oxidant standard, and since the 1977 Clean Air Act calls for the attainment of all Federal ambient air standards by 1982, with possible extension to 1987, most state implementation plans (SIPs, see Chapters 2 and 3) call for significant reductions in HC emissions. Motor vehicles are a major source of HC emissions. Consequently, the results of the HC emissions burden analysis for an individual proj-

ect can be very important with regard to conformity with the SIP. Note that projects which are not consistent with the SIP generally do not get built. Some have argued that consistency with the SIP with regard to the photochemical oxidant standard attainment should not be made on a project-by-project basis but rather for the highway program as it relates to an entire region. In this manner the net HC emission benefits of some projects can be used to offset the negative impacts of projects which might make a positive contribution to the regional HC emissions burden.

As previously mentioned, HCs are generally considered important as air pollutants only as they relate to the photochemical oxidant cycle. For this reason HC emissions burden analyses should probably be performed for nonmethane HC on a 6 a.m. to 9 a.m. basis for the warmer months of the year (i.e., the photochemical oxidant season). However, due to limitations in the availability of traffic data, HC emissions burden analyses are usually performed on an *annual* basis, and since most regional HC emissions inventories are performed on a *total* HC basis, most highway projects are evaluated on a total HC basis instead of a strict nonmethane HC basis. This approach facilitates comparisons between project emissions and total regional emissions which tend to be expressed in terms of kilograms of total HC emissions per year. Note also that the methane–nonmethane fraction makes little difference with regard to the comparison between two highway alternatives since the function of nonmethane HC should be compatible between the two alternative scenarios.

CO mesoscale analyses for the various project alternatives serve three purposes when performed for the year of analysis, the year of completion, and twenty years after project completion. First, the results of the mesoscale analysis can be used to adjust background data to reflect future reductions expected as a result of vehicle turnover. For example, if mesoscale CO emissions were expected to be 20 percent lower than the current levels by the time the highway is completed, one might choose to adjust background values accordingly and thus move the analysis "in the direction of reality." The same principle holds for the analysis of scenarios representing the future (e.g., ten years after completion). If the combined effects of in-

---

*Many of the EPA guidelines and recommendations assume that this is the case. For example, the ambient HC standard is actually not a standard but a guideline to be used in meeting the photochemical oxidant standard. The standard is 160 $\mu g/m^3$ of nonmethane HC between 6 a.m. and 9 a.m. The assumption behind this regulation is that 160 $\mu g/m^3$ of nonmethane HC between 6 a.m. and 9 a.m. will produce an equivalent amount of photochemical oxidant later in the day. However, the EPA has recently released (July 1978) its "EKMA Model" (EPA-600/8-78-014a, *User's Manual for Kinetics Model and Ozone Isopleth Plotting Package*) which does consider the nitrogen oxides/nonmethane HC ratio in formulating its predictions.

creased traffic and decreased emission rates per vehicle suggest that background levels will increase or decrease (usually decrease), it is appropriate to adjust background levels to correspond to these expectations.

Second, one may choose to perform a microscale analysis of the various project alternatives for a single worst-case year and thereby demonstrate compliance with the CO standard with a minimum of effort. The results of the CO mesoscale analysis provide a convenient indicator as to when (i.e., which year) maximum emissions can be expected. (Usually maximum emissions occur during the year of project completion.)

Finally, mesoscale CO analyses provide regulatory agencies with data that may be comparable with their own emission inventories. Some states actually base the SIPs for CO on total emissions (i.e., if statewide CO emissions decrease by 10 percent, statewide CO concentrations will decrease by 10 percent). Of course, it is not possible to tell from this type of analysis what might happen at any given receptor—some may decrease, others may increase.

Mesoscale nitrogen dioxide (NO_2) emissions analyses provide the reviewer with some indication as to which project alternatives can be expected to generate the most nitrogen oxides (NO_x). Usually it is the alternative that generates the most vehicle miles traveled (VMT) at the highest speed. However, this information is seldom used to draw conclusions. (Note that the alternative which generates the most NO_x often generates the least CO and HC.) As always, the analyst should contact the state air pollution agency regarding the need for a NO_x mesoscale analysis before deciding whether to perform one.

Lead Analysis

In 1978 the EPA promulgated an ambient air quality standard of 1.5 μg/m^3 of lead averaged over a calendar quarter. To date the EPA has yet to develop some long-term line source dispersion model for lead.* Development of such a model would seem to be a relatively straightforward task. One could adopt a long-term model such as

*At one time (April 1979) the EPA was about to release a highway lead model (PBLSQ). However, as of December of 1980 it has yet to appear, purportedly due to problems with the deposition algorithm.

AQDM, CDM, or any number of models that have been available for almost a decade and, employing a sector average-type dispersion algorithm (use a stability wind rose, the so-called STAR output, as input), model line sources as a series of point sources. This would leave only the deposition problem, which could be "solved" by leaving the choice of a deposition velocity to the user. The resulting model would be rather crude—partly because of the deposition problem: the larger particles settle near the source and thus lead to a decrease in average deposition velocity with increasing distance from the source —but certainly better than nothing. As a very conservative first approximation it could be assumed that deposition of lead particulates does not even occur.

Given that the EPA has still not formulated and distributed an ambient lead model, it may be possible to demonstrate compliance with the lead standard by using an hourly line-source dispersion model together with a series of assumptions regarding the nature of "average" conditions. An example of this type of analysis is contained in Appendix 6D.

Construction Impacts

The air quality impacts from highway (or in some circumstances, airport) construction activities arise from three basic sources. The first is the fugitive dust problem. When land is cleared of vegetation and the soil dries out, fine-grained soil material can be picked up by the wind to become fugitive dust (suspended and/or settleable particulates). This problem is of course more acute for some soils than for others. The U.S. Department of Agriculture, Soil Conservation Service (SCS) has mapped much of the nation's soil. These maps (actually reports) are usually available through the county SCS office and contain information regarding the susceptibility of the various soil types to wind erosion. By consulting these references and knowing something about the construction schedule, the analyst can obtain some estimate of the magnitude of the potential fugitive dust problem and therefore recommend mitigation techniques. Examples include minimization of the amount of land cleared; minimization of the interval between clearing and replanting; the use of dust suppression methods such as watering; application of calcium chloride; and the use of mulches that also serve to retard water erosion. These types of controls are usually part of the standard specifications for most transportation projects. Currently there are no techniques (models) available for the routine estimation of fugitive dust concentrations in the vicinity of construction activities.

A second category of construction air quality impacts involves the generation of traffic congestion when access to existing highways must be restricted during construction. The impacts of these diversions can be assessed in much the same manner as any other highway project; however, due to the temporary nature of these impacts, they are usually determined to be insignificant.

The third air quality impact associated with construction involves emissions from construction equipment and/or the burning of any waste material. Emission rates for construction equipment can be found in EPA AP-42, *Compilation of Air Pollution Emission Factors*, and impacts can be analyzed using conventional modeling techniques. Open burning of waste material is banned in almost every locality and is therefore not a factor for most projects.

In most states construction impacts are usually considered temporary and/or insignificant. Thus they are accorded minimal discussion in most air quality impact reports. These discussions often commit the responsible agency to undertake all appropriate mitigation measures. As always, contact with the appropriate state agency is advisable before an analysis of the impacts is begun.

Contents of Air Quality Reports

An air quality report should be written for the professional reviewer. It should contain all the information necessary for the reviewer to assess the air quality impacts of the proposed project and should contain sufficient information for another professional to reconstruct the entire analysis, thereby enabling the second analyst to testify regarding the accuracy of the conclusions expressed. This does not mean that the report needs be a tome which relates the thinking behind every assumption made in developing the analysis; rather, the information regarding the model inputs, receptor locations, one/eight-hour

conversions, and so on, should simply be made available to the reader in a convenient format (e.g., figures, tables, appendices containing computer printouts). The report should also contain a summary suitable for inclusion in an EIS, written in terms readily understood by the layman, relating the main conclusions of the analysis. A checklist of items that should be contained in an air quality analysis is contained in Appendix 6E. The FHWA's views on the contents of air quality reports are contained in a discussion paper, which has been reproduced here as Appendix 6F.

Special Considerations for Airport Analyses

Most of the principles discussed in connection with the assessment of air quality impacts of highways apply equally to airports. In fact, the most significant source of CO associated with airport operation usually involves the highway network; aircraft emissions are often too far removed from potential receptor sites to generate violations of the CO standards.

Microscale CO analyses for airports are best carried out with the aid of a Gaussian Plume-type model such as AVAP. A box model can be used, if one wants to demonstrate that on the average (i.e., throughout the entire volume of the box), CO concentrations generated by the airport will be infinitesimal. However, the question as to whether the ambient CO standard will be violated at some specific receptor point on or near the airport cannot be answered using this modeling approach. Thus, from a technical standpoint, the FAA box model is essentially useless as a tool for the assessment of CO impacts.

In using a model such as AVAP, it is important to monitor exactly where the various receptor points in the receptor grid are with respect to the various airport sources. Otherwise one might locate a receptor at the source, thereby predicting concentrations not likely to occur.

Note also that for airports, as opposed to highways, the specification of a mixing height can exert an influence on predicted pollutant concentrations at some distance downwind from the airport. In this case a low mixing height can actually prevent emissions aloft from reaching ground level.

A mesoscale (HC emissions burden) analysis should also be conducted for airport projects.

Airplanes seldom seem to generate violations of the CO standards; however, they do tend to be significant sources of HC emissions. As previously noted, the change in the HC emissions burden between the null and the build alternatives can be a critical factor with regard to SIP consistency. Mesoscale analyses are also sometimes performed for nitrogen oxides, sulfates, and particulates. However, these analyses usually serve only to show how insignificant airport emissions are when considered in relation to region-wide emissions for these pollutants.

The pollutant sources associated with airport operations include aircraft, ground transportation, ground service vehicles, aircraft maintenance services, and evaporation of HCs associated with the storage and handling of fuels. EPA APTD-1470, *An Air Pollution Impact Methodology for Airports*, January 1973, remains one of the more useful references on the subject of airports and air pollution. The U.S. DOT publication P 5600.5, *Environmental Assessment Notebook Series: Airports*, 1978, and available through the U.S. Government Printing Office (Stock No. 050-000—138-5), contains more guidance regarding the preparation of airport EISs.

In preparing an airport air quality analysis it is important to coordinate and consult with FAA officials. Continued coordination with state and local pollution control agencies is also important.

BIBLIOGRAPHY

American Meteorological Society, Second Joint Conference on Applications of Air Pollution Meteorology, *Session 8: Complex Terrain—I*, Boston, MA, March 1980.

Beaton, J. L., et al., *Mathematical Approach to Estimating Highway Impact on Air Quality*, FHWA-RD-72-36, April 1972.

Benesh, F., and Midurski, T., *Carbon Monoxide Hot Spot Guidelines*, vol. 2, *Rationale*, GCA/Technology Division, Bedford, MA, prepared for EPA, Research Triangle Park, NC, EPA-450/3-78-034, August 1978.

Benesh, F., *Carbon Monoxide Hot Spot Guidelines*, vol. 4, *Documentation of Computer Programs to Generate Volume I Tables and Curves*, GCA/Technology Division, Bedford, MA, prepared for EPA, Research Triangle Park, NC, EPA-450/3-78-036 (see also Midurski).

Benesh, F., *Carbon Monoxide Hot Spot Guidelines*, vol. 5, *Users Manual for the Intersection Midblock Model*, GCA/Technology Division, Bedford, MA, prepared for EPA, Research Triangle Park, NC, EPA-450/3-78-037, August 1978.

Benesh, F., *Carbon Monoxide Hot Spot Guidelines*, vol. 6, *Users Manual for the Modified ESMAP Model*, GCA/Technology Division, Bedford, MA, prepared for EPA, Research Triangle Park, NC, EPA-450/3-78-040, August 1978.

Benkley, C. W., and Shulman, L. L., Estimating Hourly Mixing Depths from Historical Meteorological Data, *J. Appl. Meteor.*, 18:772–780, June 1979.

Benson, P. E., and Squires, B. T., *Validation of the CALINE 2 Model Using Other Data Bases*, Caltrans, FHWA-CA-TL-79-09, May 1979.

Benson, Paul E., *Caline 3—A Versatile Dispersion Model for Predicting Air Pollutant Levels Near Highways and Arterial Streets*, FHWA/CA/TL-79/23, November 1979.

Bibbero, R. J. and Young, I. G., *Systems Approach to Air Pollution Control*, Wiley, New York, 1974.

Briggs, G. A., Momentum and Buoyancy Effects. In D. H. Slade, ed., *Meteorology and Atomic Energy*, U.S. Atomic Energy Commission, 1968.

Brachaczek, W. W., Sulphal Emissions from Catalyse-Equipped Automobiles on the Highway, *J. Air Pollution Assoc.*, 29:255.

Brubaker, K. L., Brown, P., and Cirillo, R. R., *Addendum to User's Guide for Climatological Dispersion Model*, EPA 45-/3-77-015, Research Triangle Park, NC 27711, May 1977.

Burt, E., *Valley Model User's Guide*, EPA-450/2-77-018, EPA, Research Triangle Park, NC, September 1977.

Busse, A. D., and Zimmerman, J. R., *User's Guide for the Climatological Dispersion Model*, EPA-RA-73-024, (NTIS PB 227346/AS), EPA, Research Triangle Park, NC, December 1973.

Cadle, S. H., Chock, D. P., Monson, P. R., and Heuss, J. M., General Motors Sulfate Dispersion Experiment: Experimental Procedures and Results, *J. Air Pollution Control Assoc.*, 27:33, 1977.

Cadle, S. H., Chock, D. P., Heuss, J. M., and Monson, P. R., *Results of the General Motors Sulfate Dispersion Experiments*, General Motors Research publication, GMR-2107, 1976.

Carpenter, W. A., and Clemaña, *Analysis and Comparative Evaluation of AIRPOL-4*, Virginia Highway and Transportation Research Council Report, VHTRC75-R55, 1975.

Chock, D. P., A Simple Line-Source Model for Dispersion Near Roadways, *Atmos. Environ.*, 12:823, 1978.

Chock, D. P., *The General Motors Sulfate Dispersion Experiment: Assessment of the EPA HIWAY Model*, General Motors Research Laboratories, GMR-2126, April 1976.

Chock, D. P., General Motors Sulfate Dispersion Experiment: Assessment of the EPA HIWAY Model, *J. Air Pollution Control Assoc.*, 27:39, 1977.

Cole, H. S., and Summerhays, J. E., A Review of Techniques Available for Estimating Short-Term NO_2 Concentrations, *J. Air Pollution Control Assoc.*, **29**:8, 812–817, August 1979.

de Nevers, N., and Morris, J. R., Rollback Modeling: Basic and Modified, *J. Air Pollution Control Assoc.*, **25**:9, 943–947, 1975.

Danard, M. B., Numerical Modeling of Carbon Monoxide Concentrations Near a Highway, *J. Appl. Meteor.*, **11**: 947, 1972.

Draxler, R. R., Determination of Atmospheric Diffusion Parameters, *Atmospheric Environment*, **10**:2, 99–105, 1976.

Egan, B. A., *Turbulent Diffusion in Complex Terrain*, Lectures on Air Pollution and Environmental Impact Analyses, American Meteorological Society, Boston, MA, September 1975.

Ellis, George W., et al, *The Determination of Vehicular Cold and Hot Operating Conditions for Estimating Highway Emissions*, DOT, FHWA, September 1978.

Eskridge, R. E., and Hunt, J. C. R., Highway Modeling: Part I—Prediction of Velocity and Turbulence Fields in Wake of Vehicles, *J. Appl. Meteor.*, **36**:387, 1979.

Eskridge, R. E., Binkowski, F. S., Hunt, J. C. R., Clark, T. L., and Demerjian, K. E., Highway Modeling: Part II—Advection and Diffusion of SF_6 Tracer Gas, *J. Appl. Meteor.*, **36**:401, 1979.

Gifford, F. A., Jr., An Outline of Theories of Diffusion in the Lower Layers of the Atmosphere. In D. H. Slade, ed., *Meteorology and Atomic Energy*, U.S. Atomic Energy Commission, 1968.

Gifford, F. A., Jr., Statistical Properties of a Fluctuating Plume Dispersion Model. In *Atmospheric Diffusion and Air Pollution*, F. N. Frenkeil and P. S. Sheppard, eds., Academic Press, NY, 1980, pp. 117–137.

Goody, R. M. and Walker, J. C. G., *Atmospheres*, Prentice-Hall, Englewood Cliffs, NJ, 1972.

Green, N. J., et al., Dispersion of Carbon Monoxide from Roadways at Low Wind Speeds, *J. Air Pollution Control Assoc.*, **29**:1057–1061, 1979.

Hanna, S. R., A Simple Method of Calculating Dispersion from Urban Area Sources, *J. Air Pollution Control Assoc.*, **21**:774–777, 1971.

Hanna, S. R., et al., AMS Workshop on Stability Classification Schemes and Sigma Curves—Summary of Recommendations, *Bull. Am. Meteor. Soc.*, **58**:12, 1305–1309, December 1977.

Harbaugh, J. W., and Bonham-Carter, G., *Computer Simulation in Geology*, Wiley-Interscience, New York, 1970.

Hayes, S. R., *Performance Measures and Standards for Air Quality Simulation Models*, EPA-450/4-79-032, EPA, Research Triangle Park, NC, October 1979.

Highway Research Board, *Highway Capacity Manual*, Special Report 87, National Academy of Sciences, National Research Council, Washington, D.C., 1965.

Hillyer, M. J., Reynolds, S. D., and Roth, P. M., *Procedures for Evaluating the Performance of Air Quality Simulation Models*, EPA-450/4-79-033, EPA, Research Triangle Park, NC, October 1979.

Holland, J. Z., *A Meteorological Survey of the Oak Ridge Area: Final Report Covering the Period 1948-52*, USAEC Report ORO-99, Weather Bureau, Oak Ridge, TN, 1953.

Holzworth, G. C., *Mixing Heights, Wind Speeds, and Potential for Urban Air Pollution Throughout the Contiguous United States*, AP-101, EPA, Research Triangle Park, NC, 1972.

Johnson, W. B., Dabbert, W. F., Ludwig, F. L., and Allen, R. J., *Field Study for Initial Evaluation of an Urban Diffusion Model for Carbon Monoxide*, Comprehensive Report for Coordinating Research Council and EPA, Contract CAPA-3-68 (1-69), Stanford Research Institute, Menlo Park, CA, 240 pp., National Technical Information Service PB 203469, 1971.

Kalpasanov, Y. and Kurchatova, G., A Study of the Statistical Distribution of Chemical Pollutants in Air, *J. Air Pollution Control Assoc.*, **26**:981, 1976.

Kincannon, B. F., Castaline, A. H., *Information Document on Automobile Emissions Inspection and Maintenance Programs*, EPA-400/2-78-001, February 1978.

Koch, R. C., et al., *Power Plant Plumes in Complex Terrain: An Appraisal of Current Research*, EPA-600/7-77-020, EPA, Research Triangle Park, NC, March 1977.

Larsen, R. I., An Air Quality Data Analysis System for Interrelating Effects, Standards, and Needed Source Reductions, *J. Air Pollution Control Assoc.*, **23**:933, 1973.

Larsen, R. I., An Air Quality Data Analysis System for Interrelating Effects, Standards, and Needed Source Reductions—Part 2, *J. Air Pollution Control Assoc.*, **24**:551, 1974.

Larsen, R. I., An Air Quality Data Analysis System for Interrelating Effects, Standards, and Needed Source Reductions: Part 4, A Three-Parameter Averaging Time Model, *J. Air Pollution Control Assoc.*, **27**: 454–459, 1977.

Larsen, R. I., *A Mathematical Model for Relating Air Quality Measurements to Air Quality Standards*, AP-89, EPA, Research Triangle Park, NC, 1971.

Larsen, R. I., A New Mathematical Model of Air Pollutant Concentration, Averaging Time, and Frequency, *J. Air Pollution Control Assoc.*, **19**:24, 1969.

Larsen, R. I., et al., Analyzing Air Pollutant Concentration and Dosage Data, *J. Air Pollution Control Assoc.*, **17**:85, 1967.

Little, P., and Wiffen, R. D., Emission and Deposition of Lead from Motor Exhausts, *Atmospheric Environment*, **12**:1331–1341, 1978.

Lorang, P., *Review of Past Studies Addressing the Potential Impact of CO, HC, and NO Emissions from Commercial Aircraft on Air Quality*, EPA, AC-78-03, 1978.

Lowry, William P., *Weather and Life—An Introduction to Biometeorology*, Academic Press, New York, 1967.

Ludwig, F. L., et al., *User's Manual for the APRAC-2 Emissions and Diffusion Model*, prepared for the EPA, Contract No. 68-01-3807, Stanford Research Institute, Menlo Park, CA, June 1977.

Ludwig, F. L., and Dabberdt, W. F., *Evaluation of the APRAC—1A Urban Diffusion Model for Carbon Monoxide*, Final Report, Contract CAPA-3-68 (1-69), Stanford Research Institute, Menlo Park, CA, 167 pp. (NTIS-PB 210 819), 1972.

Lyons, W. A., *Turbulent Diffusion and Pollutant Transport in Shoreline Environments*, Lectures on Air Pollution and Environmental Impact Analyses, American Meteorological Society, Boston, September 1975.

Mancuso, R. L., and Ludwig, F. L., *User's Manual for the APRAC-1A Urban Diffusion Model Computer Program*, EPA-650/3-73-001, Research Triangle Park, NC, September 1972.

McMahon, T. A., and Denison, P. J., Empirical Atmospheric Deposition Parameters—A Survey, *Atmospheric Environment*, 13:571–585, 1979.

McVoy, G. R., Monte Carlo Simulation Techniques Applied to Air Quality Impact Assessment, *J. Air Pollution Control Assoc.*, 29:843–845, 1979.

Midurski, T., *Carbon Monoxide Hot Spot Guidelines*, vol. 1, *Techniques*, GCA/Technology Division, Bedford, MA, prepared for EPA, Research Triangle Park, NC, EPA-450/3-78-033, August 1978 (see also Benesh).

Midurski, T., *Carbon Monoxide Hot Spot Guidelines*, vol. 3, *Workbook*, GCA/Techology Division, Bedford, MA, prepared for EPA, Research Triangle Park, NC, EPA-450/3-78-035, August 1978.

Midurski, T., *Carbon Monoxide Hot Spot Guidelines*, vol. 7, *Example Applications at Waltham/Providence/Washington, D.C.*, GCA/Technology Division, Bedford, MA, prepared for EPA, Research Triangle Park, NC, EPA-450/3-78-041, August 1978.

Midurski, T. and Castaline, A. H., *Determination of Percentages of Vehicles Operating in the Cold Start Mode*, EPA-450/3-77-023, Research Triangle Park, NC, August 1977.

Mihram, G. A., *Simulation: Statistical Foundations and Methodology*, Academic Press, New York, 1972.

National Cooperation Highway Research Program, *Monitoring Carbon Monoxide in Urban Areas*, Final Report, HR20-14, March 1978.

Noll, K. E., et al., A Comparison of Three Highway Line Source Dispersion Models, *Atmospheric Environment*, 12:1323–1329, 1978.

Norco, J. E., et al., *An Air Pollution Impact Methodology for Airports—Phase 1*, EPA, APTD-1470, 1973.

Pasquill, F., *Atmospheric Diffusion*, 2nd ed., D. Van Nostrand, London, 1975.

Pasquill, F., *Atmospheric Diffusion: The Dispersion of Windborne Material from Industrial and Other Sources*, Van Nostrand, London, 1962, p. 297.

Pasquill, F., Atmospheric Dispersion Modeling, *J. Air Pollution Control Assoc.*, 29:117–119, 1979.

Pasquill, F., *Atmospheric Dispersion Parameters in Gaussian Plume Modeling*, EPA-600/4-76-0306, June 1976.

Patel, N. R., Comment on a New Mathematical Model of Air Pollution Concentration, *J. Air Poll. Control Assoc.*, 23:291, 1973.

Patterson, R. M., et al., *Validation Study of an Approach for Evaluating the Impact of a Shopping Center on Ambient Carbon Monoxide Concentrations*, GCA-TR-74-4, GCA/Technology Division, Bedford, MA, 1974.

Petersen, W. B., *A Pilot Study on Dispersion Near Roadways*, EPA-600/4-78-044, 1978.

Petersen, W. B., *User's Guide for HIWAY-2: A Highway Air Pollution Model*, EPA-600/8-80-018, EPA, Research Triangle Park, NC, May 1980.

Pierce, T. E., and Turner, D. B., *User's Guide for MPTER: A Multiple Point Gaussian Dispersion Algorithm with Optional Terrain Adjustment*, EPA-600/8-80-016, EPA, Research Triangle Park, NC, April 1980.

Pollack, R. I., *Studies of Pollutant Concentration Frequency Distributions*, EPA-650/4-75-004, Research Triangle Park, NC, 1975.

Rao, S. T., Chen, M., Keenan, M., Sistla, G., Peddada, R., Wotzak, G., and Kolak, N., *Dispersion of Pollutants Near Highways—Experimental Design and Data Acquisition Procedures*, EPA-600/4-78-037, 1978.

Rao, S. T., Sedefian, L., and Czapski, U. H., Characteristics of Turbulence and Dispersion of Pollutants Near Major Roadways, *J. Appl. Meteor.*, 36:283, 1979.

Rao, S. T., Sistla, G., Keenan, M. T., and Wilson, J. S., An Evaluation of Some Commonly Used Highway Dispersion, *J. Air Pollution Control Assoc.*, 30:239, 1980.

Remsburg, E. E., et al., The Nocturnal Inversion and Its Effect on the Dispersion of Carbon Monoxide at Ground Level in Hampton, Virginia, *Atmospheric Environment*, 13:443–447, 1979.

Rote, D. M., and Wangen, L. E., *A Generalized Air Quality Assessment Model for Air Force Operations*, Air Force Weapons Laboratory Report No. AFWL-TR-740304, Kirland Air Force Base, NM 87117, 1975.

Rubino, R. A., et al., Ozone Transport, *J. Air Pollution Control Assoc.*, 26:972–975, 1976.

Sistla, G., Samson, P., Keenan, M., and Rao, S. T., A Study of Pollutant Dispersion Near Highways, *Atmospheric Environment*, 13:669, 1979.

Slade, D. H., ed., *Meteorology and Atomic Energy 1968*, U.S. Atomic Energy Commission, NTIS No. TID-24190, Lib. of Cong. No. 68-60097, 1968.

Smith, D. G., Validation Studies of Air Quality Models at Dulles Airport, *J. Air Pollution Control Assoc.*, 29:110–113, 1979.

Smith, D. G., Yamartino, R. J., Benkley, C., Isaacs, R., Lee, J., and Chang, D., *Corcorde Air Quality Monitoring and Analysis Program at Dulles International Airport*, FAA-AEQ-77-14, 1977.

Stern, A. C., ed., *Air Pollutants, Their Transformation and Transport* (vol. 1 of 5 vols.), Academic, New York, 1976.

Sutton, O. G., The Problem of Diffusion in the Lower Atmosphere, *Quart. J. Roy Met. Soc.*, 17:257–281, 1947.

TRW Systems Group, *Air Quality Display Model*, prepared for National Air Pollution Control Administration Contract No. PH-22-68-60 (NTIS PB 189194),

HEW, Public Health Service, Washington, D.C., November 1969.

Turner, D. B., Air Quality Frequency Distributions from Dispersion Models Compared with Measurements, in *Proceedings of the Symposium on Statistical Aspects of Air Quality Data*, EPA 650/4-74-038.

Turner, D. B., Atmospheric Dispersion Modeling, A Critical Review, *J. Air Pollution Control Assoc.*, 29:502–519, 1979.

Turner, D. B., A Diffusion Model for an Urban Area, *J. Appl. Meteor.*, 3:83–91, 1964.

Turner, D. B., and Novak, J. H., *User's Guide for RAM*, EPA, Research Triangle Park, NC, 1978.

Turner, D. B., *Workbook of Atmospheric Dispersion Estimates*, Public Health Service, 999-AP-26 (NTIS PB 191482), EPA, Research Triangle Park, NC, 1969.

U.S. Dept. of HEW, *Air Quality Criteria for Particulate Matter*, AP-49, 1969.

U.S. Dept. of HEW, *Air Quality Criteria for Sulfur Oxides*, AP-50, 1970.

U.S. Dept. of HEW, *Air Quality Criteria, Carbon Monoxide*, AP-62, 1970.

U.S. Dept. of HEW, *Air Quality Criteria, Photochemical Oxidants*, AP-63, 1970.

U.S. Dept. of HEW, *Air Quality Criteria, Hydrocarbons*, AP-64, 1970.

U.S. Dept. of HEW, *Air Quality Criteria, Nitrogen Oxides*, AP-84, 1970.

U.S. Dept. of Transportation, FAA, *Revision of the Box Model Method for Ascertaining Aircraft Emissions at Airports*, Washington, D.C., Issuing Office Ref. No. AAS-410, February 1976.

U.S. EPA, *Air Pollution Technical Publications of the USEPA*—A periodic listing prepared by the EPA Air Pollution Technical Information Center, Research Triangle Park, NC 27711.

U.S. EPA, *Compilation of Air Pollution Emission Factors*, AP-42, 1975, (2nd ed. and 10 supplements as of 1980).

U.S. EPA, *EPA Guideline Series, Supplementary Guidelines for Lead Implementation Plans*, EPA-450/2-78-038, OAQPS No. 1.2-104, August 1978.

U.S. EPA, *Guidelines for Air Quality Maintenance Planning and Analysis*, vol. 9, revised, *Evaluating Indirect Sources*, EPA-450/4-78-001, 1978.

U.S. EPA, Guidelines on Air Quality Models, *Federal Register*, 45:61, 20157–20158, Washington, D.C., March 1980.

U.S. EPA, *Guidelines for the Review of the Impact of Indirect Sources on Ambient Air Quality, Guidelines for Air Quality Maintenance Planning and Analysis*, vol. 9, EPA-450/4-78-001, EPA, Research Triangle Park, NC, 1975.

U.S. EPA, *Mobile Source Emission Factors*, Office of Air and Waste Management, Washington, D.C., EPA-400/9-78-005, March 1978.

U.S. EPA, *Mobile Source Emission Factors for Low Altitude Areas Only*, EPA-400/9-78-006, March 1978.

U.S. EPA, *OAQPS Guideline Series, Guidelines on Air Quality Models*, EPA-450/2-78-027, OAQPS No. 1.2-080, April 1978.

U.S. EPA, *Procedures for Quantifying Relationships Between Photochemical Oxidants and Precursors*, EPA-450/2-77-021a, EPA, Research Triangle Park, NC, November 1977.

U.S. EPA, *Procedures for Quantifying Relationships Between Photochemical Oxidants and Precursors: Supporting Documentation*, EPA-450/2-77-021b, EPA, Research Triangle Park, NC, February 1978.

U.S. EPA, Requirements for Preparation, Adoption and Submittal of Implementation Plans; Approval and Promulgation of Implementation Plans, *Federal Register*, 45:154, 52676-52748, Washington, D.C., August 1980.

U.S. EPA, *UNAMAP (Version 3)*, NTIS, PB-277-193 (listing of some EPA dispersion models), 1978.

U.S. EPA, *User's Guide to Mobile 1*, Mobile Source Emissions Model, EPA-400/9-78-007, August 1978.

U.S. EPA, *User's Manual for Kinetics Model and Ozone Isopleth Plotting Package*, EPA-600/8-78-014a, EPA, Research Triangle Park, NC, July 1978.

U.S. EPA, *User's Manual for Single Source (CRSTER) Model*, EPA-450/2-77-013 (NTIS PB 271360), OAQPS, Research Triangle Park, NC, July 1977.

Wang, I. T., Conley, L. A., and Rote, D. M., *Airport Vicinity Air Pollution Model User Guide*, FAA-RD-75-230, 1975.

Wang, I. T., et al., *Airport Vicinity Air Pollution Study Model Application and Validation and Air Quality Impact Analysis at Washington National Airport*, Argonne National Laboratory, Argonne, IL, U.S. DOT, FAA-RF-74-132, July 1974.

Ward, C. E., Ranzieri, A. J., and Shirley, E. C., *CALINE-2 —An Improved Microscale Model for the Dispersion of Air Pollutants from a Line Source*, FHWA-RD-77-74, 1977.

Yamartino, R. J., et al., *Impact of Aircraft Emissions on Air Quality in the Vicinity of Airports*, vol. 1, *Recent Airport Measurement Programs, Data, and Sub-Model Development*, FAA-EE-80-09A, July 1980.

Yamartino, R. J., et al., *Impact of Aircraft Emissions on Air Quality in the Vicinity of Airports*, vol. II, *An Updated Model Assessment of Aircraft Generated Air Pollution at LAX, JFK, and ORD*, FAA-EE-09A, July 1980.

Zimmerman J. R. and Thompson, R. S., *User's Guide for HIWAY, A Highway Air Pollution Model*, EPA-650/4-74-008, 1975.

APPENDIX 6A

THE USE OF MOBILE
SOURCE EMISSION FACTORS
IN HIGHWAY-PROJECT
ANALYSES

NOISE AND AIR QUALITY BRANCH

OFFICE OF ENVIRONMENTAL POLICY

FEDERAL HIGHWAY ADMINISTRATION

WASHINGTON, D.C. 20590

NOVEMBER 1978

TABLE OF CONTENTS

INTRODUCTION

The mobile source emission factors have, with each successive issuance, become more difficult to understand and implement in transportation analyses. This situation stems largely from the more complex methodology and the need for additional input variables. Depending upon the data input being required, the particular input item may have an insignificant effect on emissions. In other instances, the particular input item may significantly affect emissions, but is either very difficult or impossible to obtain from existing transportation data bases. The guidance being provided here is, by necessity, rather general, and is not a substitute for the judgment of the user which should be exercised in each specific case. This guidance is directed to those analyses performed to assess the air quality impacts of proposed highway projects. This guidance document is not necessarily intended for use in transportation systems analyses or for revisions of the State implementation plans (SIP's), but the information and guidance may be of interest to persons involved in this work.

The guidance in this document is being confined to the application of the mobile source emission factors themselves, recognizing that they constitute an essential part of the overall air quality impact assessment. Since many of the other assumptions that are made in highway project microscale carbon monoxide (CO) analyses may be of equal or greater significance than those made with respect to the emission factors, the user may wish to consult a draft document titled "Considerations to Assure Adequate Air Quality Analysis for Individual Highway Sections" dated June 1977. This document provides guidance on "worst-case" analysis assumptions that are recommended for use.

The interested user may also wish to refer to an FHWA report titled "A Discussion of the Environmental Protection Agency (EPA) Mobile Source Emission Factors and Methodology" dated April 1978. This report discusses primarily the correction factors that have been developed by EPA to adjust emissions for various driving and environmental conditions that are different from those in the EPA 1975 Federal Test Procedure (FTP).

This report contains limited sensitivity analyses for most of the input parameters. The sensitivity analyses are included to provide the user with information on the basis for the recommendations and guidance that are given.

SUMMARY OF RECOMMENDATIONS

The following is a brief summary of the principal recommendations given in this report. The interested reader should consult the text for elaboration.

1. A single average speed, as opposed to the three-bag speeds, should be used for individual link analyses. If the average speed is in the low range, it should be carefully estimated.

2. In performing CO link impact analyses, only the percent catalytic vehicles operating in the cold-transient mode need be estimated. The remainder can be assumed to be hot operating.

3. Reasonably accurate estimates of cold-transient mode catalytic vehicles need to be made, particularly at lower ambient air temperatures. Simplified methodology for making estimates of hot/cold vehicle-temperature operating modes will be made available by FHWA.

4. In performing hydrocarbon (HC) and oxides of nitrogen (NOx) total burden project-corridor analyses, only rough estimates of ambient temperature and proportion of vehicles operating in various temperature modes need be made because only relative differences in emissions are of interest.

5. The selection of the appropriate ambient temperature for CO analyses is dependent on the time of year which the CO levels are the highest for a given geographical area. The selection is also dependent upon the time of day and period (1 hour or 8 hours) which is being analyzed. The selection of this parameter is critical only at low temperatures and high percentage of cold-transient mode operations.

6. The vehicle mix on a specific highway link can have a significant effect on emissions. Reasonably accurate estimates should be made. The proportion of heavy-duty gasoline (HDG) trucks is particularly significant. As a practical matter, motorcycles can be ignored. The users should use their own vehicle mix for a specific highway link in preference to the national vehicle mix. The FHWA Technical Advisory T 5040.1 dated April 3, 1978, may also be consulted for information on vehicle mixes on various types of highways.

7. Analyses performed for projects whose average elevation is greater than 4,000 feet should use the high-altitude emission factors. Otherwise, the low-altitude emission factors are applicable.

8. The following correction factors may be ignored for project analyses.

   a. Air-conditioning (A/C) correction.
   b. Trailer towing correction.
   c. LDV loading correction.
   d. NOx humidity correction.
   e. Truck characteristic correction.

9. It is recommended that the transportation agency consult with the State or local air quality agency regarding the type of Inspection/Maintenance (I/M) credit reductions that may be taken for projects located in nonattainment areas. MOBILE 1 computer program may be used to calculate the appropriate credit.

SPEED CORRECTION

The 1975 FTP's for light-duty automobiles and trucks have an overall average speed of 19.6 miles per hour (mph). The Environmental Protection Agency has developed speed-correction factors which adjust emissions for average speeds other than 19.6 mph. Speed-correction factors have also been developed for HDG and diesel trucks based upon the on-the-road emissions obtained in the San Antonio Road Route.

Average speed can have a substantial effect on emission rates. The following tabulations show the 1982 emissions of CO, HC, and NOx for individual vehicle types at various average speeds. These tabulations reveal the following:

a. Changes in average speed have a dramatic effect on CO emissions for all vehicle types. Changes in average speed have the greatest effect on CO emissions at the lower range of average speeds.

b. The HDG trucks are high emitters of CO. The lowest CO emissions occur at average speeds between 45 and 50 mph. The HDG trucks are relatively high emitters of HC's.

c. Total HC emissions decrease with increasing average speed for all types of vehicles. Changes in speed have the greatest effect on HC emissions at the lower range of average speeds.

d. The NOx emissions are higher with increased average speed for all vehicle types except heavy-duty diesel (HDD) trucks. For the latter, NOx emissions decrease up to about 30 mph, and then emissions begin to increase above this speed.

e. The HDD trucks are the highest emitters of NOx. The HDG trucks are relatively high emitters of NOx compared to light-duty vehicles (LDV).

f. Changes in average speed have only a moderate effect on NOx emissions from automobiles and light-duty trucks (LDT's).

The current EPA speed-correction methodology depends upon a separate average speed for each of the three vehicle operating conditions, i.e., cold transient (Bag 1), hot operating (Bag 2), and hot transient (Bag 3). In the FTP, the overall average speed is 19.6 mph which represents the average for all three bags. The cold- and hot-transient portions of the FTP each have an average speed of 26.6 mph while the hot-operating portion has an average speed of 16 mph.

1982 Carbon Monoxide Emissions (Grams/Mile) At
Various Average Speeds*

Average Speed (mph)	LDV	LDT 1	LDT 2	HDG	HDD
5	101.3	150.7	214.2	582.6	72.8
10	50.7	76.5	104.6	422.1	50.7
15	35.6	54.4	70.2	321.7	36.7
20	28.4	43.6	54.6	256.8	27.6
25	23.3	36.0	44.9	214.0	21.6
30	19.1	29.7	37.5	185.7	17.5
35	15.9	25.0	31.9	167.5	14.8
40	14.0	22.0	28.2	156.8	13.0
45	13.2	20.8	26.2	152.4	11.8
50	13.0	20.5	25.4	153.8	11.2
55	11.9	18.9	24.2	161.7	11.0

*100 percent hot stabilized.

1982 Total Hydrocarbon Emissions (Grams/Mile) At Various Average Speeds*

Average Speed (mph)	LDV	LDT 1	LDT 2	HDG	HDD
5	8.2	12.3	17.6	65.9	9.6
10	4.7	6.9	10.1	42.9	7.2
15	3.6	5.2	7.6	29.5	5.6
20	3.0	4.3	6.5	21.4	4.5
25	2.7	3.8	5.8	16.3	3.7
30	2.4	3.3	5.2	13.0	3.1
35	2.1	3.0	4.8	10.9	2.7
40	2.0	2.8	4.5	9.5	2.5
45	1.9	2.6	4.3	8.6	2.3
50	1.9	2.6	4.3	8.1	2.2
55	1.8	2.5	4.1	8.0	2.1

*100 percent hot stabilized.

1982 Oxides of Nitrogen Emissions (Grams/Mile) At Various Average Speeds*

Average Speed (mph)	LDV	LDT 1	LDT 2	HDG	HDD
5	1.6	1.8	3.2	8.5	36.0
10	1.6	1.7	3.0	9.0	28.1
15	1.7	1.9	3.1	9.5	23.1
20	1.9	2.1	3.4	10.0	20.1
25	2.1	2.3	3.8	10.4	18.4
30	2.2	2.4	4.1	10.9	17.8
35	2.3	2.6	4.3	11.4	18.1
40	2.4	2.7	4.5	11.9	19.4
45	2.5	2.7	4.6	12.4	22.0
50	2.6	2.8	4.8	12.9	26.2
55	2.8	3.1	5.2	13.4	33.1

*100 percent hot stabilized.

Recommendations

For highway project analyses, the use of three speeds for each of the temperature-operating modes is not necessary or practical. The average speed of vehicles on a specific transportation link is assumed to be the same irrespective of the vehicle-operating temperature condition. In other words, the average speed is independent on whether vehicle speed should be used for highway-project analyses. As the previous tabulations have shown, CO emissions are sensitive to slight changes in average speed, particularly at the lower average speeds. Care should therefore be taken in estimating present and projecting future average speeds for either existing highways or proposed improvements.

The selection of the proper average speed is particularly critical when making comparisons of total emissions or localized CO impacts between alternatives such as the "build" and "no-build."

TEMPERATURE - HOT/COLD-MODE CORRECTION

Carbon Monoxide (CO)

Two important parameters that determine the level of CO emissions from LDV's, LDT's, and motorcycles are ambient temperature and the numbers of these vehicles operating in the cold-transient mode.[1] Ambient temperature has only a slight effect on emissions from cold-operating noncatalyst vehicles. Temperature has a dramatic effect on emissions for cold-operating catalyst vehicles. Temperature has no effect on hot-operating catalyst vehicles, hot-operating noncatalyst vehicles, and catalyst vehicles operating in the hot-transient mode.[2]

The following tabulation shows a comparison of CO emissions for light-duty catalyst vehicles at two temperatures for three levels of cold-transient mode and hot-transient mode vehicle operation.

The CO emissions from LDT's which are not tabulated behave in much the same way, except the magnitude of the emissions is greater.

---

[1] For catalyst vehicles, the first 505 seconds of vehicle operation following a 1-hour engine-off period. For noncatalyst vehicles, the first 505 seconds of vehicle operation following a 4-hour engine-off period.

[2] The first 505 seconds of vehicle operation following a short engine-off period. All referred to as the hot-transient mode.

Light-Duty Catalyst Vehicle Carbon Monoxide Emissions (Grams/Mi) At 25 MPH

	1978		1982		1987		1999	
	20°F	75°	20°F	75°F	20°F	75°F	20°F	75°F
Cold Transient Mode								
0%	37.4	37.4	23.6	23.6	10.7	10.7	6.3	6.3
20%	65.8	46.2	43.7	30.3	21.7	16.0	14.5	11.3
100%	190.3	81.6	131.5	57.3	69.5	37.4	50.7	31.7
Hot Transient Mode								
0%	37.4	37.4	23.6	23.6	10.7	10.7	6.3	6.3
20%	38.1	38.1	24.2	24.2	11.3	11.3	6.9	6.9
100%	40.3	40.3	26.0	26.0	13.4	13.4	9.2	9.2

The following tabulation shows the incremental changes in LDV CO
emissions (grams/mile) for each 10 percent change respectively in
the cold-transient and hot-transient modes of vehicle operation.
The tabulated values represent the average incremental emissions
over a range of 0 to 10 percent in the cold- and hot-transient
modes.

Incremental Change in LDV Carbon Monoxide
Emissions (Grams/Mile) for a 10 Percent Change in Hot/Cold Mode

	1978	1982	1987	1999
Catalyst Cold Mode				
20°F	14.1	10.0	5.5	4.1
75°F	4.4	3.3	2.6	2.5
Non Catalyst Cold Mode				
20°F	0.7	0.2	0.0	0.0
75°F	0.3	0.1	0.0	0.0
Catalyst Hot Start				
20°F	0.3	0.2	0.3	0.3
75°F	0.3	0.2	0.3	0.3

These tabulations reveal that CO emissions from catalyst vehicles
operating in the cold-transient mode are sensitive to changes in
ambient temperature.

For example, in 1978, each 10 percent increase in the number of
cold-operating catalyst vehicles results in 14.1 grams/mile increase
in CO emissions at 20°F, and a 4.4 grams/mile increase at 75°F.
Changes in CO emissions resulting from changes in noncatalyst vehicles
and catalyst vehicles operating in hot-transient mode are insignificant.

CO Recommendations

As a practical matter for any particular highway-project analysis, the user need only determine the percent of catalyst vehicles (LDV, LDT) that are operating in the cold-transient mode. Emission changes from noncatalyst vehicles and catalyst vehicles operating in the hot-transient mode are not sensitive to changes in temperature and, therefore, can be ignored if the data is not readily available.

Hydrocarbons (HC)

The following table shows total HC emissions from light-duty catalyst vehicles at two ambient temperatures in 4 calendar years. Changes in ambient temperature have a significant effect on HC emissions from catalyst vehicles operating in the cold-transient mode. As ambient temperature increases, HC decrease. An increase in the percentage of catalyst vehicles operating in cold-transient mode substantially increases HC emissions, especially at low-ambient temperature.

Although the results are not tabulated, it can be shown that emissions from noncatalyst vehicles operating in the cold-transient mode are hardly effected by differences in ambient temperature. Increases in the percentage of noncatalyst vehicles operating in the cold-transient mode have little or no effect on HC emissions.

Also, changes in the percent of vehicles operating in the hot-transient mode has a minimal effect on emissions.

HC Recommendations

The HC analyses that might be performed for highway projects are intended to show relative rather than absolute amounts of emissions associated with various alternatives. As a result, the determination of the percentages of vehicles operating in the various temperature modes is not critical. In most cases, the assumption can be made that the percentage of vehicles operating in each temperature mode remains constant for various highway alternatives. Even if there were substantial changes in the cold operating mode for various alternatives or target years, there would still be minimal effect on HC emissions. This would be true because such emissions would be related to the ozone problem which is essentially associated with the warmer months of the year. For example, at 75°F in 1982, a change from 0 to 20 percent catalyst vehicles (LDV) operating the cold-start mode results in only a 0.4 gram/mile change (2.7 to 3.1) in the emissions rate.

Light-Duty Catalyst Vehicle Hydrocarbon Emission (Grams/Mi) At 25 MPH

	1978		1982		1987		1999	
	20°F	75°F	20°F	75°F	20°F	20°F	20°F	75°F
Cold Transient Mode								
0%	4.8	4.8	2.7	2.7	1.2	1.2	0.8	0.8
20%	6.5	5.4	3.9	3.1	2.1	1.6	1.6	1.2
100%	13.3	8.1	8.7	5.0	5.7	3.2	5.0	2.9
Hot Transient Mode								
0%	4.8	4.8	2.7	2.7	1.2	1.2	0.8	0.8
20%	4.9	5.0	2.9	2.9	1.4	1.4	1.0	1.0
100%	5.4	4.9	3.6	3.6	2.3	2.3	2.0	2.0

Light-Duty Catalyst Vehicle Oxides of Nitrogen Emissions (Gm/Mi) At 25 MPH

	1978		1982		1987		1999	
	20°F	75°F	20°F	75°F	20°F	75°F	20°F	75°F
Cold Transient Mode								
0%	2.7	2.7	2.1	2.1	1.6	1.6	1.5	1.5
20%	2.9	2.9	2.2	2.2	1.7	1.7	1.6	1.6
100%	3.7	3.7	3.0	3.0	2.3	2.3	2.2	2.2
Hot Transient Mode								
0%	2.7	2.7	2.1	2.1	1.6	1.6	1.5	1.5
20%	2.9	2.9	2.2	2.2	1.6	1.6	1.5	1.5
100%	3.6	3.6	2.5	2.5	1.9	1.9	1.7	1.7

Nitrogen Oxides (NOx)

The NOx emissions are independent of changes in ambient temperature as shown in the following tabulation. An increase in the percentage of catalyst vehicles that are either in the cold-transient or hot-transient modes of operation produces only a slight increase in the NOx emission rate. For noncatalyst vehicles, changes in percentage of cold-mode operation and changes in temperature have no effect on NOx emission rates.

In summary, it can be said that the LDV NOx emission rates are not dependent upon ambient temperature and change very little over time, especially in future years. Changes in percentages of LDV's operating in cold- and hot-transient modes have little effect on NOx emission rates.

NOx Recommendations

For highway-project analyses, NOx emissions can be calculated much in the same way as for total HC emissions previously discussed. The principal objective of these analyses is to evaluate the relative magnitude of NOx emissions from various highway-project alternatives for certain target years. The selection of input parameters discussed in this section is not critical for highway projects because NOx emissions are not highly dependent or sensitive to changes in these parameters, and by virture of the relative, rather than absolute, comparisons being made.

ESTIMATING HOT/COLD TRANSIENT MODE

The MOBILE 1 computer program has provisions for input of the percentage of hot- and cold-transient modes of vehicle operation. These input parameters are expressed as a percent of the total vehicle miles of travel (VMT) that is accumulated by catalyst and noncatalyst vehicles in these operating modes. The remaining portion of the VMT is considered to be hot stabilized operation. Some users have been misled by the MOBILE 1 computer program input data requirements into thinking that the mix of catalyst and noncatalyst vehicles must be determined and accounted for in the input data. This is not the case. MOBILE 1 computer program internally accounts for the proportional mix of catalyst and noncatalyst LDV for any given year. The determination of the required input values for vehicle temperature operating mode can be derived from Origin-Destination (O/D) surveys without the quantitative mix of catalytic and noncatalytic vehicles being considered. The percentage of VMT in each temperature operating mode which is derived from transportation data is simply dependent on the four EPA definitions involving soak (engine-off) time (1 and 4 hours) and the first 505 seconds of operation after a vehicle start. These VMT transient-mode percentages are then related to the catalytic and noncatalytic vehicle calculations within the MOBILE 1 computer program.

The user should be aware that emission calculations performed for 1975 and 1987 would have entirely different significance even though the cold-transient mode VMT percentages for catalytic (say 40%) and noncatalytic (say 30%) vehicles remained the same for these 2 years. In 1975, few catalyst vehicles were in existence so the total absolute VMT attributed to this type of vehicle was necessarily small. In 1987, a substantial number of catalytic vehicles will be present in the fleet, and the absolute VMT will be much greater. The 40 percent cold-transient VMT would then be much more significant.

Recommendation for Hot/Cold Mode Estimates

Currently, reliable methodology for estimating the percent of vehicles operating the cold mode for a specific project analysis is lacking. The FHWA has under contract the development of simplified nomographs by which estimates of the percent of vehicles operating in the cold- or hot-transient mode for specific highway link or portion of a transportation network. Procedures will be made available by which the esimates of vehicle-operating modes can be derived from transportation data (O/D surveys) by purpose of trip for any hour of the day. This report and handbook are expected to be available by the fall of 1978. It is recommended this methodology be used as applicable for highway project analysis as soon as it becomes available.

Ambient Air Temperature

The following tabulation shows the average change in LDV CO emissions
(grams/mile) which result from a 1°F change in ambient temperature.
For this comparison, it has been assumed that 20 percent of the
catalytic vehicles are operating in the cold mode at 25 mph average
speed. It is readily apparent that a 5° change in ambient temperature
between 20°F and 40°F affects CO emissions to a greater extent than a
5° change above 70°F.

The tabulation also reveals that, in future years, ambient temperature
changes have a lesser effect on CO emissions, so that temperature
assumptions are not a significant factor except for very high
percentages of catalytic cold mode at low-ambient temperatures.

Also, the user should be aware that at percentages greater than 20 for
catalytic cold-mode operations, changes in temperature will have a
greater effect on emissions. For example, in 1978, with 100 percent
of the vehicles operating in the cold mode at an ambient temperature
ranging from 20°F to 40°F, a 1°F change results in 2.5 grams/mile
change in the emission factor at an average speed of 25 mph. This
compares with 0.5 g/mi with 20 percent cold mode operations.

Average Changes in CO Emissions (Grams/Mile) Resulting
From 1°F Change in Temperature
(LDV - 20 percent cold catalyst at 25 mph)

Temperature Range	1978 g/mi	1982 g/mi	1987 g/mi	1999 g/mi
20°-40°F	0.50	0.35	0.15	0.08
40°-50°F	0.35	0.24	0.10	0.06
50°-55°F	0.3	0.2	0.08	0.06
55°-60°F	0.26	0.18	0.08	0.04
60°-65°F	0.24	0.16	0.08	0.04
65°-70°F	0.22	0.14	0.06	0.04
70°-75°F	0.20	0.12	0.06	0.04

Ambient Temperature Recommendations

Only general guidance can be provided for the selection of an
appropriate ambient temperature for use in calculating emission
factors. If there are no vehicles operating in the cold-transient
mode, then temperature is irrelevant. The so-called CO season
may not be associated with the coldest month of the year. Often
the highest CO levels are experienced in late summer and fall of the
year. The user should therefore determine the month(s) or season
when the highest levels of CO are likely to occur. This can be done
using historical monitored data. For 8-hour microscale line-source
analyses that are normally performed for highway impact assessments,
the user should determine the average temperature for the 8-hour
period in the month(s) or season during which the highest CO levels
have been found to occur.

For example, the average temperatures from 7 a.m. to 3 p.m. for a
particular month could be obtained from historical meteorological data.
If this data were not available, the user might select the average
monthly temperature. A 1-hour CO analysis which might be performed
for a 7-8 a.m. period would use monthly or seasonal average
temperatures for that time period of the day.

VEHICLE MIX

The following tabulations show the relative emissions in grams-per-
mile for each of the vehicle types. Emissions were calculated for
hot-running (no cold- or hot-transient) vehicles at an average speed
of 25 mph.

Carbon Monoxide

Year	LDV	LDT1	LDT2	HDG	HDD	MC
1978	37.5	41.6	51.1	212.5	23.4	24.7
1982	23.7	36.5	44.9	214.0	21.6	13.9
1987	10.8	25.8	32.0	141.4	21.0	4.3
1999	6.3	14.5	17.7	99.0	20.8	2.4

Total Hydrocarbons

Year	LDV	LDT1	LDT2	HDG	HDD	MC
1978	4.8	5.5	8.1	22.0	3.8	7.9
1982	2.7	3.8	5.8	16.3	3.7	3.8
1987	1.2	2.3	3.3	10.4	2.7	0.8
1999	0.8	1.4	1.8	8.7	2.3	0.3

Oxides of Nitrogen

Year	LDV	LDT1	LDT2	HDG	HDD	MC
1978	2.7	2.8	5.1	11.2	19.1	0.1
1982	2.1	2.3	3.8	10.4	18.4	0.4
1987	1.6	1.8	2.5	8.6	12.2	0.2
1999	1.5	1.6	1.8	7.1	5.4	0.1

Recommendations

It is apparent that the emissions from HDG trucks are substantial
compared to other vehicle classes even in future years. Both HDG
and HDD trucks are relatively high emitters of NOx.

As a practical matter, motorcycles can be ignored in highway project
analyses. Their total numbers are not significant and transportation
forecast data regarding this vehicle class is generally lacking.

If no other information is available regarding vehicle mix, the user
should use the national vehicle mix provided by EPA which is as follows:

LDV	80.3%
LD1	5.8%
LD2	5.8%
HDG	4.5%
HDD	3.1%
MC	0.5%
Total	100%

The split of LD1 and LD2 by EPA appears to be arbitrary. Where
specific highway project conditions are known and vary from these
values, the user should substitute the more accurate values for each
of the percentages so long as they total to 100 percent.

The user can also consult FHWA Technical Advisory T 5040.1 titled,
"Vehicle Types for Environment Design Methodologies," dated April 3,
1978, which provides data on vehicle mixes that occur on Interstate,
primary, and secondary highways during various times of the day.

TRAVEL WEIGHTING

The travel weighting factor for LDV's, LDT's, and heavy duty trucks is calculated automatically by the MOBILE 1 computer program. This is accomplished by taking into account the national averages for the fractions of vehicles registered by age (spanning 20 years) and the annual mileage accumulation rate.

Recommendations

It is recommended that the national values provided by EPA be used unless local registration data for automobiles and trucks or travel data shows significant departures from the national averages.

ALTITUDE CORRECTION

The motor vehicle emission factors have been provided by EPA for low- and high-altitude areas. The low- and high-altitude values represent vehicles tested at certification sites situated at 500-foot and 5,200 foot altitudes respectively. In the mobile source emission factor document dated March 1978, EPA stipulates the use of the high-altitude emission factors for areas situated greater than 4,000 feet in altitude. Low-altitude values should be used elsewhere.

Recommendations

For highway project analyses, it is recommended that the average project elevation be used to determine whether the high- or low-altitude emission factors are applicable. The use of interpolation between high and low-altitude is not recommended since this would involve computing two sets of emission factors and then manually interpolating values for a specific project. Reliable test data is currently lacking for vehicle emissions at altitudes other than 500 feet and 5,500 feet. For projects whose average elevation is greater than 4,000 feet, the high-altitude emission factors should be used.

LDV AIR-CONDITIONING (A/C) CORRECTION

Carbon Monoxide (CO)

Worst-case microscale CO analysis for highway projects are performed for the so-called CO season which normally occurs during the colder months of the year. Vehicle air-conditioners are either not used or usage is minimal during these months in most parts of the country.

Recommendations

For this reason and because of the lack of a means for estimating the fraction of vehicles that may have air-conditioners in operation, this correction factor need not be applied in highway project CO analyses.

HC and NOx

The calculation of the total tonnage of HC and NOx associated with various highway alternatives may be necessary for major highway projects located in some areas. These analyses are related to the ozone problem which is associated with the summer months when vehicle air-conditioners are in use. Because the analysis of alternatives within highway corridors is a relative rather than an absolute comparison of HC and NOx emissions, the A/C correction factor has no important significance. The same A/C correction factor would be applied to all alternatives under consideration. In addition, estimates of the fraction of vehicles operating air-conditioners in a specific area are uncertain.

Recommendation

Accordingly, it is recommended that the A/C correction factor not be employed for highway projects analyses.

TRAILER TOWING CORRECTION

The FTP emission factor represents a vehicle not towing a trailer. In order to account for increased emissions resulting from trailer towing, a correction factor was developed for a discrete weight of 1,000 pounds additional weight.

Recommendation

Because the numbers of LDV's towing trailers is relatively insignificant in most localities, and due to the lack of reliable forecast data regarding the fraction of vehicles towing trailer, this correction factor need not be applied in highway-project analyses.

LDV LOADING CORRECTION

The mobile source emission factor methodology provides for a correction to be applied to account for higher than average vehicle loading due to passengers and luggage. An average vehicle load of 300 pounds (driver, fuel, and other liquids) is assumed in the FTP emission factors. The load-correction factor increases vehicle pollutant emissions based on an additional 500 pounds of weight (800 pounds total).

Recommendation

Because reliable data that is necessary to apply this factor is normally unavailable for specific highway projects, it is recommended that the FTP emission factor be used without correction for additional loading.

HUMIDITY CORRECTION FOR OXIDES OF NITROGEN (NOx)

Because this correction factor is impractical to apply, and due to the fact that highway project corridor NOx analyses involve relative rather than absolute comparisons of emissions, this correction factor should be ignored.

TRUCK CHARACTERISTIC CORRECTION

The basic heavy-duty emission factors for trucks (HDG and HDD) are based on the assumptions that all trucks are half loaded. A correction factor has been developed by EPA which allows adjustment of emissions for empty trucks or fully loaded trucks. This correction factor requires data on in-use vehicle weights and engine cylinder displacements.

Recommendation

Because this type of data is not available and the basic assumption of the emission factor representing a half-loaded truck appears reasonable, this correction need not be applied in highway-project analyses.

INSPECTION/MAINTENANCE (I/M) CREDITS

In performing highway air quality impact analyses, credits may be taken for emission reductions achievable through I/M of LDV's, motorcycles, and LDT's. The amount of credit reduction is dependent upon a number of factors among which are the stringency of the emission standards, frequency of inspection, types of vehicles included, the length of time the program is in operation, the model-year vehicles included, and whether or not there is a mechanic's training program.

On May 2, 1977[3], EPA proposed regulations called Appendix N which dealt with I/M programs. The final promulgation of Appendix N has not yet been made. The EPA's MOBILE 1 computer program which calculates the latest mobile source emission factors[4] has an option which permits the calculation of I/M credits in accordance with values anticipated in the final Appendix N regulations. A User's Guide for MOBILE 1 which will be distributed soon by EPA will contain specific instructions on the appropriate input needed to exercise the I/M credit portion of the computer program. The computer program actually outputs emission factors which include I/M credits.

---

[3]Federal Register, Vol, 42, No. 84, May 2, 1977.

[4]Mobile Source Emission Factors, Final Document, U.S. EPA, March 1978.

Recommendations

Users who will be analyzing highway projects located in nonattainment areas, where an I/M program is currently being implemented or where an I/M program will be proposed for inclusion in a SIP, may take appropriate credit reductions. Because HC and NOx analyses involve comparative rather than absolute values, I/M credit reductions are not really meaningful.

It is recommended that the transportation agency consult with the State or local air quality agency regarding the type of I/M program that is or will likely be implemented so that the appropriate credit reduction can be calculated using the MOBILE 1 computer program.

Where I/M credit reductions are taken in highway-project analyses, documentation should be provided on the parameters that were used as a basis for the credit reduction. It is advisable to use the nonadjusted emission factors for the CO. line-source impact analysis, and then to apply percent credit reductions to the final concentrations of CO resulting from I/M. This will require the calculation of the the non-I/M and the I/M emission factors for a given project analysis. However, it will only be necessary to perform a complete non-I/M line-source analyses since the I/M concentrations can be expressed as a certain percent reduction from the non-I/M concentrations.

APPENDIX 6B: OFF-HIGHWAY MOBILE SOURCES*

Aircarft	Solid particulates[a]		Sulfur oxides[d]		Carbon monoxide[e]		Hydrocarbons[e]		Nitrogen oxides[d] (NO$_x$ as NO$_2$)	
	lb	kg	lb	kg	lb	kg	lb	kg	lb	kg
Jumbo jet	1.30	0.59	1.82	0.83	46.8	21.2	12.2	5.5	31.4	14.2
Long range jet	1.21	0.55	1.56	0.71	47.4	21.5	41.2	18.7	7.9	3.6
Medium range jet	0.41	0.19	1.01	0.46	17.0	7.71	4.9	2.2	10.2	4.6
Air carrier turboprop	1.1	0.49	0.40	0.18	6.6	3.0	2.9	1.3	2.5	1.1
Business jet	0.11	0.05	0.37	0.17	15.8	7.17	3.6	1.6	1.6	0.73
General aviation turboprop	0.20	0.09	0.18	0.08	3.1	1.4	1.1	0.5	1.2	0.54
General aviation piston	0.02	0.01	0.014	0.006	12.2	5.5	0.40	0.18	0.047	0.021
Piston transport	0.56	0.25	0.28	0.13	304.0	138.0	40.7	18.5	0.40	0.18
Helicopter	0.25	0.11	0.18	0.08	5.7	2.6	0.52	0.24	0.57	0.26
Military transport	1.1	0.49	0.41	0.19	5.7	2.6	2.7	1.2	2.2	1.0
Military jet	0.31	0.14	0.76	0.35	15.1	6.85	9.93	4.5	3.29	1.49
Military piston[f]	0.28	0.13	0.14	0.04	152.0	69.0	20.4	9.3	0.20	0.09

Emission Factors per Aircraft Landing-Takeoff Cycle
(lb/engine and kg/engine)
Emission Factor Rating: B

Engine and mode	Fuel rate		Carbon monoxide		Hydrocarbons		Nitrogen oxides (NO$_x$ as NO$_2$)		Solid particulates	
	lb/hr	kg/hr	lb/hr	kg/hr	lb/hr	kg/hr	lb/hr	kg/hr	lb/hr	kg/hr
Pratt & Whitney JT-9D (Jumbo jet)										
Taxi-idle	1,738	788	102.0	46.3	27.3	12.4	6.06	2.75	2.2	1.0
Takeoff	17,052	7,735	8.29	3.76	2.95	1.34	720.0	327.0	3.75	1.7
Climbout	14,317	6,494	11.7	5.31	2.65	1.20	459.0	208.0	4.0	1.8
Approach	5,204	2,361	32.6	14.8	3.00	1.36	54.1	24.5	2.3	1.0
General Electric CF6 (Jumbo jet)										
Taxi-idle	1,030	467	51.7	23.5	15.4	7.0	3.6	1.63	0.04	0.02
Takeoff	13,449	6,100	6.7	3.04	1.3	0.59	540.0	245.0	0.54	0.24
Climbout[b]	11,400	5,171	6.6	2.99	1.3	0.59	333.0	151.0	0.54	0.24
Approach	6,204	2,814	18.6	8.44	1.9	0.86	173.0	78.5	0.44	0.20
Pratt & Whitney JT-3D (Long range jet)										
Taxi-idle	872	396	109.0	49.4	98.6	44.7	1.43	0.649	0.45	0.20
Takeoff	10,835	4,915	12.3	5.60	4.65	2.11	148.0	67.1	8.25	3.7
Climbout	8,956	4,062	15.3	6.94	4.92	2.23	96.2	43.6	8.5	3.9
Approach	4,138	1,877	39.7	18.0	7.84	3.56	21.8	9.89	8.0	3.6
Pratt & Whitney JT-3C (Long range jet)										
Taxi-idle	1,198	543	92.6	42.0	92.2	41.8	2.49	1.13	0.40	0.18
Takeoff	10,183	4,619	9.04	4.10	0.855	0.388	119.0	54.0	6.50	2.9
Climbout	8,509	3,860	16.0	7.26	0.893	0.405	84.7	38.4	6.25	2.8
Approach	4,115	1,867	49.0	22.2	8.26	3.75	23.2	10.5	3.25	1.5
Pratt & Whitney JT-4A (Long range jet)										
Taxi-idle	1,389	630	62.8	28.5	64.8	29.4	2.71	1.23	1.2	0.54
Takeoff	15,511	7,036	18.8	8.53	0.674	0.306	236.0	107.0	21.0	9.5
Climbout	13,066	5,927	18.3	8.30	1.27	0.576	155.0	70.3	20.0	9.1
Approach	5,994	2,719	26.3	11.9	3.83	1.74	35.9	16.3	6.0	2.7

Modal Emission Factors
Emission Factor Rating: B

*From *Compilation of Air Pollutant Emission Factors*, third ed., August 1977, EPA.

Engine and mode	Fuel rate		Carbon monoxide		Hydrocarbons		Nitrogen oxides (NO_x as NO_2)		Solid particulates	
	lb/hr	kg/hr	lb/hr	kg/hr	lb/hr	Kg/hr	lb/hr	kg/hr	lb/hr	kg/hr
General Electric CJ805 (Long range jet)										
Taxi-idle	1,001	454	63.8	28.9	27.3	12.4	1.57	0.712	1.3	0.59
Takeoff	9,960	4,518	29.1	13.2	0.556	0.252	111.0	50.3	15.0	6.8
Climbout	8,290	3,760	28.9	13.1	0.583	0.264	74.0	33.6	15.0	6.8
Approach	3,777	1,713	42.8	19.4	2.43	1.10	17.8	8.07	5.0	2.3
Pratt & Whitney JT-8D[c] (Med. range jet)										
Taxi-idle	959	435	33.4	15.2	6.99	3.71	2.91	1.32	0.36	0.16
Takeoff	8,755	3,971	7.49	3.40	0.778	0.353	198.0	89.8	3.7	1.7
Climbout	7,337	3,328	8.89	4.03	0.921	0.418	131.0	59.4	2.6	1.2
Approach	3,409	1,546	18.2	8.26	1.75	0.794	30.9	14.0	1.5	0.68
Rolls Royce Sprey MK511 (Med. range jet)										
Taxi-idle	662	300	60.2	27.3	66.1	30.0	0.849	0.385	0.17	0.077
Takeoff	7,625	3,459	14.2	6.44	Neg	Neg	153.0	69.4	16.0	7.3
Climbout	6,355	2,883	15.3	6.94	0.242	0.110	115.0	52.2	10.0	4.5
Approach	3,052	1,384	39.1	17.7	4.22	1.91	30.4	13.8	1.5	0.68
Allison T56-A15 (Air carrier turboprop; mil. transport)										
Taxi-idle	493	224	8.74	3.96	7.39	3.35	1.23	0.560	1.6	0.73
Takeoff	2,393	1,085	3.77	1.71	0.440	0.200	27.9	12.7	3.7	1.7
Climbout	2,188	992	3.40	1.54	0.399	0.181	22.2	10.1	3.0	1.4
Approach	1,146	520	3.49	1.58	0.326	0.148	7.32	3.32	3.0	1.4
Allison T56-A7 (Air carrier turboprop; mil. transport)										
Taxi-idle	548	249	15.3	6.94	6.47	2.93	2.16	0.980	1.6	0.73
Takeoff	2,079	943	2.15	0.975	0.430	0.195	22.9	10.4	3.7	1.7
Climbout	1,908	865	3.01	1.37	0.476	0.216	21.2	9.62	3.0	1.4
Approach	1,053	478	3.67	1.66	0.517	0.235	7.78	3.53	3.0	1.4

Modal Emission Factors (cont'd.)
Emission Factor Rating: B

Engine and mode	Fuel rate		Carbon monoxide		Hydrocarbons		Nitrogen oxides (NO$_x$ as NO$_2$)		Solid particulates	
	lb/hr	kg/hr	lb/hr	kg/hr	lb/hr	kg/hr	lb/hr	kg/hr	lb/hr	kg/hr
Airesearch TPE-331[d] (Gen. aviation turboprop)										
Taxi-idle	146	66.2	3.53	1.60	0.879	0.399	0.955	0.433	0.3	0.14
Takeoff	365	166.0	0.393	0.178	0.055	0.025	3.64	1.65	0.8	0.36
Climbout	339	154.0	0.568	0.258	0.053	0.024	3.31	1.50	0.6	0.27
Approach	206	93.4	2.58	1.17	0.240	0.109	1.69	0.767	0.6	0.27
Teledyne/Continental 0-200 (Gen. aviation piston)										
Taxi-idle	7.68	3.48	7.52	3.41	0.214	0.097	0.009	0.004	NA[e]	NA
Takeoff	48.4	22.0	54.6	24.8	0.720	0.327	0.259	0.117	NA	NA
Climbout	48.4	22.0	54.6	24.8	0.720	0.327	0.259	0.117	NA	NA
Approach	21.3	9.66	23.8	10.8	0.380	0.172	0.052	0.024	NA	NA
Lycoming 0-320 (Gen. aviation piston)										
Taxi-idle	13.0	5.90	11.1	5.03	0.355	0.161	0.013	0.006	NA	NA
Takeoff	65.7	29.8	70.9	32.2	1.49	0.676	0.214	0.097	NA	NA
Climbout	63.5	28.8	65.8	29.8	1.31	0.594	0.375	0.170	NA	NA
Approach	23.1	10.5	24.3	11.0	0.496	0.225	0.051	0.023	NA	NA

Modal Emission Factors (cont'd.)
Emission Factor Rating: B

Pollutant	Average emissions[b]	
	lb/10^3 gal	kg/10^3 liter
Particulates[c]	25	3.0
Sulfur oxides[d] (SO$_x$ as SO$_2$)	57	6.8
Carbon monoxide	130	16
Hydrocarbons	94	11
Nitrogen oxides (NO$_x$ as NO$_2$)	370	44
Aldehydes (as HCHO)	5.5	0.66
Organic acids[c]	7	0.84

Average Locomotive Emission Factors Based on Nationwide Statistics

Pollutant	Engine category				
	2-Stroke supercharged switch	4-Stroke switch	2-Stroke supercharged road	2-Stroke turbocharged road	4-Stroke road
Carbon monoxide					
lb/10^3 gal	84	380	66	160	180
kg/10^3 liter	10	46	7.9	19	22
g/hphr	3.9	13	1.8	4.0	4.1
g/metric hphr	3.9	13	1.8	4.0	4.1
Hydrocarbon					
lb/10^3 gal	190	146	148	28	99
kg/10^3 liter	23	17	18	3.4	12
g/hphr	8.9	5.0	4.0	0.70	2.2
g/metric hphr	8.9	5.0	4.0	0.70	2.2
Nitrogen oxides (NO_x as NO_2)					
lb/10^3 gal	250	490	350	330	470
kg/10^3 liter	30	59	42	40	56
g/hphr	11	17	9.4	8.2	10
g/metric hphr	11	17	9.4	8.2	10

Emission Factors by Locomotive Engine Category
Emission Factor Rating: B

APPENDIX 6C: WORKBOOK OF ATMOSPHERIC DISPERSION ESTIMATES, USEPA

PREFACE

This workbook presents some computational techniques currently used by scientists working with atmospheric dispersion problems. Because the basic working equations are general, their application to specific problems usually requires special care and judgment; such considerations are illustrated by 26 example problems. This workbook is intended as an aid to meteorologists and air pollution scientists who are required to estimate atmospheric concentrations of contaminants from various types of sources. It is not intended as a complete do-it-yourself manual for atmospheric dispersion estimates; all of the numerous complications that arise in making best estimates of dispersion cannot be so easily resolved. Awareness of the possible complexities can enable the user to appreciate the validity of his "first approximations" and to realize when the services of a professional air pollution meteorologist are required.

Chapter 1 — INTRODUCTION

During recent years methods of estimating atmospheric dispersion have undergone considerable revision, primarily due to results of experimental measurements. In most dispersion problems the relevant atmospheric layer is that nearest the ground, varying in thickness from several hundred to a few thousand meters. Variations in both thermal and mechanical turbulence and in wind velocity are greatest in the layer in contact with the surface. Turbulence induced by buoyancy forces in the atmosphere is closely related to the vertical temperature structure. When temperature decreases with height at a rate higher than 5.4°F per 1000 ft (1°C per 100 meters), the atmosphere is in unstable equilibrium and vertical motions are enhanced. When temperature decreases at a lower rate or increases with height (inversion), vertical motions are damped or reduced. Examples of typical variations in temperature and wind speed with height for daytime and nighttime conditions are illustrated in Figure 1-1.

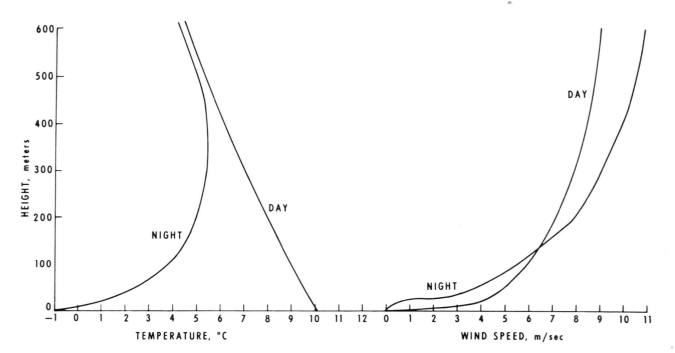

Figure 1-1. Examples of variation of temperature and wind speed with height (after Smith, 1963).

The transfer of momentum upward or downward in the atmosphere is also related to stability; when the atmosphere is unstable, usually in the daytime, upward motions transfer the momentum "deficiency" due to eddy friction losses near the earth's surface through a relatively deep layer, causing the wind speed to increase more slowly with height than at night (except in the lowest few meters). In addition to thermal turbulence, roughness elements on the ground engender mechanical turbulence, which affects both the dispersion of material in the atmosphere and the wind profile (variation of wind with height). Examples of these effects on the resulting wind profile are shown in Figure 1-2.

As wind speed increases, the effluent from a continuous source is introduced into a greater volume of air per unit time interval. In addition to this dilution by wind speed, the spreading of the material (normal to the mean direction of transport) by turbulence is a major factor in the dispersion process.

The procedures presented here to estimate atmospheric dispersion are applicable when mean wind speed and direction can be determined, but measurements of turbulence, such as the standard deviation of wind direction fluctuations, are not available. If such measurements are at hand, techniques such as those outlined by Pasquill (1961) are likely to give more accurate results. The diffusion parameters presented here are most applicable to ground-level or low-level releases (from the surface to about 20 meters), although they are commonly applied at higher elevations without full experimental validation. It is assumed that stability is the same throughout the diffusing layer, and no turbulent transfer occurs *through* layers of dissimilar stability characteristics. Because mean values for wind directions and speeds are required, neither the variation of wind speed nor the variation of wind direction with height in the mixing layer are taken into account. This usually is not a problem in neutral or unstable (e.g., daytime) situations, but can cause over-estimations of downwind concentrations in stable conditions.

REFERENCES

Davenport, A. G., 1963: The relationship of wind structure to wind loading. Presented at Int. Conf. on The Wind Effects on Buildings and Structures, 26-28 June 63, Natl. Physical Laboratory, Teddington, Middlesex, Eng.

Pasquill, F., 1961: The estimation of the dispersion of wind borne material. Meteorol. Mag. *90*, 1063, 33-49.

Smith, M. E., 1963: The use and misuse of the atmosphere, 15 pp., Brookhaven Lecture Series, No. 24, 13 Feb 63, BNL 784 (T-298) Brookhaven National Laboratory.

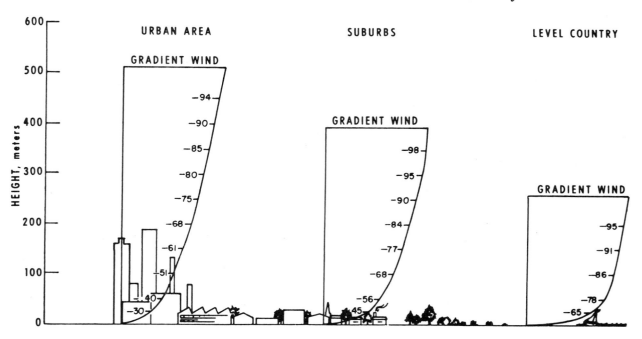

Figure 1-2.   Examples of variation of wind with height over different size roughness elements (figures are percentages of gradient wind); (from Davenport, 1963).

Chapter 2 — BACKGROUND

For a number of years estimates of concentrations were calculated either from the equations of Sutton (1932) with the atmospheric dispersion parameters C_y, C_z, and n, or from the equations of Bosanquet (1936) with the dispersion parameters p and q.

Hay and Pasquill (1957) have presented experimental evidence that the vertical distribution of spreading particles from an elevated point is related to the standard deviation of the wind elevation angle, σ_E, at the point of release. Cramer (1957) derived a diffusion equation incorporating standard deviations of Gaussian distributions: σ_y for the distribution of material in the plume across wind in the horizontal, and σ_z for the vertical distribution of material in the plume. (See Appendix 2 for properties of Gaussian distributions.) These statistics were related to the standard deviations of azimuth angle, σ_A, and elevation angle, σ_E, calculated from wind measurements made with a bi-directional wind vane (bivane). Values for diffusion parameters based on field diffusion tests were suggested by Cramer, et al. (1958) (and also in Cramer 1959a and 1959b). Hay and Pasquill (1959) also presented a method for deriving the spread of pollutants from records of wind fluctuation. Pasquill (1961) has further proposed a method for estimating diffusion when such detailed wind data are not available. This method expresses the height and angular spread of a diffusing plume in terms of more commonly observed weather parameters. Suggested curves of height and angular spread as a function of distance downwind were given for several "stability" classes. Gifford (1961) converted Pasquill's values of angular spread and height into standard deviations of plume concentration distribution, σ_y and σ_z. Pasquill's method, with Gifford's conversion incorporated, is used in this workbook (see Chapter 3) for diffusion estimates.

Advantages of this system are that (1) only two dispersion parameters are required and (2) results of most diffusion experiments are now being reported in terms of the standard deviations of plume spread. More field dispersion experiments are being conducted and will be conducted under conditions of varying surface roughness and atmospheric stability. If the dispersion parameters from a specific experiment are considered to be more representative than those suggested in this workbook, the parameter values can be used with the equations given here.

REFERENCES

Bosanquet, C. H., and J. L. Pearson, 1936: The spread of smoke and gases from chimneys. Trans. Faraday Soc., 32, 1249-1263.

Cramer, H. E., 1957: A practical method for estimating the dispersion of atmospheric contaminants. Proc. 1st Natl. Conf. on Appl. Meteorol. Amer. Meterol. Soc.

Cramer, H. E., F. A. Record, and H. C. Vaughan, 1958: The study of the diffusion of gases or aerosols in the lower atmosphere. Final Report Contract AF 19(604)-1058 Mass. Inst. of Tech., Dept. of Meteorol.

Cramer, H. E., 1959a: A brief survey of the meteorological aspects of atmospheric pollution. Bull. Amer. Meteorol. Soc., 40, 4, 165-171.

Cramer, H. E., 1959b: Engineering estimates of atmospheric dispersal capacity. Amer. Ind. Hyg. Assoc. J., 20, 3, 183-189.

Gifford, F. A., 1961: Uses of routine meteorological observations for estimating atmospheric dispersion. Nuclear Safety, 2, 4, 47-51.

Hay, J. S., and F. Pasquill, 1957: Diffusion from a fixed source at a height of a few hundred feet in the atmosphere. J. Fluid Mech., 2, 299-310.

Hay, J. S., and F. Pasquill, 1959: Diffusion from a continuous source in relation to the spectrum and scale of turbulence. pp 345-365 in Atmospheric Diffusion and Air Pollution, edited by F. N. Frenkiel and P. A. Sheppard, Advances in Geophysics, 6, New York, Academic Press, 471 pp.

Pasquill, F., 1961: The estimation of the dispersion of windborne material. Meteorol. Mag., 90, 1063, 33-49.

Sutton, O. G., 1932: A theory of eddy diffusion in the atmosphere. Proc. Roy. Soc., A, 135, 143-165.

Chapter 3 — ESTIMATES OF ATMOSPHERIC DISPERSION

This chapter outlines the basic procedures to be used in making dispersion estimates as suggested by Pasquill (1961) and modified by Gifford (1961).

COORDINATE SYSTEM

In the system considered here the origin is at ground level at or beneath the point of emission, with the x-axis extending horizontally in the direction of the mean wind. The y-axis is in the horizontal plane perpendicular to the x-axis, and the z-axis extends vertically. The plume travels along or parallel to the x-axis. Figure 3-1 illustrates the coordinate system.

DIFFUSION EQUATIONS

The concentration, χ, of gas or aerosols (particles less than about 20 microns diameter) at x,y,z from a continuous source with an effective emission height, H, is given by equation 3.1. The notation used to depict this concentration is χ (x,y,z;H). H is the height of the plume centerline when it becomes essentially level, and is the sum of the physical stack height, h, and the plume rise, ΔH. The following assumptions are made: the plume spread has a Gaussian distribution (see Appendix 2) in both the horizontal and vertical planes, with standard deviations of plume concentration distribution in the horizontal and vertical of σ_y and σ_z, respectively; the mean wind speed affecting the plume is u; the uniform emission rate of pollutants is Q; and total reflection of the plume takes place at the earth's surface, i.e., there is no deposition or reaction at the surface (see problem 9).

$$\chi \,(x,y,z;H) \quad \frac{Q}{2\pi \, \sigma_y \, \sigma_z \, u} \, \exp^* \left[-\frac{1}{2} \left(\frac{y}{\sigma_y} \right)^2 \right]$$
$$\left\{ \exp \left[-\frac{1}{2} \left(\frac{z\text{-}H}{\sigma_z} \right)^2 \right] + \exp \left[-\frac{1}{2} \left(\frac{z+H}{\sigma_z} \right)^2 \right] \right\} \tag{3.1}$$

*Note: exp —a/b $= e^{-a/b}$ where e is the base of natural logarithms and is approximately equal to 2.7183.

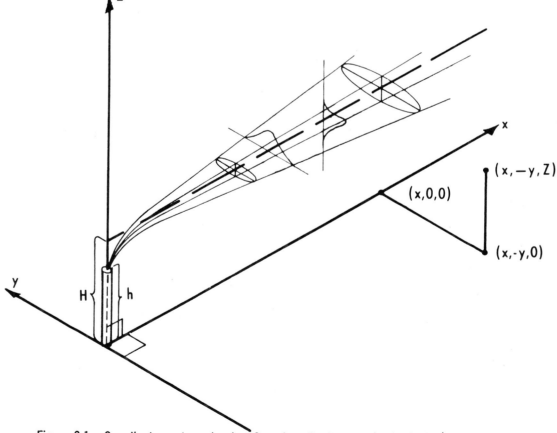

Figure 3-1. Coordinate system showing Gaussian distributions in the horizontal and vertical.

Any consistent set of units may be used. The most common is:

χ (g m^{-3}) or, for radioactivity (curies m^{-3})

Q (g sec^{-1}) or (curies sec^{-1})

u (m sec^{-1})

σ_y, σ_z, H,x,y, and z (m)

This equation is the same as equation (8.35) p. 293 of Sutton (1953) when σ's are substituted for Sutton's parameters through equations like (8.27) p. 286. For evaluations of the exponentials found in Eq. (3.1) and those that follow, see Appendix 3. χ is a mean over the same time interval as the time interval for which the σ's and u are representative. The values of both σ_y and σ_z are evaluated in terms of the downwind distance, x.

Eq. (3.1) is valid where diffusion in the direction of the plume travel can be neglected, that is, no diffusion in the x direction.

This may be assumed if the release is continuous or if the duration of release is equal to or greater than the travel time (x/u) from the source to the location of interest.

For concentrations calculated at ground level, i.e., z = 0, (see problem 3) the equation simplifies to:

$$\chi (x,y,0;H) = \frac{Q}{\pi \, \sigma_y \, \sigma_z \, u} \exp \left[-\frac{1}{2} \left(\frac{y}{\sigma_y} \right)^2 \right]$$
$$\exp \left[-\frac{1}{2} \left(\frac{H}{\sigma_z} \right)^2 \right] \tag{3.2}$$

Where the concentration is to be calculated along the centerline of the plume (y = 0), (see problem 2) further simplification results:

$$\chi (x,0,0;H) = \frac{Q}{\pi \, \sigma_y \, \sigma_z \, u} \exp \left[-\frac{1}{2} \left(\frac{H}{\sigma_z} \right)^2 \right] \tag{3.3}$$

For a ground-level source with no effective plume rise (H = 0), (see problem 1):

$$\chi (x,0,0;0) = \frac{Q}{\pi \, \sigma_y \, \sigma_z \, u} \tag{3.4}$$

EFFECTS OF STABILITY

The values of σ_y and σ_z vary with the turbulent structure of the atmosphere, height above the surface, surface roughness, sampling time over which the concentration is to be estimated, wind speed, and distance from the source. For the parameter values given here, the sampling time is assumed to be about 10 minutes, the height to be the lowest several hundred meters of the atmosphere, and the surface to be relatively open country. The turbulent structure of the atmosphere and wind speed are considered in the stability classes pre-

sented, and the effect of distance from the source is considered in the graphs determining the parameter values. Values for σ_y and σ_z are estimated from the stability of the atmosphere, which is in turn estimated from the wind speed at a height of about 10 meters and, during the day, the incoming solar radiation or, during the night, the cloud cover (Pasquill, 1961). Stability categories (in six classes) are given in Table 3-1. Class A is the most unstable, class F the most stable class considered here. Night refers to the period from 1 hour before sunset to 1 hour after sunrise. Note that the neutral class, D, can be assumed for overcast conditions during day or night, regardless of wind speed.

Table 3-1   KEY TO STABILITY CATEGORIES

Surface Wind Speed (at 10 m), m sec^{-1}	Day			Night	
	Incoming Solar Radiation			Thinly Overcast or ≥4/8 Low Cloud	≤3/8 Cloud
	Strong	Moderate	Slight		
< 2	A	A-B	B		
2-3	A-B	B	C	E	F
3-5	B	B-C	C	D	E
5-6	C	C-D	D	D	D
> 6	C	D	D	D	D

The neutral class, D, should be assumed for overcast conditions during day or night.

"Strong" incoming solar radiation corresponds to a solar altitude greater than 60° with clear skies; "slight" insolation corresponds to a solar altitude from 15° to 35° with clear skies. Table 170, Solar Altitude and Azimuth, in the Smithsonian Meteorological Tables (List, 1951) can be used in determining the solar altitude. Cloudiness will decrease incoming solar radiation and should be considered along with solar altitude in determining solar radiation. Incoming radiation that would be strong with clear skies can be expected to be reduced to moderate with broken (5/8 to 7/8 cloud cover) middle clouds and to slight with broken low clouds. An objective system of classifying stability from hourly meteorological observations based on the above method has been suggested (Turner, 1961).

These methods will give representative indications of stability over open country or rural areas, but are less reliable for urban areas. This difference is due primarily to the influence of the city's larger surface roughness and heat island effects upon the stability regime over urban areas. The greatest difference occurs on calm clear nights; on such nights conditions over rural areas are very stable, but over urban areas they are slightly unstable or near neutral to a height several times the average building height, with a stable layer above (Duckworth and Sandberg, 1954; DeMarrais, 1961).

Some preliminary results of a dispersion experiment in St. Louis (Pooler, 1965) showed that the dispersion over the city during the daytime behaved somewhat like types B and C; for one night experiment σ_y varied with distance between types D and E.

ESTIMATION OF VERTICAL AND HORIZONTAL DISPERSION

Having determined the stability class from Table 3-1, one can evaluate the estimates of σ_y and σ_z as a function of downwind distance from the source, x, using Figures 3-2 and 3-3. These values of σ_y and σ_z are representative for a sampling time of about 10 minutes. For estimation of concentrations for longer time periods see Chapter 5. Figures 3-2 and 3-3 apply strictly only to open level country and probably underestimate the plume dispersion potential from low-level sources in built-up areas. Although the vertical spread may be less than the values for class F with very light winds on a clear night, quantitative estimates of concentrations are nearly impossible for this condition. With very light winds on a clear night for ground-level sources free of topographic influences, frequent shifts in wind direction usually occur which serve to spread the plume horizontally. For elevated sources under these extremely stable situations, significant concentrations usually do not reach ground level until the stability changes.

A stable layer existing above an unstable layer will have the effect of restricting the vertical diffusion. The dispersion computation can be modified for this situation by considering the height of the base of the stable layer, L. At a height 2.15 σ_z above the plume centerline the concentration is one-tenth the plume centerline concentration at the same distance. When one-tenth the plume centerline concentration extends to the stable layer, at height L, it is reasonable to assume that the distribution starts being affected by the "lid." The following method is suggested to take care of this situation. Allow σ_z to increase with distance to a value of L/2.15 or 0.47 L. At this distance x_L, the plume is assumed to have a Gaussian distribution in the vertical. Assume that by the time the plume travels twice this far, 2 x_L, the plume has become uniformly distributed between the earth's surface and the height L, i.e., concentration does not vary with height (see Figure 3-4). For the distances greater than 2 x_L, the concentration for any height between the ground and L can be calculated from:

$$\chi \text{ (x,y,z;H)} = \frac{Q}{\sqrt{2\pi}\,\sigma_y\,L\,u}\,\exp\left[-\frac{1}{2}\left(\frac{y}{\sigma_y}\right)^2\right]$$

(3.5)

for any z from 0 to L
for x >2 x_L; x_L is where σ_z = 0.47 L

(see problem 6). Note that Eq. (3.5) assumes normal or Gaussian distribution of the plume *only* in the horizontal plane. The same result can be obtained from the following equation where σ_{zL} is an effective dispersion parameter because $\sqrt{2\pi}$ L = 2.5066 L and 0.8 πL = 2.51 L.

$$\chi \text{ (x,y,z;H)} = \frac{Q}{\pi\,\sigma_y\,\sigma_{zL}\,u}\left[\exp-\frac{1}{2}\left(\frac{y}{\sigma_y}\right)^2\right]$$

(3.6)

for any z from 0 to L
for x $>2_{xL}$; x_L is where σ_z = 0.47 L
The value of σ_{zL} = 0.8 L

EVALUATION OF WIND SPEED

For the wind speed, u, a mean through the vertical extent of the plume should be used. This would be from the height H — 2 σ_z through H + 2 σ_z. Of course, if 2 σ_z is greater than H then the wind can be averaged from the ground to H + 2 σ_z. However, the "surface wind" value may be all that is available. The surface wind is most applicable to surface or low-level emissions, especially under stable conditions.

PLOTS OF CONCENTRATIONS AGAINST DISTANCE

To gain maximum insight into a diffusion problem it is often desirable to plot centerline concentrations against distance downwind. A convenient procedure is to determine the ground-level centerline concentrations for a number of downwind distances and plot these values on log-log graph paper. By connecting the points, one may estimate concentrations for intermediate downwind distances (see problem 6).

ACCURACY OF ESTIMATES

Because of a multitude of scientific and technical limitations the diffusion computation method presented in this manual may provide *best estimates* but not infallible predictions. In the unstable and stable cases, severalfold errors in estimate of σ_z can occur for the longer travel distances. In some cases the σ_z may be expected to be correct within a factor of 2, however. These are: (1) all stabilities for distance of travel out to a few hundred meters; (2) neutral to moderately unstable conditions for distances out to a few kilometers; and (3) unstable conditions in the lower 1000 meters of the atmosphere with a marked inversion above for distances out to 10 km or more. Uncertainties in the estimates of σ_y are in general less than those of σ_z. The ground-level centerline concentrations for these

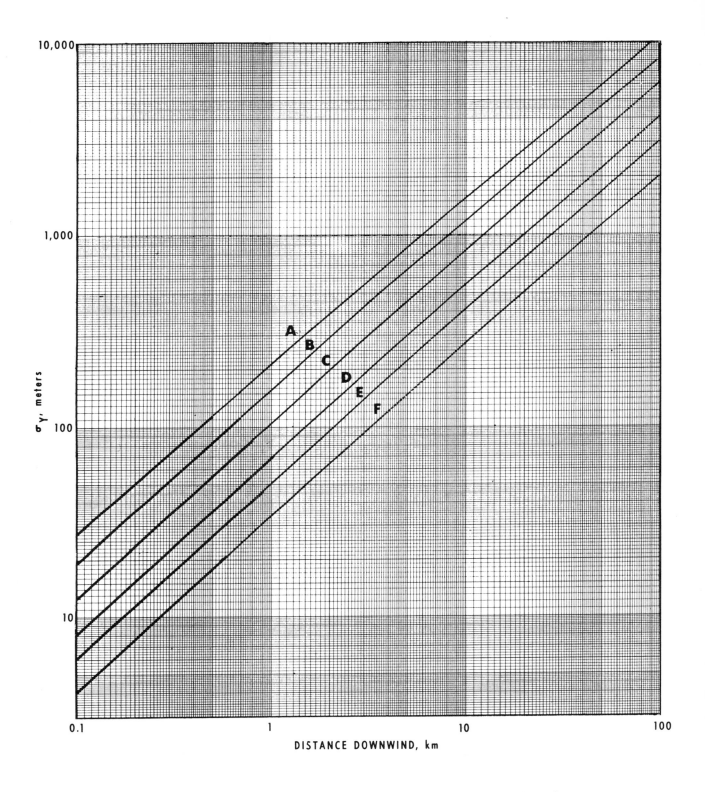

Figure 3-2. Horizontal dispersion coefficient as a function of downwind distance from the source.

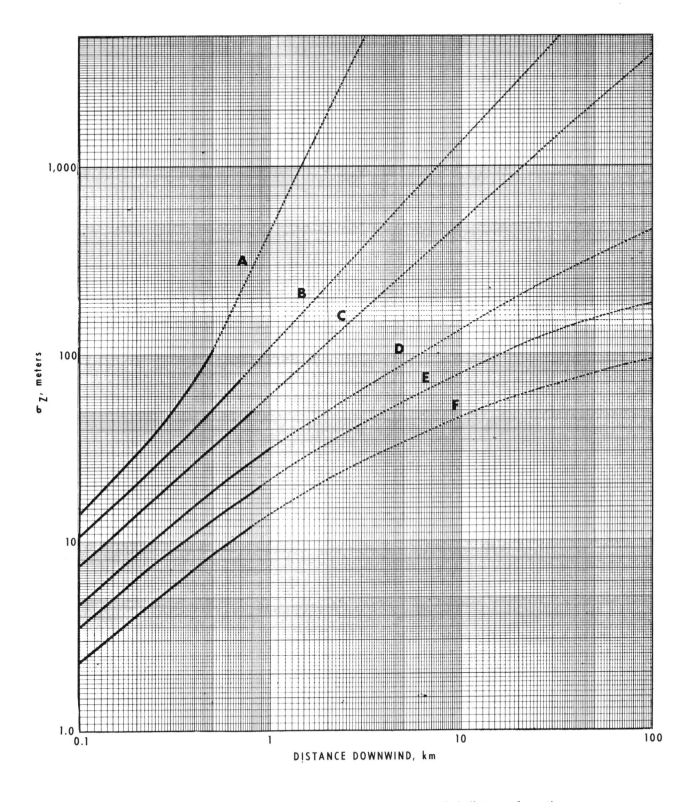

Figure 3-3. Vertical dispersion coefficient as a function of downwind distance from the source.

281

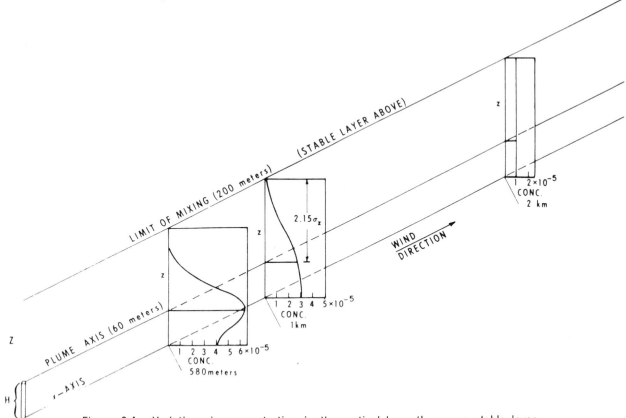

Figure 3-4.   Variations in concentration in the vertical beneath a more stable layer.

three cases (where σ_z can be expected to be within a factor of 2) should be correct within a factor of 3, including errors in σ_y and u. The relative confidence in the σ's (in decreasing order) is indicated by the heavy lines and dashed lines in Figures 3-2 and 3-3.

Estimates of H, the effective height of the plume, may be in error because of uncertainties in the estimation of ΔH, the plume rise. Also, for problems that require estimates of concentration at a specific point, the difficulty of determining the mean wind over a given time interval and consequently the location of the x-axis can cause considerable uncertainty.

GRAPHS FOR ESTIMATES OF DIFFUSION

To avoid repetitious computations, Figure 3-5 (A through F) gives relative ground-level concentrations times wind speed (χ u/Q) against downwind distances for various effective heights of emission and limits to the vertical mixing for each stability class (1 figure for each stability). Computations were made from Eq. (3.3), (3.4), and (3.5). Estimates of actual concentrations may be determined by multiplying ordinate values by Q/u.

PLOTTING GROUND-LEVEL CONCENTRATION ISOPLETHS

Often one wishes to determine the locations where concentrations equal or exceed a given magnitude. First, the axial position of the plume must be determined by the mean wind direction. For plotting isopleths of ground-level concentrations, the relationship between ground-level centerline concentrations and ground-level off-axis concentrations can be used:

$$\frac{\chi\,(x,y,0;H)}{\chi\,(x,0,0;H)} = \exp\left[-\frac{1}{2}\left(\frac{y}{\sigma_y}\right)^2\right] \quad (3.7)$$

The y coordinate of a particular isopleth from the x-axis can be determined at each downwind distance, x. Suppose that one wishes to know the off-axis distance to the 10^{-3} g m^{-3} isopleth at an x of 600 m, under stability type B, where the ground-level centerline concentration at this distance is 2.9×10^{-3} g m^{-3}.

$$\exp\left[-\frac{1}{2}\left(\frac{y}{\sigma_y}\right)^2\right] = \frac{\chi\,(x,y,0;H)}{\chi\,(x,0,0;H)} =$$

$$\frac{10^{-3}}{2.9 \times 10^{-3}} = 0.345$$

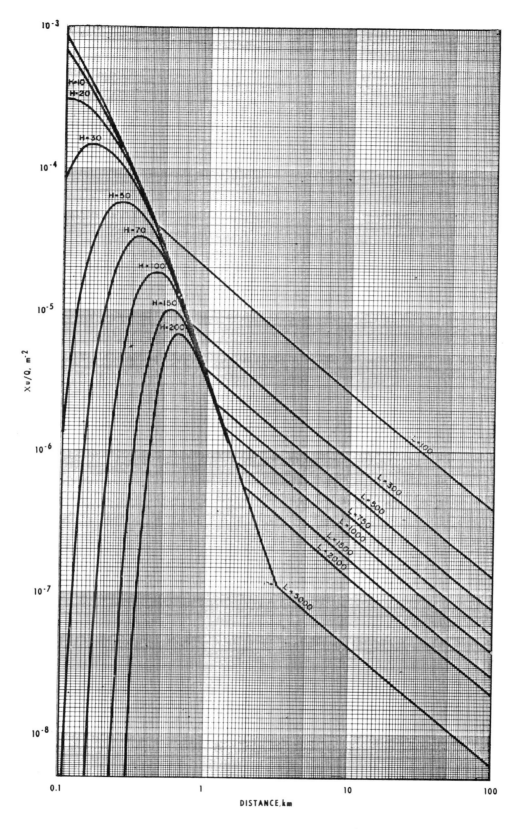

Figure 3-5A. χu/Q with distance for various heights of emission (H) and limits to vertical dispersion (L), A stability

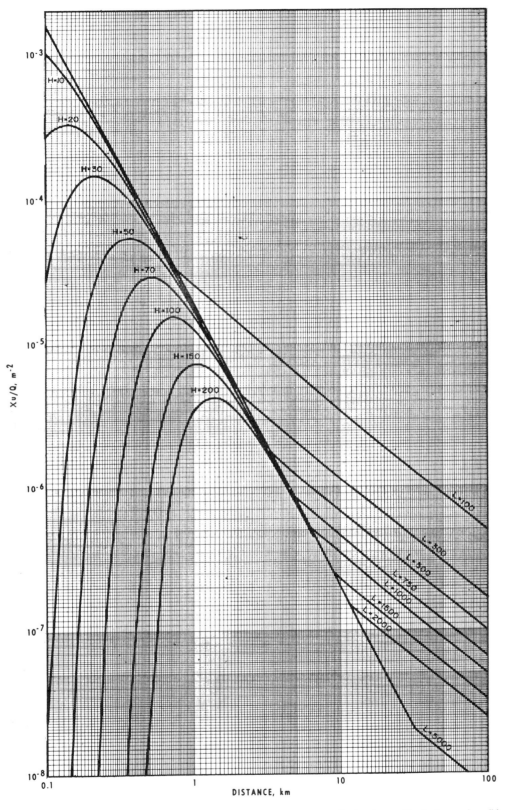

Figure 3-5B. $\chi u/Q$ with distance for various heights of emission (H) and limits to vertical dispersion (L), B stability.

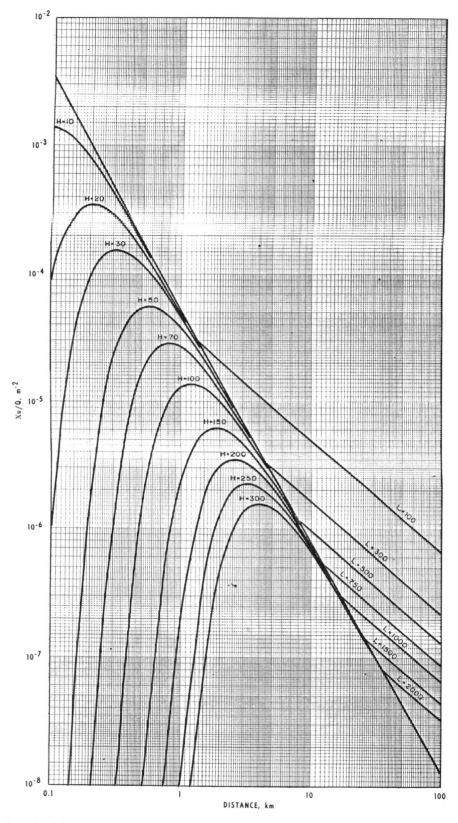

Figure 3-5C. χu/Q with distance for various heights of emission (H) and limits to vertical dispersion (L), C stability.

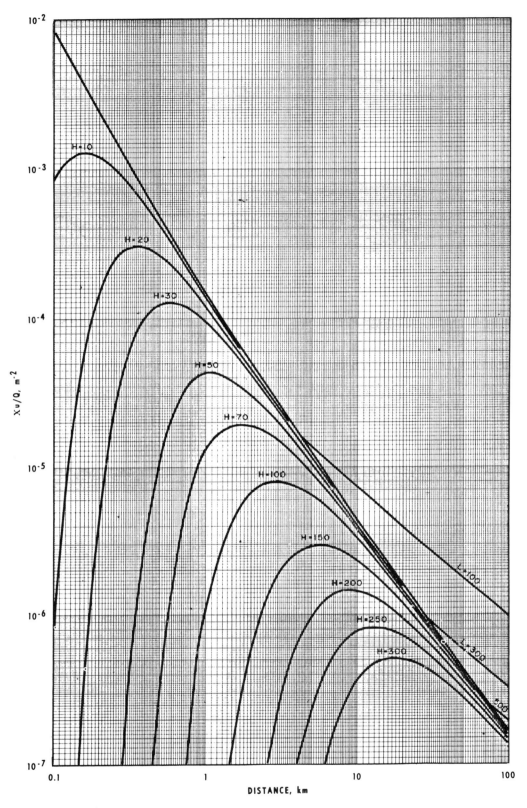

Figure 3-5D. $\chi u/Q$ with distance for various heights of emission (H) and limits to vertical dispersion (L), D stability.

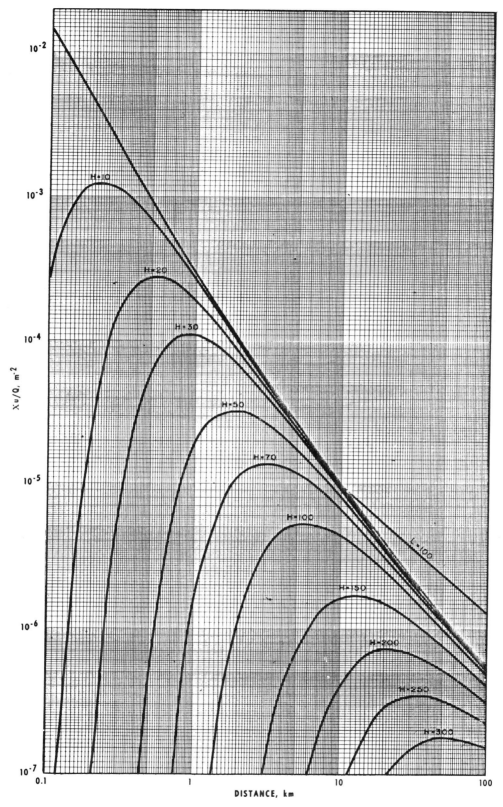

Figure 3-5E. xu/Q with distance for various heights of emission (H) and limits to vertical dispersion (L), E stability.

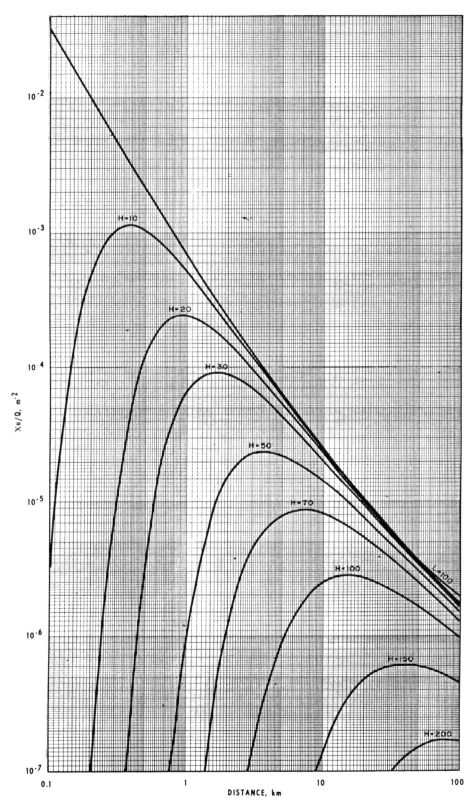

Figure 3-5F. χu/Q with distance for various heights of emission (H) and limits to vertical dispersion (L), F stability.

288

From Table A-1 (Appendix 3) when exp

$$\left[-\frac{1}{2}\left(\frac{y}{\sigma_y}\right)^2 \right] = 0.345, \; y/\sigma_y = 1.46$$

From Figure 3-2, for stability B and x = 600 m, σ_y = 92. Therefore y = (1.46) (92) = 134 meters. This is the distance of the 10^{-3} isopleth from the x-axis at a downwind distance of 600 meters.

This can also be determined from:

$$y = \left\{ 2 \ln^* \left[\frac{\chi(x,0,0;H)}{\chi(x,y,0;H)} \right] \right\}^{1/2} \sigma_y \tag{3.8}$$

The position corresponding to the downwind distance and off-axis distance can then be plotted. After a number of points have been plotted, the concentration isopleth may be drawn (see problems 8 and 26). Figures 3-6 and 3-7 give ground-level isopleths of $\chi u/Q$ for various stabilities for sources at H = 0 and H = 100 meters. For example, to locate the 10^{-3} g m^{-3} isopleth resulting from a ground-level source of 20 g sec^{-1} under B stability conditions with wind speed 2 m sec^{-1}, one must first determine the corresponding value of $\chi u/Q$ since this is the quantity graphed in Figure 3-6. $\chi u/Q$ = 10^{-3} x 2/20 = 10^{-4}. Therefore the $\chi u/Q$ isopleth in Figure 3-6B having a value of 10^{-4} m^{-2} corresponds to a χ isopleth with a value of 10^{-3} g m^{-3}.

AREAS WITHIN ISOPLETHS

Figure 3-8 gives areas within isopleths of ground-level concentration in terms of $\chi u/Q$ for a ground-level source for various stability categories (Gifford, 1962; Hilsmeier and Gifford, 1962). For the example just given, the area of the 10^{-3} g m^{-3} isopleth (10^{-4} m^{-2} $\chi u/Q$ isopleth) is about 5 x 10^4 meter^2.

CALCULATION OF MAXIMUM GROUND-LEVEL CONCENTRATIONS

Figure 3-9 gives the distance to the point of maximum concentration, x_{max}, and the relative maximum concentration, $\chi u/Q_{max}$, as a function of effective height of emission and stability class (Martin, 1965). This figure was prepared from graphs of concentration versus distance, as in Figure 3-5. The maximum concentration can be determined by finding $\chi u/Q$ as a function of effective emission height and stability and multiplying by Q/u. In using Figure 3-9, the user must keep in mind that the dispersion at higher levels may differ considerably from that determined by the σ_y's and σ_z's used here. As noted, however, since σ_y generally decreases with height and u increases with

---

*"ln" denotes natural logarithms, i.e., to the base e.

height, the product u σ_y σ_z will not change appreciably. The greater the effective height, the more likely it is that the stability may not be the same from the ground to this height. With the longer travel distances such as the points of maximum concentrations for stable conditions (Types E or F), the stability may change before the plume travels the entire distance.

REVIEW OF ASSUMPTIONS

The preceding has been based on these assumptions, which should be clearly understood:

(i) Continuous emission from the source or emission times equal to or greater than travel times to the downwind position under consideration, so that diffusion in the direction of transport may be neglected.

(ii) The material diffused is a stable gas or aerosol (less than 20 microns diameter) which remains suspended in the air over long periods of time.

(iii) The equation of continuity:

$$Q = \int_0^{+\infty} \int_{-\infty}^{+\infty} \chi \, u \, dy \, dz \tag{3.9}$$

is fulfilled, i.e., none of the material emitted is removed from the plume as it moves downwind and there is complete reflection at the ground.

(iv) The mean wind direction specifies the x-axis, and a mean wind speed representative of the diffusing layer is chosen.

(v) Except where specifically mentioned, the plume constituents are distributed normally in both the cross-wind and vertical directions.

(vi) The σ's given in Figures 3-2 and 3-3 represent time periods of about 10 minutes.

REFERENCES

DeMarrais, G. A., 1961: Vertical temperature difference observed over an urban area. Bull. Amer. Meteorol. Soc., *42*, 8, 548-554.

Duckworth, F. S., and J. S. Sandberg, 1954: The effect of cities upon horizontal and vertical temperature gradients. Bull. Amer. Meteorol. Soc., *35*, 5, 198-207.

Gifford, F. A., 1961: Use of routine meteorological observations for estimating atmospheric dispersion. Nuclear Safety, *2*, 4, 47-51.

Gifford, F. A., 1962: The area within ground-level dosage isopleths. Nuclear Safety, *4*, 2, 91-92.

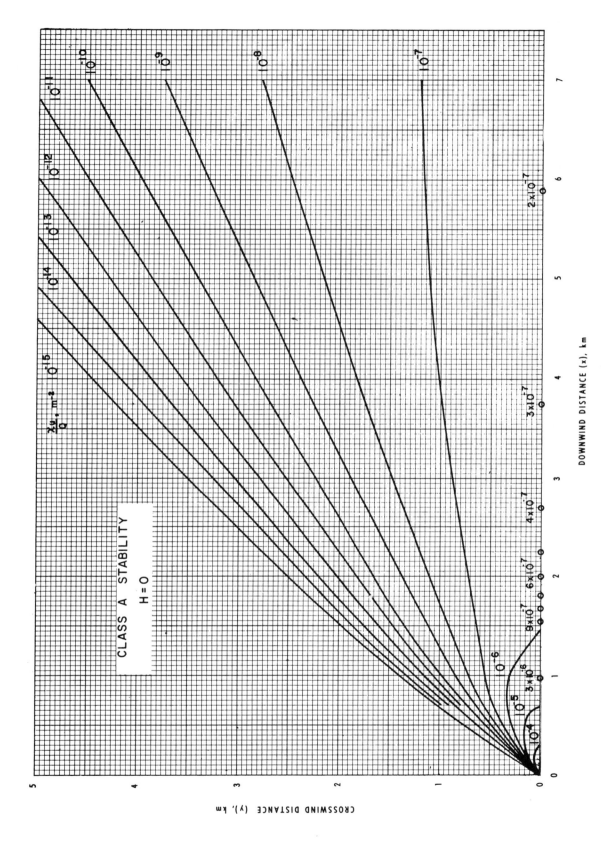

Figure 3-6A. Isopleths of $\chi u/Q$ for a ground-level source, A stability.

290

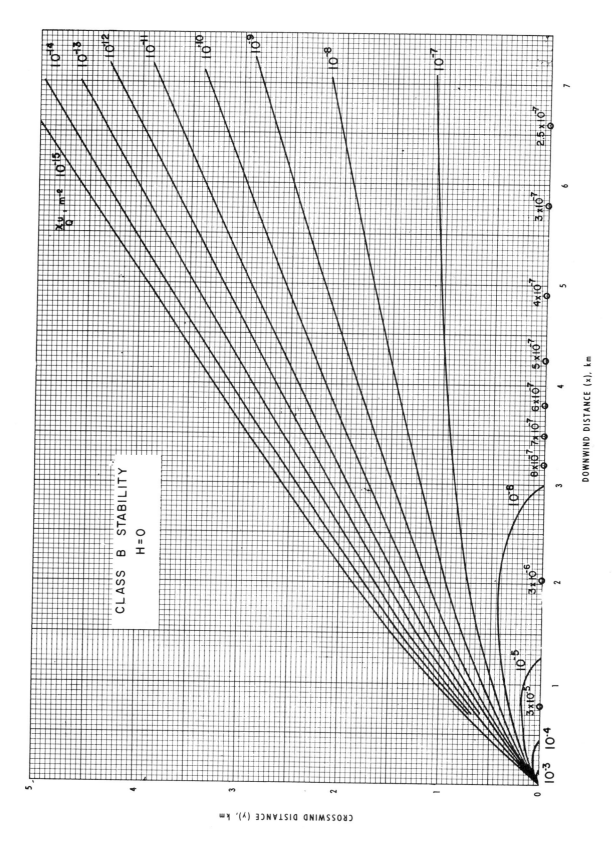

CLASS B STABILITY
H=0

$\dfrac{\chi u}{Q}$, m^{-2}

Figure 3-6B. Isopleths of $\chi u/Q$ for a ground-level source, B stability.

DOWNWIND DISTANCE (x), km

CROSSWIND DISTANCE (y), km

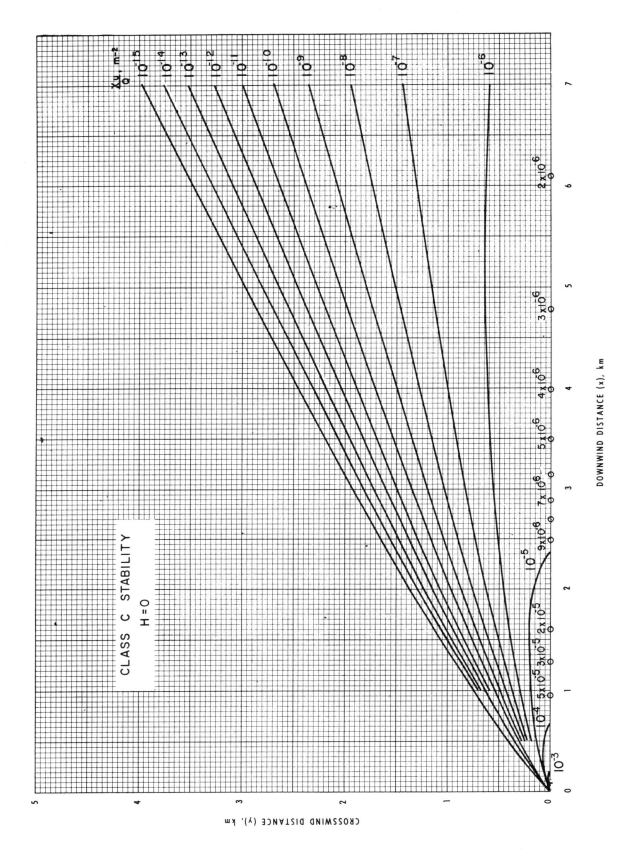

CLASS C STABILITY
H = 0

$\frac{\chi u}{Q}$, m⁻²

DOWNWIND DISTANCE (x), km

CROSSWIND DISTANCE (y), km

Figure 3-6C. Isopleths of $\chi u/Q$ for a ground-level source, C stability.

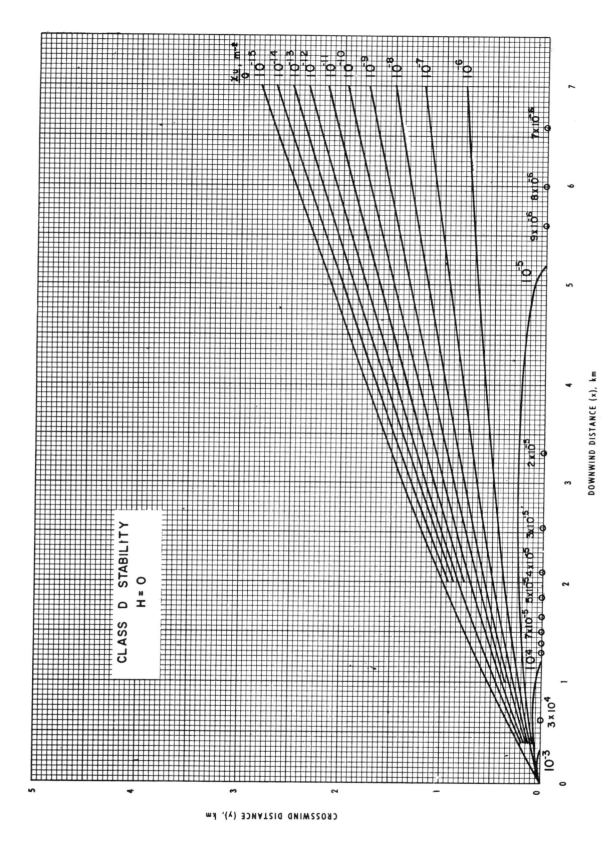

Figure 3-6D. Isopleths of $\chi u/Q$ for a ground-level source, D stability.

293

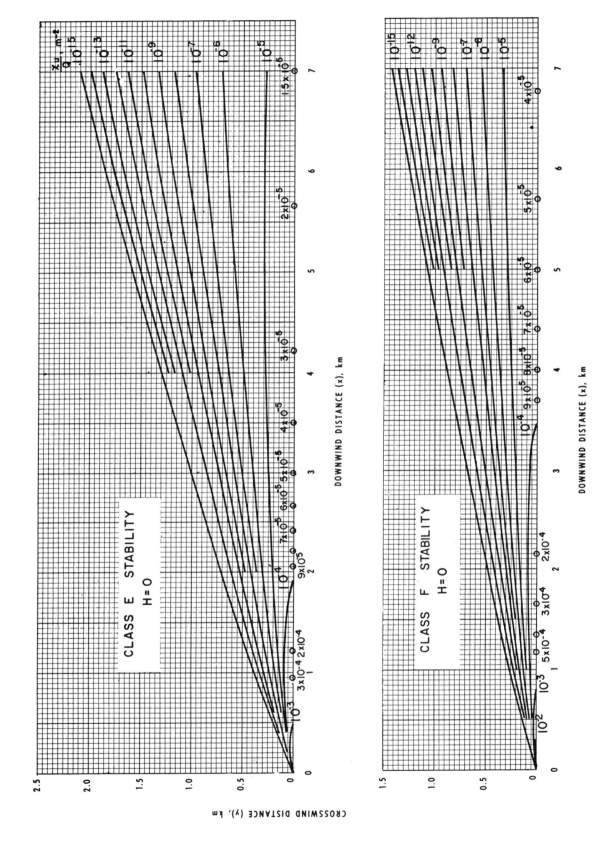

Figure 3-6E, F. Isopleths of $\chi u/Q$ for a ground-level source, E and F stabilities.

294

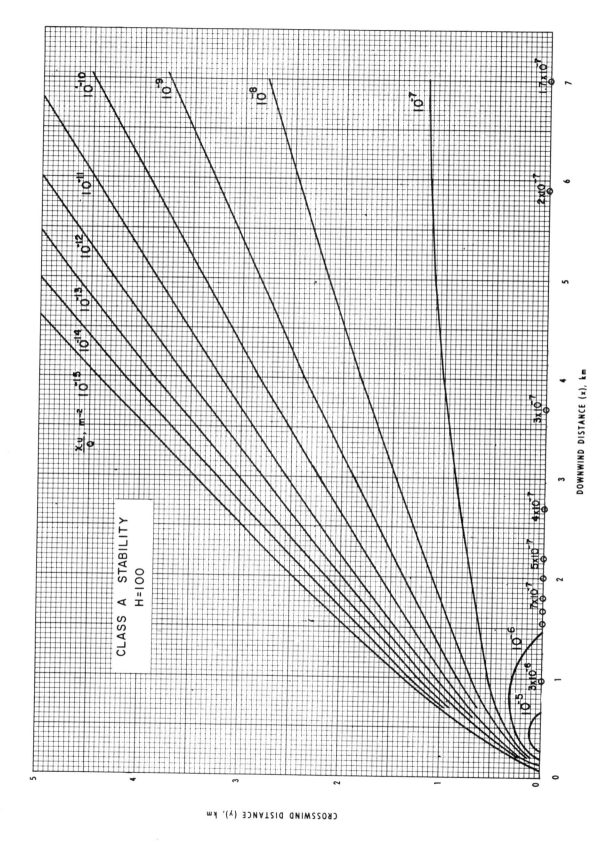

Figure 3-7A. Isopleths of χu/Q for a source 100 meters high, A stability.

295

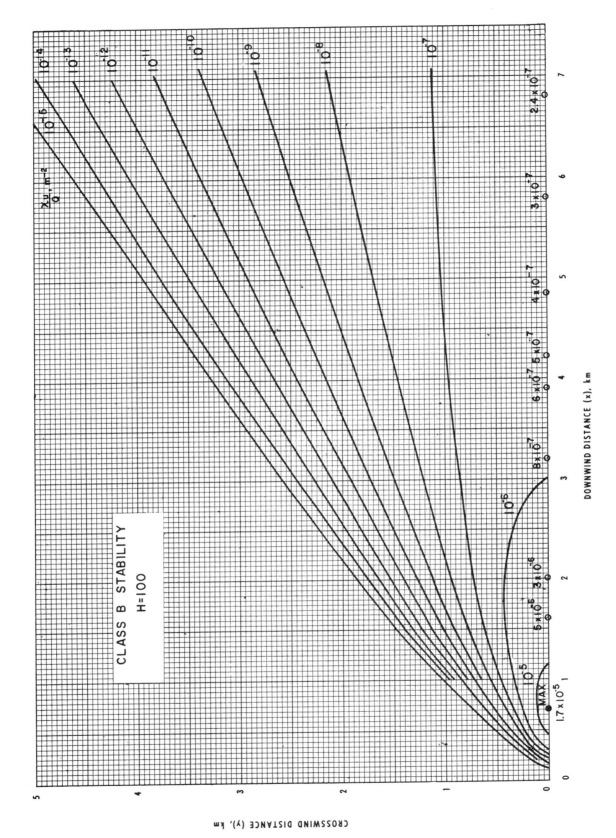

Figure 3-7B. Isopleths of $\chi u/Q$ for a source 100 meters high, B stability.

296

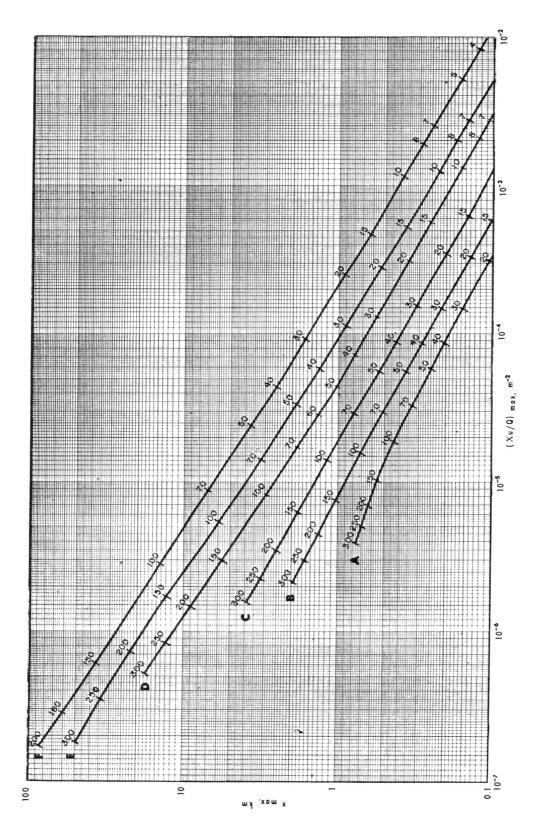

Figure 3.9. Distance of maximum concentration and maximum $\chi u/Q$ as a function of stability (curves) and effective height (meters) of emission (numbers).

Chapter 4 — EFFECTIVE HEIGHT OF EMISSION

GENERAL CONSIDERATIONS

In most problems one must estimate the effective stack height, H, at which the plume becomes essentially level. Rarely will this height correspond to the physical height of the stack, h. If the plume is caught in the turbulent wake of the stack or of buildings in the vicinity of the stack, the effluent will be mixed rapidly downward toward the ground (aerodynamic downwash). If the plume is emitted free of these turbulent zones, a number of emission factors and meteorological factors influence the rise of the plume. The emission factors are: velocity of the effluent at the top of the stack, v_s; temperature of the effluent at the top of the stack, T_s; and diameter of the stack opening, d. The meteorological factors influencing plume rise are wind speed, u; temperature of the air, T_a; shear of the wind speed with height, du/dz; and atmospheric stability. No theory on plume rise takes into account all of these variables; even if such a theory were available, measurements of all of the parameters would seldom be available. Most of the equations that have been formulated for computing the effective height of emission are semi-empirical. For a recent review of equations for effective height of emission see Moses, Strom, and Carson (1964).

Moses and Strom (1961), having compared actual and calculated plume heights by means of six plume rise equations, report "There is no one formula which is outstanding in all respects." The formulas of Davidson-Bryant (1949), Holland (1953), Bosanquet-Carey-Halton (1950), and Bosanquet (1957) all give generally satisfactory results in the test situations. The experiments conducted by Moses and Strom involved plume rise from a stack of less than 0.5 meter diameter, stack gas exit velocities less than 15 m sec^{-1}, and effluent temperature not more than 35°C higher than that of the ambient air.

The equation of Holland was developed with experimental data from larger sources than those of Moses and Strom (stack diameters from 1.7 to 4.3 meters and stack temperatures from 82 to 204°C); Holland's equation is used in the solution of the problems given in this workbook. This equation frequently underestimates the effective height of emission; therefore its use often provides a slight "safety" factor.

Holland's equation is:

$$\Delta H = \frac{v_s\,d}{u} \left(1.5 + 2.68 \times 10^{-3}\, p\, \frac{T_s - T_a}{T_s}\, d\right) \quad (4.1)$$

where:

ΔH = the rise of the plume above the stack, m

v_s = stack gas exit velocity, m sec^{-1}

d = the inside stack diameter, m

u = wind speed, m sec^{-1}

p = atmospheric pressure, mb

T_s = stack gas temperature, °K

T_a = air temperature, °K

and 2.68 x 10^{-3} is a constant having units of mb^{-1} m^{-1}.

Holland (1953) suggests that a value between 1.1 and 1.2 times the ΔH from the equation should be used for unstable conditions; a value between 0.8 and 0.9 times the ΔH from the equation should be used for stable conditions.

Since the plume rise from a stack occurs over some distance downwind, Eq. (4.1) should not be applied within the first few hundred meters of the stack.

EFFECTIVE HEIGHT OF EMISSION AND MAXIMUM CONCENTRATION

If the effective heights of emission were the same under all atmospheric conditions, the highest ground-level concentrations from a given source would occur with the lightest winds. Generally, however, emission conditions are such that the effective stack height is an inverse function of wind speed as indicated in Eq. (4.1). The maximum ground-level concentration occurs at some intermediate wind speed, at which a balance is reached between the dilution due to wind speed and the effect of height of emission. This critical wind speed will vary with stability. In order to determine the critical wind speed, the effective stack height as a function of wind speed should first be determined. The maximum concentration for each wind speed and stability can then be calculated from Figure 3-9 as a function of effective height of emission and stability. When the maximum concentration as a function of wind speed is plotted on log-log graph paper, curves can be drawn for each stability class; the critical wind speed corresponds to the point of highest maximum concentration on the curve (see problem 14).

ESTIMATES OF REQUIRED STACK HEIGHTS

Estimates of the stack height required to produce concentrations below a given value may be made through the use of Figure 3-9 by obtaining solutions for various wind speeds. Use of this figure considers maximum concentrations at any distance from the source.

In some situations high concentrations upon the property of the emitter are of little concern, but maximum concentrations beyond the property line are of the utmost importance. For first approximations it can be assumed that the maximum concentration occurs where $\sqrt{2}\,\sigma_z = H$ and that at this distance the σ's are related to the maximum concentration by:

$$\sigma_y\,\sigma_z \cong \frac{Q}{\pi\,u\,e\,\chi_{max}} \cong \frac{0.117\,Q}{u\,\chi_{max}} \quad (4.2)$$

Knowing the source strength, Q, and the concentration not to be exceeded χ_{max}, one can determine the necessary $\sigma_y\,\sigma_z$ for a given wind speed. Figure 4-1 shows $\sigma_y\,\sigma_z$ as a function of distance for the various stability classes. The value of $\sigma_y\,\sigma_z$ and a design distance, x_d (the distance beyond which χ is less than some pre-determined value), will determine a point on this graph yielding a stability class or point between classes. The σ_z for this stability (or point between stabilities) can then be determined from Figure 3-3. The required effective stack height for this wind speed can then be approximated by $H = \sqrt{2}\,\sigma_z$ (see problem 15). Since Eq. (4.2) is an approximation, the resulting height should be used with Eq. (3.3) to ensure that the maximum concentration is sufficiently low. If enough is known about the proposed source to allow use of an equation for effective height of emission, the relation between ΔH and u can be determined. The physical stack height required at the wind speed for which H was determined is H — ΔH. The same procedure, starting with the determination of $\sigma_y\,\sigma_z$, must be used with other wind speeds to determine the maximum required physical stack height (see problem 16).

EFFECT OF EVAPORATIVE COOLING

When effluent gases are washed to absorb certain constituents prior to emission, the gases are cooled and become saturated with water vapor. Upon release of the gases from the absorption tower, further cooling due to contact with cold surfaces of ductwork or stack is likely. This cooling causes condensation of water droplets in the gas stream. Upon release of the gases from the stack, the water droplets evaporate, withdrawing the latent heat of vaporization from the air and cooling the plume. The resulting negative buoyancy reduces the effective stack height (Scorer, 1959).

EFFECT OF AERODYNAMIC DOWNWASH

The influence of mechanical turbulence around a building or stack can significantly alter the effective stack height. This is especially true with high winds, when the beneficial effect of high stack-gas velocity is at a minimum and the plume is emitted nearly horizontally. The region of disturbed flow surrounds an isolated building, generally to at least twice its height and extends downwind 5 to 10 times its height. Building the stack 2.5 times the height of the highest building adjacent to the stack usually overcomes the effects of building turbulence (Hawkins and Nonhebel, 1955). Ensuring that the exit velocity of the stack gas is more than 1.5 times the wind speed will usually prevent downwash in the wake of the stack. Most of the knowledge about the turbulent wakes around stacks and buildings has been gained through wind tunnel studies (Sherlock and Lesher, 1954; Strom, 1955-1956; Strom, et al, 1957; and Halitsky, 1962). By use of models of building shapes and stacks, one may determine the wind speeds required to cause downwash for various wind directions. With a wind tunnel the meteorological variables most easily accounted for are wind speed and wind direction (by rotation of the model within the tunnel). The emission factors that may be considered are the size and shape of the plant building; the shape, height, and diameter of the stack; the amount of emission; and the stack-gas velocity.

Through wind tunnel studies, the critical wind speeds that will cause downwash from various directions can be determined for a given set of plant factors. The average number of hours of downwash per year can then be calculated by determining the frequency of wind speeds greater than the critical speeds for each direction (Sherlock and Lesher, 1954) if climatological data representative of the site are available.

Maximum downwash about a rectangular structure occurs when the direction of the wind is at an angle of 45 degrees from the major axis of the structure; minimum downwash occurs with wind flow parallel to the major axis of the structure (Sherlock and Lesher, 1954).

Halitsky (1961, 1963) has shown that the effluent from flush openings on flat roofs frequently flows in a direction opposite to that of the free atmospheric wind, owing to counter-flow along the roof in the turbulent wake above the building. In addition to the effect of aerodynamic downwash upon the release of air pollutants from stacks and buildings, one must also consider the effects of aerodynamic downwash when exposing meteorological instruments near or upon buildings.

Where the pollution is emitted from a vent or opening on a building and is immediately influenced by the turbulent wake of the building, the pollution is rapidly distributed within this turbulent wake. To account for mixing in the turbulent wake, one may assume binormal distributions of concentrations at the source, with horizontal and vertical standard deviations of σ_{y_0} and σ_{z_0}. The standard deviations are related to the width and height of the building, for example, letting $4.3\,\sigma_{y_0}$ equal the width of the building and $2.15\,\sigma_{z_0}$ equal

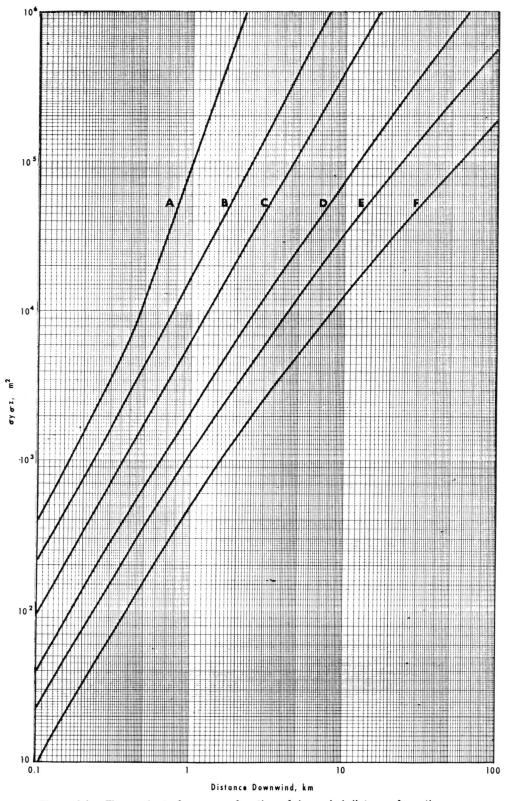

Figure 4-1.   The product of $\sigma_y\sigma_z$ as a function of downwind distance from the source.

the height. Values other than 4.3 and 2.15 can be used. When these values are used 97% of the distribution is included within these limits. Virtual distances x_y and x_z can be found such that at x_y, $\sigma_y = \sigma_{y_0}$ and at x_z, $\sigma_z = \sigma_{z_0}$. These x's will differ with stability. Equations applicable to point sources can then be used, determining σ_y as a function of $x + x_y$ and σ_z as a function of $x + x_z$.

REFERENCES

Bosanquet, C. H., W. F. Carey, and E. M. Halton, 1950: Dust from chimney stacks. Proc. Inst. Mech. Eng., *162*, 355-367.

Bosanquet, C. H., 1957: The rise of a hot waste gas plume. J. Inst. Fuel, *30*, 197, 322-328.

Davidson, W. F., 1949: The dispersion and spreading of gases and dust from chimneys. Trans. Conf. on Ind. Wastes, 14th Ann. Meeting, Ind. Hygiene Found. Amer., 38-55.

Halitsky, J., 1961: Wind tunnel model test of exhaust gas recirculation at the NIH Clinical Center. Tech. Rep. No. 785.1, New York Univ.

Halitsky, J., 1962: Diffusion of vented gas around buildings. J. Air Poll. Cont. Assoc., *12*, 2, 74-80.

Halitsky, J., 1963: Gas diffusion near buildings, theoretical concepts and wind tunnel model experiments with prismatic building shapes. Geophysical Sciences Lab. Rep. No. 63-3. New York Univ.

Hawkins, J. E., and G. Nonhebel, 1955: Chimneys and the dispersal of smoke. J. Inst. Fuel, *28*, 530-546.

Holland, J. Z., 1953: A meteorological survey of the Oak Ridge area. 554-559 Atomic Energy Comm., Report ORO-99, Washington, D.C., 584 pp.

Moses, H., and G. H. Strom, 1961: A comparison of observed plume rises with values obtained from well-known formulas. J. Air Poll. Cont. Assoc., *11*, 10, 455-466.

Moses, H., G. H. Strom, and J. E. Carson, 1964: Effects of meteorological and engineering factors on stack plume rise. Nuclear Safety, *6*, 1, 1-19.

Scorer, R. S., 1959: The behavior of plumes. Int. J. Air Poll., *1*, 198-220.

Sherlock, R. H., and E. J. Lesher, 1954: Role of chimney design in dispersion of waste gases. Air Repair, *4*, 2, 1-10.

Strom, G. H., 1955-1956: Wind tunnel scale model studies of air pollution from industrial plants. Ind. Wastes, Sept. - Oct. 1955, Nov. - Dec. 1955, and Jan. - Feb. 1956.

Strom, G. H., M. Hackman, and E. J. Kaplin, 1957: Atmospheric dispersal of industrial stack gases determined by concentration measurements in scale model wind tunnel experiments. J. Air Poll. Cont. Assoc., *7*, 3, 198-203.

Chapter 5 — SPECIAL TOPICS

CONCENTRATIONS IN AN INVERSION BREAK-UP FUMIGATION

A surface-based inversion may be eliminated by the upward transfer of sensible heat from the ground surface when that surface is warmer than the overlying air. This situation occurs when the ground is being warmed by solar radiation or when air flows from a cold to a relatively warm surface. In either situation pollutants previously emitted above the surface into the stable layer will be mixed vertically when they are reached by the thermal eddies, and ground-level concentrations can increase. This process, called "fumigation" was described by Hewson and Gill (1944) and Hewson (1945). Equations for estimating concentrations with these conditions have been given by Holland (1953), Hewson (1955), Gifford (1960a), Bierly and Hewson (1962), and Pooler (1965).

To estimate ground-level concentrations under inversion break-up fumigations, one assumes that the plume was initially emitted into a stable layer. Therefore, σ_y and σ_z characteristic of stable conditions must be selected for the particular distance of concern. An equation for the ground-level concentration when the inversion has been eliminated to a height h_i is:

$$\chi_F (x,y,0;H) =$$

$$\frac{Q \left[\int_{-\infty}^{p} \frac{1}{\sqrt{2\pi}} \exp (-0.5 \, p^2) \, dp \right]}{\sqrt{2\pi} \, \sigma_{yF} \, u \, h_i}$$

$$\exp \left[-\frac{1}{2} \left(\frac{y}{\sigma_{yF}} \right)^2 \right] \tag{5.1}$$

where $p = \dfrac{h_i - H}{\sigma_z}$

and σ_{yF} is discussed below.

Values for the integral in brackets can be found in most statistical tables. For example, see pages 273-276, Burington (1953). This factor accounts for the portion of the plume that is mixed downward. If the inversion is eliminated up to the effective stack height, half of the plume is presumed to be mixed downward, the other half remaining in the stable air above. Eq. (5.1) can be approximated when the fumigation concentration is near its maximum by:

$$\chi_F (x,y,0;H) = \frac{Q}{\sqrt{2\pi} \, u \, \sigma_{yF} \, h_i} \exp \left[-\frac{1}{2} \left(\frac{y}{\sigma_{yF}} \right)^2 \right] \tag{5.2}$$

$$h_i = H + 2 \, \sigma_z = h + \Delta H + 2 \, \sigma_z \tag{5.3}$$

A difficulty is encountered in estimating a reasonable value for the horizontal dispersion since in mixing the stable plume through a vertical depth some additional horizontal spreading occurs (see problem 12). If this spreading is ignored and the σ_y for stable conditions used, the probable result would be estimated concentrations higher than actual concentrations. Or, using an approximation suggested by Bierly and Hewson (1962) that the edge of the plume spreads outward with an angle of 15°, the σ_{yF} for the inversion break-up fumigation equals the σ_y for stable conditions plus one-eighth the effective height of emission. The origin of this concept can be seen in Figure 5-1 and the following equation, where the edge of the plume is the point at which the concentration falls to 1/10 that at the centerline (at a distance of $2.15 \, \sigma_y$ from the plume center).

$$\sigma_{yF} = \frac{2.15 \, \sigma_y \, (\text{stable}) + H \tan 15°}{2.15}$$

$$= \sigma_y \, (\text{stable}) + H/8 \tag{5.4}$$

A Gaussian distribution in the horizontal is assumed.

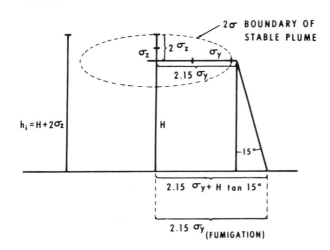

Figure 5-1. Diagram showing assumed height, h_i and σ_y during fumigation, for use in equation (5.2).

Eq. (5.4) should not be applied near the stack, for if the inversion has been eliminated to a height sufficient to include the entire plume, the emission is taking place under unstable not stable conditions. Therefore, the nearest downwind distance to be considered for an estimate of fumigation concentrations must be great enough, based on the time required to eliminate the inversion, that this portion of the plume was initially emitted into stable air. This distance is $x = u t_m$, where u is the mean wind in the stable layer and t_m is the time required to eliminate the inversion from h, the physical height of the stack to h_1 (Eq. 5.3).

t_m is dependent upon both the strength of the inversion and the rate of heating at the surface. Pooler (1965) has derived an expression for estimating this time:

$$t_m = \frac{\rho_a \, c_p}{R} \cdot \frac{\delta\Theta}{\delta z} \, (h_1 - h) \left(\frac{h + h_1}{2}\right) \quad (5.5)$$

where t_m = time required for the mixing layer to develop from the top of the stack to the top of the plume, sec

ρ_a = ambient air density, g m^{-3}

c_p = specific heat of air at constant pressure, cal g^{-1} °K^{-1}

R = net rate of sensible heating of an air column by solar radiation, cal m^{-2} sec^{-1}

$\frac{\delta\Theta}{\delta z}$ = vertical potential temperature gradient, °K m$^{-1} \sim \frac{\delta T}{\delta z} + \Gamma$ (the adiabatic lapse rate)

h_1 = height of base of the inversion sufficient to be above the plume, m

h = physical height of the stack, m

Note that $h_1 - h$ is the thickness of the layer to be heated and $\left(\frac{h + h_1}{2}\right)$ is the average height of the layer. Although R depends on season, and cloud cover and varies continuously with time, Pooler has used a value of 67 cal m^{-2} sec^{-1} as an average for fumigation.

Hewson (1945) also suggested a method of estimating the time required to eliminate an inversion to a height z by use of an equation of Taylor's (1915, p. 8):

$$t = \frac{z^2}{4 \, K} \quad (5.6)$$

where: t = time required to eliminate the inversion to height z, sec

z = height to which the inversion has been eliminated, m

K = eddy diffusivity for heat, m^2 sec^{-1}

Rewriting to compare with Eq. (5.5),

$$t_m = \frac{h_1^2 - h^2}{4 \, K} \quad (5.7)$$

Hewson (1945) has suggested a value of 3 m^2 sec^{-1} for K.

PLUME TRAPPING

Plume trapping occurs when the plume is trapped between the ground surface and a stable layer aloft. Bierly and Hewson (1962) have suggested the use of an equation that accounts for the multiple eddy reflections from both the ground and the stable layer:

$$\chi \, (x,0,z;H) = \frac{Q}{2\pi \, u \, \sigma_y \, \sigma_z} \Bigg\{$$
$$\exp\left[-\frac{1}{2}\left(\frac{z - H}{\sigma_z}\right)^2\right]$$
$$+ \exp\left[-\frac{1}{2}\left(\frac{z + H}{\sigma_z}\right)^2\right]$$
$$+ \sum_{N=1}^{N=J} \left[\exp - \frac{1}{2}\left(\frac{z - H - 2\,NL}{\sigma_z}\right)^2 \right.$$
$$+ \exp - \frac{1}{2}\left(\frac{z + H - 2\,NL}{\sigma_z}\right)^2$$
$$+ \exp - \frac{1}{2}\left(\frac{z - H + 2\,NL}{\sigma_z}\right)^2$$
$$\left. + \exp - \frac{1}{2}\left(\frac{z + H + 2\,NL}{\sigma_z}\right)^2 \right]\Bigg\} (5.8)$$

where L is the height of the stable layer and $J = 3$ or 4 is sufficient to include the important reflections. A good approximation of this lengthy equation can be made by assuming no effect of the stable layer until $\sigma_z = 0.47 \, L$ (see Chapter 3). It is assumed that at this distance, x_L, the stable layer begins to affect the vertical distribution so that at the downwind distance, $2 \, x_L$, uniform vertical mixing has taken place and the following equation can be used:

$$\chi \, (x,y,z;H) = \frac{Q}{\sqrt{2\pi} \, \sigma_y \, L \, u} \exp\left[-\frac{1}{2}\left(\frac{y}{\sigma_y}\right)^2\right]$$
$$(5.9)$$

For distances between x_L and $2 \, x_L$ the best approximation to the ground-level centerline concentration is that read from a straight line drawn between the concentrations for points x_L and $2 \, x_L$ on a log-log plot of ground-level centerline concentration as a function of distance.

CONCENTRATIONS AT GROUND LEVEL COMPARED TO CONCENTRATIONS AT THE LEVEL OF EFFECTIVE STACK HEIGHT FROM ELEVATED CONTINUOUS SOURCES

There are several interesting relationships between ground-level concentrations and concentrations at the level of the plume centerline. One of these is at the distance of maximum concentration at the ground. As a rough approximation the maximum ground-level concentration occurs at the distance where $\sigma_z = \dfrac{1}{\sqrt{2}}$ H. This approximation is much better for unstable conditions than for stable conditions. With this approximation, the ratio of concentration at plume centerline to that at the ground is:

$$\frac{\chi\,(x,0,H)}{\chi(x,0,0)} = \frac{\dfrac{1}{2}\left[1.0 + \exp -\dfrac{1}{2}\left(\dfrac{2H}{\sigma_z}\right)^2\right]}{\exp -\dfrac{1}{2}\left(\dfrac{H}{\sigma_z}\right)^2}$$

$$= \frac{\dfrac{1}{2}\,[1.0 + \exp -0.5\,(2\,\sqrt{2})^2]}{\exp -0.5\,(\sqrt{2})^2}$$

$$= \frac{\dfrac{1}{2}\,(1.0 + 0.0182)}{0.368}$$

$$= 1.38$$

This calculation indicates that at the distance of maximum ground-level concentration the concentration at plume centerline is greater by about one-third.

It is also of interest to determine the relationship between σ_z and H such that the concentration at ground-level at a given distance from the source is the same as the concentration at plume level. This condition should occur where:

$$\exp -\frac{1}{2}\left(\frac{H}{\sigma_z}\right)^2 = \frac{1}{2}\left[1.0 + \exp -\frac{1}{2}\left(\frac{2H}{\sigma_z}\right)^2\right]$$

The value $H/\sigma_z = 1.10$ satisfies this expression, which can be written as $\sigma_z = 0.91$ H (see problem 10).

TOTAL DOSAGE FROM A FINITE RELEASE

The total dosage, which is the integration of concentration over the time of passage of a plume or puff, can be obtained from:

$$D_T\,(x,y,0;H) = \frac{Q_T}{\pi\,\sigma_y\,\sigma_z\,u}\exp\left[-\frac{1}{2}\left(\frac{y}{\sigma_y}\right)^2\right]$$

$$\exp\left[-\frac{1}{2}\left(\frac{H}{\sigma_z}\right)^2\right] \qquad (5.10)$$

where D_T = total dosage, g sec m^{-3}
and Q_T = total release, g

The σ's should be representative of the time period over which the release takes place, and care should be taken to consider the x-axis along the trajectory or path of the plume or puff travel. Large errors can easily occur if the path is not known

accurately. The estimate of this path is usually increasingly difficult with shorter release times. D_T can also be given in curie sec m^{-3} if Q_T is in curies.

CROSSWIND-INTEGRATED CONCENTRATION

The ground-level crosswind-integrated concentration is often of interest. For a continuous elevated source this concentration is determined from Eq. (3.2) integrated with respect to y from $-\infty$ to $+\infty$ (Gifford 1960a) giving:

$$\chi_{\text{CWI}} = \frac{2\,Q}{\sqrt{2\pi}\,\sigma_z\,u}\exp\left[-\frac{1}{2}\left(\frac{H}{\sigma_z}\right)^2\right] \quad (5.11)$$

In diffusion experiments the ground-level crosswind-integrated concentration is often determined at particular downwind distances from a crosswind line or arc of sampling measurements made at this distance. When the source strength, Q, and average wind speed, u, are known, σ_z can be estimated indirectly even though no measurements were made in the vertical. If any of the tracer is lost through reaction or deposition, the resulting σ_z from such estimates will not represent the vertical dispersion (see problem 18).

ESTIMATION OF CONCENTRATIONS FOR SAMPLING TIMES LONGER THAN A FEW MINUTES

Concentrations directly downwind from a source decrease with sampling time mainly because of a larger σ_y due to increased meander of wind direction. Stewart, Gale, and Crooks (1958) reported that this decrease in concentration follows a one-fifth power law with the sampling time for sampling periods from about 3 minutes to about half an hour. Cramer (1959) indicates that this same power law applies for sampling times from 3 seconds to 10 minutes. Both of these studies were based on observations taken near the height of release. Gifford (1960b) indicates that ratios of peak to mean concentrations are much higher than those given by the above power law where observations of concentrations are made at heights considerably different from the height of release or considerably removed from the plume axis. He also indicates that for increasing distances from an elevated source, the ratios of peak to average concentrations observed at ground level approach unity. Singer (1961) and Singer, et al. (1963) show that ratios of peak to mean concentrations depend also on the stability of the atmosphere and the type of terrain that the plume is passing over. Nonhebel (1960) reports that Meade deduced a relation between calculated concentrations at ground level and the sampling time from "a study of published data on lateral and vertical diffusion coefficients in steady winds." These relations are shown in Table 5-1.

Table 5-1 VARIATION OF CALCULATED CONCENTRATION
WITH SAMPLING TIME

Sampling Time	Ratio of Calculated Concentration to 3-minute Concentration
3 minutes	1.00
15 minutes	0.82
1 hour	0.61
3 hours	0.51
24 hours	0.36

This table indicates a power relation with time: $\chi \propto t^{-0.17}$. Note that these estimates were based upon published dispersion coefficients rather than upon sampling results. Information in the references cited indicates that effects of sampling time are exceedingly complex. If it is necessary to estimate concentrations from a single source for the time intervals greater than a few minutes, the best estimate apparently can be obtained from:

$$\chi_s = \chi_k \left(\frac{t_k}{t_s} \right)^p \qquad (5.12)$$

where χ_s is the desired concentration estimate for the sampling time, t_s; χ_k is the concentration estimate for the shorter sampling time, t_k, (probably about 10 minutes); and p should be between 0.17 and 0.2. Eq. (5.12) probably would be applied most appropriately to sampling times less than 2 hours (see problem 19).

ESTIMATION OF SEASONAL OR ANNUAL AVERAGE CONCENTRATIONS AT A RECEPTOR FROM A SINGLE POLLUTANT SOURCE

For a source that emits at a constant rate from hour to hour and day to day, estimates of seasonal or annual average concentrations can be made for any distance in any direction if stability wind "rose" data are available for the period under study. A wind rose gives the frequency of occurrence for each wind direction (usually to 16 points) and wind speed class (9 classes in standard Weather Bureau use) for the period under consideration (from 1 month to 10 years). A stability wind rose gives the same type of information for each stability class.

If the wind directions are taken to 16 points and it is assumed that the wind directions within each sector are distributed randomly over a period of a month or a season, it can further be assumed that the effluent is uniformly distributed in the horizontal within the sector (Holland, 1953, p. 540). The appropriate equation for average concentration is then either:

$$\overline{\chi} = \frac{2\,Q}{\sqrt{2\pi}\,\sigma_z\,u \left(\frac{2\pi\,x}{16} \right)} \exp \left[-\frac{1}{2} \left(\frac{H}{\sigma_z} \right)^2 \right]$$

$$= \frac{2.03Q}{\sigma_z\,ux} \exp \left[-\frac{1}{2} \left(\frac{H}{\sigma_z} \right)^2 \right] \qquad (5.13)$$

or

$$\overline{\chi} = \frac{Q}{L\,u \left(\frac{2\pi\,x}{16} \right)} = \frac{2.55\,Q}{L\,u\,x} \qquad (5.14)$$

depending upon whether a stable layer aloft is affecting the distribution.

The estimation of χ for a particular direction and downwind distance can be accomplished by choosing a representative wind speed for each speed class and solving the appropriate equation (5.13 or 5.14) for all wind speed classes and stabilities. Note that a SSW wind affects a receptor to the NNE of a source. One obtains the average concentration for a given direction and distance by summing all the concentrations and weighting each one according to its frequency for the particular stability and wind speed class. If desired, a different effective height of emission can be used for various wind speeds. The average concentration can be expressed by:

$$\chi\,(x,\Theta) = \sum_S \sum_N \left\{ \frac{2\,Q\,f\,(\Theta,S,N)}{\sqrt{2\pi}\,\sigma_{zS}\,u_N \left(\frac{2\pi\,x}{16} \right)} \right.$$

$$\left. \exp \left[-\frac{1}{2} \left(\frac{H_u}{\sigma_{zS}} \right)^2 \right] \right\} \qquad (5.15)$$

where $f\,(\Theta,\,S,\,N)$ is the frequency during the period of interest that the wind is from the direction Θ, for the stability condition, S, and wind speed class N.

σ_{zS} is the vertical dispersion parameter evaluated at the distance x for the stability condition S.

u_N is the representative wind speed for class N.

H_u is the effective height of release for the wind speed u_N.

Where stability wind rose information cannot be obtained, a first-order approximation may be made of seasonal or annual average concentrations by using the appropriate wind rose in the same manner, and assuming the neutral stability class, D, only.

METEOROLOGICAL CONDITIONS ASSOCIATED WITH MAXIMUM GROUND-LEVEL CONCENTRATIONS

1. For ground-level sources maximum concentrations occur with stable conditions.

2. For elevated sources maximum *"instantaneous"* concentrations occur with unstable conditions when portions of the plume that have undergone little dispersion are brought to the ground. These occur close to the point of emission (on the order of 1 to 3 stack heights). These concentrations are usually of little general interest because of their very short duration; they *cannot* be estimated from the material presented in this workbook.

3. For elevated sources maximum concentrations for time periods of a few minutes occur with unstable conditions; although the concentrations fluctuate considerably under these conditions, the concentrations averaged over a few minutes are still high compared to those found under other conditions. The distance of this maximum concentration occurs near the stack (from 1 to 5 stack heights downwind) and the concentration drops off rapidly downwind with increasing distance.

4. For elevated sources maximum concentrations for time periods of about half an hour can occur with fumigation conditions when an unstable layer increases vertically to mix downward a plume previously discharged within a stable layer. With small ΔH, the fumigation can occur close to the source but will be of relatively short duration. For large ΔH, the fumigation will occur some distance from the stack (perhaps 30 to 40 km), but can persist for a longer time interval. Concentrations considerably lower than those associated with fumigations, but of significance can occur with neutral or unstable conditions when the dispersion upward is severely limited by the existence of a more stable layer above the plume, for example, an inversion.

5. Under stable conditions the maximum concentrations at ground-level from elevated sources are less than those occurring under unstable conditions and occur at greater distances from the source. However, the difference between maximum ground-level concentrations for stable and unstable conditions is only a factor of 2 for effective heights of 25 meters and a factor of 5 for H of 75 m. Because the maximum occurs at greater distances, concentrations that are below the maximum but still significant can occur over large areas. This becomes increasingly significant if emissions are coming from more than one source.

CONCENTRATIONS AT A RECEPTOR POINT FROM SEVERAL SOURCES

Sometimes, especially for multiple sources, it is convenient to consider the receptor as being at the origin of the diffusion coordinate system. The source-receptor geometry can then be worked out merely by drawing or visualizing an x-axis oriented upwind from the receptor and determining the crosswind distances of each source in relation to this x-axis. As pointed out by Gifford (1959), the concentration at (0, 0, 0) from a source at (x, y, H) on a coordinate system with the x-axis oriented upwind is the same as the concentration at (x, y, 0) from a source at (0, 0, H) on a coordniate system with the x-axis downwind (Figure 5-2). The total concentration is then given by summing the individual contributions from each source (see problem 20).

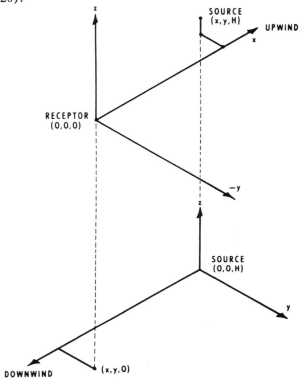

Figure 5-2. Comparison of source-oriented and receptor-oriented coordinate systems.

It is often difficult to determine the atmospheric conditions of wind direction, wind speed, and stability that will result in the maximum combined concentrations from two or more sources; drawing isopleths of concentration for various wind speeds and stabilities and orienting these according to wind direction is one approach.

AREA SOURCES

In dealing with diffusion of air pollutants in areas having large numbers of sources, e.g., as in urban areas, there may be too many sources of most atmospheric contaminants to consider each source individually. Often an approximation can be made by combining all of the emissions in a given area and treating this area as a source having an initial horizontal standard deviation, σ_{yo}. A virtual distance, x_y, can then be found that will give this standard deviation. This is just the distance that will yield the appropriate value for σ_y from Figure 3-2. Values of x_y will vary with stability. Then equations for point sources may be used, determining σ_y as a function of $x + x_y$, a slight variation of the suggestion by Holland (1953). This procedure treats the area source as a cross-wind line source with a normal distribution, a fairly good approximation for the distribution across an area source. The initial standard deviation for a square area source can be approximated by $\sigma_{yo} \simeq s/4.3$, where s is the length of a side of the area (see problem 22).

If the emissions within an area are from varying effective stack heights, the variation may be approximated by using a σ_{zo}. Thus H would be the *mean* effective height of release and σ_{zo} the standard deviation of the initial vertical distribution of sources. A virtual distance, x_z, can be found, and point source equations used for estimating concentrations, determining σ_z as a function of $x + x_z$.

TOPOGRAPHY

Under conditions of irregular topography the direct application of a standard dispersion equation is often invalid. In some situations the best one may be able to do without the benefit of *in situ* experiments is to estimate the upper limit of the concentrations likely to occur.

For example, to calculate concentrations on a hillside downwind from and facing the source and at about the effective source height, the equation for concentrations at ground-level from a ground-level source (Eq. 3.4) will yield the highest expected concentrations. This would closely approximate the situation under stable conditions, when the pollutant plume would be most likely to encounter the hillside. Under unstable conditions the flow is more likely to rise over the hill (see problem 21).

With downslope flow when the receptor is at a lower elevation than the source, a likely assumption is that the flow parallels the slope; i.e., no allowance is made for the difference between ground-level elevations at the source and at the receptor.

Where a steep ridge or bluff restricts the horizontal dispersion, the flow is likely to be parallel to such a bluff. An assumption of complete reflection at the bluff, similar to eddy reflection at the ground from an elevated source, is in order. This may be accomplished by using:

$$\chi(x,y,0;H) = \frac{Q}{\pi \, \sigma_y \, \sigma_z \, u} \left\{ \exp\left[-\frac{1}{2}\left(\frac{y}{\sigma_y}\right)^2\right] + \exp\left[-\frac{1}{2}\left(\frac{2\,B\text{-}y}{\sigma_y}\right)^2\right] \right\} \left\{ \exp\left[-\frac{1}{2}\left(\frac{H}{\sigma_z}\right)^2\right] \right\} \tag{5.16}$$

B is the distance from the x-axis to the restricting bluff, and the positive y axis is defined to be in the direction of the bluff.

The restriction of horizontal dispersion by valley sides is somewhat analogous to restriction of the vertical dispersion by a stable layer aloft. When the σ_y becomes great enough, the concentrations can be assumed to be uniform across the width of the valley and the concentration calculated according to the following equation, where in this case Y is the width of the valley.

$$\chi = \frac{2Q}{\sqrt{2\pi} \, \sigma_z \, Y \, u} \exp\left[-\frac{1}{2}\left(\frac{H}{\sigma_z}\right)^2\right] \tag{5.17}$$

LINE SOURCES

Concentrations downwind of a continuously emitting infinite line source, when the wind direction is normal to the line, can be expressed by rewriting equation (12) p. 154 of Sutton (1932):

$$\chi(x,y,0;H) = \frac{2\,q}{\sqrt{2\pi} \, \sigma_z \, u} \exp\left[-\frac{1}{2}\left(\frac{H}{\sigma_z}\right)^2\right] \tag{5.18}$$

Here q is the source strength per unit distance, for example, g sec^{-1} m^{-1}. Note that the horizontal dispersion parameter, σ_y, does not appear in this equation, since it is assumed that lateral dispersion from one segment of the line is compensated by dispersion in the opposite direction from adjacent segments. Also y does not appear, since concentration at a given x is the same for any value of y (see problem 23).

Concentrations from infinite line sources when the wind is not perpendicular to the line can be approximated. If the angle between the wind direction and line source is ø, the equation for concentration downwind of the line source is:

$$\chi(x,y,0;H) = \frac{2\,q}{\sin\phi \, \sqrt{2\pi} \, \sigma_z \, u} \exp\left[-\frac{1}{2}\left(\frac{H}{\sigma_z}\right)^2\right] \tag{5.19}$$

This equation should not be used where ø is less than 45°.

When estimating concentrations from finite line sources, one must account for "edge effects" caused by the end of the line source. These effects will of course extend to greater cross-wind distances as the distance from the source increases. For concentrations from a finite line source oriented cross-wind, define the x-axis in the direction of the mean wind and passing through the receptor of interest. The limits of the line source can be defined as extending from y_1 to y_2 where y_1 is less than y_2. The equation for concentration (from Sutton's (1932) equation (11), p. 154), is:

$$\chi(x,0,0;H) = \frac{2\ q}{\sqrt{2\pi}\ \sigma_z\ u}\ \exp\left[-\frac{1}{2}\left(\frac{H}{\sigma_z}\right)^2\right]$$

$$\int_{p_1}^{p_2} \frac{1}{\sqrt{2\pi}}\ \exp(-0.5\ p^2)\ dp \qquad (5.20)$$

$$\text{where}\ p_1 = \frac{y_1}{\sigma_y},\ p_2 = \frac{y_2}{\sigma_y}$$

The value of the integral can be determined from tabulations given in most statistical tables (for example, see Burrington (1953), pp. 273-276; also see problem 24).

INSTANTANEOUS SOURCES

Thus far we have considered only sources that were emitting continuously or for time periods equal to or greater than the travel times from the source to the point of interest. Cases of instantaneous release, as from an explosion, or short-term releases on the order of seconds, are often of practical concern. To determine concentrations at any position downwind, one must consider the time interval after the time of release and diffusion in the downwind direction as well as lateral and vertical diffusion. Of considerable importance, but very difficult, is the determination of the path or trajectory of the "puff." This is most important if concentrations are to be determined at specific points. Determining the trajectory is of less importance if knowledge of the magnitude of the concentrations for particular downwind distances or travel times is required without the need to know exactly at what points these concentrations occur. Rewriting Sutton's (1932) equation (13), p. 155, results in an equation that may be used for estimates of concentration downwind from a release from height, H:

$$\chi(x,y,0;H) = \frac{2\ Q_T}{(2\pi)^{3/2}\ \sigma_x\ \sigma_y\ \sigma_z}\ \exp\left[-\frac{1}{2}\right.$$

$$\left(\frac{x-ut}{\sigma_x}\right)^2\right]\ \exp\left[-\frac{1}{2}\left(\frac{H}{\sigma_z}\right)^2\right]$$

$$\exp\left[-\frac{1}{2}\left(\frac{y}{\sigma_y}\right)^2\right] \qquad (5.21)$$

(The numerical value of $(2\pi)^{3/2}$ is 15.75.)

The symbols have the usual meaning, with the important exceptions that Q_T represents the *total mass* of the release and the σ's are *not* those evaluated with respect to the dispersion of a continuous source at a fixed point in space.

In Eq. (5.21) the σ's refer to dispersion statistics following the motion of the expanding puff. The σ_x is the standard deviation of the concentration distribution in the puff in the downwind direction, and t is the time after release. Note that there is no dilution in the downwind direction by wind speed. The speed of the wind mainly serves to give the downwind position of the center of the puff, as shown by examination of the exponential involving σ_x. Wind speed may influence the dispersion indirectly because the dispersion parameters σ_x, σ_y, and σ_z may be functions of wind speed. The σ_y's and σ_z's for an instantaneous source are less than those for a few minutes given in Figure 3-2 and 3-3. Slade (1965) has suggested values for a σ_y and σ_z for quasi-instantaneous sources. These are given in Table 5-2. The problem remains to make best estimates of σ_x. Much less is known of diffusion in the downwind direction than is known of lateral and vertical dispersion. In general one should expect the σ_x value to be about the same as σ_y. Initial dimensions of the puff, i.e., from an explosion, may be approximated by finding a virtual distance to give the appropriate initial standard deviation for each direction. Then σ_y will be determined as a function of $x + x_y$, σ_z as a function of $x + x_z$, and σ_x as a function of $x + x_x$.

Table 5-2   ESTIMATION OF DISPERSION PARAMETERS FOR QUASI-INSTANTANEOUS SOURCES (FROM SLADE, 1965)

	x = 100 m		x = 4 km	
	σ_y	σ_z	σ_y	σ_z
Unstable	10	15	300	220
Neutral	4	3.8	120	50
Very Stable	1.3	0.75	35	7

REFERENCES

Bierly, E. W., and E. W. Hewson, 1962: Some restrictive meteorological conditions to be considered in the design of stacks. J. Appl. Meteorol., *1*, 3, 383-390.

Burington, R. S., 1953: Handbook of Mathematical Tables and Formulas. Sandusky, Ohio, Handbook Publishers, 296 pp.

Cramer, H. E., 1959: Engineering estimates of atmospheric dispersal capacity. Amer. Ind. Hyg. Assoc. J., *20*, 3, 183-189.

Gifford, F. A., 1959: Computation of pollution from several sources. Int. J. Air Poll., 2, 109-110.

Gifford, F. A., 1960a: Atmospheric dispersion calculations using the generalized Gaussian plume model. Nuclear Safety, 2, 2, 56-59, 67-68.

Gifford, F. A., 1960b: Peak to average concentration ratios according to a fluctuating plume dispersion model. Int. J. Air Poll., 3, 4, 253-260.

Hewson, E. W., and G. C. Gill, 1944: Meteorological investigations in Columbia River Valley near Trail, B. C., pp 23-228 in Report submitted to the Trail Smelter Arbitral Tribunal by R. S. Dean and R. E. Swain, Bur. of Mines Bull 453, Washington, Govt. Print. Off., 304 pp.

Hewson, E. W., 1945: The meteorological control of atmospheric pollution by heavy industry. Quart. J. R. Meteorol. Soc., 71, 266-282.

Hewson, E. W., 1955: Stack heights required to minimize ground concentrations. Trans. ASME 77, 1163-1172.

Holland, J. Z., 1953: A meteorological survey of the Oak Ridge area, p. 540. Atomic Energy Comm., Report ORO-99, Washington, D. C., 584 pp.

Nonhebel, G., 1960: Recommendations on heights for new industrial chimneys. J. Inst. Fuel, 33, 479-513.

Pooler, F., 1965: Potential dispersion of plumes from large power plants. PHS Publ. No. 999-AP-16, 1965. 13 pp.

Singer, I. A., 1961: The relation between peak and mean concentrations. J. Air Poll. Cont. Assoc., 11, 336-341.

Singer, I. A., K. Imai, and R. G. Del Campos, 1963: Peak to mean pollutant concentration ratios for various terrain and vegetation cover. J. Air Poll. Cont. Assoc., 13, 40-42.

Slade, D. H., 1965: Dispersion estimates from pollutant releases of a few seconds to 8 hours in duration. Unpublished Weather Bureau Report. Aug. 1965.

Stewart, N. G., H. J. Gale, and R. N. Crooks, 1958: The atmospheric diffusion of gases discharged from the chimney of the Harwell Reactor BEPO. Int. J. Air Poll., 1, 87-102.

Sutton, O. G., 1932: A theory of eddy diffusion in the atmosphere. Proc. Roy. Soc. London, A, 135, 143-165.

Taylor, G. I., 1915: Eddy motion in the atmosphere. Phil. Trans. Roy. Soc., A, 215, 1-26.

Chapter 6 — RELATION TO OTHER DIFFUSION EQUATIONS

Most other widely used diffusion equations are variant forms of the ones presented here. With respect to ground-level concentrations from an elevated source (Eq. 3.2):

$$\chi(x,y,0;H) = \frac{Q}{\pi\,\sigma_y\,\sigma_z\,u}\,\exp\left[-\frac{1}{2}\left(\frac{y}{\sigma_y}\right)^2\right]$$

$$\exp\left[-\frac{1}{2}\left(\frac{H}{\sigma_z}\right)^2\right] \tag{3.2}$$

Other well-known equations can be compared:

Bosanquet and Pearson (1936):

$$\chi(x,y,0;H) = \frac{Q}{\sqrt{2\pi}\,pq\,x^2\,u}\,\exp\left[-\frac{1}{2}\right.$$

$$\left(\frac{y}{qx}\right)^2\right]\,\exp\left[-\frac{H}{px}\right] \tag{6.1}$$

where p and q are dimensionless diffusion coefficients.

Sutton (1947):

$$\chi(x,y,0;H) = \frac{2\,Q}{\pi\,C_y\,C_z\,x^{2-n}\,u}\,\exp\left[-\frac{1}{x^{2-n}}\right.$$

$$\left(\frac{y^2}{C_y{}^2} + \frac{H^2}{C_z{}^2}\right)\right] \tag{6.2}$$

where n is a dimensionless constant and C_y and C_z are diffusion coefficients in $m^{n/2}$.

Calder (1952):

$$\chi(x,y,0;H) = \frac{Q\,u}{2\,k^2\,a\,v_x{}^2\,x^2}\,\exp\left[-\frac{u}{k\,v_x\,x}\right.$$

$$\left(\frac{y}{a} + H\right)\right] \tag{6.3}$$

where $a = \dfrac{v'}{w'}$, the ratio of horizontal eddy velocity to vertical eddy velocity, k is von Karman's constant approximately equal to 0.4, and $v_x = \dfrac{k\,u}{\ln\left(\dfrac{H}{z_0}\right)}$ where z_0 is a roughness parameter, m.

NOTE: Calder wrote the equation for the concentration at (x, y, z) from a ground-level source. For Eq. (6.3) it is assumed that the concentration at ground level from an elevated source is the same as the concentraton at an elevated point from a ground-level source.

Table 6-1 lists the expressions used in these equations that are equivalent to σ_y and σ_z (continuous source) in this paper.

Table 6-1   EXPRESSIONS EQUIVALENT TO σ_y AND σ_z IN VARIOUS DIFFUSION EQUATIONS.

Equation	σ_y	σ_z
Bosanquet and Pearson	$q\,x$	$\sqrt{2}\,p\,x$
Sutton	$\dfrac{1}{\sqrt{2}}\,C_y\,x^{\frac{2-n}{2}}$	$\dfrac{1}{\sqrt{2}}\,C_z\,x^{\frac{2-n}{2}}$
Calder	$\dfrac{\sqrt{2}\,a\,k\,v_x\,x}{u}$	$\dfrac{\sqrt{2}\,k\,v_x\,x}{u}$

REFERENCES

Bosanquet, C. H., and J. L. Pearson, 1936: The spread of smoke and gases from chimneys. Trans. Faraday Soc., 32, 1249-1263.

Calder, K. L., 1952: Some recent British work on the problem of diffusion in the lower atmosphere, 787-792 in *Air Pollution*, Proc. U. S. Tech. Conf. Air Poll., New York, McGraw-Hill, 847 pp.

Sutton, O. G., 1947: The problem of diffusion in the lower atmosphere. Quart. J. Roy. Met Soc., 73, 257-281.

Chapter 7 — EXAMPLE PROBLEMS

The following 26 example problems and their solutions illustrate the application of most of the techniques and equations presented in this workbook.

PROBLEM 1: It is estimated that a burning dump emits 3 g sec^{-1} of oxides of nitrogen. What is the concentration of oxides of nitrogen, averaged over approximately 10 minutes, from this source directly downwind at a distance of 3 km on an overcast night with wind speed of 7 m sec^{-1}? Assume this dump to be a point ground-level source with no effective rise.

SOLUTION: Overcast conditions with a wind speed of 7 m sec^{-1} indicate that stability class D is most applicable (Statement, bottom of Table 3-1). For x = 3 km and stability D, $\sigma_y = 190$ m from Figure 3-2 and $\sigma_z = 65$ m from Figure 3-3. Eq. (3.4) for estimation of concentrations directly downwind (y = 0) from a ground-level source is applicable:

$$\chi (x,0,0;0) = \frac{Q}{\pi \sigma_y \sigma_z u} = \frac{3}{\pi \, 190 \, (65) \, 7}$$

= 1.1 x 10^{-5} g m^{-3} of oxides of nitrogen.

PROBLEM 2: It is estimated that 80 g sec^{-1} of sulfur dioxide is being emitted from a petroleum refinery from an average effective height of 60 meters. At 0800 on an overcast winter morning with the surface wind 6 m sec^{-1}, what is the ground-level concentration directly downwind from the refinery at a distance of 500 meters?

SOLUTION: For overcast conditions, D class stability applies. With D stability at x = 500 m, $\sigma_y = 36$ m, $\sigma_z = 18.5$ m. Using Eq. (3.3):

$$\chi (x,0,0;H) = \frac{Q}{\pi \sigma_y \sigma_z u} \exp \left[-\frac{1}{2} \left(\frac{H}{\sigma_z} \right)^2 \right]$$

$$= \frac{80}{\pi \, 36 \, (18.5) \, 6} \exp [-0.5 \, (60/18.5)^2]$$

$$= 6.37 \times 10^{-3} \exp [-0.5 \, (3.24)^2]$$

The exponential is solved using Table A-1 (Appendix 3).

$$= 6.37 \times 10^{-3} \, (5.25 \times 10^{-3})$$
$$\chi = 3.3 \times 10^{-5} \text{ g } m^{-3} \text{ of } SO_2$$

PROBLEM 3: Under the conditions of problem 2, what is the concentration at the same distance downwind but at a distance 50 meters from the x-axis? That is: $\chi (500, 50, 0; 60) = ?$

SOLUTION: Using Eq. (3.2):

$$\chi (x,y,0;H) = \frac{Q}{\pi \sigma_y \sigma_z u} \exp \left[-\frac{1}{2} \left(\frac{y}{\sigma_y} \right)^2 \right]$$

$$\exp \left[-\frac{1}{2} \left(\frac{H}{\sigma_z} \right)^2 \right]$$

All but the exponential involving y has been found in the preceding problem. Therefore:

$$\chi (500, 50, 0; 60) = 3.3 \times 10^{-5}$$
$$\exp [-0.5 \, (50/36)^2]$$

$$= 3.3 \times 10^{-5} \, (0.381)$$

$$= 1.3 \times 10^{-5} \text{ g } m^{-3} \text{ of } SO_2$$

PROBLEM 4: A power plant burns 10 tons per hour of coal containing 3 percent sulfur; the effluent is released from a single stack. On a sunny summer afternoon the wind at 10 meters above ground is 4 m sec^{-1} from the northeast. The morning radiosonde taken at a nearby Weather Bureau station has indicated that a frontal inversion aloft will limit the vertical mixing to 1500 meters. The 1200-meter wind is from 30° at 5 m sec^{-1}. The effective height of emission is 150 meters. From Figure 3-9, what is the distance to the maximum ground-level concentration and what is the concentration at this point?

SOLUTION: To determine the source strength, the amount of sulfur burned is: 10 tons hr^{-1} x 2000 lb ton^{-1} x 0.03 sulfur = 600 lb sulfur hr^{-1}. Sulfur has a molecular weight of 32 and combines with O_2 with a molecular weight of 32; therefore for every mass unit of sulfur burned, there result two mass units of SO_2.

$$Q = \frac{64 \text{ (molecular weight of } SO_2)}{32 \text{ (molecular weight of sulfur)}}$$

$$\times \frac{600 \text{ lb } hr^{-1} \, (453.6 \text{ g } lb^{-1})}{3600 \text{ sec } hr^{-1}}$$

$$= 151 \text{ g } sec^{-1} \text{ of } SO_2$$

On a sunny summer afternoon the insolation should be strong. From Table 3-1, strong insolation and 4m sec^{-1} winds yield class-B stability. From Figure 3-9, the distance to the point of maximum concentration is 1 km for class-B stability and effective height of 150 meters. From Figure 3-3 at this distance $\sigma_z = 110$ m. This is much less than 0.47 L. Therefore, at this distance, the limit of mixing of 1500 meters will not affect the ground-level concentration. From Figure 3-9, the maximum $\chi u/Q$ for B stability and this effective height of 150 m is 7.5 x 10^{-6}.

$$\chi_{max} = \frac{\chi u}{Q_{max}} \frac{Q}{u} = \frac{7.5 \times 10^{-6} \times 151}{4}$$

$$= 2.8 \times 10^{-4} \text{ g } m^{-3} \text{ of } SO_2$$

PROBLEM 5: For the power plant in problem 4, at what distance does the maximum ground-level concentration occur and what is this concentration on an overcast day with wind speed 4 m sec^{-1}?

SOLUTION: On an overcast day the stability class would be D. From Figure 3-9 for D stability and H of 150 m, the distance to the point of maximum ground-level concentration is 5.6 km, and the maximum $\chi u/Q$ is 3.0 x 10^{-6}.

$$\chi_{max} = \frac{3.0 \times 10^{-6} \times 151}{4}$$

$$= 1.1 \times 10^{-4} \text{ g m}^{-3}$$

PROBLEM 6: For the conditions given in problem 4, draw a graph of ground-level centerline sulfur dioxide concentration with distance from 100 meters to 100 km. Use log-log graph paper.

SOLUTION: The frontal inversion limits the mixing to L = 1500 meters. The distance at which $\sigma_z = 0.47$ L = 705 m is x_L = 5.5 km. At distances less than this, Eq. (3.3) is used to calculate concentrations:

$$\chi (x,0,0;H) = \frac{Q}{\pi \sigma_y \sigma_z u} \exp \left[-\frac{1}{2} \left(\frac{H}{\sigma_z} \right)^2 \right]$$

At distance equal to or greater than $2 x_L$, which is 11 km, Eq. (3.5) is used:

$$\chi (x,0,0;H) = \frac{Q}{\sqrt{2\pi} \sigma_y L u}$$

Solutions for the equations are given in Table 7-1. The values of concentration are plotted against distance in Figure 7-1.

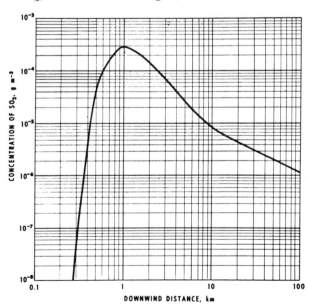

Figure 7-1. Concentration as a function of downwind distance (Problem 6).

Table 7-1   CALCULATION OF CONCENTRATIONS FOR VARIOUS DISTANCES (PROBLEM 6)

x, km	u, m sec^{-1}	σ_y, m	σ_z, m	H/σ_z	$\exp\left[-\frac{1}{2}(H/\sigma_z)^2\right]$	χ, g m^{-3}
0.3	4	52	30	5.0	3.73 x 10^{-6}	2.9 x 10^{-8}
0.5	4	83	51	2.94	1.33 x 10^{-2}	3.8 x 10^{-5}
0.8	4	129	85	1.77	0.209	2.3 x 10^{-4}
1.0	4	157	110	1.36	0.397	2.8 x 10^{-4}
2.0	4	295	230	0.65	0.810	1.4 x 10^{-4}
3.0	4	425	365	0.41	0.919	7.1 x 10^{-5}
5.5	4.5	720	705	0.21	0.978	2.1 x 10^{-5}

x, km	u, m sec^{-1}	σ_y, m	L, m	χ, g m^{-3}
11.0	4.5	1300	1500	6.9 x 10^{-6}
30	4.5	3000	1500	3.0 x 10^{-6}
100	4.5	8200	1500	1.1 x 10^{-6}

PROBLEM 7: For the conditions given in problem 4, draw a graph of ground-level concentration versus crosswind distance at a downwind distance of 1 km.

SOLUTION: From problem 4 the ground-level centerline concentration at 1 km is 2.8 x 10^{-4} g m^{-3}. To determine the concentrations at distances y from the x-axis, the ground-level centerline concentration must be multiplied by the factor $\exp \left[-\frac{1}{2} \left(\frac{y}{\sigma_y} \right)^2 \right]$

σ_y = 157 meters at x = 1 km. Values for this computation are given in Table 7-2.

Table 7-2   DETERMINATION OF CROSSWIND CONCENTRATIONS (PROBLEM 7)

y, m	$\frac{y}{\sigma_y}$	$\exp\left[-\frac{1}{2}\left(\frac{y}{\sigma_y}\right)^2\right]$	χ (x,y,0)
± 100	0.64	0.815	2.3 x 10^{-4}
± 200	1.27	0.446	1.3 x 10^{-4}
± 300	1.91	0.161	4.5 x 10^{-5}
± 400	2.55	3.87 x 10^{-2}	1.1 x 10^{-5}
± 500	3.18	6.37 x 10^{-3}	1.8 x 10^{-6}

These concentrations are plotted in Figure 7-2.

PROBLEM 8: For the conditions given in problem 4, determine the position of the 10^{-5} g m^{-3} ground level isopleth, and determine its area.

SOLUTION: From the solution to problem 6, the graph (Figure 7-1) shows that the 10^{-5} g m^{-3} isopleth intersects the x-axis at approximately x = 350 meters and x = 8.6 kilometers.

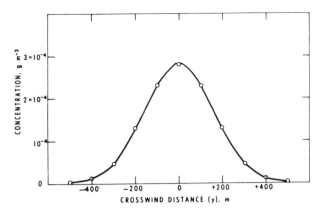

Figure 7-2. Concentration as a function of crosswind distance (Problem 7).

The values necessary to determine the isopleth half widths, y, are given in Table 7-3.

Table 7-3   DETERMINATION OF ISOPLETH WIDTHS (PROBLEM 8)

x, km	σ_y, m	χ (centerline), g m^{-3}	$\dfrac{\chi \text{ (isopleth)}}{\chi \text{ (centerline)}}$	y/σ_y	y, m
0.5	83	3.8×10^{-5}	0.263	1.64	136
0.8	129	2.3×10^{-4}	4.35×10^{-2}	2.50	323
1.0	157	2.8×10^{-4}	3.53×10^{-2}	2.59	407
2.0	295	1.4×10^{-4}	7.14×10^{-2}	2.30	679
3.0	425	7.1×10^{-5}	1.42×10^{-1}	1.98	842
4.0	540	4.0×10^{-5}	0.250	1.67	902
5.0	670	2.4×10^{-5}	0.417	1.32	884
6.0	780	1.8×10^{-5}	0.556	1.08	842
7.0	890	1.4×10^{-5}	0.714	0.82	730
8.0	980	1.1×10^{-5}	0.909	0.44	432

The orientation of the x-axis will be toward 225°. close to the source, curving more toward 210° to 215° azimuth at greater distances because of the change of wind direction with height. The isopleth is shown in Figure 7-3.

Since the isopleth approximates an ellipse, the area may be estimated by π ab where a is the semimajor axis and b is the semiminor axis.

$$a = \frac{8600 - 350}{2} = 4125 \text{ m}$$

$$b = 902$$

$$A \text{ (m}^2) = \pi \, (4125) \, (902)$$

$$= 11.7 \times 10^6 \text{ m}^2$$

or A = 11.7 km^2

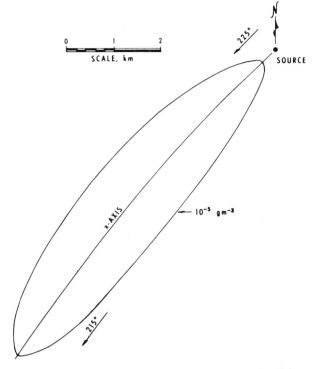

Figure 7-3. Location of the 10^{-5} g m^{-3} ground-level isopleth (Problem 8).

PROBLEM 9: For the conditions given in problem 4, determine the profile of concentration with height from ground level to z = 450 meters at x = 1 km, y = 0 meters, and draw a graph of concentration against height above ground.

SOLUTION: Eq. (3.1) is used to solve this problem. The exponential involving y is equal to 1. At x = 1 km, σ_y = 157 m, σ_z = 110 m. (From problem 4).

$$\frac{Q}{2\pi \, \sigma_y \, \sigma_z \, u} = \frac{151}{2\pi \, 157 \, (110) \, 4} = 3.5 \times 10^{-5} \text{ g m}^{-3}$$

Values for the estimation of $\chi(z)$ are given in Table 7-4.

PROBLEM 10: For the conditions given in problem 4, determine the distance at which the ground-level centerline concentration equals the centerline concentration at 150 meters above ground. Verify by computation of χ (x,0,0) and χ (x,0,150).

SOLUTION: The distance at which concentrations at the ground and at plume height are equal should occur where σ_z = 0.91 H (See Chapter 5). For B stability and H = 150 m, σ_z = 0.91 (150) = 136 m occurs at x = 1.2 km. At this distance σ_y = 181 m.

Table 7-4 DETERMINATION OF CONCENTRATIONS FOR VARIOUS HEIGHTS (PROBLEM 9)

a. z, m	b. $\frac{z \cdot H}{\sigma_z}$	c. $\exp\left[-\frac{1}{2}\left(\frac{z \cdot H}{\sigma_z}\right)^2\right]$	d. $\frac{z+H}{\sigma_z}$	e. $\exp\left[-\frac{1}{2}\left(\frac{z+H}{\sigma_z}\right)^2\right]$	f. c. + e.	g. $\chi^{(z)}$, g m^{-3}
0	—1.36	0.397	1.36	0.397	0.794	2.78 x 10^{-4}
30	—1.09	0.552	1.64	0.261	0.813	2.85 x 10^{-4}
60	—0.82	0.714	1.91	0.161	0.875	3.06 x 10^{-4}
90	—0.55	0.860	2.18	0.0929	0.953	3.34 x 10^{-4}
120	—0.27	0.964	2.45	0.0497	1.014	3.55 x 10^{-4}
150	0.0	1.0	2.73	0.0241	1.024	3.58 x 10^{-4}
180	0.27	0.964	3.00	1.11 x 10^{-2}	0.975	3.41 x 10^{-4}
210	0.55	0.860	3.27	4.77 x 10^{-3}	0.865	3.03 x 10^{-4}
240	0.82	0.714	3.54	1.90 x 10^{-3}	0.716	2.51 x 10^{-4}
270	1.09	0.552	3.82	6.78 x 10^{-4}	0.553	1.94 x 10^{-4}
300	1.36	0.397	4.09	2.33 x 10^{-4}	0.397	1.39 x 10^{-4}
330	1.64	0.261	4.36	7.45 x 10^{-5}	0.261	9.14 x 10^{-5}
360	1.91	0.161	4.64	2.11 x 10^{-5}	0.161	5.64 x 10^{-5}
390	2.18	0.0929	4.91	5.82 x 10^{-6}	0.093	3.26 x 10^{-5}
420	2.45	0.0497	5.18	1.49 x 10^{-6}	0.050	1.75 x 10^{-5}
450	2.73	0.0241	5.45	3.55 x 10^{-7}	0.024	8.40 x 10^{-6}

These values are plotted in Figure 7-4.

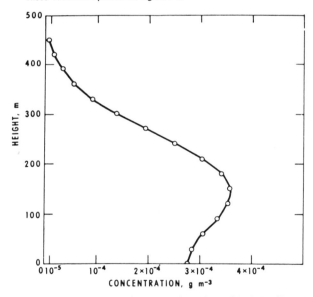

Figure 7-4. Concentration as a function of height (Problem 9).

Verifying:

$$\chi(x,0,0) = \frac{Q}{\pi\,\sigma_y\,\sigma_z\,u}\exp\left[-\frac{1}{2}\left(\frac{H}{\sigma_z}\right)^2\right]$$

$$= \frac{151}{\pi\,181\,(136)\,4}\exp\left[-\frac{1}{2}\left(\frac{150}{136}\right)^2\right]$$

$$= 4.88 \times 10^{-4}\exp\left[-\tfrac{1}{2}\,(1.10)^2\right]$$

$$= 4.88 \times 10^{-4}\,(0.546)$$

$$= 2.7 \times 10^{-4}\text{ g m}^{-3}$$

$$\chi(x,0,150) = \frac{Q}{2\pi\,\sigma_y\,\sigma_z\,u}\left\{\exp\left[-\frac{1}{2}\left(\frac{z-H}{\sigma_z}\right)^2\right]\right.$$

$$\left. + \exp\left[-\frac{1}{2}\left(\frac{z+H}{\sigma_z}\right)^2\right]\right\}$$

$$= \frac{151}{2\pi\,181\,(136)\,4}\left\{\exp\left[-\frac{1}{2}\left(\frac{0}{136}\right)^2\right]\right.$$

$$\left. + \exp\left[-\frac{1}{2}\left(\frac{300}{136}\right)^2\right]\right\}$$

$$= 2.44 \times 10^{-4}\left\{1.0 + \exp\left[-\frac{1}{2}\,(2.21)^2\right]\right\}$$

$$= 2.44 \times 10^{-4}\,(1.0 + 8.70 \times 10^{-2})$$

$$= 2.44 \times 10^{-4}\,(1.087)$$

$$= 2.7 \times 10^{-4}\text{ g m}^{-3}$$

PROBLEM 11: For the power plant in problem 4, what will the maximum ground-level concentration be beneath the plume centerline and at what distance will it occur on a clear night with wind speed 4 m sec^{-1}?

SOLUTION: A clear night with wind speed 4 m sec^{-1} indicates E stability conditions. From Figure 3-9, the maximum concentration should occur at a distance of 13 km, and the maximum $\chi u/Q$ is 1.7 x 10^{-6}

$$\chi_{max} = \frac{\chi u}{Q} \times \frac{Q}{u} = \frac{1.7 \times 10^{-6} \times 151}{4}$$

$$= 6.4 \times 10^{-5}\text{ g m}^{-3}\text{ of SO}_2$$

PROBLEM 12: For the situation in problem 11, what would the fumigation concentration be the next morning at this point (x = 13 km) when superadiabatic lapse rates extend to include most of the plume and it is assumed that wind speed and direction remain unchanged?

SOLUTION: The concentration during fumigation conditions is given by Eq. (5.2) with the exponential involving y equal to 1. in this problem.

$$\chi_F(x,0,0;H) = \frac{Q}{\sqrt{2\pi}\,u\,\sigma_{yF}\,h_i}$$

For the stable conditions, which were assumed to be class E, at x = 13 km, σ_y = 520 m., and σ_z = 90 m. Using Eq. (5.3) to solve for h_i:
h_i = H + 2 σ_z = 150 + 2 (90) = 330 m.
From the horizontal spreading suggested by Eq. (5.4):

$$\sigma_{yF} = \sigma_y \text{ (stable)} + H/8 = 520 + 19 = 539$$

$$\chi_F = \frac{151}{\sqrt{2\pi}\ 4\ (539)\ 330}$$

$$= 8.5 \times 10^{-5} \text{ g m}^{-3} \text{ of SO}_2$$

Note that the fumigation concentrations under these conditions are about 1.3 times the maximum ground-level concentrations that occurred during the night (problem 11).

PROBLEM 13: An air sampling station is located at an azimuth of 203° from a cement plant at a distance of 1500 meters. The cement plant releases fine particulates (less than 15 microns diameter) at the rate of 750 pounds per hour from a 30-meter stack. What is the contribution from the cement plant to the total suspended particulate concentration at the sampling station when the wind is from 30° at 3 m sec⁻¹ on a clear day in the late fall at 1600?

SOLUTION: For this season and time of day the C class stability should apply. Since the sampling station is off the plume axis, the x and y distances can be calculated:

$$x = 1500 \cos 7° = 1489$$

$$y = 1500 \sin 7° = 183$$

The source strength is:

$$Q = 750 \text{ lb hr}^{-1} \times 0.126 \frac{\text{g sec}^{-1}}{\text{lb hr}^{-1}} = 94.5 \text{ g sec}^{-1}$$

At this distance, 1489 m, for stability C, $\sigma_y = 150$ m, $\sigma_z = 87$. The contribution to the concentration can be calculated from Eq. (3.2):

$$\chi (x,y,0;H) = \frac{Q}{\pi\ \sigma_y\ \sigma_z\ u} \exp\left[-\frac{1}{2}\left(\frac{y}{\sigma_y}\right)^2\right]$$

$$\exp\left[-\frac{1}{2}\left(\frac{H}{\sigma_z}\right)^2\right]$$

$$= \frac{94.5}{\pi\ 150\ (87)\ 3} \exp\left[-0.5\left(\frac{183}{150}\right)^2\right]$$

$$\exp\left[-0.5\left(\frac{30}{87}\right)^2\right]$$

$$= \frac{94.5}{1.23 \times 10^5} \quad \exp\left[-0.5\ (1.22)^2\right]$$

$$\exp\left[-0.5\ (0.345)^2\right]$$

$$= 7.68 \times 10^{-4}\ (0.475)\ (0.943)$$

$$= 3.4 \times 10^{-4} \text{ g m}^{-3}$$

PROBLEM 14: A proposed source is to emit 72 g sec⁻¹ of SO₂ from a stack 30 meters high with a diameter of 1.5 meters. The effluent gases are emitted at a temperature of 250°F (394°K) with an exit velocity of 13 m sec⁻¹. Plot on log-log paper a graph of maximum ground-level

concentration as a function of wind speed for stability classes B and D. Determine the critical wind speed for these stabilities, i.e., the wind speed that results in the highest concentrations. Assume that the design atmospheric pressure is 970 mb and the design ambient air temperature is 20°C (293°K).

SOLUTION: Using Holland's effective stack height equation:

$$\Delta H = \frac{v_s\ d}{u}\left[1.5 + 2.68 \times 10^{-3}\ p\ \frac{T_s - T_a}{T_s}\ d\right]$$

$$= \frac{13\ (1.5)}{u}\left[1.5 + 2.68 \times 10^{-3}\ (970)\right.$$

$$\left.\left(\frac{394 - 293}{394}\right)\ (1.5)\right]$$

$$= \frac{19.5}{u}\left[1.5 + 2.6\left(\frac{101}{394}\right)1.5\right]$$

$$= \frac{19.5}{u} \cdot [1.5 + 2.6\ (0.256)\ 1.5]$$

$$= \frac{19.5}{u}\ [1.5 + 1.0]$$

$$= \frac{19.5\ (2.5)}{u}$$

$$= \frac{48.8}{u}$$

The effective stack heights for various wind speeds and stabilities are summarized in Table 7-5.

Table 7-5   EFFECTIVE STACK HEIGHTS (PROBLEM 14)

u, m sec⁻¹	Class D ΔH, m	Class D h + ΔH, m	Class B 1.15 ΔH, m	Class B h + 1.15 ΔH, m
0.5	97.6	127.6	112.2	142.2
1.0	48.8	78.8	56.1	86.1
1.5	32.6	62.6	37.5	67.5
2	24.4	54.4	28.1	58.1
3	16.3	46.3	18.7	48.7
5	9.8	39.8	11.3	41.3
7	7.0	37.0	8.0	38.0
10	4.9	34.9		
20	2.4	32.4		

By use of the appropriate height, H, the maximum concentration for each wind speed and stability can be determined by obtaining the maximum $\chi u/Q$ as a function of H and stability from Figure 3-9 and multiplying by the appropriate Q/u. The computations are summarized in Table 7-6, and plotted in Figure 7-5.

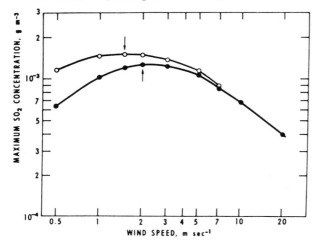

Figure 7-5. Maximum concentration as a function of wind speed (Problem 14).

Table 7-6   MAXIMUM CONCENTRATION AS A FUNCTION OF WIND SPEED (PROBLEM 14)

Stability Class	u, m sec^{-1}	H, m	$\chi u/Q_{max}$, m^{-2}	Q/u, g m^{-1}	χ_{max}, g m^{-3}
B	0.5	142.2	8.0 x 10^{-6}	144	1.15 x 10^{-3}
	1.0	86.1	2.0 x 10^{-5}	72	1.44 x 10^{-3}
	1.5	67.5	3.1 x 10^{-5}	48	1.49 x 10^{-3} ←
	2	58.1	4.1 x 10^{-5}	36	1.48 x 10^{-3}
	3	48.7	5.7 x 10^{-5}	24	1.37 x 10^{-3}
	5	41.3	7.8 x 10^{-5}	14.4	1.12 x 10^{-3}
	7	38.0	8.7 x 10^{-5}	10.3	8.96 x 10^{-4}
D	0.5	127.6	4.4 x 10^{-6}	144	6.34 x 10^{-4}
	1.0	78.8	1.42x10^{-5}	72	1.02 x 10^{-3}
	1.5	62.6	2.47x10^{-5}	48	1.19 x 10^{-3}
	2	54.4	3.5 x 10^{-5}	36	1.26 x 10^{-3} ←
	3	46.3	5.1 x 10^{-5}	24	1.22 x 10^{-3}
	5	39.8	7.3 x 10^{-5}	14.4	1.05 x 10^{-3}
	7	37.0	8.2 x 10^{-5}	10.3	8.45 x 10^{-4}
	10	34.9	9.4 x 10^{-5}	7.2	6.77 x 10^{-4}
	20	32.4	1.1 x 10^{-4}	3.6	3.96 x 10^{-4}

The wind speeds that give the highest maximum concentrations for each stability are, from Figure 7-5: B 1.5, D 2.0.

PROBLEM 15: A proposed pulp processing plant is expected to emit ½ ton per day of hydrogen sulfide from a single stack. The company property extends a minimum of 1500 meters from the proposed location. The nearest receptor is a small town of 500 inhabitants 1700 meters northeast of the plant. Plant managers have decided that it is desirable to maintain concentrations below 20 ppb (parts per billion by volume), or approximately 2.9 x 10^{-5} g m^{-3}, for any period greater than 30 minutes. Wind direction frequencies indicate that winds blow from the proposed location toward this town between 10 and 15 per cent of the time. What height stack should be erected? It is assumed that a design wind speed of 2 m sec^{-1} will be sufficient, since the effective stack rise will be quite great with winds less than 2 m sec^{-1}. Other than this stipulation, assume that the physical stack height and effective stack height are the same, to incorporate a slight safety factor.

SOLUTION: The source strength is:

$$Q = \frac{1000 \text{ lb day}^{-1} \times 453.6 \text{ g lb}^{-1}}{86,400 \text{ sec day}^{-1}} = 5.25 \text{ g sec}^{-1}$$

From Eq. (4.2):

$$\sigma_y \sigma_z = \frac{0.117 \, Q}{\chi_d \, u} = \frac{0.117 \, (5.25)}{(2.9 \times 10^{-5}) \, 2}$$

$$= 1.06 \times 10^4 \text{ m}^2$$

At a design distance of 1500 meters (the limit of company property), $\sigma_y \sigma_z = 1.06 \times 10^4$ gives a point from Figure 4-1 about 0.2 from Class C to Class D along the line x = 1500 m. From Figure 3-3, $\sigma_z = 80$ for this stability. $H = \sqrt{2} \, \sigma_z = 113$ meters

PROBLEM 16:   In problem 15 assume that the stack diameter is to be 8 ft, the temperature of the effluent 250° F, and the stack gas velocity 45 ft sec^{-1}. From Holland's equation for effective stack height and the method used in problem 15, determine the physical stack height required to satisfy the conditions in problem 15. In estimating ΔH, use $T_a = 68°F$ and $p = 920$ mb.

SOLUTION: First determine the relation between ΔH and u from Holland's equation.

$v_s = 45 \text{ ft sec}^{-1} = 13.7 \text{ m sec}^{-1}$

$d = 8 \text{ ft} = 2.44 \text{ m}$

$T_s = 250°F = 121°C = 394°K$

$T_a = 68°F = 20°C = 293°K$

$p = 920 \text{ mb}$

$$\Delta H = \frac{v_s \, d}{u} \left[1.5 + 2.68 \times 10^{-3} \, p \, \frac{T_s - T_a}{T_s} \, d \right]$$

$$= \frac{13.7 \, (2.44)}{u} \left[1.5 + 2.68 \times 10^{-3} \, (920) \, \frac{394 - 293}{394} \, (2.44) \right]$$

$$= \frac{33.4}{u} [1.5 + (2.46)\ 0.256\ (2.44)]$$

$$= \frac{33.4}{u} (1.5 + 1.54)$$

$$\Delta H = \frac{102}{u}$$

The relation between $\sigma_y\ \sigma_z$ and u is:

$$\sigma_y\ \sigma_z = \frac{0.117\ Q}{\chi_d\ u} = \frac{0.117\ (5.25)}{2.9 \times 10^{-5}\ u} = \frac{2.12 \times 10^4}{u}$$

The required computations using Figure 4-1 are summarized in Table 7-7:

Table 7-7   REQUIRED PHYSICAL STACK HEIGHT AS A FUNCTION OF WIND SPEED (PROBLEM 16)

u, m sec^{-1}	ΔH, m	$\sigma_y\ \sigma_z$, m^2	Stability to Give $\sigma_y\ \sigma_z$ at 1500 m	σ_z, m	$H' = \sqrt{2}\ \sigma_z$, m	$h = H'-\Delta H$, m
0.5	204	4.24 x 10^4	0.9 from A to B	190	269	65
1.0	102	2.12 x 10^4	0.6 from B to C	120	170	68
1.5	68	1.41 x 10^4	0.9 from B to C	96	136	68
2.0	51	1.06 x 10^4	0.2 from C to D	76	108	57
2.5	41	8.48 x 10^3	0.4 from C to D	64	91	50
3.0	34	7.06 x 10^3	0.6 from C to D	56	79	45
5.0	20	4.24 x 10^3	D	42	60	40
7.0	15	3.03 x 10^3	0.5 from D to E	34	48	33
10.0	10	2.12 x 10^3	E	28	40	30
15.0	7	1.41 x 10^3	0.5 from E to F	23	33	26

The required physical height is 68 meters.

PROBLEM 17:   A dispersion study is being made over relatively open terrain with fluorescent particles whose size yields 1.8×10^{10} particles per gram of tracer. Sampling is by membrane filters through which 9×10^{-3} m^3 of air is drawn each minute. A study involving a 1-hour release, which can be considered from ground-level, is to take place during conditions forecast to be slightly unstable with winds 5 m sec^{-1}. It is desirable to obtain a particle count of at least 20 particles upon membrane filters located at ground-level 2.0 km from the plume centerline on the sampling arc 8 km from the source. What should the total release be, in grams, for this run?

SOLUTION: The total dosage at the sampler is determined by the total sample in grams divided by the sampling rate:

$$D_T\ (g\ sec\ m^{-3}) = \frac{20\ particles}{1.8 \times 10^{10}\ particles\ g^{-1}}$$

$$\frac{60\ sec\ min^{-1}}{9 \times 10^{-3}\ m^3\ min^{-1}}$$

$$= \frac{1200}{16.2 \times 10^7}$$

$$D_T = 7.41 \times 10^{-6}\ g\ sec\ m^{-3}$$

The total dosage is given in g sec m^{-3} from

$$D_T\ (x,y,0;0) = \frac{Q_T}{\pi\ u\ \sigma_y\ \sigma_z} \exp \left[-\frac{1}{2} \left(\frac{y}{\sigma_y} \right)^2 \right]$$

where Q_T is the total release in grams.

Therefore $Q_T = \dfrac{\pi\ u\ \sigma_y\ \sigma_z\ D_T}{\exp \left[-\dfrac{1}{2} \left(\dfrac{y}{\sigma_y} \right)^2 \right]}$

For slightly unstable conditions (Class C) at x = 8 km, σ_y = 690 m, σ_z = 310 m; y = 2000 m, u = 5 m sec^{-1}

$$Q_T = \frac{\pi\ 5\ (690)\ 310\ (7.41 \times 10^{-6})}{\exp \left[-\frac{1}{2} \left(\frac{2000}{690} \right)^2 \right]}$$

$$= \frac{24.9}{\exp [-0.5\ (2.90)^2]}$$

$$= \frac{24.9}{1.49 \times 10^{-2}}$$

$$Q_T = 1670\ g$$

No correction has been made for the facts that the release is for 1 hour and the standard deviations represent time periods of 3 to 15 minutes.

PROBLEM 18:   A release of 2 kg of fluorescent particles is made based on the results of the computation in problem 17. The conditions are class C stability and wind speed 5 m sec^{-1}. The crosswind-integrated ground-level dosage along the 8-km arc is determined from the samplers along this arc to be 8.2×10^{-1} g sec m^{-2}. What is the effective σ_z for this run?

SOLUTION: The crosswind-integrated dosage is given by:

$$D_{CWI} = \frac{2\ Q_T}{\sqrt{2\pi}\ \sigma_z\ u} \exp \left[-0.5 \left(\frac{H}{\sigma_z} \right)^2 \right]$$

Since the source is at ground-level, the exponential has a value of 1. Solving for σ_z:

$$\sigma_z = \frac{2\ Q_T}{\sqrt{2\pi}\ D_{CWI}\ u}$$

$$= \frac{2\ (2000)}{\sqrt{2\pi}\ (0.82)\ 5}$$

$$= \frac{4000}{10.28}$$

$$\sigma_z = 389\ m$$

PROBLEM 19:   At a point directly downwind from a ground-level source the 3- to 15-minute concentration is estimated to be 3.4×10^{-3} g m^{-3}. What would you estimate the 2-hour concentration to be at this point, assuming no change in stability or wind velocity?

SOLUTION: Using Eq. (5.12) and letting k = 3 min, s = 2 hours, and p = 0.2:

$$\chi_{\text{2 hour}} = \left(\frac{3}{120}\right)^{0.2} \quad 3.4 \times 10^{-3}$$

$$= \frac{1}{40^{0.2}} (3.4 \times 10^{-3})$$

$$= \frac{3.4 \times 10^{-3}}{2.09} = 1.6 \times 10^{-3} \text{ g m}^{-3}$$

Letting k 15 min, s = 2 hours, and p = 0.17

$$\chi_{\text{2 hour}} = \left(\frac{15}{120}\right)^{0.17} 3.4 \times 10^{-3}$$

$$= \frac{1}{8^{0.17}} (3.4 \times 10^{-3})$$

$$= \frac{3.4 \times 10^{-3}}{1.42} = 2.4 \times 10^{-3} \text{ g m}^{-3}$$

The 2-hour concentration is estimated to be between 1.6×10^{-3} and 2.4×10^{-3} g m^{-3}.

PROBLEM 20:   Two sources of SO_2 are shown as points A and B in Figure 7-6. On a sunny summer afternoon the surface wind is from 60° at 6 m sec^{-1}. Source A is a power plant emitting 1450 g sec^{-1} SO_2 from two stacks whose physical height is 120 meters and whose ΔH, from Holland's equation, is ΔH (m) = 538 (m^2 sec^{-1})/u (m sec^{-1}). Source B is a refinery emitting 126 g sec^{-1} SO_2 from an effective height of 60 meters. The wind measured at 160 meters on a nearby TV tower is from 70° at 8.5 m sec^{-1}. Assuming that the mean direction of travel of both plumes is 245°, and there are no other sources of SO_2, what is the concentration of SO_2 at the receptor shown in the figure?

SOLUTION: Calculate the effective height of Source A using the observed wind speed at 160 meters.

$$\Delta H = \frac{538}{8.5} = 63.3$$

$$H_A = 120 + 63 = 183 \text{ m}$$

$$Q_A = 1450 \text{ g sec}^{-1}$$

$$H_B = 60 \text{ m}$$

$$Q_B = 126 \text{ g sec}^{-1}$$

For a sunny summer afternoon with wind speed 6 m sec^{-1}, the stability class to be expected is C. The equation to be used is Eq. (3.2):

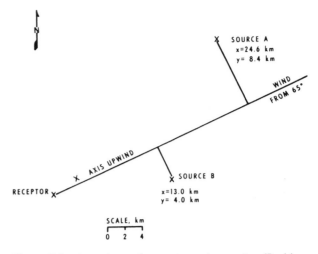

Figure 7-6.   Locations of sources and receptor (Problem 20).

$$\chi (x,y,0;H) = \frac{Q}{\pi \sigma_y \sigma_z u} \exp\left[-\frac{1}{2}\left(\frac{y}{\sigma_y}\right)^2\right]$$

$$\exp\left[-\frac{1}{2}\left(\frac{H}{\sigma_z}\right)^2\right]$$

For Source A, x = 24.6 km, y = 8.4 km

$\sigma_y = 1810$ m, $\sigma_z = 1120$ m, u = 8.5 m sec^{-1}

$$\chi_A = \frac{1450}{\pi \, 1810 \, (1120) \, 8.5} \exp\left[-0.5\right.$$

$$\left.\left(\frac{8400}{1810}\right)^2\right] \exp\left[-0.5 \left(\frac{183}{1120}\right)^2\right]$$

$$= \frac{1450}{5.42 \times 10^7} \exp[-0.5 \, (4.64)^2]$$

$$\exp[-0.5 \, (0.164)^2]$$

$$= 2.67 \times 10^{-5}) \, (2.11 \times 10^{-5}) \, (0.987) .$$

$$\chi_A = 5.6 \times 10^{-10} \text{ g m}^{-3}$$

For Source B, x = 13.0 km, y = 4.0 km.

$\sigma_y = 1050$ m, $\sigma_z = 640$ m, u = 7.0 m sec^{-1}

$$\chi_B = \frac{126}{\pi \, 1050 \, (640) \, 7} \exp\left[-0.5 \left(\frac{4000}{1050}\right)^2\right]$$

$$\exp\left[-0.5 \left(\frac{60}{640}\right)^2\right]$$

$$= \frac{126}{1.48 \times 10^7} \exp[-0.5 \, (3.81)^2]$$

$$\exp[-0.5 \, (0.0938)^2]$$

$$= 8.5 \times 10^{-6} \, (7.04 \times 10^{-4}) \, (0.996)$$

$$\chi_B = 6.0 \times 10^{-9} \text{ g m}^{-3}$$

$$\chi = \chi_A + \chi_B = 0.56 \times 10^{-9} + 6.0 \times 10^{-9}$$

$$= 6.6 \times 10^{-9} \text{ g m}^{-3}$$

PROBLEM 21: A stack 15 meters high emits 3 g sec^{-1} of a particular air pollutant. The surrounding terrain is relatively flat except for a rounded hill about 3 km to the northeast whose crest extends 15 meters above the stack top. What is the highest 3- to 15-minute concentration of this pollutant that can be expected on the facing slope of the hill on a clear night when the wind is blowing directly from the stack toward the hill at 4 m sec^{-1}? Assume that ΔH is less than 15 m. How much does the wind have to shift so that concentrations at this point drop below 10^{-7} g m^{-3}?

SOLUTION: A clear night with 4 m sec^{-1} indicates class E stability. Eq. (3.4) for ground-level concentrations from a ground-level source is most applicable (See Chapter 5). At 3 km for class E, $\sigma_y = 140$ m, $\sigma_z = 43$ m.

$$\chi = \frac{Q}{\pi \, \sigma_y \, \sigma_z \, u} = \frac{3}{\pi \, 140 \, (43) \, 4}$$

$$\chi = 3.97 \times 10^{-5} \text{ g m}^{-3}$$

To determine the crosswind distance from the plume centerline to produce a concentration of 10^{-7} g m^{-3} Eq. (3.8) is used:

$$y = \left[2 \ln \frac{\chi \, (x,0,0)}{\chi \, (x,y,0)} \right]^{1/2} \sigma_y$$

$$= \left[2 \ln \frac{3.97 \times 10^{-5}}{10^{-7}} \right]^{1/2} (140)$$

$$= (2 \ln 397)^{1/2} \, 140$$

$$= (2 \times 5.98)^{1/2} \, 140$$

$$= 3.46 \times 140$$

$$= 484 \text{ m.}$$

$$\tan \Theta = \frac{484}{3000} = 0.1614$$

$$\Theta = 9.2°$$

A wind shift of 9.2° is required to reduce the concentration to 10^{-7} g m^{-3}.

PROBLEM 22: An inventory of SO_2 emissions has been conducted in an urban area by square areas, 5000 ft (1524 meters) on a side. The emissions from one such area are estimated to be 6 g sec^{-1} for the entire area. This square is composed of residences and a few small commercial establishments. What is the concentration resulting from this area at the center of the adjacent square to the north when the wind is blowing from the south on a thinly overcast night with the wind at 2.5 m sec^{-1}? The average effective stack height of these sources is assumed to be 20 meters.

SOLUTION: A thinly overcast night with wind speed 2.5 m sec^{-1} indicates stability of class E.

(It may actually be more unstable, since this is in a built-up area.) To allow for the area source, let $\sigma_{y0} = 1524/4.3 = 354$. For class E the virtual distance, $x_y = 8.5$ km. For x = 1524 m, $\sigma_z = 28.5$. For x + x_y = 10,024 m, $\sigma_y = 410$ m.

$$\chi = \frac{Q}{\pi \, \sigma_y \, \sigma_z \, u} \exp \left[- \frac{1}{2} \left(\frac{H}{\sigma_z} \right)^2 \right]$$

$$= \frac{6}{\pi 410 \, (28.5) \, 2.5} \exp \left[- \frac{1}{2} \left(\frac{20}{28.5} \right)^2 \right]$$

$$= 6.54 \times 10^{-5} \, (0.783)$$

$$\chi = 5.1 \times 10^{-5} \text{ g m}^{-3}$$

PROBLEM 23: An estimate is required of the total hydrocarbon concentration 300 meters downwind of an expressway at 1730 on an overcast day with wind speed 4 m sec^{-1}. The expressway runs north-south and the wind is from the west. The measured traffic flow is 8000 vehicles per hour during this rush hour, and the average speed of the vehicles is 40 miles per hour. At this speed the average vehicle is expected to emit 2×10^{-2} g sec^{-1} of total hydrocarbons.

SOLUTION: The expressway may be considered as a continuous infinite line source. To obtain a source strength q in grams sec^{-1} m^{-1}, the number of vehicles per meter of highway must be calculated and multiplied by the emission per vehicle.

Vehicles/meter =

$$\frac{\text{Flow (vehicles hour}^{-1})}{\text{Average speed (miles hour}^{-1}) \, 1600 \, (\text{m mile}^{-1})}$$

$$= \frac{8000}{40 \times 1600} = 1.25 \times 10^{-1} \text{ (vehicles m}^{-1})$$

q = 1.25×10^{-1} (vehicles m^{-1}) $\times 2 \times 10^{-2}$ (g sec^{-1} vehicle^{-1})

q = 2.5×10^{-3} (g sec^{-1} m^{-1})

Under overcast conditions with wind speed 4 m sec^{-1} stability class D applies. Under D, at x = 300 meters, $\sigma_z = 12$ m. From Eq. (5.18):

$$\chi \, (300,0,0;0) = \frac{2q}{\sqrt{2\pi} \, \sigma_z \, u}$$

$$= \frac{2 \, (2.5 \times 10^{-3})}{2.507 \, (12) \, 4}$$

$$= 4.2 \times 10^{-5} \text{ g m}^{-3} \text{ of total hydrocarbons.}$$

PROBLEM 24: A line of burning agricultural waste can be considered a finite line source 150 m long. It is estimated that the total emission of organics is at a rate of 90 g sec^{-1}. What is the 3- to 15-minute concentration of organics at a distance of 400 m directly downwind from the center of the line when the wind is blowing at 3 m sec^{-1} perpendicular to the line? Assume that it is 1600 on a sunny fall afternoon. What is the concentration directly downwind from one end of the source?

SOLUTION: Late afternoon at this time of year implies slight insolation, which with 3 m sec^{-1} winds yields stability class C. For C stability at $x = 400$ m, $\sigma_y = 45$ m, $\sigma_z = 26$ m.

$$q = \frac{Q}{150} = \frac{90}{150} = 0.6 \text{ g sec}^{-1} \text{ m}^{-1}$$

Eq. (5.20) is appropriate.

$$\chi(x,0,0;0) = \frac{2q}{\sqrt{2\pi}\,\sigma_z\,u} \int_{p_1}^{p_2} \frac{1}{\sqrt{2\pi}}$$

$$\exp(-0.5\,p^2)\,dp$$

$$p_1 = \frac{y}{\sigma_y} = \frac{-75}{45} = -1.67, \quad p_2 = \frac{y}{\sigma_y} = \frac{75}{45}$$
$$= +1.67$$

$$\chi(400,0,0;0) = \frac{2(0.6)}{\sqrt{2\pi}(26)3} \int_{-1.67}^{+1.67} \frac{1}{\sqrt{2\pi}}$$

$$\exp(-0.5\,p^2)\,dp$$

$$= 6.14 \times 10^{-3}\,(0.91)$$

$$= 5.6 \times 10^{-3}\text{ g m}^{-3}$$

For a point downwind of one of the ends of the line:

$$p_1 = 0, \quad p_2 = \frac{y}{\sigma_y} = \frac{150}{45} = +3.33$$

$$\chi(400,0,0;0) = 6.14 \times 10^{-3} \int_{0}^{+3.33} \frac{1}{\sqrt{2\pi}}$$

$$\exp(-0.5\,p^2)\,dp$$

$$= 6.14 \times 10^{-3}\,(0.4995)$$

$$= 3.1 \times 10^{-3}\text{ g m}^{-3}$$

PROBLEM 25: A core melt-down of a power reactor that has been operating for over a year occurs at 0200, releasing 1.5×10^6 curies of activity (1 second after the accident) into the atmosphere of the containment vessel. This total activity can be expected to decay according to $\left(\dfrac{t}{t_0}\right)^{-0.2}$. It is estimated that about 5.3×10^4 curies of this activity is due to iodine-131, which has a half-life of 8.04 days. The reactor building is hemispherically shaped with a radius of 20 meters. Assume the leak rate of the building is 0.1% day^{-1}.

The accident has occurred on a relatively clear night with wind speed 2.5 m sec^{-1}. What is the concentration in the air 3 kilometers directly downwind from the source at 0400 due to all radioactive material? due to iodine-131?

SOLUTION: Source strength = leak rate x activity (corrected for decay)

$$\text{Leak rate} = \frac{0.001 \text{ day}^{-1}}{86400 \text{ sec day}^{-1}}$$

$$= 1.157 \times 10^{-8} \text{ sec}^{-1}$$

Source strength of all products

$$Q_A \text{ (curies sec}^{-1}) = 1.157 \times 10^{-8}\,(1.5 \times 10^6)$$

$$\left[\frac{t \text{ (sec)}}{t_0 \text{ (sec)}}\right]^{-0.2}$$

$$= 1.74 \times 10^{-2} \left(\frac{t}{1}\right)^{-0.2}$$

To determine decay of materials with the half-life given, multiply by $\exp\left(\dfrac{-0.693\,t}{L}\right)$ where t is time and L is half-life.

Source strength of I^{131}.

$$Q_I \text{ (curies sec}^{-1}) = 1.157 \times 10^{-8}\,(5.3 \times 10^4)\,\exp$$
$$\left(\frac{-0.693\,t}{L}\right)$$

For I_{131} $L = 6.95 \times 10^5$ sec

$$Q_I = 6.13 \times 10^{-4}\,\exp\left(\frac{-0.693\,t}{6.95 \times 10^5}\right)$$

For a clear night with wind speed 2.5 m sec^{-1}, class F applies. Approximate the spreading at the reactor shell by $2.15\,\sigma_{y0} = 2.15\,\sigma_{z0} =$ the radius of the shell = 20 m $\sigma_{y0} = \sigma_{z0} = 9.3$ m. The virtual distances to account for this are: $x_y = 250$ m, $x_z = 560$ m.

At $x = 3000$ m. $x + x_y = 3250$ m, $\sigma_y = 100$ m. $x + x_z = 3560$ m, $\sigma_z = 29$ m.

$$\chi(x,0,0;0) = \frac{Q}{\pi\,\sigma_y\,\sigma_z\,u} = \frac{Q}{\pi\,100\,(29)\,2.5}$$

$$= 4.4 \times 10^{-5}\,Q$$

For concentration at 0400, 3000 m downwind due to all radioactivity, $t = 7200$ seconds.

$$\chi_A = 4.4 \times 10^{-5}\,(1.74 \times 10^{-2})\,(7200)^{-0.2}$$
$$= 7.66 \times 10^{-7}\,(0.17)$$

$$\chi_A = 1.3 \times 10^{-7} \text{ curies m}^{-3}$$

The concentration at 0400, 3000 m downwind due to I^{131} is:

$$\chi_I = 4.4 \times 10^{-5}\,(6.13 \times 10^4)\,\exp\,[-0.997 \times 10^{-6}\,(7200)]$$

$= 2.7 \times 10^{-8}$ (1.0) The decay of I^{131} is insignificant for 2 hours

$\chi_I = 2.7 \times 10^{-8}$ curies m^{-3}

PROBLEM 26: A spill estimated at 2.9×10^6 grams of unsymmetrical dimethyl hydrazine occurs at 0300 on a clear night while a rocket is being fueled. A circular area 60 meters in diameter built around the launch pad is revetted into squares 20 feet on a side to confine to as small an area as possible any spilled toxic liquids. In this spill only one such 20- by 20-foot area is involved. At the current wind speed of 2 m sec^{-1}, it is estimated that the evaporation rate will be 1100 g sec^{-1}. The wind direction is predicted to be from $310° \pm 15°$ for the next hour. Table 7-8 gives the emergency tolerance limits for UDMH vapor.

Table 7-8   EMERGENCY TOLERANCE LIMITS FOR UDMH VAPOR VERSUS EXPOSURE TIME

Time, minutes	Emergency Tolerance Limits, g m^{-3}
5	1.2×10^{-1}
15	8.6×10^{-2}
30	4.9×10^{-2}
60	2.5×10^{-2}

What area should be evacuated?

SOLUTION: From Table 3-1, the stability class is determined to be Class F. This is not a point source but a small area source. Allowing 4.3 σ_{yO} to equal the width of the wetted area, 6.1 meters (20 feet), $\sigma_{yO} = 1.4$ meters. In attempting to determine the virtual distance, x_y, it is found to be less than 100 meters, and will be approximated by 40 meters. The release will take:

$$\frac{2.9 \times 10^6 \text{ g}}{1.1 \times 10^3 \text{ g sec}^{-1}} = 2.64 \times 10^3 \text{ sec} = 44 \text{ min.}$$

Therefore the concentration for an exposure time of 1 hour (2.5×10^{-2} g m^{-3}) is of main concern.

The equation for calculation of downwind concentrations is Eq. (3.4):

$$\chi (x,0,0;0) = \frac{Q}{\pi \, \sigma_y \, \sigma_z \, u} \text{ where } \sigma_y \text{ is a function of } x + x_y.$$

Values of the parameters and of χ are given in Table 7-9.

Table 7-9   DETERMINATION OF CONCENTRATION AS A FUNCTION OF DISTANCE (PROBLEM 26)

x, km	σ_z, m	$x + x_y$, km	σ_y, m	χ, g m^{-3}
0.1	2.3	0.14	5.5	13.9
0.3	5.6	0.34	12.5	2.5
0.6	9.7	0.64	22	8.2×10^{-1}
1	14	1.04	35	3.6×10^{-1}
3	27	3.04	93	7.0×10^{-2}
6	37	6.04	175	2.7×10^{-2}
10	47	10.04	275	1.4×10^{-2}

These values of χ are graphed as a function of x in Figure 7-7. The downwind concentration drops below the critical value of 2.5×10^{-2} at a distance of 6.5 km.

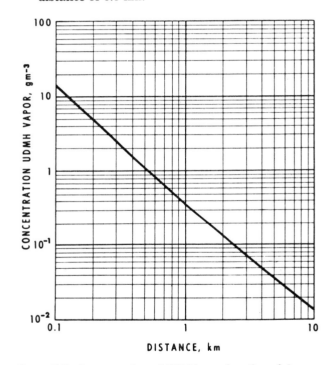

Figure 7-7. Concentration of UDMH as a function of downwind distance (Problem 26).

Calculated widths within a given isopleth are summarized in Table 7-10.

The maximum width of the area encompassed by an isopleth is about 140 meters from the downwind position. Since the wind direction is expected to be from $310° \pm 15°$, the sector at an azimuth of $115°$ to $145°$ plus a 140-meter rectangle on either side should be evacuated. See Figure 7-8.

Table 7-10   DETERMINATION OF WIDTHS WITHIN ISOPLETHS (PROBLEM 26)

x, km	x + x_y, km	σ_y, m	χ (centerline), g m⁻³	$\dfrac{\chi \text{ (isopleth)}}{\chi \text{ (centerline)}}$	$\dfrac{y}{\sigma_y}$	y, m
0.1	0.14	5.5	13.9	1.8×10^{-3}	3.55	20
0.5	0.54	19	1.1	2.27×10^{-2}	2.75	52
1.0	1.04	35	3.6×10^{-1}	6.94×10^{-2}	2.31	80
2.0	2.04	66	1.3×10^{-1}	1.92×10^{-1}	1.82	120
3.0	3.04	93	7.0×10^{-2}	3.57×10^{-1}	1.44	134
4.0	4.04	120	4.8×10^{-2}	5.20×10^{-1}	1.14	137
5.0	5.04	149	3.5×10^{-2}	7.14×10^{-1}	0.82	122
6.0	6.04	175	2.7×10^{-2}	9.26×10^{-1}	0.39	68

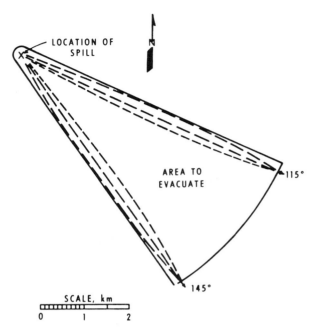

Figure 7-8. Possible positions of the 2.5×10^{-2} g m⁻³ isopleth and the evacuation area (Problem 26).

APPENDICES

Appendix 1: ABBREVIATIONS AND SYMBOLS

Abbreviations

cal   calorie
g   gram
°K   degrees Kelvin
m   meter
mb   millibar
sec   second

Symbols

a ratio of horizontal eddy velocity to vertical eddy velocity

c_p specific heat at constant pressure

C_y Sutton horizontal dispersion parameter

C_z Sutton vertical dispersion parameter

d inside stack diameter at stack top

$D_T(x,y,0;H)$ Total dosage

e 2.7183, the base of natural logarithms

$f(O,S,N)$ frequency of wind direction for a given stability and wind speed class

h physical stack height

h_i height of the base of an inversion

H effective height of emission

H_u effective height of emission for a particular wind speed

k von Karman's constant, approximately equal to 0.4

K eddy diffusivity

L two uses: 1. the height of an air layer that is relatively stable compared to the layer beneath it; a lid
     2. the half-life of a radioactive material

n Sutton's exponent

N an index for wind speed class

p three uses: 1. Bosanquet's horizontal dispersion parameter
     2. atmospheric pressure
     3. a dummy variable in the equation for a Gaussian distribution.

q two uses: 1. Bosanquet's vertical dispersion parameter
     2. emission rate per length of a line source

Q emission rate of a source

Q_T total emission during an entire release

R net rate of sensible heating of an air column by solar radiation

s the length of the edge of a square area source

S an index for stability

t_k a short time period

t_m time required for the mixing layer to develop from the top of the stack to the top of the plume

t_s a time period

T_a ambient air temperature

T_s stack gas temperature at stack top

u wind speed

u_N a mean wind speed for the wind speed class N.

v' horizontal eddy velocity

v_s stack gas velocity at the stack top

v_x a velocity used by Calder

w' vertical eddy velocity

x distance downwind in the direction of the mean wind

x_d design distance, a particular downwind distance used for design purposes

x_L the distance at which $\sigma_z = 0.47L$

x_x a virtual distance so that $\sigma_x(x_x)$ equals the initial standard deviation, σ_{xo}

x_y a virtual distance so that $\sigma_y(x_y)$ equals the initial standard deviation, σ_{yo}

x_z a virtual distance so that $\sigma_z(x_z)$ equals the initial standard deviation, σ_{zo}

y crosswind distance

z height above ground level

z_o roughness parameter

$\dfrac{\delta()}{\delta z}$ the rate of change of potential temperature with height

ΔH the rise of the plume centerline above the stack top

$()$ two uses: 1. wind direction azimuth or sector
     2. potential temperature

π 3.1416

ρ_A ambient air density

σ_A the standard deviation of azimuth (wind direction) as determined from a wind vane or bi-directional vane

σ_E the standard deviation of wind elevation angle as determined from a bi-directional vane

σ_x the standard deviation in the downwind direction of a puff concentration distribution

σ_{xo} an initial downwind standard deviation

σ_y the standard deviation in the crosswind direction of the plume concentration distribution

σ_{yo} an initial crosswind standard deviation

σ_z the standard deviation in the vertical of the plume concentration distribution

σ_{zL} an effective σ_z equal to 0.8 L

σ_{zo} an initial vertical standard deviation

σ_{zS} the vertical standard deviation of the plume concentration at a particular downwind distance for the stability, S.

ϕ the angle between the wind direction and a line source

χ concentration

χ_{CWI} crosswind-integrated concentration

χ_d a ground-level concentration for design purposes

χ_F inversion break-up fumigation concentration

χ_k concentration measured over a sampling time, t_k

χ_{max} maximum ground-level centerline concentration with respect to downwind distance

χ_s concentration measured over a sampling time, t_s

$\dfrac{\chi}{Q}$ relative concentration

$\dfrac{\chi u}{Q}$ relative concentration normalized for wind speed

$\chi\,(x,y,z;H)$ concentration at the point (x, y, z) from an elevated source with effective height, H.

$\chi\,(x,\Theta)$ the long-term average concentration at distance x, for a direction Θ from a source.

APPENDIX 6D: NEW YORK STATE DOT INTERIM LEAD ANALYSIS FOR HIGHWAY AIR QUALITY IMPACT ASSESSMENTS (DECEMBER 12, 1979)

On October 5, 1978, the EPA promulgated an ambient air quality standard for lead of 1.5 $\mu g/m^3$ averaged over a calendar quarter. Since vehicles which use leaded gasoline are a significant source of airborne lead, it is incumbent upon the NYSDOT to devise a procedure for the assessment of lead impacts. Unfortunately, there exists no readily available dispersion model designed for the calculation of an average three-month concentration of an air pollutant in the vicinity of a line source (such as a highway). However, by adapting available methods for the calculation of one-hour pollutant concentrations we can obtain a conservative estimate of the emission rates required to produce a violation of the ambient lead standard in the vicinity of a highway.

Currently available methods of modeling pollutant dispersion from line sources, such as HIWAY or CALINE-2, were designed to yield one-hour CO concentration estimates. In using these models to address lead impacts we are faced with two problems. One problem stems from the fact that lead is emitted in particulate form and these particulates have a settling velocity which is greater than the settling velocity of CO molecules. This problem can be dealt with by assuming that the settling velocity of lead particulates is negligible, (i.e., that the particulates will remain suspended and downwind concentrations will not be reduced through deposition). In this manner we can arrive at a conservative approximation of the dispersion mechanism.

The second problem to be faced in estimating lead concentrations for subsequent comparison with the ambient standard involves the averaging time. The CO models mentioned above were designed to yield a one-hour average concentration for a specified set of conditions (e.g., wind speed, wind direction, stability, receptor location, emission rate, etc.) which are assumed to remain constant for one hour. Since parameters such as wind speed and wind direction obviously do not remain constant for a calendar quarter, we can not apply models such as HIWAY or CALINE-2 directly to the problem of estimating a three-month average lead concentration in the vicinity of a highway. However, we can make some estimate of what the average one-hour concentration will be at a given receptor point.

Following this line of reasoning, we can proceed to select average parameters for wind speed, stability, mixing height, and emission rate in the hope of arriving at an unbiased estimate of the average one-hour lead concentration at a given receptor. However, the concept of applying an average condition in the calculation of an average one-hour concentration breaks down in the case of the wind direction parameter. The selection of any particular wind direction leads to a result in which downwind receptor locations exhibit inordinately high concentrations and upwind receptors exhibit zero (or some background) concentration. One method which could be used to overcome this problem would be to multiply the concentration calculated for the downwind receptor point under each specified wind direction by its average frequency of occurrence. However, this method would necessitate repetition of the dispersion calculation for all possible wind directions that would yield nonzero concentration estimates, and the subsequent summation of the results of each calculation. A less tedious, though less precise, ap-

1983 Lead Emissions from Various Roadway Types

Roadway Type	Lanes	Speed (mph)	ADT	Emission Rate (g/m-sec) $\times 10^{-5}$
Rural limited access	4	60	50,000	0.158
Residential	2	30	5,000	0.008
Urban expressway	6	48	118,000	0.268
City street	4	16	28,000	0.034
Urban expressway	6	38	108,000	0.189
City street	4	FTP	28,000	0.119
Acceleration ramp	1	0–60	24,300	3.01
Highway	8	60	80,000	

proach would be to assume that on the average winds will be neither parallel nor perpendicular to the highway and that the receptor will always be downwind from the highway. This last stipulation should cause our typical estimate to be higher than the true average one-hour concentration by a factor of two.

Thus, we can apply HIWAY as presented in *Volume 9** in an attempt to estimate the emission rate associated with a violation of the ambient lead standard using the following input parameters.

1. Constant wind/roadway angle of 45°.
2. Constant wind speed of 4 m/sec. (The annual average wind speed in New York State is approximately 4.4 m/sec.).
3. Constant D stability. (D or neutral stability is the most common the various stability categories.)
4. An initial σ_z of 5 m.
5. A straight highway of infinite length.
6. A source-receptor separation of 10 m.

Using figure 9d on page 68 of Volume 9, and solving for Q (emissions in g/m/sec) it is noted that a concentration of 1.5 μg/m^3 will be generated by an emission rate of 3×10^{-5} g/m-sec under the assumptions listed above, assuming a zero background concentration.

If we assume a background lead concentration of 0.5 μg/m^3, (the statewide annual arithmetic average lead concentration was approximately 0.2 μg/m^3 in 1976—according to the 1977 NYS

---

*EPA, Guidelines for Air Quality Maintenance Planning and Analysis, vol. 9 (revised), Evaluating Indirect Sources, EPA-450/4-78-001, September 1978.

Air Quality Report published by the New York State Department of Environmental Conservation), then the average lead emission rate expected to generate concentrations which might produce a violation of the standard under the conditions specified is 2×10^{-5} g/m-sec.

The EPA Guideline Series document, EPA-450/2-78-038, *Supplementary Guidelines for Lead Implementation Plans*, August 1978, lists the following projected emission rates for the year 1983 in Table 6, pages 149–152. Table 7, page 148 of this document indicates that vehicular lead emission rates will be markedly reduced in the years after 1983 (a date we consider to be a reasonable year of completion for any major highway project currently undergoing an air quality analysis). By 1987 lead emission rates will be on the order of one half the 1983 values presented below. (See also Attachment 6 of an FHWA Memorandum on this subject dated January 31, 1978 which illustrates the impact of the EPA's lead phase-out schedule.)

Comparing the 1983 emission rates listed above with the 2×10^{-5} g/m-sec value derived from the Volume 9 analysis, we note that only one of the highways listed above could be expected to generate a lead concentration approaching the ambient standard.

Therefore we propose not to undertake quantitative analyses of lead impacts for highway projects involving less than 50,000 AADT. This proposal is, we believe, consistent with a December 11, 1978 FHWA memorandum on the subject of highway lead impacts which states ". . . detailed analysis would not be warranted for low volume facilities." For highways with AADT's of greater than 50,000 we feel that an analysis of the type presented herein should suffice in most cases.

APPENDIX 6E: CONTENTS OF AIR QUALITY REPORTS

Project Description
Map showing location
SMSA?
Nature of Project, e.g., New ROW, Modification of existing Current and projected volumes
Alternatives to proposed activity
Unusual topographic features

Ambient Air Quality
Monitoring?
   If so
      when
      where
      how (instrument type, sampling frequency
        . . .)
      results
Future background concentrations
   1 hr. CO
   8 hr. CO
Method of projection

Microscale Analysis
Emission Calculation
   Specification of
      traffic volumes
      vehicle mix
      speed

      operating modes
      ambient temperature
      year of analysis
Dispersion Calculation for critical receptors
   Model used
   Receptor locations and how determined
   Wind direction
   Wind speed
   Stability
   Emission height
   Receptor height
   1 hr. results
   8 hr. results
   Comparison with standards

Lead Analysis

Mesoscale Analysis (Regional Emissions Burden)
Emissions Calculation Assumptions
CO
HC—6 a.m.–9 a.m. nonmethane
NO_x
Definition of analysis area
Analysis for year of completion

SIP Conformance

Construction Impacts

Discussion of Alternatives

Conclusions

APPENDIX 6F: PROJECT-LEVEL AIR QUALITY ANALYSES, A DISCUSSION PAPER*

FHWA BULLETIN
JUNE 18, 1980
ATTACHMENT

INTRODUCTION

Air quality analyses for individual highway projects have been performed for about a decade now. The purpose of this paper is to discuss the current status of project analyses as performed by State highway agencies (SHA). The information presented is based primarily on the results of discussions with Federal Highway Administration (FHWA) and SHA field personnel during visits to the following nine States: Arizona, Colorado, Georgia, Kansas, Michigan, New Jersey, Oregon, Pennsylvania, and Texas. Some of the information is based on our review of air quality analyses included in environmental impact statements (EIS's). The principal emphasis of this discussion paper is on technical issues rather than on administrative or policy issues.

Our observations are by no means exhaustive. Because the experiences of individual States may differ from those described in this paper, there may be some differences of opinion about what is said. We would appreciate receiving any reactions, comments, and/or suggestions from interested readers.

Air quality analyses vary considerably in content and level of detail from one project to another. There are several reasons for these variations. First, the FHWA Air Quality Guidelines (FHPM 7-7-9) allow for considerable flexibility in performing these analyses. The regulations rely heavily on the required consultation between the SHA and the State/local air quality control agency to define the scope, content, assumptions, and the level of technical detail for a particular project.

Second, air quality analyses are performed by different groups with varying levels of expertise. Some States rely heavily on consultants. Some States have centralized operations where all analyses are performed, and others have decentralized operations that vary in their technical capability to do project analyses. Therefore, it is not surprising to find considerable variation in the content and quality of the work performed throughout the Nation.

Third, project location, local topography, and meteorological conditions influence the level of detail required. Large projects located in urban areas usually require analyses that are quite detailed and that involve a substantial amount of effort, time, and cost. Controversial projects involved in litigation, or which are otherwise challenged, are almost always analyzed in greater detail. Projects located in geographical areas with unique topography or adverse meteorology may also require a detailed investigation.

Fourth, State environmental laws such as Indirect Source Review (ISR), which require a permit before a highway can be constructed, usually have an overriding influence on the scope, content, and

*Jesse R. Chaves, *FHWA Bulletin*, June 19, 1980, Attachment.

level of detail of the analyses performed for EIS's. This is
especially true when the SHA attempts to satisfy the ISR
and EIS requirements with the same analysis. In some cases, the
ISR permit is secured after EIS approval. A more elaborate
analysis than the one performed for the EIS may be required to
obtain a permit.

Fifth, in response to critical comments received from review
agencies, additional or more detailed analyses are often required.

Traffic Data

Traffic data used in air quality analyses is derived from complex
travel forecasting models. As a general rule, air quality
analysts use the traffic data provided by transportation planning
departments for particular years of interest. In most instances,
traffic for a particular year of interest is simply linearly
interpolated from particular key years for which traffic,
population, land use, and other data are available.

Projected traffic volumes and speeds produced by traffic assignment
models for traffic system links require interpolation for project-
level air quality analysis. Unadjusted forecasts have often
been challenged, particularly when the project is controversial.
At one time the use of unadjusted traffic volumes was fairly common.
This problem is less frequent now, but care still needs to be
exercised to prevent the use of unadjusted volumes.

The forecasting of traffic mixes, especially estimating the proportion
of heavy-duty gasoline and diesel trucks, is largely a matter of
judgment.   The procedures for making these forecasts are, at best,
questionable. However, determining the percentage of heavy-duty
gasoline trucks is important in air quality analyses because of
the relatively high rates of carbon monoxide (CO), hydrocarbons (HC),
and oxides of nitrogen (NOx) emitted from this class of vehicles.
Even though improved truck forecasting procedures are needed to
enable more reliable environmental analyses to be made, present
indications suggest that such procedures will not be developed in
the near future.

There have been several instances reported where the data (including
traffic data) being fed into project analyses from transportation
planning (metropolitan planning organization (MPO)) has been delayed
because the MPO's cannot respond fast enough. In addition, traffic
projections made for the same highway project by the MPO and the
State transportation agency did not agree. These discrepancies
seem mainly due to differences in population forecasts and assumptions
regarding population distribution within the urban area. Inconsistencies in traffic forecasts such as these present problems in
an EIS and can cause delay.

In most of the States visited, the transportation agency is generally
acknowledged as having expertise in traffic forecasting. Therefore,
the opinion of the transportation agency has prevailed in instances
of a disagreement with others over traffic projections.

Microscale Models

There are a number of line-source dispersion models routinely used in performing microscale CO analyses. The two most widely used models are CALINE 2, developed by the California Department of Transportation (CALTRANS), and HIWAY, developed by the Environmental Protection Agency (EPA). A few State transportation agencies have developed and use their own models, but, in general, the models in use have had some form of field verification and are accepted by environmental agencies. There is little or no controversy regarding which models to use for project-level assessments.

Existing models in use today have several disadvantages. For example, CALINE 2 and HIWAY models substantially overpredict for low-wind speed, parallel wind, and very stable atmospheric conditions. Models based on the Gaussian formulation are not designed for complicated geometry such as street canyons in a central business district. The more sophisticated numerical models require elaborate and costly input data and the results may only be slightly better than from the more generalized Gaussian models. The expenditure of large sums of money in developing and validating more sophisticated and accurate line-source models is not justified. The greatest uncertainty in estimating future air quality levels comes from the assumptions to predict future traffic, vehicle emissions, and meteorology, and not from any inherent inaccuracy of the models themselves.

Recently, CALTRANS completed the development of a new line-source model called CALINE 3. This model is not an update of CALINE 2, but represents a new formulation which provides for a greater flexibility and accuracy than the old model. The FHWA is preparing to distribute CALINE 3 to all State transportation agencies.

A number of State transportation agencies have developed simplified procedures in the form of nomographs (and in one case, a circular slide rule) to perform microscale CO analyses. The FHWA Technical Advisory T6640.4 contains a nomographic procedure based on CALINE 2. These simplified procedures have been quite popular and extensively used, especially by agencies that have no computers and those that have a limited computer capability.

One State transportation agency uses a simple proportional model to determine microscale CO impacts because it believes line-source models do not adequately represent "worst-case" conditions. This method relies on field monitoring at receptor sites and the calculation of local CO emissions for a base year and the years of interest. The monitored concentrations are adjusted in proportion to the total local calculated CO emissions. The EPA has been critical of this method and prefers the use of line-source models. The FHWA believes that line-source models are adequate to represent "worst-case" conditions for CO.

FHWA BULLETIN
JUNE 18, 1980
ATTACHMENT

Field Monitoring

Field monitoring is sometimes performed to determine the background
levels of CO along a proposed project corridor. Measured background
levels are added to the expected contribution from the proposed
facility to determine the total concentration of CO at a particular
site.

Field monitoring practices vary from one State to another. Some
State transportation agencies do not monitor but rather make estimates
of the existing background levels. One State spends as much as
4 months at one site to determine background levels for the larger
projects. Some States conduct their monitoring operations throughout
the year, while others restrict field measurements to the "CO season,"
which occurs roughly from November through January in most areas.
Monitoring performed "off season" is usually adjusted for "worst-
case" conditions by using long-term continuous CO data from permanent
monitoring stations. Monitoring done during the "CO season" needs
no adjustment.

A variety of equipment is used. Bag sampling is used in conjunction
with Ecolyzer or Nondispersive Infrared (NDIR) instruments in the
laboratory. Ecolyzers with and without recorders are used on site,
and NDIR instruments are also used on site for continuous sampling.

We find that monitoring is performed mainly for urban highway projects,
and often this is done even when CO background levels are not anticipated to be high. Monitoring is sometimes done to enhance credibility
with the public or an environmental agency. Often monitoring is
performed at the insistence of an air quality agency. One State
transportation agency expressed the view that project monitoring
is a complete waste of time and money, and plans in the future to
do only that field monitoring that is absolutely essential. State
transportation agencies do try to take advantage of existing CO
data derived from other monitoring programs. More often than not,
such data may be of limited value because it is affected by local
streets and does not represent the project background level.

States are finding that off-season monitoring with adjustment for
"worst-case" is of doubtful value, even if such monitoring is
conducted over an extended period of time. The obvious advantage
of year-round monitoring is the greater flexibility it offers
States by distributing workloads. Also, many States find that
continuous monitoring for more than 30 days during the winter
(worst-case CO season) does not provide any additional useful
data. A period of 2 weeks of monitoring may be sufficient to
obtain "worst-case" levels if adverse meteorological conditions
occur during this period. The NCHRP Report No. 200, titled
"Monitoring Carbon Monoxide Concentrations in Urban Areas," provides
the latest guidance on monitoring for highway projects. One State
transportation agency indicated it had evaluated this methodology
and was adopting the recommendations.

FHWA BULLETIN
JUNE 18, 1980
ATTACHMENT

When properly conducted, monitoring will reveal existing CO background levels. Care should be taken in determining expected future background levels where these levels represent a substantial part of the total concentration from the proposed highway for specific years of interest.

Generally, adjustments to obtain future CO background levels are based on expected total CO emissions within the project corridor. These emissions are dependent primarily on future tailpipe emission factors, vehicle miles of travel, and vehicle speeds within the corridor.

Because a CO monitoring program may be expensive, time-consuming, and difficult to schedule, some SHA's prefer to use models to simulate CO levels along the proposed project for the specific years of interest. Sometimes such simulations calculate background levels throughout an entire urbanized area. Such an approach, if carefully carried out, will yield satisfactory results.

As a general rule, most of the State transportation agencies monitor only CO for project-level assessments. A few States may monitor ozone (O3), HC, and NOx, but these monitoring efforts are not related to specific highway projects. Collected data is usually made available to the State air quality agency. Summaries of existing local/State/Federal long-term ambient air quality data for HC, NOx, and O3 within the region are often included in the air quality section of an EIS.

Mesoscale Corridor Analyses

A wide variety of practices are encountered from State to State regarding mesoscale corridor analyses. A number of States perform corridor burden analyses only on major projects in urban areas, and some States do not perform corridor analyses at all.. The mesoscale project corridor analyses that are performed usually involve calculating the tons or pounds of HC and NOx generated per day from the build and no-build alternatives for specific years of interest within the proposed corridor. One State transportation agency performs mesoscale analyses for 95 percent of its projects. The HC contributions from each individual project (difference between build and no-build) are summed up and tabulated in a "balance sheet." In these instances, State highway agencies are not taking advantage of the regional transportation planning analyses.

Several of the State transportation agencies visited indicated that they do not use the results of regional transportation emissions analyses performed either by MPO's or their own planning departments. They prefer instead to do a separate mesoscale corridor analysis for each project. This duplication is viewed by FHWA as unnecessary and nonproductive.

FHWA BULLETIN
JUNE 18, 1980
ATTACHMENT

One State transportation agency indicated it had made a regional
transportation HC emission analysis for a major city, including
the surrounding counties. The analysis included the build and
no-build alternatives in the region for the existing and projected
network for 4 target years of interest. The State air quality
agency concurred in the report. As a result, the transportation
agency does not perform mesoscale corridor analyses for individual
projects. For those projects located in other urbanized areas
that do not have regional analyses, individual corridor analyses
are still performed. It is interesting to note that in this
State the group responsible for project analyses also did the
transportation analyses.

Some States expressed the view that individual corridor mesoscale
analyses are of practically no value from a technical standpoint.
They feel that these analyses are done to enhance public credibility
and because the environmental agencies almost always ask for them
in their letters of comment.

In one State where the air quality agency has indirect source
review permit authority, the transportation department does a
mesoscale corridor burden analyses on all projects for CO, NOx,
HC, TSP , and lead. If the relative difference in emissions
from the build and no-build alternatives shows decreases in all
pollutants from the build alternative, no further analyses are
performed. If one or more of these pollutants increases due to
the build alternative, a detailed CO microscale analysis is
performed for the "primary" as well as "secondary" impact areas.
In this instance, the burden analysis is used as a basis for
performing or not performing the CO microscale analysis.

Reviews of corridor mesoscale analyses performed for individual
projects show the following:

(a) The corridor limits are often picked arbitrarily and may
    not represent the "traffic drainage shed" affected by
    the proposal. The results of these analyses are questionable.

(b) In most cases, there is less than a 1 percent difference
    between the pollutant emissions for the build and no-build
    alternatives in the years of interest.

(c) The corridor emissions from an individual project
    represent a very small fraction of the total transportation
    emissions in the urban area.

(d) Individual highway links in a transportation network
    cannot always be easily isolated and analyzed for build/
    no-build comparisons.

There is a growing recognition that results of individual project
corridor analyses are of very limited value in providing information
regarding the potential HC/NO_2/O_3 impact. As a result of the
1977 Clean Air Act Amendments, greater emphasis has been placed

on transportation system (regional) air quality analyses, which include emissions from all the major individual links in the transportation network. In the past, individual highway corridor analyses (HC and NOx) were performed largely because acceptable regional transportation emission analyses were lacking. Today, most urban areas with air quality problems either now or soon will have detailed transportation emission inventories and analyses.

We find that some of the personnel working on project air quality analyses have little knowledge regarding the work performed at the system level. This lack of awareness is reflected in project EIS discussions. The work done at the **system level** (3C transportation planning and/or State Implementation Plan (SIP) revisions) is seldom referenced. It is obvious that full advantage has not been taken of work already performed. In several cases, EIS approval was delayed because reference to the results of the system level analysis was not made.

Lead Analysis

A few States perform the lead corridor burden analysis for major projects for comparative evaluation of **build/no-build emissions**. The national lead standard of 1.5 micrograms per cubic metre quarterly average is not expected to be exceeded in the future along major highways and streets. The increased use of unleaded gasoline in catalyst-equipped cars and the required general reduction in the lead content of leaded gasolines will contribute to lower lead levels in the ambient air. The overall average lead content of gasoline in 1974 was 2 grams per gallon and is expected to be 0.05 gram per gallon in 1990. Therefore, the analysis of lead for proposed highway projects, in most instances, does not appear to be necessary. Because a lead standard has been promulgated by EPA, a few air agencies have either suggested or requested that lead analyses be made for highway projects.

Validated line-source models for estimating lead concentrations along highway corridors are not available. The development, validation, and use of such models for determining lead concentrations for proposed highway projects do not appear necessary or justified in view of the continued decrease in lead emissions from gasoline powered vehicles and the increased use of diesel vehicles.

"Worst-Case Assumptions"

Because the 1- and 8-hour standards are expressed in concentrations that are not to be exceeded more than once per year, "worst-case" analysis is usually performed for the 1- and 8-hour periods covered by the standards. Both traffic and meteorological conditions are considered since the condition of interest involves maximum vehicle emissions combined with poor dispersion of the pollutants near the appropriate receptor sites.

FHWA BULLETIN
JUNE 18, 1980
ATTACHMENT

Often, overly conservative "worst-case" parameters are selected
to simplify the analysis. The presumption here is that if these
conditions do not result in exceeding the CO standard, the
air quality analysis can be terminated with the conclusion that
there are no air quality problems. This approach often leads to
problems at later stages of a project where traffic conditions,
emission factors, background levels, or other conditions change.
While the analyst may know that concentrations have been substantially overpredicted due to the overly conservative assumptions,
it becomes difficult to do a creditable job of convincing others
that there is no cause for concern when subsequent analyses
approach or exceed the standards. In the past, this situation
was compounded by the fact that under "worst-case" meteorological
conditions, CALINE 2 and HIWAY models substantially overpredict
actual concentrations. CALINE 3, which is being distributed,
does not suffer this deficiency. Overly conservative analyses
which result in substantial overpredictions may cause unjustified
concern over the potential adverse air quality impacts of the
project.

In almost all cases, State transportation agencies are using
reasonable "worst-case" assumptions. A commonly used assumption
in urban areas for the 1-hour analysis is parallel wind, 1 meter-
per-second wind speed, and atmospheric stability class D or E.
The 8-hour level is normally derived from the 1-hour concentration
by applying a 0.6 meteorological persistence factor and an adjustment
for the difference between peak hourly traffic volume and the
average hourly volume throughout the 8-hour period. Some States
have analyzed historical meteorological data for a 5- or 10-year
period to determine the frequency of occurrence of wind direction,
wind speed, and atmospheric stability for any hour of the year.
Such data is used for the "worst-case" analysis.

In many States, agreements have been reached between the transportation
and air quality agency regarding project-level analyses. These
agreements usually describe the level of detail that will be addressed
on different categories of projects and the acceptable "worst-case"
assumptions that will be used.

Results of CO "worst-case" analysis at receptor sites are usually
reported as a single concentration to the nearest 0.1 or even
0.01 of a part per million (ppm). This practice continues despite
the fact that such accuracy in estimating CO levels is impossible.
It would be far more informative and realistic if results of analyses
were reported over a range of reasonable "worst-case" conditions
reported to the nearest whole ppm.

Motor Vehicle Emission Factors

Periodically, EPA publishes and distributes a set of motor vehicle
emission factors along with methodology for their use. The latest
of these issuances is the Mobile Source Emission Factors dated
January 1978. The computerized version of this document is known
as MOBILE 1. The methodology is intended for a variety of
applications involving air quality analyses and is not specifically
intended for highway project analyses.

FHWA BULLETIN
JUNE 18, 1980
ATTACHMENT

Because highway project analyses do not require the use of all the capabilities of the MOBILE 1 computer methodology, FHWA issued Technical Advisories T6640.1 and T6640.3 in 1978 to simplify implementation of EPA's methodology. Technical Advisory T6640.1 consists of emission factor tables for various years and vehicle types over a range of conditions. Technical Advisory T6640.3 provides a discussion of the EPA methodology and includes specific simplifying recommendations for highway project analyses. For future EPA issuances of the emission factors, FHWA intends to continue to provide simplified procedures for project-level implementation. The next EPA issuance of mobile source emission factors, called MOBILE 2, is expected some time in mid-1980.

Two of the States objected to the FHWA suggested phase-in schedule for MOBILE 1. They indicated the schedule was unreasonable and required unnecessary reanalysis of air quality. This causes a problem to some highway agencies because their air quality analyses and reports are often completed 9 to 12 months prior to the completion of the draft EIS. One particular project was caught up in three issuances of EPA emission factors. The reanalysis of projects is costly and causes delay, especially when these analyses have been performed under consultant contracts. This reanalysis rarely has any significant effect on the final decision for the project. The FHWA will minimize or eliminate the need for reanalysis due to any future revisions of emission factors.

One State that has made extensive measurements of CO near highways in recent years indicated that its data shows that EPA's MOBILE 1 underpredicts emissions by a factor ranging from 1.5 to 5. There is no evidence from other States to corroborate this finding.

Signalized Intersection Analysis

Signalized intersections are often the subject of interest since these are locations near which CO levels are expected to be the highest. When intersection analyses are performed, they are often accomplished using MOBILE 1 emission factors based on low-average speeds and available line-source diffusion models. On occasion, this procedure has been criticized because it is alleged to underpredict CO concentrations. Some highway agencies have been under some pressure from air quality agencies to use alternative techniques which consider the modal operation (idle, acceleration, deceleration, and steady state) of vehicles at intersections and the detailed traffic lane flows. States which have attempted to use the EPA Indirect Source Review (ISR), Volume 9 Procedures, have found:

(a) The method is complex and time-consuming and has not been computerized;

(b) The method has not been adequately validated to provide confidence in its results;

(c)   The method substantially overestimates concentrations when compared to limited field data
that is available.

There are currently at least five State transportation agencies
which are conducting field investigations to evaluate existing
methods for intersection analyses and possibly developing improved
ones. One State environmental agency has also just concluded
such a study. CALINE 3, which was recently distributed, has the
capability to handle dispersion of CO at intersections. The
major problem in using dispersion models for intersection analyses
is that the emission rates must be determined and be put into the
model by the user. It appears that there is a current need to
develop a series of realistic emission rates for signalized
intersections that could be implemented without going through
complicated traffic engineering or modal emissions analysis.

Because of the unreliable state-of-the-art, FHWA does not recommend
the use of the ISR, Volume 9, or the EPA Hot Spot Guideline
intersection analysis methods for analyzing highway projects for
EIS's.

Coordination and Consultation

One of the most significant parts of the FHWA Air Quality Guidelines
is that they require consultation between the SHA and the air
quality agency regarding project analyses. The consultation that
takes place varies widely from State to State. In some places,
written agreements and understandings have been developed regarding
levels of analysis and other details for each type of project.
Some SHA's have not developed formal agreements, but have
learned what the air quality agency expects.

In one State, the technical air quality report is distributed to
FHWA Division, EPA, and the State air quality agency for comment
prior to preparation of the draft EIS. Another State having ISR
simply follows the requirements of the State's ISR regulations.
One State uses an "Air Quality Work Program," which consists of
an elaborate checklist which is used to determine, prior to the
draft EIS, the details of the project analysis and any concerns
by the State air quality agency and EPA.

In yet another State, the SHA coordinates on each of the smaller
projects by means of a letter indicating the level of analysis
detail planned and gets concurrence from the air quality agency.
For larger projects, an early coordination meeting between the
FHWA Division and the State air quality agency is held to determine
the general plan and design of the air quality analysis.

A number of States have developed rather detailed and elaborate
"guidelines" for conducting project-level analyses. In almost
all instances, these have been developed in consultation with
FHWA, EPA, and the State air quality agency. At least two
States interviewed were revising "guidelines" that were developed
several years ago.

FHWA BULLETIN
JUNE 18,1980
ATTACHMENT

"Guidelines" have been found very useful to the SHA's,
particularly those with decentralized operations and those
which have the work done by consultant firms.

Written agreements vary in scope and complexity. In one FHWA
Region, each of the SHA's had some sort of written
agreement with the State air quality agency. In most instances,
these agreements specify the level of analysis required for
each type of project. In almost all cases, low-traffic volume
projects are exempt from analysis. Criteria for such exemptions
and the levels of analysis required for different types of
projects are based on local consultation and thus vary from
State to State. It is clear that the FHWA Guidelines are generally
accomplishing the desired results of obtaining technically adequate
air quality analyses while at the same time permitting sufficient
flexibility for dealing with the more localized concerns.

Training and Workshops

All the SHA's interviewed expressed the need for continuation
of FHWA's basic air quality courses. The need for these basic
courses is most critical where there is a turnover in personnel
or where new people are added. Some States expressed no need for
this training at the present time. These States have people who
have had considerable experience with project air quality analysis.
In a number of SHA's, the technical people feel somewhat
isolated. They were interested in finding out what is going on
in other States and discussing more advanced technical topics and
exchanging ideas. In fact, some have attended the basic air quality
course two or three times mainly to interact with technical people
from other SHA's. The States indicated that a series of short,
"regional" workshops would best fulfill this need because of limitations on long distance travel by some States.

One SHA and one FHWA division office indicated there was a critical
need by cities and counties for training in air quality and other
environmental disciplines. It is not clear from our overall
discussions whether this need is more universal or unique to this
particular State.

Photochemical Models

Only one SHA interviewed had used a photochemical model
in an attempt to quantify the ozone impact of a major proposed
highway in an urban area. Results of the analysis which were
performed several years ago showed this method of modeling insensitive to potential emissions from a major proposed facility. It
seems clear, based on this and other experiences, that photochemical
models are inappropriate tools for assessing the potential incremental
effects of individual highway segments on ozone levels in an urban
area. In addition, photochemical models are complex, require users
who have specialized skills, and are very costly to implement.

FHWA BULLETIN
JUNE 18, 1980
ATTACHMENT

Some Closing Observations

Within the last several years, the emphasis and interest have shifted away from project-level to transportation planning and SIP-related air quality analyses. The Clean Air Act Amendments of 1977 helped establish this trend, but other factors are involved. For example, project-microscale analyses for future years seldom show potential violation of CO standards except at some signalized intersections where CO can still be a problem. After about a decade of doing highway project corridor HC/NO_2 analyses as a surrogate for the ozone problem, we have found inadequacies. It is evident that such analyses are being and should be conducted at the system level. Full advantage has not been taken by some SHA's of analysis already performed at the system level.

We find that in some SHA's there is a tendency to do too much, or in some cases, perform project analyses that do not appear necessary. Frequently, this is in response to requests from State or Federal air quality agencies. The great majority of States are performing adequate project analyses at a level of effort which appears reasonable.

A number of SHA's interviewed felt that the results of air quality analyses are not really used for decisionmaking. No project has ever been stopped on the basis of air quality alone. A few projects have been modified because of the incorporation of mitigation measures, but these decisions were not based primarily on air quality reasons or technical analyses. Basic transportation policy currently has an overriding influence on the incorporation of mitigation measures; therefore, the results of technical air analyses are not depended upon for decisionmaking.

FHWA BULLETIN
JUNE 18, 1980
ATTACHMENT

Conclusions and Recommendations

(1) The FHWA Air Quality Guidelines (FHPM 7-7-9) require consultation between the SHA and air quality control agency. This is probably the most important part of the regulation. Because of the flexibility allowed, one finds considerable variation from State to State in the content and scope of highway project air quality analyses.

(2) Over the last several years, emphasis and interest have shifted from project-level to transportation system-level analyses. This shift is the result of several factors:

    (a) The 1977 Clean Air Act Amendments place emphasis on system-level air quality planning;

    (b) Project CO analyses rarely show potential exceedances of National Ambient Air Quality Standards (NAAQS);

    (c) HC, NO_2, and O3 can best be analyzed at the regional scale;

    (d) Recent transportation policy decisions provide for Transportation Control Measure (TCM) type measures;

(3) The CO field monitoring for projects should be done only when background levels are expected to be high. Monitoring should be done during the "CO season" and generally should cover a period of less than 30 days. The NCHRP Report No. 200 provides the latest guidance on this subject.

(4) Simplified analysis procedures such as nomographs and emission factor tabulations are very popular. The FHWA feels that they are suitable for use for most project-level analyses and plans to continue distribution of these simplified techniques to the States.

(5) Lead analyses need not be performed for projects because of the decreasing future lead emissions from vehicles. Validated lead dispersion models are not available and future development of such models may not be justified.

(6) Photochemical models are inappropriate for use in project analysis because they are insensitive to HC/NOx emission changes resulting from major highways. The FHWA does not recommend their use for project analysis.

(7) With the passage of time, there is less technical justification for performing corridor mesoscale analyses (HC and NO_2) for individual highway projects. Reliance should be placed on the results of emission analyses performed at the system level such as those used in the development of SIP revisions. The FHWA recommends the discontinuance of corridor mesoscale burden analyses for individual projects.

(8) Current EPA methodologies for assessing CO levels at signalized intersections (Volume 9, ISR, and Hot Spot Guidelines) are inadequate for project analyses because these methods are complicated and substantially overpredict CO levels. The FHWA does not recommend their use. An improved simplified technique is needed to realistically estimate CO emissions at signalized intersections. Until such simplfied techniques become available, existing line-source dispersion models can be used for estimating CO concentrations.

(9) Long lead times are required for mobile source implementing each new issuance of emission factors. The FHWA will recommend a reasonable phase-in schedule for MOBILE 2 which will eliminate or minimize the need for project reanalysis.

CHAPTER 7

Terrestrial and Aquatic Impacts

The impacts of transportation systems on hydrology, water quality, and the local ecosystem are discussed here in a single chapter to stress their interrelationships. Unlike air quality and noise impacts, few standard techniques are available for the assessment of hydrologic, water quality, or ecologic impacts, and quantitative standards which express permissible degradation levels generally do not exist. This is not to suggest that these impacts are uncontrolled; on the contrary; recent state and Federal wetlands laws* have elevated wetlands (hydrologic, water quality, or ecologic) impacts to the point that many transportation projects have been and will be stopped, modified, or delayed as a result of these concerns.

In this chapter a brief introduction to some of the fundamentals of hydrology and ecology is presented together with suggestions as to how these fundamental principles can be applied to environmental impact assessment. In the assessment of hydrologic, water quality, or ecologic impacts, standard "cookbook" impact analysis techniques are neither available nor desirable. Virtually every project is unique in some respect and analysis procedures suitable for one project are often inappropriate for another, due to differences in geology, geography, location, vegetation type, hydrologic regime, habitat type, climate, and sometimes, politics. Hence, every

*For example the Corps of Engineers 404 permit process applies to many, if not most, major transportation projects. This and state fresh and tidal wetlands laws require careful consideration of hydrologic, water quality, and ecologic impacts and the implementation of extensive mitigating measures for those activities permitted in wetlands. See Chapter 3.

analysis must be tailored to meet the needs of the project under consideration. Whenever possible, impact study design should be accomplished by an interdisciplinary team, with input from those agencies and groups with a role to play in project development. Note that impact analysis should *not* begin after project design has been finalized and alternative designs which might mitigate impacts, are difficult to integrate into project plans. The development of a balanced plan in cooperation with review/regulatory agencies is a key to timely project impelementation.

Transportation systems can affect local hydrology and water quality as well as aquatic and terrestrial ecosystems in a number of ways. Highway, railway, and runway embankments can restrict surface or groundwater flow. Highway and airport apron runoff may contain harmful pollutants. The filling of floodplains or paving of permeable soil can aggravate local flooding problems, and construction activities can create serious erosion and sedimentation problems. Also, the construction of a transportation facility may induce growth in the form of residential development, manufacturing and commercial facilities, wastewater treatment plants, and so on, and the impacts of this induced development may be more serious than the direct impacts of the transportation project itself. Unfortunately, induced growth is difficult to predict, and even though many of the techniques discussed here are applicable to assessments of other types of projects, it is difficult to be specific regarding the potential impacts of vaguely defined developments which may be induced by the project in question at some time in the future.

As previously suggested, standard procedures for the quantitative assessment of hydrologic and water quality impacts comparable to those employed in the assessment of air quality and noise impacts have generally not evolved.* There are several possible reasons for this failure of the environmental analysis profession to produce a cookbook approach to hydrologic, water quality, and ecologic impacts. First, there is a lack of applicable standards which can be applied to a transportation project for the purpose of determining whether the impacts associated with its implementation may be deemed acceptable or unacceptable. For example, if the construction of a roadbed might constrict the flow of water through an underlying aquifer and one were somehow able to quantify an expected change in groundwater flow, one would still be left with the difficult problem of assessing the significance of the change. In the case of noise or air quality impacts one can compare expected sound levels or pollutant concentrations with a numerical standard, and significance is easily judged. Yet how could a standard for changes in groundwater be developed? Unlike air and noise, where there are perceived impacts upon the human condition associated with defined levels of pollution which can be used in defining acceptable and unacceptable impacts, hydrologic, water quality, and ecologic impacts often do not lend themselves to the establishment of precise numerical standards.

Another issue is the lack of uniformity between projects. In the case of air quality and noise assessment, levels of impact can be determined in the same general manner for virtually any project and the acceptable impacts are generally the same in all locations. However, returning to the groundwater example, a 1-m change in water table level at one location might not produce a discernable effect, while the most subtle change in another nearby location might generate marked changes in the ecology at that area.

Still another difficulty associated with the assessment of hydrologic/water-quality impacts has to do with the nature of the impacts. Air and noise impacts are only assessed with respect to their effects upon human health and welfare; other types of impacts are usually considered

*Exceptions in this regard have to do with chloride (salt) and flooding, both of which may pose a direct impact upon human health and welfare.

unimportant. While transportation-induced changes in hydrology or water quality may occasionally affect people through flooding or chloride (salt) impacts, changes in hydrology or water quality may induce a whole range of changes in the ecosystem. Unfortunately those changes are quite difficult to predict. One can rarely state with precision which plant species might die out as the result of ill-defined changes in water table levels, and, even if these changes in vegetation species composition could be anticipated, it would still be very difficult, if not impossible, to predict what effects these changes might have upon local flora and fauna. Similarly, it is difficult to predict turbidity levels that might be associated with highway construction and still more difficult to specify what effects changes in turbidity levels might have upon the ecology of a stream, lake, or coastal area.

Problems related to the acquisition of baseline data also tend to be more troublesome for the assessment of hydrologic, water quality, and ecologic impacts than for air and noise analyses. Background air pollutant levels can be determined from existing monitoring stations (area or site monitoring efforts lasting a few months), or background pollutant levels may simply be assumed since they usually constitute only a small fraction of the total pollutant impact expected from the proposed facility. Similarly, noise measurements can often be successfully accomplished over a relatively short period of time, usually at any time of the year. Unfortunately, an understanding of existing hydrologic, water quality, or ecologic conditions is often of critical importance in the assessment of impacts; and while meaningful information is relatively easy to obtain, the acquisition of precise, detailed background data is often difficult and time-consuming.

The desire to get the data by spending time and money appears to be very strong among some regulatory agencies charged with the responsibility for approving transportation projects. This is quite understandable given the rather imprecise tools available for the prediction of most impacts and a sometimes compelling desire for something substantive upon which to base a decision. Unfortunately, unless one has the time and money to monitor a number of water quality or ecological variables together with flow rates and atmospheric conditions at several locations over all seasons of the year, sometimes for several years, one can end up with what might at best be an incomplete description of the subject area. For example, just because dissolved oxygen levels of one point in a stream on one day were found to be capable of supporting all manner of aquatic life, one cannot assume that this favorable level is constant throughout the year, and that dissolved oxygen levels might not fall later in the year to a point where virtually every fish in the stream will die.

If it is determined that on-site field sampling must be performed for water quality or ecologic parameters, the services of an expert should be utilized. It is very easy to spend a great deal of time and effort collecting data which will later prove useless. However, one should not be dissuaded from conducting informal field investigations to get "the lay of the land." It can also be embarrassing to have to concede under oath that the analyst performing the environmental impact analysis never saw the site in question.

In assembling data for an analysis of hydrologic, water quality, or ecological impacts, one should contact the regional offices of the U.S. Geological Survey,* the FWS, the EPA, and the Soil Conservation Service (Dept. of Agriculture), as well as the state environmental agency, for published data on the area (geologic, topographic, and soils maps; aerial photos; endangered species habitats; water quality data; stream gage data; etc.). These agencies often have a considerable volume of data available for the asking. Note that this also provides the analyst with a chance to talk to people who know the local area and who may someday be reviewing the completed work product.

THE HYDROLOGIC CYCLE

Most people are familiar with the general workings of the hydrologic cycle whereby water is

evaporated from the earth's surface to return as various forms of precipitation.

When precipitation falls upon the ground surface it can follow a variety of pathways, depending upon the circumstances. A light rainfall upon dry surfaces (e.g., vegetation) may evaporate directly back into the atmosphere without raising antecedent moisture levels (the degree of surface wetness) beyond the point where runoff (flowing water) may begin. Runoff may find its way directly into a stream or collect as depression storage (puddles) from which it may evaporate or soak into the soil to become soil moisture (for subsequent intake by plants) or into an aquifer† to become part of the groundwater system (See Figure 7-1).

The distinction between groundwater and surface water is somewhat arbitrary and at times serves to obscure the workings of the hydrologic cycle to the layman who seeks to classify the movement of water into one or the other of these two modes. Figure 7-1 depicts some of the relationships between groundwater and surface water in a cross section view of a hypothetical river bed. Note that many, if not most, river valleys contain thick deposits of permeable alluvium which transmit a considerable volume of groundwater. As suggested by the figure, normal stream flow is sustained at least in part by local groundwater flow derived from upland areas, and the stream may be characterized as an influent stream. However, under flood conditions stream levels may exceed local water table levels, resulting in a temporary discharge to permeable bank sediments, and the same stream may function as an effluent stream during flood stages. This bank storage accumulated in valley sediments during flood stages may subsequently be rereleased to the stream as floodwaters recede (see Figure 7-2), thus sustaining the flow of what will again be an influent stream. At some point farther downstream this same water may percolate down through river bed sediments in influent reaches of the same river to follow regional groundwater flow patterns down the valley. One way to picture this type of variation between influent and effluent reaches of a stream is to think not in terms of stream flow but in terms of valley flow. In those portions of the valley in which the ground surface happens

---

*In addition to the geologic maps, stream gage records, and other materials available from regional USGS offices, an incredible array of aerial photographs can be obtained from the U.S. Geological Survey's EROS Data Center in Sioux Falls, South Dakota, 57198, phone (605) 594-6511. This office is generally able to supply stereo infrared color photographs and other mappings of virtually any area at any scale in a reasonable time at nominal cost.

†Water-bearing formation.

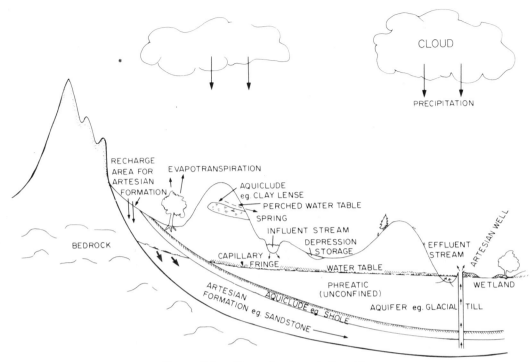

Figure 7-1.   Groundwater relationships.

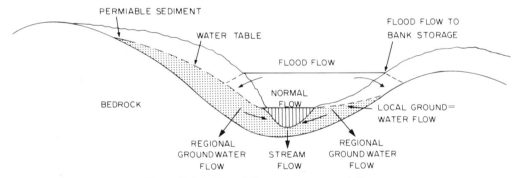

Figure 7-2.   Flood flow versus normal flow.

to dip below the water table (the upper limit of the saturated zone) lakes, wetlands, and streams are present. In other areas regional aquifers may be recharged by surface waters percolating down through sediments of variable permeability. If water is prevented from percolating down to the regional water table by an impermeable layer, a perched water table may result (see Figure 7-1).

Groundwater

As suggested by the preceding discussion, groundwater does not flow in mysterious under-

ground conduits or rivers.* Rather it is driven by the force of gravity to percolate through the pore spaces of permeable materials like sandstone, gravel, glacial till, and so on or through cracks in impermeable material (granite, gneiss, etc.). Flow through porous media is described by Darcy's Law, which states that the velocity of flow through a permeable medium is propor-

*An exception to this occurs in regions of Karst (limestone) topography where water *does* move through underground caverns formed by the dissolution of limestone.

tional to the pressure forcing the liquid through the medium.

The movement of groundwater through a phreatic* aquifer can be likened to the movement of water through a bowl of sand. As the bowl is tipped the water will percolate down through the sand to rest in the lowest portion of the bowl. The greater the degree of tilt (i.e., the steeper the hydrolic gradient), the more rapidly the water will flow through the sand. If the hypothetical bowl were filled with gravel instead of sand (i.e., if the permeability were increased) then the water would flow more rapidly through the medium. The height of the water level in the sand, that is, the height of the "water table," can be changed by adding more water to the bowl (recharge) or removing water from the bowl (discharge). If layers of sand were separated by layers of impermeable material and the bowl then turned on its edge, the water would be trapped under some hydrostatic pressure between the two impermeable layers (aquacludes) and would behave as in an artesian foundation. Similarly, if a depression were scooped out of the sand to intersect the "water table" in the bowl, the water-filled depression would be analogous to a wetland, stream, or lake.

Linsey, Kohler, and Paulhus represent Darcy's Law as

$$v = ks \qquad (7\text{-}1)$$

where v = velocity of flow
s = hydraulic gradient (head or pressure)
k = a constant related to the permeability of the medium having units of velocity.

Thus if one increases the pressure forcing the fluid through the medium, the velocity of flow will increase accordingly. Similarly, if the permeability of the medium is increased (e.g., flow through gravel instead of sand), the velocity of flow will also increase. Discharge, q, through a unit cross-section area (e.g., 1-ft² area through which the flow passes) is proportional to the velocity of the fluid (e.g., if water flows twice as fast through the same size pipe, twice as much water will be discharged). Thus,

$$q = vA \qquad (7\text{-}2)$$

where q is the volume of flow and A is the cross section of the aquifer under consideration. Note that the larger (e.g., thicker) the aquifer the more flow it can transmit. The U.S. Geological Survey defines transmissibility, T, as discharge in gallons per day through a 1-ft wide (vertical) section of an aquifer, under unit head. Thus total discharge through an aquifer can be expressed as

$$Q = TIL \qquad (7\text{-}3)$$

where Q = discharge, T - transmissibility, I is the hydraulic gradient (head or pressure), and L = the width of the aquifer. If construction activities are to modify groundwater flow, at least one term in this expression must be affected; that is, the activity must change the permeability (T, transmissibility) of the aquifer, the pressure (I, hydraulic gradient—water table slope or elevation) forcing the water through the aquifer, or the cross-section area (L, width) of discharge.

The transmissibility of an aquifer can be reduced by compressing the aquifer with an embankment. This would tend to cause the water table to rise upstream from the embankment and to fall downstream from the embankment.† Road cuts or ditches can intersect the water table causing artificial springs or seeps by which groundwater becomes surface water, thereby causing a reduction in local water table height. Extensive paving, sewering, or regrading can lead to increased runoff which will no longer percolate down into the aquifer to become groundwater. By the same token, ponding of surface waters behind embankments can lead to an increase in aquifer recharge.

Impacts of transportation projects upon groundwater flow are easy to imagine but exceedingly difficult to quantify. In order to make quantitative predictions regarding groundwater flow it is necessary to acquire a great deal of information concerning the area under consideration. About the only way to get this type of information is to conduct a systematic boring study of the area taking core samples of the strata, noting the depth of the water table, and determining the permeability of the various samples. Given this type of detailed information concerning the geometric and petrographic na-

---

*i.e., unconfined, not bounded from above, as in the case of an artesian aquifer.

†For reasons discussed later in this chapter, this impact is usually not as serious as it might appear to be.

ture of the local strata it is possible to apply models which simulate flow through porous media. Unfortunately the application of these models often requries the services of an expert who has access to a powerful computer and a rather large budget. Until someone develops an inexpensive way to investigate what is beneath the earth's surface and a simple method of applying Darcy's Law in three dimensions to inhomogeneous media, the assessment of groundwater impact will continue to be performed in rather gross and unsatisfactory terms.

Groundwater quality problems can be meaningfully addressed only after flow regimes have been defined, and only then can the additional complications of pollutant dispersion, adhesion, and degradation be addressed. Note that groundwater tends to move very slowly (feet per year); consequently, once an aquifer becomes polluted it stays polluted, making groundwater contamination a serious matter. Fortunately, with the exception of toxic spills, transportation systems rarely pollute groundwater. However, deicing (salting) of highways does carry with it the potential for groundwater contamination, though few serious occurrences of this type of impact have been reported. A rather crude technique for assessing impacts is discussed later in this section.

Surface Water Flow

Most people think of hydrologic and water quality impacts in terms of lakes, rivers, and streams. These forms of surface water flow are a manifestation of the geographic, geologic, and climatic conditions which prevail in a particular region. While complete description of all the factors which influence the spacial and temporal characteristics of a particular surface water body is virtually impossible, an understanding of some of the basics of surface water hydrology can be easily presented through analogy.

A simple way to visualize surface water flow is to imagine an inclined table top with a raised edge covered with a tablecloth. For purposes of this discussion, the table with its edges correspond to the boundaries of a hypothetical watershed. If water is sprinkled on the table top it will saturate the tablecloth and begin to flow down the face of the table. After sprinkling (precipitation) stops, water will continue to drip from the

saturated cloth for some time in somewhat the same manner that groundwater sustains the base flow of a stream. The amount of water flowing off the hypothetical table depends upon the type of cloth covering the table. A heavy cloth will absorb more water than a light cloth just as a watershed covered with pervious forest soil will tend to hold more water than will an urbanized watershed characterized by suburban lawns and impermeable pavement. The degree of "table cloth wetness" prior to sprinkling (antecedent moisture conditions) also affects the volume of runoff from a particular "storm." A dry table cloth (low antecedent moisture) will absorb more of the total volume of precipitation before "runoff" begins than will a wet one. Similarly, a basin in which it has just rained (high antecedent moisture) will tend to produce more runoff for a particular storm than would be generated in the same basin under low antecedent moisture conditions. One inch of rain over a larger basin (or table) can be expected to produce more total runoff than the same storm over a smaller basin. A gentle rain over a long time period can produce as much total runoff as an intense shower over a short time period. However, a more intense shower can be expected to produce higher peak flows.

Another way in which timing can influence runoff has to do with the relationship between storm duration and the time required for water to travel from the farthest reaches of a basin to its outfall (the basin's time of concentration). If rainfall stops before the precipitation that fell in the farthest reaches of the basin can make its way to the basin outfall, water from remote parts of the basin will still be "on its way" while other portions of the basin have stopped contributing a significant volume of runoff. Thus, if all portions of the basin are to contribute to stream flow at the same time (thereby producing peak flow) the storm must last longer than the basin's time of concentration. Note that a basin's time of concentration depends upon a number of factors including its size, shape, slope, channel type, cover type, antecedent moisture levels, and so on. In general, the smaller and steeper a basin, the shorter its time of concentration.

A basin with a short time of concentration tends to produce higher peak flows per unit area than a basin with a longer time of concentration. One of the reasons for this is that very intense rainfall rates (as experienced during thunder-showers) tend to cover a relatively small area for a relatively short time. The shorter a basin's time of concentration, the more likely it is that an intense storm will persist for a period equal to or greater than its time of concentration. Thus a basin with a short time of concentration has the potential to experience a higher average rainfall intensity (intensity is measured in inches of rainfall per unit time) for a duration exceeding its time of concentration that a basin with a long time of concentration. Referring back to the table top analogy, a foot of water falling on the table top in one minute would be expected to produce a higher "peak flow" than the same foot of water sprinkled on the table top at a uniform rate over a one-hour period.

A hyrdograph is a graphical representation of the outflow characteristics of a particular basin (see Figure 7-3). As noted in the figure, discharge begins to increase as rainfall begins to fall; this first increase is a result of rain falling directly into the stream. As the basin becomes wetted and runoff begins to accumulate from the near portions of the watershed the hydrograph rises until runoff [in cubic feet per second (cfs)] from all portions of the basin has reached the point of discharge. At this point (peak outflow) discharge will remain more or less constant as long as rainfall intensity (inches of rainfall per

hour) remains constant. When precipitation stops, basin discharge will start to decrease as the near portions of the watershed stop contributing runoff to the stream. The shape of the falling limb of the hydrograph reflects the effects of basin size, shape, slope, and so on. Flow represented by the falling limb of the hydrograph, will continue to decrease until there is no longer any runoff from the remote reaches of the watershed still in the "pipeline." Recession may require only hours or even minutes for a small basin with a short time of concentration or it may take days for a large river basin receiving precipitation from a major storm. The final portion of the falling limb of the hydrograph can also reflect the contribution of additional groundwater flow caused by a temporary increase in local water tables (see Figure 7-3). The base flow of a stream represents groundwater contributions from an average water table situation and is represented by the base of the hydrograph.

Figure 7-4 illustrates the technique for combining hyrdographs from tributary streams. The derivation and combination of hydrographs is one of the basic methods of predicting stream flow in response to a particular stream type. Note the importance of timing in the generation of peak flow conditions. For example, a small tributary with a short time of concentration may not

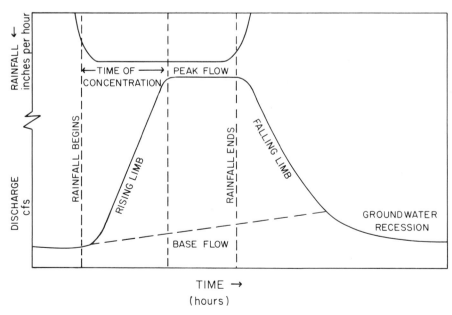

Figure 7-3.   A theoretical hydrograph.

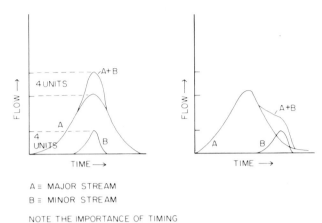

A ≡ MAJOR STREAM
B ≡ MINOR STREAM

NOTE THE IMPORTANCE OF TIMING

Figure 7-4. Combining hydrographs.

add significantly to the peak flow of the receiving stream if the receiving stream has a longer time of concentration. By the same token, streams which happen to have similar peaking characteristics may combine to give rise to dramatic peak flows. One method of flood control, involving the use of retention ponds, takes advantage of this phenomenon by changing the peaking characteristic of a stream (see Figure 7-5). Note that it is also possible to mitigate flooding problems by changing the peaking characteristics of a tributary stream through channelization or construction of retention facilities.

Rainfall intensity plays an important part in the generation of peak flow in streams. A severe thundershower lasting only ten minutes may produce dramatic flooding in urban streets, parking lots, and other basins with a short time of con-

centration. The same storm, however, might produce barely perceptable effects on the flow of a major river. As previously mentioned, the maximum rainfall intensity likely to affect an entire basin is inversely proportional to the basin's size (time of concentration), and unless precipitation persists for a time period equal to, or greater than, the basin's time of concentration, all portions of the basin will not simultaneously contribute peak flow to the main stream, and thus will not generate maximum flow at the basin outfall.

The time of concentration for a particular basin, especially a small basin, varies from storm to storm. For example, a storm of low intensity in a basin with a low antecedent moisture regime may require more time to generate flow from all portions of the basin than an intense storm occurring the next day while the basin still exhibits a high antecedent moisture level. Overland flow (time required for precipitation to find its way from the land into a stream channel) varies from several minutes to perhaps an hour depending upon antecedent moisture conditions and basin geometry, as well as other factors such as season of the year, land-use practices, and cover type.

Channel flow is described by the Manning Formula

$$q = \frac{1.49}{n} A R^{2/3} s^{1/2} \qquad (7\text{-}4)$$

Where q = flow, in cubic feet per second
n = "Manning's n" a roughness coefficient between 0 and 1
A = the channel cross section area

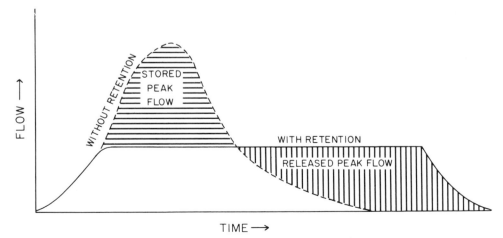

Figure 7-5. Effect of a retention pond.

R = the hydraulic radius at the channel which is equal to the cross-section area divided by the length of the wetted perimeter.

s = hydraulic gradient (approximates channel slope).

Values for n can be obtained from Chow (1964), Linsley, Kohler, and Paulhus (1975) or from almost any civil engineering handbook.

In inspecting the Manning equation, note the interrelationship of the variables. As channel roughness increases, that is, n goes from some low value, for example, 0.02 for a gravel channel, to a higher value, for example, 0.112 for a weed-choked channel, the volume of flow decreases. As the cross section of the channel increases, it can accomodate more flow. A deep "V"-shaped channel will accommodate more flow (have a larger hydraulic radius) than a very shallow channel of the same cross-section area. As the slope of the channel increases, the volume of flow accommodated increases. Note that the Manning formula can be used to determine stream velocity for a given volume of flow by dividing both sides of the equation by cross-section area. In this manner the equation can be used in estimating the channel flow component of the time of concentration for a basin.

Many techniques have been developed for the quantification of rainfall–runoff relationships. One of the simplest (and least accurate) is the so called "rational formula" used mainly for the design of small structures such as ditches or culverts draining up to several acres. This formula may be expressed as

$$Q = CIA \qquad (7\text{-}5)$$

where Q = runoff in acre inches per hour* or cubic feet per second

C = fraction of rainfall which will appear as runoff

I = rainfall intensity in inches per hour for a duration equal to or greater than the basin's time of concentration

A = basin area in acres.

Values for C, the runoff coefficient, vary between 0 and 1. One would expect areas such as parking lots, rooftops, and water bodies to ex-

*The volume of water which would cover 1 acre of area 1 in. deep (see also acre-feet); 1 acre-in. of water per hour is approximately equal to 1 ft^3/sec (1 cfs).

hibit high C values; conversely, dry sandy soils covered by vegetation tend to exhibit low C values. Note that the value for C varies with antecedent moisture conditions. Tables for C values for various land-use types can be found in Chow (1964), Linsley, Kohler, and Paulhas (1975), and most civil engineering handbooks.

Maximum rainfall intensity, I, is a function of geographic location (some areas have higher rainfall intensities than others), basin size (smaller basins tend to have shorter times of concentration, and storms of shorter duration tend to exhibit higher maximum intensities; also, larger basins are subject to lower average basin-wide rainfall intensities), and return period. The return period of a storm associated with a particular rainfall intensity is the average length of time between successive occurrences of storms of equal or greater magnitude. For example, a rainfall intensity over a 10-acre area of 1 in./hr persisting for a 4-hr period in a particular region might have a return period of 5 years. Note that this five-year storm" might actually occur twice in one week. However, storms of this or greater intensity would, on the average, be expected to occur 20 times per century.

Values for peak rainfall intensity across various parts of the country as a function of return period and storm duration may be found in references such as *Rainfall Frequency Atlas of the U.S. for Durations from Thirty Minutes to Twenty-four Hours and Return Periods from One to One Hundred Years*, compiled for the U.S. Weather Bureau by D./M. Hershfield (1961).

While the rational formula is not particularly accurate, it is easy to use and it does illustrate some important concepts. By inspection of the equation it is apparent that larger basins can in general be expected to generate higher peak flows. The greater the rainfall intensity, the greater the prospect of flooding. Finally, basins associated with high C values, for example urban basins with extensive paved area or forested basins saturated by previous rainfall, can be expected to produce more runoff than rural basins with low antecedent moisture conditions.

Besides the rational formula, there are several other methods of predicting changes in the stream flow in response to development. The U.S. Geological Survey (USGS) has developed empirical relationships (e.g., Zembrzuski and Drum, 1979) relating stream flow to factors such as location, basin area, slope, channel length, rainfall, land-use type, and so on for various parts of the country. The U.S. Army Corps of Engineers* has developed the HEC Model Series primarily for the purpose of flood analyses, and the U.S. Department of Agriculture, Soil Conservation Service (SCS) has developed a technique for the estimation of stream flow based upon soil type. The SCS approach is actually quite useful in dealing with small to medium-sized watersheds (i.e., up to several square miles). The methodology, described in SCS TR-55 of the SCS Engineering Field Manual and summarized by Chow (1964), is actually quite powerful in that it provides the users with not only peak flow information but outflow hydrograph(s) as well. Of course, the SCS methodology is more difficult to use than the rational formula in that it requires more input data. For larger basins it is advisable to divide the watershed into sub-basins and combine their hydrographs through routing. [Routing is a technique for describing the progress of a flood wave down a channel which involves the repeated application of Manning's formula together with information regarding stream channel cross section area, slopes, roughness, etc. See Chow (1964) or other standard texts for details.] The repeated application of the SCS methodology to many sub-basins, together with the number of calculations required to complete a nontrivial routing problem, make application at the hand calculation version of the SCS methodology quite burdensome for more than a few sub-basins. Fortunately, the SCS has developed TR-20, which is essentially a computerized version of the techniques described in TR-55. The TR-20 model is available from the National Technical Information Service (NTIS).

There are other techniques available for the prediction of stream flow. Among these is the Stanford Watershed Model developed at Stanford University by Linsley and others [Linsley, Kohler, and Paulhus (1975) and Crawford and Linsley (1966)]. This model and its spin-offs, such as the Kentucky Watershed Model [a direct spin-off (Ross, 1970; Lion, 1970)] and the USGS Model [an indirect spin-off (Dawdy et al.,

*The U.S. Army Corps of Engineers, Hydraulic Engineering Center at 609 Second Street, Davis, CA 95616, (916) 756-1104, is actively involved in the development and dissemination of hydrologic modeling material.

1972)] take a holistic approach to stream flow prediction by simulating the entire hydrologic cycle using subroutines or subprograms to simulate evapotranspiration, groundwater recharge, rainfall, snow melt, and so on. This approach has many advantages in that once calibrated for a particular basin (a task which can require considerable effort and a large volume of data), changes in the watershed can be simulated by changing various model parameters to determine their effects on stream flow.

Other hydrologic models such as the STORM Model developed by the Corps of Engineers and the Storm Water Management Model (SWMM) developed by the EPA have the capability to simulate water quality as well as quantity in urban areas. See Brown et al. (1974), EPA-600/2-76-175a (1976), or Overton and Meadows (1976), for a discussion of the relative merits of the models.

Hydrologic and Water Quality Impacts

The construction or operation of transportation facilities can generate hydrologic and water quality impacts in a number of ways. Flushing spilled fuel on an airport apron into the nearest storm sewer before it catches fire can generate an oil slick detectable for miles downstream. Highways and railroads which connect developed areas usually follow valleys where topography tends to be less rugged and construction of the transportation facility is less expensive. Consequently, transportation facilities are often in close proximity to streams, lakes, and wetlands. Until recently, hydrologic features in the path of a proposed roadway were seen primarily as obstacles to be bridged, filled, or moved at least cost. Consequently, streams were often channelized and/or bridged with low-cost structures which constricted flow, occasionally causing upstream flooding. Lakes and wetlands were destroyed or disrupted by the indiscriminate use of fill. With the advent of Federal, state, and local wetlands regulations and with the expansion of the U.S. Army Corps of Engineers Section 404 permit program, as well as the Fish and Wildlife Coordination Act (see Chapters 2 and 3), acquisition of permits for the construction of highways, railroads, or airports in wetlands, lakes, or streams has become difficult, and sometimes nearly impossible, regardless of the impacts.

Assessment of the impact associated with construction in areas defined as wetlands has assumed increased importance in recent years.

In assessing the hydrologic or water quality impacts of a transportation project it is often convenient to consider construction-related impacts separately from impacts associated with the operation of the completed facility. Erosion and sedimentation impacts are perhaps the most familiar of the various construction impacts and will not be treated at length here. The various techniques of erosion control include minimization of clearing, especially during rainy periods; quick reestablishment of vegetative cover; use of protective mulches; minimization of exposed slope length; restriction of construction vehicle movements to paved areas whenever possible; avoidance of erodable soils; and management of on-site drainage through construction and use of channels, pipes, sedimentation ponds, filter fabrics, silt curtains, and so on. These techniques are well known and are part of the standard contract specifications for virtually all major highway, railway, or airport construction projects. Readers interested in the details of erosion control procedures are invited to study any of the many references published by the U.S. Department of Agriculture, SCS, and others listed at the end of this chapter.

Techniques for the prediction of the amount of erosion, turbidity, or sedimentation associated with transportation project construction are uncertain at best. The "universal soil loss equation" (Howell et al., 1976; Myer et al., 1975; Clyde et al., 1978, and others) is an empirical formula which relates soil loss per unit area to rainfall intensity, soil erodability, slope length and steepness, vegetative cover, and erosion control practices. Unfortunately, no one can predict the types of storms which will (or will not) occur between the time an area is cleared and the time it is revegetated or otherwise protected. Consequently, predictions made with the universal soil loss equation (which is not noted for its accuracy) are quite uncertain. Use of the results of soil loss estimates to predict aquatic impacts involves additional uncertainties. To begin with, one must estimate what percentage of the eroded soil will be redeposited before reaching the stream of interest. Given the mass of material that might reach the stream, there remains the problem of determining how

much of this material will be suspended and in how much water and how much of the material will be deposited where in the watercourse. Given this information one is still faced with the problem of determining how these turbidity and sedimentation impacts might affect aquatic biota. To begin to make such a determination one should know which species will be present together with their tolerance, the timing of the impact, the duration of the impact, and the availability of refuge areas.

Though worst-case turbidity estimates are sometimes developed using the universal soil loss equation or other method, the usual solution to construction-related turbidity impacts is to call for extensive erosion control and treatment measures (e.g., siltation ponds) in sensitive areas. In some instances it is appropriate to ban construction activities during the spawning periods of important species.

Among the more subtle and probably most serious of the hydrologic impacts associated with roadway construction are changes in local hydrologic patterns which change the level of the local water table, which can in turn lead to dramatic changes in important vegetation. Most everyone has noted a forest of dead trees along one side of a highway. As will be discussed later in this chapter, individual species are usually present on a site because they are better suited to the precise conditions present at the site than any other species. Soil moisture is among the conditions which influence the suitability of a given site for a given plant. If soil moisture conditions change as the result of highway construction, a change in vegetative patterns can be anticipated.

Roadway construction can change soil moisture conditions in a number of ways. If the roadway embankment restricts the flow of surface water, storm water will tend to pond upslope from the embankment, thereby increasing the average moisture content of the affected soil. Also, roadway drainage facilities can direct runoff to concentrate in an area which previously did not receive runoff from such an extensive area. If construction of a roadway embankment significantly compacts (i.e., reduces the porosity) of the underlying strata, the ability of the strata to conduct groundwater flow may be reduced, thus causing an increase in water table elevation upslope from the embankment. Construction of sloped drainage ditches which intersect the water table (thereby causing groundwater to be lost from groundwater storage) can lower the local water table as well as create a possible ponding problem elsewhere downstream.

Note that in assessing the hydrologic and water quality impacts of a construction project, one should not confine the investigation to just the site of the proposed facility. Significant impacts may also be associated with the acquisition of fill from borrow pits or, conversely, with the disposal of excess or unsuitable materials removed from the construction site. There may also be impacts associated with induced development.

Severe groundwater impacts from transportation systems are rare. Changes in aquifer recharge rates due to the paving of what was once permeable soil can be roughly assessed by assuming that the recharge rate of the aquifer is limited by the percolation rate of the surface strata. If this is the case (generally true for periods of intense precipitation, less so for a light rain), then the amount of recharge "lost" to the system will be roughly approximated by the percentage of recharge area to be rendered impermeable (paved).

Note that recharge lost to the system as runoff from paved surfaces may still percolate into the groundwater system at some later time. With regard to possible reductions in aquifer transmissiblity due to compaction under an embankment, permeability tests that subject samples of the material to be compacted to ambient pressures with and without the proposed project can provide some insights as to the expected degree of possible flow constriction. In general one would expect "clean" (i.e., permeable materials such as unconsolidated alluval material) to compact less than "dirtier" materials of low permeability containing a large fraction of silt or organic material. Fortunately, those materials which tend to make good aquifers also tend to resist compaction due to the construction of embankments.

Assessment of changes in surface hydrology expected to result from project construction can be performed as necessary using one or more of the models discussed previously. As discussed later in this section, flood impact studies for the 50- and 100-year storms are regularly performed for major projects using the Hydrologic Engineering Center (HEC) models (U.S. Army Corps of Engineers). Flooding studies for floods of

shorter return periods (e.g., mean annual flood) can also be performed. Though the results are often inconclusive, it is sometimes helpful to know what effect the proposed project will have upon the mean annual flood for ecologic impact analysis. If it can be shown that the additional (or reduced) flooding expected as the result of the project is insignificant in comparison to year-to-year variations in flood level, then one can assume that the project will not generate much in the way of changes in vegetation as the result of altering its annual flood patterns. If impacts upon short-term flooding are significant, additional analysis of the areas to be affected may be in order.

In assessing surface water impacts, it is important to avoid the interruption of natural drainage patterns. Failure to place a culvert where an embankment crosses even the smallest intermittent stream may cause ponding that will disrupt local vegetation and wildlife. The extent of ponding can be estimated using the SCS models and rainfall intensity data. However, given the ease with which this type of problem can be anticipated and solved, the need to perform this type of analysis should occur only rarely.

Another type of impact upon surface water has to do with the construction of bridges and culverts in such a way as to impede the movements of fish and other aquatic organisms. Again the solution to this type of problem is usually simple. Culverts and bridges should be designed to provide an ample depth of water for fish movements under low flow conditions. It is also important not to create a waterfall at the downstream end of the structure which might impede fish movements (see McClellan, 1970, 1980 for details).

The impacts of roadway construction on major floods are most often considered in connection with bridge design. Of particular concern, especially in light of recent Federal floodway regulations, is the potential for channel constriction by a too-short bridge structure which could cause flooding upstream from the constriction. Those impacts are usually quantified using the U.S. Army Corps of Engineers HEC Models. Note that construction of a channel constriction that may cause flooding upstream may also reduce flooding problems downstream where they are sometimes more worrisome. However, the potential for mitigating flood impacts through the careful design of highway structures (e.g., small to medium-sized bridges and culverts) to retain flood waters in upland areas is all but forbidden by current regulations (see Chapter 3).

Transportation projects may also contribute to flooding by directly and indirectly causing a net increase in runoff due to an increase in impervious area, especially if local storm water facilities have already reached capacity. Note that as a basin becomes more urbanized, higher peak flows can be expected. With increasing urbanization, the value of the average runoff coefficient C tends to increase as impermeable area increases and forested areas give way to lawns. The basin's time of concentration may also decrease, thus increasing maximum potential runoff intensity expected in a particular basin.

Factors which may reduce a basin's time of concentration include the construction of storm sewers; channelization of streams (performed ostensibly to *reduce* flooding in a particular area); and removal of vegetation and forest litter which tends to slow overland flow. The most practical means of mitigating problems of increased runoff due to increases in impervious area is usually to design storm drainage in such a way as to retain the runoff on site. Examples of such means would include letting a portion of the facility flood occasionally by deliberately undersizing storm sewers, or through the construction of retention ponds which may also serve to mitigate water quality problems associated with the first flush of pollutants from a paved area. However, the design of retention facilities must be done in accordance with the hydraulics of the receiving waters. Recalling the hydrographs presented in Figure 7-3, note that it is possible to retain storm runoff on-site for gradual release in such a way as to *increase* the peak flow of the receiving waters.

Water Quality

Transportation projects can affect water quality during construction through the generation of erosion, turbidity, and sedimentation problems together with increases in COD (chemical oxygen demand) and nutrient levels that may be associated with increases in turbidity levels. Clearing operations that remove stream bank vegetation which shades the stream can also cause

a serious impact as the attendant increase in water temperatures disrupts the aquatic ecosystem. (Note that the solubility of oxygen in water varies inversely with temperature.) Operational impacts of transportation systems usually involve the washing of pollutants from pavement surface into a watercourse or from the accidental spillage of toxic materials.*

The amounts and type of pollutants washed from pavements depends upon several factors. For example, pollutants derived from vehicular traffic (oil, grease, asbestos, rubber, lead, and other trace materials plus fallout of a general nature) tend to build up with time. Thus, as time increases between successive storms (or street cleaning operations), the concentration of pollutants present in the first flush of runoff from the paved surface also tends to increase. Loading factors (grams of pollutant per vehicle-miles traveled) are extremely difficult to predict due at least in part to the highly variable nature of the amount of deposition and reentrainment that can occur with changes in atmospheric conditions, emission rates, and the variability in the general levels of air pollution from all sources found in different parts of the country at different times. The *Users Manual* (1977) for the EPA's Storm Water Management Model contains some general values for loading factors, as do Sarten and Boyd (1975) and Shaheen (1975). However, before attempting to calculate pollutant loadings from a highway, it is wise to consult with the local "208" agency (a state water pollution control authority, usually associated with the state environmental agency, concerned with nonpoint discharges) for guidance on loading factors which may have been developed for the location of interest.

One method of assessing the probability of toxic spills from highway (or for that matter from railway, or even airport) accidents, involves estimating the joint probabilities of the various circumstances required to produce a toxic spill. For example, an estimate of the probability that a tanker truck loaded with toxic material will rupture during an accident thus polluting a stream located adjacent to x miles of highway could be performed as follows.

*As previously mentioned, spilled fuel can be a serious problem at airport fueling areas, even though most are supposed to have oil traps in their drainage systems. Of course oil traps only function when properly maintained.

1. Estimate the total VMT (Vehicle Miles Traveled) for trucks along the proposed highway segment during a given year, for example, year of maximum VMT.
2. Multiply total truck VMT by the accident rate per VMT for trucks for the facility type under consideration.
3. Multiply the value obtained in 2 by the percentage of trucks carrying toxic materials.
4. Finally, multiply the value obtained in 3 by the probability that the tank will rupture upon impact.

While the result of such a rough calculation can by no means be considered exact, it does represent a best guess regarding the probability of a toxic spill and might in unusual circumstances suggest the need for extraordinary design measures to contain, or at least retard, the flow of toxic spill.

Another source of transportation water quality impacts has to do with road salting. When assessing the impacts of road salting (airports generally do not use salt, due to its corrosive nature) one is interested in the resultant chloride concentration.* Chloride is toxic to plants and has harmful effects on humans as well, especially those with high blood pressure. (Sodium from road salting usually does not present a problem in that it tends to displace calcium ions in the soil thereby becoming immobile.) Note that the chloride ion is extremely mobile and can be transported by groundwater as well as surface water.

To assess the impacts of a water pollutant one usually begins by estimating its concentration. In the case of salt, Toler (1973) suggests that chloride concentrations can be assessed on an annual average basis using a mass-balance approach (total mass of pollutant divided by total volume of water). This method assumes that after about five years of normal application chloride concentration has reached equilibrium and that subsequent applications of salt will be washed into local watercourses. Thus, one can determine chloride concentrations using one of

*The Federal drinking water secondary standard for chloride is 250 milligrams per liter (mgl). There is no standard for sodium. Note also that road salt may contain trace amounts of other materials, like cyanide, which may be added to prevent the salt from caking.

the following equations:

$$\frac{T \times M}{I \times A} \times K = C \qquad (7\text{-}6)$$

where T = tons of salt per lane-mile
M = number of lane-miles
I = inches of runoff (annual inches of rain $\times$ 0.4)
A = drainage area in square miles
K = 8.37 if concentration of chloride is desired, or 13.79 if concentration of sodium chloride is desired
C = annual average concentrations in milligrams per liter (ppm)

or

$$\frac{T \times M}{R \times A} \times k = C \qquad (7\text{-}7)$$

where T = tons of salt per lane-mile
M = number of lane-miles
R = runoff in cubic feet per second per square mile (see below)
A = drainage area in square miles
k = 0.61 if concentration of chloride is desired, or 1.02 if concentration of sodium chloride is desired
C = annual average concentration in milligrams per liter (ppm).

This approach does, of course, ignore problems relating to the first flush phenomena in which much of the total amount of pollutant present is diluted by only a small volume of water. To account for this problem, Toler (1973) provides a figure in his paper which indicates that for small basins, that is, a few square miles, maximum daily concentrations appear to be on the order of twice average annual concentrations. Note that as basin size increases the number of sources and, more importantly, the volume of water (and the opportunity for mixing) increases. Thus, chloride concentration levels tend not to be as variable as those measured in smaller basins. With regard to groundwater impacts from road salting, Toler suggests that a similar approach might be adopted whereby chloride concentration is estimated by dividing total mass of salt applied by total volume of recharge.

The most effective method of mitigating water pollution impacts from transportation systems is obviously to prevent the pollutants from reaching the watercourse. This is the idea behind erosion and sedimentation control measures designed in connection with project construction. Failing prevention, the most effective mitigation measure is to dilute pollutants to the maximum practical extent. This may be accomplished in a number of ways. First of all, storm water drainage facilities should be designed to avoid concentration of runoff for discharge at a single outfall. If possible it is often preferable not to construct ditches or storm sewers at all, but rather to allow water to drain from the paved area and soak into the adjacent soil or make its way to a natural stream via overland flow. Should conditions dictate that storm sewers must concentrate flow, it is often advisable to construct a retention facility at the outfall to act as a settling basin as well as to provide for dilution of the first flush of pollutants, thereby reducing the shock effect upon the receiving waters.

ECOLOGY

Ecology is a rather new and developing branch of biology dealing with terrestrial, marine, and freshwater systems. The following pages present a brief overview of some of the fundamental concepts of ecology which have proven useful in the assessment of transportation impacts. For a more comprehensive treatment of the subject than can be offered here, the reader is urged to consult *Fundamentals of Ecology* by Eugene P. Odum or other standard works.

Natural Selection

While the concept of natural selection is most often discussed in connection with dissertations on evolution, it is also germane and fundamental to ecology. All species possess an inherent potential to reproduce an infinite number of their kind; however, there exist in nature forces which limit the number of similar individuals of any given type. Forces which restrict the number of similar individuals include limits on resources such as energy (food or sunlight), nutrients, water, and suitable shelter or cover. Other factors such as disease, fire, climatic conditions, actions of predators, and so on, influence the type of individual that can inhabit a given area. Given an infinite capacity for population growth in an area which can accommodate only a limited number of individuals, it is clear that not all members of a particular group of similar individuals will survive to produce large numbers of their type. Those who survive tend to be best suited to the conditions which prevail, and the offspring of these fittest of individuals tend to inherit the characteristics of their forebears. There is, however, some potential for variability in the reproductive process; not all offspring will be exact duplicates of their immediate ancestors. Hence there are always some differences between members of the same species. These intraspecific differences will of course effect an individual's chances for survival. Those individuals possessing a favorable combination of characteristics will tend to survive and generate more of their type than less fortunate individuals. Hence each species is endowed with some capacity for change and adaptation. This capacity leads to the development of highly specialized species capable of exploiting a particular set of conditions (habitat) more successfully than any other species.

The process of succession provides a good illustration as to how species specialization works in nature. The first plants to beocme established on a newly cleared site will usually be annuals (weeds). Barring subsequent disturbances, the growth and decay of the annual plants will eventually improve soil conditions to the point where grasses can become established. With the establishment of grasses (perennial plants, i.e., ones that do not die after one year), conditions will be such that seeds from annual plants will have difficulty becoming established and the annuals will become more and more scarce. As time passes, seeds from woody plants will start to become established and seedlings will grow above the grasses, shading them from the sun. As more woody plants become established, less light will be available to the grasses and soon conditions will have changed to the point where grasses are no longer suited to the site, which will be completely shaded by brush. At this point, the only plant species which can now become established are those which can endure the low light conditions which limit plant growth at ground level. It just so happens that certain plant species, for example, beech, maple, oak, and so on, can endure extended low light periods during the seedling stage. This is one reason why these species are found in climax forests which characterize the final stable stage of plant succession. Once the supply of light above the soil layer has been effectively shut out by a closed canopy of vegetation, only those plant species which can tolerate this limiting factor will survive. Then as mature trees die off, their place in the canopy will be taken by individuals growing under the low light conditions which characterize the climax forest floor.

There are, of course, other factors besides light which influence the type of vegetation that will be present on a particular site. Edaphic factors such as soil texture, moisture availability, nutrient supply, and so on, also play a role in the determination of which plant species is best suited for survival on a particular site. In general, if there exists a species which is more aptly suited for survival on a particular site than the species which occupies the site, eventually the new species will displace the present type. Site conditions need not change drastically before a different species will be favored, because each species of plant has slightly different requirements. With hundreds of different species having the potential to occupy a certain site, the assemblage of plants on a given site often represents a high degree of fine tuning which has taken place over many years. For example, a look at virtually any tall mountain will reveal distinct differences in vegetative type as elevation increases. The perceptive observer will also note differences in vegetative type between northern and southern slopes in most areas. These differences in vegetation are the result of the subtle differences in microclimate which drive the forces of natural selection to favor one species over another.

The same forces which cause different plants to inhabit different types of sites are also at work in the animal kingdom, though the larger animals, due to their ability to move about, are somewhat less sensitive to changes in microclimate. Still, one finds few alligators in Maine, and few moose in Florida.

The point of this discussion is that each species is adapted for survival under a specific set of conditions which define its habitat or environment. Within this environment, the species will secure the energy required for reproduction and survival. Of course, survival of the species is dependent on its ability to reproduce. The special conditions necessary for reproduction often dictate which areas are suitable for a given species; for example, adult mosquitoes can survive in many areas, but reproductive requirements tend to restrict their range to wetter areas suitable for survival of the larval stage.

One of the fundamental tenets of ecology is that no two species can coexist if they require exactly the same resources for survival; that is, they occupy the same niche. Natural selection dictates that the fitter species will exploit its environment and increase its numbers until constrained by some limiting factor, to the exclusion of any other species which might be less well adapted to exploit the niche in question.

The phenomenon of adaption and specialization is not limited to the species level. Particular strains, varieties, and even individual members of the same species may exhibit a degree of specialization which enables them to survive at the expense of others who may be less fit. For example, trees growing within a dense stand compete for light. The microclimate within dense tree stands is such that the danger of wind throw (being blown down) is rather slight compared with more exposed areas. Consequently, those individual trees which grow straight and tall, putting most of their productivity into an effort to secure a supply of solar energy for themselves, tend to dominate the forest canopy, shutting out the sun's energy to less well adapted individuals. However, when some action, such as highway construction, opens up a dense forest stand, trees along the newly created edge tend to be highly subject to wind throw, an environmental stress to which their tall, straight trunks, concentration of branches at canopy level, and underdeveloped root systems render them poorly adapted.

Trophic Levels

The definition of an organism's trophic level refers to the mechanisms through which the organism derives the *energy* needed to maintain its life functions. Organisms at the first level (primary producers, i.e., plants) obtain their energy directly from the sun. Organisms of the second trophic level (secondary producers or herbivores) obtain their energy (food) from primary producers. Organisms of the third trophic level (carnivores) feed on herbivores, and so on. Since the laws of thermodynamics dictate that the transfer of energy from one trophic level to the next cannot be 100 percent efficient, the total number of sustainable trophic levels is limited. At each transfer between trophic levels, an amount on the order of 90 percent of the total available energy is lost. Thus, the total amount of biomass which can be sustained at each trophic level tends to decrease with each successive level. Consequently, the maximum number of trophic levels in an ecosystem (energy pyramid) seldom exceeds four or five.

Diversity

Ecologists generally speak of two types of diversity; species diversity and habitat diversity. An ecosystem or trophic level containing, for example, ten species in which a single species accounted for 90 percent of the total biomass would be said to exhibit lower diversity than a similar system containing the same number of organisms with a more balanced species mix. Various indexes have been developed to describe species diversity. At one time it was thought that systems which exhibit high species diversity were more stable (less prone to disruption) than systems characterized by low species diversity. In recent years this concept has lost favor with the scientific community and is not nearly as popular as it once was. Species diversity is also used by some as a measure of the intrinsic value of a particular ecosystem.

Habitat diversity refers to the heterogeneity of habitat types (e.g., forest, field, mudflat, mud bottom, rocky bottom, etc.) present in a particular area. In general, the greater the diversity of a particular area the greater its value as wildlife habitat. Like people, wildlife have definite food and shelter (or cover) requirements. While a forest may provide excellent cover and shelter for deer, a field habitat may provide a greater food resource, at least during particular parts of the year. Thus transition areas between different habitat types (edges or ecotones) from which wildlife can avail itself of a variety of habitat types depending upon its needs (food, rest, breeding, rearing of young, etc.) are especially valuable to wildlife. The aggregation or concentration of wildlife in ecotones is referred to as the edge effect.

Nutrient Cycling

Nutrients such as nitrogen, phosphorous, potassium, and a myriad of trace elements often act as limiting factors to plant growth (primary productivity). As anyone who has ever done any serious gardening can attest, the availability of nutrients on a particular site is limited and the removal of biomass (harvesting) can deplete the available nutrients within a few years. Soil depletion in a garden can be counteracted by a program of artificial fertilization designed to replace depleted nutrients, thus preventing nutrient availability from becoming a limiting factor. With adequate nutrients some other factor such as soil moisture will then become limiting. If this is the case, watering the garden will increase productivity by eliminating moisture availability as a limiting factor. Note that when one speaks of limiting factors one is generally referring to a single factor, for example, a single nutrient such as phosphorus, that restricts productivity. A limiting factor limits productivity somewhat like the slowest bucket handler in a bucket brigade limits the output of the entire work force.

In nature, just as in a garden, there is a limited supply of essential nutrients. While the weathering of rock material does liberate new supplies of nutrients and sedimentation does remove nutrients from the biosphere, the most important source of nutrients in natural systems comes from the cycling of the same nutrients through the biosphere in a manner somewhat analogous to the movement of money through an economic system. For example, phosphate leached from rocks may be taken up by plants which are eaten by insects that might in turn be eaten by birds to be eaten by carnivores. This same phosphate will be present in each of these organisms and somewhere along this chain an organism will die to be decomposed by bacteria which will return the phosphate to the soil where it will again be available to plants.

In a climax community, nutrients that might be limiting tend to be tied up in the biomass and productivity tends to continue at a relatively constant rate. Other systems such as wetlands, estuaries, and flood plans receive an influx of nutrients from external sources enabling productivity to proceed at a much higher rate.

Ecologic Impact Analysis and Mitigation

The assessment of ecologic impacts is an exceedingly difficult and uncertain task with few standard techniques to guide the analyst. Part of the problem lies in the importance of secondary, tertiary, or even less direct impacts of development. Construction of a highway will obviously result in what might be euphemistically termed "severe disruption" of the vegetation within the right of way. Assessment of this direct impact is simple. Whatever is in the path of the proposed project will cease to exist after construction. Yet construction of the linear embankments characteristic of transportation system developments (e.g., highway rights of way, railroad beds, pipelines, runways, etc.) have also been known to change surface water and groundwater flows and disrupt wildlife movements. These impacts can in turn cause other effects, which may manifest themselves far beyond the project limits. For example, improper construction of a highway embankment can impede surface flows and cause ponding of water upslope from the embankment. This ponding may well lead to a shift in vegetative type and a consequent change in habitat type, thereby impacting wildlife. Transportation system developments have also been known to interfere with wildlife migration, introduce undesirable plant species, degrade water quality, and restrict the movement of fish and other aquatic species.

The most common problem with respect to impacts upon animal migrations has to do with deer. Unfortunately, techniques for the assessment and mitigation of potential interference in the movement of deer (or other mammals such as bear) are far from standardized, although literature is available and research is being conducted (see bibliography). One school of thought opts for the construction of the facility without regard for animal migrations and the imposition of "fixes," for example, fences, mirrors to frighten deer away, signs, and so on, after problem areas have been identified (usually, and unfortunately, through accidents). This approach, though crude and dangerous, has worked for many years in many locations and may be preferable to the indiscriminate construction of expensive deer crossing structures which may or may not be used by the deer.

Perhaps a more reasonable approach to the problem of accommodating deer movements involves the use of judgment and experience together with some field verification (which should be done for each season) in an attempt to assess potential deer problems. If done early in project design, it is often possible to accommodate deer (or bear) movements at stream crossings. Note that deer often avail themselves of the extensive cover and gentler topography of bottom lands in deciding (if deer decide) how to conduct their movements. Thus, it is often possible to accommodate deer movements at stream crossings by preserving natural cover, providing at least several feet of vertical and horizontal clearance, making sure the substrate is of a natural material (as opposed to paving or riprap), and occasionally by installing deer fence to direct the animals toward the available passage.

In attempting to keep deer out of a right of way, it should be noted that deer tend to be attracted to pastures such as areas along highways, especially in heavily forested areas where grazing opportunities are limited. Thus the installation of anything less than a 9-ft deer fence between the forest and the pasture would tend to be less effective in keeping deer out of the road than an alternate design that allowed the deer use of at least some of the grassy area by placing the fence closer to the highway.

One of the major problems associated with attempts to fence deer out of highway rights of way is that the same fences that keep deer out also keep them in the right of way should they somehow find their way into the pasture area, as they frequently do. One-way deer gates (Erickson et al., 1978) which let deer escape the right-of-way area have been shown to be of some use in this regard.

One of the basic precepts of ecological impact analysis is that everything is connected to everything else. For example, changes in surface hydrology can cause changes in groundwater hydrology which can alter vegetative patterns which can change wildlife habitats which can change wildlife which can affect vegetation which may change groundwater patterns, which can change surface hydrology, and so on. As one attempts to predict the effects of some perturbation through an ecosystem the uncertainties associated with prediction increase dramatically with the number of steps involved in the analysis. To further complicate matters, effects do not tend to restrict themselves to a single academic discipline. The world's foremost botanist, for example, would find it difficult to predict the impacts of ponding upon a forest stand upslope from an impermeable embankment without consulting a hydrologist who could predict the exact nature of the changes in soil moisture in time and space expected to result from project construction. The hydrologist in turn might require assistance from project engineers, geologists, or meteorologists, who in turn might have to conduct lengthy on-site investigations before supplying needed data.

It should be noted that while it is obviously important to describe the site and its environs in preparing an ecological impact analysis, it is not possible to analyze impacts by simply collecting and presenting large amounts of data, regardless of how much time and money may have been spent on site description. In general, unless a particular data set will be of some *direct* use in answering questions as to *how* an ecosystem might change as the result of project initiation, time and money should not be committed to its acquisition. It should also be noted that the acquisiton of *meaningful* ecological data is often a difficult and time-consuming task. For example, if one wishes to obtain fish-spawning data, it will be necessary for experts to collect the data during that portion of the year when the fish in question might spawn. Even then, unless special techniques are employed every year for several years at all river locations, the resultant data will always be considered incomplete. One should always apply the "so what" test before setting out to collect environmental data. Similarly, one should not be impressed by vast amounts of raw data purporting to describe existing conditions when one is really interested in potential changes that might result from the proposed project.

Wetlands

Serious discussions concerning ecological impacts of transportation projects occur most often in connection with the acquisiton of tidal wetlands, inland (freshwater) wetlands, or section 404 permits. Note that most of the agencies involved in issuing wetlands permits have limited missions and objectives; their job is not to build projects but to protect the environment. Note also that many major projects involve regulated wetlands of some form or another. At times it seems that developable land, people, transportation facilities, and water all seem to occur in the same place. In any event, it is always wise for the developers to consult with state and Federal regulatory agencies early in the project development process to determine where wetlands are located, and the plan to avoid encroaching upon these areas if at all practical.

If there is no viable alternative to wetlands encroachment, every effort should be made to involve the regulatory agencies in project design *from the very beginning*. Otherwise, the regulators will tend not to believe that there are no real alternatives to encroachment upon the wetlands within their jurisdictions, and their demands with regard to studies and mitigation will reflect this attitude. With early regulatory agency involvement, appropriate impact studies can be performed during project design (while changes in design can easily be accommodated) *before* an adversary relationship has developed. With regulatory involvement in the design of required impact studies, as well as in design of the project itself, the chances for timely issuance of the necessary permits are greatly enhanced.

The word *mitigation* often means different things to different people. To project developers it apparently means "to lessen the impact of a project," for example, preventing erosion. To regulatory agencies, it often involves *paying the price for environmental impacts*, for example, purchasing lands to be maintained in their natural state to replace those disrupted by construction. Unfortunately, the transportation developer seldom has the funds or the legal mandate to purchase and maintain replacement lands.* Given these two different interpretations, the potential for misunderstanding concerning an appropriate degree of mitigation is obvious.

One technique for the replacement of wetlands destroyed by transportation projects involves the imaginative acquisition of material for the construction of embankments. Given that project design already incorporates such obvious "avoidance" features as careful alignment, restriction of median widths, and careful construction practices, one can create new wetlands, for highway purposes, by excavating borrow pits in areas where the water table is close to the surface and then lining the excavation with organic materials taken from other sections of the project. Those man-made wetlands can be placed in the right of way or located at selected borrow

---

*Note the development of FHWA Policy (July 31, 1980 *Federal Register* 50-728-50731, 23 CFR Part 777) authorizing replacement of privately owned wetlands in certain circumstances on an acre-for-acre basis. However, state transportation agencies are often forbidden to spend public monies for nontransportation purposes. Note contrasts between this policy and the Department of the Interior FWS mitigation policy which calls for replacement of equivalent *habitat value* which may well involve more than an acre-for-acre replacement of wetlands.

sites. Note that wetlands can also be intentionally created by using highway, runway, or railway embankments as dams. It should be noted, however, that the creation of wetlands will require the destruction of the site's previous habitat and environment. This type of value judgment seems to be implied by the mandates given to regulatory agencies.

In dealing with the Corps of Engineers and other Federal agencies, principally the FWS, concerning wetlands it is usually necessary to classify the wetlands involved according to criteria outlined in U.S. Department of Interior, FWS publication FWS/OBS-79/31 *Classification of Wetlands and Deepwater Habitats of the United States*, December 1979. While relatively straightforward in its classification of marine, estuarine, riverine, lacustrine, and paulstrine habitats into various subgroups, the document is rather vague in its definition of what constitutes a wetland. The document defines wetlands as

lands which are covered by shallow water, or support predominantly hydrophytes (plants that are typically found in wet habitats), [or contain] hydric (wet) soil.

Unfortunately there are no standard listings as to which plants are hydrophytes or which soils are considered hydric. The best way out of this dilemma has proven to involve the judgment of a competent botanist as to which areas are dominated by hydrophytes, with written concurrence by the FWS.

Another technique brought to bear on wetland questions by the FWS is the Habitat Evaluation Procedure (HEP) (1980). This procedure involves the assignment of arbitrary numerical values to various habitat units for various species in the project area by a team of biologists. Acres impacted together with their present and projected value are then tabulated as a quantitative measure of habitat destruction. The implication is that the developer should mitigate by acquiring, or upgrading habitat until a balance is achieved between value lost and value gained. Thus it would seem that the FWS has devised a "scientific" scheme for the objective evaluation of mitigation plans.

In assessing the results of HEP one should keep in mind that the results hold *only* for those species considered in the analysis. Mitigation plans given a high rating under HEP may still be detrimental to species not considered in the analysis, or have severe aesthetic, recreational, or water quality impacts. For example, if one were conducting an HEP analysis for upland game species, a program of clear-cutting and burning selected sections of forest should receive a favorable HEP rating. However few would implement such a program or the basis of HEP alone.

Rare and Endangered Species

Species that are truly rare or endangered tend to be associated with habitats that are rare or endangered. Other species considered rare in a particular area are simply at the margins of their natural range; for example, alligators might be rare in parts of Georgia. Other species may be simply becoming extinct as the result of natural evolution in much the same way dinosaurs became extinct. Lists of rare and endangered species are of course maintained by state and Federal environmental agencies.

One of the problems with assessing impacts upon rare or endangered species is that they tend not to be detected by ordinary sampling procedures, sometimes because they are rare in the area in question and sometimes because they do not exist in the area in question. Note that if something cannot be found it does not mean that it does not exist.

Usually habitats are easier to identify than rare species are to collect. Thus the best procedure for evaluating rare or endangered species is to consult with the state and/or Federal environmental agencies to check whether the habitat types to be impacted by the project might support rare or endangered species. If it appears that rare species might be affected by the project, a program of study and possibly of mitigation or avoidance should be undertaken in cooperation with the cognizant regulatory agencies, notably the rare and endangered species group of the FWS.

BIBLIOGRAPHY

Allen, R. E., and McCullough, D. R., Deer-Car Accidents in Southern Michigan, *J. Wildl. Manage.* 40:317–325, 1976.

American Association of State Highway Officials (AASHO), *Guidelines for Hydraulic Considerations in*

Highway Planning Location, vol. I, *Highway Drainage Guidelines*, 1973, 341 National Press Building, Washington, D.C. 20004.

AASHO, *Guidelines for Hydrology*, vol. II, *Highway Drainage Guidelines*, 1973, 341 National Press Building, Washington, D.C. 20004.

AASHO, *Guidelines for Erosion and Sediment Control in Highway Construction*. vol. 3, *Highway Drainage Guidelines*, 1973, 341 National Press Building, Washington, D.C. 20004.

AASHO, *Guidelines for the Hydraulic Design of Culverts*, vol. IV, *Highway Drainage Guidelines*, 1975, 341 National Press Building, Washington, D.C. 20004.

AASHTO, *A Design Guide for Wildlife Protection and Conservation for Transportation Facilities*, 1976, 341 National Press Building, Washington, D.C. 20004.

American Public Health Association, American Water Works Association, and Water Pollution Control Federation (APHA, et al.), *Standard Methods for the Examination of Water and Wastewater*, 14th ed., 1976, 1015 Eighteenth Street, N.W., Washington D.C. 20036.

American Society of Civil Engineers and the Water Pollution Control Federation, Joint Committee, *Design and Construction of Sanitary and Storm Sewers*, 1969.

Arner, D. H., *Transmission Line Rights-of-Way Management*, U.S. Department of Interior, FWS, Office of Biological Services, 1451 Green Road, Ann Arbor, MI 48105.

Baker, H. G., Characteristics and Modes of Origin of Weeds. In H. G. Baker and G. L. Stebbins, eds., *The Genetics of Colonizing Species*, Academic, New York, 1965, pp. 147–172.

Barton, B. A., Short-Term Effects of Highway Construction on the Limnology of a Small Stream in Southern Ontario, *Freshwater Biol.*, 7:99–100, 1977.

Barton, J. R., and Winger, P. V., *Stream Rehabilitation Concepts*, Utah State Department of Highways, Salt Lake City, UT, 1974.

Bear, Jacob, *Dynamics of Fluids in Porous Media*, Elsevier, New York, 1975.

Beard, L. R., *Statistical Methods in Hydrology*, H.S. Army Engineer District, Corps of Engineers, Sacramento, CA, 1962.

Bellis, Edward D., and Graves, H. B., III, *Highway Fences as Vehicle-Deer Collision Deterrents*, Institute for Research on Land and Water Resources, Penn. State Univ., University Park, June 1976.

Bellis, E. D., and Graves, H. B., III, Deer Mortality on a Pennsylvania Interstate Highway, *J. Wildl. Manage.* 35:232–237, 1971.

Bellis, E. D., and Graves, H. B., III, Carbaugh, B. T., and Vaughan, J. P., *Behavior, Ecology and Mortality of White-tailed Deer along a Pennsylvania Interstate Highway*, Institute for Research on Land and Water Resources, Penn State Univ., University Park, Publ. 71, 1971.

Bramble, W. D., and Byrnes, W. R., Evaluation of the Wildlife Habitat Values of Rights of Way, *J. Wildl. Manage.*, 43:642–649, 1979.

Brandstetter, A., *Comparative Analysis of Urban Stormwater Models*, Battelle Northwest, August 1974.

Brandstetter, A., *Assessment of Mathematical Models for Storm and Combined Sewer Management*, EPA-600/2-76-175a, Municipal Environmental Research Laboratory, Office of Research and Development, EPA, Cincinnati, OH, August 1976.

Brown, J. W., et al., *Models and Methods Applicable to Corps of Engineers Urban Studies*, U.S. Army Corps of Engineers, August 1974.

Bryan, Hal, *The Effects of Herbicides Used By the Kentucky DOT of the Ecosystem*, Department of Transportation, Commonwealth of Kentucky, Frankfort, August 1976.

Button, E. F., Rubins, E. J., Woodward, M. A., and Griffin, G. F., *Effects of Deicing Salts and Lead Upon Trees, Shrubs and Soils in Connecticut*, Department of Transportation, State of Connecticut, Wolcott Hill Road, Wethersfield, CT 06109, January 1977. (Also available from NTIS).

Carbaugh, B. T., *Activity and Behavior of White-tailed Deer (Odocoileus virginianus) Along an Interstate Highway in a Forest Region of Pennsylvania*, D. Ed. Thesis, Penn. State Univ., University Park, 1970.

Carbaugh, B. T., Vaughan, J. P., Bellis, E. D., Graves, H. B., III, Distribution and Activity of White-tailed Deer along an Interstate Highway, *J. Wildl. Manage.*, 39:570–581, 1974.

Chow, Ven Te, *Handbook of Applied Hydrology*, McGraw-Hill, New York, 1964.

Chow, V. T., and Yen, B. C., *Urban Storm Water Runoff: Determination of Volumes and Flow Rates*, EPA Municipal Environmental Research Laboratory, EPA-600/2-76-116, May 1976.

Clewell, Andre F., Gainey, Louis F., Jr., Harlos, David P., and Tobi, Enola R., *Biological Effects of Fill-Roads Across Salt Marshes*. Florida Department of Transportation, Tallahassee, FL 32304, March 1976.

Clyde, C. G., et al., *Manual of Erosion Control Principles and Practices During Highway Construction*, Utah Water Research Laboratory, Hydraulics and Hydrology Series, UWRL/H-78/02, College of Engineering, Utah State Univ., Logan, UT 84322, 1978.

Colston, Newton V., and Tafuri, Anthony N., Urban Land Runoff Considerations. In William Whipple Jr., ed., *Urbanization and Water Quality Control*, American Water Resources Association, Minneapolis, MN, 1975, pp. 120–128.

Convisser, M., Mitigation of Transportation Impacts. In G. A. Swanson, tech. coordinator, *The Mitigation Symposium: A National Workshop on Mitigating Losses of Fish and Wildlife Habitats*, USDA, Gen. Tech. Rep. RM-65, 1979, pp. 71–74.

Cowardin, L. M., Carter, V., Golet, F. C., and LaRoe, E. T., *Classification of Wetlands and Deepwater Habitats of the United States*, U.S. Dept. of the Interior, FWS, Biological Services Program, FWS/BS-79-31, 1979.

Crawford, N. H., and Linsley, R. K., *Digital Simulation in Hydrology: Stanford Watershed Model IV*, Tech. Rep. 39, Stanford Univ. CA, 1966.

Darnell, R. M., *Impacts of Construction Activities in Wetlands of the United States*, EPA-600/3-76-045, Environmental Research Laboratory, Office of Research and Development, EPA, Corvallis, OR 97330, 1976.

Davis, Phillip B., and Humphrys, Clifford R., *Ecological Effects of Highway Construction Upon Michigan Woodlots and Wetlands*, Environmental Liaison Unit, Michigan Dept. of State Highways and Transportation, Box K, Lansing, MI 48904, August 1977.

Dawdy, D. R., Lichty, R. W., and Bergmann, J. M., *A Rainfall-Runoff Simulation Model for Estimation of Flood Peaks for Small Drainage Basins*, U.S. Geological Survey Professional Paper 506-B, U.S. Government Printing Office, Washington, D.C., 1972.

DesJardins, C. R., Ecological Mitigation: A Viable Option in the Federal-Aid Highway Program. In G. A. Swanson, tech. coordinator, *The Mitigation Symposium: A National Workshop on Mitigating Losses of Fish and Wildlife Habitats*, USDA, Gen. Tech. Rep. RM-65, 1979, pp. 562-565.

Doucet, G. T., Sarrazin, J. R., and Bider, J. R., Use of Highway Overpass Embankments by the Woodchucks, *Marmota monax*, Can. Field Nat., 88:187-190, 1974.

Drysdale, Frank R., and Benner, David K., *The Suitability of Salt-Tolerant Species for Revegetation of Saline Areas Along Selected Ohio Highways*, Ohio DOT, Box 899, Columbus, OH 43216, August 1973.

Edmunson, George C., *Plant Materials Study: A Search for Drought-Tolerant Plant Materials for Erosion Control, Revegetation, and Landscaping Along California Highways*. California DOT, Office of Landscape and Architectural Design, 1120 N. Street, P.O. Box 1499, Sacramento, CA 95814, June 1976. (Also available from NTIS).

Erickson, P. A., Camougis, G., and Robbins, E. J., *Highways and Ecology: Impact Assessment and Mitigation*, DOT, FHWA, Washington, D.C., 1978.

Epsey, W. H., Jr., and Winslow, D. E., Urban Flood Frequency Characteristics, *Proc. ASCE*, 100, HY2, 179-293, 1974.

Evans, Willis A. and Johnston, F. Beryl, *Fish Migration and Fish Passage—A Practical Guide to Solving Fish Passage Problems*, Forest Service Region 5, USDA, March 1974.

Farnworth, E. G., Nichols, M. C., Vann, C. N., Wolfson, L. G., Bosserman, R. W., Hendrix, P. R., Golley, F. B., and Cooley, J. L., *Impacts of Sediment and Nutrients on Biota in Surface Waters of the United States*, EPA-600/3-79-105, Office of Research and Development, 1979.

Ferris, C. R., Effect of Interstate-95 on Breeding Birds in Northern Maine, *J. Wildl. Manage.*, 43:421-427, 1979.

Franklin Institute Research Laboratories, *Investigation of Porous Pavements for Urban Runoff Control*, EPA, U.S. Gov. Print. Office, Washington, D.C., 1972.

Fried, J. J., *Groundwater Pollution Theory, Methodology, Modelling and Practical Rules*, Elsevier Scientific, New York, 1975.

Getz, L. L., Cole, F. R., and Gates, D. L., Interstate Roadsides as Dispersal Routes for *Microtus Pennsylvanicus*, *J. Mamm.*, 49:208-212, 1978.

Gosselink, J. G., Reimold, R. F., Gallagher, J. L., Windom, H. L., and Odum, E. P., *Spoil Disposal Problems for Highway Construction Through Marshes*, Georgia DOT, Atlanta, GA, 1972.

Graves, H. B., Bellis, E. D., and Knuth, W. M., Censusing White-tailed Deer by Airborne Thermal Infrared Imagery, *J. Wildl. Manage.* 36:875-884, 1972.

Hanes, R. E., Zelazny, L. W., and Blaser, R. E., *Effects of Deicing Salts on Water Quality and Biota*, Literature Review and Recommended Research, National Cooperative Highway, Res. Prog. Rep. 91, 1970.

Hershfield, D. M., *Rainfall Frequency Atlas of the United States*, Weather Bureau TP-40, U.S. Department of Commerce, Weather Bureau, Washington D.C., 1961.

Hershfield, D. M., Extreme Rainfall Relationships, *Proc. ASCE*, **88**, HY6, 73-92, 1962.

Howell, R. B., *Heavy Metals in Highway Runoff and Effects on Aquatic Biota*, paper presented at Comission of European Communities, et al., Heavy Metals in the Environment International Conference, London, September 1979.

Howell, R. B., Shirley, E. C., and Kerri, K. D., *Water Quality Manual*, Vol. 2, *Hydrologic and Physical Aspects of the Environment*, Implementation Package 77-1, Federal Highway Administration, Washington, D. C., October, 1976.

Huber, et al., *SWMM: Users Manual Version II*, EPA-670/2-75-017, 1975.

Hunt, W. A., and Graham, R. J., *Preliminary Evaluation of Channel Changes Designed to Restore Fish Habitat*, Planning and Research Bureau, Dept. of Highways, State of Montana, Helena, MT, 1972.

Hutchinson, G. E., *A Treatise on Limnology*, Vol. 1, *Geography, Physics, and Chemistry*, Wiley, New York, 1951.

Hutchinson, G. E., *A Treatise on Limnology*, Vol. 2, *Introduction to Lake Biology and the Limnoplankton*, Wiley, New York, 1967.

Hutchinson, G. E., *A Treatise on Limnology*, Vol. 3, *Limnological Botany*, Wiley, New York, 1975.

Hynes, H. B. N., *The Ecology of Running Waters*, Univ. of Toronto Press, Toronto, 1970.

Iwamoto, R. N., Salo, E. O., Madej, M. A., McComas, R. L., and Rulifson, R. L., *Sediment and Water Quality: A Review of the Literature Including a Suggested Approach for Water Quality Criteria with Summary of Workshop and Conclusions and Recommendations*, EPA-910/9-78-048, 1978.

Jackson, J. A., Rights-of-Way Management for an Endangered Species: The Red-cockaded Woodpecker. In R. Tillman, ed., *Proceedings of the First National Symposium on Environmental Concerns in Rights-of-*

Way Management, Mississippi State Univ., 1976, pp. 247-252.

Jackson, J. A., Highways and Wildlife—Some Challenges and Opportunities for Management. In G. A. Swanson, tech. coordinator, The Mitigation Symposium: *A National Workshop on Mitigating Losses of Fish and Wildlife Habitats*, USDA, Gen. Tech. Rep. RM-64, 1979, pp. 556-571.

Jackson, T. J., and Ragan, R. M., Hydrology of Porous Pavement Parking Lots, *Proc. ASCE.* **100**, HY12, 1739-1752, 1974.

Joselyn, G. B., Warnock, J. E., and Etter, S. L., Manipulation of Roadside Cover for Nesting Pheasants—A preliminary Report, *J. Wildl. Manage.*, **32**:217-233, 1968.

King, R., and Carlander, D., *A Study of the Effects of Stream Channelization and Bank Stabilization on Warmwater Sport Fish in Iowa: Sub-project No. 3. Some Effects of Short-Reach Channelization on Fishes and Food Organisms in Central Iowa Warm Water Streams*, Iowa Cooperative Fishery Research Unit, Iowa State Univ., Ames, IA 50011, April 1976.

Leclerc, G., and Schaake, J. C., Jr., *Methodology for Assessing the Potential Impact of Urban Development on Urban Runoff and the Relative Efficiency of Runoff Control Alternatives*, Massachusetts Institute of Technology, Dept. of Civil Engineering, Ralph M. Parsons Laboratory, Rep. No. 167, March 1973.

Leedy, D. L., *Highway-Wildlife Relationships*, vol. I, *A State-of-the-Art Report;* vol. 2, *An Annotated Bibliography*, Offices of Research and Development, DOT, FHWA, Washington, D.C., 1975.

Leedy, D. L., Franklin, T. M., and Hekimian, E. C., *Highway-Wildlife Relationships*, vol. 2, *An Annotated Bibliography*, Offices of Research and Development, DOT, FHWA, Washington, D.C. 20590, December 1975. (Also available from NTIS).

Leopold, L. B., *Hydrology for Urban Land Planning—A Guidebook on Hydrologic Effects of Urban Land Use*, USGS Circular 554, 1968.

Leopold, B., *Water—A Primer*, W.H. Freeman, San Francisco, 1974.

Linsley, R. K., and Franzini, J. B., *Water Resources Engineering*, 2nd ed., McGraw-Hill, New York, 1972.

Linsley, R. K., Jr., Kohler, M. A., and Paulhus, J. L. H., *Hydrology for Engineers*, 2nd ed., McGraw-Hill, New York, 1975.

Liou, E. Y., *OPSET: Program for Computerized Selection of Watershed Parameter Values for the Stanford Watershed Model*, Univ. of Kentucky Water Resources Inst. Res. Rep. No. 34, Lexington, KY, 1970.

McCaffery, K. R., Deer Trail Counts as an Index to Populations and Habitat Use, *J. Wildl. Manage.*, **40**:308-316, 1976.

McClellan, Thomas J., *Fish Passage Through Highway Culverts*, Office of Engineering, DOT, FHWA, Washington, D.C. 20590, 1970. (Repr. 1980.)

Meade, J. A., Guidelines for Herbicide Use, *Pub. Works*, **107**:7, 48-53, July 1976.

Metcalf and Eddy, Inc., *Stormwater Management Model*, vol. III, *User's Manual*, NTIS No. PB-203 291, 1971.

Meyer, G. J., Schoeneberg, P. J., and Huddleston, J. H., Sediment Yields from Roadsides: An Application of the Universal Soil Loss Equation, *Soil Water Conserv.* **30**:6, November-December 1975.

Michael, E. D., Ferris, C. R., and Haverlock, E. G., Effects of Highway Rights-of-Way on Bird Populations. In R. L. Tillman, ed., *Proceedings of the First National Symposium on Environmental Concerns in Rights-of Way Management*, Mississippi State Univ. 1976, pp. 254-261.

Miller, J. F., et al., *Precipitation Frequency Atlas of the Western U.S.* National Oceanographic and Atmospheric Administration, U. S. Dept. of Commerce, 1973.

Moxley, Luther, and Davidson, Harold, *Salt Tolerance of Various Woody and Herbaceous Plants*. Dept. of Horticulture, Michigan State Univ., East Lansing, MI, Horticultural Rep. No. 23, 1973. Reprinted by DOT, FHWA, 1974.

Muncy, R. J., Atchison, G. J., Bulkley, R. V., Menzel, B. W., Perry, L. G. and Summerfelt, R. C., *Effects of Suspended Solids and Sediment on Reporduction and Early LIfe of Warmwater Fishes: A Review*, EPA-600/3-79-042, Office of Research and Development, 1979.

Nakao, D. L., Hatano, M. M., Howell, R. B., and Shirley, E. C., *Highway Operation and Plant Damage*. California DOT, Sacramento, CA 95807 (Interim Rep. CA-DOT-TL-7134-1-76-13).

Odum, E. P., *Fundamentals of Ecology*. 3rd ed., W. B. Saunders, Philadelphia, PA, 1971. 574

Oetting, R. B., and Cassel, J. F., Waterfowl Nesting on Interstate Highway Right-of-Way in North Dakota, *J. Wildl. Manage.*, **35**:774-780, 1971.

Overton, D. E., and Meadows, M. E. *Stormwater Modeling*, Academic, New York, 1976.

Oxley, D. J., Fenton, M. B., and Carmody, G. R., The Effects of Roads on Populations of Small Mammals, *J. Applied Ecol.*, **11**:51-59, 1974.

Page, R. D., and Cassel, J. F., Waterfowl Nesting on a Railroad Right-of-Way in North Dakota, *J. Wildl. Manage.*, **35**:554-549, 1971.

Peek, F., and Bellis, E. D., Deer Movements and Behavior Along an Interstate Highway, *Highway Res. News*, **36**:36-42, 1969.

Pojar, T. M., Prosence, R. A., Reed, D. F., and Woodward, T. N., Effectiveness of Lighted, Animated Deer Crossing Sign, *J. Wildl. Manage.*, **39**:87-91, 1974.

Pojar, T. M., Reseign, T. C., and Reed, D. F., "Deer Crossing" Signs may Prove Valuable in Reducing Accidents and Animal Deaths, *Highway Res. News*, **46**:20-23, 1972.

Puglisi, M. J., Lindzey, J. S., and Bellis, E. D. Factors Associated with Highway Mortality of White-tailed Deer, *J. Wildl. Manage.*, **38**:799-807, 1974.

Raudkivi, J. J., *Hydrology, An Advanced Introduction to Hydrological Processes and Modeling*, Pergamon Press, New York, 1979.

Reed, D. F., *Techniques for Determining Potentially Critical Deer Highway Crossings*, Colorado Div. of Game, Fish, and Parks, Game Inf. Leafl. 73, 1969.

Reed, D. F., Pojar, T. M., and Woodward, T. N., Use of One-Way Gates by Mule Deer, *J. Wildl. Manage.* **38**: 9-15, 1974.

Reed, D. F., Pojar, T. M., and Woodward, T. N., Mule Deer Responses to Deer Guards, *J. Wildl. Manage.*, **27**:111-113, 1974.

Reed, D. F., Woodward, T. N., and Pojar, T. M., Behavioral Response of Mule Deer to a Highway Underpass, *J. Wildl. Manage.*, **39**:361-367, 1975.

Reed, J. P., Jr. *Stream Community Response to Road Construction Sediments*, Virginia Water Resources, Res. Center Bull. No. 97, 1977.

Reilley, R. E., and Green, H. E., Deer Mortality on a Michigan Interstate Highway, *J. Wildl. Manage.*, **38**: 16-19, 1974.

Richardson, E. V., Simons, D. B., Karaki, S., Mahmood, K., and Stevens, M. A., *Highways in the River Environment: Hydraulic and Environmental Design Considerations*, Training and Design Manual prepared for the DOT, FHWA, 1975.

Ross, G. A., The Stanford Watershed Model: The Correlation of Parameter Values Selected by a Computerized Procedure with Measurable Physical Characteristics of the Watershed, Univ. of Kentucky Water Resources Inst. Res. Rep. No. 35, 1970.

Roth, D., and Wall, G., Environmental Effects of Highway Deicing Salts, *Soil Water Conserv.*, **31**(2):71, 1976.

Russel-Hunter, W. D., *Aquatic Productivity*, Macmillan, New York, 1970.

Sarton, J. D., and Boyd, G. B., Water Quality Improvements through Control of Road Surface Runoff. Jewell and Swan, eds. In *Water Pollution Control in Low Density Areas*, Univ. Press of New England, Hanover, NH 1975, pp. 301-316,

Schulz, E. F., and Lopez, O. G., *Determination of Urban Watershed Response Time*, Colorado State Univ. Hydrol. Papers No. 71, 1974.

Schaheen, D. G., *Contributions of Urban Roadway Usage to Water Pollution*, EPA-600/2-75-004. Office of Research and Development, Washington D.C. 20460, April 1975.

Sorenson, D. L., McCarthy, M. M., Middlebrooks, E. J., and Porcella, D. E., *Suspended and Dissolved Solids Effects on Freshwater Biota: A Review*, EPA-600/3-77-042, Office of Research and Development, 1977.

Sucoff, E., *Effects of Deicing Salts on Woody Vegetation along Minnesota Roads*, Minnesota Agricultural Experimental Station, College of Forestry, Tec. Bull. 303, Forestry Ser. 20, 1975.

Swanson, G. A., tech, coordinator, *The Mitigation Symposium: A National Workshop on Mitigating Losses of Fish and Wildlife Habitats*, Rocky Mountain Forest and Range Experiment Station, Forest Service, USDA, Fort Collings, CO, Gen, Tech, Rep. RM-65, 1979.

Taub, S. H., Clark, C. F., Mayhew, D. A., and Lisiecki, J. B., *Suitability of Ohio Interstate Highway Borrow Pit Ponds for Sport Fishing*, Ohio Agricultural Res. and Devel. Center, Res. Bull. 1064, Wooster, OH, January 1974.

Teskey, R. O., and Hinckley, T. M., *Impact of Water Level Changes on Woody Riparian and Wetland Communities*, Vol I, *Plant and Soil Responses*, FWSIOBS 77-58, U.S. Dept. Int., FWS Biological Services Program, 1977.

Thomas, W. E., Computer Modeling of Rivers: HEC-1-6. In H. W. Shen, ed., *Modeling of Rivers*, River Mechanics Institute, Colorado State Univ., 1977.

Thomas, D. M., and Benson, M. A., *Generalization of Streamflow Characteristics from Drainage-Basin Characteristics*, U.S. Geological Survey Water Supply Paper No. 1975, 1970.

Tillman, R., ed., *Proceedings of the First National Symposium on Environmental Concerns in Rights-of-Way Management*, Mississippi State Univ., 1976, p. 335.

Toler, L., *Effect of Deicing Chemicals on Surface and Ground Water*, USGS-MOPW-003, U.S. Geological Survey, Water Resources Division, 99 Worchester Street, Wellesley Hills, MA   02181, 1973.

U.S. Army Corps of Engineers, *HEC-1 Flood Hydrograph Package User's Manual*, Hydrologic Engineering Center, Davis, CA, January 1973.

U.S. Army Corps of Engineers, *HEC-2 Water Surface Profiles, User's Manual*, Hydrologic Engineering Center, 1976.

U.S. Department of Agriculture (USDA), Soil Conservation Service (SCS), *A Method for Estimating Volume and Rate of Runoff in Small Watersheds*, SCS TP-149, January 1968.

USDA, SCS, *National Engineering Handbook*, Part IV, Hydrology, 1972.

USDA, SCS, *Procedures for Computing Sheet and Rill Erosion on Project Areas*, SCS TR-51, September 1972.

USDA, SCS, *Urban Hydrology for Small Watersheds*, SCS TR-55, January 1975.

USDA, SCS, *Procedures for Determining Peak Flows in Colorado*, includes and supplements TR-55, March 1977.

U.S. Department of the Interior (DOI), FWS, Endangered and Threatened Wildlife: Plants, *Federal Register*, **41**: 117, 24524-24572, June 16, 1976.

U.S. DOI, FWS, *Habitat Evaluation Procedures (HEP)*, ESM 102, Division of Ecological Services, 1980.

U.S. DOI/USDA, *Environmental Criteria for Electrical Transmission Systems*, Government Printing Office, Washington, D.C.   20402, 1971.

U.S. DOT, FHWA, *Highways in the River Environment, Hydraulic and Environmental Design Considerations*, Washington, D.C.   20590, May 1975.

U.S. DOT,, FHWA, *Implementation Package 77-1*, vol. 1-5, *Water Quality Manual*, 1976.

U.S. EPA, *Assessment of Mathematical Models for Storm and Combined Sewer Management*, Environmental Protection Services, EPA-600/2-76-175a, 1976.

U.S. EPA, *Control of Erosion and Sedimentation Deposition from Construction of Highways and Land Development*, Office of Water Programs, September 1971.

U.S. EPA, *The Control of Pollution from Hydrographic Modifications*, Government Printing Office, Washington, D.C. 20402, 1973.

U.S. EPA, *Ground Water Pollution from Subsurface Excavations*, Office of Air and Water Programs, EPA-430/9-73-012, Government Printing Office, 1973.

U.S. EPA, *Methods for Chemical Analysis of Water and Wastes*, Methods Development and Quality Assurance Research Laboratory, National Environmental Research Center, EPA-625/6-74-002, Cincinnati, OH 45268, 1974.

U.S. EPA, *Processes, Procedures, and Methods to Control Pollution Resulting from All Construciton Activity*, Office of Air and Water Programs, Government Printing Office, EPA-430/9-73-C07, October 1973.

U.S. EPA, *Processes, Procedures, and Methods to Control Pollution Resulting from Silvicultural Activities*, Office of Air and Water Programs, Government Printing Office, October 1973.

U.S. EPA, *Storm Water Management Model User's Manual*, 1977.

U.S. Geological Survey, *Guidelines for Determining Flood Flow Frequency*, U.S. Water Resources Council Bull. 17, 1976.

U.S. Geological Survey, *Guidelines for Determining Flood Frequency*, U.S. Water Resources Council Bull. 17a, 1977.

Voorhees, D., *Waterfowl Nesting: Highway Right-of-Way Mowing Versus Succession*, North Dakota State Highway Department, Capitol Grounds, Bismarck, ND 58505, January 1977.

Ward, A. L., Cupal, J. J., Goodwin, G. A., and Morris, H. D., *Effects of Highway Construction and Use on Big Game Populations*, Office of Research and Development, DOT, FHWA, 1976.

Wischmeier, W. H., Johnson, C. B., Cross, B. V., Soil Erodibility Nomograph for Farmland and Construction Sites, *J. Soil Water Conserv.*, **26**, 1971.

Wischmeier, W. H., and Smith, D. D., *Predicting Rainfall-Erosion Losses from Cropland East of the Rocky Mountains*, Soil and Water Conservation Research Division, Agricultural Research Service, May 1965.

Yevjevich, V., *Probability and Statistics in Hydrology*, Water Resources Publication, Fort Colling, CO, 1972.

Zembruzski, T. J., and Dunn, B., *Techniques for Estimating Magnitude and Frequency of Floods on Rural Unregulated Streams in New York State Excluding Long Island*, U.S. Geological Survey, Water Resource Investigation 79-83.

Zimmer, David W., and Bachmann, Roger W., *A Study of the Effects of Stream Channelization and Bank Stabilization on Warmwater Sport Fish in Iowa: Subproject No. 4. The Effects of Long Reach Channelization on Habitat and Invertebrate Drift in Some Iowa Streams*, Iowa Cooperative Fishery Research Unit, Iowa State Univ., Ames, IA 50011, May 1976.

Index